# The Routledge Dictionary of Cultural References in Modern French

*The Routledge Dictionary of Cultural References in Modern French* reveals the hidden cultural dimension of contemporary French, as used in the press, going beyond the limited and purely lexical approach of traditional bilingual dictionaries.

Even foreign learners of French who possess a good level of French often have difficulty in fully understanding French articles, not because of any linguistic shortcomings on their part but because of their inadequate knowledge of the cultural references.

This cultural dictionary of French provides the reader with clear and concise explanations of the crucial cultural dimension behind the most frequently used words and phrases found in the contemporary French press. This vital background information, gathered here in this innovative and entertaining dictionary, will allow readers to go beyond a superficial understanding of the French press and the French language in general, to see the hidden yet implied cultural significance that is so transparent to the native speaker.

Key features:

- a broad range of cultural references from the historical and literary to the popular and classical, with an in-depth analysis of punning mechanisms.
- over 3,000 cultural references explained
- a three-level indicator of frequency
- over 600 questions to test knowledge before and after reading.

*The Routledge Dictionary of Cultural References in Modern French* is the ideal reference for all undergraduate and postgraduate students of French seeking to enhance their understanding of the French language. It will also be of interest to teachers, translators and Francophiles alike. French students in khâgne, Sciences-Po and schools of journalism will also find this valuable and relevant for their studies.

**Michael Mould** has taught and translated in France for over 40 years. Previous publications include *L'Anglais des Ressources Humaines* (2003) and *Corporate English* (1995).

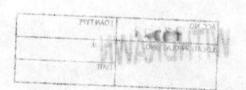

# The Routledge Dictionary of Cultural References in Modern French

Michael Mould

Routledge
Taylor & Francis Group

LONDON AND NEW YORK

First edition published 2011
by Routledge
2 Park Square, Milton Park, Abingdon, OX14 4RN

Simultaneously published in the USA and Canada
by Routledge
711 Third Avenue, New York, NY 10017

*Routledge is an imprint of the Taylor & Francis Group, an informa business*

*British Library Cataloguing in Publication Data*
A catalogue record for this book is available from the British Library

*Library of Congress Cataloging in Publication Data*
Mould, Michael.
 The Routledge dictionary of cultural references in modern French / Michael
Mould. – 1st ed.
  p. cm.
 1. French language–Dictionaries. 2. Popular culture–France–Dictionaries. I.
Title. II. Title: Dictionary of cultural references in modern French.
 PC2766.M68 2011
 443'.21–dc22
              2010033838

ISBN: 978-0-415-59792-0 (hbk)
ISBN: 978-0-415-59794-4 (pbk)
ISBN: 978-0-203-83092-5 (ebk)

Typeset in Times New Roman by
Taylor & Francis Books

MIX
Paper from
responsible sources
FSC® C004839
www.fsc.org

Printed and bound in Great Britain by
CPI Antony Rowe, Chippenham, Wiltshire

To my wife, Danielle, and to my son, Francis

# Contents

Even while they teach, men learn.

Seneca, the Younger

# Preface

Many years ago, as an intermediate-level student of French, I was frequently puzzled by certain sentences I read in the press. Although I understood the individual components of the phrase, I was still at a loss to understand the global meaning behind the words. At best, I was aware of this; at worst, highly significant allusions simply passed me by unnoticed. Certain words I used in conversation would frequently provoke smiles on the face of my interlocutor for a reason that escaped me. There was a sense beyond the words, I was missing it, and my bilingual dictionary was of no help.

A case in point is the word *atmosphère* that appeared, and still appears, frequently in newspaper and magazine headlines. My bilingual dictionary gave me extensive translations of the word – 'polluted atmosphere', 'upper and lower atmospheres', 'sterile atmosphere' – but absolutely no mention of the hidden cultural significance of the word that is so transparent to the French native speaker. My bilingual dictionary did not tell me that *atmosphère*, as it is frequently used in the press, is part of:

a   one of the most famous retorts in the history of French cinema
b   the most famous line ever said by the French actress, Arletty
c   the most famous line from the film *Hôtel du Nord*.

It is precisely this hidden cultural dimension that this book wishes to unveil.

In this dictionary, students will find a broad range of high frequency cultural references with a three-level ranking that will enable them to rationally allocate their study time and concentrate their effort more effectively.

This book is primarily aimed at the English-speaking academic community. It may be used by university students as a self-study tool or by lecturers and teachers as a source of course material and as a testing tool. It should prove to be a useful *vade mecum* for the general reader of the French press (native or non-native) and I believe that it could constitute a useful reference manual for translators and journalists alike. I would like to think that this dictionary fills a gap in the current commercial offering of dictionaries.

There are over 3,000 cultural references within these pages and it is hoped that they will not only enable students to solve many of the culture-bound comprehension problems they are certain to encounter, but that they will also convey something of the essence of French culture in the broadest sense of the word.

# Acknowledgements

I should like to extend my warmest thanks to the various newspapers and magazines for having courteously granted permission to reproduce the hundreds of quotations taken from their respective publications. My thanks go to *Le Canard Enchaîné, Les Dossiers du Canard, Les Echos, L'Express, Le Figaro, Marianne, Le Monde, Le Nouvel Observateur, Le Point,* and *Libération.* All of the quotations taken from these publications are protected by copyright. All rights reserved.

For their precious help in reading the early proofs and for giving so much constructive criticism, my sincere thanks also go to Malcolm Raddan J.P. M. ès L. M.Ed., formerly Head of the Modern Foreign Languages Department at Guilsborough School, Northamptonshire and Gerald Lees BA (Oxon) Cert. Ed. MCIL, Director of Company Languages, Colchester. Thank you, Liliane Périé, Marc Daniel and Noëlle Graziani for having served as guinea pigs for the test section and Anne Paquette for having re-read the texts with eagle eyes.

It has been said that 'teachers affect eternity; they can never tell where their influence stops'. I should like to take this opportunity to thank and remember those people whom I had the honour, joy and good fortune to have as my teachers over the years: Patrick J. Larkin, Marjorie Riding, Dr William Bryant, my numerous teachers at the Alliance Française who gave me their love of the French language, my lecturers at Paris IV Sorbonne and especially Dr Luce Bonnerot and Professor Alain Jumeau. The fruit of my work is the fruit of theirs.

I am indebted to all of my students at France Telecom who, over the years, taught me so much.

I should also like to express my gratitude to Samantha Vale Noya, my enthusiastic editor at Routledge, for having been such a lovely person to work with over the period of our project; her enthusiasm was a constant encouragement. My thanks also go to the many people behind the scenes and particularly to my patient and meticulous copy-editor Kris Wischenkämper.

Lastly, I should like to express my limitless thanks to my wife, Danielle, for her support and patience ... and particularly for her consummate IT skills without which this book would have been more than a challenge for me to produce.

To all, I express my deepest gratitude.

Michael Mould

# Abbreviations

| | | |
|---|---|---|
| abr. | abréviation | abbreviation |
| AD | Anno Domini | in the year of our Lord |
| adj. | adjectif | adjective |
| adv. | adverbe | adverb |
| ax. | axiome | axiom |
| BC | avant Jésus-Christ | Before Christ |
| c. | circa | for approximate historical dates |
| cf. | confer | compare with |
| cit. | citation | quotation |
| conjug. | conjugaison | conjugation |
| dev. | devise | motto |
| dict. | dicton | saying |
| e.g. | exempli gratia | for example |
| etc. | et caetera/cetera | and the rest, and so forth |
| excl. | exclamatif | exclamatory |
| exp. adv. | expression adverbiale | adverbial expression |
| i.e. | idem est | that's to say |
| imp. | impératif | imperative |
| interj. | interjection | interjection |
| interr. | interrogatif | interrogative |
| IT | informatique | information technology |
| loc. adj. | locution adjectivale | adjectival phrase |
| loc. adv. | locution adverbiale | adverbial phrase |
| loc. nom. | locution nominale | noun phrase |
| loc. jurid. | locution juridique | legal phrase |
| loc. prov. | locution proverbiale | proverb |
| loc. verb. | locution verbale | verb phrase |
| loc. subj. | locution subjonctive | subjunctive phrase |
| NB | nota bene | note well |
| nf. | nom féminin | feminine noun |
| nfpl. | nom féminin pluriel | plural feminine noun |
| nm. | nom masculin | masculine noun |

| | | |
|---|---|---|
| nm/f | nom masculin/féminin | masculine/feminine noun |
| nmpl. | nom masculin pluriel | plural masculine noun |
| nmfpl. | nom masculin/féminin pluriel plural masculine/feminine noun | |
| prép. | préposition | preposition |
| qqn. | quelqu'un | somebody |
| sb. | idem | somebody |
| st | quelque chose | something |
| vi. | verbe intransitif | intransitive verb |
| vt. | verbe transitif | transitive verb |

# Introduction

The research for this book was prompted by two observations. First, even degree-level students and readers of the French press, frequently miss significant elements for the comprehension of a text not because of their linguistic short-comings as such, but rather because of their inadequate knowledge of the cultural references used. The second observation concerns the fact that this dimension of understanding is inadequately addressed by bilingual dictionaries.

The objective of this book is to provide the readers with a comprehensive list of the high frequency cultural-linguistic references that they will meet, not only in press articles but in idiomatic oral French and to help them go beyond the words in order to appreciate the full cultural significance of what is so obvious to the French native speaker.

The research period to prepare this book ran from January 2007 to June 2010. Over that period, four national news magazines and *Le Canard Enchaîné* were analyzed on a weekly basis. As for the dailies, each was sampled on a periodic basis (three or four times a week). The titles chosen, *Le Canard Enchaîné, Les Dossiers du Canard, Les Echos, L'Express, Le Figaro, Marianne, Le Monde, Le Nouvel Observateur,* and *Le Point*, provide a broad political spectrum ranging from the right wing to the left, and in terms of style range from the serious world of finance to the humorous and satirical. Nearly 400 issues of the magazines and newspapers above were analyzed during this period. Each chapter is a linguistic 'snapshot' of expressions found during the research period of two and a half years and does not claim to be an exhaustive list of elements in a given field.

The reader will find over 3,000 cultural-linguistic references. Each entry, in Chapters 5, 6, 7 and 8, is accompanied by a full explanation of its origin. There is a related newspaper quote or pun on the entry, as well as an explanation of the context in which the quote was used. In all cases, each entry has been flagged for frequency using asterisks:

* **low to medium** frequency
** **high** frequency
*** **very high** frequency.

It needs to be emphasized that a weekly eight-page broadsheet, *Le Canard Enchaîné*, frequently contains a higher proportion of cultural references than a 60-page weekly news magazine and that the magazine *Marianne* is much richer in cultural references (particularly historical) than any of the other news magazines that were studied. It should also be understood that the three-asterisk example taken to illustrate 'bouc émissaire' (scapegoat) taken from *Le Nouvel Observateur,* indicates that the cultural reference is very high for *all* the various publications and that the quote from *Le Nouvel Observateur* was used quite simply because of the clarity of the example.

This book is primarily, although not exclusively, intended for the English-speaking student of French; however, I sincerely believe that many French and other foreign students and readers have a lot to learn from it. It follows that certain English words, used in French, have been explained in detail as have many other entries that pose no problem for the native English reader. I did not wish to make too many ethno-centric assumptions about the knowledge of the reader and consequently, I would ask English-speaking readers to bear with me on such points; I understand that they might find certain explanations irritatingly obvious.

The fun factor has been addressed by the inclusion of over 600 questions related to the contents of the various chapters and bearing on the whole spectrum of French culture as seen in the press. This could be useful for both student and teacher. I hope that this book will contribute to making good the current deficit in the commercial offering of dictionaries, but it is by no means the destination; it is rather a warm invitation to the reader to pursue this fascinating journey.

Carro, August 2010

# Chapter 1

# Popular cultural references

In this chapter the reader will find a host of terms taken from a broad spectrum of sources mentioned in the French press: advertising slogans, film titles, lyrics from famous songs, music hall classics, and children's playground lore. Such references rarely get a mention in classical bilingual dictionaries and are rarely, if ever, mentioned in university language courses; and yet they are a very significant part of the French linguistic landscape. As with all of the entries in this book, these expressions are used as such or frequently punned upon or modified in some way. A translation has been proposed for those general-interest readers who might appreciate a little help in this area. Politicians' nicknames are frequently those given by *Le Canard Enchaîné*.

**'abreuver nos sillons d'un sang impur'** `**`
These are words from the national anthem *La Marseillaise*. A 'sillon' is a furrow, while 'abreuver' means 'to drench' or 'to soak'. The exact words are 'Qu'un sang impur abreuve nos sillons'.

**affinité. Et plus si** `**`
'And possibly more.' These are the words included in a typical ad in the lonely hearts section of a newspaper. After mentioning the possibilities of travel, music and cinema, this expression concludes the ad implying that the relationship could develop into much more than sharing hobbies if a true affinity can be found between two people.

*Affreux, sales et méchants* `**`
The French title of the Ettore Scola film (1976) *Brutti, sporchi e cattivi*.

*Allô maman, bobo* `**`
One of the great successes of the singer, composer and actor Alain Souchon (1944–). A 'bobo' in children's language is a 'pain' or a 'sore' etc. See Chapter 14 'Bobo'.

## 'Alsace et la Lorraine. l" ⬚ *

These are the words from a jingoistic song of 1930 affirming that the Germans would not take Alsace and Lorraine, as they did in 1871. It was annexed by the Germans in 1940.

## *Amoureux des bancs publics. Les* ⬚ **

'Lovers on a public bench.' The words come from a song written and sung in 1977 by Georges Brassens (1921–81) which juxtaposes the spontaneity of young lovers kissing in public with the reprobation of the priggish, bourgeois passers-by.

## Approchez Mesdames, Messieurs! ⬚ *

'Come closer, ladies and gentlemen', 'Step right up'. This expression is the typical banter of a salesperson at a stand trying to attract customers or the equivalent of 'roll up' when used by sb. trying to attract people to a show.

## *Arroseur arrosé. L'* ⬚ **

The meaning of this expression resembles the English 'hoist with one's own petard'. It is the title of the second of two films by Louis Lumière (1864–1948) made in 1895 and constituting the first slapstick comedy in the history of French cinema. Lasting 49 seconds, it features a gardener watering the garden. A little rascal puts his foot on the hose and the water stops flowing. The gardener takes a close look at the nozzle of the hose; it is then that the rascal takes his foot off the hose and the gardener is drenched and runs after the mischievous boy.

## Arsène Lupin ⬚ **

The gentleman burglar, a fictitious character created by Maurice Leblanc in a collection of short stories, the first of which appeared in 1905 in the newspaper *Je sais tout*. Over the years, various actors have played the television and cinema role.

## Asnières. Le 22 à ⬚ **

Famous words from one of the most well-known sketches by the comic Fernand Raynaud (1926–73). It is a reference to the time when the French telecommunications network was a national disgrace. In the sketch, 'le 22 à Asnières' is a number that is impossible to reach. Asnières is on the north-west outskirts of Paris in the *département* of the Hauts-de-Seine (92). Before 1974, comics used to quip that 'half of the French population was waiting for a telephone to be installed, and the other half was waiting for the dialling tone'.

## Atmosphère … atmosphère … ⬚ ***

This is one of the most famous retorts in French cinema history. It was made by Arletty, real name Léonie Bathiat (1898–1992), acting opposite

Louis Jouvet (1887–1951) in the film *Hôtel du Nord* (1938) and said with the Parisian equivalent of a cockney accent. She was responding to her partner who had just complimented her on her face having 'atmosphère'. The exact line she spoke was: 'Atmosphère, atmosphère, est-ce-que j'ai une gueule d'atmosphère?' 'Gueule' is the slang term for gob or mug.

### *Autant en emporte le vent* ⟨ ** ⟩
This is the French translation of the American film title *Gone with the Wind* by Victor Flemming, made in 1939, and based on the novel by Margaret Mitchell (1900–49). The words of the French title come from *La Balade des pendus* by the poet François Villon (1431–63).

### *banlieue. Elle court, elle court la* ⟨ * ⟩
The title of a Franco-Italian film that came out in 1973 which satirically describes the hellish life of 'banlieusards' using public transport to go to work in Paris and to return to the far-flung suburbs in the evening. It is important to realize that in France, rich people live in the inner cities whereas the less well-heeled live in the suburbs. 'Suburb' is thus an extremely difficult word to translate given the fact that between England, the USA and France the connotation of the same word 'banlieue' refers to two diametrically opposite social realities.

### barbichette. Je te tiens par la ⟨ *** ⟩
This is a nursery rhyme *cum* game where two children hold each other's chin; the first child who laughs, receives a little smack. The text goes: 'Je te tiens, tu me tiens par la barbichette, le premier de nous deux qui rira aura une tapette.' It is used today to describe two politicians who each have some dirt on the other and have concluded a pact of non-agression in their mutual interest. It is basically reciprocal blackmail.

### bateau. Pince-me et Pince-moi sont sur un ⟨ * ⟩
This is a game that young children play. Child 'A' says 'Pinch Me' and 'Pinch You' are in a boat; 'Pinch You' falls overboard, who is left?' Child 'B' replies 'Pinch Me', upon which child 'A' pinches child 'B'.

### bave du crapaud n'atteint pas la blanche colombe. La ⟨ * ⟩
This is a French saying. 'Toad slime cannot besmirch the pure dove', i.e. calumny cannot damage sb. who is blameless.

### beauf nm ⟨ *** ⟩
This was originally a comic character created by Cabu (a famous cartoonist) and is now defined as a petty bourgeois, narrow-minded, conservative, male chauvinist pig.

### Bébé Cadum. Le                                             [ * ]

'Cadum' is the registered trademark of the French soap company set up in 1907 which was later to organize an annual competition (from 1924 onwards) to elect 'Le Bébé Cadum' of the year. The expression used by schoolchildren today tends to refer to a weak mummy's boy.

### Bécassine                                                  [ * ]

This is the name of a comic strip character who appeared in a young girl's magazine in 1905. She represents the simple-minded, ill-dressed, Breton maid. See Chapter 9 'Royal, Ségolène'.

### Belle Hélène. La                                           [ * ]

The name of an *opéra bouffe* by Jacques Offenbach first put on in 1864 and including many satirical references to the Second Empire (1852–70) and Napoleon III. He was frequently called 'le nain' (the dwarf) because of his short stature.

### 'Bernadette, elle est très chouette'                       [ * ]

'Bernadette is a real nice person.' This is the first line of the song written and sung by Nino Ferrer (1934–98) in 1967, entitled 'Le Téléfon' in which various forenames are rhymed with physical or moral qualities, e.g. 'Noémie est très jolie', 'Mon cousin, il est malsain', etc. 'Chouette' is familiar in terms of linguistic register. Bernadette is also the forename of former President Jacques Chirac's wife. Notice too that a 'chouette' is a night bird similar to the 'hibou'. Both are translated in English by the generic term 'owl'.

### Bernadette Soubirous                                       [ * ]

This is the name of a Catholic saint. She was a French farm girl (1844–79) who, when she was fourteen, had visions of the Virgin Mary in a cave not far from her native village, Lourdes. The pilgrimages to Lourdes date from this period. She entered the religious order of the Sisters of Charity in Nevers in 1866. She was beatified in 1925 and canonized in 1933 by Pope Pius XI.

### besoin de personne en Harley-Davidson. Je n'ai            [ *** ]

'I don't need anybody when I'm on my Harley-Davidson.' *Harley-Davidson* was a song created by lyricist and composer Serge Gainsbourg (1928–91). It was sung by Brigitte Bardot in 1967 and became one of her greatest successes. Harley-Davidson is the legendary motorbike brand name.

### beurre, l'argent du beurre (et le sourire de la crémière.) Le   [ * ]

The saying is: 'The butter, the money to buy the butter, and the smile of the dairy maid [to boot].' This refers to sb. who wants too much. The French saying is 'tu ne peux pas avoir le beurre et l'argent du beurre'. This is a saying equivalent to the English 'you can't have your cake and eat it'.

## 'bicyclette. À'                                              [ * ]

'By bicycle' or 'on a bicycle'. The very words 'à bicyclette', inevitably bring to mind a song recorded in 1968 by Yves Montand, the actor, singer and music hall artist (1921–91) as does the first line 'Quand on partait de bon matin' ('When we used to set out early in the morning').

## Bidochon. Les                                              [ * ]

Les Bidochon are comic strip characters representing a typical working-class couple and the everyday problems that they face in the consumer society. They appeared for the first time in 1977 in the magazine *Fluide Glacial* created by Christian Binet. NB: 'classe moyenne' in French is NOT 'middle class'.

## Bisounours                                              [ * ]

This is the name of a children's cuddly teddy bear. It is the French name of the American fluffy toy popularized in the 1980s, corresponding to the 'Care Bear'. The Care Bear was originally created by the company American Greetings in 1981 as a greeting card character. In French, the word 'bisou' is children's language for a 'kiss'.

## 'Bizarre!, vous avez dit bizarre?'                    [ ** ]

'Moi, j'ai dit bizarre? Comme c'est bizarre!' ('I said "bizarre", did I? How bizarre!'). These are the famous words spoken by Louis Jouvet in the play by Marcel Carné *Drôle de Drame* (1937). Jouvet (1887–1951) was one of the greatest actors of his time, a director and teacher of dramatic art. This line has since become a cult phrase.

## bizutage nm                                              [ * ]

In a British university, 'Rag Week' tends to be used to describe the week of events organized early in one's first term to raise money for charity (and involving practical jokes on new students). The term, in French, is much more related to the idea of the 'initiation' of a new student or freshman. It frequently involved some form of degrading humiliation inflicted on the new student. In this respect, 'bizutage' more closely resembles the American term 'hazing' which is a rite of initiation that can go to extreme limits. This type of 'bizutage' was made illegal in France in 1998. The terms 'bizut' or 'bizuth' refer to the first-year students or freshmen who undergo such treatment.

## black, blanc, beur                                      [ * ]

This expression came into vogue in the 1990s to describe the multi-ethnic character of France. It is an echo of 'bleu, blanc, rouge' the colours of the French flag. A 'beur' is a second-generation North African, born and living in France.

7

### 'Boire ou conduire, il faut choisir'                ★★★
'One must choose between drinking and driving.' A publicity slogan of *Le Comité de la Sécurité Routière* to combat drink-driving.

### 'Bon sang, mais c'est bien sûr ... '                ★
This was the pet phrase used by Inspector Bourrel in the highly successful television series *Les Cinq Dernières Minutes* first broadcast in 1958. The series starred Raymond Souplex in the lead role. It was aired on French TV until 1973. In each episode, on discovering the culprit, the police inspector would exclaim, 'Good God, but of course'. In fact 'Bon sang' was never used by the famous inspector; he used the expression 'Bon Dieu'.

### Bonheur est dans le pré. Le                ★★
*Happiness is in the Meadow.* This is the title of a film by Etienne Chatiliez (1995). It is also the first line of a poem by the French poet Paul Fort (1872–1960) entitled *Le Bonheur*.

### Boum. La                ★★
Sophie Marceau, the French actress (1966–), made her name with the film *La Boum* in 1980. A *boum* is a youngsters' party. The word is also an echo of one of the greatest hits of the singer Charles Trenet (1913–2001), 'Mon cœur fait boum'.

### 'bu? Tu t'es vu quand t'as'                ★
'Have you seen yourself when you've been drinking?' This was the 1991 slogan of the campaign launched by *Le Comité français d'éducation pour la santé* in the fight against alcohol abuse. See below 'verre'.

### bureaucrates de Courteline. Les                ★★★
Georges Courteline (1858–1929) was a French writer and playwright who frequently poked fun at the pettifogging bureaucrat at the service window. This is typified in his work entitled *Messieurs les Ronds-de-Cuir* published in 1893. The term 'un rond-de-cuir' means a 'pen-pusher'.

### 'Buvez, éliminez!'                ★
'Drink, eliminate.' The advertising slogan for the mineral water Vittel launched in 1979 and composed by the French entertainer, singer and comic, Richard Gotainer (1948–).

### café du Commerce. Le                ★★
This is a very frequent name for a café or bar in France. Discussions of the 'café du Commerce' type are political, vain and even ridiculous. The debates are the debates of the common man in the street that are full of clichés and

truisms and lacking in subtlety. It thus refers to a debate of low intellectual quality.

## Ça eût payé     ***

'It could have been profitable.' This is another expression that we owe to the comic Fernand Raynaud in one of his songs. It is to be pointed out that in the song, the original text reads 'ça a eu payé', this being the tense (only used orally) known as *le passé surcomposé*. See above 'Asnières'.

## Capitaine Haddock     ***

See below 'sparadrap'.

## Carabosse     **

The is the name of a wicked and hunchbacked fairy in children's fairy tales.

## carré blanc. Le     *

The white square was used on French television between 1961–8 to warn the general public that the programme in question was not suitable for all categories of viewer. It has now been replaced by a digit referring to age suitability.

## 'Carrefour, le pays où la vie est moins chère'     *

The slogan of the Carrefour supermarket chain is 'Carrefour, the country where the cost of living is lower'. See below 'positive'.

## Cave se rebiffe. Le     **

This is the title of a film by Gilles Grangier (1961), starring Jean Gabin and Bernard Blier. *Un cave*, in criminal slang, is a man who is naïve and who does not know the codes of the underworld. This is the second part of the trilogy which includes *Les Tontons Flingueurs* and *Touchez pas au grisbi*. See below.

## Cercle des poètes disparus. Le     *

This is the French title of the award-winning, American film *Dead Poets Society* that was released in France in 1989. Directed by Peter Weir and starring Robin Williams, the story is about an unconventional teacher in a highly conventional school in the USA. The teacher invites his students to 'seize the day' and not to over-concentrate on tomorrow. The leitmotiv of the film is the Latin expression *carpe diem*. See Chapter 13 'carpe diem'. NB Poets does not have a possessive apostrophe.

## César. Une compression de     *

César Baldaccini, was a French sculptor (1921–98) who is particularly remembered for his compressions of metallic objects. A 'César' is also the name of the annual French cinema award, the equivalent of the American Oscar. The trophy is a statuette-compression of César's creation.

### C'est bon pour le moral     `**`
This is the title of a song recorded by the French West Indian group La Compagnie Créole that was a great success in 1983. It has become a cult phrase.

### C'est celui qui dit, qui l'est     `***`
A schoolchild's reply to an insult: 'It's the person who says it, who is it.'

### 'C'est facile, c'est pas cher et ça peut rapporter gros!'     `*`
In 1976, the national lottery called Loto was launched with this ungrammatical slogan ('It's easy, it's not expensive and it can bring in a packet!'). The text should have been 'ce n'est pas cher'.

### 'Chante rossignol'     `*`
These words come from a traditional French love song *À la claire fontaine*. 'Chante rossignol chante (sing, skylark, sing)/Toi qui as le cœur gai (Thou who art blithe-hearted)/Tu as le cœur à rire (Thy heart is mirthful)/Moi je l'ai à pleurer' (mine is tearful). It is, in fact, a lover's lament. See below 'Il y a longtemps que je t'aime'.

### Charivari. Le     `*`
An anti-clerical and republican magazine founded in 1832 during the reign of Louis Philippe (1830–48). The satirical magazine was constantly in opposition to the 'July Monarchy' and was often taken to court at a time when the freedom of the press had no legal foundation. Honoré Daumier (1808–79) was one of the most famous caricaturists who contributed to the magazine. It was last published in 1937. See Chapter 6 'Monarchie de Juillet'.

### Charme discret de la bourgeoisie. Le     `*`
This is the title of a film by Luis Buñuel that came out in 1972 and won an Oscar for the best foreign film.

### chasseur sachant chasser doit savoir chasser sans son chien. Un     `*`
This is a well-known French tongue-twister.

### 'Chassons le gaspi de chez nous'     `*`
'Let's drive out wastage.' This was the slogan of a government publicity campaign to make energy savings in the wake of the second oil crisis in the mid 1970s.

### Chaud devant!     `***`
In a crowded café, this is the waiter's traditional cry to make people get out of his way and warn them that he is carrying something hot. It is the French catering equivalent of 'mind your backs'.

## Chauffe Marcel!

[ * ]

This is an expression originating from a comic sketch of the 1960s in which a man is serenading a woman under her balcony while an accomplice plays the accordeon. Each time the music stopped, the seducer would encourage the musician with the words 'Chauffe Marcel!' ('Get to it, Marcel!'). It is sometimes used in the interrogative mode to ask sb. if their work (particularly physical labour) is progressing well.

## chocolat. Être

[ ** ]

The expression refers to sb. who has been taken in, taken for a ride, is victim of an injustice or thwarted. 'Footit and Chocolat' were a well-known music hall act in the late 1890s in Paris. They were clowns. 'Chocolat' was a Senegalese, who was always being beaten by the white man. The racist remarks were always sure to raise a laugh. He was sketched by Toulouse Lautrec, his fellow drinker in the cabarets of Montmartre. He died an alcoholic in total poverty in 1917 (cf. 'être marron').

## 'Ciel mon mari!'

[ ** ]

'Heavens, my husband!' A hackneyed theatrical line used by the unfaithful spouse, Lucienne, spoken to her lover on being taken by surprise by her husband. It comes from the vaudeville *Le Dindon* by Georges Feydeau (1862–1921). This is as well known and humorous in French as is the stock English expression 'We can't go on meeting like this'.

## Cinq colonnes à la une

[ *** ]

This is a newspaper expression. In newspapers, text is spread across five columns. The article on the front page has a headline covering the width of the five columns indicating that it is very important front page news. The expression gave its name to one of the most famous news magazines in the history of French television that went on the air for the first time in 1959. It was produced by the legendary team of Pierre Desgraupes, Pierre Dumayet, Pierre Lazareff and Igor Barrère. The last programme went on the air in 1968.

## *Clochemerle*

[ * ]

This is the name of a humorous and satirical novel, written by Gabriel Chevallier (1895–1969) and published in 1934, about a typical French village and the ludicrous quarrels of its inhabitants. The point at issue in the novel is the mayor's project to build a public urinal next to the parish church. The term 'Clochemerle' is used today in relation to petty, parochial squabbling.

## Cocorico!

[ ** ]

This is an onomatopoeic word which resembles the sound that a cock is supposed to make when crowing. It is the French version of 'cock-a-doodle-do'. It is also is a cry of victory. To be 'cocorico' is to be chauvinistic. See below 'coq gaulois'.

### colonies de vacances. Les jolies

Title and words of a song by Pierre Perret (1934–) that was a hit in the summer of 1966 and was a satirical presentation of children's holiday camps in France. This song was contemporary with the big American hit by Allan Sherman (1924–73) on the same subject, 'Hello Mother, Hello Father', that also topped the charts in the English-speaking world in 1966.

### 'comme on nous parle'

'The way they speak to us', are words from one of the biggest hits by Alain Souchon, *Foule sentimentale*. The song ridicules the consumer society and criticizes the ad men for the way in which they address the general public. It was released in 1993. See above *Allô maman, bobo*.

### 'contrat de confiance. Le'

The advertising slogan of the Darty electrical and household appliances chain.

### Copains d'abord. Les

'Chums come first.' This is one of the most famous titles of the songs of George Brassens (1921–81) that came out in 1964. It was composed for the film *Les Copains* by Yves Robert and is seen as a hymn to friendship.

### coq gaulois. Le *

The reason why the French sports emblem is a cock derives from the play on words between 'gallus' ('the cock' in Latin) and 'Gallus' ('the Gaulois' in Latin).

### corneille. La *

'La corneille, sur la racine de la bruyère, boit l'eau de la fontaine Molière.' 'The crow on the root of the briar drinks the water from the fountain of Molière.' A useful mnemonic technique thanks to which French children can easily remember their greatest writers: Corneille, Racine, La Bruyère, Boileau, La Fontaine and Molière.

### 'Crac, boum, hue!'

The trivial words from a song by the actor/singer Jacques Dutronc (1943–) that deals with a secret method for picking up girls: 'un joujou extra qui fait crac, boum, hue'. The song was entitled *Les Playboys*, and was one of the great hits in 1966 in the heyday of the 'yé-yé' era. The music was composed by Jacques Dutronc and the lyrics by Jacques Lanzmann.

### Crime était presque parfait. Le

'The crime was almost perfect.' This is the French translation of the title of the Hitchcock film *Dial M for Murder* that came out in 1954 and starred Grace Kelly.

### Croix de bois, croix de fer      `**`
'Croix de bois, croix de fer, si je mens, je vais en enfer'. A playground expression used when trying to persuade others that one is not lying. 'Cross made of wood, cross made of iron, if I am lying, I will go to hell.' This is equivalent to the English 'cross my heart and hope to die'.

### Croix de Lorraine nf      `*`
The cross of Lorraine, otherwise known as the cross of Anjou, is a cross with two horizontal bars, the upper one being shorter than the lower. On 1 July 1940 it became the official symbol of the free French forces under General Charles de Gaulle. See Chapter 2 'Croix de Lorraine'.

### CRS-SS      `*`
This is one of the memories of the unrest of 1968. The CRS are the anti-riot police (Compagnies Républicaines de Sécurité). Faced with the violence of police tactics, the students in the Latin quarter chanted CRS = SS.

     SS was the notorious German term for 'Schutzstaffel', the protection squad set up by Hitler in 1927.

### 'Debout, les damnés de la terre'      `**`
'Arise, damned of the earth.' These are the words of the first line of the *Internationale*. See below 'lutte finale'.

### 'décarcasse. A quoi ça sert que Ducros se'      `**`
These are the words of Pierre Mirat, French actor, in the advertising campaigns for Ducros spices during the 1970s and 1980s. The slogan is 'What's the point in Ducros going to all that trouble?'

### 'Demain j'enlève le bas'      `**`
In August 1981, advertising posters could be seen all over Paris showing the picture of a beautiful girl in a bikini. The slogan was 'On 2 September, I shall take off the top'. Indeed, a few days later, the same beautiful girl was shown topless, this time the slogan being 'On 4 September, I shall take off the bottom'. A few days later, indeed the girl had taken off the lower part of her bikini but was shown photographed from the back only. This was in fact an impressive demonstration of the power of advertising to get people's attention. It is an example *par excellence* of the 'teasing' principle. The campaign was launched by the advertising company Avenir, 'the company that always keeps its promises'.

### 'déménage! Ça'      `*`
This is a famous advertising slogan of the 1980s of the company Ducros, for its strong Dijon mustard. The slogan can be translated by 'It's a bit strong', or 'It takes the roof off your mouth!'

## Devine qui vient dîner?  **

The French title of the American, Oscar award-winning film, *Guess Who's Coming to Dinner*. The film was directed by Stanley Kramer, and starred Spencer Tracy (1900–67), Katharine Hepburn (1907–2003) and Sidney Poitier. It was released in 1967. No question mark in English Title.

## Dites 33  *

This is the French doctor's equivalent of 'Say ah' when examining a patient's throat.

## Don Camillo et Pépone  *

These fictional characters were created in 1948 by the Italian writer Giovannino Guareschi. Don Camillo is an Italian village priest and Pépone is the communist mayor. A series of films was made about these short stories and starred the French actor Fernandel. Although Don Camillo and Pépépone frequently fight, they both have a certain respect for each other, although this is never openly expressed. The films are remembered for the frequent conversations that the priest has with Christ on the cross in the village church. Don Camillo is one of the best-loved characters in French cinema history. One such conversation with Christ was used in a very successful TV advertising campaign by the pasta company Panzani.

## Dur, dur, d'être un bébé  **

'It's hard being a baby.' This was the title of a hit song by Jordy Lemoine, a French child-singer (1988–) recorded in 1992. It had considerable chart success for several months and has become a cult phrase.

## École des fans. L'    *

This was one of the most popular Sunday TV programmes that went on the air for the first time in 1977. It was hosted by the French comedian, journalist and radio/TV compère, Jacques Martin (1933–2007). The name of the programme evokes the play by Molière *L'École des femmes*.

## écureuil, l' nm    **

A stylized squirrel is the logo of the French savings bank La Caisse d'Épargne.

## éléphant ça trompe énormément. Un    ***

'The elephant is extremely deceptive.' This is the title of a film by Yves Robert that came out in 1976. Given that the word 'elephants' is the familiar term to designate the socialist old guard, this title is frequently punned upon in the press. NB *Une trompe* is an elephant's trunk.

### 'Elle est pas belle la vie!' (sic)

'Isn't life beautiful?' This is an advertising slogan of the pork meat products company Fleury Michon. Grammatically speaking, it should have been 'Elle n'est pas belle la vie?' or 'N'est-t-elle pas belle la vie?'

### Emmaüs

A charity organization founded in 1953 by the late Abbé Pierre (Henri Groués 1912–2007) to give shelter and employment to the homeless. Also has the function of an Oxfam-type shop. See Chapter 9 'Abbé Pierre'.

### *Enfants du paradis. Les*

A cult film produced in wartime by Marcel Carné between 1943 and 1945. The dialogues were written by Jacques Prévert. This film is considered, by some, to be the best French film ever made. One of the stars of the film, Arletty, was arrested at the end of the war and accused of 'collaboration with the enemy' because of her relationship with a German officer (this was known as 'horizontal collaboration'). In the dock, she defended herself by saying to the judge 'my heart is French, but my ass is international'.

### *Enfants du marais. Les*

The title of a film by Jean Becker that came out in 1999 starring Jacques Gamblin, Jacques Villeret, Michel Serrault and André Dussolier that describes the simple joys of friendship and life in the country. 'Marais' means 'marsh' or 'marshland'.

See Chapter 12 Geographical names 'Le Marais'.

### Enfer. L'

'Hell.' Organized in 1844, this was the part of the Bibliothèque Nationale to which nobody could have access given that it contained all of the books considered to be 'contraires aux bonnes mœurs' (contrary to accepted standards of good behaviour). In 1969, the ban came to an end and such books could be consulted on request.

### *entreprise (ne) connaît pas la crise. Ma petite*

The title of one of the hits of the singer and composer Alain Bashung (1947–2009) ('My little firm is unaffected by the recession'). This song was later used in a TV ad for a light commercial vehicle produced by Citroën, the Berlingo.

### 'Entrez dans la danse'

See below 'Nous n'irons plus'.

### Épinal. Images d'

Originally, they were coloured prints on popular themes such as religion, military uniforms, battles, etc. and intended for the illiterate population. The printer Jean-Charles Pellerin (1756–1836) was the first to publish such prints at the time of the French Revolution. He lived in the town of Épinal. Today, the expression refers to a naïve and idealized vision of the world.

### Espion venu du froid. L'
⸨ * ⸩
The French title of the Jean le Carré novel about the Cold War, *The Spy Who Came in from the Cold.* The novel was published in 1963 and a film version came out in 1965 starring Richard Burton and Claire Bloom.

### Et moi et moi et moi
⸨ *** ⸩
These are the words and title of a hit song recorded by 'yé-yé' star Jacques Dutronc in 1967. The first line begins 'Sept cent millions de chinois (sic), et moi et moi et moi'. It could be punned upon with the word 'émoi' (emotion, excitement, turmoil, etc.). See above 'J'y pense'.

### Été meurtrier. L'
⸨ ** ⸩
This is the title of a Jean Becker film (1983) starring Isabelle Adjani and Alain Souchon. Frequently used in the press after the announcement of traffic deaths at the end of the summer vacation or any other violent events in July and August.

### éternel second. L'
⸨ * ⸩
Raymond Poulidor, former cyclist who arrived second on several occasions but never won the Tour de France. He never tested positive for drugs and is still alive and well, contrary to several of his more illustrious colleagues who died at a relatively young age.

### Eurodisney (Disneyland Paris)
⸨ * ⸩
The name of the European Disneyland theme park located 32 km east of Paris near the new town of Marne-la-Vallée in the *département* of Seine-et-Marne (77).

### Facteur sonne toujours deux fois. Le
⸨ ** ⸩
The French translation of the American film title *The Postman Always Rings Twice.* Originally a crime novel written by James Cain in 1934 but generally remembered as the 1981 film by Bob Rafelson starring Jack Nicholson and Jessica Lange.

### Facteur Cheval. Le
⸨ * ⸩
Joseph Ferdinand Cheval (1836–1924) was a French postman who spent 33 years of his life building his 'ideal palace' in his home town of Hauterives in the *département* of the Drôme (26) which is part of the Rhone-Alpes region. His work was classified as an historic monument in 1969. It is considered to be a masterpiece of naïve architecture.

### Fanfan la Tulipe

A cloak-and-dagger film made in 1952 starring Gérard Philipe and Gina Lollobrigida and set against the backdrop of seventeenth-century France. If it is frequently referred to today it is because it was one of Nicolas Sarkozy's favourite films when he was a child. The hero is pure and incorruptible.

### Fauchon

Located at 24–26, place de la Madeleine in the eighth *arrondissement* of Paris, Fauchon is the ultimate luxury catering and pastry shop in France.

### fève nf.

*Une fève* (broad bean) is always hidden in either the *galette des rois* or the *gâteau des rois* that are traditionally eaten on Twelfth Night (*La Nuit des Rois, l'Epiphanie*). The *galette* is a flaky pastry tart filled with marzipan, whereas the *gâteau* is a crown-shaped bun covered with glacé fruits and coarse sugar. The person who has the portion of the cake bearing the *fève* is declared king or queen and wears the cardboard crown for the day … and pays for the next cake!

### flagrants délires. Le Tribunal des

This was the title of a satirical radio programme, featuring Pierre Desproges (1939–88) that was a great success between 1980–3 on the radio station France Inter. The title is a pun on the legal term 'en flagrant délit' (*in flagrante delicto*). To be caught 'en flagrant délit' is to be caught during or immediately after the committing of a crime, i.e. 'red-handed'.

### flics. 22 v'là les

It is the tradition, on seeing policemen, to say '22 v'la les flics' ('22, here they come', or '22, there they are'). It has been suggested that this expression originated in the typesetting department of a printing works. The workers worked in absolute silence in order to avoid typographical errors known in French as 'coquilles'. If one forgets the 'q' in this word, the result is catastrophic. When the foreman was absent, the workers would begin to chatter, but as soon as he returned sb. would shout the warning '22'. It would appear that 22 = C+H+E+F, i.e. the third, eighth, fifth and sixth letters of the alphabet, respectively. If one adds the values, one finds 22.

### fluctuat nec mergitur

This is the motto of the city of Paris. See Chapter 13 'fluctuat'.

### Folie des grandeurs. La

*Delusions of Grandeur* was the title of a comic film directed by Gérard Oury that came out in 1971 and starred Louis de Funès (1914–83), Yves Montand and Alice Sapritch (1916–90). It was inspired by *Ruy Blas* by Victor Hugo and the action takes place against the backdrop of imperial Spain. One of the most famous lines from this cult film is 'Qu'est ce que je vais devenir? Je suis ministre, je ne sais rien faire!' 'What is to become of me? I am a minister. I'm no good at anything!'. See above 'bicyclette'.

## Fouquet's

`[ *** ]`

The 'bling-bling' restaurant *cum* bar situated on the Champs Élysées (99) in the eighth *arrondissement*. It was here on 6 May 2007 that Nicolas Sarkozy celebrated his victory in the presidential election along with his showbiz and industrialist friends. Many people, of all political colours, were shocked by this vulgar display of 'fric et frime'. This restaurant belongs to the Barrière group, the leader in France in the field of casinos. Recently, a law was passed legalizing on-line gambling.

## France profonde. La

`[ ** ]`

This is a term that refers to the heartland of France, i.e. the rural areas where traditions are tenacious and people are conservative in their outlook.

## 'furet du bois joli. Le'

`[ * ]`

This comes from a children's song *Il court, il court le furet*, which tells the story of a ferret that is rather like the Loch Ness Monster in that some people say they have seen it but nobody can prove its existence. In debates about unemployment, the old argument of 500,000 jobs that have not been filled is regularly brought out for airing but so far nobody knows where they are nor who was in charge of drawing up the related statistics. Some of the words of the song 'Il est passé par ici … il repassera par là' were used in an advertising campaign for a small parcel delivery service in the 1980s.

## Goncourt. Le

`[ ** ]`

'Le Goncourt' is the most prestigious French literary prize awarded by the Académie Goncourt set up by the will and testament of Edmond de Goncourt (1822–96). The Académie was officially founded in 1902 and the first prize was awarded in 1903. The prize is awarded in early November by the ten members of the Académie who meet regularly at the Parisian restaurant Le Drouant. The prize is awarded for the best prose work of imagination written in the French language.

## *Gorille vous salue bien. Le*

`[ ** ]`

'Gorille' is a slang term for a 'heavy' and is the last line of the film of the same name directed by Bernard Borderie in 1957 and starring Lino Ventura (1919–87), one of France's best-loved actors. The expression evokes an ironic goodbye. 'La potiche vous salue bien' was used in an article written by the former prison hospital doctor of La Santé, Véronique Vasseur, to describe her disgust at having been 'used' purely as a figurehead by Nicolas Sarkozy, and her disillusionment with politics in general.

## Grands Boulevards. Les

Although the Grands Boulevards are not uniquely the work of Haussmann (1809–91) under the Second Empire, it was during this period that the centre of gravity of the boulevards of Paris moved from the east to the west and thus to the more affluent quarters of the capital. The Grands Boulevards bring to mind the boulevard des Capucines (second *arrondissement*), the boulevard des Italiens (second and ninth), the boulevard Haussmann (eighth and ninth) and the boulevard de la Madeleine (first, eighth and ninth). It is in the area of the Grands Boulevards that the major department stores can be found.

### *Grande Vadrouille. La*

A cult Franco-British comedy, directed by Gérard Oury in 1966 which tells of the misfortunes and peregrinations of two Frenchmen in occupied France who, in spite of themselves, help three British RAF officers shot down over Paris during the Second World War. The film starred Bourvil, Louis de Funès and Terry-Thomas. This film held the French box office record (over 17 million cinema entries) until it was beaten by *Bienvenue chez les Ch'tis* in 2008.

### *Guerre des Boutons. La*

Another cult film made by Yves Robert in 1961 based on the novel by Louis Pergaud (1882–1915) published in 1913. It is a simple story of the 'war' between two gangs of young boys where the victims are robbed of their laces, belts and buttons. The most famous line in the film (not in the book) is the famous, ungrammatical 'si j'aurais su, j'aurais pas venu', which in correct French should read 'si j'avais su, je ne serais pas venu'.

## Harlequin. Éditions

Specializing in sentimental stories for a female readership, this collection is looked down upon by the literary community. However, one paperback in three sold is a Harlequin book. Over 130 million copies have been sold worldwide. The collection includes 700 titles and is fuelled by over one 1,000 writers, all Anglo-American.

## histoire d'un mec. C'est l'

'It's a joke about a bloke' This was the expression used by the comedian and actor Coluche (Michel Colucci 1944–86) when starting a joke. It became his catchphrase.

### *Homme qui aimait les femmes. L'*

This is the title of a film by François Truffaut (1932–84) that came out in 1977 and starred Charles Denner. The expression is frequently used to describe the sexual mores of French presidents, irrespective of their political colour.

### *Homme qui murmurait à l'oreille des chevaux. L'*     ` *** `
The French title of the film *The Horse Whisperer*, that came out in 1998, directed by and starring Robert Redford.

### *Hulot. Les Vacances de Monsieur*     ` *** `
This is the title of the classic prize-winning film of Jacques Tati that came out in 1953 and relates the holiday of a rather clumsy but well-meaning man who is always putting his foot in it. The name is frequently used and punned upon in relation to the ecology defence leader, Nicolas Hulot.

### 'Il se passe toujours quelque chose aux Galeries Lafayette!'     ` * `
This was the advertising slogan of the famous Parisian department store in the 1970s.

### 'Il y a longtemps que je t'aime'     ` * `
This is the first line of the chorus of a traditional song *À la claire fontaine*. 'Il y a longtemps que je t'aime Jamais je ne t'oublierai.' See above 'Chante rossignol'.

### instituteur nm.     ` ** `
Although the denotation of the word can be translated adequately by 'primary school teacher', the connotation is far richer in French. It must be understood that after the separation of church and state in France in 1905, the 'instituteur' was seen as a lay soldier in the service of the Republic, fighting against superstition and obscurantism. He is the hero in the works of Marcel Pagnol and 'les instituteurs' were collectively called the 'hussards noirs' of the Republic. See Chapter 6 'hussards noirs'.

### irréductibles. Un village peuplé d'     ` * `
'One small village of indomitable Gauls still holds out against the Roman invaders'. These famous words introduce each story in the comic strip series of *Astérix le Gaulois*, created in 1959 by René Goscinny (story) and Albert Uderzo (drawings).

### Jamais sans ma ...     ` * `
'Never, without my ... '. These words echo the title of a book, *Not Without My Daughter*, published in 1986 and of the film version made in 1991. It is the true story of an American woman, Betty Mahmoody, who married an Iranian doctor practising in the USA. They had a daughter. One day, the woman visited Tehran with her daughter during the holidays and found herself the prisoner of her fundamentalist husband and his family. It is the story of her fight to regain her liberty and that of her daughter.

### 'Je l'aurai un jour, je l'aurai'

This is the catchphrase used by a disgruntled client in *Palace*, a French TV comedy series, in which the director answers the criticism of the client with an absurd excuse. The scene ends with the disgruntled client vowing 'I'll get him one day, I'll get him'. The two actors playing the same scene were used by the mutual insurance company MAAF in one of their most successful advertising campaigns until 2007. The advertising sketch continues today with different actors. The sketches originally featured the late Philippe Khorsand (1948–2008) and Marcel Philippot, a well-known vaudeville actor.

### *Je t'aime, moi non plus*

This rather contradictory and ungrammatical sentence is the title of a famous song by Serge Gainsbourg sung as a duo with Jane Birkin in 1969. The song was quite 'hot' for the time in that it was a description of their love-making. Today, the words refer to a love–hate relationship and stigmatizes the hypocrisy of sentiments. It is often used to describe the rivalry between members of the same political party.

### 'Je vous parle d'un temps que les moins de vingt ans ... '

When elderly people speak about the past to a young person, it is not rare for them to prefix their remarks with these words, which are the lyrics of a song by Charles Aznavour *La Bohème* (1966), which begins with the words 'Je vous parle d'un temps que les moins de vingt ans ne peuvent pas connaître'. ('I'm speaking to you about a time that the under-twenties can have no knowledge of.')

### Jeu de main, jeu de vilain!

When children play roughly together, this is the typical warning made by an adult, equivalent to the English 'This is going to end in tears'.

### 'joli. Ah, c'est pas'

From a song entitled *Grand-Père* by Georges Brassens (1921–81) which tells the story of the funeral of a grandfather who has limited financial means. The line, referring to a kick up the backside that the priest received, goes 'C'est depuis ce temps-là, que le bon apôtre, ah, c'est pas joli, ah, c'est pas poli, a une fesse qui dit "merde" à l'autre'. ('It is since that day that the good apostle has had one buttock that says "shit" to the other'.) In French, when one has 'one eye that says "shit" to the other' it means that one is cross-eyed. Consequently, one assumes from the lyrics of this song that the priest had his backside kicked out of joint by a member of grandfather's family because he didn't give grandfather a decent burial.

### 'jolie fleur dans une peau de vache. Une'

George Brassens again. From a song entitled *Une Jolie Fleur*. 'Une jolie fleur dans une peau de vache, une jolie vache déguisée en fleur, qui fait la belle et

21

qui vous attache puis qui vous mène par le bout du cœur'. ('A pretty flower, dressed in cowhide (peau de vache is also a 'bastard' or a 'bitch'), a pretty cow dressed as a flower, she gently seduces you and ties you up and leads you by the end of your heart'.) See above 'Copains d'abord'.

### 'joujou extra. Un'
See above 'Crac'.

### 'J'y pense et puis j'oublie'
A song title by the late Claude François, and lyrics of a song by Jacques Dutronc. See above '*Et moi et moi et moi*' and 'Crac'.

### 'lave plus blanc. X'
'X washes whiter.' This is the French translation of the advertising slogan for Persil, a brand of washing powder produced by the Anglo-Dutch company Unilever.

### loi Carrez. La
The Carrez law, 23 May 1997, makes it an obligation for the vendor of a flat, in a condominium, to declare the exact surface area of the property concerned. This has to be certified by a surveyor. The law takes its name from Gilles Carrez, the UMP *député* who proposed this legislation.

### *long fleuve tranquille. La Vie est un*
The title of a film by Etienne Chatiliez that is both a comedy and social satire, which came out in 1988. It is a story in which a nurse on duty in a maternity ward (in a spirit of revenge against her lover, the obstetrician of the hospital) switches the identity bracelets of two newborn babies. One comes from an extremely wealthy, Catholic family (the Le Quesnoy family), the other from a poor and semi-criminal one (the Groseille family). Each family unknowingly brings up the child of the other. Thirteen years after the event, the nurse announces the news in an anonymous letter when she realizes (on the death of her lover's wife) that he will never marry her. That's when the fun begins!

### Lucky Luke ***
Lucky Luke is a comic strip and cartoon character created in 1946 by the Belgian, Maurice de Bévère (1923–2001), whose pen name was Morris. Lucky Luke is a 'poor lonesome cowboy' accompanied by his dog Rantanplan and his faithful steed Jolly Jumper. His sworn enemies are the Dalton brothers. He has given the French language an immortal expression 'Il tire plus vite que son ombre' ('He is so quick on the draw that he beats his own shadow') generally translated by 'the fastest draw in the West'. Each story ends with Lucky Luke riding off into the sunset. To conform to anti-smoking

legislation in France, the cigarette hanging from his lips has been replaced by a stalk of grass.

### 'lutte finale. C'est la'

This is the first line of the chorus of the 'Internationale' which is the anthem of the international socialist movement. It was originally a poem written by Eugène Pottier (1816–87) during the bloody weeks of the Commune in 1871. The music was later composed by a Belgian, Pierre De Geyter (1848–1932). See above 'Debout, les damnés de la terre'.

### Madame Michou

This is a pejorative term designating the very basic, middle-aged, unsophisticated French woman in the street. It was a term of abuse used by Claude Allègre referring to Ségolène Royal. See Chapter 9.

### mai. Le premier

May 1 is Labour Day in France. See below 'muguet'.

### 'Maille qui m'aille. Il n'y a que'

Maille is a famous trademark of mustard, mayonnaise and pickled gherkins, and the advertising slogan is a play on the conjugation of the verb 'aller' in the third person singular, in the subjunctive mood, 'aille'. 'Maille is the only one that suits me.'

### marièrent et eurent beaucoup d'enfants. Ils se

This is the classic ending to a French fairy tale. In English 'They lived happily ever after' whereas in the French version, worried as the French always have been about negative demographic trends, 'They got married and had lots of children'.

### 'Margot dégrafait son corsage. Quand'

'When Margot unbuttoned her blouse to breastfeed her little cat' These are words from a song by Georges Brassens that tells the story of a shepherdess who breast-feeds an orphan kitten! See above '*Copains d'abord. Les*' and '*jolie fleur dans une peau de vache. Une*'.

### Mélodie du bonheur. La

The French translation of the American film title, *The Sound of Music*, the Robert Wise film of 1965 that was showered with nominations and film awards.

### Même pas mal!
'It didn't even hurt.' The typical schoolboy reply to an agressor in the playground after receiving a punch.

## Mère Denis. La                                                    [ * ]

Jeanne Marie Le Calvé (1893–1989) called 'la Mère Denis' was one of the most emblematic characters appearing in French advertising during the 1970s. She was the star of an ad for the washing machine company Vedette. With her old washer-woman style and country accent she was known by everyone. Her advertising text has now become a cult phrase in French: 'Ch'est bahn vrai cha' ('c'est bien vrai, ça', 'that's absolutely true').

### Mère Michel. La                                                   [ * ]

'C'est la Mère Michel qui a perdu son chat.' This is one of the most well-known French nursery rhymes telling the story of Old Mother Michel who has lost her cat. Michèle Alliot Marie is sometimes presented as 'l'amère Michèle' (bitter Michèle).

## midinettes. Les                                                    [ * ]

This word refers to the young female workers in the Paris dressmaking industry, so called because many of them originally came from the Midi, i.e. the south of France. It can be pejorative. If a girl has the tastes of a 'midinette' it implies that she is immature and simple-minded.

## Mille tonnerres/sabords                                            [ * ]

'Ten thousand thundering typhoons' or any of the other insults cum exclamatory remarks made by Captain Haddock in the comic strip series *The Adventures of Tintin*, created by the Belgian artist and story-teller Hergé (pen name of Georges Remi 1907–83). See above 'capitaine Haddock'.

## Milou                                                              [ * ]

See below 'Tintin'.

### minuit Dr Schweitzer. Il est                                      [ ** ]

This was the title of a French play (1950) by Gilbert Cesbron, later made into a film by André Haguet (1952) starring Pierre Fresnay and Jeanne Moreau and telling the story of Albert Schweitzer. In this play, the nurse says 'It's midnight, Dr Schweitzer, it's time for you to go to bed'. Dr Schweitzer is supposed to have replied 'At this time, the sun is rising in Alsace, it is Angelus'. The real Dr Schweitzer, on learning this, levelled some ironic criticism against the French who are obsessed with theory at the expense of reality. He retorted: 'If Cesbron had even bothered to come here before writing his play, he would have realized that the Gabon and Guns-bach are on the same international dateline.' From another angle, Louis Schweitzer is a former CEO of the car company Renault and former president of the Halde. See Chapter 14 'Halde'.

24

## Môme. La

The was the nickname of Edith Piaf (1915–63) the music hall artiste. She was born Edith Giovanna Gassion and took the nickname 'Piaf' which is French for 'sparrow', a typically Parisian bird.

## *Mon truc en plumes*

This is the title of a song sung by Zizi Jeanmaire (Renée Marcelle) in 1961. A classical dancer by training, she was in fact famous for being a music hall dancer, singer and chorus-girl captain. 'Truc' is a 'whatsit', a 'widgit', and the ambiguity leaves a lot of room for double entendre. 'Zizi' is the children's word for a penis.

## Monsieur est trop bon.

A hackneyed phrase from the theatre. It is the servant's stereotypical (and rather fawning) reply to a master who has shown him a certain degree of generosity.

## Monsieur Loyal

The ringmaster.

## Monsieur Propre

A household cleaning product produced by Proctor & Gamble, an American multinational company. The advert features a muscular and bald genie used in US adverts since 1958. Widely known in France since its launch in 1972, the name is sometimes used to describe an honest magistrate fighting organized crime.

## muguet. Le

Lily of the valley is a flower that one gives to one's friends and family on 1 May as a charm to bring good luck. In France, and only on 1 May, anybody is allowed to sell lily of the valley in the streets without a licence. See above 'mai. Le premier'.

## 'My tailor is rich'

This sentence is known by every Frenchman. They are the very first words of the original 'Assimil' self-tuition language course in English *l'Anglais sans peine* ('English without tears') that first appeared in 1929. The complete sentence is 'My tailor is rich but my English is poor'.

## Ni putes, ni soumises                                                          ***

The translation of this movement 'neither whore nor submissive' contains a pun; 'une fille soumise' may be interpreted as a registered prostitute. It is the name of the French feminist movement founded by Fadela Amara in 2003 with the objective of fighting all forms of violence towards women: rape, forced marriage, conjugal violence, pressure to give up studying, pressure to wear the Islamic veil, etc.

### Noir c'est noir        ( * )

French adaptation of the song *Black is black* recorded by the Spanish group Los Bravos in 1966 that went to no. 2 in the UK charts, topping 1 million in worldwide sales. The French version was recorded by Johnny Hallyday in the same year.

### Non, je ne regrette rien       ( ** )

Title of one of Piaf's most famous successes. This song came out in 1960. See above 'Môme'.

### Nous n'irons plus au bois ...      ( *** )

This is the title and first line of a children's song. The original text reads: 'Nous n'irons plus au bois, les lauriers sont coupés, la belle que voilà ira les ramasser. Entrez dans la danse, voyez comme on danse, sautez, dansez, embrassez qui vous voudrez'. It is unlikely that the people who sing this song are aware of its origin. This text refers to the sexual practices prevalent at the court of Versailles of Louis XIV. The thousands of workers employed to build the château brought in their wake hordes of prostitutes. It was said that the forest of Versailles was like an open-air brothel with as many prostitutes as there were trees. Their activity was restricted by royal order but they simply took to exercising their trade in special houses. Braids of laurel were a common feature on the walls of such buildings in the grounds of Versailles. Louis XIV, who was alarmed at the spread of venereal disease, had these establishments closed, hence the words of the song!

### nouveau est arrivé. Le 'X'      ( ** )

'The new "x" has arrived.' This is a reference to the publicity surrounding the first sale of the young red wine, Beaujolais nouveau, which traditionally takes place on the third Thursday in November. The Beaujolais vineyards lie north of Lyons.

### Nouvelle Vague nf         ( * )

'New wave.' A short-lived movement in the French cinema world (late 1950s and early 1960s). The word was first used in an article by Françoise Giroud in *L'Express* in 1957. The names that come to mind in relation to this movement include François Truffaut, Jean-Luc Godard, Claude Chabrol, Roger Vadim and Claude Berri.

### Obélix            ( * )

He is the fictional cartoon character created in 1961 by Goscinny and Uderzo in the series called *Astérix le Gaulois*. Given that Obélix had fallen into the cauldron of magic potion as a child, he is never allowed a supplementary dose because he has had enough to last him a lifetime. He is always hungry and ready for a fight.

### On achève bien les chevaux
`***`

The French title of the Sydney Pollack film *They Shoot Horses, Don't They?* which came out in 1970 and starred Jane Fonda and Susannah York.

### On a gagné!
`**`

This is the football supporters' ritual chant following the victory of their team.

### 'On est foutu, on mange trop'
`*`

'We're done for, we're overeating.' Words of a satirical song entitled *Papa Mambo* about obesity, composed and recorded by Alain Souchon in 1978. See above *Allô maman, bobo* and 'comme on nous parle'.

### On ira tous au paradis
`*`

'We will all go to heaven.' The title of a famous song (1972) written and sung by the French composer and singer Michel Polnareff that provoked quite a scandal in the early 1970s by suggesting that even prostitutes would have their place in paradise.

### On nous cache tout on (ne) nous dit rien
`**`

This is the typical paranoid refrain indicating the man in the street's distrust of the government, since e.g. the cover-up of the Tchernobyl accident during which the French authorities maintained that France had not been contaminated ... the radioactive clouds having either stopped at the French frontier or bypassed the country.

### Paname
`*`

This is the affectionate slang term used by Parisians to refer to Paris. It is said to come from the fashion of wearing the Panama hat by the workers of Paris in the early days of the twentieth century.

### pantoufle nf., pantoufler vi., pantouflard nm., pantouflage nm.
`***`

'Pantouflage' is a scheme whereby senior civil servants can go into the private sector, at a much higher salary, while retaining the security of their old job position, to which they can return whenever they want.

### 'Parce que tu le vaux bien'
`***`

'Because you're worth it.' This is the advertising slogan of l'Oréal, the cosmetic products company. Originally, 'parce que je le vaux bien'.

## pari de Pascal. Le

⎡ * ⎤

Briefly put, 'Pascal's wager' says that one had better say that one believes in God, since if God exists, one wins, and if God doesn't exist then one has lost nothing. Hence the advantage in believing.

## Parigot tête de veau

⎡ ** ⎤

There has always been long-standing contempt between Parisians and people from the provinces. This insult against Parisians can be heard in the provinces all over France. 'Parigot' is slang for Parisian while 'tête de veau' is literally 'calf's head' and is one of the most common of the famous French dishes of offal.

## *Paris brûle-t-il?*

⎡ * ⎤

This is the title of a René Clément film that was released in 1966. It was based on the book by Larry Collins and Dominique Lapierre that was published in 1964. It tells the story of the last days of the German occupation of Paris, particularly the 25 August 1944. The title is the question that Hitler is supposed to have asked General Dietrich von Choltitz. The French capital, its bridges and monuments, had been mined by the German army with the intention of blowing up the city on evacuation. General von Choltitz refused to obey the order to destroy the city.

## Passe ton bac d'abord!

⎡ ** ⎤

'Pass your high school exams first.' This is the traditional advice or order of parents to their children, particularly in the case where the children have plans for their future which differ from those of their parents.

## *Pépé le Moko*

⎡ * ⎤

This is the title of a French cinema classic by Julien Duvivier starring Jean Gabin, that came out in 1937. It tells the story of a gangster who has taken refuge in the Kasbah.

## Père Fouettard. Le

⎡ *** ⎤

The term 'bogeyman' is as close as we can come to a translation of this term which is very well known in north-eastern France, Holland and Germany. On St Nicolas' Day, 6 December, 'Père Fouettard' accompanies St Nicolas on his rounds. St Nicolas distributes gifts to well-behaved children, whereas 'Le Père Fouettard' whips the children who have been naughty. He is always dressed in black, with horns and a devil's tail.

## Perfide Albion

⎡ *** ⎤

'Perfidious Albion.' This is an eighteenth-century expression referring to England's habitual treachery in its dealings with other countries in general, and France in particular. 'Albion' (Celtic in origin) is said to be the name the

Roman soldiers gave England on approaching the south coast and on seeing the chalky White Cliffs of Dover for the first time, *albus* being Latin for 'white'.

### Petit Papa Noël

Title and opening line of the chorus of a Christmas song first recorded in 1946 by Tino Rossi (1907–83). This is as much of a classic at Christmas time in France as 'White Christmas' by Bing Crosby is in England and the USA.

### Petit Nicolas

A character in the children's story created in 1959 by René Goscinny (1926–77) and illustrated by Jean-Jacques Sempé. It tells the story of a child brought up in an urban environment with all of the classic aspects of a child's life, friendship at school, first love, etc. Inevitably this has become the nickname of President Sarkozy given his small stature and the nickname given to him by Bernadette Chirac.

### p'tit quinquin. Le

A 'quinquin' is a small child in 'ch'ti'. It is the name of a lullaby written in 1853 by Alexandre Desrousseaux. 'Dors min p'tit quinquin, Min p'tit pouchin, Min gros rogin! Tu m'fras du chagrin Si te n'dors point j'qu'à d'main'. ('Sleep my little one, my little chick, my big grape, I shall be upset if you don't sleep until tomorrow.') The Ch'tis are the inhabitants of the *départements* of the Nord (59) and the Pas-de-Calais (62).

### petit rapporteur. Le

A 'telltale'. The title of a satirical television programme that was broadcast between 1975 and 1976 and launched by Jacques Martin, featuring Daniel Prévost, Pierre Desproges, Pierre Bonte, Piem and Stéphane Collaro. This programme was a pioneer in the area of political satire on French television.

### petits chanteurs de la croix de bois. Les

The name of a young boys' choir founded in 1907. Today, it is not only a choir but a boarding school providing education from the primary up to the mid-secondary level. The choir is internationally famous and gives concerts all over the world.

### Petits meurtres entre amis

This is the French title of the British film *Shallow Grave*, a crime thriller directed by Danny Boyle that came out in 1995. It is frequently used to refer to the political infighting among politicians of the same party.

### 'petits trous, des petits trous. Des'

Words from the song by Serge Gainsbourg *Le Poinçonneur des Lilas* which underlines the soul-destroying job of the ticket inspector punching holes into metro tickets. See above 'Je t'aime, moi non plus'. See below 'Poinçonneur des Lilas. Le'.

### 'pétrole, mais on a des idées. En France, on n'a pas de'

'In France, we don't have any oil, but we do have ideas.' Slogan first used in a TV publicity campaign in the wake of the first oil crisis in 1974.

### Pieds Nickelés. Les

Originally the name of the three characters (Croquignol, Filochard and Ribouldingue) in a comic strip series created by Louis Forton and first published in 1908. They are small-time swindlers and lazy good-for-nothings who are not very intelligent.

### plombier. C'est le

This is the punch line of one of the most famous sketches of the French comic Fernand Raynaud (1926–73). A plumber comes to visit a client. He knocks at the door but the client is absent. However, from within, the client's parrot asks 'Who is it? to which the plumber replies 'It's the plumber'. Everytime the plumber says 'It's the plumber', the parrot repeats the question 'Who is it?' Finally, the plumber has a heart attack and collapses on the staircase. Two elderly ladies come down the stairs and see the dead body. One asks the other 'Who is it?' The parrot in the flat cries out 'It's the plumber'. The term 'plombier' has not been a neutral term since the French secret service (DST) tried to bug the premises of *Le Canard Enchaîné* in 1973. This constituted a Watergate-type scandal, and is often referred to in the press. 'Un plombier' now refers to a secret agent who bugs a room. See also 'Asnières', 'Pourquoi tu tousses, Tonton?', and 'Va là bas voir si j'y suis'.

### 'poids des mots, le choc des photos. Le'

The slogan of the popular news magazine *Paris Match*: 'the weight of the words, the shock of the photos'.

### *Poil de Carotte*

This is the name of the character of the autobiographical novel written by Jules Renard (1864–1910) that was published in 1894. It tells the tale of the unloved, ginger-headed boy, the victim of parental humiliation and indifference.

### *poinçonneur des Lilas. Le*

This is the title of a famous song by Serge Gainsbourg about the idiotic job of a *métro* ticket inspector punching holes into the then card-board tickets at the metro station La Porte des Lilas, in the north-east of Paris.

### 'positive, avec Carrefour. Je'
*

'With Carrefour, I positivize.' This was the highly successful advertising slogan launched by the Carrefour supermarket chain in 1988, coining the verb 'positiver'.

### *poupée qui fait 'non'. La*
*

Title and words from a song by Michel Polnareff, one of the most controversial figures of the French pop scene. The song was a great success in 1966. See above *On ira tous au paradis*.

### 'Pourquoi faire simple quand on peut faire compliqué?'
***

'Why choose an easy solution, when there is a more complicated one?' One of the mottos of the cartoon characters 'Les Shadoks'. (The French are incorrigible Shadoks). See below 'Shadoks'.

### 'Pourquoi tu tousses Tonton?'
***

One of the most famous lines in a sketch by the French comedian Fernand Raynaud. The simple-minded nephew is stopped at the customs desk and has to explain the presence of 'white powder' found in his suitcase. He phones his mafioso uncle and every time he mentions the word 'powder', his uncle coughs to cover up his embarassment. Invariably, when sb. coughs in France, it is followed by the question 'Pourquoi tu tousses?' See above 'Asnières', 'Ça eût payé' and 'plombier. C'est le'.

### *Prends l'oseille et tire-toi*
***

This is the French translation of the comedy *Take the Money and Run* co-written by, directed by and starring Woody Allen. The film was released in 1969. 'Oseille' is slang meaning 'loot', 'dough', 'dosh', etc.

### Professeur Tournesol
**

He is one of the main characters in Hergé's *Adventures of Tintin*. He is the absent-minded professor.

### Prolonger le métro jusqu'à la mer
*

Eternal candidate at presidential elections under the Third Republic, the comedian Ferdinand Lop (1891–1974) suggested extending the métro as far as the sea, as an election promise.

### *Quai des Brumes*
**

See below 'T'as de beaux yeux, tu sais!'

### 'Qu'est-ce qu'elle a, ma gueule?'
*

'What's wrong with my gob?' Words of a song by Johnny Hallyday recorded in 1980, called *Ma gueule*.

## quille! C'est la ⟨ * ⟩
This was the expression that used to be shouted out by newly demobilized soldiers after their national service. 'La quille' is a skittle but was used as a synonym for 'demob'. National service was abolished in France under Jacques Chirac in 1996.

## 'rate qui se dilate. J'ai la' ⟨ ** ⟩
These are the words of a music hall song *Je ne suis pas bien portant* which is one of the classics of French comedy that was a great success in 1932. It was sung by the comic singer Gaston Ouvrard (1890–1981). The music is by Géo Koger and the lyrics by Vincent Scotto. It relates the health problems of a newly conscripted soldier. Each part of the body is mentioned and rhymes with a particular complaint. 'J'ai la rate qui se dilate, j'ai le foie qui n'est pas droit', etc. ('My spleen is swollen, my liver is not straight', etc.)

## Ravi. Lou ⟨ ** ⟩
This is the Provençal term for 'the village idiot'. He is depicted at the Christmas crèche as the simple-minded boy whose arms are always raised in admiration of the infant Jesus. See Chapter 9 'Gaudin, Jean Claude'.

## *Razzia sur la chnouf* ⟨ * ⟩
This is the title of a film by Henri Decoin that came out in 1955 and dealing with drug peddling in the Parisian underworld. It starred Jean Gabin (1904–76) and Lino Ventura (1919–87). 'Chnouf' is slang for 'junk' in the narcotics meaning of the term.

## Rantanplan ⟨ * ⟩
See 'Lucky Luke'

## *Recherche Susan désespérément* ⟨ * ⟩
The French translation of the American film title, *Desperately Seeking Susan*, directed by Susan Seidelman, that was released in 1985.

## *Repos du guerrier. Le (sexual relaxation)* ⟨ ** ⟩
A film by Roger Vadim made in 1958 and part of the French 'new wave' movement starring Brigitte Bardot and Robert Hossein.

## République-Bastille ⟨ ** ⟩
This is the route frequently followed by demonstrators when there is a large public demonstration, e.g. against the government. Place de la République is in the third *arrondissement* while Place de la Bastille is in the fourth.

## *Rififi à Paname. Du* ⟨ ** ⟩
'Aggro in Paris.' A gangster film by Denys de la Patellière made in 1965, starring Jean Gabin. One of the French cinema classics. See above 'Paname'.

### Salut l'artiste                                                    `**`
The title of a film by Yves Robert (1973) now frequently used to salute the passing away of a cinema or theatre star.

### Salut les copains                                                 `***`
The title of a pop music radio programme on Europe 1 in the yé-yé period and then a teenage newspaper created in 1962.

### Sapeur Camember. Le                                               `***`
The pranks of 'le Sapeur Camember' were one of the first examples of French comic strips (1896) written by George Colomb alias 'Christophe' (1856–1945). Camember is a simple-minded soldier who tries to speak very good French but usually ends up by uttering absurdities. He belongs to the corps of 'génie militaire' that can be translated either by 'military engineering' or more ironically by 'military genius'.

### sardine qui boucha le Vieux Port. La                              `**`
This expression refers to the tendency of the Marseillais to exaggerate. In fact, it is a 'true' story. In 1779, the English released some French prisoners (during the Anglo-French conflict in India) who were then put on board a French frigate 'Sartine'. The ship was named after a minister of the navy under Louis XVI. The ship was sailing under a flag of truce but for some unknown reason, it was attacked by the English navy off Cape St Vincent, off the coast of Portugal. Badly damaged, the ship succeeded in reaching the port of Marseilles but could not reach a normal mooring position. It was stranded at the entrance to the port. Its size effectively blocked maritime traffic for a few days. The locals seized upon this story and it has since become the 'sardine' that blocked the port of Marseilles.

### 'Sautez, dansez, embrassez qui vous voudrez'                      `*`
Words accompanying a traditional children's 'rondo'. 'Jump, dance, and kiss whom you will.' This comes from the song 'Nous n'irons plus aux bois'. See above 'Nous n'irons'.

### schmilblick. Faire avancer le                                     `**`
This expression means 'to help move things forward'. It was the name of a famous TV game in which contestants had to make guesses about a mystery object.

### Sea, sex and sun                                                   `*`
Title of a song by Serge Gainsbourg (1928–91) recorded in 1978. It is used today to give a humorously succinct description of a successful holiday, according to the criteria of some people. See above 'besoin de personne en Harley-Davidson. Je n'ai', 'Je t'aime, moi non plus' and 'Poinçonneur des Lilas. Le'.

### Sévère mais juste     [ * ]

A famous expression used to describe one's old teacher who was 'hard but fair'. It is also one of the punchlines of a sketch by Raymond Devos, the famous Belgian comedian (1922–2006).

### Shadoks     [ *** ]

'The Shadoks' is the name given to the TV cartoon characters created by Jacques Rouxel (1931–2004). They are plump birds with long legs and very small wings whose motto is 'Why choose an easy solution, when there is a more complicated one?' The programme of three-minute episodes went on the air on French TV between 1968 and 1973.

### Si tu vas à Rio     [ * ]

Title and first line of a song written in 1958 by the Turkish tenor Dario Moreno (1921–68) who was a star of light opera.

### Si Versailles m'était conté     [ ** ]

A Franco-Italian film written and directed by Sacha Guitry that came out in 1954 and told the fabulous story of Versailles and the characters associated with it.

### 'sinon rien. Un X'     [ *** ]

The famous advertising slogan for the aniseed-based apéritif 'Ricard'. The slogan was based on the reply to the question 'What will you have?' The answer being 'A Ricard, if not, nothing'. The advertising campaign was launched in 1984 by the agency Young and Rubicam.

### Sois belle et tais-toi     [ ** ]

'Be beautiful and keep quiet.' The title and lyrics of a song by Serge Gainsbourg, the French composer and singer. See above *'besoin de personne en Harley-Davidson. Je n'ai'*, *'Je t'aime, moi non plus'*, *'Sea, sex and sun'* and *'Poinçonneur des Lilas. Le'*. It is also the title of a film by Marc Allégret that came out in 1958.

### souris dansent. Les     [ * ]

'Quand le chat n'est pas là, les souris dansent.' The French equivalent of 'when the cat's away, the mice will play'.

### souris verte. La     [ ** ]

This is the title of a nursery rhyme in which 'la souris verte' is a well-known character. The nursery rhyme begins 'La souris verte, qui courait dans l'herbe'. It can be punned upon in texts dealing with the ecologist or 'green' movement.

### Sous vos applaudissements Mesdames Messieurs!     [ * ]

'With a warm round of applause, ladies and gentlemen.' The typical phrase of a compère at the end of an artiste's act.

### Souvenirs, souvenirs          `[ * ]`
'Memories, memories.' The first recording success of Johnny Hallyday (1960) at the beginning of what was later to be called the 'yé-yé' period.

### sparadrap du Capitaine Haddock. Le     `[ *** ]`
A reference to the character in the comic strip album by Hergé, *The Adventures of Tintin*. Sparadrap is an adhesive medical dressing, for small cuts and abrasions which is difficult to get rid of because it sticks to the fingers. This is a reference to an episode in *L'Affaire Tournesol* in which Captain Haddock becomes more and more short-tempered given the impossible task of getting rid of the sticky plaster. Today, it refers to any embarassing affair that will just not go away.

### St Cyrien             `[ * ]`
Either an inhabitant of St Cyr (in the *département* of the Yvelines [78]) or a student or former student of the prestigious military academy *cum* high school located a few km west of Versailles, some 20 km from the heart of Paris. It used to house the officer training school (1804–1940) but this was relocated to Coëtquidan in Brittany in 1945.

### sulpicien(ne) adj           `[ * ]`
Today, this term is generally reserved to describe the religious art shops and their wares around the church of St Sulpice in the sixth *arrondissement* of Paris. It generally implies objects of bad taste.

### Sur le pont d'Avignon, on y danse ...     `[ * ]`
The title and first words of a well-known children's song about the bridge of Avignon.

### Tanguy. Le Syndrome         `[ ** ]`
From the film *Tanguy* by Etienne Chatiliez made in 2001 and dealing with the problem posed by a brilliant lecturer who finds that he is better off in all respects staying with the parents he adores rather than facing the world standing on his own two feet. The film deals with his parents' attempts to get him to leave. With the housing crisis in France, unemployment and divorce, many young people are being forced to return to live with their parents.

### 't'ar ta gueule à la récré'         `[ * ]`
'T'ar' is a contracted form of 'tu vas voir' while 'gueule' is the slang term for 'gob' or 'mug'. The complete expression is a schoolboy threat made to a classmate and referring to injury to the face (gob) that the classmate is going to suffer come playtime. The words come from the song by Alain Souchon *J'ai dix ans* (1974). Sometimes written as 'gare ta gueule'. See above, 'Allô maman, bobo', 'comme on nous parle', and 'On est foutu'.

### 'T'as de beaux yeaux, tu sais'                    ***

Immortal words from the film by Marcel Carné in 1938 *Quai des Brumes*, based on a novel by Pierre Mac Orlan *Le Quai des Brumes* published in 1927. This phrase remains one of the most famous lines in the history of French cinema spoken by Jean Gabin to Michèle Morgan.

### Tati                    *

A store originally located in the boulevard Barbès in the poor eighteenth *arrondissement* of Paris and selling cheap fabrics and clothes. There are now several branches elsewhere.

### Téléphone pleure. Le                    *

This is the title of one of the greatest hits of the late Claude François (1939–78) that topped the charts in 1974. Recently used in the context of the wave of suicides which has shaken the company Orange, the French telephone operator. Between January 2008 and March 2010, 40 employees committed suicide, most of them at their place of work.

### Temps des cerises. Le                    **

Although this song was written by Jean-Baptiste Clément in 1866, (consequently, well before the French defeat at Sedan in the Franco-Prussian War of 1870) it has since become the song intimately associated with the 'Commune,' the insurrection of Paris that was savagely crushed by the army during the bloody week of 22–28 May 1871. See Chapter 6 'Commune' and 'Sedan'.

### tendresse, bordel! Et la                    **

'What about tenderness, for Christ's sake!' This was the title of a comedy film that came out in 1979 directed by Patrick Schulmann. This is frequently used in the press, the word 'tendresse' being replaced by another word according to the context.

### tentation de Venise. La                    *

The temptation of Venice is a dream that each of us is said to have. It is by no means an impossible pipe dream, but for various reasons we refuse to make the dream turn into reality. The temptation comes when things are going badly. It was the title of a book written in 1993 by the former prime minister Alain Juppé after he had been found guilty of corruption by the French courts and after receiving a suspended 14-month prison sentence and one year's ineligibility in politics. He is now minister of defence.

### tête et les jambes. La                    *

The head represents the intellectual capacity, while the legs represent physical skill. This was the name of a TV game programme during which two contestants took part, one answering questions on a given subject, the other accomplishing some physical feat to 'bail out' the 'head' for giving a wrong answer. The programme ran for over twenty years, from 1960 to 1980.

### 'tétons. Elle avait des tout petits'

[ * ]

'Valentina had very little nipples.' Lyrics from the song *Valentina* (1925) made famous by the music hall star Maurice Chevalier (1888–1972). (The British mind can only boggle at the things the French write songs about!)

### Tintin

[ *** ]

The name of the comic strip character created by Hergé in 1929 in the series entitled *The Adventures of Tintin and Milou*. Other characters include Captain Haddock, Professor Tournesol and the detective duo Dupont and Dupond. NB: 'tintin' is also an exclamatory term meaning 'nothing doing' or 'no way'. 'Faire tintin' means 'to go without'.

### tirez pas sur le pianiste. Ne

[ * ]

'Don't shoot the pianist.' This can be a request for indulgence towards sb. who is doing his/her best, or a request not to accuse the fall guy, but to accuse the real guilty party instead. In his book *Impressions of America*, Oscar Wilde (1854–1900) reports having seen a sign in a saloon in the town of Leadville that read 'Don't shoot the pianist. He is doing his best'. ('Merci de ne pas tirer sur le pianiste. Il fait de son mieux'.)

### tombé dedans quand il était petit. Il est

[ * ]

See above 'Obélix'.

### 'Tonnerre de Brest!'

[ * ]

One of the exclamations of Captain Haddock in the series of Tintin, created by Hergé. See above 'sparadrap', 'Professeur Tournesol' and 'Tintin'.

### Tontons Flingueurs. Les

[ *** ]

This is the title of another cult film, made by George Lautner in 1963 and starring Bernard Blier (1916–89), Lino Ventura (1919–87) and Francis Blanche (1921–74). This film contains many of the most famous lines in French cinema history. 'Tonton' is the child's word for uncle (nunky) and a 'flingueur' is 'a contract killer' or 'hit man'. In this film, two rival gangs do their best to eliminate each other. The verb 'flinguer' is frequently used in French politics in the figurative sense of the term, i.e. 'to shoot sb. down in flames'. See above *'Cave se rebiffe. Le'*.

### 'Touche pas à mon pote'

[ *** ]

'Don't touch my pal.' This is the slogan of 'SOS Racisme' an association founded in 1984 by Julien Dray and Harlem Désir which fights all forms of racism. The logo of the association is the yellow palm of a hand with these words written on it.

### Touchez pas au grisbi $\qquad$ ***
A film by Jacques Becker starring Jean Gabin and Lino Ventura that came out in 1972. 'Grisbi' is the slang term for money, i.e. loot, dosh, dough. See above '*Cave se rebiffe. Le*' and '*Tontons Flingueurs*'. The title should read *Ne touchez pas* ....

### Toute ressemblance ... $\qquad$ **
'Toute ressemblance avec des personnes existant ou ayant existé est purement fortuite.' ('Any resemblance to any person living or dead is purely accidental.') This is the standard legal disclaimer that is mentioned in a film of fiction.

### Toujours plus $\qquad$ **
'Never enough.' The title of a book written by the journalist and writer François de Closets in 1984 which highlights what is wrong with France, the French and French politicians.

### Tout le monde il est beau, tout le monde il est gentil $\qquad$ *
The title of a satirical film (1972) by the late Jean Yanne (1933–2003). It is used ironically to describe political correctness and the hypocrisy of the media.

### Tout va très bien, Madame la Marquise $\qquad$ ***
'Everything is quite alright, Madame La Marquise.' One of the greatest successes of Ray Ventura (1908–79), songwriter and band leader. In this song, the Marquise is away on holiday and phones home to the château for news. Her butler begins by saying that everything is OK and then says 'apart from one tiny thing' ... and there follows an account of the series of catastrophes that has befallen the château during her absence. When sb. is optimistic in a critical situation, this sentence is used ironically. In 2008, the then minister of finance Christine Lagarde said that France would only be marginally affected by the US subprime mortgage disaster. She has since been nicknamed Mme la Marquise de Bercy. See Chapter 12.

### train peut en cacher un autre. Un $\qquad$ ***
'The passage of one train may hide the passage of another', meaning that just because one train has passed doesn't mean that there is not another one coming. This notice is always displayed at a railway level crossing in France and is frequently punned upon.

### tranquille comme Baptiste $\qquad$ *
This expression apparently dates from the time of the French Revolution and was the forename given to the simpleton in a farce who remained impassive even while being jeered at.

### 'trois petits tours et puis s'en vont'          [ ** ]

The words of a famous nursery rhyme: 'Ainsi font, font, font, les petites marionettes, ainsi font, font, font, trois petits tours et puis s'en vont'. ('This is what the three little puppets do, three little turns and off they go'.)

### ... un peu, beaucoup, passionnément          [ ** ]

This is the French equivalent of 's/he loves me, s/he loves me not', said while plucking off the petals of a flower.

### Un 'x', un          [ *** ]

In the crowded and noisy café, the waiter shouts the customer's order to the bar and repeats the number of beers or coffees concerned just in case the barman has not heard the first part of the order, e.g. 'Un demi, un'.

### Va voir là bas si j'y suis          [ * ]

'Go over there and see if I'm there.' Famous words from one of the sketches of the French comic, Fernand Raynaud. See above 'Asnières', 'plombier. C'est le', 'Pourquoi tu tousses Tonton'.

### Vélib          [ ** ]

Launched by the Paris town hall in July 2007, (and managed by the industrial group JC Decaux) vélib (vélo + liberté) is a self-service bike rental scheme which allows a biker the possibility of hiring a bike in one part of Paris and of leaving it at another 'station' in another part of Paris. The service operates 24/7. It is a great success.

### 'verre, ça va, deux verres, bonjour les dégâts. Un'           [ *** ]

'One glass is OK, two glasses means trouble.' The 1984 slogan of a publicity campaign launched by *Le Comité français d'éducation pour la santé* (1972–2002) to combat drink-driving.

### *Vie en rose. La*           [ ** ]

'Life seen through rose-coloured spectacles.' One of the most famous songs by Edith Piaf recorded in 1946.

### *Vincent, François, Paul, et les autres*           [ ** ]

This is the title of the film by Claude Sautet 1974 telling the story of a group of friends who meet to spend their weekends in a country house belonging to one of the group. Hence the quip about the socialists involved in the contest for the candidacy for the presidential elections: 'Vincent (Peillon), François (Hollande), Bertrand (Delanoë), Martine (Aubry), Pierre (Moscovici) et les autres'.

## Vous prendrez bien un peu de ...                       [ * ]
The classic formula of the hostess asking the guests if they would like some more of a given dish.

## X en a rêvé, Y l'a fait                                [ *** ]
The sentence was first used in connection with Napoleon's decision in 1802 to build the Ourcq canal. This project involved deviating the water of the river Ourcq (north-east of the capital) in order to provide Paris with good quality water. 'Ils en ont rêvé, Bonaparte l'a fait', 'They dreamed about it, Bonaparte made it happen'. This expression has been used in a variety of situations. It was used by Sony as an advertising slogan: 'J'en ai rêvé, Sony l'a fait.'

## 'Y'a bon Banania'                                      [ * ]
This was the advertising slogan, in pidgin French, for the chocolate milk drink Banania. Colonial racism was very much a part of late nineteenth-century France and a part of early television and cinema advertising. This advertising slogan was accompanied by the picture of the smiling caricature of a colonial Senegalese infantryman. See above 'chocolat. Être'.

## Y'a d'la joie                                          [ * ]
One of the biggest successes of Charles Trenet (1913–2001). The song was one of the great hits of 1937.

## Y-a-t-il un médecin dans la salle?                     [ * ]
'Is there a doctor in the house?' The typical question asked when sb. is in need of a doctor in a cinema or theatre.

## 'Y-a-t-il un pilote dans l'avion?'                     [ *** ]
This question is frequently asked when the press has the impression that the government has lost control. It comes from the title of a satirical American comedy, directed by Jim Abrahams and David and Jerry Zucker. The original title of this Paramount film was *Airplane*, and starred the late Leslie Nielson. It was a box office hit in France in 1980.

## Yé-yé                                                   [ ** ]
This is the abbreviation of the 'yeah yeah', of the Anglo-American music fashion of the early 1960s. It was first used in 1963 by Edgar Morin in *Le Monde* to describe the French new wave in music, with its idols such as Françoise Hardy and Johnny Hallyday.

## Zéro de conduite                                       [ * ]
'Zero for behaviour.' This is the typical remark of a teacher on a pupil's end of term report. It should be noticed that 'conduite' may be understood as

'behaviour' or as 'driving'. It is also the title of a film by Jean Vigo (1933). Considered, at the time, to be 'anti-French', its projection was forbidden until 1945.

NB: Several other film titles are also culturally significant for the French, e.g. *Les Valseuses*, *Le Père Noël est une ordure*, *Le Diner de cons*, *Les Bronzés*, *Papy fait de la résistance*; however, they are not mentioned here for the simple reason that they did not come up in the texts studied during the research.

# Chapter 2

# Famous words

This chapter contains expressions, both old and new, certified and apocryphal, coming from a broad variety of sources. They are constantly used in the press and in everyday oral exchanges either re-quoted verbatim or punned upon. Several of them are not French but are frequently used in the French language. Certain entries listed in this chapter could quite legitimately have been included in Chapter 6, but such entries have been cross-referenced. Translations have been proposed where it was thought that this would help the general interest reader. Here again, this is far from being a comprehensive list of such words and is merely a reflection of those words found during the research.

### abracadabrantesque
`***`

This term was coined by Arthur Rimbaud (1854–91), the French poet. It came back into the limelight on 21 September 2000. During a television interview, the then President of the Republic, Jacques Chirac, used the term to describe the posthumous accusations of Jean Claude Méry, (the Rassemblement pour la République (RPR) fund manager) concerning the illegal funding of the president's party, the RPR (it has since been renamed the Union pour un mouvement populaire [UMP]). The term itself means a preposterous, cock and bull story.

### adversaire, celui de la France, n'a jamais cessé d'être l'argent. Mon
`*`

Charles de Gaulle, president of the Fifth Republic (1959–68).

### agrégé qui sache écrire. Trouvez-moi un (often misquoted)
`*`

In 1962, when de Gaulle was looking for a successor to the prime minister, Michel Debré, he is said to have ordered his staff to 'find me *un normalien* who knows how to write'. Soon after, Georges Pompidou (*agrégé de lettres classiques*) was appointed as prime minister (1962–8).

## 'Allons enfants'

**

The first two words of the French national anthem *La Marseillaise*.

## anomalie démocratique. Le Sénat est une

*

The French Upper Chamber, the Senate, is not elected by direct universal suffrage. It has always been held by the right-wing parties although this may change in 2011. This is the reason why Lionel Jospin, the socialist prime minister (1997–2002), called the Senate 'an anomaly in a democratic society'. See Chapter 10 'Sénat'.

## Après moi le déluge

**

Attributed to Louis XV (1710–74) but also in the form 'après nous, le déluge' attributed to Madame de Pompadour (1721–64). During the Seven Years War, the army of Louis XV suffered a severe defeat at the hands of the Prussian army led by Frederic II at the battle of Rossbach on 5 November 1757. While he was posing for the artist, Quentin de La Tour, Louis had a sad expression on his face. To comfort him, his favourite of the moment, Madame de Pompadour, said 'Il ne faut point s'affliger: vous tomberiez malade. Après nous, le déluge.' See also Chapter 8 'Déluge'.

## audace. L' nf.

*

See Chapter 6 'audace. encore de l''.

## Au secours, la droite revient

*

'Help! the right (wing party) is coming back.' This was the socialist party's election slogan in the late 1980s.

## 'Aux armes citoyens'

*

These are the first two words of the chorus of the French national anthem *La Marseillaise*.

## Aux grands hommes …

***

The first words of the inscription on the pediment of the Panthéon. 'Aux grands hommes, la patrie reconnaissante.' ('To great men, the homeland is grateful.') See Chapter 10 'Panthéon'.

## Aux innocents les mains pleines

**

An old French saying meaning that the simple-minded will find success in their undertakings. This expression echoes the Beatitudes, and is also the title of a vaudeville written by Lambert Thiboust, a French playwright (1826–67), and presented in 1849.

## bâton de maréchal nm.

**

During a speech to the cadets of the military academy of St Cyr, on 9 August 1819, King Louis XVIII, who reigned between 1814–24, said: 'Il n'y en a pas dans vos rangs qui n'ait dans sa giberne le bâton de Maréchal de France de Monsieur le Duc de Reggio et il ne tient qu'à vous de l'en faire sortir.' ('Remember that there is not one of you in your ranks who does not carry in his cartridge pouch the marshal's baton of the Duke of Reggio; it is up to you to bring it forth.') It has now come to mean the supreme accolade.

### beurre ou des canons. Du
`*`

'Butter or guns.' Used by Goebbels (1897–1945) during a speech in Berlin on 17 January in 1936. Also used by Goering (1893–1946) during a speech in Hamburg in the same year.

### bonheur, une idée neuve en Europe. Le
`*`

These were words said by Saint Just (1767–94), a French politician, during the Revolution, addressing the Convention on 3 March 1794. See below 'droit au bonheur'.

### bordel peuplé de nains. Un
`*`

'A brothel populated with dwarves.' The words of Victor Hugo referring to the Élysée after the *coup d'état* of Louis Napoleon in 1851.

### brioche! S'ils n'ont pas de pain, qu'ils mangent de la (apocryphal)
`**`

The words attributed to Marie-Antoinette (1755–93). 'If they have no bread, let them eat cake.' NB 'brioche' is a bun-like cake.

### Ça m'en touche un sans faire bouger l'autre
`***`

An extremely obscene expression used by Jacques Chirac, former president of France, who was well known for his barrack-room language. Referring to his testicles, he said 'this affair touches one without making the other move', meaning 'It doesn't affect me in the slightest'.

### calice de la trahison jusqu'à la lie. Boire le
`**`

'To drain the cup of treason to the dregs.' These were the words of Talleyrand, the French politician (1754–1838). He served the Ancien Régime, the Revolution, Napoleon and the Restoration Monarchy. See below 'trahison'.

### Calomniez, calomniez, il en restera toujours quelque chose
`*`

'Throw dirt enough and some of it will stick.' Attributed to Francis Bacon (1561–1626) and to Beaumarchais (1732–99).

### caisses sont vides. Les
`***`

'There's no money in the coffers.' Words spoken by Nicolas Sarkozy soon after arriving at the Élysée after the presidential elections of 2007. In spite of this, he gave a €15 billion tax break to the richest taxpayers in France, and awarded himself a 170 percent salary increase.

### cash, Monsieur le Président. Je vous le dis très

'I'm telling you straight up Mr President.' These words were spoken during a cabinet meeting by Fadela Amara in 2007, a junior minister of immigrant origin, in charge of urban policy. The use of the youngster's slang shocked some of the people who were present. See Chapter 9 'Amara, Fadela'.

### Casse-toi, pauvre con!
'Bugger off, you poor sod.' These words were said by Nicolas Sarkozy, president of France, during a visit to the Paris Agricultural Show in 2008, in response to a man who didn't want to shake his hand.

### 'certaine idée de la France. Je me suis fait une'
The words come from *Mémoires de Guerre* by Charles de Gaulle (Volume 1, Plon 1954). The text reads 'Toute ma vie, je me suis fait une certaine idée de la France. Le sentiment me l'inspire aussi bien que la raison.' ('Throughout my life I have had a certain conception of France. Sentiment inspires it just as much as reason.')

### cerveau disponible. Ce que nous vendons à Coca Cola, c'est du temps de
'What we sell to Coca Cola is available human brain time.' These are the words of Patrick Le Lay, in 2004, the then chairman and CEO of TF1, the leading TV channel in France, on how he saw the advertising role of his channel.

### C'est tout de même extraordinaire!
This is one of the verbal tics of Nicolas Sarkozy when speaking on television.

### 'change. Il faut que tout change pour que rien ne'
'If we want things to stay as they are, we shall have to change everything.' These words come from the novel *Le Guépard* (*The Leopard*) by Giuseppe Tomasi di Lampedusa (1896–1957), a Sicilian aristocrat and Italian writer. It describes the gradual disappearance of the old order in a changing world in Sicily.

### 'changement dans la continuité. Le'
This was the slogan of the new President Giscard d'Estaing in 1974.

### charbon. Aller au
'To roll up one's sleeves and set to work.' These words were spoken by the late Raymond Barre (1924–2007), former prime minister (1976–81), on

announcing his intention to stand for election in the legislative elections of 1978.

### charbonnier est maître chez lui. Le (apocryphal)

'Each person is free to act as he wishes in his own home.' Legend has it that François I<sup>er</sup> got lost in the forest of Fontainebleau while hunting. Night fell, and he had lost touch with the rest of the hunt. Seeing a light in the distance, he approached and knocked at the door of a small cottage. He was welcomed by the wife of the coal merchant but she didn't recognize him. The king sat down in a chair near the fireplace. Soon after, the coal merchant returned and on seeing someone in his favourite chair told the stranger to sit somewhere else. The king accepted this discourteous conduct and is said to have added 'le charbonnier est maître chez lui' ('the coal merchant is master in his own home').

### Chassez le naturel et il revient au galop

See Chapter 5.

### Cherchez la femme

These were the words of Alexander Dumas (the elder) (1802–70) in his book *Les Mohicans de Paris* (1864) in which the detective invites his colleagues to look for the woman in the affair.

### chienlit non. La réforme, oui, la

'Reform, yes, havoc, no.' Words spoken by General de Gaulle, president of the Republic, in response to the mass demonstrations in Paris in May 1968.

### Circulez (il n') y a rien à voir

This is the typical phrase pronounced by the police to disperse onlookers at the scene of an accident. 'Move along there, there's nothing to see.' It is used in the press to indicate that a scandal has been hushed up and that the press is being told not to poke its nose into the affair.

### cirer! La Bourse, j'en ai rien à

'The stock exchange, I couldn't give a tinker's cuss.' These ungrammatical and vulgar words were spoken by Édith Cresson, the first woman socialist prime minister of the Republic shortly after her appointment in May 1991. The infinitive of the verb is 'n'en avoir rien à cirer'. See Chapter 9 'Cresson, Édith'.

### clair n'est pas français. Ce qui n'est pas

'What is unclear is not French.' These are the words of French writer Antoine le Comte de Rivarol (1753–1801) in his work entitled *Discours sur l'universalité de la langue française*, published in 1784.

### cœur a ses raisons. Le

See Chapter 5.

### comité Théodule. Un

The expression 'comité Théodule' is a pure invention of de Gaulle who said 'L'essentiel pour moi, ce n'est pas ce que peuvent penser le comité Gustave, le comité Théodule ou le comité Hippolyte, c'est ce que veut le pays.'

### commission. Quand je veux enterrer un problème, je nomme une

'When I want to bury a problem, I set up a commission.' Words of Clémenceau (1841–1929), head of the French government (1917–19).

### Comparaison n'est pas raison

A proverb of the thirteenth century which states that comparison is not equivalent to reason.

### concierge est dans l'escalier. La
This is the classic notice that a *concierge* used to put on her door when she was absent from her *loge*. It meant that she was on the staircase. NB: 'une concierge' is also the translation of 'a gossip'.

### connaissance (acquaintance or consciousness)

On 16 February 1899, Félix Faure, president of the Third Republic, telephoned his mistress and asked her to come to the Élysée. He died after his sexual exertions. Legend has it that a priest was called for and Faure's mistress was shown out by the back door. On arriving in the room, the priest asked the valet 'Le Président a-t-il toujours sa connaissance? ('is the president still conscious?') The valet, having understood 'Is his acquaintance still with him?' replied 'Ah non, Mon Père, on l'a fait sortir par derrière' ('No, Father, we showed her out via the service exit'). See Chapter 6 'Félix Faure'.

### Construisons les villes à la campagne
'Let's build the towns in the country.' This is a witticism of Alphonse Allais, French writer and humorist (1854–1905).

### copains et les coquins. Les

This alliteration was an attack launched by Michel Poniatowsky (1922–2002), the leading supporter of Giscard d'Estaing, against the 'buddies and the brigands' of Jacques Chirac's party, the RPR, which had within its ranks an alarming number of people who were known to be less than honest!

### corbeille. La politique de la France ne se fait pas à la  [ * ]
The words of Charles de Gaulle. 'The policy of France is not decided upon at the trading floor of the stock exchange.' The 'corbeil' used to be the old trading floor, or pit, at the Paris stock exchange, that was surrounded by a handrail and used by companies trading at the Bourse. See above 'cirer'.

### crime, c'est une faute. C'est pire qu'un  [ ** ]
These were the words of Antoine Boulay de la Meurthe (1761–1840) on hearing of the execution of the Duc d'Enghien (1772–1804). Louis Antoine Henri de Bourbon-Condé was the last of the Condé heirs. Although he had left France, Napoleon had him kidnapped abroad and brought back to France. He was shot at the Château of Vincennes. Napoleon hoped that this would put an end to any royalist hopes of a restoration. This quotation is equally attributed to Talleyrand.

### croissance avec les dents. J'irai chercher la  [ *** ]
'I shall go and fetch economic growth with my bare hands.' A promise made by Nicolas Sarkozy after becoming president in 2007.

### Croix de Lorraine. La  [ *** ]
'De toutes les croix que j'ai dû porter, la croix de Lorraine est la plus lourde.' ('Of all the crosses I have had to bear, the cross of Lorraine is the heaviest.') Attributed to Winston Churchill because of his reputedly difficult relations with General de Gaulle.

### culture, c'est ce qui reste quand on a tout oublié. La  [ *** ]
'Culture is what is left when we have forgotten everything else.' This is commonly attributed to Edouard Herriot (1872–1957), the French writer and politician. It is in fact a shortened version of what he originally said: 'La culture – a dit un moraliste oriental – c'est ce qui reste dans l'esprit quand on a tout oublié.'

### dégraisser le mammouth. Il faut  [ ** ]
Referring to overstaffing in the ministry of education (teachers included), Claude Allègre, minister of education, research and technology in the first Jospin government (1997–2000), said 'we must downsize the mammoth'. His remarks eventually led to his resignation.

### Demain, on rase gratis  [ ** ]
'Tomorrow we shave for free.' This is the French equivalent of 'jam yesterday, jam tomorrow, never jam today' from *Alice in Wonderland* by Lewis Carroll (1832–98) and usually referring to politicians' empty promises.

### démissionne. Un ministre ça ferme sa gueule ou ça  [ ** ]
'A minister shuts his trap, or if he wants to open it, he resigns.' These are the words of Jean-Pierre Chevènement, minister of research and technology, on

resigning from the socialist government in 1983 because of what he saw as a move towards economic liberalism.

### Descends, si t'es un homme!

During the presidential visit to a Brittany fishing village, Guivinec, in November 2007, a fisherman shouted an insult to Nicolas Sarkozy accusing him of being an 'enculé'. In French, this can be translated by 'a dickhead' 'an asshole' or 'a wanker'. He insulted the president for having awarded himself a 170 percent wage increase at a time when the fishermen were going through hard times. President Sarkozy replied 'Come down here, if you are a man', to which the heckler replied 'If I come down there, I'll give you a Glasgow kiss (un coup de boule) so I had better not come down'.

### détail de l'histoire de la Deuxième Guerre mondiale. Ce n'est qu'un point de     \*\*\*

During a radio programme *Grand Jury RTL Le Monde* on 13 September 1987, Jean-Marie Le Pen, President of the French National Front, referred to the Nazi gas chambers as 'a point of detail in the history of the Second World War'. See Chapter 6 'poujadisme'.

### Dieu n'existait pas, il faudrait l'inventer. Si     \*\*

'If God didn't exist, it would be necessary to invent Him.' The words of François-Marie Arouet, alias Voltaire, the French writer and philosopher (1694–1778), as part of an epistle to the author of an atheistic work entitled *The Three Impostors*. It was also written in a letter to Prince Frederick William of Prussia.

### Dieu y pourvoira     \*\*

See Chapter 8 'Dieu y pourvoira'.

### Dieu reconnaîtra les siens (apocryphal)     \*\*

During the crusade launched by Pope Innocent III against the Albigensian heretics in the south west of France, the town of Béziers was besieged by papal troops in 1209. Within the city walls were both heretics as well as devout Catholics. When Arnaud Amalric, the papal legate leading the attack, was asked what was to be done about the Catholics as opposed to the heretics of the town, he is said to have answered 'Tuez-les tous. Dieu reconnaîtra les siens' ('Kill them all, God will recognize his own'). Over 30,000 people were massacred including women and children. This quote is sometimes misattributed to Simon de Montfort. See Chapter 6 'Cathare'.

### don de ma personne. Je fais     \*\*

The words of Maréchal Pétain on assuming total power in France, after the débâcle. The radio broadcast speech was made on 17 June 1940 and it was during this speech that he asked the French army to cease hostilities. His exact words were 'Je fais à la France le don de ma personne pour atténuer son malheur'. ('I give myself to France in order to alleviate her distress.') The following day, General de Gaulle made his famous call to arms from London via the BBC exhorting the French to continue the fight.

### Donnez-moi dix hommes sûrs et je tiens l'État       `*`
'Give me ten men in whom I can place my trust and I can control the State.' Napoleon Bonaparte (1769–1821).

### droit au bonheur. Le       `*`
Louis Antoine de Saint-Just (1767–94), member, of the Committe of Public Safety (along with Robespierre and Couthon), overthrown in the Thermidor reaction and guillotined with Robespierre. See above 'bonheur'. The 'right to happiness' may be considered in the light of the American Declaration of Independence which mentions 'Life, liberty and the pursuit of happiness', thus echoing a widespread philosophical idea of the eighteenth century in the USA and in Europe.

### droit dans mes bottes. Je suis       `***`
See Chapter 11 'Juppé, Alain'.

### droit d'ingérence. Le       `*`
A concept born of the Biafran War (1967–70) and developed by the French writer and philosopher Jean-François Revel (1924–2006), the idea being that in certain extreme cases, national sovereignty could be violated. The Biafran crisis saw the creation of *Médecins Sans Frontières* and the 'droit d'ingérence' was a concept popularized by one of its founders, Bernard Kouchner. See Chapter 9 'Kouchner, Bernard'.

### Élections, piège à cons       `***`
'Elections are a trap for assholes.' This is one of the slogans chanted by the students during the riots in Paris in May 1968.

### emmerdes volent toujours en escadrille. Les       `***`
'Bloody hassles always fly in squadrons.' Jacques Chirac. See Chapter 9 'Chirac, Jacques'.

### Encore une minute, Monsieur le Bourreau (apocryphal)
'Just one more minute, executioner.' These words were attributed to Madame du Barry, one of Louis XV's mistresses, who died at the guillotine on 8 December 1793.

### enfer, c'est les autres. L'
The words of Jean-Paul Sartre (1905–80), writer and philosopher in his play *Huis Clos* (1943).

### Enfin, les difficultés commencent!
The words of the leader, Léon Blum, on the electoral success of the Popular Front in 1936.

### Enrichissez-vous!
François Guizot (1787–1874) was a French politician who occupied several ministerial posts and was prime minister from 1847–48. Some historians suggest that this quote was aimed at people who were not rich enough to vote, others that his internal policy was designed to enrich the bourgeoisie. These words were said before the *Chambre des Députés* on 1 March 1843. Quoted out of context, these words give the impression that Guizot was a wheeler-dealer. In fact, his words were an invitation to the opposition to use their new political rights to reinforce the institutions and enhance the material and moral conditions of France.

### Ensemble, tout devient possible
'Together, everything becomes possible.' Campaign slogan of Nicolas Sarkozy in the 2007 presidential election.

### Entre ici, Jean Moulin!
With these words, Andre Malraux (1901–76), the then minister of culture, began his tribute to Jean Moulin (the hero of the French Resistance) during the transfer of the latter's ashes to the Panthéon on 19 December 1964. See Chapter 12 'Caluire'.

### équipe qui gagne. On ne change pas une
This is a common saying, often used ironically. 'One doesn't change a winning team.'

### erreur est humaine (persévérer est diabolique). L'
This philosophical proverb has been variously attributed to Titus-Livi, Cicero and Seneca the younger. The original phrase is *errare humanum est, perseverare diabolicum*.

### Et pourtant, elle tourne (apocryphal)
See Chapter 13 'Eppur se muove'.

### État ne peut pas tout. L'
'The State is not all powerful.' Words of Lionel Jospin, on 13 September 1999, admitting on television the State's impotence faced with factory closures.

### État, c'est moi. L' (apocryphal)    ( ** )
This is generally attributed to Louis XIV (1638–1715) who said these words in a speech before the *Parlement de Paris* on 13 April 1655.

### faillite. Je suis à la tête d'un état en    ( * )
'I am at the head of a state that is bankrupt.' These words were said by the Prime Minister François Fillon in 2007. Notice the constitutional error: the head of the State is the president, not the prime minister.

### Familles, je vous hais    ( *** )
'Families! I hate you.' André Gide, French writer (1869–1951).

### feignons d'en être les organisateurs. Puisque ces
   mystères nous dépassent,    ( *** )
'Since these mysteries are beyond us, let's pretend that we are the organizers.' Jean Cocteau (1889–1963) from the play *Les Mariés de la Tour Eiffel*. In fact, the exact words were: 'Puisque ces mystères me dépassent, feignons d'en être l'organisateur.'

### femme est l'avenir de l'homme. La    ( * )
'Woman is the future of man.' The words of Louis Aragon, poet and writer (1897–1982), and leitmotiv of a song by the late Jean Ferrat (1930–2010) based on the poem of Aragon 'Les Yeux d'Elsa'.

### femme, on le devient. On ne naît pas    ( ** )
'A woman is not born a woman; she becomes one.' Simone de Beauvoir (1908–86) feminist writer, philosopher and companion of Sartre.

### fluidifier les relations sociales    ( *** )
See Chapter 11 'Gautier-Sauvagnac, Denis'

### force tranquille. La    ( ** )
'Calm force.' This was the presidential campaign slogan of François Mitterrand in 1981 created by the publicity and communications specialist, Jacques Séguéla.

### France d'en bas. La    ( ** )
These are the words of Jean-Pierre Raffarin, prime minister (2002–5) in three successive governments under Jacques Chirac. This expression refers to the people at the lower end of the social scale.

### France qui se lève tôt. La    ( ** )
'The France of the early-risers.' One of the presidential campaign expressions of Nicolas Sarkozy in 2007.

## France s'ennuie. La

'France is bored.' Words written in the newspaper *Le Monde* by Pierre Viansson-Ponté just before the outbreak of violence in May 1968 echoing the words of Lamartine who, speaking to the Chambre des Députés in 1839, said 'La France est une nation qui s'ennuie'.

## fusillés pour l'exemple

The background of this expression is the trenches of the First World War during which 600 French soldiers were executed by firing squad for various offences: disobedience, self-mutilation and mutiny. In fact, it goes back to Voltaire who, commenting on the execution of the British admiral John Byng, said 'il faut quelquefois fusiller un amiral pour encourager les autres' ('from time to time one should shoot an admiral in order to encourage the others').

## garde meurt mais ne se rend pas. La (apocryphal)

'The guards die but do not surrender.' This was attributed to General Cambronne (1770–1842) who commanded the last of the Old Guard at Waterloo against the British General, Colville, on 18 June 1815. On Colville's insistence that he surrender, Cambronne is said to have replied 'La garde meurt mais ne se rend pas'. Colville insisted, and Cambronne is said to have shouted back 'Merde' ('shit'). He later denied having said either of the phrases attributed to him! Today, 'le mot de Cambronne' is a euphemism for 'merde'. 'La garde meurt mais ne se rend pas' are the words that were engraved on Cambronne's monument in his home town of Nantes when it was erected in 1845, thus reinforcing the apparent authenticity of the quote.

## gardez-moi de mes amis, mes ennemis, je m'en charge! Mon Dieu,

'God protect me against my friends, I'll take care of my enemies myself.' These are the words of Voltaire (1694–1778). Frequently attributed to Maréchal de Villars (1653–1734), one of Louis XIV's most brilliant soldiers.

## girouette qui tourne, mais le vent. Ce n'est pas la

Edgar Faure, a French politician (1908–88) was accused by his enemies of being an opportunist with very flexible political opinions. He was accused of being a 'weather vane', to which he replied, 'It is not the weather vane that changes direction, but the wind', thus plagiarizing the words of Camille Desmoulins (1760–94). The term 'weather cock' may also be used as a translation for 'girouette'.

## 'gloire est arrivé. Le jour de'

The second line of the French national anthem, *La Marseillaise*.

### guerre lasse. De                                              `**`
'Weary with war.' An expression that was both the title of a novel by Françoise Sagan (1935–2004) and a film by Robert Enrico.

### guerre est une affaire trop sérieuse … La                   `***`
The words of Georges Clémenceau (1841–1929) who said 'La guerre est une affaire trop sérieuse pour être confiée à des militaires' ('War is too serious a matter to entrust to military men'). These words are also attributed to Talleyrand.

### guêtre. Jusqu'au dernier bouton de                           `**`
In 1870, the minister of war, Maréchal Edmond Le Bœuf, assured Napoleon III that 'il ne manque pas un bouton de guêtre à nos soldats' ('the army is ready down to the last gaiter button'). The French lost the ensuing war against the Prussians, capitulating at Sedan on 1 September 1870.

### Heureux comme Dieu en France                                 `**`
'As happy as God in France.' A German saying: 'Glücklich wie Gott in Frankreich.'

### homme africain n'est pas assez entré dans l'histoire. L'      `***`
'African man has not sufficiently entered history.' This was a sentence in the speech made by President Sarkozy at the University of Dakar on 26 July 2007. He went on to say that the African man would never think of inventing his own destiny. The speech was written by the president's ghostwriter and advisor Henri Guaino. Many people found the words insulting, paternalistic, and tinged with colonial condescension. In 2009, soon after the Dakar speech, President Chirac, who is passionately fond of primary African art, quipped 'Non seulement l'homme africain est entré dans l'histoire, il y est même entré le premier!' ('Not only did African man enter history, he was even the first to do so!')

### homme est un loup pour l'homme. L'                            `*`
See Chapter 13 'homo homini lupus'.

### Ici Londres (les Français parlent aux Français)               `*`
'London calling. Frenchmen speak to the French.' These were the words of General de Gaulle during the first BBC transmission to France in 1940, beginning with the call to arms of 18 and 22 June. These words were used at each subsequent transmission. This is frequently punned upon in the form of 'ici, l'ombre', 'the shadow speaking'.

### Il faut savoir terminer une grève                            `*`
Maurice Thorez (1900–64), secretary general of the French communist party and minister for the civil service (1945–7), said these words on 11 June 1936

after the signing of the Matignon agreements giving the workers, among other things, a 40-hour week and two weeks' paid holiday.

NB: the word *grève* literally means 'shore', 'bank' or 'strand' and was the place where unemployed workers used to gather (at the place now occupied by the Hôtel de Ville de Paris) while waiting to be hired by an employer. It was the original labour exchange. When a conflict about wages broke out, workers would leave the factory and assemble on the *grève* in order to find a new employer, hence the verb 'faire grève'.

### Ils ne passeront pas

Originally the words of General Nivelle (1856–1924) throughout the defence of Verdun. Nivelle's Orders of the Day, in late June, were 'vous ne les laisserez pas passer' ('you shall not let them pass'). This was later taken up by the republican forces in the Spanish Civil War in the form of '¡No pasarán!'

### Ils n'ont rien appris ni rien oublié

These were the words of Talleyrand in 1815 referring to the *émigrés* returning from Koblenz who acted as if nothing had happened since they had fled France. They are also attributed to Napoleon who, on his return from Elba on 1 March 1815, speaking about the Bourbons said: 'Depuis le peu de mois qu'ils règnent, ils vous ont convaincus qu'ils n'ont rien oublié ni rien appris'. ('In the few months that they have reigned, they have convinced you that they have neither forgotten anything, nor learned anything'.)

### instituteur ne pourra jamais remplacer le curé ou le pasteur. L'

'The primary school teacher will never be able to replace the priest or the pastor.' Words of Nicolas Sarkozy at the Lateran Palace during his visit to the Vatican on 21 December 2007. These words mark a break with the position of all previous presidents of the republic, i.e. not to make any comments about the place of religion in the affairs of the city. Traditionally, the primary school teachers were the lay soldiers whose role it was to fight clerical influence. Since the law of 1905, religious instruction has been forbidden in French state schools, except in Alsace and Lorraine. See Chapter 6 'hussards noirs'.

### insu de mon plein gré. À l'

'Unbeknown to my full consent.' In the wake of the Festina doping scandal involving cyclists of the 'Tour de France' in 1998, Richard Virenque, after denying taking drugs, admitted that he had been given drugs without his being aware of it. This barbaric French phrase was popularized by the caricature of Virenque in the satirical *Guignols de l'Info*, a TV programme on Canal+, the equivalent of the British TV programme *Spitting Image*.

**interdit d'interdire. Il est**                                                 ` ** `
'It is forbidden to forbid.' One of the slogans painted on the walls of Paris during the student riots of 1968.

**J'aime la justice, mais je préfère ma mère**                                   ` * `
'I love justice but I prefer my mother.' These somewhat enigmatic words were spoken by Albert Camus on 13 December 1957, a few days after he had received the Nobel Prize for literature.

**J'ai survécu**                                                                 ` * `
'I survived.' This was the reply of Emmanuel Joseph Sieyès (1748–1836) the French politician, on being asked what he had done during the French Revolution. This quotation is frequently attributed to Talleyrand.

**Je décide, il exécute**                                                        ` ** `
'I decide, he carries out the decision.' A jibe made by President Chirac against his then minister of economy and finance, Nicolas Sarkozy, during an interview on 14 July 2004. He was responding to petty attacks made against him by Sarkozy. What is interesting is the unconstitutionality of the then president's words. According to the French constitution, the government fixes and implements policy and the prime minister leads the action of the government, not the president.

**J'écris ton nom, Liberté**                                                     ` ** `
See Chapter 5 'J'écris ton nom, Liberté'.

**Je n'ai pas rencontré beaucoup d'entre vous à Londres**                        ` * `
These were the words of Charles de Gaulle addressing the French equivalent of the employers' association after the liberation of France: 'I didn't come across many of you in London.'

**Je ne partage pas vos idées**                                                  ` ** `
'Je ne partage pas vos idées mais je me battrai pour que vous puissiez les exprimer.' ('I do not share your ideas, but I will fight for your right to express them.') Generally attributed to Voltaire (1694–1778).

**Je pense, donc, je suis**                                                      ` *** `
*Cogito ergo sum.* René Descartes, French mathematician and philosopher (1596–1650). His name gives us the adjective 'cartésien' meaning methodical and rational.

**Je serai le président du pouvoir d'achat**                                     ` * `
'I shall be the president of buying power.' An election promise made by Nicolas Sarkozy in the run-up to the presidential election of 2007.

## Je suis contre les femmes, tout contre.

'I am against women. Right up against women.' The words of Sacha Guitry (1885–1957) playwright, cinema director and wit, famous for his misogynistic jibes.

## Je te vois Sarkozy

Words said by a passer-by in February 2008 at the main-line station in Marseilles, la gare Saint-Charles. As he passed some policemen, who were carrying out ID checks on the public, he shouted 'Sarkozy, I can see you'. He was arrested and later charged with insulting breach of the peace. The case was ultimately dismissed. This expression is now used by the satirical press whenever telephone tapping or videosurveillance cameras are the topic of conversation. See Chapter 13 'Big Brother'.

## Je vous ai compris

These were the first words of a speech given by General de Gaulle in Algiers at the Place du Forum on 4 June 1958, when he seemed to be reassuring the faction of 'French Algeria'. When independence was granted to Algeria in 1962, under the terms of the Evian agreement of 18 March, the words of de Gaulle seemed retrospectively to have been doublespeak. Many supporters of the idea of 'French Algeria' were embittered and an attempt was made on the life of de Gaulle at Petit Clamart on 22 August of the same year.

## Jouir sans entraves

*

'Pleasure without constraints.' One of the student slogans of 1968.

## J'y étais

After the battle of Austerlitz in 1805, one of Napoleon's most brilliant victories, he spoke to his soldiers and said 'Il vous suffira de dire, "j'étais à la bataille d'Austerlitz", pour que l'on réponde "Voilà un brave".' ('You will only have to say "I was at the battle of Austerlitz" for people to reply "There is a courageous man".') In the concluding words of his speech of thanks to Queen Elizabeth II on 27 February 2008 at the dinner at Windsor Castle given in his honour, Nicolas Sarkozy said 'Je pourrai dire que j'y étais'. ('I will be able to say, "I was there".)

## J'y suis, j'y reste

***

'Here I am, and here I stay.' These were the words of Comte de Mac-Mahon (1808–93), Maréchal de France, president of the Republic (1873–9). He said these words after taking the fortress of Malakoff during the Crimean War (1854–86) on 8 September 1855 and in response to the question of Lord Raglan's envoy, asking if Mac-Mahon was capable of holding on to the newly captured fortress.

### laisser (donner) du temps au temps. Il faut     \*\*\*
'Give time, the time' (*dar tiempo, al tiempo*). These are the words of Miguel de Cervantes (1547–1616), later to be taken up by François Mitterrand (1916–96) president of the Republic from 1981 to 1995.

### Lafayette, nous revoilà     \*
'Lafayette, here we are, once again.' These are the words of Lt Colonel Charles E. Stanton. He served in the First World War as an aid to General Pershing. Stanton said these words at the grave of General Lafayette in the cemetery of Picpus on 4 July 1917. Marie Joseph de la Fayette (1757–1834) was a hero for the Americans whom he helped in their fight for independence against the British.

### liberté de la presse ne s'use que quand on ne s'en sert pas. La     \*\*\*
'The freedom of the press only becomes worn when it isn't used.' This is the motto of the satirical weekly newspaper *Le Canard Enchaîné*, written below the title on the back page.

### liberté, que de crimes on commet en ton nom! Ô     \*\*
The words of Madame Roland de la Platière (1754–93), the muse of the Girondins, who died crying these words at the guillotine as she looked towards the Statue of Liberty that then decorated the Place de la Revolution, re-named Place de la Concorde in 1795.

### loin. Le tact dans l'audace, c'est de savoir jusqu'où on peut aller trop     \*
'Being tactful in audacity, is knowing just how far one can go too far.' These are the words of Jean Cocteau (1889–1963), French artist, poet and film director.

### Lui c'est lui, moi c'est moi     \*\*
'He is who he is, and I am who I am.' Words spoken by Laurent Fabius, socialist prime minister (1984–6) in order to put a certain distance between himself and the then President François Mitterrand.

### machin. Un     \*\*
'A thingamajig.' The scornful words of General de Gaulle describing the United Nations Organization, said in Nantes in September 1960.

### magnifical. It is     \*\*\*
The words of Nicolas Sarkozy to Queen Elizabeth II on his official visit to Great Britain in 2008. He did not pass his exam at Sciences Po, because he was disqualified by his low mark in English.

## maison brûle. La
From a speech made by Jacques Chirac in Johannesburg in 2002 on climate change and ecology. 'La maison brûle et nous regardons ailleurs' ('The house is on fire and we are looking elsewhere').

## Malheur aux vaincus
'Woe to the vanquished.' From the Latin expression 'Vae victis'; words that were said by Brennus, the leader of the Gauls on seizing Rome in 390 BC after having defeated the Romans on the Allia.

## 'Maréchal, nous voilà'
The patriotic hymn of the Vichy regime, to the glory of Maréchal Pétain. It was created in 1941 by André Montagard and Charles Courtioux but was in fact a plagiarism of the musical work of Casimir Oberfeld, a Jewish composer who died in deportation to Auschwitz in 1945.

## meilleur d'entre nous. Le
'The best among us.' These were the words of Jacques Chirac referring to Alain Juppé whom he had considered as his possible successor.

## Merde. *
See above 'garde'

## merde dans un bas de soie. De la *
'Shit in a silk stocking.' Such were the words used by Napoleon when referring to Talleyrand. See Chapter 6 'Talleyrand'.

## Métro, boulot, dodo
'Tube, graft, shut-eye.' The monotonous rhythm of most Parisians' lives. Inspired by a verse written by Pierre Béarn, a French man of letters. His original line reads 'Métro, boulot, bistrot, mégots, dodo, zéro' ('tube, graft, café, fag ends, shut-eye, zero'). The quote comes from a collection of poems entitled *Couleurs d'usine*, published in 1951.

## mieux disant culturel. Le
In 1987, during the privatization of the first French TV channel, the then minister of culture François Léotard said that the channel would be attributed to the bidder with the 'highest bid in terms of culture'. TF1 has since moved into the area of trash TV and reality shows. TF1 belongs to the Bouygues consortium.

## misère du monde. La France ne peut accueillir toute la
'France cannot take on board the poverty of the world.' These were the words of former socialist prime minister Michel Rocard on 24 August 1996 referring to France's inability to open up the gates to immigration.

## mon général. Les deux                    &#x2b50; **

The flippant reply given to an 'either or' question, where both answers can apply. It is the punchline of a famous joke involving a conscript and his commanding officer. Before a selection interview, the conscript has been told the answers to the questions that his officer will ask him. Unfortunately, the sequence is not the same and the answers are totally inappropriate. Infuriated, the General says to the conscript 'Do you think I'm an idiot or a madman?' to which the conscript gives the reply he has been told to use for the last question 'Both Sir'.

## Nationaliser les pertes, privatiser les profits          **

Criticism of liberalism.

## Nettoyer au karcher          **

'To clean with a high-pressure hose.' The then minister of the interior Nicolas Sarkozy, during a walkabout on 21 June 2005 in the poor suburb of La Courneuve (in the *département* of the Seine-Saint-Denis [93]), promised the inhabitants that he would clean up the 'Cité des 4000' with a high pressure hose. His words concerning the riff-raff of the council estates provoked a heated reaction which led to more urban violence.

## odeur. Le bruit et l'          **

'The din and the stench.' During his visit to the poor Goutte d'Or area of Paris in 1991, Jacques Chirac spoke about social parasites, citing the case of the head of an immigrant family with his four wives and scores of children, who earns 50,000 francs in social allowances per month, 'naturally without doing a stroke of work ... and if you add to that the din and the stench'. He was elected president in 1995. See Chapter 1 'furet du bois joli'.

## Omar m'a tuer          ***

'Omar killed me'. Omar Raddad was the name of the gardener who worked for the rich widow, Ghislaine Marchal, who was found dead in the boiler room of her house in Mougins (Alpes Maritimes [06]) in 1991. The police found the inscription, in Madame Marchal's own blood, on one of the walls of the boiler room: 'Omar m'a tuer'. The grammatical mistake (it should have read 'Omar m'a tuée') is unlikely to have been made by the well-educated Madame Marchal. The police suspected Omar. In actual fact, in 1996, Omar was granted a presidential pardon. He is now fighting for a retrial.

## On préfère toujours l'original à la copie          **

The words of the National Front leader, Jean-Marie Le Pen, referring to the right-wing party's attempts, during election time, to poach his anti-immigration and national preference themes.

## Où ne montera-t-il pas? \*

'To what heights may he not rise?' This was the motto of the French politician Nicolas Fouquet (1615–80?). He was the finance minister under Louis XIV. He provoked the jealousy of the Sun King by an ostentatious party given at his new château Vaux le Vicomte, located in today's *département* of the Seine-et-Marne (77). He was arrested and spent the rest of his life in prison in Pinerolo, in Italy. The circumstances of his death are unclear. See Chapter 13 'Quo non ascendet'.

## Ouvrez une école et fermez une prison \*

'Open a school and close a prison.' This was the credo of Victor Hugo (1802–85).

## Parce que c'était lui, parce que c'était moi \*\*\*

This was the reply of Montaigne (1533–92) on being asked the reason for his friendship with Etienne de la Boétie (1530–63). 'Because it was him, because it was me.'

## Paris outragé, Paris brisé, Paris martyrisé, mais Paris libéré \*\*\*

'Paris violated, Paris crushed, Paris martyrized, but Paris liberated.' These were the words of General de Gaulle on the evening of 25 August 1944 at the Hôtel de Ville on the liberation of Paris.

## Paris vaut bien une messe (apocryphal) \*\*\*

These words are attributed to Henry III of Navarre (1553–1610) on his conversion to the Catholic faith (for the second time) which enabled him to become King of France as Henri IV. The date is not certain but 1593 is the most frequently given date. NB: his nickname was 'le Vert Galant'.

## parité quand une femme, notoirement incompétente, sera nommée à un poste de très haute responsabilité. Les femmes auront atteint la \*

'Women will have achieved parity the day when a notoriously incompetent woman is appointed to a post of great responsibility.' The words of the late Françoise Giroud, journalist and writer (1916–2003).

## parlez jamais, pensez-y toujours. N'en \*\*

'Never speak of it, think of it always.' Raymond Poincaré (1860–1934), president of the III Republic (1913–20). He was referring to the ultimate aim of France to repossess Alsace and Lorraine which had been lost to the Prussians in the Franco-Prussian War in 1870–1.

### participer. L'important est de   `*`
'The important thing is taking part.' The words of Pierre de Frédy, Baron de Coubertin (1863–1937) who was responsible for reviving the Olympic Games. The first modern Olympics took place in Athens in 1896.

### peine de naître. La   `***`
'Vous vous êtes donné la peine de naître, et rien de plus' ('You took the trouble to be born, and nothing else.') The words of Beaumarchais (1732–99) in *Le Mariage de Figaro* in which he denounces the archaic privileges of the nobility. They are the words of Figaro addressed to le Comte Almaviva. The play was written in 1778.

### poubelles de l'histoire, les   `**`
The words of Leon Trotsky addressed to his former allies, the revolutionary socialists, during the Moscow show trials of the early 1920s. 'Votre rôle est fini. Allez donc à la place qui est la vôtre dans les poubelles de l'histoire.' ('Your role is over. Consequently, go to the place which is yours in the dustbins of history.')

### Pourvu que ça dure!   `***`
When everything is going well, one is frequently prompted to say 'Let's hope it lasts'. These are words attributed to Napoleon's mother, Letizia, in relation to her son's military victories.

### printemps sera chaud, chaud, chaud. Le   `**`
'Springtime will be hot, hot, hot.' This is a chanted threat made by students and trades unionists alike since May 1968 to indicate that there will be industrial unrest in spring.

### promesses n'engagent que ceux qui y croient. Les   `*`
'Promises are binding only on those who believe them.' This is a very old French adage.

### pschitt! Ce n'est pas qu'elles se dégonflent, c'est qu'elles font   `***`
'It's not that these accusations just go pear-shaped, it's that they disappear into thin air.' The words of President Jacques Chirac during a television interview on 14 July 2001, on being questioned about the illegal funding of his political party.

### Quand il y en a un ça va, c'est quand ils sont nombreux que ça pose des problèmes   `***`
These were the words of Brice Hortefeux, minister of the interior, during the *Université d'été* of the UMP in Seignosse on 5 September 2009 referring to

Arabs. 'When there is just one of them, it's OK, it's when there are lots of them that they cause problems.' He was found guilty of racial abuse and fined. He has appealed.

### Quand je m'examine

'Quand je m'examine, je m'inquiète, quand je me compare, je me rassure.' ('When I look at myself, I'm worried, when I compare myself to others, I'm reassured'.) Talleyrand. This also exists in the version 'Quand je me contemple, je me désole, quand je me compare, je me console.'

### Quand j'entends le mot culture ...

This is a reference to a much misquoted and misattributed sentence. The original phrase was in German: 'Wenn ich (das Wort) Kultur höre, entsichere ich meinen Browning.' ('When I hear the word "culture", I release the safety catch on my Browning.') The words were in fact spoken by Friedrich Thiemann, a character in a play called *Schlagete* written by a dyed-in-the-wool Nazi named Hans Johst (1890–1978) and put on in Berlin in 1933. Over time, it has been attributed to several people, among them, Hermann Göring and Baldur von Schirach.

### Quand la Chine s'éveillera, le monde tremblera

Napoleon Bonaparte is said to have predicted 'When China awakes, the world will tremble.' These words were used as the title of a book by Alain Peyrefitte (1925–99), politician, *normalien* and writer, for his *essai* entitled *Quand la Chine s'éveillera* published in 1976, reprinted in 2006.

### Quand le bâtiment va, tout va

This aphorism indicates that when the building industry is flourishing, the whole of the economy is in good shape.

### quarteron de généraux. Un

On 22 April 1961, a military putsch took place in Algeria, organized by four generals, Challe, Salan, Zeller and Jouhaud, backed by a parachute regiment, in an attempt to stop the process of Algerian self-determination initiated by General de Gaulle. In his speech to the nation the following day, 23 April 1961, de Gaulle used these words about the putschists: 'Ce pouvoir a une apparence: un quarteron de généraux en retraite. Il a une réalité: un groupe d'officiers partisans, ambitieux et fanatiques.' ('This power has an appearance: a bunch of retired generals. It has a reality: a handful of partisan, ambitious and fanatical officers.') 'Quarteron' is in fact 25, i.e. the quarter of 100. It is now used pejoratively to indicate a small number, a handful.

## Que d'eau, que d'eau!

**\*\*\***

'So much water, so much water.' These words were said by Mac-Mahon, president of the Republic, on 26 June 1875, on visiting the city of Toulouse which had been severely damaged by floods.

## Qui connaît M. Besson?

**\*\***

The words of Ségolène Royal on learning of the defection of the socialist, Eric Besson, to join the Sarkozy camp just before the presidential elections in 2007. Besson was later to publish a book entitled *Qui connaît Madame Royal?*

## Qui va garder les enfants?

**\***

When Ségolène Royal announced her intention to stand for the French presidency in 2007, while her husband was first secretary of the Parti Socialiste, Laurent Fabius, a fellow socialist, retorted 'Who is going to look after the children?'

## racaille. La

**\*\*\***

See Chapter 12 'Argenteuil'.

## Ralliez-vous à mon panache blanc

**\*\*\***

See Chapter 6 'panache blanc'.

## Rendre à César

**\*\***

See Chapter 8 'César (rendre à)'.

## Responsable mais pas coupable

**\*\*\***

'Responsible but not guilty.' So pleaded Georgina Dufoix, minister of social affairs in the government of Laurent Fabius, when she was charged with manslaughter in 1993 along with Laurent Fabius in the AIDS-contaminated blood scandal. They were both acquitted by *La Cour de la République* in 1999.

## révolte? Est-ce une

**\*\*\***

These are the words of Louis XVI. On the evening of 14 July 1789, the Bastille had fallen and the prison governor's head was being paraded at the end of a pike in the gardens of the Palais Royal. La Rochefoucauld-Liancourt came to inform the king. The latter asked him 'Is it a revolt?', to which the duke replied 'No Sire, it is a revolution'.

## Rien ne se crée, rien ne se perd, tout se transforme

'Nothing is created, nothing is lost, everything is transformed.' These were the words attributed to the French chemist Antoine Laurent de Lavoisier (1743–94), father of modern chemistry, guillotined during the Terror of the French Revolution.

### Rien ne va plus, les jeux sont faits    [ ** ]

The croupier's words to players at roulette indicating that it is now too late to place any other bets.

### Rolex à 50 ans, c'est que l'on a raté sa vie. Si l'on n'a pas de    [ ** ]

'If one hasn't got a Rolex watch by the time one is 50, one has made nothing of one's life.' Jacques Séguela, communication specialist, replying to criticism of the ostentatious watch of Nicolas Sarkozy.

### roquet nm.    [ * ]

During a television debate in 1986, Laurent Fabius, the then prime minister, kept on interrupting Jacques Chirac. The latter said that the former was behaving like a 'roquet', i.e. a nasty, snappy little dog.

### Salauds de pauvres!    [ ** ]

'The bloody poor.' One of the most famous lines in the film by Claude Autant-Lara, *La Traversée de Paris* (1956) that is based on the book by Marcel Aymé (1902–67). The film co-starred Bourvil, Louis de Funès and Jean Gabin and deals with the subject of the black market in Paris during the Second World War.

### sang et des larmes. Du    [ *** ]

The famous declaration by Winston Churchill made to the House of Commons on 13 May 1940: 'I have nothing to offer but blood, toil, tears and sweat' is often quoted in French. It is generally abbreviated in French to 'du sang et des larmes' (blood and tears) or 'de la sueur et des larmes' (sweat and tears).

### Sans la liberté de blâmer il n'est point d'éloge flatteur.    [ *** ]

'Without the freedom to criticize, there can be no flattering praise.' This is the motto written beneath the title of the daily newspaper *Le Figaro* which took its name from the character in the play *The Marriage of Figaro* by the writer and playwright Pierre-Augustin Caron de Beaumarchais (1732–99).

### sauvageon nm.    [ * ]

Jean-Pierre Chevènement used the term 'sauvageon' (little savage) in 1998, before the National Assembly when referring to the young murderers of a grocer.

### Science sans conscience n'est que ruine de l'âme.    [ ** ]

'Science without conscience is the soul's perdition.' From *Pantagruel* by François Rabelais (1494–1553).

### S'il n'en reste qu'un, je serai celui-là.    [ *** ]

The words of Victor Hugo in *Ultima verba* from the collection *Les Châtiments*, written in 1853, two years after the *coup d'état* of Napoleon III. An amnesty was being prepared for those 'outlaws' who would agree to submit to the authority of Napoleon III. Hugo was among those who refused the amnesty, with this poem and these words. The last four lines of the poem read 'Si l'on n'est plus que mille, eh bien, j'en suis. Si même ils ne sont plus que cent, je brave encore Sylla (sic). S'il en demeure dix, je serai le dixième; Et s'il n'en reste qu'un, je serai celui-là.' ('If there are only a thousand of us remaining, well, I shall be among them. Even if there are only one hundred left, I shall still defy Scylla. If there should remain ten, I shall be the tenth. And if there should remain only one, that one shall be me.') See Chapter 7 'Charybde en Scylla.'

### Silence dans les rangs! $\boxed{*}$
'Silence in the ranks' is an order given to soldiers to be quiet. Today, it is used as an order to obey and keep one's mouth shut.

### Soldats, du haut de ces pyramides, quarante siècles vous contemplent. $\boxed{**}$
'Soldiers, from the summit of these pyramids, 40 centuries look down upon you.' Words spoken by Napoleon to his troops during the Egyptian campaign, on 21 July 1798, just before the battle of the Pyramids.

### Sous les pavés la plage. $\boxed{**}$
'Beneath the paving stones, the beach.' One of the student phrases painted on Parisian walls during the unrest of May 1968.

### souvenirs que si j'avais 1 000 ans. J'ai plus de $\boxed{**}$
This is the title of a poem by Charles Baudelaire (1821–67) 'Spleen'. This is also the title of a book written by Jacques Vergès, the famous lawyer, in 1999.

### Souvent femme varie … (probably apocryphal) $\boxed{**}$
The full text is 'Souvent femme varie. Et bien fol qui s'y fie.' ('Woman is often fickle and truly mad is he who trusts her.') It is attributed to François I$^{er}$ (1494–1547) who is said to have engraved these words on a window in the Château of Chambord around 1520. This is originally the text of Virgil (70–19 BC): 'varium et mutabile semper femina' ('fickle and changeable always is woman').

### Soyons réalistes, demandons l'impossible! $\boxed{*}$
'Let's be realistic, let's ask for the impossible'. Another example of 1968 student graffiti.

### spirituel ou il ne sera pas. Le 21ème siècle sera (apocryphal)
'The 21st century will be spiritual, or there will be no 21st century.' The words were attributed to André Malraux (1901–76), General de Gaulle's minister of culture. The word 'spirituel' is sometimes replaced by 'religieux'.

### suite d'un arrêt de travail. Par

'Following a work stoppage.' The phrase known by all French commuters is the stock announcement made during a strike, announcing disruption of the tube or railway network.

### Tel est notre bon plaisir

'Such is our wish.' Royal phrase inaugurated by François Ier and today used to describe the arbitrary and despotic behaviour of the president. It is frequently punned upon with 'télé'.

### terre ne ment pas. La

'The soil doesn't lie.' Words spoken by Maréchal Pétain during a speech made in June 1940.

### têtes vont tomber. Les

Paul Quilès, former socialist minister during the socialist congress of Valence in 1981, taking Robespierre's words, said 'It is not enough to say "heads will roll", we must specify which heads.' He was immediately nicknamed 'Robespaul'.

### tirez les premiers, Messieurs les Anglais

These words were said at the battle of Fontenoy in 1745, during the war of the Austrian Succession, by a French officer, le Comte d'Anterroche(s) in answer to the English officer's request that the French should begin hostilities. Today, it is frequently used to express the fact that the English have beaten the French to it! For example, 'Messieurs les Anglais ont encore tiré les premiers.'

### toi aussi mon fils (probably apocryphal)

'You too my son.' These are supposed to have been the last words of Caesar on being assassinated in the Senate in 44 BC, having seen that Brutus, his protégé (and possibly his biological son) was among the assassins. The words epitomize betrayal. See Chapter 13 'tu quoque, fili'.

### tous les matins en me rasant. J'y pense

'I think about it (becoming president) every morning while shaving.' Words of Nicolas Sarkozy when asked, some years ago, whether he ever thought about becoming president of the Republic.

### Tout va pour le mieux dans le meilleur des mondes
See Chapter 5 '*Meilleur des mondes. Le*'.

### trahi que par les siens. On n'est jamais si bien
'One is never so well betrayed as one is by one's own.' An old proverb.

### trahison est souvent question de dates. La     ( * )
'Treason is often a question of dates.' Charles Maurice de Talleyrand Périgord, French politician (1754–1838), an expert in this area.

### 'Travailler plus pour gagner plus'     ( *** )
'Work more to earn more'. Election slogan of Nicolas Sarkozy in 2007.

### 'Trop d'impôts tuent l'impôt'     ( *** )
'Excessive taxes, kill taxes.' A slogan that has been in the air since the time of Adam Smith and popularized by President Chirac in the 1990s.

### Tu l'as dit bouffi     ( * )
'Too bloody right.' 'Too true!'

### Tuez-les     ( ** )
See above 'Dieu reconnaîtra'.

### Un pour tous, tous pour un     ( ** )
'One for all and all for one.' This was the motto of *The Three Musketeers*, the novel by Alexandre Dumas (1802–70). It is to be noted in passing that this is the traditional (if not official) motto of Switzerland *Unus pro omnibus, omnes pro uno*. In the nineteenth century this became a popular motto throughout Europe: *Uno per tutti, tutti per uno* and *Einer für alle, alle für einen*.

### valise ou le cerceuil. La     ( ** )
'The suitcase or the coffin.' This was the threat used by the 'Front de libération nationale' (FLN) in Algeria after the declaration of independence in 1962. It was directed towards the French colonials, i.e. 'pieds noirs'. They were given the choice of leaving Algeria (the suitcase) or of being assassinated (the coffin).

### Vaste programme!     ( *** )
General de Gaulle, responding to a heckler who cried out 'Mort aux cons' ('Death to the assholes'), quipped 'Vaste programme'.

### veaux. Les Français sont des     ( ** )
'Veaux' are literally 'calves' that we would translate by 'sheep' given the fact that the expression implies that the French are mindless and will follow anyone, anywhere. These are the words of General de Gaulle.

### Vérité en deçà des Pyrénées, erreur au-delà     ( *** )
'What is considered truth on this side of the Pyrenees is considered false beyond them.' From *Les Pensées* by Blaise Pascal (1623–62).

### vice appuyé sur le bras du crime. Le   `**`

These are the words of Chateaubriand (1768–1848) on seeing Talleyrand, leaning on Fouché as they both went in to see Louis XVIII following his return from temporary exile after the defeat of Napoleon at Waterloo. Both men survived the various regimes. Talleyrand was the minister of foreign affairs and Fouché head of the police. They both survived (after having served) the revolution and the restoration. Talleyrand was considered immoral and Fouché had voted for the execution of Louis XVI, the brother of the king to whom he was going to pledge allegiance when Chateaubriand witnessed the scene on 16 July 1815.

### vieillard meurt en Afrique, c'est une bibliothèque qui brûle. Quand un   `**`

'When an old man dies in Africa, it is a library that burns down.' One of the translations of the words from the speech made by Amadou Hampâté Bâ (1900–91) to the United Nations Educational, Scientific and Cultural Organization (UNESCO) in 1960.

### vieillesse est un naufrage. La   `**`

'Old age is a disaster.' *Naufrage* is a 'shipwreck'. Charles de Gaulle in his book *Mémoires de Guerre. L'Appel.* It is a remark said to have been suggested to him by the visible decline of Maréchal Pétain with whom de Gaulle had worked closely before the Second World War.

### Vingt fois sur le métier remettez votre ouvrage   `**`

Nicolas Boileau (1636–1711), *l'Art poétique*. The advice given here is to a writer about his work. He should add to it sometimes, erase things often, but above all polish and polish the work.

### violon, acheter au son du canon. Vendre au son du   `*`

This is an old stock market adage that suggests that one should sell when things are calm and buy when things are tumultuous. The word 'clairon' sometimes replaces 'canon'.

### vrai-faux passeport nm.   `***`

See Chapter 11 'vrai-faux'.

### 'yes' needs the 'no' to win against the 'no'. The   `*`

Perhaps the most famous 'raffarinade', said in English, made during the speech of Jean-Pierre Raffarin in 2005 during the debate on France's ratification of the European Constitutional Treaty. If any readers understand this phrase, they are kindly invited to contact the publisher.

# Chapter 3

# Figurative expressions

This chapter is aimed at completing the translation of the bilingual dictionary. To know that 'dès potron-minet' means 'at the break of day', is one thing; to know the origin of the term is quite another. If students make do with the bilingual dictionary translation, they are missing a lot! The expressions below represent a highly colourful aspect of the French language and help us to appreciate some quintessential aspects of the nature of French culture. The expressions below were those found during the research and are by no means a comprehensive list of such expressions.

**aile (avoir du plomb dans l')**      **\*\***
'To be in a bad way' or in a perilous situation. This is an image from shooting, when a bird has been wounded and has lead shot in its wing.

**aile (battre de l')**      **\*\***
This has a similar meaning to the expression above where a wounded bird flaps its wings helplessly.

**anges (les discussions sur le sexe des)**      **\***
See Chapter 7 'byzantinisme'.

**ardoise nf.**      **\*\*\***
When one has an 'account' with the café owner, one does not pay for each consumption but pays the overall amount at the end of the week. The various drinks, for example, are marked on a slate. The English term 'to put it on the slate' is identical in origin. 'Ardoise' is frequently used to refer to a debt in the broadest meaning.

**armes et bagages (avec)**      **\*\***
This means 'totally'. When a soldier surrenders, he gives himself up along with his weapons and equipment.

## assiette (ne pas être dans son)

Although the meaning of this expression is to be 'out of sorts', 'off colour' or 'under the weather' and is thus related to health, the expression 'assiette' is in fact used to refer to how well a rider sits in the saddle, as well as to the horizontality of an aircraft. 'Assiette' also has a fiscal meaning, i.e. the base of the population upon which a tax is levied, hence great punning possibilities.

## auberge espagnole nf.

Curiously, Spanish inns have had a bad reputation in France since the eighteenth century. It is an inn where you find only the food and drink that you bring yourself. It also implies that people do what they want, when they want and how they want, hence the American translation of the term, 'a madhouse'.

## ballets bleus/roses

In 1959, a scandal hit the headlines involving André Le Troquer, former president of the National Assembly, and various *notables*. They were tried and sentenced for organizing erotic parties and engaging in sexual relations with under-age girls. The term *ballet* was used since the young girls in question were dressed in ballet skirts. By extension, the term *ballets bleus* was later used to describe the same kind of orgiastic parties involving adults and underage boys.

## ban et l'arrière ban (convoquer le)

See Chapter 6.

## bât blesse (c'est là où le)

The 'bât' is the 'packsaddle' which, if mounted badly, can provoke a sore on the mule's body. To know where the *bât blesse* is to know where there is a hidden wound or problem. Today, it is used in the sense of the English expression 'there's the snag'.

## battre en brèche

An artillery term indicating a violent attack aimed at breaching a defensive wall. Today, it refers to destroying an argument, reducing it to nothing. 'Monter' or 'être sur la brèche' is to be in the thick of the fighting. The bravest of the brave would fight at the point where the wall had been breached, i.e. the most dangerous and exposed position. See Chapter 8 'brèche (s'engouffrer dans la)'.

## baudet (crier haro sur le)

See Chapter 5 'crier haro sur le baudet'.

## blanchi sous le harnais/harnois

> **

The 'harness' in question is in fact that of the armour worn by a soldier. To be 'blanchi sous le harnais' means 'to be a seasoned soldier', and by extension, any experienced and competent person in a given field. *Blanchi* would seem to refer to the white hairs of old age, and thus 'experience'.

## bois dont on fait des flûtes nm.

> *

The implication here is of being a 'yes-man', who is only a passive instrument playing the tune of those who use it.

## boisseau (mettre sous le)

> *

See Chapter 8.

## boucliers (une levée de)

> ***

This means 'a public outcry'. It comes from Roman history. When Roman soldiers raised their shields, it was an expression of their resistance to an order.

## boulets rouges (tirer à)

> ***

'To attack violently.' This meant to attack the enemy with canon balls that had previously been heated to the point of being red-hot, the intention being to set fire to the ships or buildings under attack.

## branle-bas de combat nm.

> ***

This is an old naval expression which meant to take down the 'branles', i.e. the hammocks between decks, with a view to clearing them for action. It thus refers to the hasty preparations to make a warship ready for battle. Today, it refers to any hasty and often disorderly measures taken to prepare for action. It can be likened to the English 'action stations'.

## bride abattue (courir à)

> **

'To ride flat out.' *La bride* (the bridle) is that part of the horse's harness enabling the rider to control it. The horse is given total freedom to run if the bridle is left 'abattue', i.e. totally slack.

## brûle pourpoint (à)

> **

This is a seventeenth-century expression which means 'at point blank range', i.e. the barrel of the gun is placed so close to the victim as to burn his doublet ('pourpoint'). It is used today in the sense of asking a question 'point blank'. See below 'but en blanc'.

## brûler ses vaisseaux

> *

This means to undertake a task or make a decision with no possibility of going back. It was a military tactic used by several great military leaders, including William the Conqueror, who burned his boats on the shores of Hastings to encourage his companions to fight, since there was literally no going back. The idea may be translated by 'burning one's bridges/boats'.

### but en blanc (de)                                        `**`
There are two ways of firing an arrow at a target. Either the shot is fired ballistically, tracing an arc as it moves towards the target, or it is fired 'de but en blanc', i.e. directly from the mound upon which the bowman is firing, to the 'blanc', i.e. the centre of the target – the bull's eye. To ask a question 'de but en blanc' is to ask a question very frankly, without beating about the bush, i.e. 'point blank'. See above 'brûle pourpoint'.

### catimini (en)                                            `**`
This means 'on the sly' or on the quiet. This expression has been in use since the thirteenth century. The substantive *catimini* was used in the fifteenth century to indicate menstruation, 'catimini' deriving from the Greek 'kata-mênia' meaning 'each month'. This expression is one of the many under-scoring the inferiorization of women via language.

### cor et à cri (à)                                         `**`
This term comes from hunting and refers to the sound of the hunting horn and the cries of the hunters. 'Demander à cor et à cri' is to demand something with clamour and insistence. NB: 'la chasse' is generally understood to be 'shooting' while 'la chasse à courre' is hunting with hounds.

### coup de pieds de l'âne nm.                               `***`
See Chapter 5 'coup de pied de l'âne'.

### coupes claires/sombres (des) nfpl.                       `***`
A lumberjack is said to make 'coupes claires' when he cuts down many trees in order to increase the amount of light passing through the branches, to encourage the growth of the saplings. 'Coupes sombres' on the other hand, are cuts where very few trees are felled, hence very little light passes through. 'Coupes sombres' is a term that is frequently misused in the press as meaning 'excessive cuts', 'sombre' having a negative connotation. If job cuts are drastic, the term should be 'coupes claires', if they are not too drastic, the term should be 'coupes sombres'. French journalists frequently confuse these two expressions.

### cousu de fil blanc                                       `***`
White thread is used to each sew pieces of cloth together before the final sewing is done with more discreetly coloured thread. 'Cousu de fil blanc' means 'blatantly'.

### crible (passer au)   ***

See Chapter 8 'crible. passer au'.

### damer le pion à qqn.   *

This expression 'to get the better of sb.' comes from chess. When a pawn succeeds in reaching the eighth row (i.e. the row along which the opponent's king, queen, bishops, castles, and knights are situated), the pawn is immediately transformed into any piece of the player's choice, except a king. This expression therefore means to gain a sudden and critical advantage over the opponent.

### deux temps trois mouvements (en)   **

'Very rapidly.' This refers to the speed with which the manipulation of weapons is carried out, in two phases and three movements. It would appear that this is an expression of the late eighteenth century.

### estoc et de taille (frapper d')   *

This is a term from the thirteenth century and indicates the two ways a sword may be used in fighting; *estoc* being the point, while *taille* refers to the cutting edge. It implies a violent combat which in English can be translated by 'cut and thrust'.

### fagots (de derrière les)   *

This is said of the very best wine that is kept to age in the cellar. The expression dates from the eighteenth century and has now come to mean something that one keeps preciously. A 'fagot' is a bundle of sticks that one keeps near the fireplace as kindling to start the fire.

### feu (faire long) nm.  

The term comes from the vocabulary of artillery. It means that the charge burns too slowly to ignite the powder in the canon and thus means 'to fail' or 'to fizzle out'. The term 'ne pas faire long feu' has come to mean 'not to last long'.

### figue mi raisin (mi)   *

This means half and half, neither one nor the other. It implies a certain degree of ambiguity. Figs and raisins are frequently associated in French since they are both dried fruits that were eaten during Lent. It should be noticed that in English, Adam and Eve used fig leaves to cover their private parts, whereas in French these parts were hidden with 'feuilles de vigne', 'vine leaves'.

### filer à l'anglaise   **

The French expression is equivalent to the English 'to take French leave'. This seems to be part of the long history of difficult Anglo-French relations. See Chapter 1 'Perfide Albion'.

## flanc (tirer au)

This means 'to shirk or skive.' It comes from the vocabulary of the army. The most dangerous part of the corps of the army for a soldier to be in is the front. The sides are known as the flank, and it is less dangerous to be on the flank than at the front. The term *tirer* has nothing to do with 'firing' but is a verb that means 'to move towards'. Consequently, sb. who *tire au flanc* is sb. who is trying to move away from danger and into a less exposed position.

## fleurets mouchetés (s'affronter à) nmpl.

This means that the opponents are not committed 100 percent to the fight since they are fighting with buttoned foils, verbally jousting and nothing more. This expression is the opposite of 'se battre à fer émoulu', i.e. with sharpened swords. The latter is thus a fight to the death with no quarter, but is extremely rare when used in the figurative sense.

## franc du collier

This means 'frank'. It originally referred to a horse that would pull in a straight line without the whip having to be used. It was subsequently used to describe a valliant soldier but is now used to qualify sb. who is 'as straight as a die'.

## gaz (il y a de l'eau dans le)

This expression indicates the imminence of a dispute between two parties who have hitherto been in harmony. The expression refers to water vapour that was used in the early gas distribution systems. When the vapour turned into water there was a danger of explosion. It was initially used to refer to domestic clashes.

## guigne (s'en soucier comme d'une)

In this expression, a 'guigne' is a sour Morello cherry, i.e. a thing of very little importance. Thus the expression means 'not to care a fig about something'.

## hallali (sonner l') nm.

'To blow the mort.' This is the sound of the hunting horn that indicates that the dogs are going 'in for the kill'.

## honte bue (toute)

This expression dates from the fifteenth century and implies that one has lost all sense of self-esteem and that one is beyond shame.

## hue et à dia (tirer à)

This means 'to pull in opposite directions'. The words correspond to the shouted command of the coach driver: *hue* to make the horse turn to the right and *dia* to make the horse turn to the left.

### index (mettre à l') nm.                           **

See Chapter 6.

### jambe (ça lui fait une belle)                      *

'A fat lot of good that will do him.' The expression 'faire une belle jambe' dates from the sixteenth century when shoes and stockings made their appearance. Men were proud of their legs; thighs and calves were part of the arsenal of seduction and they were frequently decorated with ribbons. The expression seems to mean that this will not change the beauty of one's leg, i.e. it is without consequence.

### Jarnac (un coup de)                                ***

See Chapter 6 'Jarnac'.

### jeu ne vaut pas la chandelle (le)                  *

'Not worth a light.' This is an expression that dates from the sixteenth century. Evenings were spent playing cards or games of chance and consequently this expression simply means that the gains in playing cards will not be sufficient to cover the cost of burning the candles.

### lice (entrer en) nf.                               ***

In the Middle Ages, the area in which a tournament was to take place was enclosed by a fence or barrier called 'lice'. It was also the name of the specific area where the fighting took place, a corridor along which two horsemen would ride towards each other, either side of a fence or barrier. 'Entrer en lice' is 'to enter the lists'.

### lisière (tenir en) nf.                             *

'To keep under one's control'. It is the harness that used to be employed to make sure that young children did not wander. Not to be confused with 'lisière' in the sense of the edge of a village or forest.

### maille à partir avec qqn. (avoir) nf.             **

'Maille' derives from a word meaning 'half'. The original verb was 'départir', i.e. to share. Une 'maille' meant the half of a denier (a low-value seventeenth-century coin). It thus meant a quarrel arising from the impossible task of sharing into two equal halves something of very low value. Today, it refers to a dispute or a 'brush' with sb.

### Message reçu cinq sur cinq                         **

This term comes from military radio communications. The quality of the reception was graded on a five-point scale. 'Cinq sur cinq' indicates that a message has been received 'loud and clear'.

### miroir aux alouettes nm.

This term refers to any very attractive but phoney enterprise that attracts by its glitter, i.e. a decoy or lure. The 'miroir aux alouettes' (literally 'a mirror for skylarks') was a device made of wood and bearing many small mobile mirrors and wires. Fascinated by their reflection, the skylarks were attracted by the mirrors and became trapped in the wires.

### mors aux dents (prendre le)

'To take the bit between one's teeth.' 'To get carried away', 'to fly off the handle.' A horse that gets the bit stuck between its teeth does not respond to the directions of the rider. It bolts and cannot be reined in.

### odeur de sainteté (ne pas être en) nf.

'To die in the odour of sanctity' is to die in a state of spiritual perfection. Certain dead saints are said to have given off a sweet smell, a smell that distinguished them from other corpses. This is more often than not used in the negative in which case it means 'to be in sb.'s bad books'.

### oignons (soigné aux petits) nmpl.

This refers to the great care that has been taken in preparing or carrying out any operation and evokes the loving care taken in cooking a dish slowly with little onions.

### oiseau de mauvais augure nm.

See Chapter 7 'augures' and 'oiseau de mauvais augure'.

### oiseau-lyre nm.

The lyrebird has the particularity of being able to imitate many sounds, natural or otherwise. Figuratively, it refers to sb. who is servile towards the powers that be. See above 'bois dont on fait des flûtes'.

### orfraie (pousser des cris d') nf.

This literally means to screech like a white-tailed eagle. There seems to be a confusion between two paronymous words – 'orfraie' and 'effraie' (respectively a bird of prey and a kind of owl), and 'effraie' and 'effroi' (dread). The expression means to shriek at the top of one's voice, in panic. It is frequently used to describe the arguments of people defending their vested interests.

### panne (être en) nf.

'To have broken down', or 'to be immobilized'. There are three possible origins. To *mettre en panne* a boat is to make the boat list to one side during the time it takes to repair a leak on the opposite side. It is also the name of a *manœuvre* whereby the sails are set to simultaneously push and restrain the boat in order to mark time. In a harbour for pleasure craft, the boats are moored along the 'panne', a sort of jetty that is perpendicular to the harbour wall. If they are *en panne* they are, by definition, immobilized.

### passer l'arme à gauche    **

This is a euphemism and nineteenth-century military slang for 'to die'. Death is often equated with eternal rest. The phrase comes from the military expression 'at ease' ('repos') a position in which the soldier's rifle is placed vertically next to the left foot. The word 'gauche' frequently has a negative connotation in French. See Chapter 7 'augures'.

### pavé (tenir le haut du)    ***

'To occupy a socially superior position', 'to be a big wig'. The 'haut du pavé' was that part of the street that was closest to the wall of the houses. It was raised and sloped away to the gutter in the middle of the street so as to evacuate the sewage and rain water. People of a high social class would walk on this part, whereas the lower classes would walk either near or in the gutter.

### payer sur la bête (se)    **

This means to beat sb. who refuses to pay back a debt. The idea is that one vents one's anger on the bad payer. There is also an idea of being paid 'in kind' directly, with no go-between.

### pied (prendre son) nm.    *

Initially, this was a synonym of 'to experience intense sexual pleasure'. Aristophanes mentions the fact that women would often 'prendre leur pied' at the moment of orgasm. This had the effect of shortening the vagina and accentuating the penetration. It is used post-1968 as a popular expression and now means to have great pleasure, i.e. to reach an orgasm or to get one's pleasure.

### pignon sur rue (avoir) nm.    ***

'To own a house or shop in town'. 'To be a well-known, respectable and socially superior member of the community.' The gable ('pignon') is the most visible part of the house and was the symbol of the possession of property and thus, of respectability.

### planche (avoir du pain sur la)    **

'To have one's work cut out.' The idea being that the baker has made the dough into loaves but that the cooking process remains to be completed.

### poire et le fromage (entre la)    ***

This expression indicates a moment, towards the end of the meal, when the diners are full, and can give their attention to general conversation in a relaxed manner.

## Polichinelle (un secret de)                    `***`

Although this is translated by 'an open secret' this translation lacks nuance. Punchinello is a character from the *Commedia dell'arte*. In order to take revenge on one of the lords at court, Punchinello tells the king that the lord in question has a body covered in feathers. The king is sworn to secrecy, as is each of the individual courtiers to whom Punchinello tells the same secret. Consequently, everyone knows the secret *individually* but nobody knows that everyone else is in the know.

## potron-minet (dès) loc. adv.                    `*`

This is a delightful, if somewhat old-fashioned way of saying 'at the break of day', 'at the crack of dawn'. It comes from an earlier expression 'dès potron-jacquet'. In Norman French, 'jacquet' is a 'squirrel' while 'potron' comes from the Latin *posterio* indicating 'the backside'. In the nineteenth century 'jacquet' was replaced by 'minet' (pussy cat). Consequently, the expression means 'as soon as the cat shows its arse', i.e. in the very early morning.

## poudre aux yeux (jeter de la)                    `**`

'To put on a show'. 'To deceive sb. by using a flattering approach'. It implies that the victim is impressed by the brilliance of the show.

## poudre d'escampette (prendre la)                    `**`

'To take to one's heels.' 'Escampette' is a diminutive of the sixteenth-century word 'escampe' which means 'flight', the substantive of 'to flee'. The powder can be interpreted as gunpowder, the explosion of which makes people run away, or indicates the dust provoked by running feet.

## puce à l'oreille (mettre la)                    `***`

Today, this means 'to have suspicions' or 'to start thinking'. In the past, it meant to be worried or agitated or even to have a sexual itch. La Fontaine wrote 'fille qui pense à son amant absent toute la nuit, dit-on, a la puce à l'oreille' ('a girl who thinks of her absent lover the whole night, is said to have a flea in the ear'). This has nothing to do with the English expression 'flea in the ear'.

## Rabelais (le quart d'heure de)                    `*`

This refers to the disagreeable moment when one has to settle one's debts or the bill at the end of a meal. In *Gargantua*, the story is told of a man who has eaten at an inn but cannot pay the bill. He makes three small packets upon which he writes 'poison for the king', 'poison for the queen' and 'poison for the dauphin'. The inn-keeper is immediately convinced that there is a regicide in his inn, and has the man arrested and taken to Paris. Not only does the man not pay the inn keeper's bill but he is also transported to

Paris free of charge. The king laughed at this story and invited the culprit to dinner. Today, the expression means to experience a nasty moment.

### repartir comme en 14 `***`

Let's remember the ardour, enthusiasm and naivety with which the young recruits, from all over Europe, went to war in 1914. 'It would all be over by Christmas!' 'Repartir comme en quatorze' means to start again with vigour and enthusiasm.

### revenir bredouille `**`

In the seventeenth century, this expression was used to describe a woman who left the ball without having been invited to dance. It is frequently used today to describe a hunter or angler who returns home without having caught anything, i.e. empty-handed.

### roses (découvrir le pot aux) nfpl. `***`

The original sense is unclear but could refer to 'découvrir' in the meaning of 'to uncover' or 'to take off the lid'. 'Rose' in French is not without strong erotic connotations and 'pot' is an old French term for 'arse'. The basic idea is to discover a secret.

### rubis sur l'ongle (payer) nm. `***`

This means 'to pay cash, down to the last centime'. It was originally the fact of drinking wine down to the last drop, and this drop was small enough to stay on the thumbnail of the drinker.

### schmilblick (cela fait avancer le) `**`

See Chapter 1 'schmilblick'.

### sérail (élevé dans le) `***`

The 'sérail' was the palace of an Ottoman sultan. It implies having been brought up in a high social class from which it is possible to know all of the mechanisms and codes of the inner circle of the establishment.

### singe (payer en monnaie de) nm. `**`

This means 'to pay with empty promises'. It comes from the time when the buffoons and tumblers paraded their monkeys in front of the tollgate keeper in exchange for a free passage. The expression has been in use since the time of Saint Louis who imposed a toll on people wishing to cross the bridge from Île de la Cité, in Paris, to rue Saint-Jacques just on the other side of the Seine.

### sonnantes et trébuchantes (en espèces) adj. `***`

This refers to metallic money whose sterling quality can be judged by the sound that it makes on falling. The debasing of the coin would affect its ring, and it would not be 'sonnante'. 'Trébuchante', on the other hand, indicates the right weight and comes from the expression to weigh gold or silver on a pair of small, but very accurate, scales called 'un trébuchet'. Such a pair of scales was used by goldsmiths and chemists. It is generally used today to denote a payment in cash as opposed to a payment by credit card or cheque.

### sortir du bois
*To come out into the open'. There can be the connotation of danger given the metaphor of the wolf coming out of the forest.

### soucier comme de l'an 40 (s'en)
This means 'not to care less'. The year '40' is a mystery. The expression may come from a Norman saying 'je m'en moque comme l'Alcoran' (the Koran) but the expression 'comme de l'an quarante' dates from the French Revolution and can be found in the texts of *Le Père Duchesne*, one of the principal publications of the time that appeared between 1790–4.

### sucre sur le dos de qqn. (casser du)
This means 'to speak ill of people behind their backs'. 'Casser du sucre' is an old expression meaning 'to gossip', whereas 'sur le dos' implies that the person in question will bear the burden of the attack.

### Suisse (boire en)
'Like a Swiss person' and not 'in Switzerland'. This means to drink alone, on the sly. Gaston Auguste Esnault (1874–1971), specialist of French slang, suggests that this might refer to a socio-cultural difference between the Germanic countries, where it is normal that people pay for their own drinks, as in the expression 'to go Dutch' ('chacun paie son écot'), as opposed to the more Latin habit of paying for a round of drinks.

### tabac (passer à) nm.
'To beat up'. The term 'tabac' is a slang term for a beating or a thrashing. 'Donner du tabac' used to be a euphemism for 'to fight'. This is frequently used in cases involving police brutality.

### tailler des croupières
'To force sb. to flee'. The idea was that the pursuant was close enough behind the person in flight to make cuts into the hindquarters of the fleeing person's horse. It has now come to mean 'to put a spoke in sb.'s wheel'.

### tambour battant
'Rapidly and energetically'. Military marches and charges were always accompanied by the beating of drums.

## tante (chez ma)    \*

'In pawn', at the pawnbroker's. 'Je l'ai laissée chez ma tante' was the reply of the prince de Joinville, Prince François-Ferdinand d'Orléans (Louis-Philippe's son) when asked by his mother where his watch was. He had pawned his watch in order to honour a debt. Other synonymous terms are 'le crédit municipal', 'au Mont de Piété' and 'au clou'.

## tapisserie (faire) nf.    \*

Young women at a ball are said to 'faire tapisserie' since they are not invited to dance and are therefore reduced to a decorative role such as a character in the tapestry. In English the equivalent expression is 'to be a wallflower'.

## tire-larigot (à) loc. adv.    \*

'In enormous quantities'. It was initially used with the verb 'boire'. *Larigot* is a popular refrain in old drinking songs. The verb *tirer* is associated with wine as is the English equivalent 'to draw'. This expression has been known since the sixteenth century.

## tirer son épingle du jeu   

'To get out of a difficult situation without any loss'. It can refer to the game such as 'Mikado' or refer to a slang sexual metaphor where the 'épingle' is the sex of the male and 'jeu' is the female organ.

## tomber dessus comme la vérole sur le bas clergé    \*

Abruptly and with violence, like an epidemic of pox or syphilis. This expression reflects the anti-clericalism prevalent throughout French history.

## tourner casaque   

'To change one's opinion radically and quickly'. The 'casaque' in question is a valet's livery or military uniform. To 'tourner casaque' therefore means to change livery or party. This could be compared to the English expression 'to be a turncoat'. 'Tourner casaque' is synonymous with 'retourner sa veste'.

## trêve des confiseurs nf.    \*

A time when political and diplomatic conflicts are suspended during the end-of-year celebrations, i.e. a Christmas/New Year truce; the time during which confectioners do not work.

## Turc (une tête de)    \*

This means 'a whipping boy' or 'whipping post'. The Turks or the Moors have traditionally been represented as 'the enemy'. Heads made out of cardboard representing the Turk were used in the past for shooting practice. At the end of the nineteenth century, it was the name given to a game at the funfair which consisted of punching a head (depicting a Turk) to register one's physical strength. Turk also has the connotation of great strength.

### vache enragée (manger de la)     ( ** )
This expression means 'to live through hard times.' An early eighteenth-century expression, it used to mean to be in such desperate circumstances as to be prepared to eat meat from a diseased animal that had been killed for reasons of hygiene.

### vau l'eau (aller à) loc. adv.     ( * )
A sixteenth-century expression indicating 'to follow the current', i.e. to descend, to go to the dogs, to be on the road to ruin.

### veiller au grain     ( *** )
'To be vigilant' and to keep an eye open for trouble. *Grain* in this context is a nautical term that means 'a squall', i.e. a sudden, violent, if short-lived, blast of wind, and has nothing to do with cereals.

### vendre la mèche     ( * )
'To give the game away,' 'to let the cat out of the bag'. The verb 'vendre' and the past participle 'vendu' are frequently associated with betrayal (cf. 'sold down the river').

### vessies pour des lanternes (prendre des) nfpl.     ( ** )
'To think that the moon is made of cheese,' 'to have the wool pulled over one's eyes,' 'to be really mistaken.' *Lanternes* in the sixteenth-century sense meant 'absurdities' while the verb *vessier* meant to 'blow up like a balloon'. That said, lampshades are often made out of 'vessie de porc', i.e. pig's bladder.

### virer casaque     ( * )
See above 'tourner casaque'.

### virer sa cuti     ( * )
This term comes from the skin test to screen for tuberculosis. 'Virer sa cuti' means to come up positive on the test. It has now come to mean 'to change one's lifestyle or sexual orientation completely. See Chapter 14 'BCG'.

### volée de bois vert nf.     ( * )
'A flurry of blows.' The idea here is that wood that is 'green' is still full of sap and therefore will be less likely to snap than dry wood, while the punishment is being inflicted. Green is also a colour frequently associated with a reprimand.

### volet (trié sur le)

'Selected according to very strict criteria'. This expression dates from the sixteenth century. A *volet* was a small sieve-type appliance enabling the user to sort the grain. This can be compared to the expression 'passer au crible'. See Chapter 8 'crible. passer au'.

### yeux (ne pas avoir froid aux)

'To be plucky to the point of impudence'. It is always used in the negative form. To be cold in one part of the body used to be synonymous with being cowardly or backing out at the last minute. 'Avoir froid au cul' in this respect can be compared with the English 'to have cold feet'.

# Chapter 4

# Headline punning

Given the flexibility of the French language and the fertile minds of French journalists, it would seem impossible, at first sight, to 'teach' the principles of punning or draw out any rules that could be useful to the student or reader. On closer examination, however, we can find certain constants that will help a reader understand and even anticipate certain puns. Such mechanisms are often used in conjunction with famous historical phrases, literary quotations, advertising slogans, proverbs, etc., hence the importance of possessing a good literary, classical and historical background. A certain degree of skill in punning is mandatory in order to understand the French press. To begin with, puns may be broken down into several categories:

1 Punning on well-known names
2 Homophones
3 Homonyms
4 Telescoping
5 Vowel changes
6 Consonant changes

## I Punning on well-known names

Given the frequency with which these names appear in the press, the reader would do well to be aware of their punning potential. This section is to be read in conjunction with Chapter 9 Who's who.

### Allègre, Claude
'Allègre' means 'jaunty' or 'light-hearted'. Other associated words include 'allegro', 'allégrement', 'allégresse'. 'Allegro ma non troppo' in reference to the musical direction.

### Arnault, Bernard
'Arnault limite', no limit.

## Attali, Jacques

'Attali' is an anagram of 'Attila'.

## Aubry, Martine, *Aubry vaut Delors.*

We can understand *Martine vaut de l'or*, 'Martine is worth gold', or 'Martine is as good as her father'. Martine Aubry's maiden name is Delors. She is the daughter of the former socialist Minister of Finance, Jacques Delors. Given the frequency of the word 'gold' in French, punning potential is high. Her married name 'Aubry' also lends itself to punning. We can find *Aubry bus*–Abribus is the registered trademark of a bus shelter. *Martine fait de l'Aubry collage* (bricolage), *les sans-Aubry* ('les sans abris' are 'the home-less'). *Aubry de vaisselle* ('bris' is breakage or breaking e.g. of crockery), *Urbi et Aubry* which is a play on the words of the Pope's blessing 'Urbi et orbi'. See Chapter 13 'Urbi et orbi'.

## Bachelot, Roselyne

Her surname can be punned upon with the word 'lot' as in 'lot de consolation' (consolation prize). The number of expressions using the word 'l'eau' opens up many punning possibilities. A 'lot' is a 'batch' in everyday French and IT jargon.

## Bayrou, François

*Un farouche des tracteurs* (*détracteur*). Bayrou owns a farm in the south-west of France and also has business interests in breeding racehorses. The motto of *The Three Musketeers* 'Un pour tous, tous pour un' can thus be changed into 'Un pour tous, tous bourrin'. *Bourrin* is 'an old nag'. *Bayrou n'a pas de Pau*. He was unsuccessful in his attempt to win the town of Pau in the leg-islative elections of 2008. *Pot* is a homophone of *Pau* and is also a slang term for 'luck'. *Peau* means 'skin' or 'animal hide'. *Avoir la peau de qqn.* is 'to have sb.'s hide'.

## Benoît XVI, Pope

Benoît XIII et III: Benedict thirteen plus three, *treize et trois = très étroit*, i.e. very narrow-minded.

## Bergé, Pierre

*Les bâtons du Bergé. Le bâton du berger* is the shepherd's staff or crook, and is also a famous trademark of *saucisson*. A *bâton* is the former slang for 10,000 francs. Pierre Bergé is financing Ségolène Royal's political activities. *L'étoile du berger* is 'the evening star'. Punning potential is thus high.

## Besson, Eric

*Bes(son) et lumière*, sound and light.

## Blanc, Christian

The colour *blanc* is so frequent in French that the punning possibilities here are almost limitless, e.g. *Christian n'est pas blanc comme neige*, i.e. he is not as pure as the driven snow.

## Borloo, Jean-Louis

The end of his surname being 'loo' (pronounced 'low') we can find the same punning potential as for 'Bachelot' (see above) with 'l'eau' and 'lot'.

## Boutin, Christine

*Boutin train*, i.e. *un boute-en-train*, is 'a live wire' or 'the life and soul of the party'. *Tintin* is a slang term for 'nothing doing'. *Faire tintin* is 'to go without'.

## Bouton, Daniel

*Bouton* is a 'button'. One of the most famous films in the history of the French cinema is *La Guerre des boutons*. There is also the possibility of telescoping *Bouton train* as above. *Ton* is also the 'tone', e.g. of sb.'s voice.

## Courroye, Philippe

There are several punning possibilities here. The surname brings to mind *courroie* in the expression *courroie de transmission*, a technical term for 'a fan belt'. The idea in 'transmission' is 'passing along or conveying'. He is the Public Prosecutor of Nanterre. Courroye is close to Nicolas Sarkozy and he wrapped up the investigation into the scandal of Nicolas Sarkozy's flat in Île de la Jatte with 'indecent haste'. Hence the pun 'On Nanterre', i.e. 'on enterre' 'we are burying' or 'covering up' an affair. Recently he was accused of not having transmitted a certain document in the dossier concerning the Angolagate scandal; hence the pun 'Nouveaux problèmes de transmission pour Courroye'. © *Le Canard Enchaîné* 4603.

The pun can also bear on 'cour' for 'court' in the royal sense of the word and 'roye' which is the old French spelling for 'king'.

## Darcos, Xavier

The surname contains the word *os*, i.e. 'bone' with all of the resulting possibilities. *Cos* may also be construed as *causes*, the second person singular of the verb *causer*, the familiar form of 'to speak'. Hence *Darcos toujours*, i.e. 'keep talking, it won't make a blind bit of difference'. The telescopic form *un Darcos à ronger* gives *un os à ronger*, i.e. 'a bone to be gnawed', or something to keep sb. occupied.

## Dassault, Serge

Dassault is a homophone of *d'assaut*; *prendre d'assaut* is 'to take by storm'. *Le Beau Serge* (1958) is also the name of the new wave film of Claude Chabrol.

### d'Estaing, Valéry Giscard

*d'Estaing* is a homophone of *destin*, i.e. fate or destiny, with all of the accompanying possibilities, e.g. *d'Estaing cruel*. See below Giscard.

### Fillon, François

The pronunciation of the surname is 'feeyong'. *Fion* is slang for 'arse' and the expression *Courage, fuyons*, i.e. 'take heart, let's scarper' comes to mind. This was the title of an Yves Robert film in 1979. *Filon* is also 'a seam' in a mine and can also mean 'a sector of activity'. Consequently, punning potential is high.

### Giscard, Valéry

The end of the name gives us 'quart'. *Giscard de tour*, i.e. *un quart de tour*. For an engine to start *au quart de tour* means that the engine starts first time while the driver has hardly touched the ignition. It can also refer to sb. who has a short fuse.

### Hortefeux, Brice

The number of expressions that include the word *feu* and *feux* afford - limitless possibilities for punning, e.g. the telescopic *Brice Hortefeux à volonté*, i.e. 'fire at will' and *Hortefeux d'artifice*, i.e. 'a firework display'.

### Hue, Robert

Two expressions immediately come to mind. *Tirer à hue et à dia* means 'to pull in opposite directions' while the name also reminds one of the trivial words of a song by Jacques Dutronc 'Crac, boum, hue'. See Chapter 1 'Crac, boum, hue'.

### Kouchner, Bernard

*Kouchner du temps*, i.e. *air du temps*, 'to be in the air' and *Bernard de vivre*, i.e. 'the art of living'. His name also provides the sound of the word *nerf* 'nerve'. After threatening Iran with war, he was nicknamed 'Kouchner de la guerre'.

### Lagarde, Christine

*Garde* can be used in many different ways and consequently the punning potential is very high. One of the most famous and recurrent puns is the phrase attributed to Cambronne: *La garde meurt mais ne se rend pas.* See Chapter 2 'garde'.

### Lagardère, Arnaud

The forename 'Arnaud' provides lots of possibilities with 'no'. See Chapter 5 'Lagardère'.

## Lang, Jack

'Langue' is another of those words frequently used in figurative expressions and opens up great punning possibilities, e.g. *langue de vipère*, i.e. 'a spiteful gossip', *je donne ma langue au chat* 'I give up' in a guessing game. There is also *Jack Pote*, i.e. 'jackpot', *pote* being a slang term for chum, pal, mate. A tongue is used for licking but 'lécher' can also mean 'to bootlick' or 'to suck up to'.

## Larcher, Gérard

*L'archer* can mean 'the archer' or 'the bow' of a violin or cello. There are many expressions in French using the word 'violon', so consequently punning potential is high.

## Le Pen, Jean-Marie

The surname can evoke either a verb *peiner*, e.g. 'je peine', 'I toil'. The appropriate conjugations of the verb could be the singular conjugations including the third person singular form, e.g. *on peine à le croire*, i.e. 'one has difficulty in believing it'. There are also all of the possibilities with the use of the noun *peine* in the meaning of the sentence of a court, or moral pain. Nor should we forget the homophones *un pêne*, i.e. 'a lock bolt' and *une penne* which means 'a large feather' or quill. Jean-Marie Le Pen's political career is over but his daughter 'Marine' will take up the succession. See Chapter 6 'poujadisme'.

## Mamère, Noël

This can be construed as *ma mère* 'my mother' or *mammaire* the adjective 'mammary' or the noun *mémère*, i.e. 'an old biddy' or the adjective 'frumpy'.

## Minc, Alain

*Un Minc à gagner*, i.e. *un manque à gagner* which is 'a shortfall'. *Mince* is also used as an exclamation 'drat', 'blow it' (UK) or 'darn it' (US).

## Moscovici, Pierre

The last verb in Caesar's declaration, *veni, vidi, vici* comes to mind. Thus, Moscovici can be construed as 'Mosco conquered'. 'Mosco' is the affectionate term by which this politician is known. All of the expressions using 'Moscow' can, of course, be punned upon.

## Obama, Barack

In French 'barraque' is a slang term for 'house', 'place', 'pad'. It is frequently used in the expression *casser la barraque*, i.e. 'to bring the house down', or *casser la barraque à qqn.*, i.e. 'to mess things up for somebody'.

### Pinault, François
The last part of the surname evokes 'no' and thus *Pinault comment* (no comment).

### Royal, Ségolène
This name opens up quite a few possibilities. The use of the feminine definite article with a family name is reserved for exceptional stars, e.g. *La Piaf, La Callas*. These are two of the rare examples. La Royal(e) is the name given to the French navy (in spite of France's republican regime). There is also the famous North African dish *couscous royal* and *gelée royale*, i.e. 'royal jelly'. *Ségocentric* is another punning possibility.

### Sarkozy, Nicolas
*Sarkophage*, i.e. 'sarcophagus' can be construed as sb. who criticizes Sarkozy. In French *bouffer* 'to guzzle' or 'to scoff' can mean 'to criticize violently' as in *bouffer du curé* which means to be violently anti-clerical.

### Strauss-Kahn, Dominique
Known as DSK, this enables the telescopic pun (with the French pronunciation of the letter 'k') *DSK de conscience*, i.e. 'a moral dilemma'. Johann Strauss (father and son) come to mind and their famous musical genre, the waltz. In French, the verb *valser* and the noun *valse* can be used pejoratively. *Une valse* can be the slang for a 'thrashing', *les valseuses* is slang for 'testicles'. The recent case of DSK's adulterous affair was exploited to the full in this meaning! The verb *valser* can also be the slang for 'to be thrown', e.g. *il a envoyé valser le vase*, i.e. 'he sent the vase flying'. *Envoyer valser qqn.*, is 'to send somebody packing', *faire valser l'argent* is 'to throw money around'. *Faire valser les étiquettes* means 'to jack up the prices', which is rather comic given that DSK is the head of the International Monetary Fund!

### Tapie, Bernard
The homophone *tapis* (mat, floor, carpet, etc.) can be punned upon in many ways. *Tapie vert* could mean 'an envious Bernard Tapie' or evoke the *tapis vert*, i.e. the green baize of the casino table. *Tapie volant* could refer to 'Bernard stealing' or to the 'magic carpet'. There are also many expressions using *tapis*, e.g. *envoyer au tapis*, i.e. 'to floor sb'. Nor should we forget the verb *tapir* and the past participle *tapi* which can mean 'lurking' or 'nestling'.

### Trichet, Jean-Claude
It is indeed unfortunate that the head of the Central European Bank should have a name that is a homophone of the infinitive of the verb 'to cheat'

*tricher* or the imperfect *trichait* or the past participle *triché*. 'Jean-Claude was cheating' is indeed funny for a man who was Governor of the Bank of France at the time of the crash of the Crédit Lyonnais bank when he was accused of presenting financial accounts knowing that they were not fair and honest! He was acquitted.

## Valls, Manuel

The surname is a homophone of the noun *valse*, 'waltz'. See above Strauss-Kahn. *Manuel* can be understood as either 'manual' in the sense of 'good with one's hands' or 'manual' in the meaning of a schoolbook or book of technical instructions.

## Villepin, Dominique de

Punning possibilities here are double. *Ville*, i.e. 'town', *vil*, 'vile' i.e. 'worthless, cheap, base' and *pin* the homophone of *pain*, i.e. 'bread', and the word for 'pinewood'. Given the number of French expressions using the word 'bread' or 'pine', punning potential is high: *Villepin complet* (wholemeal bread). *Le sapin* can mean the Christmas tree, but it can be associated with 'death' or 'the end' in the expression *ça sent le sapin*, i.e. the smell of the wood from which cheap coffins are made.

## Weil, Simone

The surname is pronounced 'vay' and evokes the verb *veiller*, i.e. 'to be watchful' or 'to take care'. *Simone Weil* can thus mean 'Simone is vigilant'.

## 2 Homophones

Some of the puns are recurrent, the most famous of them coming from *Tartuffe* by Molière: 'Cachez ce sein que je ne saurais voir'. As is often the case with quotations, this quote does not correspond to the original. In *Tartuffe* the verb is 'couvrir' and not 'cacher'. Any word rhyming with *sein* ('breast') will do for the pun; *train, gain, pain, main, saint, teint*, etc. The reader would do well to remember this one. Other frequent homophones used in newspaper punning include the following:

### a. 'Faim' (hunger) for 'fin' (end)

| | |
|---|---|
| *le mot de la faim* | the last word |
| *générique de faim* | the credits at the end of the film |
| *la faim du monde* | the end of the world |
| *la faim d'une époque* | the end of an age, era, epoch |
| *la faim est proche* | the end is nigh |

## b. Ère, air, Eire, hère, aire.

| | |
|---|---|
| *un changement d'air* | air |
| *un changement d'ère* | epoch |
| *un changement d'Eire* | Eire |
| *un hère connu* | a well-known tune or a well-known, miserable wretch |

## c. sceaux, seaux, saut, sot *seals, champagne buckets, jump, idiot*

| | |
|---|---|
| *le Garde des Seaux* | the keeper of the champagne buckets |
| *le Garde des Sceaux* | the Minister of Justice |
| *un sot dans le vide* | 'an idiot in the void' for 'a leap into the void' |
| *le saut du secret* | 'the jump of the secret' for 'the seal of secrecy' |

## d. coût *for* coup

| | |
|---|---|
| *tous les coûts sont permis* for *tous les coups sont permis* | no holds barred |
| *un coût dans l'aile* for *un coup dans l'aile* | to be in a bad way |
| *des coûts bas* for *des coups bas* | punches below the belt |

## e. mère, maire, mer  *mother, mayor, sea*

| | |
|---|---|
| *La fête des mères* | mother's day |
| *La fête des maires* | mayor's day |
| *La fête des mers* | the festival of the seas |

## f. Miscellaneous homophones

| | |
|---|---|
| *la mère, l'amère* | the mother/the bitter one |
| *Anvers, envers, en vers* | Antwerp/towards/in verse |
| *au Quai, OK* | at the Ministry of Foreign Affairs/all right |
| *aumônes, hormones* | alms/hormones |
| *balais, ballet* | broom/ballet |
| *ce braquet, se braquer* | this bike gear/to dig one's heels in |
| *chant, champ* | song, singing/field |
| *chaud, show* | hot/spectacle |
| *de boue, debout* | made of mud/standing up |
| *Delhi, délit* | Delhi, the capital of India/an offence |
| *fait, fée* | fact/fairy |
| *faucon, faux con* | falcon/false, stupid bastard |
| *faux taux, photos* | false rates/photos |
| *fois, foi, foie* | time/faith/liver |
| *gêne, gène* | embarrassment, discomfort/gene |
| *hasch, hache* | pot, grass/axe |
| *heures, heurts* | hours/clashes |

| | |
|---|---|
| *d'hiver, divers* | of winter/miscellaneous |
| *mâle, mal* | virile, male/evil, pain |
| *maux, mots* | ills/words |
| *ras, rat* | close-cropped/rat |
| *saint, sein, sain, ceint* | saint/breast/healthy, wholesome/encircled |
| *tante, tente* | aunt/tent |
| *toit, toi* | roof/you (thou) |
| *tromper, tremper* | to mislead/to temper metal/to soak |
| *vert, verre, ver(s), vers* | green/glass/worm(s)/verse/towards |
| *voit, voie, voix* | (s)he sees/track, way, path/voice or voices |

## 3 Homonyms

| | |
|---|---|
| *remonter les bretelles* | 'to give sb. a telling off' or 'to drive up motorway slip roads'. |
| *traites* | 'regular credit repayments' or 'milking of a cow'. |
| *actions* | 'conduct', 'state of movement' or 'shares' in the financial sense of the term. |
| *bidon* | 'bogus' or 'an oil drum'. |
| *train* | 'carriages pulled by a locomotive' or 'the speed at which one walks', e.g. *un train de Sénateur*, i.e. ponderously. |
| *noir* | 'a black person' or 'the dark'. |

## 4 Telescoping

| | |
|---|---|
| *Cynique ta mère* | Cynical. *Nique ta mere* NTM 'F ... your mother', a French rap group. |
| *Borloo de consolation* | *lot de consolation*, a consolation prize. |
| *Dassault périlleux* | *saut périlleux* is 'a somersault'. |
| *Emmaüs et coutumes* | *us et coutumes*, customs. See Chapter 9 'Abbé Pierre'. |
| *encens unique* | incense, the oriental fragrance, *une voie en sens unique* is 'a one-way street'. |
| *Bulgare au Villepin* | *gare au Villepin*, beware of Villepin. |
| *Hongrois rêver* | *on croit rêver*, the mind boggles. |
| *Facho devant* | 'Fascist in front'. *Chaud devant*, mind your backs. See Chapter 1 'Chaud devant'. |

| | |
|---|---|
| *Massacre de Reims* | *Le sacre de Reims.* The coronation in Reims. French kings were traditionally crowned in Reims cathedral. The socialist party congress of November 2008 held in Reims was not a model of unity. |
| *L'amer du nord* | 'the bitter man of the north', i.e. *la mer du nord*, 'the North Sea'. |
| *à Likoud au coude* | *être coude à coude*, to be neck and neck. (Likoud is the right-wing party in Israel.) |
| *tête de containeur* | *tête de con*, 'dickhead'. |

# 5 Vowel change

| | |
|---|---|
| *prometteurs immobiliers* | *promoteurs immobiliers*, property developers. *Prometteur* can be construed as 'promiser' or 'promising'. |
| *abattu en plein viol* | *abattu en plein vol*, shot down in full flight. Viol is 'rape'. |
| *leur part du ghetto* | *leur part du gâteau*, their part of the cake. |
| *nos meilleurs vieux* | *Nos meilleurs vœux*, 'our best wishes' becomes 'our best old folk'. |
| *l'évité d'honneur* | *l'invité d'honneur* is 'the guest of honour', *l'évité* is sb. who is avoided. |
| *renseignements généreux* | *généraux*, 'general', and *généreux* 'generous'. See Chapter 14 'RG'. |
| *Sarko réforme l'odieux visuel* | *odieux*, 'odious' for 'audio'. *Audio-visuel* can have the meaning of 'audio-visual' or 'broadcasting'. |
| *guichet inique* | *guichet inique*, 'iniquitous service window' for *guichet unique*, i.e. 'a single service window or point of contact with a one-stop-shopping philosophy'. |

# 6 Consonant change

| | |
|---|---|
| *à poil et à vapeur* | *à poil* is 'starkers' whereas *à voile et à vapeur* (literally 'sail and steam') means *bisexuel*. |
| *ballet des congrès* | *Palais des Congrès*. See Chapter 10 'Palais des Congrès'. |

| | |
|---|---|
| *coup de camif dans le contrat* | *La Camif* is a mail order company that recently went into liquidation. *Coup de canif* is 'an adulterous affair', i.e. 'a penknife cut in the marriage contract'. |
| *doigt dans le deuil* | *se fourrer le doigt dans l'œil* is 'to be sadly mistaken', 'to have another think coming' while *deuil* is 'bereavement' or 'mourning'. |
| *les Japonais ont du sushi à se faire* | *avoir du souci à se faire* means 'to have something to worry about'. |
| *fan de ménages* | *femme de ménage* is 'a cleaning lady' while *fan de ménages* refers to someone who likes doing extras at the weekend to earn more money, i.e. inaugurating a new supermarket, acting as compère at a conference, etc. |
| *flot et usage de flot* | *faux et usage de faux* means 'falsifying and using forged documents'. *Flot*, in the plural, is an old poetic term for 'waves'. |
| *il y a encore du goulot* | *goulot* is 'the neck of a bottle', *goulot d'étranglement* is 'a bottleneck' in the traffic sense of the term. *Goulot* here replaces *boulot* the slang term for work, i.e. 'graft'. |
| *frime de fin d'année* | *frime* is 'showing off'. *Prime de fin d'année* is a 'Christmas bonus'. |
| *fromage de dette* | *fromage de tête* is 'brawn', the dish. |
| *glandeur de la France* | *grandeur de la France*. *Un glandeur* is a 'shirker'. |
| *homme des casernes* | An echo of *l'homme des cavernes*, 'caveman'. The expression reads 'the man of the barracks'. |
| *lutte de glaces* | *lutte des classes*, class war. 'The combat of the ice'. |
| *Sarko n'en finit pas de bomber la Corse* | *bomber le torse* is 'to stick out one's chest, to swagger'. The bombs refer to Corsican violence. |
| *Tôt devant* | *Chaud devant!* Typical shout of the café waiter. *Tôt* means early. See Chapter 1 'Chaud devant!' |

A specific group of nouns and names, ending with an [ɑ:] sound are frequently telescoped i.e. Bernard, Collard, Cagoulard, cumulard, taulard, etc. These names and nouns ending in 'ard' are frequently used in conjunction with *de vivre* and *de la pêche*. Hence, we have *Bernard de vivre, cumulard de la pêche, Richard et métiers.*

## 7 Some headline examples
## taken from Le Canard Enchaîné and Les Dossiers du Canard

These quotations are protected by copyright. All rights reserved.

I Context: *Sarkozy complaining about the world butter shortage*

Pun: *Sarkozy a le beurre et le canon*

Explanation: Literally, this means that 'he has the butter and the canon'. 'Canon' can mean an extremely beautiful woman, and is the familiar French term for a 'stunner'. It reminds us of the French proverb *Tu ne peux pas avoir le beurre et l'argent du beurre* ('You can't have your cake and eat it') and echoes the historical words of Göring and Himmler about the choice between butter and canon. (See Chapter 2 'beurre').

2 Context: *The fishermen's strike in France over the high price of fuel oil*

Pun: *Les pêcheurs français ne veulent pas finir à l'armée du chalut*

Explanation: Literally, this translates as 'the French fishermen do not want to end up at the army of trawl', the pun being on the quasi-homophony of *salut* (salvation) and *chalut*, the French word for 'trawl'; this makes one think of the 'Salvation Army'.

3 Context: *Political instability in the Middle East*

Pun: *Hamas critique*

Explanation: The pun is on the scientific term 'masse critique', i.e. critical mass.

4 Context: *The former trainer of the French world swimming champion Laure Manaudou has been charged with theft*

Pun: *L'entraineur de la nageuse Laure Manaudou, va-t-il plonger?*

Explanation: *Plonger* is the verb 'to dive' but in French slang it can mean 'to go down', 'to get busted', 'to be put in clink'.

**5** Context: *President Sarkozy's visit to the Rungis wholesale market south of Paris*

Pun: *Sarkozy à Rungis, le coup d'étal permanent.*

Explanation: *Étal* is a market stall, and echoes the title of an essay by the late President François Mitterrand *Le Coup d'État permanent* written in 1964 during the presidency of Charles de Gaulle, in which Mitterrand attacked the abuse of personal power of the president in the Fifth Republic. The verb *étaler* is also associated with 'putting on a show' or 'exhibiting' which is a reference to Nicolas Sarkozy's tendency to show off.

**6** Context: *France's foreign policy regarding Africa*

Pun: *Sarkozy ne veut pas se faire Angolais*

Explanation: The pun is on the similarity of the word 'Angolais' (Angolan) and 'engueuler'. *Se faire engueuler* means 'to get a rocket'.

**7** Context: *How to get the Greeks to swallow the austerity package*

Pun: *Euro qui comme Ulysse a fait un beau naufrage*

Explanation: See Chapter 5 'Heureux qui comme Ulysse'.

**8** Context: *The adultery of the head of the IMF, Dominique Strauss-Kahn*

Pun: *The Wall Street Journal rêve de voir DSK dans la position du démissionnaire*

Explanation: The classical position for making love to a woman is known in French as *la position du missionnaire*, 'the missionary position'. The term *démissionnaire* refers to somebody who is on the point of resigning or who has resigned. There was talk of DSK's resignation in the wake of his adulterous affair with a colleague at the IMF.

**9** Context: *The in-fighting among the socialist leaders*

Pun: *Mes gnons, allons voir si la rosse*

Explanation: This is a pun on one of the most famous quotations from French classical literature. (See Chapter 5 'Mignonne, allons voir si la rose'). *Gnon* is the slang term for a 'bash' while the rose is the symbol of the French socialist party. *Une rosse* is a slang term for 'a thrashing'.

10 Context: *The massive bailouts given to the French banks*

   Pun: *Le Bonheur est dans le prêt* (*Happiness is in the loan*)

Explanation: Play on the homophone *prêt* (loan) and *pré* (meadow). The title of a French film by Etienne Chatiliez. See Chapter 1 *Bonheur est dans le pré*.

11 Context: *The banning of commercial ads on state TV*

   Pun: *Ni pub ... mais soumise*

Explanation: 'No advertising but submissive'. An echo of the women's defence association Ni putes, ni soumises founded by Fadela Amara. See Chapter 1 'Ni putes'. NB: *une femme soumise* is a euphemism for a registered prostitute. The submission referred to is that of French TV under government control.

12 Context: *On their first meeting, 14 November 2007, Sarkozy asked Carla Bruni if she would dare give him a kiss on the mouth*

   Pun: *De Gaulle est resté célèbre pour l'Appel du 18 juin; Sarkozy restera dans l'histoire pour la pelle du 14 novembre*

Explanation: 'L'Appel' was the call to arms made by de Gaulle in June 1940, whereas *une pelle* is the slang term for 'a French kiss'.

13 Context: *The former Mayor of Paris Jean Tibéri and his wife are currently on trial for enrolling false electors on the electoral register in their* arrondissement. *Their first deputy has started to spill the beans about the fraudulent system*

   Pun: *Les Tibéri redoutent moins le glaive que la balance*

Explanation: Justice is represented as a woman holding a sword (*glaive*) and the scales of justice (*balance*). *Balance* is also the slang term for a 'grass'. *Balancer* is 'to grass'. Thus the Tibéris are more afraid of the 'grass' than they are of 'the sword of justice'. NB *se prendre/ramasser une pelle* means 'to come a cropper'.

14 Context: *France will rejoin NATO (OTAN) in the near future*

   Pun: *OTAN en emporte le vent*

Explanation: This is a pun on the French translation of the American film title 'Gone with the Wind' '*Autant en emporte le vent*'. See Chapter 1 *Autant en emporte le vert*.

15 Context: *'Libéralisme responsable' is an oxymoron*

    Pun: *Oxymore où est ta victoire?*

Explanation: this is a pun on a famous biblical quotation *Ô mort où est ta victoire, Ô mort où est ton aiguillon?* 'O death, where is thy victory, O death, where is thy sting?' See Chapter 8 'Ô mort'.

# Chapter 5

# Literary references

French newspaper and magazine articles are peppered with French literary references. One cannot go far in reading the press without encountering the whole time span of French literature from du Bellay to Sartre. The centralization of the French educational system has resulted in the French sharing a very homogeneous cultural foundation and consequently the quotes below are part of the average French person's cultural heritage. One needs to know the most famous quotes of the main authors to be able to read the French press with ease. A small number of the quotes below are not French but are so frequently used in the French press that it seemed logical to include them in the list.

### Adieu, veau, vache, cochon, couvée    ***
*Adieu vis, clous et plaques en métal* © *Le Monde 20 089*. This quote refers to the possibility of using a product similar to the secretions of a sea worm (which enables it to 'weld' sand) to mend bone fractures. The text echoes the words from *La Laitière et le Pot de lait*, a famous fable by La Fontaine (1621–95) of which the moral is not to count one's chickens. The dairy maid is going to market to sell the pitcher of milk. With the proceeds, she intends to buy some eggs which, when they hatch, will be sold and the proceeds used to buy a pig. She plans on buying a cow and a calf and ultimately on having a herd of cattle. Unfortunately, she trips over and the milk is lost and she must abandon her project of making a big profit. See below 'lait tombe'.

### Aide-toi, et le ciel t'aidera    **
*Le RSA s'inscrit ainsi dans une vision active de solidarité, encourageant le travail, selon le principe 'aide-toi, l'État t'aidera'.* © *Libération 8722*. This is an echo of the words of La Fontaine in the fable *Le Chartier embourbé*. This may be likened to the English saying 'God helps those who help themselves'.

### Animaux malades de la peste. Les    ***
*La RATP malade de la Poste*. © *Le Canard Enchaîné 4635*. This text refers to the plan by the Paris transport authority (RATP) to distribute recorded

delivery mail on the platforms of certain *métro* stations. *Les Animaux malades de la peste* is the title of the most frequently quoted fable by La Fontaine. In this fable the animals, faced with the plague, make a confession about their sins in order to clear their conscience. The lion mentions that during his life, he has eaten innocent sheep and even a shepherd. When it comes to the turn of the little ass to confess, he admits to having eaten a few blades of grass in a field. Immediately every one of the animals picks on the ass and treats him as a scapegoat. *À ces mots on cria haro sur le baudet.* See below 'crier haro sur le baudet'.

### Anne, ma sœur Anne, ne vois-tu rien venir?

These words come from *La Barbe Bleue* (1697) by Charles Perrault (1628–1703) and are spoken by Barbe Bleue's wife to her sister, asking if the latter, at the top of the tower, can see help coming. The sister answers: 'Je ne vois que le soleil qui poudroie, et l'herbe qui verdoie.' ***Anne, ma sœur Anne, ne vois-tu rien venir? Je ne vois que la politique qui verdoie et l'écologie qui merdoie.*** © *Les Dossiers du Canard 115*. The context of this quote is the sorry state of French ecological reform. NB: 'merdoyer' is the slang intransitive verb for 'to cock up', 'to screw up'.

### appétit vient en mangeant. L'

This is a quotation from *Gargantua* by François Rabelais (1494–1553). ***L'appétit vient en mangeant.*** *Le Canard Enchaîné 4650*. This was the first line of an article about food safety.

### Apprenti sorcier. L'

*The Sorcerer's Apprentice* (*Der Zauberlehrling*) (1797) was originally a poem written by Goethe (1749–1832). ***Vieille dame indigne, La Caisse [d'Épargne] gémit … que les banques rament désormais sur un fleuve d'argent virtuel, infesté de produits toxiques. Piètre jérémiade d'apprenti sorcier.*** © *Le Point 1884*. See Chapter 8 'jérémiades'. This is a reference to the delicate situation in which many banks found themselves in the wake of the US subprime mortgage crisis.

### apprivoiser? Qu'est-ce que signifie

In the book *Le Petit Prince* by Antoine de Saint-Éxupéry (1900–44) and published in 1943, the little prince asks the fox to play with him. The fox replies that he cannot, because, as a fox, he is not tame. *Le petit prince* asks the fox. 'What does "to tame" mean?' The latter replies *apprivoiser c'est créer des liens.* **'Océans est un film grandiose. En dépit de son introduction et de sa conclusion un rien nunuche, nous montrant l'émerveillement très Petit Prince d'un garçonnet qui demande: "l'océan c'est quoi?"'** © *Le Monde 20 220*. The quote above refers to a review of the film *Océans*, the introduction and conclusion of which are a little childish. See below 'Dessine-moi' and '*Petit Prince*'.

### Arlésienne. L'    `**`

This literally means a woman from the town of Arles. It is the title of a short story by Alphonse Daudet (1840–97), taken from *Les Lettres de mon moulin* (1869), which Bizet later turned into an opera. This is an allusion to the opera by Bizet in which the character of the Arlésienne is frequently spoken about but never seen. *Une Arlésienne annoncée à plusieurs reprises et jamais mise en ligne.* © *L'Express 3037.* The context of this quote is the setting up of a platform for the legal downloading of the Beatles' music. Such a platform has just seen the light (November 2010).

### badine pas avec l'amour. On ne    `***`

This is the name of a play by Alfred de Musset (1810–57). The play was written in 1834 and produced at the *Comédie Française* in 1861. The play has quite an anti-clerical slant. Camille has announced to her childhood love that all men are wicked and that she is going to return to the convent. In a wonderful diatribe her lover speaks of the ideas that have poisoned her mind and says 'J'ai souffert souvent, Je me suis trompé quelques fois, mais j'ai aimé'. 'Badiner' means 'to banter', 'to jest' or 'to treat lightly'. *Poutine, ne badine pas avec l'amour.* © *Marianne 575.* This text was written in the light of the ferocious criticism by Vladimir Putin of the Russian press which had announced his divorce and remarriage to a young Russian gymnast.

### bataille d'Hernani. Une    `**`

Hernani is the name of the hero in the play of the same name by Victor Hugo (1802–85) that broke with the classical tradition of the three unities of time, place and action. It provoked a fierce reaction from the classicists. During its first performance at the *Comédie Française* on 25 February 1830, a cabal of the classical school tried to wreck the performance with whistles and cat-calls. The newspaper critics were merciless in their criticism of the play by the young romantic. Ultimately, the play won through. 'Une battle d'Hernani' is thus one between the avant-garde and the conservative moralists. *Leur [the agricultural seed industry] lobby n'est pas pour rien dans la bataille d'Hernani suscitée par l'amendement du député PC qui voulait protéger les AOC des OGM.* © *Le Canard Enchaîné 4565.* See Chapter 14 'AOC' and 'OGM'.

### Bâteau ivre. Le    `***`

This is the title of a poem by Arthur Rimbaud (1854–91) written in 1871 and based on the theme of evasion. 'Comme je descendais des Fleuves impassibles,/Je ne me sentis plus guidé par les haleurs.' These lines express the feeling of the author as he goes downriver, with the impression that the boat haulers are no longer guiding his boat. *Pour l'instant, la Société Générale est devenue une sorte de bateau ivre qui rebondit de mur en mur.* © *Le Nouvel Observateur 232.* This text reflects the misfortunes of the French bank which not only suffered from the financial crisis but also lost billions of euros because of rogue trading by one of its brokers.

### Brave New World

The title of a book by Aldous Huxley (1894–1963) that is frequently quoted in the French press either in English or in its French title *Le Meilleur des mondes*. ***Le brave new world multipolaire et onusien qui tient lieu de "vue du monde" à une partie des décideurs européens se révèle être une illusion.*** © *Le Figaro 20 166*. It is interesting to note that the English title comes from *The Tempest* by Shakespeare, while the French title comes from Voltaire's *Candide*. See below '*Candide*'.

### 'Cachez ce sein'

***Cachez ces délits.*** © *L'Express 3037*. The heading of an article about 'fixing' the crime statistics. See below 'Couvrez ce sein'.

### Candide

***À Capitol Hill, en cette froide journée de janvier, on joue 'Candide'.*** © *L'Express 3059*. This text refers to the bankers giving evidence in front of the commission of enquiry into the financial crisis who have innocently invoked the cyclical nature of financial and economic activity, without mentioning the word 'toxic' or the word 'speculation'. The chairman of the commission said with a certain degree of irritation, 'I hope that you are not going to invoke the will of God'! *Candide* is the title of a philosophical tale published by Voltaire in 1759, to a certain extent in response to the reaction of society to the Lisbon earthquake of 1755. Voltaire (1694–1778) reacted against the theory of 'divine providence'. The character Pangloss is ingenuous and naïve. See below 'Pangloss'. See Chapter 8 'cavaliers de l'Apocalypse'.

### Caves du Vatican. Les

This is the title of a novel written by André Gide (1869–1951) in 1914 and describes a gratuitous murder. 'Cave' can be punned upon in that it can mean 'cellar' or, in the language of criminals, sb. who is honest, and doesn't know the mores of the underworld. ***Sympa pour Benoit XVI et ses caves du Vatican.*** © *Le Canard Enchaîné 4630*. Recently ejected from the Fillon Government, Christine Boutin refused the post of Ambassador to the Vatican (she is a devout Catholic). She said 'Je n'ai pas l'intention d'entrer dans une caverne.'

### chair est triste, hélas! La

These are the first words of the first line of a poem by Stéphane Mallarmé (1842–98) *Brise Marine*. 'La chair est triste, hélas! et j'ai lu tous les livres.' ***La chair est triste hélas, et j'ai lu tous mes mails.*** Words of a character in the latest novel by Marc-Edouard Nabe, quoted in © *L'Express 3053*.

## Chassez le naturel et il revient au galop  ⸢***⸣

This is a verse from the comedy *Le Glorieux*, III (1732) by Philippe Néricault (1680–1754), whose pen name was Destouches, which in turn comes from Horace. It can be rendered in English by the saying 'What's bred in the bone, comes out in the flesh'. *L'artiste [Sarkozy] a un peu modifié son numéro. Un poil moins abrupt et arrogant. … Mais le naturel revient au galop.* © *Le Canard Enchaîné 4607.*

## chatouille ou ça vous gratouille? (Ça vous)  ⸢**⸣

'Does it tickle you or does it itch?' These words are from the play *Knock* by Jules Romains (1885–1972). The patient has just told his doctor that his throat tickles and itches. With great seriousness the doctor replies: 'Ne confondons pas; est-ce que ça vous chatouille ou est-ce que ça vous gratouille?' The subtitle of the play is 'The triumph of medical science'. These lines were immortalized by the actor Louis Jouvet. *'Ça vous élance ou ça vous relance'.* © *Marianne 614.* This is a reference to the actions of the minister in charge of kick-starting the economy in the wake of the financial crisis.

## Chimène (les yeux de) nmpl.  ⸢***⸣

To look at sb. with the eyes of Chimène is to look amorously at sb. with hidden passion. Chimène, one of the female characters in the play *Le Cid*, by Pierre Corneille (1606–84), is desperately in love with Rodrigue. *Il est des dirigeants du Medef qui, pour Laurence, gardent les yeux de Chimène.* © *L'Express 3054.* Laurence Parisot, head of the French employers' confederation, the Medef, was being challenged for the leadership although some executives of this organization have great admiration for her. See below 'Cid', 'cœur' 'combat cessa', 'cornélien', 'Ô rage!', 'Ôte-moi d'un doute', 'Pour' and 'Va'.

## Chronique d'une mort annoncée nf.  ⸢**⸣

The title of a novel published in 1981 by Gabriel García Marquez, the Colombian novelist and Nobel Prize winner (1982), in which an assassination is programmed. *Blu-ray: chronique d'une mort annoncée.* © *Le Monde 19 800.* This headline was used in the context of the introduction of 'Blu-ray,' a disc format enabling the viewer to see high definition films. Experts in the field do not predict a long life for this technology, given the technical possibilities of internet and new television sets.

## Cid. Le  ⸢**⸣

*Le Cid* was a play in verse written by Corneille and first produced in 1636/7. Many literary allusions come from this play. *En France, quand on désire méditer sur les ambitions qu'un père nourrit pour son fils, il suffit d'ouvrir 'Le Cid' de Corneille.* © *L'Express 3041.* This was a reference to the polemical proposition of Nicolas Sarkozy to 'nominate' his son as head of the Epad.

See Chapter 14 'Epad'. See above 'Chimène'. See below 'cœur' 'combat cessa', 'cornélien', 'Ô rage!', 'Ôte-moi d'un doute', 'Pour' and 'Va'.

### Cigale et la Fourmi. La

*La Cigale et la Fourmi* is one of La Fontaine's best-known fables. It contrasts the prudential and industrious behaviour of the ant who spends summer gathering food to prepare for winter, and the frivolous grasshopper who spends her time singing but finds herself in difficulty when winter comes. She goes to see her neighbour the ant, to tell her that she is hungry ('Elle alla crier famine chez la fourmi sa voisine'). The ant asks her how she has spent summer, to which the grasshopper replies 'I spent summer singing'. The ant replies 'J'en suis fort aise. Eh bien dansez maintenant'. ***Dans un pays où les ménages sont plus fourmis que cigales, décideront-ils [the Germans] de dépenser plus ou d'épargner davantage?*** © *Le Nouvel Observateur 2347.* This is a reference to the effects that Angela Merkel's new tax package will have on spending patterns in Germany.

### cœur a ses raisons que la raison ne connaît point. Le

This is the famous quotation from *Les Pensées* (1670) by Blaise Pascal, French scientist, writer and philosopher (1623–62). ***La rancœur a ses raisons que le cœur ignore.*** © *Le Canard Enchaîné 4580.* This refers to Cécilia Sarkozy's vengeful attitude on her return from her escapade in New York, towards those of her friends who, during her flight to the USA, had chosen to disown her and side with her husband.

### cœur? Rodrigues, as-tu du

The famous words of Don Diègue to his son in the play, *Le Cid*, by Pierre Corneille (1606–84). Having suffered an affront at the hands of the Comte de Gormas, and being too old to fight, Don Diègue asks his son whether he has the courage to avenge his father. 'Heart' in this context is a synonym of 'courage'. ***On ne sait pas si cet enfant a du cœur comme Rodrigue, mais une chose est sûre: il a de sacrés réflexes.*** © *Marianne 633.* This text came from a general news story about the quick thinking of a young boy who managed to keep the family car under control after his father had lost consciousness at the wheel. See above 'Chimène' and '*Cid*'. See below 'combat cessa', 'cornélien', 'Ô rage!', 'Ôte-moi d'un doute', 'Pour' and 'Va'.

### cœur. Tu me fends le

This is one of the best-loved lines in French cinema history and of Marseilles folklore. It comes from *Marius*, the first of the plays from the trilogy by Marcel Pagnol (1895–1974), *Marius, Fanny, César.* The words are spoken by César to Panisse during the famous card game. César is trying to give Escartefigue (his partner) a hidden message that he should play hearts as trump ('couper à cœur'). In response to Panisse's accusation that César is cheating. César pretends to be hurt and says that Panisse is 'breaking his heart'. By the time Escartefigue has understood the message, Panisse has detected the trickery and leaves the card table, throwing his cards in the air. *C'est surtout le dernier ministre qui me fend le cœur.* © *Le Canard Enchaîné 4569.*

### combat cessa faute de combattants. Et le
These are the words of Rodrigue in *Le Cid* by Corneille. It refers to a battle that peters out without any great result because of a lack of combatants. *La bataille des européennes n'a pas eu lieu, faute de combattants.* © *Marianne 633.* This quote is a reference to the massive rate of abstention in the European elections of 2009. See above 'Chimène', '*Cid*', 'coeur'. See below 'cornélien', 'Ô rage', 'Ôte-moi d'un doute', 'Pour' and 'Va'.

### Comédie humaine. La
In 1845, Balzac (1799–1850) decided to gather the whole of his works under the single title of *La Comédie humaine*, the title being a reference to Dante and *La Comédie divine*. *La Comédie Hymen.* © *Le Canard Enchaîné 4571.* This headline is a pun related to the case of the annulment of a marriage between a Muslim boy and a Muslim girl on the grounds that she was not a virgin. NB also known as *La Divine Comédie*.

### cornélien (un dilemme)
The character 'Rodrigue', in the play *Le Cid* by Corneille (see above), is faced with the choice between love and honour and finds himself on the horns of a dilemma, i.e. the choice between avenging his father or of keeping Chimène. ... *le déficit 2009 de la Sécurité Sociale va imposer un nouveau choix cornélien.* © *Les Echos 20 431.* See above 'Chimène', '*Cid*', 'coeur', and 'combat cessa'. See below 'Ô rage!, Ôte-moi d'un doute' and 'Va'.

### Cosette
Cosette is the name of the little girl in the novel *Les Misérables* by Victor Hugo (1802–85). Her mother sends her to board and lodge with the Thénardiers who exploit her mercilessly. *L'histoire de Gabrielle dite 'Coco' Chanel, vue par la réalisatrice Anne Fontaine, c'est Cosette en couseuse'* © *Les Echos 20 410.* The film *Coco avant Chanel*, directed by Anne Fontaine (2009), tells the story of the hard times that Coco Chanel went through in her early life.

### coup de pied de l'âne. Le
When a great man is old and weak, his vassals of the past no longer respect him and are the first to kick him once he is down. The expression comes from the fable by La Fontaine *Le Lion devenu vieux*, published in 1668. *Joaquin Almunia, aujourd'hui commissaire européen aux affaires économiques*

*lui a infligé le coup de pied de l'âne en mettant l'Espagne dans le même sac que la Grèce.* © *Le Point 1952.* This is a reference to the martyrdom of José Luis Zapatero, the Spanish prime minister, who has become highly unpopular. His old enemy, Almunia, as one of the European Commissioners, has recently added to his problems by downgrading the economic status of Spain.

### coup d'État permanent. Le      `***`

*Avec Sarko, c'est le coup d'étal permanent.* © *Le Canard Enchaîné 4570.* Apart from the obvious reference to Sarkozy's tendency to show off ('faire étal') this article was about supermarket chains and mass distribution. It is an echo of the *essai* written by the late François Mitterrand in 1964 protesting aginst the excessive personal powers of de Gaulle under the Constitution of the Fifth Republic. The book was entitled *Le coup d'État permanent.*

### courtelinesque      `***`

Georges Courteline, real name Georges Moineaux (1858–1929), was a novelist and playwright who came to fame through his work that depicted the petty human comedies of everyday life. His name evokes the pettifogging civil servant at the service window who has an over-inflated opinion of his own importance and who is both the servant and the slave of ridiculous rules and regulations. His behaviour gives rise to absurd situations. *Voilà cette ex-préfète de 55 ans suspendue et astreinte à un strict contrôle judiciaire comme un vulgaire voleur de Mobylette. Une histoire courtelinesque.* © *L'Express 3067.* This text refers to a woman *préfet* who has been charged with the theft of property belonging to the State.

### Couvrez ce sein que je ne saurais voir      `***`

This quotation from the play *Tartuffe* (1664) by Molière (1622–73) is perhaps the most frequently (mis)quoted and punned upon sentence in the French press. The play was forbidden by the court and it was only in 1669 that the ban was lifted. Tartuffe is a hypocritical character and says these words in the scene in which he is confronted with a lady wearing a low-cut dress. *Cachez ce minaret…* © *L'Express 3047.* This text refers to the result of the Swiss referendum on the construction of minarets in Switzerland. This phrase is always quoted as 'cachez' but in the text of Molière it is 'couvrez'.

### crier famine chez la fourmi sa voisine. Elle alla      `***`

*Canal+, seule chaine du PAF à avoir enregistré une hausse de ses recettes publicitaires [+5%] quand l'ensemble de ses concurrents crie famine.* © *L'Express 3053.* The TV channel Canal+ is doing well financially while the other channels are in difficulty. See above *Cigale et la Fourmi, La.*

### crier haro sur le baudet

*Haro sur les paradis fiscaux*. © *Le Nouvel Observateur 2295*. This was a remark made in the wake of the financial crisis of 2008. Today it means to make a hue and cry. See above *Animaux malades de la peste*.

### cultiver son jardin. Il faut

In the story of *Candide* (1759) by Voltaire (1694–1778), we learn that work helps us avoid three things: boredom, vice and need. The concluding words of the novel *Candide* are 'Il faut cultiver notre jardin'. *Le patron de la Caisse d'Epargne, lui, va devoir aller cultiver son jardin*. © *L'Express 2990*. This is a reference to Charles Milhaud, the chairman of the national savings bank *La Caisse d'Épargne*, who was forced to resign after the bank posted a loss of €600 million.

### Dansez maintenant!

*Vous chantiez au son du carillon subventionné, à l'abri du monopole de la Poste, rassasiés par la gamelle de l'Etat Providence, eh bien riez maintenant.* © *Marianne 577*. This text refers to the imminent privatization of the French Post Office and echoes the words of La Fontaine. See above *Cigale et la Fourmi*.

### Demain, dès l'aube … **

This is one of the best known lines of French literature. 'Demain, dès l'aube, à l'heure où blanchit la campagne,/Je partirai. Vois-tu, je sais que tu m'attends/J'irai par la forêt, j'irai par la montagne./Je ne puis demeurer loin de toi plus longtemps'. These lines come from a poem written by Victor Hugo (1802–85) four years after the accidental death of his daughter, Léopoldine, who was drowned in a boating accident on the Seine. Newly married, she died with her husband in 1843 at the age of 19. The lines above are taken from *Contemplations*. *Hier matin, donc, à l'heure où blanchit la campagne, je fais tout comme lui, tout comme il a fait. … Résultat: travail hors connexion*. © *Marianne 576*. This text refers to the trials and tribulations faced by micro-computer users who are not very gifted in this field.

### dépourvue **

In the fable *La Cigale et la Fourmi* we can read 'La cigale ayant chanté tout l'été se trouva fort dépourvue quand la bise fut venue'. *Certains quotidiens régionaux se moquaient de la cigale Manaudou fort dépourvue maintenant que l'échec est venu*. © *Marianne 591*. This is a reference to the former French Olympic swimming champion who neglected her training to spend more time with her boyfriend. She won no medals at the Peking Olympics. See above *Cigale et la Fourmi*.

## 'Dessine-moi un mouton!'    `***`

The words of *le petit prince* from the work of the same name by Antoine de Saint-Exupéry. ***Dessine-moi un redressement judiciaire*** © *L'Express 3063*. The studio MKO Game is developing a video game called *Le Petit Prince* and is running into financial difficulties and there is a danger of the company going into receivership ('redressement judiciaire'). See above 'apprivoiser'.

## Diafoirus    `***`

This is the name of a character in the play *Le Malade Imaginaire* by Molière. He is pedantic and fond of pseudo-scientific expressions but is not particularly interested in his patients' welfare. His usual recommendation to the patient was 'pugare, saignare' (purges and blood-letting). ***Les Diafoirus de la performance économique ne comprennent pas l'utilité sociale d'hommes et de femmes dont le métier est une vocation avant d'être une fonction.*** © *Marianne 575*. This text refers to the decline in the appreciation, by the general public, of the teaching community in an age where the transmission of a cultural heritage has little or no market value. See above 'Couvrez'.

## Discours de la Méthode    `**`

The most famous work written by the French philosopher René Descartes (1596–1650). ***Discours de la méthode fiscale tenu par le ministre du Budget, Eric Woerth.*** © *Le Canard Enchaîné 4585*. These words refer to the explanations of Eric Woerth when he was minister of budget.

## Dulcinée. Sa    `***`

This word is often used ironically to refer to the beloved woman, the sweetheart. It comes from *Don Quichotte*, the story written by Miguel de Cervantes (1547–1616). ***Le vrai monde est dans les films, voilà ce que nous dit 'Cinéman' quand il revient dans sa classe et ne rêve que de repartir dans 'Barry Lindon', retrouver sa dulcinée.*** © *Le Point 1936*. This was a review by Bernard Henri Lévy of the film *Cinéman* by Yann Moix in which the characters can choose to escape reality by entering their favourite film. See below 'moulins à vent'.

## Éducation sentimentale. L'    `*`

A novel by Gustave Flaubert (1821–80) published in 1869. ***Il flotte dans cette Éducation sentimentale à l'envers, un parfum fitzgeraldien.*** © *Marianne 598*. This was a comment on the book *Ce que nous avons eu de meilleur* by Jean-Paul Enthoven. 'Fitzgeraldien' refers to the American novelist F. Scott Fitzgerald (1896–1940) the author of (among others) *Tender is the Night* and *The Great Gatsby*.

## Exercice de style    `***`

This is the title of the most famous work by the writer Raymond Queneau (1903–76), published in 1947. Students of the French language should, at some stage of their studies, read this unique book. The author tells the same story in dozens of different ways, each version having its own literary style and register. Queneau was a precursor of this creative mode and co-founder of the 'Oulipo' association with François Le Lionnais in 1960. 'Oulipo' stands for 'Ouvroir de Littérature Potentielle'. It was an association made up of writers and mathematicians. Georges Perec, one of the great names of this association, wrote a novel in 1969 entitled *La Disparition*. It was a novel written without once using the letter 'e'. Each creation was the result of a self-imposed constraint of some kind, 'la contrainte oulipienne'. *Exercice de style. L'Express 3056*. This was the heading of an article by the film critic Eric Libiot.

### Faust, Faustien                                                                [ ** ]

Christopher Marlowe (1564–93) was the first playwright to exploit the tale of Dr Faustus, a sixteenth-century alchemist who, in return for knowledge, sells his soul to the devil, Mephistopheles. Goethe (1749–1832) also produced a play of the same name. ***Schröder, c'est Faust [...] Il a vendu son âme pour une seconde vie.*** © *Le Nouvel Observateur 2360*. This was a comment about the ex-Chancellor of Germany, Gerhard Schröder, and his newly formed business activities and his connections with President Putin, China and Iran. His commercial interests have provoked the indignation of German opinion.

### feignons d'en être les organisateurs. Puisque ces mys-
### tères nous dépassent,                                                    [ ** ]

A quote from the play *Les Mariés de la Tour Eiffel* by Jean Cocteau (1889–1963) produced for the first time at the Théatre des Champs-Élysées in 1921. ***Le président feignant d'organiser ce mystère qui le dépasse, l'audience est suspendue.*** © *Le Figaro 20 091*. This refers to the adjournment decided upon by a judge who was visibly puzzled by the court case he was supposed to be trying. See Chapter 2 'feignons'.

### flatteur vit aux dépens de celui qui l'écoute. Tout            [ * ]

*Tous ces flatteurs qui vivent aux dépens de ceux qui les écoutent.* © *Marianne 654*. This text refers to the flatterers at the court of President Sarkozy. Nobody dared to voice the slightest objection against the president's controversial wish to impose his son as the head of the Epad. See Chapter 14 'Epad'. This was the moral of the fable of *Le Corbeau et le Renard*. See below 'Maître'.

### *Fleurs du mal. Les*                                                       [ * ]

*Les Fleurs du mal* is the title of a collection of poems by Charles Baudelaire (1821–67) published in 1857 and the heading of an article bearing on the multiplicity of currents within the French socialist party and the large number of contributions to the congress of the PS. ***Les 21 contributions pour le congrès du PS ne surprennent pas François Hollande. 'Il est normal que de multiples fleurs s'épanouissent; mais ensuite il faut qu'il y en ait qui*** *rassemblent le bouquet'.* © *Marianne 586.* The symbol of the French socialist party is the rose in a clenched fist.

### Foire aux vanités. La

*Vanity Fair* was a novel written by William Makepeace Thackeray (1811–63). The term comes from the allegorical book by John Bunyan (1628–88) published in 1678, *The Pilgrim's Progress,* which tells of Christian's journey from the 'City of Destruction' to the 'Celestial City'. ***Entreprises: la foire aux vanités.*** © *Le Nouvel Observateur 2357.* This quote was the heading of an article dealing with the boomerang effect of the self-congratulatory prize-givings among corporate entities for 'Top Employer of the Year' and everything that they are doing for the environment and the personal development of their staff. France Telecom was mentioned for its work in the area of staff stress management. No mention was made of the 25 people who had committed suicide between mid-2008 and late 2009. The suicide figure stood at 58 in July 2010.

### fourmi. La
***
*Ce qui suppose que les fourmis, principalement l'Allemagne, se portent au secours des cigales.* © *Le Figaro 20 057.* Germany has always been considered as an industrious 'ant' in terms of economic and financial policy, and the other European nations as 'grasshoppers'. See above *Cigale et la Fourmi, La.*

### fourmi n'est pas prêteuse. La
**
'La fourmi n'est pas prêteuse, c'est là son moindre défaut'. ***Fillon n'est pas prêteur.*** © *Le Canard Enchaîné 4617.* See above *Cigale et la Fourmi, La.*

### fromage. Un
***
In slang, 'un fromage' refers to a 'cushy' and very well paid job in the civil service. The expression comes from the fable by La Fontaine *Le Rat qui s'est retiré du monde.* 'Un certain rat, las des soins d'ici bas,/Dans un fromage de Hollande/Se retira loin du tracas'. ***Un parti socialiste dont les dirigeants étaient totalement 'hollandisés' obsédés par la conservation de leurs fromages.*** © *Marianne 626.* François Hollande was first secretary of the French socialist party until 2009. The quote above refers to François Hollande's supporters who are obsessed with keeping their 'cushy' jobs and privileges.

### galère? Qu'allait-il faire dans cette
***
In Molière's play *Les Fourberies de Scapin* (1671) Scapin tries to extort money from Géronte by telling him that Géronte's son has been taken prisoner by the Turks and is now on a Turkish galley pending the payment of a ransom. Géronte replies 'Que diable allait-il faire dans cette galère?' It is to be noticed that 'galère' can mean either a ship, i.e. 'a galley', or 'a nightmarish situation'. Referring to the film *Mes stars et moi* (2008) a critic, commenting on the poor scenario, wrote: ***Catherine Deneuve, Emmanuelle***

*Béart et Kad Merad, qu'êtes vous allés faire dans cette galère?* © *Le Nouvel Observateur 2295*. The question is asked 'How could such talented professionals agree to take part in such a mediocre film?' See above 'Couvrez'.

## Ganelon

*

Ganelon is the character from the epic poem of the eleventh century *La Chanson de Roland*. Ganelon is the archetypal felon and traitor who, consumed by hate, betrays Roland. *Il est sans doute temps de cesser d'accabler Ganelon-Besson: trahit-on vraiment ses convictions lorsqu'on en a si peu?* © *Marianne 613*. This is a reference to the socialist Eric Besson who, in the home straight of the presidential elections, abandoned Ségolène Royal and joined the Sarkozy camp. The quote asks the question 'Can one speak of betraying one's convictions when one has so few?'

## Gargantua

***

This is the name of one of the giants in the story by Rabelais (1494–1553), *Gargantua and Pantagruel*. Their names evoke insatiable appetites. *Le diagnostic est implacable: dérèglement climatique, besoins énergétiques gargantuesques et limites des énergies renouvelables.* © *Le Point 1882*. See below 'Pantagruel'.

## Gavroche

***

Gavroche is the name of the generous and jaunty street urchin in the novel *Les Misérables* by Victor Hugo, published in 1862. The painting by Delacroix, *Liberté guidant le peuple* (1830), is said to have been Hugo's inspiration for this character. Gavroche dies on the barricades in 1832 and is remembered for the song he sings 'Je suis tombé par terre, c'est la faute à Voltaire, le nez dans le ruisseau, c'est la faute à Rousseau.' *Il a l'allure de titi parisien; casquette de Gavroche vissée sur la tête.* © *Le Point 1876*. This text refers to Florent Dargnies who founded a company specializing in sightseeing tours of Paris in an old Citroen 2CV. He has a fleet of 30 such cars. See above 'Cosette'.

## Grandeur et décadence

**

'The rise and fall'. This was part of the title of a novel by Honoré de Balzac (1799–1850), *Grandeur et décadence de César Birotteau*, which is part of the saga of *La Comédie humaine*. *Les illusions perdues de Daniel Bouton. Détrôné. Grandeur et décadence d'un patron qui se croyait invincible.* © *Le Point 1912*. This text refers to the fall of the chairman of the French bank Société Générale who was forced to resign in the wake of phenomenal losses due to the rogue trading of one of his brokers. As an *énarque*, Daniel Bouton believed himself to be endowed with papal infallibility.

## Grenouille qui se veut faire aussi grosse que le bœuf. La

**

From the fable by La Fontaine. In his attempt to inflate his size, the frog burst. *Les banques d'affaires … ont poussé la Caisse Nationale à vouloir se faire plus grosse qu'un bœuf.* © *Le Canard Enchaîné 4591.* This is a reference to the reckless behaviour of some of France's biggest banks, and their fragile positions that came to light in the wake of the financial crisis. NB: sometimes written in modern French as 'qui veut se faire'.

### guerre de Troie n'aura pas lieu. La                    ★★★
This is the name of a play, written in 1935 by Jean Giraudoux (1882–1944), an allegory of the rise of Hitler, the danger of war and the concessions required to avoid it. *La guerre du gaz n'aura pas lieu.* © *Le Nouvel Observateur 2351.* This text refers to an agreement reached between Russia and Ukraine over gas prices.

### haro sur ...                    ★★★
See above 'crier haro'.

### Harpagon (ma cassette!)                    ★★★
Harpagon is a character in the comedy *L'Avare* (1668) by Molière (1622–73). He is constantly worried about his money box (cassette). *Domenech, lui, n'a plus ce problème, ce n'est que de la goinfrerie. [...] En somme un Harpagon moderne.* © *Le Nouvel Observateur 2359.* The excessively high salaries paid to football players can possibly be tolerated given that they have relatively short careers. In the case of the French selector Domenech, this is not the case. The French football coach has been accused of making too much money with a salary that is totally unwarranted in the light of his poor performance with the national French team.

### 'Heureux qui comme Ulysse'                    ★★★
Ulysses was the Latin name of the Greek hero Odysseus in the poem called the *Odyssey* that is ascribed to Homer and which relates the wanderings of the king of Ithaca. *Hélas, nos quatre Ulysse se font cueillir à leur arrivée par la police qui les a remis à la police des frontières. Pas sûr qu'ils finissent heureux ni qu'ils aient un beau voyage.* © *Marianne 607.* This is an echo of the title and first line of a poem by Joachim du Bellay (1522–60), 'Heureux qui comme Ulysse a fait un beau voyage'. The text refers to clandestine immigrants arrested by the border police and suggests that it is unlikely that they will have a nice trip or that they are going to be happy.

### homme est un loup pour l'homme. L'                    ★★
These are the words of Plautus (254?–184 BC), a Roman writer who wrote *homo homini lupus* (man is a wolf for man, i.e. brother will turn on brother). It was later popularized by Thomas Hobbes (1588–1679) the British philosopher in a work entitled *De Cive* (of the citizen). *Un loup pour l'homme.* © *L'Express 3015.* This was the heading of an article that deals with a novel

written by Tristan Egolf, the subject of which is the *loup-garou* (werewolf). See Chapter 13 'homo homini lupus'.

### hommes de bonne volonté. Les                                 [ \*\*\* ]
This is the title of a saga written by Jules Romains, poet and writer (1885–1972) and including 27 volumes covering the years 1908 to 1933. It was a description of all the layers making up French society. *Les hommes de bonne volonté. Marianne 619.* The context of this quote is the work done by a group of social workers in Palestine to stop the corruption surrounding the distribution of international aid.

### Ils ne mouraient pas tous, mais tous étaient frappés        [ \*\*\* ]
This is taken from the fable *Les Animaux malades de la peste* by La Fontaine. *Toutes ne sont pas mortes, mais toutes sont malades.* © *Marianne 578.* This refers to the banks and the fallout of the US subprime mortgage crisis. See above *Animaux malades de la peste, Les* and 'crier haro'. See below 'selon'.

### inventaire à la Prévert nm.                                 [ \*\*\* ]
Jacques Prévert (1900–77), a French poet, used the 'Inventaire' as a poetic art form. As its name implies, it is just one long succession of items. It is synonymous with an endless list or litany. His poem begins 'Une pierre, deux maisons, trois ruines, quatre fossoyeurs, un jardin des fleurs, un raton laveur'. *L'inventaire à la Prévert des actions menées par les clubs Rotary ... peut prêter à sourire.* © *Les Echos 20 448.* This text suggests that one might be tempted to smile when reading the long list of good works carried out by the Rotary clubs.

### Invitation au voyage                                        [ \*\* ]
One of the most famous of the poems in the collection *Les Fleurs du Mal* written by Charles Baudelaire (1821–67). *Du nord au sud, d'ouest en est, invitation au voyage dans trente stations balnéaires françaises.* © *Le Figaro 20 215.* The text is an announcement giving ideas for summer holiday destinations. See below 'luxe, calme et volupté'.

### ivresse. Pourvu que l'on ait l'                             [ \*\* ]
Alfred de Musset (1810–57) wrote 'Qu'importe le flacon pourvu que l'on ait l'ivresse'. *Qu'importe le terminal, pourvu qu'on ait la connexion.* © *Le Point 1949.* This text refers to the advances made in the field of mobile telephone handsets. The handset is of little importance as long as we have the connection.

### Je plie, et ne romps pas                                    [ \*\* ]
These words, spoken by the reed, come from the fable by La Fontaine *Le Chêne et le Roseau. Cela ne veut pas dire qu'il laisse tomber la*

*rupture. Juste qu'il sait aussi plier quand il ne rompt pas.* © *Le Canard Enchaîné 4665*. This is a reference to the fact that Nicolas Sarkozy, in the wake of the severe defeat of his party in the regional elections, has had to make some concessions, without changing anything fundamental in his policy.

### Jean qui pleure et qui rit

*Mais dans le domaine du crédit immobilier, l'autre talon d'Achille du secteur bancaire, c'est Jean qui rit et Jean qui pleure.* © *Les Echos 20 598*. This refers to two opposite sides of the same coin and comes from a collection of *Petits poèmes* by Voltaire, this particular one dating from 1772. The poem contrasts Jean in the morning, who contemplates the ills of the world and is depressed, and Jean in the evening who, thanks to wine, women and good food, sees life from the opposite angle. See Chapter 7 'Achille'.

### J'écris ton nom, Liberté

From the litany 'Liberté' in *Poésie et Vérité* (1942) by Paul Eluard (real name Eugène Grindel 1895–1952). This poem was very successful in occupied France and thousands of tracts bearing this poem were dropped over France by the RAF. The poem is three pages long and begins: 'Sur mes cahiers d'écolier/Sur mon pupitre et les arbres/Sur la sable sur la neige/J'écris ton nom … Liberté'. *Liberté, j'écris ton nom.* © *Le Canard Enchaîné 4572*. This quote refers to a book published in 2009 on the slave trade in the eighteenth century.

### jeter un pavé dans la mare

This means to create a big surprise in an otherwise peaceful situation and is said to come from the fable by La Fontaine, *Les Grenouilles qui demandent un Roi*. *Bruno Masure jette un sacré pavé.* © *Marianne 614*. This is a reference to a TV newsreader who published a book in 2009 *Journalistes à la niche* in which he reveals the 'incestuous' relationship between French journalists and politicians. 'À la niche' is the command the owner gives to a dog to lie down in its kennel and reflects the submission of French TV journalists/newsreaders to the political powers that be.

### jeune fille rangée nf.

*Les Mémoires d'une jeune fille rangée* (*Memoirs of a Dutiful Daughter*) is the title of the first book in the autobiographical trilogy by Simone de Beauvoir (1908–86) published in 1972. *Pour une jeune fille rangée, fraîchement sortie de pension, le café est le chemin royal de la liberté.* © *Le Canard Enchaîné 4557*. Once outside the boarding school, the café is the royal path to freedom for a young girl.

## Jourdain. M.                                                                          [ ** ]
*Mais connaissez-vous le dernier concept à la mode, dont vous usez comme M. Jourdain faisait de la prose?* © *L'Express 3047*. In the play *Le Bourgeois Gentilhomme*, Molière ridicules M. Jourdain, the bourgeois, who wants to imitate the nobles in every aspect of their lives. He thus takes fencing lessons, dancing lessons and philosophy lessons and is informed by his *maître de philosophie* that the language he is speaking is called 'prose'. It is then that M. Jourdain says the famous line 'Par ma foi! Il y a plus de quarante ans que je dis de la prose sans que j'en susse rien.' This is a reference to 'cloud computing' that not many of us know about but that we all use without realizing it when we download, when we play in network games, where we use virtual resources. 'Cloud computing' is translated by 'informatique distribuée'.

## Lagardère                                                                              [ ** ]
In the novel *Le Bossu* (1862) by Paul Féval and Anicet Bourgeois, the hero is called Lagardère. His friend Nevers is killed by the latter's own cousin Gonzague, and Lagadère vows to avenge his death. He says 'Si tu ne viens pas à Lagardère, Lagardère ira à toi.' *Tu ne viens pas à Lagardère.* © *Le Canard Enchaîné 4553*. This is a reference to the refusal of the tennis player, Jo Tsonga, to join the Lagardère tennis team. See Chapter 9 'Lagardère, Arnaud'.

## lait tombe. Le                                                                         [ * ]
This line is quoted in an article by André Glucksmann about the crisis of capitalism. *Jean de la Fontaine dénonçait à l'avance l'empilement des crédits et l'optimisme naïf … Voire la mutation d'un pot au lait en produit financier toxique.* © *Le Figaro 20 137*. Seeking profit at any price resulted in the creation of toxic financial instruments. See above 'Adieu'.

## langage … lui tint à peu près ce                                                       [ * ]
*Sarko coupe court à ses états d'âme [de Xavier Bertrand] en lui tenant à peu près ce langage.* © *Le Canard Enchaîné 4598*. Xavier Bertrand was the secretary general of the UMP presidential party. These words come from the fable by La Fontaine *Le Corbeau et le Renard*. See below 'Maître'.

## Lettres persanes                                                                       [ * ]
*Lettres persanes* is the title of a satirical novel in epistolic form through which Montesquieu (1689–1755) ridiculed the social mores of eighteenth-century France, playing guide to a naïve Persian visitor. *Un étranger, peu au courant des affaires françaises, qui arriverait à Paris comme les Persans de Montesquieu … considérerait à coup sûr la chute de Sarkozy comme inéluctable.* © *Le Figaro 20 144*. This text refers to the fact that any foreign visitor to Paris would think that Sarkozy's fall is inevitable.

## Liaisons dangereuses. Les     [ ** ]

A novel written by Pierre Choderlos de Laclos (1741–1803) published in 1782 and the title of a film directed by Stephen Frears in 1988. *Les liaisons dangereuses. Le Monde 20 130.* It is the heading of a text describing the possible conflicts of interest on the part of politicians who also earn their living as lawyers. A special system allows French politicians (who are not obliged to take the bar exam) to become lawyers. They have to prove that they are senior civil servants who have exercised their profession for at least eight years in the civil service or international organizations. Nobody has yet been refused. Such politicians include Jean-François Copé, Dominique de Villepin, Frédéric Lefebvre and Noël Mamère. The latest candidate to ask for such an admission is the former minister of justice, Rachida Dati.

## Lièvre. Le     [ * ]

*Le bio en France, c'est l'histoire du lièvre qui démarre la course en tête, s'essouffle, ralentit, s'arrête et se fait dépasser par tous ses concurrents.* © *Le Point 1914.* The image comes from the fable by La Fontaine, *Le Lièvre et la Tortue.*

## Lison     [ * ]

*Les roulants de la SNCF, qui partent à la retraite à 50 ans ... avaient obtenu cet avantage à l'heure de la machine à vapeur. Et pourtant les locos qu'ils conduisent aujourd'hui n'ont plus rien à voir avec la 'Lison' chère à Zola.* © *Le Point 1954.* This text highlights one of the great inequalities of pension schemes in France. There is really no reason why railway train drivers should retire 15 years before anyone else given that their working conditions today bear no resemblance to the working conditions prevalent at the time this advantage was granted to this sector. The reference is to the name of the locomotive 'Lison' in the novel by Emile Zola (1840–1902), *La Bête Humaine,* which is one of the twenty novels written by Zola between 1871 and 1893 in the series *Rougon-Macquart.* NB: 'roulants' refers to train crews in general, but here, the term refers specifically to train drivers.

## Loup et le Chien. Le     [ * ]

*Le Loup et le Chien* is the fable by La Fontaine telling the story of the famished wolf who prefers his liberty to being well fed at the price of a collar around his neck. *Ce n'est pas parce que j'ai des petites marques au cou que je ne pense pas avoir la plus belle pâtée.* © *L'Express 3056.* This is a reference to the fact that Frédéric Mitterrand has been 'captured' by Nicolas Sarkozy but feels that the marks on his neck do not mean that he does not have the best 'dog food'. 'La pâtée' (a thick soup) is a dog's dinner. Ironically, 'soupe' is the name given to the attractive positions and benefits of people who accept to work for the government generally in return for some sacrifice involving their principles.

### *Loup et l'Agneau* and *Le Loup et le Renard. Le*                    〔 * 〕

Two more fables by La Fontaine. The first fable is remembered thanks to the opening line 'La raison du plus fort est toujours la meilleure'. *...dans l'affaire Clearstream ... ce n'est pas le loup et l'agneau, c'est le loup et le renard.* © *L'Express 3037.* The text refers to the trial of Dominique de Villepin, who stands accused of conspiracy to defame. Nicolas Sarkozy, as the victim, is associated with the public prosecutor against Dominique de Villepin. In the first fable, the wolf kills the lamb, whereas in the second fable, the fox outwits the wolf.

### luxe, calme et volupté                    〔 *** 〕

The poem by Charles Baudelaire *Invitation au voyage* comes from the book *Les Fleurs du Mal.* 'Là, tout n'est qu'ordre et beauté, luxe, calme et volupté.' *Tout est luxe calme et richesse.* © *Le Point 1936.* A reference to Sidi Bou Saïd, the seaside resort of Tunisia. It is to be noted that this line of the poem is frequently misquoted as 'calme, luxe et volupté'.

### Madame de La Fayette                    〔 * 〕

*Un inculte qui prend Mme de La Fayette pour une marque de lingerie.* © *Marianne 631.* This was a disparaging remark about Nicolas Sarkozy's low level of general knowledge. He is described as 'uneducated' and thinks that the name La Fayette refers to a brand name of women's lingerie. See below '*Princesse de Clèves*'.

### madeleine de Proust. La                    〔 *** 〕

The French writer Marcel Proust (1871–1922) in the first volume of *À la recherche du temps perdu* (*Du côté de chez Swann*), speaks of a little cake called *une madeleine* which he used to dunk in his tea as a child. 'Je portai à mes lèvres une cuillerée du thé où j'avais laissé s'amolir un morceau de madeleine.' This simple memory triggered a surge of childhood reminiscences. Today, it can be a smell, a taste or anything else that suddenly takes us back to our childhood. *Il [John Updike] trempe aussi sa madeleine dans le thé limpide des réminiscences enfantines.* © *Le Point 1912.* See below 'Proust'.

### Maître Corbeau                    〔 *** 〕

One of the most famous of the fables by La Fontaine, *Le Corbeau et le Renard*, begins: 'Maître Corbeau, sur un arbre perché,/Tenait en son bec un fromage./Maître Renard par l'odeur alléché,/Lui tint à peu près ce langage.' The sly fox flatters the crow asking him to sing. The crow does so and lets the cheese fall from his beak. *Maître Renard sur un bras perché, faisait un jogging.* © *Marianne 604.* This was a general news story about a woman being attacked by a fox that bit her arm and would not let go.

### Malade imaginaire. Le                                    ⬚ *

*Les réformes actuelles sur l'école me font penser à la proposition de Toinette pour guérir Argan dans 'Le Malade Imaginaire'. 'Vous avez mal à l'œil? Supprimez l'autre! Mal à un bras? Pareil!'* Jacques Lang quoted in © *Le Nouvel Observateur 2321.* In the play, Toinette is Argan's maid. The doctor advises an absurd remedy: if your eye hurts, get rid of the other one!

### mallarméen adj.                                    ⬚ **

Étienne dit 'Stéphane' Mallarmé (1842–98) *Mais comme le cygne mallarméen, il s'est laissé emprisonner dans la glace. Il peut toujours battre des ailes. Du vent.* © *Marianne 598.* Mallarmé wrote several poems in which the swan is present. This is a reference to the poem entitled *Le Vierge, le vivace et le bel aujourd'hui.* The quote above was a critical appraisal of the novelist Michel Houellebecq written by Bernard Henri Lévy, a French intellectual. There is no love lost between them. In this context, 'Du vent' is a contemptuous term for 'hot air'. It can also mean 'away with you'.

### marivaudage nm.                                    ⬚ ***

This term refers to the rather superficial and affected manner of paying court to a woman that was typical in the plays of Pierre Carlet de Chamblain de Marivaux, journalist, novelist and playwright (1688–1763). There is also the verb 'marivauder'. *'In the Air' ne se résume pas aux seuls marivaudages d'un chevalier errant des multinationales.* © *Le Monde 20 220.* This is part of the review of the film *In the Air* starring George Clooney about a cost-killer who spends his time flying from one site to another to downsize the workforce.

### Meilleur des mondes. Le                                    ⬚ ***

The French title of the book by Aldous Huxley, *Brave New World. Aux Etats-Unis ... le secteur financier, dans le meilleur des mondes possibles, en sortira diminué.* © *Les Echos 20 421.* See above '*Brave New World*' and below 'Pangloss'.

### Mère Courage                                    ⬚ ***

*Mother Courage* is a play by Bertolt Brecht (1898–1956), the full title of which is *Mother Courage and her Children (Mutter Courage und ihre Kinder).* It was written in 1938 while Brecht was in exile. The action takes place against the backdrop of the Thirty Years War and constitutes a denunciation of the absurdity of war. ***Mercedes Yusta analyse, elle, le panthéon de ces martyres du franquisme, vierges guerrières et Mère Courage.*** © *Le Monde 20 224.* This is a reference to the fact that although historians have neglected the heroines of history, the record is now being put straight with the publication of a number of books and articles. Among them are those of Mercedes Yusta, a lecturer at the University of Cergy-Pontoise, and a specialist of nineteenth- and twentieth-century Spanish history. She has written extensively about the question of the anti-Franco resistance, and the role that women played in it. See Chapter 7 'panthéon' and Chapter 10 'Panthéon'.

### Mignonne, allons voir si la rose ...

`***`

'Sweetheart, let us go and see if the rose ...' Words of the French poet Pierre de Ronsard (1524–85). The title and first line of a poem having as its theme *carpe diem*. The poem ends with an exhortation to 'cueillez, cueillez, vostre jeunesse'. ***Mignonne, allons voir.*** A heading in © *Marianne 656.* See Chapter 13 'carpe diem'.

### Mon père, ce héros au sourire si doux

`***`

These words come from a poem by Victor Hugo entitled *Après la bataille* (1859). ***Son père, ce héros.*** © *Le Figaro 20 059.* The journalist, Philippe Labro, thus refers to the son (Claude-Pierre) of the war hero, Pierre Brossolette. Pierre was one of the main organizers of the French Resistance but was arrested after being betrayed. He was taken to the notorious address in Paris, 84 avenue Foch, where he was tortured for two days by the Gestapo. He never talked. On 22 March, taking advantage of the inattention of his guards, he jumped from the window of the room in which he was being interrogated. He died from his injuries later at the Hôpital de la Salpêtrière. See Chapter 12 'Foch. 84 avenue'.

### Montagne qui accouche d'une souris. La

`**`

This fable by La Fontaine was inspired by Horace in *Ars Poetica*, but is equally known as a fable by Aesop. 'Une montagne en mal d'enfant/Jetait une clameur si haute/Que chacun au bruit accourant/Crut qu'elle accou-cherait sans faute,/D'une cité plus grosse que Paris:/Elle accoucha d'une souris.' ***Ses ennuis judiciaires? Dans le feuilleton Vivendi, les juges d'instruction n'ont toujours pas remis leur ordonnance. Qu'importe! Messier est convaincu que la montagne accouchera d'une souris.*** © *L'Express 300.* Jean-Marie Messier is currently on trial for his responsibility in relation to the problems of the company Vivendi. He was acquitted by a popular jury in the USA but he was found guilty of spreading false financial information by the Tribunal de Grande Instance and given 3 year suspended prison sentence and fined 150,000€. He has appealed.

## morne plaine

See below 'Waterloo'.

## moulins à vent

This comes from the tale *El ingenioso hidalgo don Quijote de la Mancha* by Miguel de Cervantes in which Don Quixote tilts at windmills. Le PS *'charge allègrement des moulins à vent ce qui témoigne d'un anachronisme digne de Don Quichotte'*. © *Marianne 597*. This remark suggests that the PS is still out of touch with reality. See above 'Dulcineé'.

## Musset

*Les Nuits* by Alfred de Musset (1810–57) describes the pain of a man betrayed by love. This work was written between 1835–37, after de Musset's separation from George Sand. Sarkozy is described as *un vrai héros romantique du XIX siècle sorti des 'Nuits' de Musset*. This rather toadying phrase was quoted in © *Le Canard Enchaîné 4566*.

## Novlangue

'Newspeak' in English. This was the official language of Oceania in the novel *1984* by George Orwell (1903–50). The novel was published in 1949. The language was invented by Big Brother in order to control the masses. *Action irresponsable, comme on dit dans la novlangue syndicale*. © *Marianne 646*. This text refers to the redundant workers of the company Continental who vandalized the *préfecture* of the town in which their factory was located and were criticized by their own union leaders.

## Ô rage! Ô désespoir!

This must be as famous in French as 'To be or not to be' is in English. They are the opening words in the monologue of Don Diègue in the tragi-comedy *Le Cid* by Pierre Corneille. An old man, Don Diègue has just been insulted by a young man and is unable to fight. He vociferates 'Ô rage! Ô désespoir! Ô vieillesse ennemie!,/N'ai-je donc tant vécu que pour cette infamie?' *'Orages, ô désespoirs sociaux'*. © *Les Dossiers du Canard 114*. This was the pun heading of an article about the deteriorating industrial relations climate in France in 2009. See above 'Chimène', '*Cid*', 'cœur', 'combat cessa' and 'cornélien'. See below 'Ôte-moi d'un doute' 'Pour' and 'Va'.

## Ô Rome, unique objet de mon ressentiment

This quote comes from what is known as the 'imprécations de Camille' from the play *Horace* by Pierre Corneille. Camille bewails the death of her husband at the hands of her own brother. She curses the town for the war that has destroyed her family (*Horace* IV, 5, v 1301). *Ô Rome, unique objet*. © *Marianne 652*. The heading of an article about the decadence of the French Republic. 'Ô' is not part of the original quote.

## Ô temps, suspends ton vol …                    `***`

'Ô temps, supends ton vol et vous, heures propices,/Suspendez votre cours!/ Laissez-nous savourer les rapides délices/Des plus beaux de nos jours.' From *Le Lac* by Alphonse de Lamartine (1790–1869). A poem that is an expression of time rushing by and of fleeting happiness. *OTAN, suspends ton vol.* © *Le Canard Enchaîné 4608*. A pun concerning NATO forces.

## On m'assassine                    `**`

These are the words of Harpagon, in the play *L'Avare* by Molière. *Le lobby bancaire a aussitôt poussé des cris d'orfraie sur l'air bien connu du 'on me tue, on m'assassine'*. © *Marianne 660*. This is a reference to the decision of the British government to impose an exceptional tax on bank bonuses and the consequent shrieks of protest by the banks. See Chapter 3 'orfraie'.

## Ôte-moi d'un doute                    `**`

From *Le Cid* by Corneille. These are the words of Rodrigue when he addresses Chimène's father, le Comte de Gormas. 'Ôte-moi d'un doute,/ Connais-tu bien Don Diègue?' *Ce qui n'empêche pas Goujon et Lefrère, éminents universitaires, d'enfoncer le clou avec 'Ôte-moi d'un doute. L'énigme Corneille-Molière.* © *L'Express 3015*. This was used as the title of a book *Ôte-moi d'un doute* which discusses the enigma surrounding the authorship of some of Molière's plays. Corneille is thought to have been the author of some of them. At the very least, Molière is said to have received a lot of help from Corneille in writing his plays. See above 'Chimène', 'Cid, 'cornélien' 'combat cessa', 'cœur', 'Ô rage!'. See below 'Pour' and 'Va'.

## ouest, rien de nouveau. À l'                    `*`

This is the French title of the First World War novel by Erich Maria Remarque, published in 1929 *All Quiet on the Western Front* (*Im Westen nichts Neues*). *Du nouveau à l'Est*. © *Marianne 680*. This text deals with the agreement between Moscow and Kiev on gas prices and the renewal of the lease of the Russian naval base in the Crimea.

## outre-tombe                    `**`

Pierre Méhaignerie, a politician who is past his prime, referred to the UMP as a cathedral. *Marianne* suggests that he has been in the crypt for some time now with the heading *Vu d'outre-tombe*. © *Marianne 661/662*. *Les Mémoires d'outre-tombe* is an autobiographical work by François René de Chateaubriand (1768–1848).

## Ouvroir de littérature potentielle                    `**`

*Avait-il [the columnist] observé la pleine lune trop longtemps? Appliqué une recette inédite de l'Ouvroir de littérature potentielle?* © *Le Monde 20 230*. This is a comment on a typographical error in an article in which the journalist spoke about the creation of ten million jobs instead of the correct figure which was 300,000. See above *Exercice de Style*.

## Pangloss

**\*\***

In *Candide*, the philosophical tale by Voltaire, Dr Pangloss represents the naïve optimist to whom we owe the words 'Tout est pour le mieux dans le meilleur des mondes possibles'. Voltaire wrote this as an ironic response to the popular reaction to the Lisbon earthquake of 1755 which destroyed the city. *Le héros [Pantagleize] est un prof de philo ... une sorte de Pangloss candide, égaré sur la terre.* © *Marianne 57*. This is a reference to the play *Pantagleize* written in 1927 by the Belgian playwright Michel de Ghelderode.

## Pantagruel

**\***

Pantagruel is the name of the giant in the second book by Rabelais (1494–1553) published in 1532. 'Pantagruelian' is a synonym of gigantic, worthy of a giant and the appetite to go with it. *Quant à Jacques Chirac, il incarne mieux qu'aucun autre 'La France du terroir' ... dans sa générosité et ses ripailles dignes de Pantagruel.* © *Marianne 615*. Jacques Chirac enjoys the reputation of having a solid appetite ('un bon coup de fourchette'). See above 'Gargantua'.

## Panurge (moutons de) nmpl.

**\*\*\***

In *Quart Livre* by Rabelais, there is a character called Panurge who has been insulted by the sheep merchant Dindenault. To take his revenge, Panurge buys a sheep and throws it into the sea. All of the merchant's sheep follow. Dindenault, who is holding on to the last ram, is also drowned as the ram jumps into the sea, blindly following the flock. *...saisi de panurgisme aigu, les boursicoteurs et spéculateurs ont l'intelligence des moutons de Rabelais, et ne sont capables que de penser avec leurs jambes qu'ils prennent d'ailleurs à leur cou.* © *Le Point 1882*. This is a reference to the panic of investors in the wake of the financial crisis of 2008. In spite of the State's guarantees, the herd instinct seems to have prevailed over reason, hence the collapse of the financial markets. NB: 'prendre ses jambes à son cou' means 'to take to one's heels'.

## panurgisme nm.

**\***

*Comme chez les ruminants, le panurgisme est souvent mortel sur les marchés [financiers]* © *Les Echos 20 448*. See above 'Panurge'.

## par l'odeur alléché

**\***

*Le 5 juillet, face à des Sénateurs, par l'odeur du sang alléchés, la garde des Sceaux se plante magistralement.* © *Le Nouvel Observateur 2309*. This is a reference to the presentation made by the then Minister of Justice, Rachida Dati, in front of the senators, on the subject of second or habitual offenders. She completely flunked the presentation. The senators were there in number sensing that there was going to be 'blood'. See above 'Maître'.

### part du lion. La                              ***

Although it means the biggest part, it originally meant the whole. In La Fontaine's fable of *La Génisse, la Chèvre et la Brebis en société avec le Lion*, the four animals, after having decided in advance to divide their possible 'gain' into four equal parts, succeed in catching a stag. The lion divides the prey into four equal parts but attributes each part to himself, invoking the 'droit du plus fort'. This is often used today as 'la loi du plus fort' (might is right). *Eurovanille se taille la part du lion sur le marché de la vanille.* © *Les Echos 20 431.*

### patte blanche. montrer                        ***

'Montrer patte blanche' is to give sb. proof of one's identity in order to gain entry to a given place, or to prove that what one is saying is true. In La Fontaine's fable *Le Loup, la Chèvre et le Chevreau*, the mother goat leaves her young kid at home and tells her not to open the door until she hears the code. The wolf has overheard the code. In the mother's absence, he knocks at the door and gives the code but the suspicious kid is not taken in and says 'Montrez-moi patte blanche ou je n'ouvrirai point'. *Célibataires, veufs, divorcés: vous devrez montrer patte blanche pour bénéficier, comme l'an dernier, d'une demi-part supplémentaire du quotient familial.* © *Le Point 1959.* This refers to the new tax rules that have come into force since the law on finance of 2009 which requires tax payers to provide proof of their entitlement to a tax reduction.

### pavé de l'ours. Le                            **

La Fontaine's fable of *L'Ours et l'Amateur des jardins* tells the tale of a bear who sees a fly on his sleeping friend's nose and decides to kill the fly by striking it with a huge stone; in doing so, he kills his friend. The moral of the fable is 'It is better to have a wise enemy than a stupid friend'. *Il sait que, pour l'Élysée, Dassault est l'ami catastrophe comme l'ours dans la fable de La Fontaine.* © *Marianne 611.* This is a reference to Serge Dassault who is very close to the Élysée but who sometimes proves to be a great embarrassment. See Chapter 9 'Dassault, Serge'.

### *Peau de chagrin. La*                         ***

'Chagrin', comes from the Turkish word *çâgri* which means 'rump' or 'hindquarters' of a mule. This is the title of a novel by Balzac (1831). The ruined hero finds a magic piece of hide which enables him to realize his every wish. But with every wish, the piece of hide shrinks. With the last wish, the hero will die. It is frequently used today to describe dwindling budgets. *Au début du siècle, le déclin s'amorce. La culture du safran nécessitant une forte main d'œuvre, se réduit comme une peau de chagrin.* © *Point 1874.* This refers to the decline in saffron production because of the fact that its production is highly labour-intensive.

### peau de l'ours (ne vendez pas la)           [ \* ]
This is a very old French proverb corresponding to the English 'Don't count your chickens'. *Il ne faut pas vendre la peau de l'ours des Pyrénées.* © *Le Canard Enchaîné 4622.* The context of this quotation is the tendency of some UMP *députés* to write off the political future of François Bayrou. Bayrou comes from the region of the Pyrenees. Recently, some bears from Eastern Europe have been set free in this region to stem the decline in the bear population.

### Persan? Comment peut-on être           [ \* ]
Charles Louis de Secondat, Baron de la Brède et de Montesquieu (1689–1755) wrote *Lettres persanes* in 1721 as a satire of the France of the eighteenth century. He did not publish it under his own name. It is one of the first works to underscore cultural relativism and makes very topical reading. In letter no. 30 we can read, 'Ah! ah! Monsieur est Persan? C'est une chose bien extraordinaire! Comment peut-on être Persan?' *Montesquieu, s'il nous revenait, serait fort surpris des changements en l'esprit de ses compatriotes. Lorsqu'il écrivait ses 'Lettres persanes', les meilleurs esprits se figuraient difficilement les mœurs et les idées qui avaient cours sous d'autres latitudes.* © *Marianne 663.* This is a reflection on the attitude of the French towards the violent protests in Iran, as if, by some form of inevitability, Iran has to be under the rule of religion in one way or another. See above 'lettre'.

### Père Goriot. Le           [ \* ]
See below 'Rastignac'.

### Petit Poucet. Le           [ \*\*\* ]
This is the title of one of the most famous fairy tales by the French writer Charles Perrault (1628–1703) which is the equivalent tale to that of *Hansel and Gretel* by the brothers Grimm. The following image is that of the children leaving a trail of pebbles behind them as they were taken into the woods by their father. *Égrenant, tel un 'Petit Poucet', aux responsabilités mondiales, des dizaines de formules soigneusement choisies pendant une tournée d'Europe destinée à planter le décor du nouveau rapport de l'Amérique au monde.* © *Le Figaro 20 129.* This is a reference to the messages of the 'extended hand' policy that Obama left behind him during his trip to Europe in 2009.

### Petit Prince. Le          
This is the title (and main character) of a novella written in 1943 by Antoine de Saint-Exupéry. *C'est l'histoire d'un petit prince russe désœuvré*

*qui demande à son père: 'S'il te plaît, achète-moi un journal français'.* © *Les Echos 20 437*. The context of this quote is the buyout of the French evening newspaper *France Soir* by the son of a Russian multi-billionaire said to be close to Putin. It echoes the words of *le petit prince*: 'S'il te plait, dessine-moi un mouton.' See above 'Dessine-moi' and 'apprivoiser'.

## phénix des hôtes de ces bois. Le                          `***`

In the fable by La Fontaine, *Le Corbeau et le Renard*, we can read 'Que vous êtes joli, que vous me semblez beau!/Sans mentir, si votre ramage/Se rapporte à votre plumage,/Vous êtes le phénix des hôtes de ces bois.' *Avec R Karoutchi, Nicolas Sarkozy est toujours le phénix des hôtes de ces bois.* © *Les Dossiers du Canard 111.* 'Hôtes' should be understood in the sense of 'inhabitants'. This was part of the flattery of the fox towards the crow. See above 'Maître'.

## picrocholine adj.                                         `***`

*Le voisinage avec les bons vieux notables du centrisme n'ira pas sans chamailleries picrocholines.* © *Marianne 611*. This term derives from the Greek *pikros* meaning 'prickly' or 'bitter' and *kholê* meaning 'anger' or 'bile'. 'Une guerre picrocholine' refers to a war whose origin is obscure and ridiculous. It comes from the name of the Rabelasian character Picrochole who wages war against Grandgousier in the book *Gargantua*. It is in fact a satire against the war waged by Charles V of Spain, who had the delirious ambition of establishing a universal monarchy.

## plus petit que soi. On a souvent besoin de                `**`

The opening lines of the fable *Le Rat et le Lion* are: 'Il faut autant qu'on peut, obliger tout le monde:/On a souvent besoin d'un plus petit que soi.' The moral of the story being that we should be polite and agreeable towards everyone because we often need the help of people who are less important than we are. *Donc, on a effectivement besoin de plus petit que soi.* © *Marianne 606*. This fable was used in a highly successful advertising campaign for tinned peas, some years ago, with the slogan 'On a toujours besoin de petits pois chez soi.'

## Pomponette                                                `*`

Pomponette is the name of the female cat in the novel by Pagnol (1895–1974) *La Femme du Boulanger*. It is certainly one of the most famous scenes in all of Pagnol's work and certainly one of the most touching. The baker's wife leaves her husband and has an adulterous affair with a much younger man. Realizing her mistake, she returns to the family fold. Instead of calling his wife names and insulting her, the baker takes his anger out on the cat,

'Pomponette', calling it a slut who stays out all night on the tiles etc. ... his wife is within hearing distance. *Après avoir batifolé outre-Atlantique, Cécilia Pomponette était revenue au bercail sarkozyen depuis le printemps 2006.* © *Marianne 585.* This refers to the return of Cécilia Sarkozy after her adulterous New York escapade with her lover. NB: 'batifoler' means 'to flirt, to frolic' or 'to lark about'.

### Poule aux œufs d'or. La

This comes from another fable by La Fontaine. It is the fable of a greedy man who had a hen which laid golden eggs. He was so greedy that he killed the hen in order to get at the eggs. But there were none. *Les acteurs du marché dénoncent la vision à court terme du gouvernement qui, pour préserver ses recettes fiscales, prendrait le risque de tuer dans l'œuf la poule aux œufs d'or.* © *Les Echos 20 438.* This is a reference to the high rates of taxation to be levied in the area of on-line gaming profits with the danger of killing off the money-spinner.

### Pour grands que soient les rois ...

Famous lines from *Le Cid* by Corneille. *Pour grands que soient les rois, ils sont ce que nous sommes. Marianne 641.* This text refers to the battle of ruffled egos between President Sarkozy and President Obama. See above 'Chimène', '*Cid*', 'cœur', 'cornélien, 'Ô rage!' 'Ôte-moi d'un doute'. See below 'Va'.

### pourri dans le royaume de ... Il y a quelque chose de

The translation of the lines from Shakespeare's *Hamlet* is frequently used in French. *Il y a quelque chose de pourri dans le royaume de l'argent.* © *Le Point 1882.*

### Précieuses ridicules. Les

A one-act comedy by Molière, written in prose and presented for the first time in 1659. It is a story about vanity. *Précieuse mais pas ridicule.* © *Les Echos 20 627.* This was the heading of an article reviewing the American film *Precious* by Lee Daniels that came out in 2010, based on the best-selling book *Push* published in 1966 by a Harlem social worker.

### Princesse de Clèves. La

This is the title of what many people consider to be the first truly modern French novel (published in 1678) written by Marie Madeleine Pioche de La Vergne, otherwise known as Madame de La Fayette (1634–93), a French woman of letters. The title hit the headlines when Nicolas Sarkozy spoke disparagingly about the choice of this book for one of the competitive civil service examinations in France. He said that the person who chose this book must be either 'un sadique ou un imbécile'. Since his remarks were made, sales of this book have sky-rocketed. ***Nous voici donc tous en train de lire La Princesse de Clèves, transformant une lecture en acte politique.*** © *Libération 8716*. Buying the book has become an act of political defiance.


## prose, sans le savoir                                    `**`

See above 'Jourdain'.


## Proust                                                   `**`

*Il a traversé son époque comme un personnage de Proust, une sorte de Charles Swann à l'héroïsme muet; celui que l'on porte en soi plutôt qu'à la boutonnière.* © *Le Nouvel Observateur 2359*. This text is a comment on a book *Georges Boris, trente ans d'influence* which relates the very discreet life of Georges Boris, a member of the resistance and close adviser to de Gaulle, Blum and Mendès-France. The book was written by Jean-Louis Crémieux-Brilhac. See above 'madeleine'.


## quand la bise fut venue                                  `***`

This comes from the fable *La Cigale et la Fourmi*. 'La cigale, ayant chanté tout l'été, se trouva fort dépourvue quand la bise fut venue.' ***La bise automnale de la crise financière venue, voilà Delanoë fort dépourvu.*** © *Marianne 600*. Some months before the financial crisis in 2008, the socialist mayor of Paris proclaimed that he was a free marketeer. He is now in a tricky position in the fight for the leadership of the socialist party in the wake of the financial crisis. See above 'Cigale et la Fourmi'.


## quand tu nous tiens! X                                   `***`

*Indépendance, quand tu nous tiens ...* © *Le Canard Enchaîné 4672*. This was a remark made about the elogious review of a film that was quite mediocre. The journalist who wrote the review, is president of one of the companies that financed the film! 'Amour, amour quand tu nous tiens/On peut bien dire "Adieu prudence"'. These are the last two lines of the fable by La Fontaine *Le Lion amoureux*.


## Questionnaire de Proust nm.

*Henri Loyrette [Director of the Paris Louvre] se soumet au questionnaire de Proust.* © *Le Point 1962*. This questionnaire was originally an English game dating from the middle of the nineteenth century. Proust modified some of the questions. It was popularized by Bernard Pivot during his literary and cultural magazine programme *Bouillon de Culture*, on the French TV channel Antenne 2. The idea was taken up by James Lipton (an admirer of Bernard Pivot) in the USA, during his own TV programme *Inside the Actors Studio* during which he gave this questionnaire to his movie star guests. Among the many questions from *Le Questionnaire de Proust* one could cite the following: 'Le principal trait de mon caractère; La qualité que je préfère chez l'homme; La qualité que je préfère chez la femme; Ce que j'apprécie chez mes amis; Mon principal défaut; Mon occupation préférée; Ce que je déteste par-dessus tout'. Both Pivot and Lipton added a question to the original list: 'What would you like to hear God to say to you when you arrive in paradise?'

## Qu'importe      `**`
See above 'ivresse'.

## rabelaisien adj.      `*`
*Il s'y passe toujours quelque chose. Soirées branchées et buffets rabelaisiens.* © *Le Point 1910.* This was written in the context of the Motor Show in Grenoble where the champagne flows and the *petits fours* are abundant. See above 'Gargantua' and 'Pantagruel'. See Chapter 1 'Il se passe'.

## Rastignac      `***`
Eugène de Rastignac was one of the characters in the novel by Honoré de Balzac (1799–1850) *Le Père Goriot.* He has no money but is bitterly ambitious about 'arriving' in high society, and to this end he uses women to gain entrance to the world he admires. *Les ambitieux ordinaires font carrière; les plus frénétiques se vouent à l'arrivisme avec l'ivresse d'un Rastignac.* © *Le Nouvel Observateur 2358.*

## Rat de ville, et le Rat des champs. Le      `**`
This fable by La Fontaine tells the story of a mouse that lives in the town and a mouse that lives in the country. *Moi, je suis un Picard des villes, je suis né à Amiens, toi, tu es un Picard des champs.* © *Le Monde 20 246.* The words of François Scellier, the former UMP party boss referring to his colleague Francis Delattre and their respective origins.

## révolte qui gronde. La      `*`
Aristide Bruant (1851–1925) wrote a revolutionary poem called *La Chanson des canuts* in 1894 of which one of the lines reads: 'car on entend déjà la révolte qui gronde'. *Entends-tu, Victor Hugo, la révolte qui gronde, l'immense clameur qui gonfle les poitrines des seniors.* © *Marianne 608.* This is a reference to a study conducted on school textbooks to see how they might be the vehicles of 'ageism'. From Ronsard and Corneille to Hugo one can find many instances of negative attitudes towards old age. See Chapter 6 'canuts'. Hugo frequently used the apostrophe 'entends-tu' in his poems.

## Rien ne sert de courir; il faut partir à point      `*`
This is the moral of the fable *Le Lièvre et la Tortue* which states that there is no point in running; one should leave on time. *Rien ne sert de titrer, il faut écrire à point.* © *Marianne 606.* The newspaper *Le Figaro* had predicted (in a

headline) the defeat of Chavez in the Venezuelan elections. Chavez, in fact, won the election.

### roc. un                                                        `**`

This comes from the famous monologue ('la tirade du nez') of Cyrano de Bergerac in the play of that name by Edmond Rostand (1868–1918). 'C'est un roc! ... C'est un pic! C'est un cap! Que dis-je, c'est un cap? C'est une péninsule.' *S'il n'y avait pas ce sentiment que le petit n'était que le nez – quel nez, un pic, un roc, une péninsule [sic] – émergé de l'iceberg du favoritisme et du clanisme cher au chef de l'Etat.* © *Marianne 652.* The text above refers to the outcry against the nepotism of Nicolos Sarkozy and the proposed 'election' of his son as head of the Epad. The latter was recently elected 'administrateur' of the Epad. He has just failed his law examinations. See Chapter 14 'Epad'.

### Rossinante                                                     `**`

The name of Don Quixote's horse in the story written by Miguel de Cervantes (1547–1616). *Il [Jean Sarkozy] enfourche une vielle Rossinante, chevauchée par tous les 'fils de' qui parviennent sans aucun mal à se faire une place au soleil en couinant que leur patronyme était le plus effroyable de tous les handicaps.* © *Marianne 652.* This refers to the children of famous people who, effortlessly, have achieved prominence while whining that the name of their parent was a severe obstacle to their success. See above 'Dulcinée' and 'moulins à vent'.

### Rousseau                                                       `*`

*Nous croyons, sans être pour autant rousseauistes, que l'homme peut être bon.* © *Le Canard Enchaîné 4589.* Jean-Jacques Rousseau (1712–78) wrote *Émile* in which he presented his ideas on education and upbringing. His contention was that man is inherently good but that life in society corrupts him. He is not the writer who first wrote about the concept of the 'noble savage' but his name is often erroneously associated with the origin of the idea.

### *Saison en enfer. Une*                                         `*`

This is the title of a collection of poems in prose form written in 1873 by Arthur Rimbaud (1854–91). *En tant que premier secrétaire du PS, je vais vous lire deux poèmes 'une saison en enfer' et 'le bateau ivre'.* © *Le Canard Enchaîné 4595.* These were the words of François Hollande in a cartoon showing the ship of the socialist party sinking. In 2008 and 2009, the socialist party seemed to have lost direction and was in a sorry state without an electoral platform but with the eternal battle of egos among the future contenders for the presidential nomination. See above *Le Bateau ivre.*

## Shéhérazade       (  *  )

Betrayed by his wife, the King of Persia decides to wed a virgin every day and kill her the morning after the wedding night. Shéhérazade, the vizir's daughter, volunteers to stop the massacre and she does so by telling the king a long story. Every night, she stops the story at a highly critical point, which obliges the king to pospone her execution until he has heard the end of the story. She succeeds in holding out for 1001 nights at which point, the king decides not to execute her. ***Comme la Shéhérazade des Mille et Une Nuits qui sauve sa tête à chaque aube en charmant son bourreau par ses histoires.*** © *Le Nouvel Observateur 2292.* This is a reference to Gordon Brown saving his skin with a speech. Also spelt Schéhérazade.

## selon que vous serez puissant ...       (  *\*\**  )

These words come from the last two lines of the fable *Les Animaux malades de la peste.* ***Selon que vous serez puissant ou misérable,/Les jugements de cour vous rendront blanc ou noir.*** In short, depending on whether you are poor or powerful, the judgement of the court will declare that you are either black or white. La Fontaine quoted in *L'Express 3041.* The context of this quote is the arrest of Roman Polanski and his defence by the intellectual elite of France. See above *Animaux malades de la peste* and 'crier haro'.

## serpents qui sifflent sur nos têtes? Pour qui sont ces    (  *  )

This is a famous verse of Racine from the play *Andromaque.* It is a well-known tongue-twister. ***Ces serpents mutants n'ont pas fini de siffler sur les têtes des chercheurs.*** © *Marianne 649.* The context of this quote is the danger constituted by cross-breeding in serpents that produces venom unknown to science.

## Sganarelle       (  *  )

He is a recurrent character in Molière's plays. This quotation is an allusion to the play *Dom Juan* (1665) which ends in tragedy. Sganarelle's master has been taken to hell, but all the comic character Sganarelle can shout about is his lost wages. 'Mes gages, mes gages.' The context is the financial crisis and the bosses of certain ruined institutions crying out for their bonuses and stock options amid the disaster. ***Alors qu'un immense drame vient de se jouer sous leurs yeux, ils demeurent comme Sganarelle sur la scène vide à scander: nos gages! nos gages!*** © *Nouvel Observateur 2321.* This quote is interesting from two points of view. It illustrates the spelling connection between English words beginning with 'w' and their French equivalent beginning with 'g': la guerre, le garde-robe, la guêpe, gaspiller, Guillaume (war, wardrobe, wasp, to waste, William, etc.) and the word 'gages' which is just one of the many words that the French language possesses to refer to various types of remuneration, each word having a specific nuance, e.g. la solde (soldier), le salaire, (employee), les appointements (civil servant), la rémuneration (general term), le cachet (actor), les gages (domestic servant), les honoraires (member of the professions doctor, lawyer, etc.).

### souris verte. La                                                  *

This is the title of a nursery rhyme in which 'la souris verte' is a well-known character. The nursery rhyme begins 'La souris verte, qui courait dans l'herbe'. *La souris verte qui lui courait sur l'herbe, n'avait aucune chance.* © *Marianne 574.* These words refer to the opinion of the outgoing mayor of Montreuil (a suburb of Paris) about the 'green' candidate in the municipal elections, implying that she didn't stand a chance. Dominique Voynet, the green candidate, in fact won.

### Splendeurs et misères des courtisanes                         *

This is the title of a novel by Honoré de Balzac that was published in 1847 as part of the collection *La Comédie humaine*. *Rastignac chez les yuppies. Splendeur et misère d'un jeune banquier américain.* © *L'Express 3064.* This sums up the book by the American writer Adam Haslett entitled *Intrusion* about the rise and fall of a young American banker. See above 'Rastignac'.

### Statue du Commandeur. La                                      **

The Statue of the Commendatore. *Dom Juan* was put on for the first time on 15 February 1665 at the *Théâtre du Palais Royal*. In the play, the ghost of *le Commandeur*, a man whom Dom Juan has killed in a duel a few months before, finally comes to take Dom Juan to hell as a punishment for his evil ways. *L'oncle François [Mitterrand], la Statue du Commandeur, est l'être aimé, la référence absolue.* © *Le Point 1952.* This is a reference to the relationship between Frédéric Mitterrand and his famous uncle, the socialist president, the late François Mitterrand. François Mitterrand was liked but also feared by his nephew.

### sur un arbre perché                                            *

*Mais comme dans le film avec Louis de Funès 'Sur un arbre perché', le conducteur coincé n'a d'autre choix que d'attendre des secours.* © *Marianne 609.* This text refers to a scene in a film with Louis de Funès where the car he was driving is dangerously perched on a cliff edge and he cannot move for fear of upsetting the delicate balance of the car. See above 'Maître'.

### Tartuf(f)e, tartuf(f)erie                                      ***

Tartuffe is the character in the play of the same name by Molière and represents the arch hypocrite, particularly in the field of religion. In this play, Molière attacks the excesses of the *Compagnie du Saint Sacrement*, thus provoking the ire of the religious cliques. The king forbade public performances of the play and one priest even demanded death at the stake for Molière. It is to Tartuffe that we owe two of Molière's most famous quotations 'Couvrez ce sein que je ne saurais voir' and 'Ah! pour être dévôt, je n'en suis pas moins homme'. In the trial of Yvan Colonna, the man accused of assassinating the *Préfet* Erignac, the counsel for the prosecution referred to the testimony and retractions of Colonna's friends as *Le tango des tartuffes au milieu d'un bal de parjures.* © *Le Figaro 20 111.* See above 'Cachez' and 'Couvrez'.

### Tartarin       [ ** ]

Tartarin is the name of the naïve hero of Alphonse Daudet (1840–97) in the book *Tartarin de Tarascon.* He is a braggart. *Il lance, émule de Tartarin: je devrais me présenter. Dans cette ville, quand j'étais étudiant, j'ai baisé 40% des Toulousaines.* © *L'Express 3056.* This text refers to the boast of the late Georges Frêche, president of the *Conseil Général* of Languedoc-Roussillon, that he should have been the socialist candidate in Toulouse in 2007 since he had had great success as a Latin lover with nearly half the feminine population of Toulouse in his student days! He died in December 2010.

### temps perdu (À la recherche du)       [ ** ]

This is the name of the seven-volume novel by Marcel Proust (1871–1922). *À quoi cette dénudation pourra-t-elle servir? À quelque recherche du temps perdu?* © *Le Point 1884.* This quote refers to the confessions of Sister Emmanuelle, published just after her death. *Le Point* asks 'What is the point in this baring of the soul? Is she trying to recapture the past?'

### Thénardier       [ *** ]

In the novel by Victor Hugo, *Les Misérables,* published in 1862, the Thénardiers are the money-grabbing couple who run the inn 'The Sargeant of Waterloo' and who exploit Cosette. *Malgré le fond de racisme qui persiste dans la classe moyenne américaine et sur lequel les nouveaux Thénardier de la politique américaine, Hilary et Bill Clinton, n'ont pas manqué d'appuyer lors de la campagne pour la désignation du candidat, il y a trois raisons ... qui font que la victoire a de moins en moins de chance d'échapper au sénateur de l'Illinois.* © *Le Point 1882.* The context of this quote was the inevitable victory of Obama in spite of the Clintons' speeches. Notice that even when used in the plural, family names in French are invariable, e.g. 'the Smiths' in English gives 'Les Smith' in French. See above 'Cosette'.

### tirer les marrons du feu       [ *** ]

In the fable by La Fontaine, *Le Singe et le Chat,* the cat takes the chestnuts from the fire, burning itself in the process, whereas the monkey eats the chestnuts that the cat has taken out of the fire, without burning itself. It implies that one takes advantage of a situation at the expense of one's associates. *Tout le monde déguste, mais eux ne pensent qu'à tirer les marrons du feu.* © *Marianne 618.* NB: 'déguster' in this context means to 'suffer' not to 'savour'.

### Tour d'ivoire [***]

This comes from *Pensées d'août à M. Villemin* by Charles Augustin Sainte-Beuve (1804–69). This quote refers to Alfred, comte de Vigny, the French writer (1797–1863). 'Et Vigny, plus secret, comme en sa tour d'ivoire, avant midi, rentrait.' *J'ai des capteurs, je ne suis pas enfermé dans une tour d'ivoire.* © *Le Nouvel Observateur 2367.* The words of Nicolas Sarkozy following the poor results of the first round of the regional elections of 2010. He spoke about the candidates who had not given their best. This was a veiled threat that they might lose their ministerial positions.

### Tout vient à point à qui sait attendre [*]

Everything comes at the opportune moment for the person who knows how to wait. Words of the poet Clément Marot (1496–1544). La Fontaine (1621–95) also wrote a similar phrase 'Tout vient à point à qui sait bien attendre'. *Tout vient à point. Les Echos 20 497.* The context of this quote is the strong financial position of GDF-Suez after it had patiently worked towards stability.

### Ubu [***]

*Arto Paasilinna ne lésine pas sur la gaudriole, mais il nous amuse malgré tout avec cette bonne grosse farce où un clone du Père Ubu piétine la sottise ambiante, sans faire dans la dentelle.* © *L' Express 3019.* Ubu was the name of a fictional and absurd character created by the French writer and poet Alfred Jarry (1873–1907). 'Ubu' appeared in several works and was the trusted dragoon captain of the King of Poland. Paasilinna is a Finnish writer. 'Sans faire dans la dentelle' means without precision or refinement.

### Ubuesque [***]

*Français immigrés de la deuxième génération ou Français nés à l'étranger, doivent s'embarquer dans un combat ubuesque pour prouver leur nationalité française.* © *Le Nouvel Observateur 2360.* This text refers to the difficulty encountered by Anne Sinclair (a famous TV star and the wife of Dominique Strauss-Kahn, president of the IMF) in getting her ID papers renewed. She was born in New York of French parents. The irony of the story is that she was a model for the bust of 'Marianne' (the symbol of the French Republic) some years ago. 'Ubuesque' is a synonym of 'grotesque'.

### un seul être vous manque et tout est dépeuplé [**]

This line was written by Alphonse de Lamartine (1790–1869). *Une seule Carla vous manque et le carnet de commandes est dépeuplé.* © *Le Canard Enchaîné 4553.* This refers to the fact that Nicolas Sarkozy went to Delhi unaccompanied by his wife, Carla, and came back without having sold a single nuclear power station or a high-speed train; he returned with an empty order book in 2008.

## Va, je ne te hais point
*

These are the words of Chimène, in *Le Cid* by Corneille, as she talks to Rodrigue, the man she loves and yet the man who has killed her own father. In Scene 3 Act IV she cannot bring herself to say that she loves him and consequently, she uses this famous understatement. *Entre les lignes, on devine qu'avant guerre, les Sarkozy de Nagy Bocsa, avec leurs terres et leur château ne haïssaient point le régime du 'régent' Horthy, qui deviendra l'allié de Hitler.* © *Le Canard Enchaîné 4666.* This is a remark made about the book published by Nicolas Sarkozy's father, Pal Sarkozy, entitled *Tant de vie.* See above 'Chimène', '*Cid*', 'cœur' 'combat cessa', 'cornélien', 'Ô rage!', 'Ôte-moi d'un doute', 'Pour'.

## Valjean
**

Valjean is one of the main characters in the novel *Les Misérables* by Victor Hugo. He was sentenced to five years in a penal colony. *Oubliez le bagne de Toulon et vos souvenirs de Jean Valjean ou de Vidoq.* © *Le Point 1954.* This text refers to the opening of a model prison in Toulon which, while not being a four-star hotel, is a far cry from most other prisons in France. See Chapter 6 'Vidocq'.

## vieux lion rugit encore. Le
*

This is an allusion to the old lion in the fable *Le Lion devenu vieux* who cannot roar. 'Le malheureux Lion, languissant, triste, et morne,/Peut à peine rugir' *Le vieux lion rugit encore.* © *Marianne 629.* This is the title of an article devoted to the war speeches of Winston Churchill. See above 'coup de pied'.

## Voltaire. Je suis tombé par terre, c'est la faute à
*

See above 'Gavroche'.

## *Voyage au bout de la nuit*
*

*Voyage au bout de la nuit* is the title of the first novel by Louis Ferdinand Auguste Destouches (1894–1961) better known as 'Céline', published in 1932 and evoking the mad slaughter of the First World War. *Ses deux fils avaient disparu un an plus tôt, comme autrefois son mari, parti en voyage dit-elle pudiquement. Un voyage au bout de la nuit qui a emporté des centaines d'hommes de tous âges de Kirumba.* © *Le Nouvel Observateur 2327.* This text refers to the child soldiers fighting in the Congo.

## Waterloo, Waterloo, Waterloo, morne plaine
***

These words come fom *Les Châtiments* written by Victor Hugo in 1852 and refers to the gloomy and dismal plain on which the battle of Waterloo was fought and lost by the French. *Le Parti Socialiste, morne plaine.* © *Marianne 581.* This is a comment about the sorry state of the French socialist party.

# Chapter 6

# Historical references

From the intercultural point of view, it is important to realize that some cultures attach much more importance to the past than others. For the French, the weight and importance of the past is enormous and has to be taken into account when approaching French culture in general. The importance of the past reaches far beyond the confines of history proper, with its references to the Sun King, Napoleon and Waterloo. A few references are not accompanied by a quotation but are important and mentioned frequently without being used figuratively.

### Action Française
( * )

In 1898, at the height of the Dreyfus affair, Henri Vaugeois founded the political movement known as *L'Action Française*. It was nationalistic, royalist and anti-Semitic and was largely influenced by the ideas of Charles Maurras (1868–1952) and closely related to *Les Camelots du Roi*. See below 'Camelots du Roi' and 'Cagoule'.

### Alésia
( * )

This was the name of a Gallic fort situated on Mount Auxois in what is today the *département* of the Côte d'Or (21). It was to this place that Vercingétorix retreated with his army before surrendering to Caesar after a two-month siege in around 52 BC. *Se voiler la face: un sport national depuis Alésia.* © *Marianne 577*. This is a reference to the French habit of not facing up to facts.

### Alexandre
( * )

This is a reference to Alexander the Great (356–323 BC), King of Macedonia, one of the greatest military conquerors of all time, and his warhorse Bucephalus, which literally means 'ox-headed' from the Greek *bous* 'ox', and *kephale* 'head'. Nicolas Sarkozy *a bien saisi ... que Barack Obama serait le héros et, s'il réussit, le maître de ce nouveau monde; mais il compte bien, lui, être l'Aristote de cet Alexandre, voire, si c'est nécessaire, son Bucéphale.* © *L'Express 3015*. Aristotle was Alexander's tutor and friend.

## Allez dire

> *

These were the words pronounced by Mirabeau on 23 June 1789 having received the order from the king to disband. 'Allez dire au Roi que nous sommes ici par la volonté du peuple et que nous n'en sortirons que par la force des baïonnettes.' 'Go and tell the King that we are here by the will of the people and we shall be expelled only by the force of bayonets.' *Allez dire à celui qui vous envoie que nous sommes ici élus régionaux, par la volonté du peuple.* © *Le Canard Enchaîné 4651.* The president of the *région* of PACA addressed these words to the minister of the interior during the congress of the Association des Régions de France in 2009. This was part of the *fronde* between the central state and the presidents of the regions. See Chapter 14 'PACA'.

## Anastasie

> *

The history of censorship is long, and one of the first instances of censorship dates back to 1559 and the *Index librorum prohibitorum* of the Catholic Church. Since 1874, the satirical press in France has represented censorship as an old shrew, with long finger nails and bearing a pair of gigantic scissors. *Anastasie: une des premières apparitions de la mégère pas apprivoisée représentée griffue par le dessinateur André Gill* [1840–85]. © *Les Dossiers du Canard 105.*

## ancien régime nm.

> ***

The *ancien régime* historically refers to pre-revolutionary France, the France of the divine right of kings and absolute monarchy, the world as it was before 1789. *On se croirait revenu à l'ancien régime. Le roi s'amuse, le roi dilapide … pendant que le peuple s'appauvrit.* © *Marianne 586.* These were the words of the socialist Ségolène Royal criticizing Nicolas Sarkozy.

## année 1793 nf.

> *

*Cette tentation naturelle de refaire en permanence 1793.* The words of the UMP *député* Jean-François Copé quoted in © *Marianne 623.* The years 1792–93 marked a period of riots, turmoil and the inability of the government to control prices. It was in 1793 that the last seigneurial rights were abolished without compensation. Mr. Copé has frequently expressed his equal dislike of the night of 4 August 1789, i.e. the famous event known as the 'abolition of privileges'. His remarks were made in the wake of public indignation at the abusive privileges of the banking world that came to light during the financial crisis 2008/9. See Chapter 9 'Copé, Jean-François'.

## années de plomb nfpl.

> **

The phenomenon in question stretches roughly from the 1960s to the 1980s and affected most western European countries. Italy had its *Brigate Rosse*, Germany had the *Baader-Meinhof* and France had *Action Directe*. These were years of political violence perpetrated by groups at both extremes of the political spectrum. *Les années de plomb, cette période de violences politiques* [*de droite et de gauche*] *qui fit 362 morts entre 1969 et 1980.* © *L'Express 2989.* This text is related to France's refusal to extradite Marina Petrella to Italy. She is one of the former *Brigate Rosse* leaders who had settled in the Paris region.

### antisémite nm.                                                              ***

Siné is the name of the former cartoonist of the weekly, satirical newspaper *Charlie Hebdo*. He was dismissed from his post for having written an article about the engagement of Jean Sarkozy, the president's son, to the heiress of the Darty electrical appliances empire. His text was considered to be anti-Semitic. *Siné se retrouve assimilé aux pires antisémites que la France ait connus de Charles Maurras à Edouard Drumont en passant par Robert Brasillach.* ©*Marianne 590.* This comment underlines the injustice of considering Siné an anti-Semite among the notorious anti-Semites of recent French history. See Chapter 11 'Dreyfus'.

### appel du 18 juin nm.                                                        ***

*La manifestation des blouses blanches partira de la place du 18 juin, clin d'œil à l'appel du même nom et à son esprit de résistance.* © *Le Canard Enchaîné 4616.* This was the famous message broadcast by de Gaulle from the BBC in London in 1940 exhorting the French to continue the fight against the Germans. This 'call' was made soon after the call of Maréchal Pétain asking the French to lay down their arms. See Chapter 12 'blouses blanches'.

### Ateliers nationaux nmpl.                                                    *

The National Workshops were set up under Napoleon III to alleviate the social distress caused by unemployment in France in the late 1840s. *Quelques jours plus tôt, elle [Laurence Parisot] s'est gaussée du fonds d'investissement social fortement suggéré par la CFDT: 'c'est la nouvelle version des Ateliers nationaux'.* © *Marianne 619.* The head of the French employers' confederation scorned the CFDT's suggestion of setting up a social investment fund saying that it was the new version of the national workshops of the nineteenth century.

### audace. De l'audace, encore de l'                                          **

'Pour vaincre les ennemies de la France que faut-il? De l'audace, encore de l'audace, toujours de l'audace.' The words of Georges Jacques Danton (1759–94), a French politician, during his speech to the Convention on 2 September 1792 while France was on the point of being invaded by the coalition troops. 'What is required to defeat the enemies of France? Daring, more daring, ever more daring.' He was guillotined during the end phase of the Terror. *Carol Duval: de l'audace, encore de l'audace.* © *Le Figaro*

*Magazine 20 254.* This text refers to the courage and daring of a successful champagne producer who took over the reins of the family vineyard on becoming a widow in 1991.

## Aujourd'hui, rien

`*`

Words of Louis XVI in his diary on 14 July 1789. *Dans son journal à la date du 14 juillet 1789, le roi avait inscrit: 'rien'.* © *Marianne 629.* This refers to the apparent lack of perception by the present government that a storm of social discontent is brewing with the threat of widespread industrial action.

## Austerlitz

`***`

Austerlitz (located today in the Czech Republic) was one of the most brilliant battles fought by Napoleon. It took place on 2 December 1805. He defeated the combined Austro-Russian armies. Since this battle, we speak of 'the sun of Austerlitz', the sun of victory. *Si la publication de la Phénoménologie de l'esprit [1806] fut l'Austerlitz de la pensée hégélienne, … celle du livre de Rudolph Haym fut son Waterloo.* ©*Marianne 604.* See below 'Pont d'Arcole' and 'Waterloo'.

## Bad Godesberg

`**`

Bad Godesberg is a quiet suburb of Bonn and used to be the seat of the German federal government. It was the location of most of the foreign embassies and government offices. The Congress of Bad Godesberg, held in 1959, was a landmark in the history of European social democracy. It was during this congress that the German social democrats decided to break with all reference to Marxism and accept the principles of the market economy. *Le camp progressiste a accompli son Bade-Godesberg.* © *Marianne 590.* NB: there is a hyphen in Bade-Godesberg when used metaphorically.

## Badinguet

`**`

*Le Napoléon d'après Austerlitz, le Badinguet d'après Sedan.* © *Marianne 673.* This is a reflection on Nicolas Sarkozy's situation after the poor showing of his party in the regional elections of March 2010. 'Badinguet' was the nickname of Napoleon III. See below 'Napoleon III' and 'Sedan'.

## ban et l'arrière ban (convoquer le)

`**`

The feudal system was arranged as a pyramid with the king at the top, to whom his vassals pledged allegiance. Each direct vassal of the king had his own vassals in turn who had also sworn allegiance to their lord. Each vassal owed help and assistance to his respective lord, e.g. to take up arms to defend the lord when under attack. 'Convoquer le ban et l'arrière-ban' was the official proclamation whereby the lord summoned his barons and vassals to fulfil their obligation towards him. Failure to do so resulted in death by hanging. Today, it implies a request for help and support made to one's friends, family, members of the same political party, members of the same government, etc. Referring to the director of the film about the terrorist Carlos the Jackal, presented at the Cannes film Festival in 2010, the article mentions his ambition: *convoquant le ban et l'arrière-ban des années de plomb*. © *L'Express 3071*. See above 'années de plomb'.

### Bastille. La                                                                    `*`

This was the famous Parisian fortress built in 1370 by Charles V. It became a state prison under Richelieu. The prison was stormed and taken by the mob on 14 July 1789 but only a handful of prisoners were imprisoned there at the time. A symbol of oppression, it was demolished during the Revolution. In its place today, in the fourth *arrondissement*, is a vast roundabout with a statue commemorating the Revolution of 1830. *Les Bastilles ne sont pas toujours des forteresses et on ne les prend pas toujours à coups de pierres et de piques*. © *Marianne 602*.

### bataille d'Angleterre nf.                                                       `*`

What the British call 'The Battle of Britain' was waged in the summer and autumn skies of England in 1940 when the *Luftwaffe* attacked Great Britain. *EDF remporte enfin sa bataille d'Angleterre*. This is a reference to the buyout of the electricity company British Energy by the French electricity company EDF. © *Le Figaro 19 953*.

### Bataille du rail nf.                                                            `*`

*La Bataille du rail* (1946) is the title of a film by René Clément (1913–96) which tells the story of the resistance operations carried out by French railwaymen to sabotage railway rolling stock and infrastructure in Nazi occupied France. The film was quickly taken out of circulation because it showed exactly how the railwaymen went about their sabotage operations. France was at war at the time and the Vietnamese were taking inspiration from the film to attack the French railway network in Indo-China. *Son plan, Jean Louis Borloo n'hésite pas à le présenter comme une nouvelle bataille du rail. L'ennemi cette fois, c'est le $CO_2$*. © *Le Figaro 20 258*. This is a reference to the battle waged by the former minister of ecology against the greenhouse gas carbon dioxide.

### Belle Époque nf.                                                               `***`

This is generally understood to be the period around 1900 when life was agreable and lighthearted, corresponding in England to the Edwardian period, i.e. the reign of Edward VII (1901–10). *Et, comme dans tous les autres épisodes, à la Belle Epoque, au fil des pages, on tremble pour de faux et on se marre pour de vrai*. © *Le Point 1935*. This comment refers to the successful series of books known as *Les Nouveaux Mystères de Marseille*, by Jean Contrucci in which vampires and dead bodies abound.

### Berezina nf.

Berezina (or Bérézina) is the name of a river in Byelorussia (Belarus) that the retreating French army of Napoleon I crossed in 1812 during the retreat from Moscow. It is used today as a synonym of rout, catastrophe and total failure, etc. *Voyez Rungis: ce marché a été conçu pour le camion et, à la première grève ou à la première neige, c'est la Berezina.* © *L'Express 3020.* This refers to the fact that a little snow has catastrophic effects on the economic life of the country in general and on the wholesale market of Rungis in particular.

### Bonapartistes et Orléanistes

*Il y a toujours eu en France au moins deux partis de droite ... comme il y a eu Bonapartistes et Orléanistes.* © *Le Figaro 20 362.* The term *Orléaniste* dates from 1830 and referred to the descendants of the July Monarchy. In the twentieth century, the house of 'Orleans' represents the heirs to the throne of France. See below 'Monarchie de Juillet'.

### Bonnot (la bande à)

Jules Joseph Bonnot (1876–1912) was a French anarchist and head of the gang that committed a series of bank robberies and murders between 1911–12. It was the first time an automobile had ever been used in a bank robbery. *C'est nous ... suppôts de la Bande à Bonnot, qui avons contraint ces honnêtes commerçants à introduire des pastilles antivol dans les vêtements.* © *Le Canard Enchaîné 4557.* This text refers to the electronic gadgetry used in shops to prevent shoplifting, the client being considered as a potential criminal.

### boulanger nm.

'Nous ne manquerons plus de pain, nous ramenons le boulanger, la boulangère et le petit mitron.' 'We will not be short of bread, we have brought back the baker, the baker's wife and the baker's apprentice.' This was the famous refrain chanted by the mob on bringing back Louis XVI from Versailles to Paris along with his wife and the heir, in October 1789. *Le boulanger, la boulangère et le petit mitron sont au Cap Nègre.* © *Marianne 643.* This is a reference to Nicolas Sarkozy, Carla Bruni and her son spending their holidays at Carla Bruni's holiday residence in the south of France.

### bouton de guêtre nm.

See Chapter 2 'guêtre (Jusqu'au dernier bouton de)'.

### Brumaire (Le 18)

The 'foggy' month in the French Revolutionary calendar. This date corresponds to 9 November 1799, date of Napoleon I's *coup d'état* establishing the Consulate. With *the coup d'état* of 2 December 1851 Napoleon III established the Second Empire. ***Les internautes du Monde s'enflamment, on se croirait au seuil du 18 Brumaire, du 2 décembre 1851.*** © *Le Monde 19 828.* The context of this sentence is the proposition by Nicolas Sarkozy that he should be president of the eurozone for at least one year. Many saw this as an attempted putsch.

### Cagoule nf.      `**`

La Cagoule was the nickname given by the press to the secret organization the Comité secret d'action révolutionnaire which came into existence after the riots of 6 February 1934. It was an extreme right-wing, anti-republican, anti-Semitic and anticommunist organization that took part in political subversion during the 1930s. ***Inversement, des fractions non-négligeables de l'Action Française, de la Cagoule et d'autres organisations anti-juives du même type, se sont portées vers la résistance ... par un rejet instinctif de l'occupation allemande.*** © *Marianne 574.* This text refers to the fact that quite a few members of the right-wing, anti-Semitic organizations in fact joined the Resistance because of their refusal to accept the German occupation of France.

### calèches (les bombes sous les)      `*`

This is a reference to the bomb attack made on Napoleon III by an Italian nationalist Felice Orsini that took place on 14 January 1858. A bomb was thrown under the horse-drawn carriage in which Napoleon III and his wife, Eugénie, were being taken to the Paris Opera. They both escaped unharmed. ***Nos héros littéraires ont eu entre 1800–1900 plus de peur que de mal. Plus de procès sur le dos que de bombes sous leur calèche.*** © *Marianne 592.* This text refers to the fact that the literary heroes of the beginning of the century faced, at most, a court case against them rather than a terrorist attack against their person.

### Camelots du Roi (La Fédération nationale des)      `*`

La Fédération nationale des Camelots du Roi was a youth organization founded by Maurice Pujo in 1908. It was closely associated with the monarchist and anti-Semitic movement of Action Française under the leadership of Charles Maurras. It was a volunteer corps of shirted and booted street fighters and agitators entrusted with carrying out street violence, poster sticking, etc. ***Le chemin de Londres d'un camelot du roi.*** © *Le Canard Enchaîné 4633.* This is the heading of an article that describes the journey of a French nationalist, Daniel Cordier, to London, to join de Gaulle after the capitulation announced by Pétain in 1940. See above 'Cagoule'.

### Canossa     

Canossa is a small town in Italy to which the Holy Roman German Emperor, Henry IV, was obliged to go to ask Pope Gregory VII to lift his excommunication on 25–27 January 1077. The Pope kept him waiting for two days. 'Aller à Canossa' now means to capitulate in a humiliating manner in front of one's opponent. ***Juppé à Canossa.*** © *Le Canard Enchaîné 4642.* This is a reference to the fact that Alain Juppé criticized President Sarkozy over the proposed abolition of corporate tax (in October 2009) saying 'c'est tout de même se foutre du monde' ('se foutre du monde' means 'not to give a shit about' sb.). After a conversation with Nicolas Sarkozy he was forced to make a public apology by saying that one of his sentences was excessive and that he apologized to the president for any offence caused.

## canut nm.

[ * ]

The revolt of the 'canuts' was the first modern insurrection in France in the new industrial era. The 'canuts' were artisans who worked in the silk industry in Lyons. They revolted in 1831 because of the refusal on the part of the silk manufacturers to respect the minimum prices agreed upon by the industrial tribunal and the *préfet*. One of the characteristics of the revolt was machine-breaking. Another revolt took place in 1834. The revolt was put down by the army with considerable loss of life. *...on se croit tantôt revenu aux bris de machines des canuts lyonnais, ou bien aux théories des ... anarchistes de la Belle Epoque.* © *Marianne 625.* This refers to the inflammatory remarks made by certain political leaders about refounding capitalism in the wake of the US subprime mortgage disaster and financial crisis. See above 'Belle Époque'. See Chapter 2 'révolte?'.

## Carmagnole' ('dansons la)

[ * ]

The Carmagnole (1792) was originally a dance performed by a large group in ring formation. During the dance, people would stamp their feet loudly, imitating the shot of canon. During the French Revolution 'to make somebody dance the Carmagnole' was a euphemism for 'to guillotine' them. *Le Président a reparlé dans un discours au canon de la Carmagnole.* © *Marianne 598.* This means that the president's speech was made in violent and stirring terms.

## Cathare nmf.

[ ** ]

*Frêche se veut l'héritier des cathares face aux croisés de Simon de Montfort.* © *L'Express 3057.* The late Georges Frêche was the socialist president of the Languedoc-Roussillon region in the south west of France. He was mayor of Montpellier for over 25 years. His racist remarks led to his exclusion from the socialist party. He saw himself as a local politician fighting against the Parisian nomenklatura. The Cathars (from the Greek 'pure') were members of a medieval religious group that propounded absolute purity of morals and who were particularly well established in the region of Albi in the south-west of France. They were declared heretics by Innocent III in 1215 and suffered repression at the hands of the crusaders and the

Inquisition. Simon de Montfort was a rather obscure baron from the Paris region who took up the crusade against the Albigensian heresy (a part of the Cathar movement) and confiscated a great amount of land which he took from the Cathar leader, Raymond VI, count of Toulouse. See below 'Jacobin' for another angle on the Frêche affair. See also Chapter 2 'Tuez-les'.

### Cauchon (L'abbé)

Pierre Cauchon (1371–1442), Bishop of Beauvais, embraced the Burgundian party, and thus the English camp, in the Hundred Years' war. He presided at the ecclesiastical court that sentenced Joan of Arc to be burned at the stake as a heretic. *Ségolène incarne la figure mythique de Jeanne d'Arc … Pour interpréter le rôle de l'abbé Cauchon, les candidats ne manquent pas, surtout au PS.* © *Marianne 604.* This text refers to the many enemies of Ségolène Royal, especially among the socialist leaders of her own party.

### Champollion

Jean-François Champollion was the French Egyptologist (1790–1832) who (with the help of the works of the English Egyptologist Thomas Young [1773–1829]) was the first man to decipher the hieroglyphs on the Rosetta Stone. *Les médecins suisses écrivent comme des cochons. Leurs ordonnances obligent les pharmaciens, armés de grandes lunettes, à se lancer dans des opérations de déchiffrage dignes de Champollion.* © *Le Monde 20 237.* This text refers to the cost (€7 million) caused by errors of interpretation of the enigmatic prescriptions written by Swiss doctors.

### Chant du départ nm.

This is a revolutionary song and war hymn written by Etienne Méhul (music) and Marie-Joseph Chénier (lyrics) in 1794. It was the official hymn of the First Empire. It was later used (in 1914) as a song to rouse the troops leaving for the front on mobilization. It is the name of the sculpture by François Rude (1784–1855) on the Arc de Triomphe, equally known as *La Marseillaise.*

### Chemin des Dames nm.

*Royal et Aubry à la baïonnette. Après le massacre de Reims, le chemin des Dames.* © *Le Canard Enchaîné 4595.* The last two candidates for the premiership of the socialist party were two women, Ségolène Royal and Martine Aubry. There is a double reference here. Traditionally French kings were crowned in Reims – the ceremony being called 'le sacre' – and the socialist congress in Reims in 2008 was not a model of party unity. 'Le Chemin des Dames', was one of the most bloody battlefields of the First World War. It became notorious after the catastrophic attacks made by General Nivelle against the German front in the spring of 1917. Over 200,000 Frenchmen were killed within two months for no gain. It was after this attack that the first mutinies began to break out. In fact, this delightful name, 'Le Chemin des Dames', comes from the fact that Adélaïde and Victoire, two daughters of Louis XV, used to take this route from Paris to the palace of Bove in the *département* of the Aisne (02). The battle of 'Le Chemin des Dames' is also known as the second battle of the Aisne.

### chêne de Vincennes nm.

*À la fin du quinquennat je rendrai la justice moi-même sous un chêne.* These are the words of Nicolas Sarkozy in a cartoon of © *Le Canard Enchaîné 4604*. The context of this quote is the fact that the magistrature in France is being seriously called to heel. The historical reference is that of Louis IX (Saint Louis) who is said to have administered justice under an oak tree in Vincennes.

### Chouannerie nf.

**

*Philippe de Villiers a mené une véritable chouannerie pour que son principal lieutenant n'entre pas au gouvernement.* © *Le Canard Enchaîné 4604*. This politician's name is closely associated with the Vendée. 'Chouannerie' was the name given to the counter-revolutionary uprisings that took place in the west of France, and particularly in the Vendée, between 1793 and 1800. Philippe de Villiers has done everything possible to avoid his right-hand man being poached by Nicolas Sarkozy.

### Clamart. Petit

**

See Chapter 12 'Petit Clamart'. Section 'Geographical names'.

### Colbert

**

Jean-Baptiste Colbert (1619–83) was a French politician who held several positions during the reign of Louis XIV including that of minister of finance (*Intendant des Finances* 1661) and *Contrôleur Général* (1665). His steward-ship of the economic affairs of the country was associated with state inter-vention, centralization, uniformity, rigour and a constant concern for reducing state expenses. **Le poids des stabilisateurs sociaux; les vertus de la réglementation; et une vieille tradition de planification colbertiste.** © *Nouvel Observateur 2324*. The British magazine *The Economist*, in May 2009, made some elogious remarks about France, and its differences with other econo-mies, the positive aspects of which were highlighted by the financial crisis.

### colbertisme nm.

*Le 19 octobre 1939, Jean Perrin créait le Centre national de la recherche scientifique sur une idée simple: assurer, par un colbertisme du savoir, un financement ambitieux des laboratoires.* © *L'Express 3041*. See above 'Col-bert'. This text refers to the idea of creating a centralized and state-funded research organization.

## collier (L'affaire du)

***

See Chapter 11 'Collier de la Reine'.

## Commune nf

**

This was the name of the revolutionary government set up in Paris (and some provincial towns) after the successive defeats of the French army at the hands of the Prussians in 1870. The bloody week of 22–28 May saw the troops from Versailles put down the revolt by a massacre of the Communards. *La Commune de Paris 1871 fut d'abord une révolte contre la trahison de l'empereur, des généraux puis des politiciens versaillais.* © *Nouvel Observateur 2321*. See Chapter 1 'Temps des cerises, Le'.

## Conseil National de Résistance nm.

***

This was the body that directed and coordinated the actions of the various resistance organizations within France from mid-1943 onwards. Its first president was Jean Moulin, martyr and hero of the Second World War. It was also responsible for drawing up the political platform to be implemented on the liberation of France, a platform to set up social democracy in France with the creation of social security, a distributive pension scheme, a free press, etc. These are precisely the advantages that are now under threat by the right-wing government of Nicolas Sarkozy. The former president of the French employers' federation, Baron Seillière, once said *il faut défaire méthodiquement le programme du Conseil National de Résistance.* © *Le Canard Enchaîné 4554*.

## Contrat social. Le nm.

**

*Les Jacobins, tout imprégnés du Contrat Social qu'ils fussent, se sont bien gardés de suivre les lubies de son auteur et sont restés jusqu'au bout partisans du régime d'assemblée.* © *Marianne 660*. The Social Contract was written in 1762 by Jean-Jacques Rousseau (1712–78) and extolled the virtues of liberty and equality. The ideas of the book were to inspire the revolutionary forces at work in eighteenth-century France. It gave us the famous opening line in Chapter 1: 'L'homme est né libre, et partout il est dans les fers.' The text refers to the fact that the Jacobins might have read *The Social Contract* but they were far from putting its ideas into practice given their attachment to the principles of a national assembly. See below 'Jacobin'.

## contre nous de la tyrannie

*

This is a line from *La Marseillaise*. 'Contre nous de la tyrannie, L'étendard sanglant est levé.' *Contre nous la tyrannie maghrébine, l'étendard tunisien était levé.* © *Le Point 1884*. This refers to the whistling that accompanied the singing of the French national anthem at a friendly football match between France and Tunisia at the Stade de France in October 2008. The anthem was composed by a French army officer, Joseph Claude Rouget de Lisle in the night of 25 to 26 April 1792. The song had been requested by the mayor of Strasbourg, Baron de Dietrich, as a military song intended for the volunteer force of the Rhine army following the declaration of war by the king of Austria. It was originally called 'Chant de guerre pour l'Armée du Rhin, dédié au Maréchal Lükner'. The name 'La Marseillaise' comes from the fact that the song was adopted by the volunteers from the 'midi', the south of France (in this case Montpellier and Marseilles) who were the first to publish the song. They arrived in the Tuileries in 1792 singing this song. The Parisians immediately adopted the song as 'La Marseillaise'. It became the national anthem in 1795. See below 'Patrie en danger'.

### corvée nf.　　　　　　　　　　　　　　　　　**\*\***

This was the name of the work that a serf was obliged to do for his lord without being paid for it. In the army, it is the equivalent of 'fatigue duty'. Today, it means any inevitable and disagreeable chore. *La corvée européenne.* © *Le Point 1912.* The context is the obligation of the population to go to the polling stations for the European elections of June 2009.

### Coup d'état de Napoléon III　　　　　　　　　**\***

The *coup d'état* took place on 2 December 1851. *À l'image de la 'société du 2 décembre' qui accompagnait le futur Napoléon III, rassemblement d'aventuriers, et d'intéressés, de nantis inquiets et de nouveaux riches.* © *Marianne 608.* This is a reference to Nicolos Sarkozy's 'court' and the various types of people present within it. Notice that 'Le nain' was the nickname of Napoleon III and is the nickname today of President Sarkozy because of his short stature. See Chapter 2 'bordel peuplé de nains'.

### Croisades nfpl.　　　　　　　　　　　　　　**\*\***

'The Crusades' was the name given to the armed expeditions sent by the Popes to defend the holy places in the Middle East, to fight against the infidels in the name of the Christian faith. They took place during the Middle Ages essentially between 1095 and 1291. *Mieux que d'autres, il [Obama] estime donc pouvoir mettre fin à l'esprit de croisade né des attentats du 11 septembre 2001.* © *Nouvel Observateur 2327.*

### Croix de Feu (L'Association des)　　　　　　　**\*\***

This was an association of First World War veterans, war wounded and soldiers decorated for gallantry, founded in 1927 by Maurice Hanot. The leader between 1932 and 1936 was Colonel de La Rocque. It is seen by English historians as an expression of French fascism. It was dissolved in 1936 by the Front Populaire.

## cuissage (le droit de) nm.                    [ * ]

It is a common myth that in the Middle Ages, a lord had the right to have sexual relations with the bride of a vassal or serf on the wedding night. Today, it refers to the liberty taken by a manager to sexually harass his female employees. ***Chirac et Mitterrand eux, ont continué de cultiver, par la suite, une sorte de droit de cuissage.*** © *Marianne 585.* This is a reflection on the sexual mores of the two French presidents who were both known to be *chauds lapins.*

## Danton                                        [ ** ]

See below 'Robespierre'.

## Déat                                          [ * ]

***Mr X, ce n'est pas Déat comme le dit la gauche. C'est Laval.*** Quoted in © *Marianne 660.* Marcel Déat (1894–1955) started his political life as a socialist and ended up as a collaborationist. He was minister of labour and national solidarity in the Laval government. At the end of the war he escaped to Italy where he lived under an assumed name. He was sentenced to death *in absentia* in 1945. Pierre Laval (1883–1945) was the head of the Vichy government and thus the architect of the collaboration. Second only to Marchéchal Pétain, he was shot at the prison of Fresnes in 1945. This quote is part of the polemic provoked by the remarks made by the socialist Cambadelis that Mr X's political trajectory resembled that of Laval. They were both intelligent men who were not recognized by their own camp. Mr X has taken Cambadelis to court for defamation. The case is pending.

## Diên Biên Phu                                 [ * ]

This is the name of the battle in North Vietnam between the French and the Viêt Minh that raged from 13 March to 7 May 1954. Encircled and cut off from their base, the French surrendered, putting an end to French hegemony in Indo-China. The name of this battle is sometimes used as a synonym of Waterloo. ***Ce n'est pas le Diên Biên Phu du productivisme, mais avant de disposer des mines viet, la Chine devra affronter le vétéran [General Giap] du Vietminh.*** © *Marianne 637.* This text refers to the mining concessions granted to China by Vietnam but accompanied by the warnings of an ecological disaster voiced by the elderly General Giap. Viêt Minh may be written as one word or two.

## Droits de l'Homme                             [ *** ]

France has been closely identified with the Rights of Man since the Declaration of Rights made on 26 August 1789 by the Constituent Assembly. It begins by declaring that men are free and equal in rights. This was in fact the death warrant of the *ancien régime.* ***Au pays des droits de l'homme, il serait temps de mettre en concordance la réalité et les principes.*** © *Marianne*

*568.* This is a call to the French government to practise what it preaches in this area.

## Édit de Nantes      ***

The Edict of Nantes, negotiated in 1598, was the edict by which Henri IV granted Protestants freedom of conscience. Its revocation in 1685 by Louis XIV had the effect of provoking the exile of many Huguenots since their religion was forbidden and their churches closed. Serge Dassault sees a parallel between this revocation and the tax on wealth (ISF) which has forced many bankers to leave France. *L'ISF fait autant de mal que [la Révocation de] l'Édit de Nantes qui a fait partir les banquiers.* His words were quoted in © *Le Canard Enchaîné 4666.*

## Édit de Villers Cotterêts      **

See 'Villers-Cotterêts, l'Ordonnance'.

## émigrés de Coblence nmfpl.      *

Between the fall of the Bastille in 1789 and the year 1800, over 140,000 French nobles, bourgeois and priests went into exile. Many of them went to Koblenz in Rhenish Prussia. It is here that the *émigré* princes formed a counter-revolutionary army. *C'est que, parait-il, il ne faudrait pas les effrayer, ces dignes héritiers des émigrés de Coblence.* © *Marianne 643.* This text refers to the more well-off elements of the French population who are ready to move from France to England to escape the tax laws of their country. See Chapter 2 'Ils n'ont rien appris'.

## éminence grise nf.      ***

Originally applied to Cardinal Richelieu's grey-clad private secretary, Joseph François Leclerc du Trembay (1577–1638). As a Capuchin (a branch of the Franciscan order) Père Joseph exercised great power and influence over Richelieu without having any official title or post. Because of his power, he was addressed as *éminence*, a term of address usually reserved for Cardinals. Today, it refers to someone who exercises discreet power and influence without holding an official position, i.e. the power behind the throne. *Autour de Mikhaïl Saakachvili on partage cette hostilité radicale, en matière politique, à la Russie. Ainsi … Giga Bokeria, éminence grise du président.* © *Le Point 1874.* Giga Bokeria is currently first deputy foreign minister of Georgia.

## Entente Cordiale nf.      **

An agreement signed between France and England in 1904 recognizing each other's spheres of geographical influence and setting up military and naval discussions. *François Fillon et Jean-Louis Borloo rejouent l'entente cordiale.* © *Le Figaro 19 953.* The egos and political ambitions of these two men have frequently marred their relationship.

## Épinay (Congrès d') nm.

Le Congrès d'Épinay in 1971 was aimed at uniting the socialists and it was during this congress that François Mitterrand (a new member of the socialist party and former extreme right-wing politician) was elected leader of the newly created Parti Socialiste. *C'est Michel Rocard qui a amené le PS à son point le plus bas depuis sa refondation au congrès d'Épinay.* © *Marianne 578.*

## États Généraux nmpl.

This is a reference to the convocation of the States General in Versailles on 4 May 1789 aimed at finding a solution to the financial problems of the kingdom and which unwittingly accelerated the revolutionary movement. Disappointment felt by the Third Estate led it to arrogate to itself the title of National Assembly. *Les éditorialistes reviennent vendredi 3 octobre sur les États Généraux de la presse inaugurés jeudi par Nicolas Sarkozy.* © *Le Nouvel Observateur 2343.* The term is now used to describe a large gathering of people from the same professional sector who meet in order to put all of their problems on the table and thrash out solutions. See below 'Grenelle'.

## événements d'Algérie. Les nmpl.

The Algerian War of Independence (1954–62) was never called a 'war' as such by the French authorities. It was referred to as either 'les événements' or 'les opérations de maintien de l'ordre'. *Pas d'anniversaire ou de commémoration en vue, et pourtant, plusieurs auteurs de la rentrée évoquent les 'événements' d'Algérie. Un sujet douloureux jusqu'à présent peu abordé.* © *Le Figaro 20 258.* See Chapter 12 'actions de maintien de l'ordre' and 'événements'.

## Félix Faure qui périt en heureuse posture

President of the Third Republic in 1895, he is remembered above all for the farcical situation in which he died on 26 February 1899. He died 'en épectase', i.e. during an orgasm in the presence of his mistress Marguerite Steinheil, who, realizing that he was dead, left by the back door. *La pauvre Meg est surnommée 'La pompe funèbre'.* (This is a reference to fellatio and to undertakers.) And Clemenceau quipped: *Il voulait être César, il ne fut que Pompée.* In French, Pompey can be construed as the past participle of the verb 'pump'. © *Le Canard Enchaîné Dossier 108* and © *Le Canard Enchaîné 4566.* See Chapter 2 'connaissance'.

## Fille aînée de l'église nf.

Clotilde (*c.* 475–545), Queen of the Franks, was the wife of Clovis I, the first King of the Franks. She was instrumental in her husband's conversion to Christianity. History has it that as defender of Catholicism, France became known as 'the eldest daughter of the church'. Be that as it may, it was in 1896 that Cardinal Langénieux spoke about France in these terms and popularized the expression: *Le baptême légendaire célébré à Reims en 545 vaudra à la France le surnom de 'Fille aînée de l'église'.* © *Marianne 585.*

### forges (Comité des) nm.
The Comité des forges, a metallurgical employers' organization, was set up in 1864 with a view to defending their interests. This lobby was considered to be one of the most reactionary and influential forces among the large employers. *Nicolas Sarkozy ne rate jamais une occasion d'égratigner ceux [les grands dirigeants des banques] qu'en privé il compare aux seigneurs du Comité des Forges.* © *Le Point 1882.*

### forges (Maître des) nmpl.
With the Industrial Revolution emerged the great dynasties of the iron and steel works such as the Wendels and the Schneiders. These great industrialists created the new towns, houses for the workers, schools, churches, etc. It was a paternalism based on work, family and religion. Here again, the connotation is one of reaction and conservatism. *Cette plaidoirie ... est digne d'un maître des forges du XIX siècle.* © *Marianne 568.*

### Formez vos bataillons
Words from the French national anthem 'La Marseillaise'. *D'ailleurs, à part le premier couplet, tout le monde l'a oubliée. Après 'formez vos bataillons', c'est le trou.* © *Le Point 1884.* A reference to the fact that most Frenchmen are unable to remember the words of the French national anthem beyond the lines of the first chorus.

### Fouché, Joseph
Fouché (1759–1820) was the notorious minister of police in 1799 and again from 1804–10 and also during the Hundred Days. He served and outlived the Terror, Bonaparte and Talleyrand. He had an impressive network of informers and was not above fabricating false evidence against his enemies. In 1816 he was declared a regicide and went into exile. He held the title of Duke of Otranto. *On commene avec Fouché, et on finit chez les Pieds Nick-elés.* © *Le Figaro Magazine 20 254.* These lines refer to the Clearstream scandal which started out as a breathtaking affair and seems to have gone pearshaped towards the end. See Chapter 1 'Pieds Nickelés'.

### Fouquier-Tinville, Antoine Quentin
Magistrate and French politician (1746–95), he was the public prosecutor of the revolutionary court. He became the symbol of ruthlessness and cruelty during the Terror. *Iran. Le Fouquier-Tinville de Téhéran.* © *Le Point 1920.*

This heading refers to Saeed Mortazavi, the public prosecutor of Teheran, whose name has become synonymous with repression.

### France et Navarre                                               ✱✱✱
Navarre was a small kingdom straddling the Pyrenees which came into existence in the ninth century. The last king of Navarre was Henri III (Bourbon) of Navarre. He reigned between 1572–1610. On becoming King of France in 1589, as Henri IV, he merged the two kingdoms. All of the French sovereigns from Henry IV until the Revolution held the title 'King of France and of Navarre'. Today, 'France et Navarre' means 'everywhere'. *Le Crédit Agricole, la banque auprès de laquelle sont endettés tous les agriculteurs de France et de Navarre.* © *Le Canard Enchaîné 4569.* See Chapter 12 'banque verte'.

### Fronde nf.                                                     ✱✱✱
The Fronde (1648–53) is the general term used to describe the troubles and violence that agitated France while Louis XIV was under age, during the regency of Mazarin. The term is now a synonym of revolt. *Il se mêle de tout, tranche de tout, transformant les institutions démocratiques en régime du 'bon plaisir'. … C'est dans la majorité que la fronde est la plus forte.* © *Le Nouvel Observateur 2346.* This is a reference to the fact that even within his own ranks, Nicolas Sarkozy's dictatorial way of governing is provoking opposition.

### Front Populaire nm.                                            ✱✱✱
The Front Populaire was the name given to the left-wing coalition which governed France between 1936 and 1937 at a time when the country was in a financial and social crisis, and against a backdrop of fascism and anti-Semitism. Under the Matignon agreements, the workers were given a fortnight's paid holiday, the working week was reduced to 40 hours and education was made compulsory up to the age of 14. Léon Blum was the *Président du Conseil* and, as a Jew, was attacked by the right-wing parties with a violence that one can hardly imagine today. *Partir à la retraite à 56 ans après avoir cotisé 43 ans signifie que l'on a quitté l'école à l'âge de 13 ans. Ce qui est strictement impossible: depuis le Front Populaire, la scolarité est obligatoire jusqu'à 14 ans.* © *Le Canard Enchaîné 4582.*

### Gotha (Almanach de) nm.                                        ✱✱✱
Some give 1763 as the date of the first publication of the ancestor of *Who's Who*. It was the reference guide to the high nobility and European royal families between 1763 and 1944. It was always written in French. The 'gotha' today refers to high society in general. *Une ville allemande n'a-t-elle pas lancé dès 1783, un mode qui a progressivement gagné l'Europe.* © *Marianne 595.*

## Girondins nmpl.

During the French Revolution, they were the party who opposed the centralization of the government that the Jacobins defended. *La diversité des analyses [of the findings of the 'Commission Balladur' on territorial reform] révèle le prisme toujours renouvelé des vieilles oppositions entre jacobins et girondins.* © *Marianne 623.* This text highlights the eternal pressure in France between those in favour of decentralization and those in favour of powerful central control. See below 'Jacobin'.

## Grand Siècle nm.

Quintessentially, it was the seventeenth century and the period (1643–1715) of the absolute monarchy of Louis XIV (1638–1715), one of the longest reigns in history. It was a period during which France dominated the world in the arts and sciences; it was the heyday of French culture, the century of Molière, Corneille, Descartes, Fermat and Pascal. In military and demographic terms, France was also the strongest power in Europe. *Par sa position en balcon sur la Seine, ce fleuron du Grand Siècle est chéri des Parisiens.* © *Le Monde 20 230.* The 'fleuron' in question is the Hôtel Lambert on the Île Saint Louis in the heart of Paris, in the fourth *arrondissement.*

## Grenelle

Grenelle was originally the Parisian street (no. 127) in which the Ministry of Labour has been located since 1905. It was here that the agreements of Grenelle were negotiated during the unrest in Paris in May 1968. Today, it has become a noun (the 'Grenelle of the Environment') to indicate any broad-scale discussions on a particular problem where all questions are put on the table and proposals for legislation are made. See above 'États Généraux'. *L'an passé, ils se sont trouvés avant le fameux 'Grenelle de l'Environnement'.* © *Marianne 598.* This text refers to the meeting of members of the building industry who gathered to discuss the impact of sustainable development on their activities.

## Grognards nm.

This was the affectionate term used by Napoleon to refer to the soldiers of his Old Guard, the most faithful and experienced men of his *Grande Armée.* The name comes from the fact that they frequently complained about their conditions. 'Grogner' is 'to moan' or 'to grumble'. *Les grognards de Sarkozy.* © *Le Nouvel Observateur 2359.* This was the heading of an article about the president's faithful followers: Brice Hortefeux, Xavier Bertrand, Luc Chatel, Eric Woerth and Christian Estrosi.

## Guernesey nf.

Bernard Henri Lévy, the intellectual who supported Ségolène Royal in the presidential elections of 2007, *est toujours au ban de la Sarkozye. Mais il ne s'est pas encore exilé à Guernesey.* © *Le Canard Enchaîné Dossier 111.* This is a reference to Victor Hugo, a ferocious opponent of Napoleon III and the Second Empire, who went into exile to the Channel Islands. His short exile was on the island of Jersey (1852–55) and his long exile on the island of Guernsey (1855–70).

### gueules cassées nfpl.                                              ✶✶
This expression ('smashed gobs') refers to the 15,000 French soldiers who returned from the First World War with severe facial injuries. It was later the name given to a lottery. The association of the *gueules cassées* was financed by the national lottery, the first subscription being launched in 1927.

### hussards noirs nmpl.                                               ✶✶✶
It was under Jules Ferry, several times minister of education (*Instruction Publique*), that education in France was made non-denominational (1880), free of charge (1881) and compulsory (1882). The non-denominational primary school teachers (*maîtres*) were seen as an army of the Republic intended to foster tolerance, knowledge and rationalism among the pupils and to combat superstition and bigotry. Teachers were elevated to the rank of 'civil servant' of the Third Republic. Charles Peguy (1873–1914) wrote 'Nos jeunes maîtres étaient beaux comme des hussards noirs'. Black was the colour of the clothes of the *maîtres* graduating from the teacher training colleges founded by Guizot in 1833. ***Avec le livre d'Alain Refalo* [*Je refuse d'obéir*], *un air de mutinerie souffle sur les hussards noirs de la République.*** © *Le Monde 20 220.* This refers to the ever-increasing malaise among school teachers in France and the fact that many of them have simply 'had enough'.

### index (mettre à l') nm.                                            ✶✶
The expression was first used in 1559 (*Index librorum prohibitorum*) by the papal authorities to ban books considered as heretical or otherwise undesirable for Christian readers. Today, it means to condemn and exclude. ***L'allemande Hypo Real Estate n'a échappé à une mise à l'index que parce qu'elle a été, dans l'urgence, nationalisée.*** © *Marianne 598.* 'The German bank only avoided bankruptcy by being nationalized.'

### isolement splendide nm.                                            ✶✶
'Splendid Isolation'. This name characterized Britain's foreign policy towards the end of the nineteenth century under the conservative leadership of the Marquis of Salisbury. ***Les écoles [les grandes écoles] sortent de leur isolement splendide, et c'est bien.*** © *Le Point 1952.* This is a reference to the fact that the *grandes écoles* can no longer remain isolated citadels educating the elite but must open up to the world.

## Jacobin nm.

`***`

The revolutionary club of the Jacobins used to meet in the Dominican convent at the church of St Jacques in Paris (the Hebrew *Jacobus* giving us the English James and the French Jacques: cf. Jacobite Rebellion). They were the extreme partisans of a centralized state. ***Les hiérarques [du parti socialiste] voulaient jauger la force du sentiment anti-jacobin.*** © *L'Express 3060*. In an opinion poll, commissioned by the socialist party and conducted in the Languedoc-Roussillon region, interviewees were asked whether they thought that the late Georges Frêche, the socialist dissident, had been fighting against the Jacobin, Parisian socialist party machine. The findings revealed that this was indeed the general feeling. The findings of the poll were not made public. See above 'Cathares'.

## Jacquerie nf.

`***`

The 'Jacquerie' or 'Great Jacquerie' was the name given to the peasants' revolt in north eastern France in 1358 during the Hundred Years' War. There have been many such uprisings since, and the term has come to mean any form of revolt. The town of ***Pont-Saint-Esprit revit, depuis quelques semaines, le temps des jacqueries. Quand les croquants, écrasés par la taille, se soulevaient contre la noblesse et son incurie.*** © *Les Echos 20 401*. 'Croquant' is a term for 'peasant'. This is a reference to the Spiripontains (name of the inhabitants of Pont-Saint-Esprit) who have demonstrated massively to demand the resignation of the mayor. The town is practically bankrupt and the local rates have sky-rocketed by 56% because of financial mismanagement. NB: *la taille* was a tax. Every Frenchman knows the character 'Jacquou le Croquant'. See above 'Fronde'.

## Jarnac (un coup de)

`***`

This word has its origin in the duel opposing Guy Chabot, lord of Jarnac, and François de Vivonne, lord of the Châtaigneraie, on 10 July 1547. Although the blows given by Chabot (two thrusts touching the back of the left knee) were perfectly fair play, the term has come to mean an unfair and treacherous blow. This word lends itself to the play on words 'j'arnaque' meaning 'I swindle'. ***'Martine' son ancienne protégée … vient de lui faire un coup de Jarnac.*** © *Le Nouvel Observateur 2368*. This is a reference to the fact that Martine Aubry used to be Jean Gandois' right-hand woman. He was later to become the head of the CNPF; he was furious and felt betrayed by the fact that she was the architect of the 35-hour week voted for by the socialists in 1998, and implemented in 2000. The CNPF was the former name of the French employers' confederation, today known as the Medef. See Chapter 14 'Medef'.

## Jansénisme nm

`*`

A Christian doctrine developed by Cornelius Jansen (1580–1638), a Dutch theologian. Jansenism highlights predestination and denies man his free will and in this, the doctrine was in contradiction with the beliefs of the Jesuits. The word connotes severity, austerity and rigour. *Notre époque ne semble pas prête à accueillir les rudes clartés d'un nouveau jansénisme.* © *Marianne 576.* See below 'Port Royal'.

### Jeu de paume nm.

*Chamfort est l'ami de Mirabeau, il est là au serment du Jeu de paume.* © *Le Nouvel Observateur 2361.* This is a reference to the Tennis Court Oath, that was taken on 20 June 1789 in Versailles by the Third Estate not to separate until the constitution had been established. Because of a misunderstanding about the hall in which the Third Estate was to meet, the members found the hall occupied by troops and misconstrued the situation. Thinking that they were being prevented from meeting by military force, they withdrew to the largest hall nearby which happened to be the indoor tennis court. See Chapter 10 'Jeu de Paume (Paris)'.

### Lafayette, nous revoilà

See Chapter 2 'Lafayette, nous revoilà'.

### Loi du 29 juillet 1881 nf.

*Le monument législatif qu'est la loi du 29 juillet 1881 sur la liberté de la presse.* © *Marianne 574.* See Chapter 10 'Loi du 29 juillet 1881'.

### Loi 1905

*Il constitue l'article 1 de la loi 1905 ... celui qui prévoit le respect de la liberté de conscience.* © *Marianne 568.* See Chapter 10 'Loi 1905'.

### Louis XI

Louis XI, known as 'l'araignée' (1423–83) was king of France between 1462 and his death. He spent a large part of his reign bringing the nobles under control and asserting royal authority. *Vlad Tepes [a Romanian king] ... un centralisateur ferraillant contre la noblesse, un inlassable justicier: un Louis XI du Danube.* © *L'Express 3041.*

### Louis XIV

*Des réformes bling-bling comme ce conseil de la création artistique au parfum louis-quatorzien.* © *Le Nouvel Observateur 2228.* This is a reference to the fact that it was Louis XIV (1638–1715) who created the *Comédie-Française* in 1680, and Nicolas Sarkozy who created the *Conseil de la création* in February 2009.

### Lumières (le Siècle des) nm.

'The Age of Enlightenment'. 'A European philosophical movement characterized by rationalism and learning, a spirit of scepticism and empiricism in social and political thought' (Webster) and represented by writers such as Voltaire, Condorcet, Rousseau, etc. *Oui, il y a un mystère Tiepolo. Mystère d'une vie dont on ne sait rien, comme si le peintre, au Siècle des Lumières, qui était pour lui un siècle ébloui, s'était ingénié à ne laisser aucune trace, aucun écrit, aucun témoin, se contentant de courir d'une commande à l'autre pour satisfaire les riches patriciens.* © *Le Nouvel Observateur 2324*. This text refers to an essay by Robert Calasso called *Le Rose Tiepolo*, which explores the dark side of a painter about whom we know very little.

### Maginot (la Ligne)

After André Maginot, minister of war in 1930. It was the name given to a defensive line of fortifications built by France along its frontier with Luxembourg, Germany and Italy. Since the attack by the Germans through Belgium, the Maginot line has since come to mean a monumental but ineffective system of defence. *Une sorte de 'Ligne Maginot' qui pourrait même, à court terme, se trouver en porte à faux avec le droit européen.* © *Le Monde 19 972*. The initial rejection of the law by the National Assembly, on downloading from internet, is the context of this quotation.

### main invisible nf.

*Alain Greenspan paraissait sur le point de pleurer. Comme si on venait de couper cette main indicible qui est censée veiller à la richesse des nations.* © *Le Monde 19 828*. This is a reference to the words of Adam Smith in his book *The Wealth of Nations* which suggests that the economy is somehow guided by an invisible hand, and to the disillusion of Alan Greenspan, the former president of the 'Fed'.

### malgré-nous. Les nmpl.

'Against our will.' This term is used to refer to the men from Alsace-Lorraine who were enrolled by force in the German army (Wehrmacht or Waffen-SS) during the period 1942–5. *Dominique Bussereau et Xavier Darcos, depuis qu'ils ont accepté de défendre les couleurs de l'UMP aux régionales, s'appellent entre eux les 'malgré nous'.* © *Le Canard Enchaîné 4658*. Both men were reluctant to enter the fight of the regional elections. They were both subsequently defeated.

### Maréchal, nous voilà

See Chapter 2 'Maréchal, nous voilà'.

### Marthe Richard

Marthe Richard (1889–1982) was a prostitute, pilot and spy. After the armistice, she proposed a motion for the closure of brothels (*maisons closes*) and it was voted nationally on 13 April 1946. *Nous n'avons plus de bordel en*

*France depuis la loi purificatrice de Marthe Richard à la Libération.* © *Le Canard Enchaîné 4559.* It is a topical question as to whether les *maisons closes* should be reopened.

### Mazarin     **

Cardinal Richelieu (1585–1642) was the advisor, the grey eminence, to Louis XIII. Cardinal Mazarin (1602–61), having succeeded him, was the principal minister of the regency with Anne of Austria (Louis XIV was under age) and acquired an immense fortune while he was in power. *C'est Richelieu et Mazarin.* © *Les Echos 20 638.* This text refers to the extensive power of Claude Guéant, the former secretary general of the Élysée, who is known as 'le Cardinal'. See above 'éminence grise'.

### Mendès France     *

Mendès France (1907–82) was a French radical-socialist politician and, among a host of other positions, he held that of *Président du Conseil* (1954–55). He was, over time, member of the board of the International Monetary Fund and executive director of the BIRD. *Il faut une amélioration de la qualité des dépenses publiques en mettant l'accent, comme le préconisait Mendès-France, sur les dépenses productives, c'est-à-dire les investissements destinés à préparer l'avenir.* © *Marianne 598.*

### Mérovingien     *

This was the name of the first dynasty of the Frankish kings who ruled over Gaul from 481 to 751. The dynasty was founded by Clovis I, the name coming from his grandfather's name Mérovée. See below 'Rois Fainéants'. *Mitterrand oscilla à la fin de son règne entre le modèle mérovingien et la figure pharaonique.* © *Marianne 616.*

### Mers el Kébir     *

Arabic for 'the great port', it is a port in Algeria that had served as a French naval base since 1935. After the capitulation of the French in 1940, the British, afraid that the French naval force would fall into the hands of the Germans, destroyed it on 3 July 1940 in an operation code-named 'Catapult' and carried out by the British fleet. Over 1,300 French sailors died in the attack after the French had refused the options open to them. *Trafalgar, Mers-el-Kébir ... et voilà encore un navire français que les anglais vont détruire.* © *Le Canard Enchaîné 4606.* This is a reference to the fact that the French aircraft carrier *Clémenceau* has been sent to England to be dismantled.

### Monarchie de Juillet nf.     **

*À l'époque [de la III République] il y avait le réseau traditionnel issu de la Monarchie de Juillet et du Second Empire.* © *Le Nouvel Observateur 2324.*

This article deals with the various forms of power network in France. The July Monarchy (1830–48) was set up with Louis Philippe as king, after the July Revolution. There were three days of violent demonstrations in Paris (Les Trois Glorieuses) that saw the overthrow of King Charles X. See below 'Second Empire'.

## Montesquieu                                    [ ** ]

Charles Louis de Secondat, baron de La Brède et de Montesquieu (1689–1755) was a French philosopher who developed the theory of the separation of powers in government in his work entitled *De l'esprit des lois* (1748). He maintained that a government in which the separation of powers was not respected could not claim to have a constitution. *Le principe de bonne gouvernance selon Montesquieu? La séparation des pouvoirs.* © *Marianne 615.* This is a highly topical issue given Nicolas Sarkozy's plans to suppress the position of *juge d'instruction* and to put the power of investigation into the hands of the *Procureur de la République*, who is not, as the European Courts have pointed out, a member of the judicial system as such but a political appointee directly under the political influence of the executive.

## Napoleon III                                    [ ** ]

*La droite bonapartiste incarnée par Jacques Chirac, quitte Napoléon pour Louis Napoléon et le pont d'Arcole pour le cul des vaches.* © *L'Express 3057.* Napoleon III did not have the panache of Napoleon. The text refers to the lacklustre period of Jacques Chirac's presidency; there were no political landmarks, just his slogan about eating more apples and his affection for slapping cows on their hindquarters. See below 'Pont d'Arcole'.

## népotisme nm.                                    [ * ]

Nepotism. This term refers to favoritism shown to the members of one's family in appointments to desirable positions. From the Latin *nepos* meaning 'nephew' or 'grandchild'. 'Nephew' was a common euphemism used in the Middles Ages to refer to the illegitimate child of a priest. Nepotism was rife in the papal world until forbidden by a bull issued in 1692 by Pope Innocent XII. *La ville s'aligne ainsi sur le népotisme des deux communes voisines. Levallois: dirigée par les époux Balkany, et Puteaux où Joëlle Ceccaldi ... a fait élire son fils au conseil municipal.* © *Marianne 572.* This is a reference to family influence in French politics that has transformed some county councils into something resembling hereditary baronies.

## nuit des longs couteaux. La                      [ * ]

On 29/30 June 1934, the head of the SA (Sturmabteilung, i.e. Storm Division) Ernst Röhm, was liquidated by Hitler, and the SA was purged. It was the only dangerous force that could have possibly constituted a danger to

Hitler's ambitions. *Ce congrès de Reims en forme d'hallali. La nuit des longs couteaux qui a suivi: Ségolène victorieuse à minuit, miraculeusement abattue à 3 heures du matin. Et Martine Aubry sortie toute armée de la cuisse de Laurent Fabius.* © *Le Nouvel Observateur 2327.* This text refers to the suspicion surrounding the elimination of Ségolène Royal in the battle for the socialist party leadership. Electoral fraud is suspected in the nomination of Martine Aubry as leader of the socialist party. See Chapter 7 'cuisse de Jupiter' and Chapter 3 'hallali'.

### nuit du 4 août. La

Against the backdrop of 'The Great Fear' following the fall of the Bastille and increasing violence nationwide, the National Assembly adopted a series of decrees during the night of 4 August 1789 (and until 11 August) which effectively overthrew the feudal system. Feudal and ecclesiastical rights and privileges were abolished. *M. Copé s'inquiète de voir les chefs d'entreprises transformés en boucs émissaires dans une ambiance de la nuit du 4 août.* © *Marianne 624.* The recent financial crisis has led to more criticism of company bosses and bankers and their so-called indecent privileges such as golden hellos, golden handshakes and stock options, etc.

### Olympe Mancini        ( * )

La Comtesse de Soissons (1639–1708) was one of Cardinal Mazarin's nieces. She was one of the favourites of Louis XVI. Her life was a long series of intrigues and plots, ending in final disgrace. *La tentative de nos joueurs de bonneteau élyséens, de grimer la première dame de France en une hypothétique Madame de Maintenon ... comme si on passait d'Olympe Mancini à la veuve Scarron.* © *Marianne 576.* Madame de Maintenon was known as La Veuve Scarron. See below 'Veuve Scarron'. This is a commentary on Nicolas Sarkozy's attempts to transform his wife (compared with Olympe Mancini) into a distinguished and respectable person (compared to Madame de Maintenon). Her previous life is light years away from her present persona.

### Ordonnance de Villers-Cotterêts 1539 nf.      ( ** )
See below 'Villers-Cotterêts.

### oubliettes nfpl.

The *oubliettes* is a generic term designating the underground prison cells to be found in certain châteaux and fortresses. Access to such cells was generally via a ladder or rope thus making any attempt at escape impossible. Research tends to suggest that they were intially used as storehouses. Prisoners sent to the *oubliettes* were soon forgotten, hence the name. *Cette incapacité à 'refonder' va de pair avec le choix libéral européen qui renvoie la nation aux oubliettes.* © *Marianne 621.*

## paladin nm.

> *

At the time of Charlemagne (742?–814) the 'paladins' were members of his suite and in time the word came to mean a kind of knight errant. *Il [Villepin] se voit aspiré autant qu'inspiré par quelque sublime transcendance, celle d'un geste épique où il deviendrait le dernier paladin du grand roman national.* © *Le Point 1952.* Villepin has had the reputation of being a knight in shining armour since his speech to the United Nations on 14 February 2003, in which he opposed the invasion of Iraq. He feels that he has a national destiny.

## panache blanc. Le

> ***

Henri IV (1553–1610) King of France (1589–1610) and of Navarre (1572–1610). During the battle of Ivry against the Catholic forces in 1590, legend has it that he shouted to his men the famous phrase 'Ralliez-vous à mon panache blanc, vous le trouverez toujours au chemin de l'honneur et de la victoire.' *[Il faut] qu'un seul candidat amène tout le monde à rallier le panache rose du PS et de son candidat.* © *Le Figaro 20 258.* This is a comment on the fact that there are several contenders for the socialist party leadership but no single person has emerged as a federating force.

## Paris vaut bien une messe

> ***

See Chapter 2 'Paris vaut bien une messse'.

## Patrie en danger. La

> *

This was the revolutionary rallying cry launched on 11 July 1792 as the prospect of the invasion of revolutionary France by the coalition forces loomed large. *Les féroces soldats du Stade de France ont rugi. Contre nous la tyrannie maghrébine, l'étendard tunisien était levé ... La patrie, en gros, était en danger.* © *Le Point 1884.* It is to be noticed that whistling at public events in France is not supportive but critical. Notice that 'patrie' is an anagram of 'parité', a very topical pun. See above 'contre nous de la tyrannie' for the context.

## Père Joseph

> *

See above 'éminence grise'.

## Plan Marshall nm.

> **

The Marshall Plan was drawn up by the American government after the end of the Second World War with a view to rebuilding a ruined Europe. *M. Sarkozy avait promis, pendant la campagne présidentielle, un plan Marshall pour les banlieues.* © *Marianne 568.* One of Nicolas Sarkozy's 2007 election promises was a generous plan of investment for the deprived suburbs. It hasn't yet materialized.

## Poitiers (arrêter à)    [ * ]

Tradition has it that it was on 25 October 732 that Charles Martel defeated the Muslim forces between Tours and Poitiers and thus put an end to the Arab invasion of the land of the Franks. He was the de facto king of the Franks until the end of his life. Ségolène Royal was elected president of the *Conseil Général* of Poitou-Charentes in 2004. *Si le calcul est avéré, on comprend mieux que Raffarin juge qu'il y a urgence pour la droite à arrêter Ségolène à Poitiers.* © *Marianne 577.* Jean-Pierre Raffarin was president of the Conseil Général of Poitou-Charentes from 1988 to 2002. Everything was done by the right-wing party to stop the socialist Ségolène Royal winning the regional elections in Poitou-Charentes. She was re-elected with a large majority.

## Pont d'Arcole. Le    [ *** ]

Le Pont d'Arcole was the name of the battle fought between 15 and 17 November 1796 by the French against the Austrian forces in Italy. It was one of the most brilliant of Napoleon's victories. He led a heroic charge at the head of his grenadiers and defeated the Austrian forces. *Nous, Français, nous avons la culture de l'assaut à la hussarde, la fascination pour le pont d'Arcole.* © *Le Nouvel Observateur. 2358.* This is a reference to the rather 'cool' behaviour of Barack Obama towards the French way of doing things. The French way favours extravagance and panache.

## Port-Royal    [ * ]

An abbey located in the *Vallée de Chevreuse* in the *département* of the Yvelines (78) run by nuns and the heart of the Jansenist movement in France in the seventeenth century. *Pascal, le solitaire de Port Royal, exprimait sa distance à l'égard des débauches de la cour de son époque.* © *Marianne 576.* This is a reflection on the decadence of the 'court' and 'courtesans' of Nicolas Sarzozy. Pascal was nicknamed 'le solitaire du Port Royal' who had decided to retreat from the corruption of the court. NB: also the name of a famous Paris hospital particularly associated with maternity.

## poujadisme nm.    [ ** ]

This political movement takes its name from Pierre Poujade (1920–2003), a French politician whose political platform was populist, right-wing, pro-French Algeria, anti-parliamentarian and was the expression of the fear, on the part of small and medium-sized tradespeople, of the threat posed by profound economic change (e.g. the newly developing supermarkets). The heyday of the movement was in the second half of the 1950s. Many of Poujadés ideas were taken up later by the founder of the French National Front, Jean-Marie Le Pen, including a reference to the corruption of MPs *tous pourris.* Les socialistes *n'en récitent pas moins un crédo poujadiste – soft ou hard – faire payer les riches, auquel ils ne font même plus semblant de croire.*

© *Marianne 595*. Even socialists, today, no longer pretend to believe in 'making the rich pay'.

### poule au pot. La
The *poule au pot* has been a famous dish in France since Henri IV expressed the wish that everyone in his kingdom should be able to eat a *poule au pot* every Sunday. *Même s'il est peu enclin à la relance par la consommation, le chef de l'État pourrait lancer un 'Prodige de la poule au pot Sarkozy'.* © *Le Figaro 20 067*.

### Reichshoffen (la bataille de)
The battle of Froeschwiller-Woerth, otherwise known as the battle of Reichshoffen, was fought in Alsace on 6 August 1870 at the beginning of the Franco-Prussian war. It was famous for a series of charges made by the French heavy cavalry brigade. It was a useless sacrifice of human life from the military point of view but was seen as a model of heroism. *La charge est une méthode sur laquelle l'état major français comptait beaucoup avant Reichshoffen en 1870.* © *Marianne 629*. The context of this quote is a reaction to the warning made by Claude Bartelone, socialist president of the *département* of Seine-Saint-Denis (93) that François Bayrou was going to feel the effect of the socialist charge during the European elections.

### Rennes (le congrès de)
*Le monarque, François Mitterrand, fut chahuté, balloté puis déstabilisé en mars 1990 avec le congrès de Rennes.* © *Marianne 589*. The Rennes congress that took place between 15 and 18 March 1990 was the very symbol of socialist disunity.

### Retz (le Cardinal de)
Paul de Gondi, better known as *Le Cardinal de Retz* (1613–79) was a French politician, man of the church and writer. He was Archbishop of Paris (1654–62). He was imprisoned for taking part in the *Fronde* but was later pardoned by Louis XIV. He retired to the abbey of St Denis where he devoted his retirement to writing about his political experiences. His most famous work is *Les Mémoires*. *Dans ce livre en question, Morand revisite la Fronde mais en compagnie, bien sûr, du cardinal de Retz.* © *Marianne 601*.

### Robespierre
*C'est à l'affrontement entre Danton et Robespierre qu'il faut remonter pour trouver un tel duo d'adversaires.* © *L'Express 3057*. This is a comparison between the rivalry and hatred of Danton and Robespierre (who were on the same political side) and that of Nicolas Sarkozy and Dominique de Villepin who are both members of the French right-wing UMP. Robespierre (1758–94) was a lawyer and politician (as are de Villepin and Sarkozy)

whose name is associated with the Terror and the Thermidorian reaction that took him to the guillotine in July 1794. Danton (1759–94) was also a lawyer and politician. Robespierre was recognized as 'incorruptible', whereas Danton was venal and not above corruption. He had preceded Robespierre to the guillotine in April 1794. See Chapter 6 'audace'.

### Roi de Rome                                                                        ┌──────┐
                                                                                       │  *   │
                                                                                       └──────┘

*Aucun ne croit à une prochaine sortie de route sauf si le président s'entête à faire de son fils le prince de la Défense, comme jadis Napoléon a fait de son fils le roi de Rome.* © *Le Nouvel Observateur 2345*. This is a reference to the Epad scandal in which the President wanted to place his son at the head of the biggest business centre in France, La Défense. His son was absolutely unqualified to hold such a position. It was in 1810 that the decision was taken to give the heir apparent the title of *Roi de Rome*. François Joseph Charles Napoleon, known as Napoleon II, was born in 1811 and died in 1832. The nomination of the *Prince de la Défense* is seen as being just as arbitrary as the creation of the *Roi de Rome*.

### Roi Serrurier nm.                                                                  ┌──────┐
                                                                                       │  *   │
                                                                                       └──────┘

The nickname of Louis XVI (1754–93) was 'the locksmith king' because of his passion for making and repairing locks. *Nicolas Sarkozy paraît aux antipodes du roi serrurier.* © *Marianne 591*. Nicolas Sarkozy is perceived as being light years away from Louis XVI.

### Roi Soleil nm.                                                                     ┌──────┐
                                                                                       │ ***  │
                                                                                       └──────┘

Louis XIV was known as the Sun King because of the pomp and splendour of the court at Versailles. He was a great patron of the arts. He was also called Louis le Grand. It shouldn't be forgotten that he left France totally ruined. *Chaque époque a sa part d'ombre. Celle du Roi Soleil est marquée par l'affaire des poisons.* © *Le Point 1951*. This affair concerned a series of poisonings that took place (1672–82) during the reign of Louis XIV. See Chapter 11 'poisons'

### Rois Fainéants nmpl.                                                               ┌──────┐
                                                                                       │ ***  │
                                                                                       └──────┘

They were the Frankish kings of the later Merovingian dynasty who ruled over Gaul from 673 to 751. The dynasty was founded by Mérovée, the grandfather of Clovis I. They include Thierry III (673–91), Clovis III, Childebert III, Dagobert II, Chilpéric II, Thierry IV, Childeric III (743–51). The reason for their nickname is unclear but their reigns were periods of political instability and loss of territory and influence. The last of the Carolingians, Louis V, was also known as the 'idle' or 'lazy' king. This term hit the headlines recently when President Sarkozy referred to his predecessors as *les rois fainéants* to underscore their inactivity and his dynamism. *Dans l'esprit du chef de l'État, l'expression 'rois fainéants' s'applique peut-être moins à des hommes en particulier qu'à une pratique de la Ve République qui permettait au chef de l'exécutif de diluer et d'esquiver ses responsabilités.* © *Le Figaro 20 084.*

## Sacre de Reims nm.
*

*Le PS craint le massacre de Reims* © *Le Canard Enchaîné 4594.* This refers to the ceaseless infighting and divisions within the socialist leadership during the party congress in Reims on 14–16 November 2008. The pun bears on *sacre* (coronation) and *massacre.* Many French kings were crowned in Reims cathedral. See above 'Chemin des Dames'.

## Saint Barthélemy (le massacre de la)

This was the name of the massacre of Protestants by Catholics on 24 August 1572 on the order of Catherine de Médicis. The signal for the start of the massacre was the ringing of the bells of the church of Saint-Germain l'Auxerrois in Paris. *La première Saint-Barthélemy de 'traîtres tamouls' s'est déroulée en 1986 à Jaffina: 175 membres du Telo, un parti rival, ont été assassinés en vingt-quatre heures.* © *Libération 8716.*

## Saint Denis
*

Saint Denis was the first bishop of Paris (*Lutece*) and the patron saint of the city. After his martyrdom, he is said to have walked with his head under his arm as far as the village of Catolacus where he collapsed and died. *Patrick Devedjian qui, tel Saint Denis, se ballade depuis quelques mois sa tête sous le bras.* © *Marianne 589.* Patrick Devedjian is one of the most disappointed of the Sarkozy camp who thought that he would be made minister of justice, given that he was one of the historic hardliners of the RPR and UMP. His disappointment was all the more unbearable in the light of ex-socialists being given senior ministerial responsibility.

## Saint Louis (Louis IX)
*

Tradition has it that Saint Louis administered justice under an oak tree in Vincennes. *...de même que Saint Louis rendait la justice sous son chêne, le Président rendrait ses oracles sur la chaine de son choix.* © *Marianne 602.* This is a reference to the control that the State exerts over French television now that President Sarkozy has announced that he will appoint the chairman of France Television. Until now, this appointment had been the responsibility of the CSA. Hence the pun on *chêne* (oak) and *chaine* (TV channel). See Chapter 14 'CSA'. See above 'chêne de Vincennes'.

## sans-culotte nmpl.
*

*L'affiliation platonique à la gauche survit souvent comme un cache-misère, une manière de dissimuler qu'on ne croit à rien. En même temps, raidissement tactique jusqu'à une dérive sans-culottiste.* © *Marianne 618.* The 'sans-culotte' were the emblematic elements of the revolutionary crowd, generally drawn from the lower classes and lacking the more genteel hose of the nobility, hence their name. The term 'sans-culotte' was also synonymous with 'rabble' and 'uncultured'. The idea here is that the socialists have little to offer in the way of ideas, beyond the rather populist slogans of the past.

## Second Empire      **

After the *coup d'état* of Louis Napoleon in December 1851, the Second Empire came into existence and lasted until the defeat at Sedan in 1870. See below 'Sedan'.

## Sedan      **

This was the battle that put an end to the Franco-Prussian war with the capitulation of the French army and the capture of Napoleon III. The battle was fought on 31 August and 1 September 1870. *Le second Empire s'acheva, enfin, dans la honte de Sedan.* © *Marianne 620.* Unlike Waterloo, Trafalgar and Berezina, the battle of Sedan is rarely, if ever, used figuratively.

## Ségur (la Comtesse de)      *

Sophie Rostopchine (1799–1874), a French writer, was the daughter of the Governor of Moscow. She married Count Eugène de Ségur in 1819. She was famous for her books that were intended for young children, particularly young girls, and that presented the world in a rather Manichaean way such as *Les Petites Filles Modèles* 1858. *Elles portaient des petites robes en velours, des chaussettes jusqu'au genou et des nœuds dans les cheveux. Elles peuplaient les romans de La Comtesse de Ségur qu'elles lisaient quand elles n'apprenaient pas la broderie.* © *Marianne 598.* This quotation must be seen as a contrast to the young girls of today, who don't seem to read and who are more concerned with their 'looks' than their 'books'.

## sorcellerie (un procès en) nf.      *

A trial of sb. charged with witchcraft. These were not uncommon until well into the eighteenth century. *Les procès en sorcellerie ont de beaux restes en France.* © *Marianne 598.* The meaning here is that witch-hunts, figuratively speaking, have far from disappeared.

## Surcouf      *

Robert Surcouf (1773–1827) was a French corsair who captured many English ships during the Revolutionary and Napoleonic wars. Today, this is the pseudonym of an anonymous diatribe against the Sarkozy government's plans, announced in a White Paper, to drastically reduce staffing levels in the army. *C'est un texte au lance-flammes contre le Livre Blanc. Il est signé d'un groupe d'officiers généraux et supérieurs sous le pseudonyme de 'Surcouf'.* © *Marianne 586.*

## Talleyrand                                              `***`

Charles-Maurice de Talleyrand-Périgord (1754–1838) was a political chameleon *par excellence*. He served under the *ancien régime*, was an ambassador during the Revolution, he was minister of foreign affairs under the Consulate and the First Empire and served as ambassador under the Restoration and the July Monarchy. To the question 'What did you do during the Revolution?' he is said to have replied 'I survived'. See Chapter 2 'J'ai survécu'. ***Talleyrand s'est vengé cinq ans plus tard par un 18 Brumaire à l'envers.*** © *Le Canard Enchaîné 4658.* This is a reference to the hatred between Dominiqe de Villepin (a specialist of Napoleon and writer of a biography of Bonaparte) and Nicolas Sarkozy that has been heightened by the Clearstream affair. See Chapter 11 'Clearstream'.

## Terreur nf.                                              `**`

There are two periods referred to in this way: the summer of 1792 (with the threat of invasion and 'la patrie en danger') and the Great Terror lasting from June 1793 to July 1794 and the fall of Robespierre. It was a period of exceptional laws, based on repression and violence, with people being sentenced to death not by proof of guilt but by the 'intime conviction' (the gut feeling) of the jurors. Over 17,000 people are recorded as having been executed but many people were assassinated without trial. The figure could be as high as 40,000. ***C'est la Terreur. Les têtes vont tomber.*** © *Le Canard Enchaîné 4634.* This is a reference to the 'paper tiger' threats of the Government to take action against café owners who have not passed on the reduction of VAT to the end customer. See Chapter 14 'TVA'. See also Chapter 2 'têtes vont tomber, Les'.

## tête sous le bras nf.                                    `*`

This is the typical image of martyrdom based on the story of St Denis decapitated in 272. The second reference is to the painting by Puvis de Chavannes (1824–98) depicting the decapitation of John the Baptist. ***Christine Albanel ... se promène sa tête sous le bras, telle une apparition de Puvis de Chavannes.*** © *Marianne 616.* At that time, she already knew that she was going to be replaced as minister of culture in 2009. See above 'Saint Denis'.

## Thermidor                                                `*`

***Pourquoi la photo de Khomeyni? Parce que c'est leur histoire! Terreur comprise. Comme la terreur de la Révolution française fait partie de notre histoire. Ils prennent tout en bloc, et ils réclament leur Thermidor.*** © *Marianne 635.*
*Thermidor* was the 'hot-weather' month in the French Revolutionary calendar; it covered the period between 19 July and 17 August. It was on 9 Thermidor (27 July 1794) that the Convention obtained the proscription of Robespierre and his followers thereby ending the period of Terror and

Jacobin dictatorship. The context of this quote is the unrest in Iran in the wake of what appear to have been rigged elections.

### Tirez les premiers, Messieurs les Anglais    `**`
See Chapter 2 'Tirez les premiers, Messieurs les Anglais'.

### Torquemada    `*`
Although this is not related to French history, it is frequently quoted in the French press. Tomas de Torquemade was the grand inquisitor of the Spanish Inquisition from 1483 until his death in 1498. *En attendant, toujours à l'affût, les nouveaux Torquemada ne manqueront pas de se jeter sur la prochaine affaire contre lui.* © *Le Point 1935.* This text refers to the critics who have attacked Frédéric Mitterrand, the minister of culture, who confessed (in an autobiography) to having been to Thailand for sex with young men. This scandal was heightened by his defence of Roman Polanski who faces a long prison sentence in the USA for having had unlawful sexual relations with a 13-year-old girl, over thirty years ago.

### Trafalgar (un coup de)    `***`
Trafalgar was one of the greatest naval battles in which Nelson defeated the combined French and Spanish fleets on 21 October 1805. Nelson was killed during this battle. Today, *un coup de Trafalgar* refers to a disastrous, knock-out defeat. *Deux commissions d'enquête sont en cours, à la demande du ministre, afin d'établir, si possible, les responsables de ce Trafalgar.* © *Le Canard Enchaîné 4616.* This text refers to the ongoing technical problems dogging the nuclear aircraft carrier *Charles de Gaulle* which, from the time of its launch, has spent more time in dry dock for repairs than it has in carrying out its naval role.

### Travail, famille, patrie    `**`
The law of 10 July 1940 gave Maréchal Pétain full powers. 'Work, Family and Homeland' were to become the official motto of the Vichy regime and the minted money bore this motto. *La francisque ressuscitait les Francs, et Travail, Famille, Patrie, devaient effacer la trinité maudite Liberté, Egalité, Fraternité.* © *Le Canard Enchaîné 4591.* The 'francisque' was both the symbol of the Vichy regime and the personal symbol of Maréchal Pétain but also the name of a distinction. François Mitterrand was decorated by Pétain and was thus a member of the Order of the Francisque.

### Trente Glorieuses (Les)    `***`
The thirty years of strong and uninterrupted economic growth that France enjoyed between 1945 and 1973. *La France, enfin, a besoin de repreneurs d'entreprise pour faire face au vieillissement de la génération des Trente*

*Glorieuses.* © *Le Point 1950.* France needs new blood to replace those company owners who are now on the point of retirement.

## Trianon (Le)                                                            ***

The Petit Trianon was a small manor built within the grounds of the palace of Versailles by Louis XV. Louis XVI gave it to his wife, Marie-Antoinette, as a present. She had a certain taste for things rustic. An artificial hamlet was built including a small lake, cottages, an orchard, a vegetable garden, a mill and a farm to provide the Queen with fresh eggs. She herself liked to act in the plays that were produced there, but never (contrary to popular belief) as a shepherdess. The context of this quote is the reintroduction of cows in the woods of Bordeaux by the mayor Alain Juppé. *Et dire qu'on a longtemps cru Juppé obnubilé par l'Élysée! Il n'a jamais rêvé que du Petit Trianon, façon Marie-Antoinette.* © *Le Canard Enchaîné 4621.* This is a reference to Alain Juppé's presidential ambitions.

## Valmy (la bataille de)                                                   *

On 20 September 1792, the French army under Kellermann and Demouriez defeated the Prussians under the Duke of Brunswick and thus stopped the invasion of revolutionary France. This was the first military victory of the Republic. *De la bataille de Valmy à la collaboration, l'égérie au bonnet phrygien a donc reflété tous les clivages idéologiques.* © *Marianne 593.* Marianne is always depicted as wearing the Phrygian cap. From revolutionary France up to the collaboration, the bust of Marianne, wearing the Phrygian cap, has always been a symbol showing an ideological divide. The Phrygian cap was the cap worn by freed slaves in the Roman Empire. It was adopted by the French revolutionaries in 1790 as a symbol of liberty and civic spirit.

## Varennes (la fuite à)                                                    *

It was to Varennes in the Meuse that Louis XVI fled in June 1791 while attempting to join the loyalist army in Metz. In spite of being disguised, he was recognized and arrested. The Constituent Assembly suspended his functions and he was thus discredited in the eyes of the people. He was executed in 1793. *Il convient d'éviter de produire l'effet d'une fuite à Varennes.* © *Marianne 592.* This quote refers to the disappearance of de Gaulle during the unrest of 1968 and the radio blackout related to his 'flight'. See Chapter 12 'Metonymy', 'Baden-Baden'. Section 'Geographical names'.

## Vél' d'Hiv'                                                              **

On 16 and 17 July 1942, under the code name 'Wind of Spring', at least 4,000 French police took part in a raid to round up Parisian Jews. Around 13,000 people were arrested including 4,115 children. The arrest of Jewish children was a purely French decision, as the Germans had not asked for Jewish children to be arrested. The Jews were subsequently driven by bus to

Drancy or to the Vélodrome d'Hiver located in the fifteenth *arrondissement* of Paris. They remained herded in this compound for five days without food. Some were killed trying to escape, over 100 committed suicide. The number of Jews arrested in this raid amounts to more than a quarter of the 42,000 Jews deported from France to Auschwitz. *Après les rafles du Vél' d'Hiv' le 16 juillet 1942, ce genre de propos devenait insupportable.* © *Le Canard Enchaîné 4565.* This is a quote that highlights the fact that any anti-Semitic language is unacceptable in France in the light of recent French history.

### Vercingétorix                                                           ( ** )
Vercingétorix was a Gallic chief (72–46 BC). After having defeated Caesar in 52 BC, he became the recognized chief of the Gauls. He was however forced to retreat to Alésia where he was besieged for two months by the Romans. He capitulated before Caesar. He was strangled in a Roman prison in 46 BC. *César a bafoué les valeurs gauloises. L'insurrection est menée par Vercingétorix.* © *Le Point 1874.* See above 'Alésia'. Vercingétorix brings to mind the British heroine Boudicca (Boadicea).

### Verdun                                                                  ( ** )
Symbol of heroism and of senseless butchery, the Battle of Verdun was fought between 21 February and 19 December 1916. It was one of the bloodiest battles of the First World War in which 163,000 French soldiers and 143,000 German soldiers lost their lives for absolutely no gain. *250 000 emplois aux Etats Unis le mois dernier, et sans doute 750 000 au total en France en 2009. C'est une boucherie! C'est Verdun et des traders planqués au fond de la tranchée versent de nouveau dans l'euphorie.* © *Marianne 643.* The consequences of the financial crisis on employment is the context of this quote. Let it be said in passing that when the French speak of heroism, the spirit of Verdun is evoked just as the British evoke the spirit of Dunkirk or the Texans the spirit of the Alamo.

### Veuve Scarron (La)                                                       ( * )
Françoise d'Aubigny (1635–1719) alias 'La Veuve Scarron', since the death of her first husband, Paul Scarron. She is better known as Madame de Maintenon, mistress and then secret wife of Louis XIV, King of France and Navarre. See above 'Olympe Mancini'.

### Vidocq
François Eugène Vidocq (1775–1857) was sentenced to eight years' hard labour in a prison in Brest for forgery. On his release he was recruited as a police informer and then put in charge of a *brigade de sûreté* made up of newly released prisoners. They were used to infiltrate the underworld and 'grass' on former acquaintances. Vidocq was the head of this brigade from 1809 to 1827. He thus served under the first Empire and the Restoration. He

is said to have inspired Balzac for the character 'Vautrin' in the novel *Splendeurs et misères des courtisanes.*

### Villers-Cotterêts (l'Ordonnance de)                    [ ** ]

This is a small town 80 km north east of Paris, located in the *département* of the Aisne (02) in the region of Picardy. Sometimes misnamed the 'édit', the 'ordonnance' of Villers-Cotterêts issued by François I$^{er}$ in 1539 effectively made French the official language of law and the administration as opposed to Latin and the regional languages that had been used hitherto. *La défense de la langue française … constitue une urgence civique et politique comme l'a voulu l'ordonnance de Villers-Cotterêts.* © *Marianne 646.*

### Voltaire                                               [ *** ]

François-Marie Arouet, better known as Voltaire (1694–1798), was the influential French writer who was prominent among the figures of the movement of French Enlightenment, and was particularly famous for his philosophical tales. *Au pays de Voltaire et des Lumières.* © *Marianne 578.* See above 'Lumières' and Chapter 12 'pays de Voltaire et des Lumières'.

### Waterloo                                               [ *** ]

The battle of Waterloo fought on 18 June 1815 was the final defeat of Napoleon Bonaparte inflicted by the British under Wellington and the Prussians under Blücher. It is used today to refer to a crushing, terminal defeat. *Le désastre d'Abu Dhabi, Waterloo de notre industrie nucléaire.* © *Le Nouvel Observateur 2357.* This is a reference to the contract that was lost by the French consortium to build nuclear power stations in Abu Dhabi. The contract went to a Korean company.

Chapter 7

# Mythological and classical references

One could be forgiven for supposing that a chapter on mythological and classical references is redundant given that such a subject is the common heritage of both the Anglo-Americans and the French. There are, however, valid reasons for including this chapter. First, several French terms coming from the Classics do not exist as such in English translation, and there is a big difference between passive recognition of a word and active knowledge of its use. With the decline in the teaching of the Classics, this chapter should prove to be at least a useful refresher. Hands up, those who can remember the names of the various parts of the underworld! Given that part of the potential readership of this dictionary may well not be English or American, we have been careful, throughout the book, not make too many ethnocentric assumptions about the knowledge of our readers.

### Achille (le talon d') `***`
Achilles' heel. Thetis, Achilles' mother, immersed her infant son in the water of the Styx, the river encircling Hades. The water had the power to make any person who was immersed in it invulnerable. But part of the heel by which Thetis held the child was not touched by the water and hence Achilles was vulnerable in his heel. He was killed, shot in the heel, by an arrow fired by Paris, the son of Priam. Consequently, one's Achilles' heel is one's weak spot. *Les droits de mutation, le talon d'Achille de la fiscalité départementale.* © *Les Echos 20 401.* The context here is the drop in the number of real estate operations and thus a big loss in the conveyancing tax receipts of the *département.*

### Adonis (le complexe d') `*`
In Greek mythology, Adonis is described as half-man and half-god, and was considered to be perfection in terms of masculine beauty. He was so beautiful that he won the love of Aphrodite, goddess of love and beauty. *Le complexe d'Adonis s'applique aux hommes qui cherchent à tout prix à augmenter leur masse musculaire.* © *Marianne 650.* The text refers to the inherent narcissism of body-building enthusiasts.

## Aède nm.

An *aède* was a Greek bard, the greatest of them all being Homer. *Ion, devenu aveugle à force de lire, était une sorte d'aède moderne, cet Homère de la misère connaît par cœur des pages de Stendhal, Hugo ou Zola, en français dans le texte, s'il vous plaît.* © *Le Canard Enchaîné 4592.* This is the description of a character in the book *Le Masseur aveugle* by C. D. Florescu, published in 2008.

## agora nf.

An agora *

*C'est elle [La République] qui décide des comportements communs, du vivre-ensemble et de la place accordée sur l'agora aux différentes croyances.* © *L'Express 3048.* The *agora* for the Greeks was equivalent to the *forum* for the Romans, i.e. a large public place where people could meet and discuss. In modern urban environments, it implies a pedestrian precinct.

## Alcibiade

**

Alcibiades was a Greek statesman (450–404 BC). He was a very attractive and vain person. He was a student of Socrates. *Pas besoin d'être laid et haï comme Socrate pour être bon philosophe. Avec son physique de présentateur de télé [...] et son million de livres vendus, l'Allemand Richard David Precht tiendrait plutôt le rôle du bel Alcibiade.* © *L'Express 3055.* This is a reference to the young German philosopher who is very handsome and has just produced a best-seller on philosophy that was written in simple language for a general audience.

## Amazones nfpl.

*

In Greek mythology, the Amazones were a nation of female warriors living in what is now Turkey. Popular etymology claims that their name 'amazone' comes from the privative prefix 'a', and the Greek word 'mazos' meaning breast, from the fact that they cut off their right breast to facilitate the use of bows in combat. Men were either killed or blinded and reduced to sexual slavery given that the queen was said to have had an insatiable sexual appetite. Any males born were killed. *Carla Bruni-Sarkozy défend le nom de son mari avec des arguments de dame patronnesse, qui, dans cette vie antérieure où elle fut une amazone, n'aurait pas manqué de l'amuser.* © *L'Express 3055.* This is a reference to the fact that Carla Bruni was known to have had a very large number of sexual partners before marrying Nicolas Sarkozy, and that her former self would have been amused at her current attempts to seek the moral high ground.

## Antigone

**

*Antigone* is a tragedy by Sophocles that has been adapted by many dramatists including Jean Anouilh. The two brothers, Polynices and Etiocles drove Œdipus from Thebes and took over the kingdom. Eteocles went back on his promise to share power with Polynices. The latter was driven from Thebes but was later to launch an attack against the city. During the attack, both brothers died. Creon, King of Thebes, who had supported Etiocles and considered Polynices a traitor, gave the former a hero's burial but refused to allow Polynices to be buried. Polynices' sister, Antigone, in defiance of Creon's order, crept out of the city under cover of darkness and buried her brother. She was caught by Creon's soldiers and imprisoned. She committed suicide. She epitomizes the choice of one's moral conscience in defiance of human law. *Devedjian voyait une moderne Antigone, impatiente, résolue à bousculer l'ordre ancien.* © *Le Canard Enchaîné 4564*. This was a reference to the courage of Nathalie Kosciusko-Morizet, junior minister in charge of ecology under Jean Louis Borloo, when she condemned the 'competition of cowardice' between her minister and Jean-François Copé, president of the UMP group at the National Assembly. Patrick Devedjian praised her attitude. See Chapter 9 'Devedjian'.

## Apollon $\quad$ [ ** ]

Apollo was the Greek and Roman god of exceptional beauty and god of music, youth and knowledge. *Arrive Marc Allégret, jeune Apollon prometteur, quatrième fils du pasteur qui fut le précepteur de Gide.* © *Le Point 1902*. Although the homosexual Gide was infatuated by the young man, (who was the son of Gide's private tutor), the young man preferred girls.

## Arcadie. L' nf. $\quad$ [ ** ]

Arcadia is a region of Greece which is represented in mythology as a country of happiness, populated by shepherds living in harmony with nature. It represents a golden age past. *Ce voyage dans l'Arcadie mal-pensante commence logiquement par une empoignade sur les enjeux mémoriels.* © *Marianne 656*. This text refers to the political incorrectness (and historical inaccuracy) of certain statements made by President Sarkozy such as the fact that France has never been attracted to totalitarianism. Critics have pointed out that he seems to have forgotten Napoleon and Pétain.

## Ariane $\quad$ [ ** ]

Ariadne was the daughter of King Minos. She fell in love with Theseus (who had come to kill the Minotaur in the labyrinth) and gave him a spool of thread which enabled him to find his way out of the labyrinth which had only one exit. *Il est surtout question du 'USS Macon' dans ce documentaire, dont le fil d'Ariane est la quête sous-marine de l'épave du dernier des aérostats de la Navy.* © *Le Nouvel Observateur 2324*. This text refers to the search for the wreck of the US airship that was lost off the coast of California in 1935.

## Ariane

Her name is often associated with a storm at sea such as that which made Theseus forget to change the colour of the black sails of his ship to white. Aegeus, his father, was waiting for his return but when he saw the sails were not white (thus indicating the failure of Theseus' mission to defeat the Minotaur), he committed suicide by throwing himself into the sea which bears his name; this was the punishment for Theseus's betrayal of Ariadne whom he had promised to love but whom he had abandoned. ***...des marées chargées d'odeurs d'Ariane qui font claquer les draps au vent des matins.*** © *Le Canard Enchaîné 4619.* Ariane is also the name of the European space launch vehicle.

## asphodèles (les champs d') nmpl.

An asphodel is a member of the lily family. According to Greek mythology, good people, after death, go to the Elysian Fields; bad people go to Tartarus, and those people who have been neither particularly good nor particularly bad, walk in the fields of asphodel, a kind of purgatory. ***Villepin, lui, foule les champs d'asphodèles.*** © *Le Point 1952.* The context here is the fact that Dominique de Villepin will possibly stand against Nicolas Sarkozy in the 2012 presidential election but that he is without a party, without an electoral base and without funding, i.e. in a political no-man's-land.

## Atrides nmpl.

The Atridae is the name given to the two sons of Atreus, the King of Mycenae, Agamemnon and Menelaus. Their story is one of bloodshed, parricide, matricide and incest. ***Chez les Bush, on rejoue les Atrides et Œdipe est roi.*** © *Le Point 1884.* This quotation must be seen against the backdrop of the complex father-son relationship of Bush senior and Bush junior.

## Augias (les écuries d') nfpl.

The Augean stables. The fifth of the 'Twelve Labours of Hercules'. The stables of the biggest cattle owner in Greece had not been cleaned for many years. Hercules' task was to clean the stables within a day. He succeeded in cleaning out the stables by diverting the rivers Alpheus and Peneus. Today, it implies cleaning up a corrupt situation. Patrick Devedjian, president of the *Conseil Général* of the Hauts-de-Seine, ***parle de nettoyer les écuries d'Augias.*** © *Le Point 1935.* This is a reference to the corrupt practices in the *département* of the Hauts-de-Seine (92) which has always been under the rule of Charles Pasqua, Nicolas Sarkozy and Patrick Balkany. Patrick Devedjian is now politically dead.

## augures nmpl.

The augurs were the Roman soothsayers. Over time, the word came to mean the omen itself. Their predictions would always be sought before any important decision was taken. They would take the auspices, i.e. observe the flight of the birds. The Latin term *auspicium* refers to divination by looking at the flight of the birds. In the sky, an imaginary rectangle was traced. If the flight of birds entered the rectangle from the right hand side (*dextra*) this was a good sign or omen; if the flight entered from the left hand side (*sinister*) this was a bad omen. *La modestie n'étant pas la politesse des rois, il s'est fait un plaisir de rappeler les prophéties des augures qui annonçaient le coup d'arrêt brutal que la crise allait infliger à son redressement.* © *Les Echos 20 424.* This is a reference to the CEO of the Sainsbury's supermarket chain, Justin King, who has had great success in turning around the financial situation of his group, in spite of the pessimistic predictions of market specialists. See below 'auspices'.

### auspices nmpl.                                                     \*\*\*
*L'arrivée de François Pérol à la tête du groupe Caisse d'Epargne-Banques Populaires ne pouvait se faire sous de pires auspices.* © *Le Point 1914.* This is a reference to the arrival of Nicolas Sarkozy's appointee at the head of the Caisse d'Épargne. It is said that his appointment is contrary to the law which states that a civil servant may not serve in a company with which he or she had dealings when working for the government. In fact, Pérol was largely the architect of the merger of the two banks. Specialists claim that there is a conflict of interest in this case. See above 'augures'.

### Aventin. L'                                                        \*\*
The Aventine Hill. The name of one of the Seven Hills of Rome, it is associated with secession, and withdrawal from others. The proverbial expression 'se retirer sur l'Aventin' is a reference to the revolt of the plebeians against the patriciate in 494 BC and their withdrawal to the Aventine. *Aujourd'hui installé dans la position confortable du recours, il [Dominique Strauss-Kahn] rêve que le PS, la gauche – et pourquoi pas la France – le supplie de descendre de son Aventin.* © *Le Nouvel Observateur 2358.* For the moment, DSK has not entered the lists but is waiting, in splendid isolation, at the International Monetary Fund in the USA. He hopes that he will be called to stand as the socialist candidate in the presidential election in 2012.

### Bacchus                                                            \*\*\*
This is the Latinized version of Dionysus, the Greek god of wine and ecstatic delirium. *Plusieurs études ont montré que la consommation régulière, en petites quantités, de vin rouge serait associée à une diminution de la mortalité cardio-vasculaire … Sans pour autant faire de la boisson de Bacchus un élixir de jouvence.* © *Le Point 1950.* Regular consumption of moderate quantities of red wine reduces the risk of death from cardiovascular disease.

## Belle Hélène

Helen. The most beautiful of women, whose beauty was harmful. There are many different versions of her exploits. In Greek mythology, Helen (otherwise known as Helen of Sparta or Helen of Troy) was the daughter of Zeus and Leda. Her abduction by Paris led to the Trojan War. In the Homeric poems she is deemed to be a model of domestic virtue; other mythographers hold a different opinion! It is also the name of the highly successful *opéra bouffe* by Offenbach, created in 1864 and whose theme is the frivolity of Parisian mores and the eternal vices of humanity and of governments. In this *opéra-bouffe*, ***des milliers de spectateurs avaient reconnu le nain couronné.*** © *Le Canard Enchaîné 4561.* A satirical reference to Napoleon III (whose nickname was 'the dwarf') and a nickname that Nicolas Sarkozy shares.

## byzantinisme nm.

Ⓒ ***

This term originates from the Byzantine theologians who were debating about the sex of angels while their city, Constantinople, was being attacked by the Turks in 1451. It implies a taste for hairsplitting and over-nice interpretation. ***Sous les controverses byzantines monte une évidence incontournable: la maladie avérée de notre système d'enseignement, grand corps malade.*** © *Le Point 1914.* This text refers to the pitiful state of the French education system in spite of the fact that education has the biggest slice of the national budget.

## calendes grecques nfpl.

Ⓒ ***

The word calends corresponded to the first day of each month in the Roman calendar. The word calendar is derived from the word *calendarium* which designated a book of accounts. Accounts were traditionally settled on the first of the month. The Greeks did not have *calendes* and consequently 'renvoyer aux calendes grecques' means to put off indefinitely. ***Le budget israélien remis aux calendes grecques.*** © *Les Echos 20 401.*

## Caligula

Ⓒ *

Caius Caesar Germanicus (12–41 BC) was one of the most unstable of the Roman Emperors. He spent his childhood in a military camp in Germania where his wearing of tiny military boots gave him his nickname 'Caligula' meaning 'little boot'. His mental state deteriorated after he came to power and he was notorious for his megalomania, debauchery and bloodthirstiness. He loved to humiliate his consuls and threatened to make his favourite horse, Incitatus, a consul. It is to him that we erroneously attribute the phrase, 'Qu'ils me haïssent pourvu qu'ils me craignent'. ***La nomination la plus bizarre depuis celle du cheval de Caligula au poste de consul.*** © *Le Point 1882.* This quote concerns the incongruous appointment of Peter Mandelson as British minister of commerce.

## callipyge adj.      **\*\***

'Callipygian (beautifully bottomed)'. From the Greek *kallipugos*. An epithet associated with Aphrodite or Venus ('Aphrodite Kallipygos' or more commonly known in France as 'Vénus Callipyge') from *kallos* meaning beauty and *pugê* meaning 'buttocks' or 'backside'. It usually refers to a woman who has an exaggeratedly curvaceous bottom. ***Devant cette apparition callipyge, la presse à popotins se pâme et mesure nos Cul-I respectifs.*** © *Le Canard Enchaîné 4619* (notice the play on words *potin* is 'gossip', whereas *popotin* is 'bottom' or 'backside'. Note too, the pun on the French acronym QI (*quotient intellectuel*). This has the same pronunciation as *cul i ... cul* meaning 'arse'). The context here is the state visit of Nicolas Sarkozy and his wife to Spain. Most of the photographers were concentrated on the curves of the respective backsides of the two First Ladies.

## Cassandre (jouer les)      **\*\*\***

Cassandra was the daughter of Priam and Hecuba. Apollo fell in love with her and promised to give her the powers of prophecy if she would consent to be his. Once she had received the powers of prophecy she did not keep her part of the bargain. Apollo was angry and withdrew from her the art of persuasion. He decreed that whatever she said, no one was to believe her. She warned against allowing the Greek horse to enter Troy. Her warnings were disregarded and Troy was destroyed. Today, *'jouer les Cassandre'* means to be a bird of ill omen, to prophesy misfortune while one's warnings go unheeded. ***Les Cassandre qui stigmatisaient depuis une décennie la part de mirage dans le miracle de Dubaï ont fini par avoir le dernier mot.*** © *Le Monde 20171*. This text refers to the fact that Dubai is insolvent, a danger that several economists had been predicting for some time without being heeded.

## Caudines (passer sous les Fourches) nfpl.      **\*\*\***

The battle of the Caudine Forks (*Furcae Caudinae*) opposed the Romans and the Samnites in 321 BC. The Romans were lured into a very narrow passage between two mountains in Italy and were captured by the enemy near Caudium. They were subsequently obliged, unarmed and with their hands tied behind their back, to pass under an ever narrower yoke formed by the Samnite soldiers' spears. In modern French, this expression means to undergo a stinging humiliation. ***Ce texte ... est presque intégralement rédigé, après être passé sous les fourches Caudines interministérielles.*** © *Les Echos 20 401*. This text refers to the highly sensitive bill related to the privatization of the French postal administration that was drastically revised during its preparation.

## Cerbère nm.      **\*\*\***

Cerberus. In classical mythology, Cerberus was the name of the three-headed dog, chained outside the gates of Hades, to prevent anyone leaving and to stop anyone entering. Its tail was a serpent. The name is now given to any aggressive doorkeeper or secretary. **Le dogme de l'impôt sur la fortune est d'abord la niche des cerbères de l'envie.** © *L'Express 3012*. This text refers to the jealousy of those people who are recommending tax hikes on the very wealthy. NB: the pun on 'niche'. 'Niche' can be either 'niche' as in 'tax niche' (a special arrangement for enjoying tax relief) or in the meaning of 'dog kennel or house'.

### Charybde en Scylla (tomber de)    [ ** ]

In the *Odysee*, Charybdis was a sea monster who lived on a rock near Messina, the straights separating Italy from Sicily. Three times a day she ingurgitated enormous amounts of water, and in the current thus created, swallowed up all of the ships in the vicinity. On the other side of the straights, there lived another monster called Scylla. She is represented as a woman whose body was made up of ferocious dogs who devoured anyone within their reach. Six of Ulysses' companions were killed by Scylla. The expression is rendered in English by 'to fall out of the frying pan into the fire'. **Mais voilà, la presse le pousse, sitôt sauvé, de Charybde vers Scylla.** © *Le Point 1935*. This is a reference to the successive scandals surrounding the newly appointed minister of culture, Frédéric Mitterrand; first, he hit the headlines with his ill-received defence of Roman Polanski, who has been arrested on charges of having had sexual relations with a 13-year-old girl, and hardly had that row blown over than he made front page news with his admission (in an autobiography published a few years ago) to having visited Thailand to have sex with young men.

### Cheval de Troie nm.    [ *** ]

The Trojan Horse. This was an immense, hollow, wooden structure filled with Greek soldiers that was left at the gates of Troy. In spite of Cassandra's warnings, it was taken into the city by the Trojans. At nightfall, the Greek soldiers left their hiding place and opened the gates of Troy that was subsequently attacked and destroyed. Hence the words of Virgil 'Ne faites pas confiance à ce cheval, Troyens. Quoi que ce soit, je crains les Danaens même quand ils offrent des cadeaux.' In modern usage, as in English, it can refer to a computer program that breaches the security of the IT system by apparently functioning as a legitimate part of a program. **La création d'un acte d'avocat … est vue par les notaires, comme l'arrivée d'un cheval de Troie, une brèche ouverte dans leur statut.** © *Le Figaro 20 111*. This refers to the plans to give lawyers the right to establish official acts, hitherto a monopoly of solicitors (*notaires*).

### chimère nf.    [ *** ]

An illusion. A chimera. From the Latin term *Chimaera* and the Greek word *Khimaira*. In Greek mythology this was a monster, one part lion, one part goat and one part snake. It spat fire and devoured human beings. It was killed by Bellepheron, riding Pegasus. 'Le pays des chimères' is 'the land of fancy', 'courir après des chimères' is 'to chase moonbeams'. *Edimbourg ... apparaît comme une cité schizophrène hantée par les chimères perdues de la haute finance.* © *Le Monde 19 965*. This text refers to the aftermath of the financial crash in the Scottish capital and the loss of its illusions.

### ciguë nf.        ✱✱✱

Hemlock. *N'en jetez plus, la coupe de ciguë est pleine.* © *Marianne 630*. The context of this quote is the politico-financial scandals in Greece. The expression 'la coupe est pleine' means 'I've had enough' or 'that's the limit'. Socrates was sentenced to death for corrupting the youth of Athens. He was forced to commit suicide by drinking a cup of hemlock. See below 'Socrate'.

### Cincinnatus        ✱✱✱

The story concerns a person who was called Lucius Quinctius Cincinnatus (520–430 BC). He was a poor farmer who, after having exercised supreme power in Rome (he was dictator in 458 and again in 439), is said to have returned to his fields and his plough. *Alarmée, la présidente du Medef place la conquête de l'Élysée au cœur de sa nouvelle réflexion stratégique. Pour empêcher quiconque d'aller chercher, dans son champ, le Cincinnatus du patronat, Denis Kessler.* © *L'Express 3054*. The context of this quote was the challenge to Laurence Parisot's leadership of the Medef by Denis Kessler who used to be the co-president of this organization and who might well have returned to his former position. NB: Cincinnatus means 'curly-haired'.

### Circé        ✱

Circe was the enchantress who turned men into swine, in Homer's *Odyssey*. *Chez Harlequin, les femmes modernes accèdent à l'abnégation d'Esther ou à la passion de Phèdre et elles peuvent être aussi redoutables qu'une Salomé et mater le plus indomptable des mâles sans avoir recours à la magie comme Circé retenant Ulysse.* © *Marianne 589*. This quote refers to the Harlequin books (romantic love stories) that are despised by the intellectual elite but which sell millions of copies worldwide. The text suggests that far from being worthy of scorn, such books may hold some interesting lessons. Indeed, they contain the essence of all the great female figures in classical literature. See Chapter 8 'Esther' and 'Salomé'. See below 'Phèdre' and Chapter 1 'Harlequin'.

### Clio        ✱

Clio was one of the nine muses and patroness of history. *Le succès jamais démenti des Rendez-vous de l'histoire, à Blois, illustre l'engouement du public pour la muse Clio.* © *Le Figaro 19 996*. The success of events such as the one mentioned above tend to confirm that the French are very fond of their history. *Les Rendez-vous de l'Histoire*, is a three-day event which attracts 25,000 visitors to Blois every year.

## Crésus

Croesus. This was the name of the king of Lydia who possessed great wealth. The source of this wealth was the river Pactolus. *Si la téléréalité l'a enrichi [Stéphane Courbit] ... les jeux en ligne pourraient faire de lui un Crésus.* © *Le Point 1914.* Courbit has made millions from trash TV and could become far richer with his profits from his financial interests in companies working in the field of on-line betting. See below 'pactole'.

## cuisse de Jupiter (sorti de la)

In Greek mythology, Semele fell in love with Zeus (Jupiter in Roman mythology) and while contemplating him in all his glory she began to burn because of the lightning surrounding him. She was pregnant and Zeus took the child from her womb just before she was consumed by the flames and put the child inside his own thigh so that it could finish its gestation. Three months later Dionysus (Bacchus), the god of wine and revelry, was born. To think that one was born out of the thigh of Jupiter is to believe that one is God's gift to mankind. *Un homme du sérail et non un parachuté politique sorti de la cuisse de Jupiter.* © *Le Point 1884.* This text refers to the qualities of the ideal candidate for the presidency of the broadcasting watchdog CSA and is an implicit criticism of President Sarkozy's intention of parachuting a political vassal to the post.

## Cupidon

Cupid, the god of love, son of Venus, corresponding to the Greek god Eros. *Peut-être faudrait-il demander conseil au grand maître des attirances, le célèbre et redoutable Cupidon.* © Le Figaro 19 953. The text refers to the mystery of gravity (attraction) and is a flippant reply to the question 'Why do people in the southern hemisphere not walk upside down?' English-speaking readers should be careful of the French word 'cupide' which means 'greedy' or 'money-grabbing'.

## Curiaces (les trois)

According to Livy, the three Horatii and the three Curatii were the mythological champions who fought a duel in the war between Rome and Alba Longa during the reign of Tullius Hostilius (the third king of Rome 673–640 BC). The two towns decided to settle their conflict by battle, choosing three champions on either side; the outcome of their duel would settle the outcome of the war. The Horatii are believed to have been the champions of Rome, whereas the Curiatii were the champions of Alba. According to the legend, the three Curiatii were wounded very quickly and two of the Horatii killed. The third Horatii was able to escape, pursued by the three wounded

Curiatii. But the latter did not catch up with the third Horatii at the same time, thus enabling him to slay them one after the other. ***Tels les Curiaces, les pays de l'Eurogroupe s'exposent un par un: le Portugal suit la Grèce et précède l'Espagne.*** © *L'Express 3058.* This is a comment on the absence of a unified political and monetary Europe. Speculators are attacking the weaker countries in Europe one after the other, in the absence of a united European front.

### Cythère nf.

Cythera, the southernmost island of the Ionian Islands in Greece which, in literature and art, represents an idyllic country of love and pleasure. ***Pourquoi la Première Guerre Mondiale … a-t-elle éloigné Keynes de sa Cythère londonienne?*** © *Marianne 644.* The question is asked as to why Keynes (who frequented London and the intellectual Bloomsbury group) left London during the First World War. It is suggested that it was for sentimental reasons. His lover, Duncan Grant, had left him for another man.

### Damoclès (l'épée de) nf.                                          ***

Damocles (400 BC) was a courtier of the tyrant of Syracuse, Dionysius. He flattered the latter, outrageously congratulating him on being so fortunate. In fact Dionysius lived in constant fear of assassination and was annoyed by Damocles' fawning. He proposed to change places with him for one day. A feast was then given. During the feast Damocles was treated like a king, drank good wine and ate fine food. But suddenly, he looked up and saw a sword hanging just above his head, a sword that was dangling by a single horsehair. This was to illustrate the fragility of happiness and the precarity of existence. This story belongs to Greek legend rather than to Greek mythology. ***Les partis politiques ont intérêt à ce que tout cela reste caché. Un seul cas de collaboration avec la Stasi rejaillirait sur l'ensemble de ses membres C'est une épée de Damoclès qui pèse sur tous.*** © *Le Nouvel Observateur 2346.* These are the words of Ronald Lässig, spokesperson of the association of Stalinist victims, the VOS. His remarks were made in the light of new access to official records of the GDR secret police which could have catastrophic effects on the current political parties if any one example of collaboration with the secret police can be proved.

### Danaïdes (le tonneau des)                                         ***

The Danaïdes were the 50 daughters of Danaos. On their father's advice, they each killed their husband on their wedding night, except one. They were punished in Hades and were forced to pour water into a bottomless barrel. In the uselessness of the repetitive task it resembles the myth of Sisyphus but is frequently used with the connotation of a financial abyss, a bottomless pit. ***…les bonus accordés aux cadres de l'assureur AEG – véritable tonneau des Danaïdes pour le contribuable américain.*** © *Figaro 20 108.* This is a text that refers to the indecent bonuses in the private sector, paid for by public money via bailouts.

## dédales nmpl.    `***`

These were the confusing and complicated galeries in the 'Labyrinthe', the name of the mythical maze designed by Daedalus, an Athenian architect who built the maze at the request of the king of Crete, Minos. It was a structure in which the Minotaur was to be kept. In modern French, 'les dédales' refer to a complicated itinerary or the intricate subtleties of a given question. ***Des lycéens perdus dans les dédales des formations.*** © *Le Figaro 20 166*. This text refers to the jungle of available training schemes being proposed to school leavers.

## Démocrite    `*`

See below 'tentation'.

## Démosthène    `**`

Demosthenes. An Athenian orator and statesman (384–322 BC), he is reputed to have practiced speaking in public by putting pebbles in his mouth. His name implies the summit of eloquence. ***Le président du MoDem a-t-il profité de sa traversée du désert pour mâcher des cailloux? Sans être un Démosthène, ce bègue rédimé, fait en tout cas, face à son Catalina à lui*** [Nicolas Sarkozy], ***un Cicéron probant.*** © *Marianne 630*. Let it be remembered that Cataline tried to assassinate Cicero. Nicolas Sarkozy is doing his best to 'kill' François Bayrou, leader of the MoDem centre party. Bayrou used to have a bad stammer but overcame this handicap and is now proving to be a convincing orator against Sarkozy. NB: 'rédimé' is related to 'redemption'. See Chapter 8 'traversée du desert'.

## descente aux enfers nf.    `***`

***Comment empêcher les attaques menées contre les dettes souveraines par le biais des CDS*** *[credit default swaps]*. ***Depuis la descente aux enfers des obligations grecques, la question agite les autorités.*** © *Les Echos 20 631*. The descent into Hell was the last of the Twelve Labours of Hercules. The expression often implies the gradual destruction of a person because of a growing addiction to drugs or alcohol, etc.

## Diogène    `**`

Diogenes (412?–327?) was a Greek philosopher known for his asceticism and cynicism. He is said to have wandered in the city at noon with a lantern, and when asked what he was doing he replied 'I am looking for a human'. He did not believe in the ideal man. In a diatribe against Louis Napoleon, Victor Hugo wrote 'Il lui faut (à Napoléon III) ce qu'il appelle lui-même "des hommes".' *Diogène les cherchait tenant une lanterne, lui, [Napoleon III] il les cherche un billet de banque à la main. Il les trouve.* © *Marianne 620.* The comparison between Nicolas Sarkozy and Napoleon III is frequently evoked by his critics. In the same text, Victor Hugo describes Louis Napoleon as 'un homme de moyenne taille … un personnage vulgaire, puéril, théatral et vain'.

### dionysiaque adj.       ☐ *

*Joie dans les sacristies! Hosanna! Sœur Catherine se confesse! La grande prêtresse dionysiaque se fait l'apôtre de la fidélité! Thèse, antithèse et foutaise.* © *Marianne 594.* This critical text refers to Catherine Millet who became famous after the publication, in 2001, of a book entitled *La Vie sexuelle de Catherine M* which deals crudely with her very free private life. It was a best-seller. She has just published another book, *Jour de souffrance*, in which she tells of her feelings of jealousy towards her partner. The comments of *Marianne* are an echo of the well-known expression 'thesis, antithesis, synthesis' which students learn to use in philosophy lessons for the purposes of demonstration. 'Foutaise' is the French term for 'bullshit'.

### Dionysos (Bacchus)       ☐ **

Dionysus (os) was the Greek god of wine and revelry. The adjective Dionysian connotes orgiastic and frenzied pleasure. *En fait, il y a deux directions opposées: une musique chaotique, individuelle, personnelle, qui n'entre pas dans des catégories et qui appartient à Dionysos; et puis une autre, religieuse, organisée, qui est du côté de l'Institution, d'Apollon.* © *Le Nouvel Observateur 2327.* This is a reference to the work of Krzysztof Warlikowski who is part of the new wave in Polish theatre. See above 'Apollon'.

### Écuries       ☐ ***

See above 'Augias'.

### égérie nf.       ☐ ***

Egeria was the Roman nymph of springs said to have been the advisor of the devout and legendary king of Rome, Numa Pompilius. He was inspired by her and she dictated his religious policy. She was either his friend or lover, and on his death she died of sadness and was transformed into a spring. Today, an Egeria inspires or counsels an artiste. She is considered to be a muse or even an icon. *Audrey Tautou* [a fortnight after her film on Coco Chanel was released] *surgissait en égérie romanesque dans un coûteux spot de pub … consacré semble-t-il, de façon parfaitement fortuite, au jus mythique de N° 5.* © *Les Echos 20 424.* This criticism calls into doubt the 'coincidence' of the launch of the advertising campaign for Chanel No. 5 featuring Audrey

Tautou and the release of the film about Coco Chanel in which Audrey Tautou also stars.

### égide de (sous l') nf.                                        \*\*\*

'Under the aegis of'. The 'aegis' was the name of the miraculous goatskin shield used by Zeus and his daughter Athena. This expression now means 'under the protection of', or 'with the sponsorship of'. *L'Iran a confirmé hier sa participation à la conférence sur l'avenir de l'Afghanistan organisée le 31 mars sous l'égide des Nations unies.* © *Le Figaro 20 111.*

### Élysées (les champs) nmpl.                                   \*\*

'The Elysian Fields'. In Greek mythology, the word signified 'the place struck by lightning' and was a part of the underworld which was the final resting place of the heroic and the virtuous. Over time, it has become a synonym of paradise. *Chacun broute son pré carré et rumine la doxa de l'adaptation forcée au marché libéral. ... sous les ricanements des dieux élyséens.* © *Marianne 586.* This is a reference to the socialist party's acceptance of the principle of a free market economy accompanied by the 'Gods of the Élysée'. In this context the Élysée can refer to the presidential seat of power.

### empyrée nm.                                                   \*\*

Empyrean. The highest heaven or abode of the gods. *Sarkozy, depuis son empyrée présidentiel, aurait dû laisser courir la justice et s'abstenir de propos imprudents.* © *Le Point 1951.* This is a criticism of the interventions of Nicolas Sarkozy in the Clearstream affair. He even made a slip by referring to 'the accused' as 'the culprits'. Most people believe that he would have done better to stand aloof and not intervene. See Chapter 12 'Clearstream'.

### éolien nf. adj.                                               \*\*\*

From the Latin 'Aeolus' and the Greek 'Aiolus' who in Greek mythology was the god of the winds and son of Poseidon (Neptune). This is not to be confused with 'Zephyr' who is specifically the god of the west wind. A group of 'éoliennes' constitutes a wind farm. *L'énergie de l'avenir, c'est l'éolien.* © *Marianne 578.*

### épigones nmpl.                                                \*\*\*

Épigones. From the Greek word *epignos* meaning afterborn, i.e. a descendant. In Greek mythology, it was the name given to the sons of the heroes who fell in the first war against Thebes. The sons stormed and took Thebes, thus avenging their fathers who had fallen during the first siege. The word is now used to refer to a 'descendant less gifted than his ancestors, or any inferior follower or imitator' (Webster). *Cette accusation porte d'autant plus qu'elle n'émane pas d'un altermondialiste mais d'un épigone de Margaret Thatcher.* © *Marianne 581.* The 'épigone' in question is the former Icelandic prime minister who levelled severe criticism at the speculators who ruined Iceland's economy. Not so long ago, he was first in line with the implementation of Thatcherite doctrine.

## Éros                                    [ ** ]

The Greek god of love. In Roman mythology it was Cupid. 'Thanatos' is the Greek term for death but in Freudian psychology it refers to a death wish. In the Freudian context, Thanatos is used as the opposite of 'Eros', the latter referring to the impulses and drives of life. *Il en résulte cette exploration des relations entre Eros-Thanatos, aussi douloureuse que magnifique.* © *L'Express 3061*. This was a reveiw of the book *Sévère* by Régis Jauffret based on the story of the sadomasochistic murder of the French banker Edouard Stern, in 2005, who was shot by his mistress during a sadomasochistic session. His body was found dressed in a latex suit.

## feu sacré nm.                           [ * ]

Prometheus was the name of the Titan 'who stole the sacred fire from the gods for the benefit of mankind: in punishment Zeus chained him to a rock where a vulture came each day to eat his liver, which Zeus renewed each night' (Webster). *Il croyait dépasser les limites humaines, voler le feu sacré comme d'autres figures mythologiques avant lui.* © *Marianne 600*. This refers to Emil Zátopek, the fastest long distance runner in the world in 1952 at the Olympic Games in Helsinki. He won four Olympic medals and eighteen world records for the 5,000 and 10,000 metres. As a Czech, he spoke out against the Russian invasion of his country in 1968. He fell from grace and suffered from Soviet repression; he was reduced to working as a dustman in Prague and later in a uranium mine. He died in the year 2000.

## foudre divine nf.                       [ * ]

Although Zeus was, among other things, the god of lightning, it is the Roman equivalent which gives us the expression 'foudres jupitériennes'. 'Attirer les foudres' means to be the object of violent criticism, i.e. to suffer the wrath of God. *Il n'avait pas imaginé que la rénovation d'une superbe salle construite dans les années trente en plein centre-ville, déclencherait les foudres d'UGC, qui possède un multiplex en périphérie de la commune.* © *Marianne 598*. This text refers to the refurbishment of an old cinema in the town centre which has provoked the anger of the company UGC which has a multiplex cinema on the outskirts of the town. See below 'jupitérienne'.

## garde prétorienne nf.                   [ *** ]

'Praetorian guard'. A special force composed as the personal bodyguard of the Roman Emperors. The name derives from the word designating the tent of the commanding general in the field, the *praetorium* that was guarded by a special squad of men. *Le Groupement d'intervention de la Polynésie (GIP) la garde prétorienne de M. Floss. Le Monde 19 898.* Less frequent is the use of the term prétorien when related to the world of banking and loans (prêts). Hence *Un tribunal de Toulouse a récemment invoqué l'obligation prétorienne d'information et de conseil.* © *Marianne 586.* This refers to the obligation of bankers to advise the person to whom they are going to grant a loan.

### gémonies (vouer qqn. aux) nfpl.

The 'gémonies', in classical Rome, was the place where bodies of strangled criminals were exposed before being thrown into the Tiber. More precisely, it was the name of the degrees on the monumental staircase linking the Capitol and the Forum, called *scalae gemoniae* (the staircase of moaning). It was a place of horror and death. Today, it means that the person is held up to public shame and humiliation. *...l'ex directeur général de la RBS est aujourd'hui voué aux gémonies pour avoir refusé de restituer son indemnité de retraite en or et à vie de 777,000 euros par an.* © *Le Monde 19 965.* This refers to the uproar provoked by the refusal of the CEO of the Royal Bank of Scotland to give back what is seen as his obscenely high redundancy and retirement package.

### gérontes nmpl.

From the Greek *gerôn* meaning 'an elderly person'. *'S'il est deux hommes* [Obama and Sarkozy] *qui étaient faits pour s'entendre, c'est bien ces deux-là. Même génération dans des conciles accoutumés aux querelles de gérontes.* © *Marianne 641.* The 'gérontes' were members of the Spartan Senate, 28 in number, who had to be over the age of 60. The text suggests that Obama and Sarkozy should normally get along very well because they are of the same generation and only too used to attending meetings dominated by elderly politicians. 'Géronte' is a familiar character in classical theatre (Molière) and has the role of an elderly and gullible person. See Chapter 5 'galère'.

### Gordien (couper le nœud)

'To cut the Gordian knot'. The intricate knot tied by Gordius king of Gordium, was cut through by Alexander in response to the prophecy that only the future ruler of Asia could undo it. The expression means to solve a problem by force or by evading the conditions imposed. *Le Moyen-Orient, ce nœud gordien mondial, où l'Iran est engagé dans une politique d'accès à l'arme nucléaire.* © *Le Figaro 20 166.* The Middle East is compared to an inextricable problem.

### Graal (le saint)

*On dit de cette compétition, [the America Cup] née sous la reine Victoria, qu'elle est le graal de la voile.* © *Le Nouvel Observateur 2361.* Since the Middle Ages, the 'grail' has been the symbol of the search for the impossible.

It was also the name given to the cup from which Jesus is said to have drunk during the Last Supper.

### Harpies nfpl.                                                          **

*Harpyia* in Latin and in the Greek plural *Harpyiai*, is the collective name of the three spirits of devastation and revenge. Their name comes from the Greek meaning 'snatchers'. They were rapacious winged monsters in Greek mythology, with the head and trunk of a woman and the tail, legs and talons of a bird. They were supposed to be snatchers of children and of souls. Their names were Aello (sudden storm), Podarge (fleet of foot) and Ocypete (swift wing). The term has come to mean any spiteful or bitter woman. *Ce profond désaccord avec les harpies du Mouvement de libération des femmes (MLF) ... consomme la rupture avec Evelyne Sullerot, alors accusée de trahison.* © *Marianne 633*. Evelyne Sullerot has called Simone de Beauvoir's references to motherhood 'absurd' and has also defended the rights of divorced fathers who have been deprived of their children. In France, custody of the children of divorced parents is rarely granted to the father. She has thus incurred the ire of the feminist hardliners.

### hécatombe nf.                                                          *

In ancient Greece, this referred to the religious sacrifice of 100 oxen. Today, it is synonymous with slaughter, carnage or disaster *Dans le sport automobile, c'est l'hécatombe.* © *Le Figaro 20 084*. The context is that because of the recession there is a decline in sponsoring contracts with the car industry.

### Hélène de Troie                                                        *

See above 'Belle Hélène'.

### Hercule                                                                **

Hercules was the son of Zeus and Alcmene and was famous for having accomplished the Twelve Labours. *Le nouveau président va inaugurer un mandat où les défis à relever s'apparentent aux douze travaux d'Hercule.* © *Le Point 1896*. This was a reference to the extent of the task awaiting the new French President, Sarkozy, on his election in 2007.

### Hermès                                                                 **

In Greek mythology, Hermes is the god of commerce and the messenger of the gods. He corresponds, in Roman mythology, to Mercury. Pegasus was the winged horse entrusted by Zeus with the task of carrying thunder and lightning to Mount Olympus. *Le SMS, c'est le rêve d'Hermès, c'est Pégase devenu réalité: de tous temps, les hommes ont voulu envoyer des messages où qu'ils soient.* © *L'Express 3041*. This comment refers to the SMS as being the dream of Hermes come true, and that of Pegasus having become reality.

## Hermione

In the tragedy *Andromaque* by Racine, Hermione is the daughter of the king of Sparta. She is pitiless and scornful and through jealousy, hatches a plot to have her lover killed. ***Considéré comme une Messaline, elle fut surtout une Hermione de la correspondance.*** © *Marianne 642*. This quote refers to the passionate letter-writing of Mme de Staël. See below 'Messaline'.

## Hespérides

In Greek mythology, this was the name of the nymphs who guarded the golden apples given as a wedding gift by Gaea to Hera. It is also the name of the garden. The Hesperides are also known as the nymphs of twilight, the name indicating 'west' or 'evening'. ***...de nombreuses citations égaient cette promenade aux Hespérides.*** © *L'Express 3020*. The sentence refers to a recently published book on knowing how to age well. Twilight is frequently used to describe one's declining years. This being said, we would do well to remember that 'twilight' (as indeed the word suggests) is a subdued half-light that can refer to the evening or, less frequently, to the morning. Let us also remember that in spite of the title *Le Crépuscule des dieux* (The Twilight of the Gods), the first meaning of 'crépuscule' is the subdued light just before sunrise; contrary to popular belief, it is in fact a synonym of 'dawn'.

## Homérique (lutte, rire, colère) adj.

Homeric (struggle, laugh, anger). Homeric laughter is unrestrained, while a Homeric struggle is a struggle on a grand scale. Homer is the most famous of the ancient Greek poets, to whom authorship of the *Iliad* and the *Odyssey* is ascribed. ***Maurice Druon était aussi un bon vivant aux colères homériques.*** © *Le Point 1910*. Druhon (1918–2009) was a French novelist and politician, former minister of culture, capable of furious outbursts of bad temper.

## Hydre (de Lerne) nf.

The Lernaean Hydra was a multi-headed serpent whose breath was mortal. Each time one if its heads was severed, others grew in its place. To kill the Hydra was one of the twelve tasks of Hercules. ***L'hydre rouge et noire ... comme on appelle ici l'alliance redoutable du pouvoir et de la pègre.*** © *Le Nouvel Observateur 2358*. This text refers to the complicity of Chinese officials with members of the Chinese mafia.

## Icare

Icarus was the son of Daedalus. He and his father were imprisoned in the labyrinth of which Daedalus was the artist and craftsman. 'Daedalus' literally means 'artful craftsman'. They both escaped from the labyrinth thanks to the wings that Daedalus had made. They were attached to the body by wax. Before their escape, Daedalus gave some advice to his son. He advised him to fly neither too low nor too high. Icarus was a proud and over-daring young man. He didn't heed his father's words and flew too high and too close to the sun. The wax attaching his wings to his body melted and he fell to his death in the sea that bears his name, the Icarian Sea (la mer Icarienne). The adjective today refers to anyone who is foolhardy or rash. *Ce lettré [Xavier Darcos, agrégé and former minister of education] a oublié de se méfier du soleil, il s'est brûlé pour s'en être approché.* © *Marianne 609.* This is a reference to Xavier Darcos and the reform bill he tried to pass when he was minister of education. As an *agrégé* his attitude to the rank and file of the teaching profession was perceived as condescending he was seen as trying to curry favour with the high political sphere. This was seen as his undoing. He has since been replaced as minister of education.

### Iphigénie
<code>*</code>

Iphigenia was the daughter of Agamemnon and Clytemnestra who was sacrificed to the gods by her father in return for favourable winds to help the Greek fleet attack Troy. She accepted her fate with dignity, in the higher interests of the state. *C'est pourquoi il fallait que Carla Bruni-Sarkozy prît la parole pour calmer "l'affaire Dati": c'est Iphigénie montant au bûcher des vanités politiques que nous avons vue.* © *L'Express 3067.* In April 2010, rumours began circulating about the French president's marital problems. Rachida Dati was seen as the most likely source. She immediately suffered reprisals (confiscation of her mobile telephone, withdrawal of her bodyguards and chauffeur-driven car). The First Lady was obliged to speak in public to defuse this explosive situation.

### Janus
<code>***</code>

This word literally means an arched passageway. In Roman mythology, Janus was the guardian of the portals and the patron of beginnings and endings. He is portrayed as having two faces, one in front and one behind. Today, the word often refers to someone who is two-faced and deceitful. *Le PS est un Janus: un organisme national démobilisé, privé de leadership et de perspectives, un niveau local qui n'a jamais été aussi florissant'.* © *Le Monde 20 089.* This text highlights the paradox of the socialist party in 2008 without direction or unity at the top, while flourishing locally.

### Junon
<code>**</code>

Juno was the wife and sister of Jupiter in Roman mythology. She is identified with the Greek Hera and she is known for her spiteful revenge. She is the goddess of marriage and of feminine nature and the protectress of women in general. *Cécilia Sarkozy en revenant, telle une Marie de Médicis, Junon politique à l'esprit de revanche, sépara la cour entre ceux qui avaient couvert sa fuite et ceux qui l'avaient abandonnée.* © *Marianne 589.*

A reference to the revenge taken by Cécilia Sarkozy on her return from the USA after her adulterous escapade. She divided people into two categories: those who had stood by her and those who had decided to turn their backs on her and side with her husband. See Chapter 5 'coeur a ses raisons'.

### Jupiter          `***`

Alcmene was the wife of Amphitryon. She was virtuous and faithful but was seduced by Zeus/Jupiter who had taken on the appearance of her husband. The child born of this union was Hercules. *On peut s'amuser à appliquer aux nouveaux souverains français de la V^ème le schéma Jupiter-Mars/ Vénus-Junon de la royauté de l'Ancien Régime.* © *Le Point 1912.* The context of this quote is the sexual mores of politicians of the fifth Republic with their numerous mistresses and their legitimate and illegitimate offspring.

### Jupiter (la cuisse de)         `***`

*Est-ce que c'est la bonne jambe de Sarah Bernhardt … ou la cuisse de Jupiter.* © *Le Canard Enchaîné 4603.* The reference concerns a leg, preserved in formalin, that was discovered at the faculty of medicine in Bordeaux and thought to be that of Sarah Bernhardt who had her leg amputated in 1915 because of gangrene. See above 'cuisse de Jupiter'.

### jupitérienne (une colère)         `**`

Zeus was the god of lightning and thunderbolts but it is the Roman equivalent Jupiter which gives the French language the expression 'foudres' and 'colère' jupitérienne(s). Such divine wrath is terrifying. *Les colères jupitériennes du président, tétanisent.* © *Marianne 568.* President Sarkozy is well known for losing his temper and insulting his staff.

### labyrinthe nm.         `***`

This was the structure built by Daedalus for King Minos of Crete to house the Minotaur. It refers to any maze or confusing path, route or journey. *Double point de départ d'une fiction en ramifications stériles, plombée par un scénario dont la construction en labyrinthe masque mal la pauvreté d'inspiration.* © *Le Nouvel Observateur 2358.* This text is part of the negative review of a film *Mr Nobody* by Jaco Van Dormael.

### lauriers (tresser des) nmpl.          `*`

To sing sb's praises. Laurels were the classical symbol of glory and well deserved success. *Ceux qui critiquent leurs camarades en tressant des lauriers à Sarkozy n'ont rien à faire au PS.* These are the words of the then national secretary of the socialist party quoted in © *Le Point 1884.* They were directed against Manuel Valls, the MP and mayor of Evry who often formulates criticism against his own party while being, in the eyes of some people, over-indulgent towards Nicolas Sarkozy.

### Lesbos                                                    [ * ]
See below 'sapphique'.

### mânes nmpl.                                               [ ** ]
The 'mânes' were the souls of the dead in the Roman religion. *Polémique garantie quand, contre l'opposition, il [Sarkozy] convoque les mânes de Blum.* © *L'Express 3002.* A reference to Nicolas Sarkozy stealing the thunder of the socialist icons, e.g. Blum and Juarès who have been cited in several of his speeches.

### mécène nm.                                                [ *** ]
Caïus Cilnius Maecenas (69–8 BC) was a wealthy Roman citizen who treated the city to theatrical representations in the century BC. Horace and Virgil both enjoyed his patronage. Hence the term for a rich patron of the arts. *Mais sur les bords de la Loire, bien protégé derrière son pont-levis, René trouva le temps d'être un grand mécène.* © *Le Figaro 20 344.* This text refers to 'le roi René' (1409–80), king of Sicily, of Naples, and of Aragon, duke of Anjou and of Lorraine, and count of Provence, who also found the time to play the role of patron of the arts.

### Méduse nf.                                                [ *** ]
*Les Français, médusés découvrent que la banque Dexia, renflouée par les deniers des contribuables, a distribué des millions d'euros à ses anciens cadres dirigeants.* © *Le Nouvel Observateur 2321.* In Greek mythology, Medusa was one of the three Gorgons. She petrified anyone who looked at her.

### messager de mauvaises nouvelles nm.                       [ ** ]
This term can be found in *Antigone* by Sophocles. 'Personne n'aime le messager porteur de mauvaises nouvelles.' The bearer of bad news was executed. *Dans ce scandale, j'ai le sentiment d'avoir été le messager des mauvaises nouvelles, celui qu'il faut tuer après les avoir entendues.* © *L'Express 2990.* These words were written in relation to the scandal of the notebooks of the head of the RG (the political intelligence unit) Yves Bertrand. See Chapter 14 'RG'.

### Messaline                                                 [ * ]
Valeria Messalina (25–48 BC) was the third wife of the emperor Claudius. She was executed in 48 BC for her scandalous behaviour and loose living and for plotting to overthrow the emperor. *Mais c'est une Messaline sentimentale. A 59 ans, elle tombe amoureuse de Kirk McCambley, qui en a 19.* © *Le Nouvel Observateur 2361.* This quote refers to the adulterous love affair of the Irish Premier's wife. See above 'Hermione'.

## Midas

**\*\***

The legendary Greek king of Phrygia who was granted the power of turning everything that he touched into gold. Not being able to drink or eat, he asked for his wish to be cancelled. He was told to wash his hands in the river Pactolus, thus turning their sands into gold. *A sa naissance en 1973* [Gold Disc] *ce trophée n'était pas cette galette clinquante arborée par des fringants Midas qui ont transformé en or ou en platine ce qu'ils ont chanté.* © *Marianne 618*. This text deals with the attribution of Gold Discs in the music industry.

## Midas (le secret de)

**\***

To take revenge for not having won the contest judged by Midas, Apollo gave him donkey's ears. Midas tried to hide them under a Phrygian cap but a servant discovered the truth while cutting Midas's hair. Unable to keep the secret, the servant dug a hole in the sand and shouted 'King Midas has donkey's ears' and filled in the hole immediately. *Un crime a été commis. Il y a longtemps. On l'avait enfoui dans la terre comme le secret du roi Midas.* © *Le Figaro 20 275*. This was a comment on the film *Katalin Varga* (2009), a history of rape and revenge by Peter Strickland.

## mithridatisation nf.

**\***

*Le zapping nous endurcit, nous mithridatise contre les misères d'autrui.* © *Le Point 1949*. Mithridates the Great (132–63 BC) was king of Pontus in Asia Minor. He was afraid of being poisoned and so immunized himself by taking doses of poison in progressively larger quantities. The text above refers to the media coverage of the Haiti earthquake and the innoculating effect of saturation reporting.

## Morphée (dans les bras de)

**\*\***

To be 'in the arms of Morpheus' means to be asleep. Morpheus was the god of dreams. *Il s'était paisiblement abandonné dans les bras de Morphée.* © *Marianne 574*.

## Muses nfpl

**\*\***

The muses were the nine daughters of Zeus and Mnemosyne, and they presided over the arts: Calliope (eloquence and epic poetry), Clio (history), Erato (erotic, lyric poetry), Euterpe (the flute and lyric poetry), Melpomene (tragedy), Polyhymnia (sacred poetry and pantomime), Terpsichore (dancing), Thalia (comedy and pastoral poetry), Urania (astronomy). *Il fut un temps où l'évocation d'une sirène entraînait un frisson de plaisir angoissé, à la pensée des marins attirés au fond des océans par son chant vénéneux. Désormais, ni tentation, ni alarme: après Copenhague, la sirène est la muse de la cacophonie.* © *L'Express 3050*. This was written in the wake of the climate change summit in Copenhagen, the mountain having given birth to a mouse, in great confusion. See below 'sirènes'.

## Narcisse
***

Narcissus. There are several versions of the story of Narcissus, the self-admirer. For Ovid, Narcissus was a very handsome man who spurned all of those who fell in love with him. He was punished by the gods for his cruelty. One day, he went to the river to drink and saw his own reflection with which he fell deeply in love. He died of thirst and self-love. A narcissus flower grew at the spot where he died. *Ainsi Narcisse dédaignait ceux qui auraient tant aimé s'approcher de lui et le séduire.* © *Le Figaro 20 166.* The context of this quotation is the narcissism of politicians and 'the pot calling the kettle black' in the case of Martine Aubry and François Hollande. See below 'narcissique'.

## narcissique adj.
***

Martine Aubry et François Hollande dénoncent *la stratégie narcissique de M. Bayrou.* © *Le Monde 20 015.* See above 'Narcisse'.

## nectar nm.
*

Nectar. This was the mythological drink that was supposed to confer immortality. It was the drink of the gods. *Mais où donc le chroniqueur avait-il sa tête? Avait-il [...] abusé du nectar dont les fidèles de Dionysos croient qu'il leur assure l'immortalité?* © *Le Monde 20 230.* This was a comment on a typographical error in an article on job creation. Instead of writing 300,000 jobs, the figure announced in the headline was 10 million. See above 'Dionysos'. See Chapter 5 'Ouvroir de littérature potentielle'.

## Néron
**

Nero. *Je ne suis pas Néron, c'est un travail collectif.* © *Le Monde 20 224.* These are the words of the Procureur de Paris, Jean-Claude Marin, in reply to criticism of his decision to appeal against the acquittal of Dominique de Villepin in the Clearstream affair. The implication is that the decision was collegial. Nero (37–68 BC) was a Roman emperor (54–68 BC) who was removed from power by the Senate after his paranoia had pushed him to kill all of those people who had hitherto been his most faithful supporters ... including his mother Aggripine. He is said to have committed suicide after his destitution.

## Nessus (le tunique de)
*

'The Coat of Nessus'. Nessus was a centaur who acted as a ferryman on the river Eunos. One day, he ferried Hercules' wife Deianeira (Déjanire) across the river. On reaching the other side he tried to rape her. Seeing this, Hercules slew the centaur with arrows poisoned with the blood of the Lernaean Hydra. As he lay dying, the centaur tricked Hercules' wife into believing that the coat tainted with his blood would serve as a love charm and ensure that

Hercules would be faithful to her. Some time later, she became jealous and sent the coat to her husband. As soon as he put it on, he was assailed by pain and killed himself by throwing himself onto a funeral pyre. Today, the expression usually means a poisoned gift. ***Je refuse pour ma part, de regagner les abris et d'enfiler les vieux uniformes qui ne valent guère mieux, pour la gauche, que la tunique de Nessus.*** © *Le Figaro 20 166*. These are the words of Manuel Valls, socialist *député* criticizing his own party's traditional stand on deliquency and inviting them to evaluate Nicolas Sarkozy's proposals on their merits. See above 'lauriers'.

## Nike     ( * )
This is one of the nicknames of Athena, the goddess of victory. *Nikaia* means victory in Greek (hence the choice of the brand name for the sports shoe) and gives the Roman word *nicaea*, from which the town of Nice takes its name. ***N'oublions pas que Nike est l'un des surnoms d'Athéna, déesse de la victoire.*** ©*Marianne 593*. NB French pronunciation rhymes with 'like'.

## Odyssée nf.     ( *** )
Odyssey. An ancient and epic poem attributed to Homer, relating the wanderings and adventures of Ulysses during the ten years following the fall of Troy. It now refers to any long and eventful journey. ***Huit ans dans la justice internationale: une odyssée de charniers puants … et de coups fourrés.*** © *L'Express 3044*. This is the accusation levelled at the world of international justice and politics by the ex-Prosecutor of the International Criminal Tribunal, Carla Del Ponte, concerning her investigations of war crimes in the former Yugoslavia.

## Œdipienne     ( *** )
***La bombe œdipienne; en héritant de l'Epad, Jean Sarkozy redevient aussi un simple fils à papa bac + 1.*** © *Le Nouvel Observateur 2346*. Nicolas Sarkozy, as a child, suffered from the absence of his father, who abandoned the family while Nicolas was still a young boy. Sarkozy was himself an absent father. Some specialists see his efforts with his son, Jean, as an attempt to compensate for his earlier absence. 'Bac + 1' refers to an academic level one year after the school-leaving certificate, i.e. first year of university. A master's degree is thus bac + 4.

## oiseau de mauvais augure     ( *** )
***L'affaire du prince Jean devrait plomber la campagne et l'élection de Douillet Raté pour les oiseaux de mauvais augure.*** © *Le Nouvel Observateur 2346*. Many people predicted a bad result for the presidential party, the UMP, in the by-election in Poissy in 2009. In spite of all the scandals and rows surrounding the president, his candidate, the former judo world champion, won the election. See above 'augures'.

### Olympe. L'                                              `***`

Mount Olympus, the highest mountain in Greece, is traditionally known as the home of the gods. *Ces femmes-là, les conseillères, sont des déesses, elles sont sur l'Olympe.* © *Le Nouvel Observateur 2295.* This text refers to the film, *Les Bureaux de Dieu,* directed by Claire Simon, which addresses the problems of family planning, abortion, etc., the role of each abortion case being played by a famous French actress.

### oracle nm.                                              `***`

Oracle comes from the Latin word *oraculum* meaning 'word' or 'reply of a god'. Among the ancient Greeks and Romans it was either the sacred place where the gods were consulted, or the person through whom a god replied. Today, it is used to refer to anyone who speaks with great authority and who enjoys great standing. *Après une coupe de champagne et deux petits fours, l'oracle s'éclipse sous les regards enamourés de ses fans.* © *Le Nouvel Observateur 2295.* This is a reference to the Wall Street guru and speculator Jim Rogers.

### pactole nm.                                              `***`

Pactolus, the name of the river in ancient Lydia (Asia Minor), the gold-bearing sands of which provided Croesus with his immense wealth. The term *pactole* could be translated by 'a packet', 'a tidy sum' or 'a small fortune'. *La Chine dispose de 1,400 milliards d'euros de réserves de change, mais ce pactole enviable, à première vue, ne représente pas de ressources stables et sûres, comme celles des pays du Moyen-Orient.* © *Le Nouvel Observateur 2295.* See above 'Midas'.

### pain et des jeux de cirque. Du                           `***`

'Bread and circuses' from the Latin expression of Juvenal *panem et circenses.* This was at the heart of the strategy of submission of the people used by Roman emperors that consisted in providing food and entertainment. *Et pour le peuple, les jeux olympiques du cirque.* © *Le Canard Enchaîné 4582.*

### Panathénées nfpl.                                        `*`

This is the name given to the annual religious festivities held in Athens to celebrate the birth of the goddess Athena, the patron saint of the city (Minerva in Roman mythology). She was the goddess of wisdom (hence the symbol of the owl for the city of Athens) and also god of the art of war. The first festivities were held in 566 BC and were inspired by (although less important than) the Olympic Games. *Pour racoler l'imaginaire collectif depuis que le sport, par le truchement de la télé, a cessé de mimer les Panathénées pour ressusciter les jeux des cirques romains. Il focalise désormais des pulsions qui n'ont pas d'âge.* © *Marianne 601.* This article was written in the wake of the whistling that accompanied the singing of 'La Marseillaise' just before the kick-off of a friendly match between France and Tunisia in 2008.

The author suggests that the fault lies in part with the politicians who have taken sport hostage in their attempt to gain votes and provide 'circuses' for the masses.

### Pandore (boîte de) nf.                                    ***

'Pandora's box'. In Greek mythology, Pandora was the first mortal woman. She had been created as the punishment for man. Zeus had given her a jar (not a box) with the order not to open it. However, her curiosity led her to open the famous 'box', thus letting out all of the human ills. Another version suggests that all of the human blessings escaped on the same occasion and were irretrievably lost. She closed the box before 'hope', which was at the bottom of the box, could escape. Only 'hope' remained. Today, the expression 'to open Pandora's box' implies starting a process over which one risks losing control and the consequences of which may be very prejudicial. *Reste que l'émergence d'un Iran nucléaire ouvrirait la boîte de Pandore de la prolifération.* © *L'Express 3037.*

### panthéon nm.                                              ***

From the Greek *Pantheion* meaning 'of all the gods'. The Latinized form of the *Pantheon* in Rome was thus 'the temple of all the gods'. *Au panthéon de nos hommes d'État figurent tout d'abord ceux qui se sont immolés au feu de leurs convictions.* © *Le Nouvel Observateur 2358.* See Chapter 10 'Panthéon'.

### Pégase                                                    **

See above 'Hermès'.

### pénates (regagner ses) nmpl.                              ***

'To go back home'. In ancient Rome, the Penates (in the narrow sense of the term) were the gods who protected the hearth. By extension, they also protected the welfare of the household. Statuettes representing these gods were often placed in the hearth and consequently these gods were closely associated with Vesta, the god of the flames of the hearth. *Martine Aubry a rejoint ses pénates lillois.* © *Le Canard Enchaîné 4571.* Martine Aubry is the mayor of Lille.

### Pénélope                                                  ***

Penelope. This was the name of Ulysses' wife. During the years he was away fighting in the Trojan War, Penelope remained faithful to him, refusing the offers of many suitors. They became impatient with her and moved into Ulysses' palace. Penelope announced that she would choose one of them once she had finished making a shroud for her father-in-law. She spent her day weaving the shroud, but at night she undid what she had done during the day. The work of Penelope is therefore an unending task of patience. *Le président, en sage Pénélope, dénouera la broderie tissée depuis quatre ans.* © *L'Express 3063.* This is a reference to the announcement made by Nicolas Sarkozy that he will slow down the reform process and 'delegislate', i.e. cancel certain laws considered to be useless, and this with the threat of a possible socialist Senate in 2011.

### Phénix nm.                                    ***

The phoenix was a mythical bird which, at the end of its life, would build a nest of sweet smelling twigs (cinnamon) and would then ignite it. The bird and the nest were reduced to ashes from which a new and young phoenix would arise. *Les intégristes du capitalisme autorégulé, qui corrigerait de lui-même ses excès, pour renaître de ses cendres tel le Phénix, doivent se rendre à l'évidence: avec la crise actuelle, les grandes théories sur la "destruction créa-trice", ont atteint leurs limites.* © *Le Figaro 19 963.* Some liberal fundamentalists believe that the financial disaster of 2008 is creative destruction that will see the rebirth of capitalism. This text, in a right-wing newspaper, suggests that this theory has reached its limits.

### Pléiades nfpl.                                 ***

In Greek mythology, this was the name given to the seven daughters of Atlas and Pleione. The giant Orion fell in love with them and pursued them with his unwelcome advances. Zeus took pity on them and turned them into doves and thus took them out of harm's way. When they died, they were placed in heaven in the constellation of the Bull. In literary history, the Pleiades were a group of seven sixteenth-century poets who were considered to be the pre-eminent stars of their time, two of the most famous of them being Ronsard and du Bellay. In the singular, *La Pléiade* is also the name of the most prestigious collection of literary works published in France by the publisher Gallimard. To be published in this collection is the supreme accolade for a writer. In more common usage, it means an illustrious group of people. *Mais pas plus de Pléiade que de beurre en branche, comme disait l'auteur [Céline] de 'Voyage au bout de la nuit'.* © *L'Express 20 120.* This text refers to the fact that the correspondence of Céline is going to be published in *La Pléiade.*

### pomme de discorde nf.                          ***

'The bone of contention', the subject of a dispute. In Greek mythology, the goddess Discord was not invited to the wedding feast of Peleus and Thetis. To take revenge for this affront, she threw a golden apple among the wedding guests; Juno (Hera), Minerva (Athena) and Venus (Aphrodite) fought over the apple. Inscribed on the apple were the words 'for the fairest'. Zeus asked Paris to choose the fairest among them. He chose Venus, who promised him the love of Helen of Troy. He later kidnapped Helen, thus triggering the Trojan War. **Guantanamo, pomme de discorde européenne.** © *Le Figaro 20 120*.

**prométhéen adj.**                                                    [ *** ]

Promethean refers to somebody's taste for action and faith in man. The Promethean dream is of man becoming the master of his own destiny. **Il [l'inconnu] endommage un capital prométhéen fondé sur la maîtrise progressive de la nature et la domestication de ses caprices.** © *Le Point 1912*. The factor of the unknown tends to damage the Promethean idea that we can progressively master nature. See above 'feu sacré'.

**Protée**                                                    [ * ]

Proteus was a sea god who could assume various forms. In modern French it refers to people who are always changing their opinion and playing different roles. **Une vingtaine d'années plus tard, l'artiste Protée s'essaie à amadouer Betty Lagardère, l'épouse du capitaine de l'industrie.** © *L'Express 3002*. This is a reference to the highly versatile François-Marie Banier, who succeeded in obtaining €1 billion from the richest woman in France, Lilliane Bettencourt. She was not his first 'conquest'.

**Pygmalion**                                                    [ *** ]

Pygmalion was a sculptor about whom Ovide writes in the book of *Metamorphoses*. He sculpts the most perfect statue of a woman and then falls in love with his own creation. Aphrodite takes pity on him and brings the statue to life. Her name was Galatea. **Seule grande comédienne française (avec Sophie Marceau) à réussir dans le métier sans se frotter aux cours d'art dramatique. Sandrine [Bonnaire] rencontre enfin, en 1983, son Pygmalion. Il s'appelle Maurice [Pialat].** © *Le Nouvel Observateur 2366*. The Pygmalion effect is often observed in schools and corporations and highlights the fact that high expectations can indirectly influence performance.

**Pyrrhus (une victoire à la)**                                                    [ *** ]

'A Pyrrhic victory'. After his victory over the Romans at Asculum in 279 BC, Pyrrhus (319–272 BC) said 'another such victory and we are lost'. Today, it refers to a victory that is gained at too high a price. **Villepin va de nouveau se retrouver devant les tribunaux. C'est une victoire à la Pyrrhus.** © *Le Monde 20 223*. The background to this quote is the appeal lodged by the public prosecutor against the decision of the criminal court to acquit Dominique de Villepin. Dominique de Villepin will be obliged to stand trial again for complicity in defamatory denunciation in the Clearstream affair. This decision is seen as highlighting the lack of independence of the *Parquet* which is under the direct control of the minister of justice who in turn answers to the president. This has enabled Dominique de Villepin to speak about President

Sarkozy's relentless fight to see him behind bars. It is an expensive victory for Sarkozy.

### Pythie de Delphes nf.

'The Pythia of Delphi'. In Greek mythology, she was the high priestess of Delphi. Seated on a three-legged stool over a crevasse from which vapours escaped, she would go into a trance and shout incoherent phrases that were interpreted by the priests as Apollo's oracle. Because of the enigmatic responses 'Delphic' has come to mean deliberately obscure or predictive. *Las Vegas, grande pythie du numérique.* © *Le Point 1949.* This heading refers to the Consumer Electronic Show that is held in Las Vegas every year and is a good indication of where digital technology is going.

### roche Tarpéienne nf.

The Tarpeian Rock. This was the name of a mountain ridge located at the extreme south-west of the Capitol in Rome and was a place of capital punishment. Criminals were thrown to their death from the Tarpeian Rock. It is referred to in the quotation *Arx tarpeia Capitoli proxima* 'the Tarpeian Rock is close to the Capitol', i.e. after great honours one may know ignominious death. On the other hand, it can be used in the sense, albeit less frequently, that even after being out of favour, one may still rise to great honours. *Il est une vieille loi en politique: de même que la roche Tarpéienne est proche du Capitole, de même un acteur politique peut toujours revenir au sommet.* © *Le Figaro 19 861.*

### Rubicon (franchir le) nm.

'To cross the Rubicon'. The Rubicon is the name of a small river in northern Italy which, from 59 BC onwards, constituted the boundary between Cisalpine Gaul and the Roman Republic. When Caesar crossed the Rubicon in 49 BC in pursuit of Pompey, he knew that he was violating the law of the Roman Senate forbidding a general to lead his army out of his province. Caesar knew that his action was an act of war against the Senate and Pompey. On crossing the Rubicon, he is said to have pronounced the words *alea jacta est* ('the die is cast'). Today, 'to cross the Rubicon' means to take some irrevocable action the consequences of which may be risky. *La vérité, c'est que Pérol n'avait pas forcément envie de franchir le Rubicon.* © *Le Point 1909.* This refers to François Pérol's nomination as chairman of the national savings bank, *La Caisse d'Épargne et Les Banques Populaires.* He is seen as a political appointee of N. Sarkozy. See Chapter 9 'Pérol'.

### saphique adj.

Sapphic. This is a term that comes from Sappho, the Greek poetess, born on the island of Lesbos, who dedicated her love poems to other women. The term 'tribadisme' also refers to female homosexuality but is very dated and closely associated with the period of the Belle Époque. ***Croyez-nous, Sapho le détour.*** © *Marianne 577.* A pun 'ça vaut le détour' referring to the beautiful island of Lesbos as a holiday destination.

**saturnales nfpl.**

[ * ]

In ancient Rome, this was the name given to the orgiastic celebrations of Saturn during which no holds were barred and slaves behaved on an equal footing with their masters. ***Si les ouvriers découvraient chez leur patron un peu d'humanité, un peu de solidarité entre les classes sans laquelle il n'est pas de société possible, ils passeraient facilement sur ces saturnales de la richesse que nous avons connues dans la dernière période.*** © *Le Nouvel Observateur 2321.* This is a comment on the reaction of the workers faced with the excessive bonuses paid to their employers. It is not that the workers are jealous of the bosses' golden parachutes so much as insulted by the attitude of the employers who never apply to themselves the rules that they apply to everyone else in terms of tightening the belt.

**Saturne**

[ * ]

Saturn (the Romanized form of the Greek Cronus) was a mythological figure who, fearing that his children would overthrow him, ate them at their birth. ***De toute façon, Chirac est seul. Saturne aussi dévora ses enfants.*** © *L'Express 3044.* This is a reference to the fact that Chirac has no real successor since he sacrificed them all, one after the other, e.g. Juppé, de Villepin.

**satyres nmpl.**

[ * ]

Satyrs. These were the deities who attended on Bacchus. They are represented as having pointed ears, short horns, an enormous phallus, with the head and torso of a man and the legs of a goat. They were fond of merriment and lechery. Today, the term is used to refer to a lustful man, particularly an elderly one. ***Il [Bernanos] serait sans pitié pour ces brames offusqués de patronnesses en mal de satyre.*** © *Marianne 573.* 'Bramer' is 'to bawl' or 'to wail'. The words of Denis Tillinac to qualify the concert of disproportionate indignation expressed by politicians and others concerning the football match in 2008 between the PSG and RC Lens (a team from the north of France) during which a 'banderole', insulting the Ch'tis, was displayed.

**sexe des anges nm.**

[ ** ]

See above 'byzantinisme'.

**sirènes nf.**

[ *** ]

Sirens or mermaids. These were mythical sea nymphs or demons who, through their beautiful singing, drew sailors to their death. The sailors, hearing the beautiful voices, would approach the coast too closely, be shipwrecked on the rocks and were devoured by the sirens. Ulysses gave orders that his men should fill their ears with beeswax and that he himself should be tied to the mast and not be released under any circumstances. He was thus able to resist the call of the sirens. 'Céder à l'appel des sirènes' is thus 'to succumb to the lure of some attraction' (money, a ministerial post, etc.). *Nombre d'armateurs ... voient leurs meilleurs matelots céder aux sirènes – dorées – des poseurs de câbles sous-marins.* © *L'Express 3020*. This text refers to the poaching of the best sailors to work on cable-laying ships where salaries are much higher than elsewhere in the profession.

## Sisyphe                                                                                    ★★

There are several versions of the story of Sisyphus, son of Eol. For having denounced Zeus to Asopos concerning the kidnapping of Egine, Sisyphus was condemned to roll a rock up the mountainside. It systematically fell to the bottom and Sisyphus was obliged to start all over again, forever rolling the rock to the top of the mountain. Today, it refers to any hard and fruitless labour. *Le Sisyphe du budget. Comme Sisyphe, Gilles Carrez n'a pas fini de rouler son rocher.* © *Le Nouvel Observateur 2346*. See Chapter 9 'Carrez'.

## Socrate                                                                                    ★★

Socrates saw his role as that of a midwife. As a midwife delivers the child from the mother, so Socrates saw his role as delivering knowledge from the individual that the individual possesses without realizing it. The Socratic method is known as 'maieutic', (*maieutikos*) *maia* meaning 'midwife' in Greek. *Depuis 5 ou 6 ans nos professeurs, à l'instar de Socrate, nous font accoucher du kalos kagathos, du beau et du bien caché en nous.* Sister Emmanuelle quoted in © *Le Point 1884*. See Chapter 9.

## Socrate                                                                                    ★★

*Socrate est mort en laissant des dettes. A ses disciples il déclara: 'Nous devons un coq à Asclépios, payez-le, ne l'oubliez pas'. Mystérieuse recommandation, ultimes paroles rapportées par Platon dans 'le Phédon'.* © *Le Canard Enchaîné 4672*. This text discusses the problem of the European debt and evokes the story of the cock that Socrates owed Aesculapius which is mentioned in Plato's *Phaedo*.

## Sosthène                                                                                   ★

When the Argonauts wanted to cross the Bosphorous, they were prevented from doing so by Amycos. They took refuge in a small creek. It was there that they met a huge winged man who predicted that they would defeat Amycos. Encouraged by this prediction, the Argonauts attacked Amycos and defeated him. They subsequently built a sanctuary to the man who had given them reassurance and honoured him under the name of Sosthenes. Admiral Philippe de Gaulle's nickname at the French naval academy was 'Sosthène'. *Il sera l'un des derniers de sa promotion à revoir ses étoiles avant de commander l'escadre de l'Atlantique. Il s'en plaint mais rien n'y fait 'Sosthène' – c'est son surnom, joue les lanternes rouges.* © *Marianne 652*. This text highlights the difference between de Gaulle's attitude of non-interference with his son's professional advancement (his son was one of the last to obtain command of a fleet), and that of the string-pulling Nicolas Sarkozy in relation to his. 'Jouer les lanternes rouges' 'to lag behind'.

### sphinx nm.

[ * ]

The Sphinx speaks in riddles. *On l'appelle le 'sphinx'. Pour son mystère, son côté insondable.* © *L'Express 3048*. This quote refers to the introverted character of the head of the CGT trades union, Bernard Thibault.

### Tables de la Loi nfpl.

[ * ]

*Lex Duodecim Tabularum* (Law of the Twelve Tables) represent the first body of written Roman law drawn up around 450 BC. *Nous sommes entrés dans une autre ère, nous habitons une autre planète. Ce pays [USA] j'en suis témoin, a fait serment, devant les Tables de la Loi, de se métamorphoser du tout au tout.* © *Marianne 603*. This is a reflection on the change in the attitude of the USA towards the rest of the world at the moment when Obama swore his oath during the investiture ceremony. See Chapter 8 'Tables de la Loi'.

### tentation de Démocrite nf.

[ * ]

*C'est une tentation que chacun d'entre nous a connu. Qui revient parfois. La tentation de Démocrite? Celle du recours aux forêts.* © *L'Express 3047*. Democritus (460?–370? BC) was a Greek philosopher who, sickened by what he had seen of man during a long journey from Greece to India, decided to build a hut at the end of his garden and live in it. It is the temptation of 'back to the woods'.

### thébaïde nf.

[ ** ]

A solitary retreat. The classical name for the southern part of Upper Egypt. *C'est la plus extraordinaire thébaïde hexagonale pour milliardaires … la Villa Montmorency.* © *Le Canard Enchaîné 4589*. NB: the term *La Thébaïde* can also be used to refer to the enemy brothers Etiocles and Polynices in the tragedy by Racine inspired in turn by the story of Antigone. See above 'Antigone'.

### Thermopyles (Thermopylae)

[ * ]

*Mais comme aux Thermopyles, 300 contre 10 000 – la civilisation indoeuropéenne s'appuie toujours sur un petit nombre d'hommes libres contre des myriades d'esclaves.* © *Le Point 1896*. A reference to the battle in 480 BC which saw a small Greek army defeat a much bigger Persian army, the idea here being that a small army of free men is worth more than a large army of slaves.

### titanesque adj.        

Titanic. The Titans is the generic name given to the six sons of Uranus and Gaea (Gaia). They were overthrown by the Olympians in a struggle that is known as the 'Titanomachy'. Today, it refers to anything of imposing size or strength. ***FDR, toujours révéré pour avoir en cent jours remis l'Amérique au travail par des chantiers publics titanesques.*** © *L'Express 3002*. This text refers to the gigantic public works programmes thanks to which Roosevelt got Americans back to work.

### Titan (un travail/combat de)       ***

***A partir du lendemain, un boulot de titan attend les délégués envoyés à Saint Denis par les 470 comités locaux anticapitalistes.*** © *Le Nouvel Observateur 2228*. This refers to the work in store for the delegates of the new anti-capitalist party NPA.

### Toison d'or nf.       ***

The Golden Fleece was Jason's objective in his quest with the Argonauts. ***Seuls quelques intellectuels français vont s'en fâcher. Leur Toison d'Or c'est un système d'équarrissage égalitaire.*** © *Le Point 1884*. This text must be understood in the context of the crash of capitalism and the state bailouts of the banking system and the fact that the market economy is here to stay. Only leftist intellectuals will regret that fact. 'Équarrissage' is the cutting up or quartering of a slaughtered animal, or the slaughtering process itself.

### Troie       **

***Tout Cassandre veut voir Troie en cendres.*** © *L'Express 3063*. This is a remark concerning a rather pessimistic book by Eric Zemmour entitled *Mélancolie française*, published by Fayard in 2010, and dealing with the fact that the French never recovered from Waterloo and that France was demo-graphically killed by its victory in 1918. The author of this book seems to take an unhealthy delight in France's misfortunes. See above 'Cassandre'.

### Ulysse       **

***Les siens l'attendent. Les siens: sa femme Lily, son petit garçon Louis. Et son chien. Et comme au retour d'Ulysse, c'est d'abord le chien qui va jaillir.*** © *Le Nouvel Observateur 2358*. When Ulysses returned home after his wanderings, he was first recognized by his old dog Argos. These lines refer to a new novel by the writer Christian Gailly. See also Chapter 5 'Heureux qui comme Ulysse'.

## Vestales nfpl.                                                    [ * ]

*Mais Guaino [presidential ghostwriter and advisor] n'est pas que la vestale du temple des promesses.* © *Marianne 577.* The vestal virgins were priestesses of Vesta and were in charge of keeping the sacred flame alight.

## Xénophon                                                         [ * ]

Xenophon, a Greek military leader and historian (430–355 BC) who led the retreat of the Ten Thousand mercenaries after the battle of Cunaxa. *Gordon Brown ... contemplant le Parti travailliste, commençait à se demander s'il ne compterait pas bientôt, comme l'armée de Xénophon, plus de morts que de vivants.* © *Marianne 631.* The context of this quote is the scandal over certain socialist MPs and their padded expense accounts and the damage that it has done to socialist party ranks in which, like Xenophon's army, the corpses outnumber the living.

## Zeus                                                             [ * ]

The greatest of all the gods in the Hellenic Pantheon. Son of Cronus and Rhea, he is essentially the god of light, lightning storms and tempests. His Roman equivalent, Jupiter, is frequently associated with divine wrath. *Le courroux du cheik éclata tel le feu de Zeus.* © *Marianne 591.* This refers to the anger of some Gulf sheiks faced with criticism from the United Nations over the abusive treatment of children 'bought' in Pakistan and kept underweight in order to provide battalions of 'light' jockeys for horse racing.

# Chapter 8

# Biblical references

In Britain's and America's multi-ethnic society, it can no longer be taken for granted that every reader will possess good biblical knowledge. One must also remember that under the terms of the French Act of 1905 on the separation of church and state, religious instruction is forbidden in state schools (with the exception of Alsace and Lorraine). Consequently, many very highly educated French people show surprising ignorance of things biblical and this chapter should prove useful to the French reader. Translations have been included because many readers will not necessarily have a Bible to hand and this may well be the only contact they will have with the original texts. The translations of the sources have been grouped together at the end of this chapter. NB: the capitalization of nouns is not always consistent between the English and French versions of the Bible.

**Adam**                                                                              *

Adam (in Hebrew *âdâm* means 'earth') was the first man in creation. 'And the Lord God formed man of the dust of the ground and breathed into his nostrils the breath of life.' *Alors Yahvé modela l'homme avec la glaise du sol, il insuffla dans ses narines une haleine de vie.* See Genesis 2, 7. Eve (in Hebrew *hawwâh* means 'life' or possibly 'the snake') was the first woman. See Genesis 3: 20. *En somme, le capitalisme est né lorsqu'Ève a commencé à marchander la pomme maléfique avec Adam.* © *Marianne 600.*

**agapes nfpl.**                                                                    ***

Banquet, feast, spread, etc. From the Greek word signifying 'love' it was originally the name of a meal taken by the early Christian communities that was both fraternal and liturgical in character. The practice, however, degenerated into orgies and it is clearly condemned in The General Epistle of Jude (12): 'These are they who are hidden rocks in your love feasts.' *Ce sont eux les écueils de vos agapes. Ils ont fait le déplacement mais assurent le service minimum. Dîners annulés, et agapes reportées.* © *Le Point 1910.* In the morose context of the automobile industry, the exhibitors at the Geneva Car Show are cutting back on superfluous expenses such as champagne and *petits fours.*

## Aimez-vous

**\*\***

'A new commandment I give unto you, that ye love one another.' *Je vous donne un commandement nouveau: Aimez-vous les uns les autres.* See the Gospel according to St John 13: 34. ***Aimez-vous les uns les autres, ou disparaissez.*** © *Le Canard Enchaîné 4584.* These were the words of Juliette Greco.

## Alpha et l'Oméga. L'

**\*\*\***

The first and last letters of the Greek alphabet. 'I am the Alpha and the Omega, the beginning and the end.' *Je suis l'Alpha et l'Oméga, le Principe et la Fin.* See Revelation 1: 8 and 21: 6. ***Mais un individu abstrait de son milieu dont le but ultime est le bonheur, ce n'est pas l'alpha et l'oméga sur la planète.*** © *Le Point 1909.*

## Apocalypse nf.

**\*\*\***

Apocalypse, from the Greek *apokalupsis*, which in turn derives from the Hebrew *nigla* meaning 'the lifting of the veil', or 'revelation'. It is the last book of the New Testament, Revelation, which deals with the ultimate triumph of good and the destruction of evil. It is generally understood as 'the end of the world'. ***Envoi de pétitions à Bruxelles qui annoncent l'Apocalypse pour l'agriculture française.*** © *Le Point 1909.*

## apôtre nm.

**\*\***

Apostle. In Greek, *aposolos* means 'someone sent out with a message'. In the Christian church, it refers to the twelve apostles of Christ who were entrusted with spreading the good news. ***Ils écrivent 'Give peace a chance', interprété dans le brouhaha avec Timothy Leary et Allen Ginsberg, apôtres de la contestation américaine.*** © *Libération 8722.*

## appelés et peu d'élus. Beaucoup d'

**\*\***

*Multi sunt vocati pauci vero electi.* In the Gospel according to St Matthew 22: 14 we can read 'For many are called but few are chosen.' *Car il y a beaucoup d'appelés, mais peu d'élus.* The pun here is on 'élu' which can be translated by 'chosen' or 'elected' in the electoral meaning of the term. ***C'est beaucoup d'exclus et peu d'élus.*** © *Le Point 1882.* This is related to the socialist electoral infighting in the *département* of the Hérault (34). See below 'grincement des dents'.

## Arche de l'alliance. L'

The word 'ark' comes from the Hebrew *aron* that comes in turn from the root *ar* (light) and the suffix *on* (force). The Ark of the Covenant is described in the Bible as a sacred container carried by seven priests. In it were supposed to have been deposited manna, Aaron's rod and the remains of the stone tablets bearing the Ten Commandments. It is regarded as the testimony of God's covenant with the children of Israel. The Ark was seen as the strength of the people and accompanied them in battle. It is mentioned in several books of the Bible: Joshua, Exodus, Deuteronomy, Samuel, Jeremiah and Psalms. *Après tant d'avanies, l'adoption d'une nouvelle arche d'alliance peut-elle encore éviter le choc frontal?* © *Marianne 614.* The context is the refoundation of democracy in Bolivia giving more representation to the native inhabitants. The question is whether or not a 'new deal' is possible or whether there will be further confrontation.

### Arche de Noé. L'    \*\*
*Arche de Noé: Si la réalité du Déluge peut toujours faire débat, banquiers et assureurs ont désormais la certitude de son existence … l'Arche financière n'est pas encore sauvée des eaux.* © *Les Echos 20 424.* The context of this quotation is the financial crisis that has hit the banking sector and the belief that the financial world is not out of the woods yet. See 'Déluge' below.

### argent. Les trente pièces d'    \*
Judas Iscariot betrayed Jesus for thirty pieces of silver. 'Then one of the twelve, who was called Judas Iscariot, went unto the chief priests, And said "What are ye willing to give me, and I will deliver him unto you?" And they weighed unto him thirty pieces of silver.' *Alors l'un des Douze, appelé Judas Iscariot(e), se rendit auprès des grands prêtres et leur dit: 'Que voulez-vous me donner, et moi je vous le livrerai'? Ceux-ci lui versent trente pièces d'argent.* See Matthew 26: 14–15. *Sarko, pour lui [Eric Besson, the socialist turncoat] n'a même pas eu à débourser les trente deniers de Judas.* © *Le Canard Enchaîné 4584.* President Sarkozy didn't have to pay anything for Besson's betrayal: he came only too willingly.

### Armageddon    \*
In the New Testament, it is a place that symbolizes the struggle between good and evil. The term appears once in the Apocalypse, i.e. The Book of Revelation. 'And they gathered them together into the place which is called in Hebrew 'Har-Magedon'. *Ils les rassemblèrent au lieu dit en hébreu 'Harmagedôn'.* See Revelation 16: 16. Today, it implies a catastrophic battle on a planetary scale. *C'est une société dont le cours a rebondi de 100% et plus … en plein Armageddon boursier.* © *Les Echos 20 636.*

### Au commencement était le verbe    \*
'In the beginning was the Word.' *Car en maçonnerie, tous les symboles sont des outils pour retrouver la parole, les racines chrétiennes de nos rituels étant indiscutables. ('Au commencement était le verbe …').* © *L'Express 3047.* This is a remark concerning the Christian roots of freemasonry. See John 1: 1.

## Babel                                                     [ ** ]

This is the name of a city in Shinar where Noah's descendants tried to build
a high tower that would reach heaven. Until that time men had shared the
same language and the same words. God thwarted the project with confusion of tongues. Today, it is a synonym of noise and confusion. 'And the
whole earth was of one language ... And they said 'Go to, let us build us a
city, and a tower, whose top may reach into heaven'. And the Lord said 'Go
to, let us go down and there confound their language, that they may not
understand one another's speech.' *Tout le monde se servait d'une même
langue et des mêmes mots ... Ils dirent 'Allons! Bâtissons-nous une ville et une
tour dont le sommet pénètre les cieux' ... Et Yahvé dit. ... 'Allons, Descen-
dons! Et là confondons leur langage pour qu'ils ne s'entendent plus les uns les
autres.'* See Genesis 11: 1, 4, and 7. ***Babel de qualité.*** © *Libération 8716*. The
context of this quotation was the profusion of films, of greatly varying
quality, at the 2009 Cannes film festival.

## Babylone                                                  [ ** ]

Babylon. This word literally means 'the gate of God'. Capital of Babylonia,
it was a city situated on the lower Euphrates river, notorious for its wealth,
luxury and wickedness. In the book of Revelation (Apocalypse), it is compared to a harlot. 'Babylone ... the mother of the harlots and of the abominations of the earth.' *Babylone ... la mère des prostituées et des
abominations de la terre.* See Revelation 17: 5. André Glucksmann, in relation to the crisis of capitalism, speaks about ***des rebelles sans cause et des
académiciens sans emploi vitupérant la Babylone moderne.*** © *Le Figaro 20
137*. NB: *Rebel Without a Cause* was the title of the 1955 film directed by
Nicholas Ray and starring James Dean.

## baiser de Judas (le baiser qui tue)                        [ * ]

*Il n'y a pas pire que le baiser qui tue.* © *Le Canard Enchaîné 4573*. The
kiss of Judas, the kiss of death. In order that the Roman soldiers should
know whom to arrest in the garden of Gethsemene, Judas told them that he
would kiss the man they were to take. To betray with a kiss has since come
to mean to betray with an affectionate gesture. 'Now he that betrayed him
gave them a sign saying, "Whomsoever I shall kiss, that is he: take him".
And straight away he came to Jesus and said, "Hail, Rabbi"; and kissed
him.' *Or le traître leur avait donné ce signe: 'Celui à qui je donnerai un baiser,
c'est lui; arrêtez-le. Et aussitôt il s'approcha de Jésus en disant: 'Salut,
Rabbi'!, et il lui donna un baiser.* See Matthew 26: 48–49. The reader's
attention must be drawn to the fact that the verb 'baiser' in modern French
is not 'to kiss' but is equivalent to the English 'to lay' or 'to screw' and can
be used in the meaning of 'to have sb', i.e. 'to take them in'. It can thus be
said that Judas 'baisa' Jesus in every sense of the word! See above 'argent.
Les trente pièces d''.

## Béhémoth

Béhémoth is a large and powerful beast representing the dangers of the desert. 'Behold now behemoth, which I made with thee; he eateth grass as an ox. Lo now, his strength is in his loins and his force is in the muscles of his belly.' *Mais regarde donc Béhémoth, ma créature tout comme toi! Il se nourrit d'herbe, comme le bœuf. Vois, sa force réside dans ses reins, sa vigueur dans les muscles de son ventre.* See Job 40: 15–16. ***L'Iran voit bientôt surgir un spectre antique et diabolique, Béhémoth.*** © *Marianne 609.* This quote refers to the exile of the Shah of Iran in 1979 and the then looming danger represented by Khomeini.

## Belphégor

*Baal-peor* was an ancient divinity worshipped in the Middle East, and in Christian demonology appears in the form of a woman who seduces her victims by stimulating their curiosity about ways of becoming rich. 'And Moses said unto the judges of Israel, "Slay ye every one of his men that have joined themselves unto Baal-peor".' *Moïse dit aux juges d'Israël: 'Que chacun mette à mort ceux de ses hommes qui se sont commis avec le Baal de Peor.'* See Numbers 25: 5. It is also the title of a fable by La Fontaine. ***Belphégor de l'islamisme belge.*** © *Marianne 60.* This text refers to Malika el-Aroud, a Belgian Islamic fundamentalist of Moroccan origin, who, on the Internet, praised her kamikaze husband who killed Commandant Massoud the day before the attacks of 11 September 2001.

## Belzébuth

A divinity worshipped by the Philistines, he is known as the Prince of Evil, the Lord of Hell. 'And the scribes which came down from Jerusalem said "He hath Beelzebub and, By the prince of the devils casteth he out the devils".' *Et les scribes qui étaient descendus de Jérusalem disaient: 'Il est possédé de Béelzéboul' et encore: 'C'est par le prince des démons qu'il expulse les démons.'* See Mark 3: 22. ***L'acte II, qui s'écrit en ce moment, dépassera tout ce qu'on peut imaginer, promet le petit Belzébuth, ravi de se voir si présent médiatiquement.*** © *Marianne 660.* This is a reference to a comment made by the 'devilish' Eric Besson, the former minister of immigration and national identity, that his future plans will surprise everybody.

## Benjamin/Benjamine nmf

*Le benjamin de l'Assemblée est le député UMP, Edouard Courtial.* © *Le Canard Enchaîné 4584.* The youngest child of several or the younger child of two. Originally this was the youngest of the 12 children of Jacob and the second child of Rachel. Rachel died in childbirth and called her son *Ben-oni* (Hebrew for 'son of my suffering') but Jacob called him *Binyâmin* (Hebrew for 'son of my old age' or 'on the favoured side'). 'And it came to pass, as her soul was in departing (for she died), that she called his name *Ben-oni*: but his father called him 'Benjamin'. *Au moment de rendre l'âme, car elle se mourait, elle le nomma Ben-Oni, mais son père l'appela Benjamin.* See Genesis 35: 18. Benjamin is also the name of one of the 12 tribes of Israel. In the world of sport, it refers to the juniors of 12 to 13 years old.

### bercail. Le retour au                                      `**`

The return to the fold. *Du retour au bercail* [of a negationist who denies the existence of Nazi gas chambers and who is also a fundamentalist bishop], *la brebis égarée se révèle aux yeux du monde une brebis galeuse.* © *Le Canard Enchaîné 4606.* This is a reference to the return to grace of the negationist Bishop Richard Williamson. *Le Canard* suggests that the 'lost sheep' is in fact a 'black sheep'. See below 'brebis égarée'.

### Bête de l'Apocalypse nf.                                    `*`

In the review of the biography of Isaac Newton (see below 'parousie') it is said that Newton discovered the date of the Apocalypse by reading the Revelation St. John. 'He that hath understanding, let him count the number of the beast; for it is the number of a man: and his number is six hundred and sixty-six.' *Celui qui a de l'intelligence, qu'il interprète ce chiffre de la Bête: car c'est un chiffre d'homme et ce chiffre est 666.* St John quoted in © *Les Echos 20 636.* See Revelation 13: 18.

### boisseau. mettre sous le                                    `*`

'Un boisseau' is a measure of grain corresponding to the English 'bushel'. 'No man, when he hath lighted a lamp, putteth it in a cellar, neither under the bushel, but on the stand, that they which enter in may see the light.' *Personne, après avoir allumé une lampe, ne la met en quelque endroit caché ou sous le boisseau, mais bien sur le lampadaire, pour que ceux qui pénètrent voient la clarté.* See the Gospel of St Luke 11: 33. Today, 'mettre sous le boisseau' can mean 'to keep something secret' or 'to sweep under the carpet'. *Un tel exercice doit établir … si Blair … et Brown lui-même mirent délibérément sous le boisseau les rapports des services secrets sur le prétendu arsenal saddamiste pour arracher le feu vert des députés.* © *Marianne 635.* The quotation above refers to the capital question as to whether or not Tony Blair and Gordon Brown kept security reports secret so as not to weaken the theory of Saddam Hussein's weapons of mass destruction. NB: 'lampadaire' is translated by 'chandelier' in other French versions of the Bible.

### Bon Samaritain nm.                                          `**`

*L'ex-premier ministre de Thaïlande, soucieux de donner l'image d'un bon samaritain, répète à l'envi 'la nécessité d'envoyer des organisations internationales sur place'.* © *Le Figaro 20 129.* This comes from the parable of the Good Samaritan, who, coming across a wounded man, did not (as did the priest and the Levite) pass by on the other side, but stopped to help. This parable was told by Jesus in answer to the question 'Who is my neighbour?' 'But a certain Samaritan, as he journeyed, came where he was: and when he saw him, he was moved with compassion. And came to him, and bound up his wounds, pouring on them oil and wine; and he set him on his own beast, and brought him to an inn, and took care of him.' *Mais un Samaritain qui était en voyage, arriva près de lui, le vit et fut pris de pitié. Il s'approcha, banda ses plaies, y versant de l'huile et du vin, puis le chargea sur sa propre monture, le mena à l'hôtellerie et prit soin de lui.* See Luke 10: 33–34.

### bouc émissaire nm. `***`

Scapegoat (*caper emissarius*). Every year, on the Day of Atonement (Le Jour du Grand Pardon, i.e. Yom Kippur), the high priest of the ancient Jews performed the same ceremony: 'And Aron shall lay both his hands upon the head of the live goat, and confess over him all the iniquities of the children of Israel, and all their transgressions, even all their sins; and he shall put them upon the head of the goat, and shall send him away by the hand of a man that is in readiness into the wilderness. And the goat shall bear upon him all their iniquities unto a solitary land: and he shall let go the goat in the wilderness.' *Aaron lui posera les deux mains sur la tête et confessera à sa charge toutes les fautes des Israélites, toutes leurs transgressions et tous leurs péchés. Après en avoir ainsi chargé la tête du bouc, il l'enverra au désert sous la conduite d'un homme qui se tiendra prêt, et le bouc emportera sur lui toutes leurs fautes en un lieu aride.* See Leviticus 16: 21–22. Today, it refers to any innocent individual who has to take responsibility for the wrongdoings of the group. The theme of the scapegoat is often evoked in French literature; one of the most famous cases being cited by La Fontaine, see Chapter 5 'crier haro sur le baudet'. It can also be found in the children's song *Le Petit Navire* where the scapegoat is the ship's boy (*le mousse*). **Nous, les 'hedgies' nous sommes les boucs émissaires idéaux. Même l'archevêque de Canterbury nous tape dessus.** © *Le Nouvel Observateur 2295.* These are the words of a hedge fund manager.

### bouchée de pain nf.

*Pro buccella panis.* Literally, 'for a piece of bread'. This expression means 'for a song, for next to nothing'. In the biblical text, the partiality of judges is being criticized. 'To have respect of persons is not good: neither that a man should transgress for a piece of bread.' *C'est mal de faire acception de personnes, mais pour une bouchée de pain, l'homme commet un forfait.* See Proverbs 28: 21. **Tous achetés à la barre du tribunal de commerce, ou pour une bouchée de pain aux anciens investisseurs.** © *Le Nouvel Observateur 2360.* This is related to the buying up by Louis Petiet of a host of small companies that are in difficulty: DMC, Isotherma, Authentica, Isotec. All of these companies were bought either from former investors or at the *Tribunal de Commerce* (Commercial Court).

## brandons nmpl.

The story has it that Samson caught 300 foxes and attached firebrands to their tails and set them free in the Philistines' cornfields. 'And when he had set the brands on fire, he let them go into the standing corn of the Philistines and burnt up the shocks and the standing corn, and also the oliveyards.' *Il mit le feu aux torches, puis lâchant les renards dans les moissons des Philistins, il incendia aussi bien les gerbes que le blé sur pied et même les vignes et les oliviers.* See Judges 15: 5. ***Le brasier expédie ses brandons dans l'immense communauté islamique.*** © *Le Point 1896.* The context of the quotation is the war in the Gaza Strip and the effect on the Islamic community.

## brebis égarée nf.

The lost sheep. ***Qui sait qui la ramènera au sein de son troupeau, la brebis égarée.*** © *Les Echos 20 500.* A review concerning the Israeli film *Tu n'aimeras point* by Haïm Tabakman which tells the story of two homosexuals in Israel. The text above was the reaction of a rabbi. See above 'bercail'. 'What man of you, having a hundred sheep, and having lost one of them, doth not leave the ninety and nine in the wilderness, and go after that which is lost, until he find it?' *Lequel d'entre vous, s'il a cent brebis et vient à en perdre une, n'abandonne les quatre-vingt-dix-neuf autres dans le désert pour s'en aller après celle qui est perdue jusqu'à ce qu'il l'ait retrouvée?* See Luke 15: 4.

## brèche (s'engouffrer dans la)

Traditionally, the bravest of the brave would fight at the point of greatest danger, i.e. where the wall had been breached. ***La religion de la sécurité s'est engouffrée dans la brèche.*** *Le Figaro 20 254.* This text refers to the government's overreaction to the flu epidemic and the precautions being advised. 'Therefore he (God) would destroy them (the Israelites), had not Moses his chosen stood before him in the breach, to turn away his wrath lest he should destroy them.' *Il (Dieu) parlait de les supprimer (les Israélites) si ce n'est que Moïse son élu se tint sur la brèche devant lui pour détourner son courroux de détruire.* See Psalms 106: 23.

## buisson ardent nm.

This refers to the burning bush by which Yahveh (Yahweh) indicated his presence to Moses and announced his intention to free the children of Israel from Egyptian oppression. 'And the Angel of the Lord appeared unto him in a flame of fire out of the midst of a bush: and he looked, and behold, the bush burned with fire, and the bush was not consumed.' *L'Ange de Yahvé lui apparut, dans une flamme de feu, du milieu d'un buisson. Moise regarda: le buisson était embrasé mais le buisson ne se consumait pas.* See Exodus 3: 2. An Israeli telephone network operator has just issued a telephone card that is totally kosher. ***Les utilisateurs n'auront pas accès aux messageries roses, seul le buisson sera ardent.*** © *Marianne 632.* The text indicates that access will be denied to sexy chat services, the only 'ardent' subject being the burning bush.

## Cain
[   *   ]

*Pourquoi est-ce que, depuis Caïn, l'homme tue l'homme?* These are the words of Robert Badinter in © *Le Nouvel Observateur 2366.* Cain and Abel were brothers. Cain tilled the soil while Abel tended the flock. One day, each made a sacrifice to God. Abel's sacrifice found favour in God's eyes. Being jealous, Cain slew his brother in the fields, the first murder in the Bible. This story gives us the famous words of the reply of Cain to God when God asked him where Abel was: 'Am I my brother's keeper?' *Suis-je le gardien de mon frère?* See Genesis 4: 1–9.

## calice jusqu'à la lie. Boire le
[   **   ]

To drain one's cup to the bitter dregs, indicates to undergo a painful ordeal right to the end. These are the words pronounced twice by Christ in the garden of Gethsemane (Gethsémani). 'O my Father, if it be possible, let this cup pass away, except I drink it, thy will be done.' *Mon Père, dit-il, si cette coupe ne peut passer sans que je la boive, que ta volonté soit faite.* See Matthew 26: 39, and 42. *Les socialistes varois* [from the Var *département* 83] *n'en finissent plus de boire le calice jusqu'à la lie depuis plus de dix ans.* © *La Tribune du Sud* N°27. This text refers to the unending problems faced by the socialist party in the Var: internal divisions, inflated egos, the absence of a strategy to defeat the right-wing mayor of Toulon, ageing militants, etc.

## calvaire nm.
[   ***   ]

Calvary. The martyrdom of Christ or his suffering on the cross. 'Calvary' is a common noun which is the Latin translation of the Hebrew word *Golgotha* (from the Aramaic word *gulgaltha)* which is a proper noun. *Calvaire* can also refer to a roadside cross or crucifix of which there are many in Brittany. It has now come to mean any particularly long and painful ordeal. *Le long calvaire des Tamouls du Sri Lanka!* © *Le Monde 20 130.* A reference to the plight of Tamil fighters six months after the defeat of the 'Tigers'. See below 'Golgotha'.

## Cana
[   *   ]

*Il n'y a pas de joie sans vin … avant de rappeler que Jésus fut, à Cana, un formidable vigneron surnaturel.* © *L'Express 3048.* In (and only in) the Gospel according to St John, Jesus performed his first miracle at the wedding in Cana (*Les noces de Cana*). He was attending a wedding when his mother informed him that there was no more wine left. He ordered six jars to be filled with water. The water turned into wine, better than the wine that had been served until then, thus provoking the surprise of the guests; normally, the best wine was served first, not last. 'Jesus saith unto them, Fill the water pots with water. And they filled them up to the brim. And he saith unto them, Draw out now and bear unto the ruler of the feast. And when the ruler of the feast tasted the water now become wine, he knew not whence it was' *Jésus leur dit: 'remplissez d'eau ces jarres'. Ils les remplirent jusqu'au bord. Il leur dit 'Puisez maintenant et portez-en au maître de repas'. Lorsque le maître du repas eut goûté l'eau devenue vin – et il ne savait pas d'où il venait.* See John 2: 1–10.

## Carême nm.       ⌈  *  ⌉

Lent is a period of fasting of forty days that was implemented by the Catholic church in reference to the forty days that Jesus fasted in the wilderness. ***Et comme il faut quatre ou cinq kilos de céréales pour obtenir un kilo de chair fraîche, ce carême a fait inévitablement tort au blé.*** © *Le Monde 20 224.* This is a reference to the fact that people are now eating less meat, both for health and environmental reasons, but this is having a negative knock-on effect on grain prices. NB: 'une mine de carême' is 'a long, sad face'.

## cavaliers de l'Apocalypse nmpl.       ⌈  *  ⌉

The four horsemen of the Apocalypse were riding on four horses, each of a different colour and symbolizing, respectively, pride (the king of vices) on a white horse, war on a red horse, famine on a black horse and the plague on a green horse. See Revelation 6: 2–8. ***Droits dans leurs bottes, les quatre cavaliers de l'Apocalypse, rejettent les accusations, invoquent la fatalité, la nature cyclique de l'activité économique, le caractère imprévisible des crises, aussi difficiles à prévoir et à arrêter que les cyclones ou les tornades.*** © *L'Express 3059.* This quote refers to the directors of the main American banks giving testimony at the hearing of the commission of enquiry in the USA set up to investigate the cause of the financial crisis. Irritated by their faked innocence, the presiding judge sarcastically said that he didn't want to hear them talk about 'the will of God'. See Chapter 5 'Candide' and Chapter 11 'Juppé, Alain'.

## cénacle nm.       ⌈  ***  ⌉

The room where Jesus Christ met with his disciples for the Last Supper and later where the Eucharist was established. Today, it refers to a small gathering of men of letters, a literary coterie. It can sometimes be used as a synonym for the inner sanctum of power. The term is intimately associated with the French Romantic Movement and includes names such as Hugo, Vigny, Balzac, Mérimée, and Sainte-Beuve. ***Hors des cénacles de l'UMP où il ne se sent pas le bienvenu, Copé profite de sa liberté de parole pour traiter au sein de son club des sujets 'sensibles' que les politiques ont, selon lui, 'du mal à aborder'.*** © *Le Figaro 20 069.* Jean-François Copé is not well liked among the presidential inner circle in spite of the fact that he is the leader of the UMP party in the National Assembly. Having no ministerial responsibility, he is free to criticize Nicolas Sarkozy's policy of as he thinks fit.

### cendres (se couvrir la tête de) nfpl.

There are many examples in the Bible of 'ash' being used as a symbol of repentance. It is to be noticed that 'ash' is sometimes translated by 'dust'. Among many others see Jeremiah 6: 26. *Les cendres dont M. Ride s'est ensuite recouvert n'y ont rien fait.* © *Le Canard Enchaîné 4591.* This text refers to the public statement made by the *inspecteur général* working with the former controversial minister of justice, Rachida Dati. The magistrates were up in arms about the fact that an *inspecteur général* should be sent to Metz in the middle of the night to question a magistrate about his decision to send a habitual offender to prison. The prisoner in question, a 16-year-old, committed suicide soon after her arrival in prison. Ride's statement was supposed to draw the magistrates' fire. Although he had been sent by the minister of justice, he claimed that he was acting on his own initiative and that the minister was not responsible.

### Cène nf.

The Last Supper that Christ took with his disciples. See Matthew 26: 26–30, Luke 22: 1–38, and John 13: 1–38. *Pour un peu, les personnages se seraient crus dans une reconstitution de la Cène … Avant de partir, Rocard offre un dernier repas à ses disciples.* © *Le Canard Enchaîné Dossier 108.* This is a reference to the final meal to which Michel Rocard treated his team members just before leaving Matignon in 1991.

### César (rendre à)

'Render therefore unto Caesar the things that are Caesar's; and unto God the things that are God's.' *Rendez à César ce qui est à César, et à Dieu ce qui est à Dieu.* This was Jesus' reply to the Pharisees who asked him the question, 'Is it lawful to give tribute unto Caesar or not?' *Est-il permis de payer le tribut à César?* See Matthew 22: 17–21. *Rendons au Figaro ce qui lui appartient.* © *L'Express 3054.* Following a technical error in the typesetting of an article appearing in *L'Express,* the name of *Le Figaro* was erased. The quote above was the heading of an article of apology printed the following week in *L'Express.*

### chemin de croix nm.

'The Way of the Cross,' including the fourteen stations, refers to a ceremony to commemorate the Passion of Christ. Figuratively speaking, it implies a hard and uphill struggle. No mention of this as such appears in the New Testament. *L'interminable chemin de croix de l'équipe de France.* © *Le Figaro 20 252.* This refers to the poor performance of the French football team in the qualifying matches for the 2010 World Cup.

### chemin étroit nm.

*Les syndicats cherchent le chemin étroit de l'unité.* © *Les Echos 20 598.* This is a reference to the conflicting opinions of the French unions concerning the propositions of the government to deal with the major problem posed by retirement and the reform of pension schemes. 'Enter ye by the narrow gate: for wide is the gate, and broad is the way, that leadeth to destruction, and many be they that enter in thereby. For narrow is the gate and straightened the way that leadeth unto life, and few be they that find it.' *Entrez par la porte étroite. Large, en effet, et spacieux est le chemin qui mène à la perdition, et il en est beaucoup qui s'y engagent; mais étroite est la porte et resserré le chemin qui mène à la Vie et il en est peu qui le trouvent.* See Matthew 7: 13–14.

### cherchez et vous trouverez    [ * ]

'Seek and ye shall find, knock and it shall be opened unto you.' *Cherchez et vous trouverez, frappez, et l'on vous ouvrira.* See Luke 11: 9. **On a cherché et on a trouvé.** © *Marianne 626.* A text referring to the apparently impossible task of finding a straightforward, easy to use mobile telephone. *Marianne* looked for and found one.

### colombe de la paix nf.    [ *** ]

A dove bearing an olive branch is a symbol of peace, the end of God's wrath against man. It was the sign given to Noah that the flood waters of the deluge had receded. 'And the dove came in to him at eventide; and lo, in her mouth an olive leaf pluckt off: so Noah knew that the waters were abated from off the earth.' *La colombe revint sur le soir et voici qu'elle avait dans le bec un rameau tout frais d'olivier! Ainsi Noé connut que les eaux avaient diminué à la surface de la terre.* See Genesis 8: 11. The doves are opposed to the hawks in political terminology. **El-Baradei: La colombe montre ses griffes.** © *L'Express 3064.* The context is the decision by the diplomat Mohamed El-Baradei, former member of the Agence internationale de l'énergie atomique, to become an opposition spokesman in Egypt against Moubarak.

### colosse aux pieds d'argile    [ *** ]

'The idol (colossus) with feet of clay.' In the book of Daniel 2: 31–35, Daniel, the Hebrew prophet, interpreted the dreams of the King of Babylon Nebuchadnezzar (Nabuchodonosor). The king had a dream in which he saw an idol with a golden head, silver torso and arms, bronze back and thighs and feet made of iron and clay. The interpretation was that the gold represented the king whereas the other metals represented various kingdoms to come. The last kingdom, of iron and clay, would be a divided kingdom, both strong and fragile. **Le Nigéria, colosse aux pieds d'argile** © *L'Express 3054.* Nigeria is strong because of its oil production but fragile because this oil production is chaotic, the president is gravely ill, and there has been a recent heightening of religious tension.

## Commandements (les Dix) nmpl.

*

The title of a book reviewed in *Le Monde 20 258* concerning violence in schools written by a social researcher, Eric Debarbieux. See below 'Tables de la Loi'.

### crible. passer au

***

'Un crible' is a kind of sieve. This verb means to examine very closely. The expression comes from the Last Supper. 'Simon, Simon, behold Satan asked to have you, that he might sift you as wheat.' *Le Seigneur dit: Simon, Simon, Satan vous a réclamé pour vous cribler comme le froment.* It evokes the attempts by Satan to put the disciple to the test. See Luke 22: 31. *Les deux journalistes **ont passé au crible la valeur montante de la droite qui se rêve à l'Élysée en 2017, Jean-François Copé**.* © *L'Express 3053*. Jean-François Copé has already announced his intention to stand for the presidency in 2017. See Chapter 9 'Copé, Jean-François'.

### crier sur les toits

***

*Praedicate super tecta.* This means to proclaim the news, far and wide. It is how Jesus defined the task of the disciples. 'What I tell you in the darkness, speak ye in the light: and what ye hear in the ear, proclaim upon the house-tops.' *Ce que je vous dis dans les ténèbres, dites-le au grand jour; et ce que vous entendez dans le creux de l'oreille, proclamez-le sur les toits.* See Matthew 10: 27. ***Il a beau crier sur tous les toits qu'il tient sa revanche … il n'y croit pas vraiment.*** © *Le Nouvel Observateur 2363* This is a reference to the regional elections and the last time the National Front leader, Jean Marie Le Pen, will stand for election.

### Damas (le chemin de)

***

'The road to Damascus.' This expression evokes a spiritual journey during which the traveller undergoes a radical change in attitude or belief. It refers to the journey undertaken by Saul, the persecutor of the early Christians. On his way to Damascus, a bright light appeared and Jesus asked Saul why he was persecuting those who believed in him. Saul was blinded (his sight was later restored). After this incident, he changed his Hebrew name Saul into the Roman form Paul. 'And as he journeyed, it came to pass that he drew nigh unto Damascus: and suddenly there shone round about him a light out of heaven: And he fell upon the earth, and heard a voice saying unto him, "Saul, Saul, why persecutest thou me?"' *Il faisait route et approchait Damas, quand soudain une lumière venue du ciel l'enveloppa de sa clarté. Tombant à terre, il entendit une voix qui lui disait: 'Saoul, Saoul, pourquoi me persécutes-tu?'* See Acts of the Apostles 9: 3–4. ***Un nouveau miracle s'est produit sur le chemin de Damas. D'infréquentable, Bachar al-Assad a subitement muté en une sorte de 'sage' du Moyen-Orient.*** © *Marianne 591*. This is a reference to the fact that until recently, Bachar al-Assad of Syria, (capital Damascus), was considered to be *persona non grata* in western capitals. Suddenly he has become a kind of 'wise man' of the Middle East.

## David et Goliath

`***`

The story of David and Goliath is the story of the victory of the small against the strong. Goliath, the Philistine, in spite of his greater physical strength, was overcome by David, the shepherd boy, his sling and his faith in God. 'And David put his hand in his bag, and took thence a stone, and slang it, and smote the Philistine in his forehead; the stone sank into his forehead, and he fell upon his face to the earth.' *Il mit la main dans son sac, prit une pierre, la lança avec la fronde et atteignit le Philistin au front.* See Samuel (1) 17: 48–51. **Mais pour aller vraiment au bout, il faudrait enquêter en Chine. Il a l'impression de jouer à David contre Goliath.** © *Le Nouvel Observateur 2228.* This is a reference to the difficulty faced by customs officers in fighting dangerous imports from China.

## Déluge nm.

`**`

The myth of the flood is one of the most widespread of stories and can be found in many cultures. All beings perish except two. Noah's Ark is the Christian version of this story. It rained for forty days and forty nights and it was the dove, bringing an olive branch back to the Ark that indicated that the waters had receded. The Ark came to rest on Mount Ararat. The Deluge is synonymous with the beginning of the new world. See Genesis 6: 7–8. 'Fifteen cubits upward did the waters prevail; and the mountains were covered. And all flesh died that moved upon the earth.' *Les eaux montèrent quinze coudées plus haut, recouvrant les montagnes. Alors périt toute chair qui se meut sur la terre.* See Genesis 7: 20–21. **Quel sera l'état du monde 'après le déluge'? Telle est la redoutable interrogation à laquelle tente de répondre Nicolas Baverez dans son dernier essai sous-titré 'La grande crise de la mondialisation'.** © *Le Point 1936.* This text refers to the state in which the world will be, once the financial crash has been overcome. See above 'colombe de la paix'.

## demeures dans la maison de mon père. Il y a plusieurs

`*`

'In my father's house are many mansions.' See John 14: 2. **Le roi Sarkozy habite plusieurs maisons.** © *Le Canard Enchaîné Dossier 111.* This is a reference to the various residences of Nicolas Sarkozy, both official and private, and those of his wife.

## derniers seront les premiers, et les premiers seront les derniers. Les

'So the last shall be first, and the first last.' *Voilà comment les derniers seront premiers, et les premiers seront derniers.* See Matthew 20: 16. **Il y a du Matthieu chez Nicolas Sarkozy. Pour lui, comme pour l'apôtre, les premiers seront les derniers et vice versa.** © *Le Canard Enchaîné Dossier 111.* This text refers to the fact that Nicolas Sarkozy has given some of the most prestigious ministerial positions to socialist turncoats and that his own faithful followers have not been rewarded at all. This is the case of Eric Besson and Bernard Kouchner (the former socialist minister of immigration, and the former minister of foreign affairs) as opposed to Patrick Devedjian who never received an appointment in spite of being a long-standing member of the right-wing party UMP.

### deux poids, deux mesures    \*\*\*

'Double standards.' This is the very symbol of injustice. 'Diverse weights and diverse measures, both of them alike are an abomination to the Lord.' *Deux sortes de poids, deux sortes d'épha, Sont l'un et l'autre en abomination à l'Éternel.* See Proverbs 20: 10. ***Deux poids deux mesures.*** © *L'Express 3063.* This was the heading of an article underlining the silence of the CRE (the energy regulatory committeee) in the wake of the declarations made by the chairman and CEO of EDF, Henri Proglio, concerning the storm named Xynthia, which hit France early in 2010. The article highlights the fact that his predecessor, Pierre Gadonneix, when he made similar statements about the storms in the south-west in 2009, was accused of having violated the principle of the independence of network managers.

### Dieu y pourvoira    \*\*

'God will provide'. ***Ce radicalisme n'est en bref qu'un extrémisme fondé sur une pétition de principe: 'Dieu y pourvoira'.*** © *Marianne 589.* This is a comment on the way radicals evacuate all of the problems that their ideology raises. 'Faire une pétition de principe' is 'to beg the question'. To put Abraham's faith to the test, God tells him to take his son to the mountain top and slay him as a sacrifice. Abraham climbs the mountain with his son Isaac who asks, 'Behold the fire and the wood: but where is the lamb for a burnt offering?' And Abraham said 'God will provide himself the lamb for a burnt offering my son'. *Voici le feu et le bois, mais où est l'agneau pour l'holocauste? Abraham répondit: 'c'est Dieu qui pourvoira à l'agneau pour l'holocauste, mon fils'.* See Genesis 22: 7, 8. In fact, God stops Abraham, who is about to sacrifice his son. Abraham sees a ram caught by its horns in a bush; this ram was sacrificed in place of Isaac.

### Éden (le jardin d')     \*\*

The Garden of Eden, the name of the garden in which Adam and Eve began their lives. It symbolizes paradise before the fall. 'And the Lord God took the man and put him into the Garden of Eden to dress it and to keep it.' *Yahvé Dieu prit l'homme et l'établit dans le jardin d'Eden pour le cultiver et le garder.* See Genesis 2: 15. ***Les politiques nous promettaient un retour à l'Eden du Welfare State.*** © *Marianne 615.* NB: when God punished Cain for killing Abel, he sent him to the desolate land of Nod, on the east of

Eden. *East of Eden* is the title of the famous novel by John Steinbeck (1902–68).

## Épiphanie nf.     [ * ]

Epiphany comes from the Greek *epiphaneia* meaning 'appearance' and refers to Christ's presentation to the Magi on the twelfth day. It is celebrated in the Christian calendar on 6 January. 'And they came into the house and saw the young child with Mary his mother; and they fell down and worshipped him; and opening their treasures they offered unto him gifts, gold and frankincense and myrrh.' *Entrant alors dans le logis, ils virent l'enfant avec Marie sa mère, et, se prosternant, ils lui rendirent hommage; puis, ouvrant leurs cassettes, ils lui offrirent en présents de l'or, de l'encens et de la myrrhe.* See Matthew 2: 11. *Le coup de génie de la 70ème minute; un moment d'épiphanie.* © *Le Figaro 20 166.* This quotation refers to the last minute victory of Barcelona over Manchester United in the final of the European Champions' League 2009; the context suggests a 'revelation' or 'moment of grace' rather than an appearance. See Chapter 1 'fève'. NB: Shakespeare's play *Twelfth Night* is translated into French by the title *La Nuit des Rois.*

## Évangile (parole d')     [ ** ]

The gospel truth. *Alan Greenspan, dont chaque mot était attendu comme parole d'Évangile, est désormais accusé d'avoir provoqué l'explosion de la bulle immobilière.* © *Marianne 598.* Alan Greenspan was the chairman of the Federal Reserve from 1987–2006 and what he said was considered to be the gospel truth. In the wake of the US subprime mortgage disaster, he recently confessed to having made some fundamentally erroneous assumptions about the economy.

## Exode nm.     [ ** ]

Exodus is the title of the second book of the Old Testament telling the story of the children of Israel leaving Egypt and wandering in the desert on their way to the Promised Land. *Il y en a eu [English people leaving the Dordogne] mais ce n'est vraiment pas l'exode.* © *Le Figaro 20 057.* This text refers to British people living in France, suffering from the £/euro exchange rate, who have been forced to sell up and return to Great Britain. Some are leaving but not in massive numbers.

## faute originelle. La     [ * ]

'Original sin.' This term is not referred to as such in the Bible. It refers to the original disobedience of Adam and Eve who tasted the forbidden fruit in the Garden of Eden. 'And when the woman saw that the tree was good for food, and that it was a delight to the eyes, and that the tree was to be desired to make one wise, she took of the fruit thereof and did eat; and she gave also unto her husband with her, and he did eat.' *La femme vit que l'arbre était bon à manger et séduisant à voir, et qu'il était, cet arbre, désirable pour acquérir le discernement. Elle prit de son fruit et mangea. Elle en donna aussi à son mari, qui était avec elle, et il mangea.* See Genesis 3: 6. ***Aux fautes originelles – des pays convaincus de payer moins grâce à leur regroupement [ … ] se sont ajoutées les erreurs d'Airbus.*** © *L'Express 3056.* This observation was made in the light of the manufacturing problems raised by the A 400M, the European military transport aircraft that has been dogged by problems and now faces a €5 billion budget overrun.

### fils prodigue nm.

( * )

The parable of the Lost Son or Prodigal Son is only mentioned in the Gospel according to St Luke. It is the story of a young man who asks his father to give him his share of the inheritance. He then goes away and wastes his money in riotous living. He is reduced to feeding swine and decides to return to work for his father as a servant. When his father sees his son, he kills the fatted calf to celebrate his return. 'But while he was yet afar off, his father saw him, and was moved with compassion, and ran, and fell on his neck and kissed him.' *Tandis qu'il était encore loin, son père l'aperçut et fut pris de pitié; il courut se jeter à son cou et l'embrassa tendrement.* See Luke 15: 11–32. ***On ne saurait signifier plus diplomatiquement que le 'retour des fils prodigues' ne doit pas ressembler à une déculottée.*** © *Marianne 615.* This is a reference to the return of the negationist bishops after their reintegration by Pope Benedict XVI. The Bishops of France have voiced their reservations and have reminded the Pope of their attachment to Vatican II. The reintegration of the negationist bishops is seen in France as a slap in the face for the progressive wing of the Catholic church. 'Une déculottée' is a 'thrashing'. For the English-speaking reader, be careful not to confuse the adjective 'prodigue' (prodigal) with the noun 'prodige' (prodigy).

### fosse aux lions. La

( * )

The story of Daniel in the lions' den can be found in the book of the same name. 'Then the king [Darius] commanded, and they brought Daniel, and cast him into the den of lions.' *Alors, le roi donna ordre de faire venir Daniel et de le jeter dans la fosse aux lions.* Daniel 6: 1–16. ***'Sainte Martine' dans la fosse aux lions, dévorée toute crue par les fauves de Solférino.*** © *Le Nouvel Observateur 2368.* This is a reference to the violent in-party rivalry within the socialist party and the fact that the socialist leader, Martine Aubry, is surrounded by her ravenous colleagues. See Chapter 12 'Solférino'.

### Géhenne nf.

( * )

For the Jewish, Christian and Islamic religions, this word is equivalent to hell, a desert in which the fire never goes out and in which sinners suffer for eternity. It is usually translated into English as 'hell fire' or 'unquenchable fire'. See Matthew 5: 30. ***Les belles légendes s'improvisent dans la géhenne de*** *l'Histoire, pas dans les partis, les comités, les assemblées. On n'imagine pas de Gaulle en député des Vosges, Mandela ou Senghor en premiers présidents d'une Cour des Comptes quelconque, et, sans la folie d'Hitler, les zigzags de Churchill d'une circonscription à l'autre auraient tourné au fiasco.* © *Le Nouvel Observateur 2358.* This text asserts that great men emerge in extreme circumstances.

### Genèse nf.
'Genesis' is the title of the first book in the Bible from the Latin term meaning 'birth' or 'generation'. 'In the beginning God created the heaven and the earth.' *Au commencement, Dieu créa le ciel et la terre.* See Genesis 1: 1. *La Genèse d'un génie littéraire.* © *Marianne 604.* This text refers to the correspondance between Norman Mailer (1923–2007) and Jean Malaquais, the Frenchman who discovered and translated Mailer for the French audience and who was to be his mentor over the years.

### Golgotha (la première station de)
'Golgotha' is the Greek form of the Aramaic word *gulgaltha* signifying 'skull', or 'place of a skull'. It was the name of the hill outside of the old town of Jerusalem where the Romans crucified convicts. It is a synonym of 'calvary', the Latin word (*calvaria*) for skull. It was here that Jesus suffered his martyrdom. The way of the cross traditionally includes fourteen stations, the most important moments of Christ's passion. The first station is the sentencing of Christ, the fourteenth station is when he was placed in the tomb. See Matthew 27: 33. It now refers to any painful ordeal. *Aujourd'hui, ses ex-apôtres sifflent sur le passage de son chemin de croix et certains de ses ex-courtisans en viennent à rêver son ascension du Golgotha.* © *Marianne 574.* This text refers to Nicolas Sarkozy and the disillusion of many of his former followers who now wish for his downfall. See above 'calvaire' and 'chemin de croix'.

### Grand Prêtre nm.

The High Priest (*Cohen-Gadol, cohen* meaning 'dedicated' or 'devoted' in Hebrew) is a title handed down from father to son since the first high priest who was Moses' brother Aaron. A member of the Hebrew clergy, he was responsible for organizing sacrifices at the Temple of Jerusalem. Today, it refers, figuratively, to a person who has great and recognized authority. *Alain Greenspan, l'ancien président de la Réserve Fédérale Américaine et grand prêtre du marché autorégulé, foudroyé sur place.* © *Marianne 602.* This refers to Alain Greenspan's consternation at the catastrophic results of the policies he himself had propounded in the name of the liberal economy. See above 'Évangile'.

### grincement de dents nmpl.

This gives the image of anger or pain. It is the threat of Jesus referring to the suffering in hell and which is spoken about (above all) in Matthew: 'there shall be the weeping and the gnashing of teeth'. *Il y aura des pleurs et des*

*grincements de dents.* See Matthew 8: 12, and 22: 13, 25: 30. ***Les premiers grincements de dents se sont déjà fait entendre au Nouveau Parti anti-capitaliste.*** © *Le Nouvel Observateur 2321*. See above 'appelés' which follows the biblical text Matthew 22: 13 mentioning 'grincement'.

### Heureux les x, car …        [     *     ]

This is the structure of the lines from the Beatitudes, i.e. the blessing at the beginning of the Sermon on the Mount. This comes from the Latin *beatus* meaning 'blessed' or 'happy'. 'Blessed are the pure in heart, for they shall see God.' *Heureux ceux qui ont le cœur pur, car ils verront Dieu.* See Matthew 5: 8. ***Heureux, les curés purs, car ils verront le Veau d'Or.*** © *Le Canard Enchaîné 4582*. This was a reference to the rector of the sanctuaries of Lourdes who is currently being investigated by the French money laundering watchdog, Tracfin, for having amassed over €427,000 in his personal bank accounts. See below 'Veau d'or'.

### Holocauste nm.        [  ***   ]

From the Greek *holos* meaning 'totally' and *kaustos* meaning 'burnt'. It refers to a sacrificial ceremony during which the whole of an animal is consumed by the flames, i.e. 'a burnt offering'. The procedure is laid down in the book of Leviticus: 'it is a burnt offering, an offering made by fire, of a sweet savour unto the Lord'. *Cet holocauste sera un mets consumé en parfum d'apaisement pour Yahvé.* See Leviticus 1: 1–17. It has since come to be associated with the massacre of the Jews during the Second World War. ***Et la construction d'un gigantesque mémorial de l'holocauste, érigé au cœur de Berlin, à quelques pas de la porte de Brandebourg et du Reichstag, montre que l'Allemagne n'oublie rien de son histoire.*** © *Le Figaro 20 303*.

### Immaculée Conception nf.        [     *     ]

Contrary to a widely held but erroneous belief, the Immaculate Conception has nothing to do with the birth of Jesus. The Immaculate Conception is the doctrine that Mary herself was born of her mother, Anne, without the stain of original sin. The doctrine of Christ's birth, without a human father, is known as the doctrine of the 'virgin birth'. Contrary to the 'virgin birth', the 'Immaculate Conception' is not of biblical origin. It is the Catholic dogma defined in 1854 by Pope Pius IX in the papal bull *Ineffabilis Deus*. ***Bon, j'ai commencé à me poser des questions quand elle s'est quasiment prise pour l'Immaculée Conception.*** © *Marianne 657*. This text refers to the disenchantment of a former Ségolène Royal supporter in the light of Royal's tendency to think of herself as God's gift to politics.

### iota nm.        [  ***   ]

This is the smallest of the letters (i) in the Greek alphabet, Greek being the language of the Gospels. Today, 'iota' means 'a jot'. 'For verily I say unto you, till heaven and earth pass away, one jot or one tittle shall in no wise pass away from the law, till all things be accomplished.' *Car je vous le dis, en vérité: avant que ne passent le ciel et la terre, pas un i, pas un point sur l'i, ne passera de la loi que tout ne soit réalisé.* See Matthew 5: 18. ***Villepin exerce sa défense sans changer d'un iota.*** © *Le Point 1950.* This is a reference to the strategy of Dominique de Villepin in his defence against the accusations of defamation for which he is currently on trial. NB: 'mettre les points sur les i' is the equivalent of 'to dot the "i"s and cross the "t"s'.

### ivraie nf.       [ ** ]

This comes from the parable of the wheat and the tares. 'But while men slept, his enemy came and sowed tares also among the wheat, and went away.' *Or pendant que les gens dormaient, son ennemi est venu, il a semé à son tour de l'ivraie, au beau milieu du blé, et il s'en est allé.* See Matthew 13: 24–30 and 36–43. ***Séparer le bon grain de l'ivraie dans ce domaine nécessite dès lors à la fois rigueur et compétences de haut vol.*** © *Les Echos 20 448.* This text refers to the difficulty in drawing a distinction between 'real' and 'false' hedge funds.

### jérémiades nfpl.       [ *** ]

'Moaning'. This is a reference to the Old Testament prophet Jeremiah, in the book of the same name in the Old Testament, who was famous for his lamentations and complaints made to God. He was a prophet of doom and destruction. 'Jérémiades' has come to mean endless whining that ultimately becomes a nuisance to the listeners. ***Qu'est-ce que j'ai fait pour mériter cela? Jérémiade reprise à son compte par le spectateur, qui doit supporter pendant deux heures vingt ce succédané de 'Smoking/No Smoking'.*** © *Le Nouvel Observateur 2358.* This is part of a vitriolic review of the new film *Mr Nobody* by Jaco Van Dormael. See below 'prophète de malheur'.

### Job (pauvre comme)       

'As poor as Job.' Job was once a rich man and very pious. On Satan's insistence, Yaweh decided to test Job's piety by taking away his wealth and reducing him to extreme poverty. In spite of this, Job continued to worship his god as he sat among the ashes. 'And he took him a potsherd to scrape himself withal; and he sat among the ashes.' *Job prit un tesson pour se gratter et il s'installa parmi les cendres.* See Job 2. 8. ***Rappelons-nous Job. Job qui avait été si riche, et qui se retrouvait si pauvre avant de redevenir riche. Son tas de fumier l'avait amené à revoir sa relation avec les biens matériels et à reconstruire sa vie différemment.*** © *Le Figaro 20 096.* Just as Job, who had been rich, became poor and remained that way for some time before regaining his former wealth, so too, the actors in the economy, in the wake of the financial crisis, are going to have to reappraise their relationships with the material world.

## Judas

***

Judas Iscariot betrayed Jesus with a kiss. See Matthew 26: 48. Eric Besson, after having been a member of Ségolène Royal's election team, joined the Sarkozy camp in the home straight of the presidential election. His name has now become a synonym of treachery and betrayal. *Le nouveau ministre de l'immigration ne restera peut-être pas dans l'histoire pour ses réalisations gouvernementales, mais, dans le langage courant, son patronyme est décidément en passe de supplanter le nom de Judas.* © *Le Canard Enchaîné 4609.*

## Laissez venir à moi ...

*

'Suffer the little children to come unto me.' *Laissez les petits enfants venir à moi.* The words of Christ in Mark 10: 14. *Laissez venir à moi les petits paiements* © *Marianne 595.* This text refers to the secrecy surrounding the funding of the Pope's travelling expenses. Journalists accompanying the Pope to Washington in 2008 had to pay double the price of a normal, business class air ticket to travel with the Papal delegation.

## lait et de miel (un pays de)

*

God commanded Moses to lead his people to the land flowing with milk and honey – the Promised Land, the land of ease and plenty. 'Unto a land flowing with milk and honey.' *Monte vers une terre qui ruisselle de lait et de miel.* See Exodus 33: 3. *Il ne faut pas enjoliver Romainville, ce n'était pas un pays de lait et de miel.* © *Le Canard Enchaîné 4574.* These are the words of Sylvain Rossignol who wrote the story of the workers in the company Roussel-Uclaf that used to be located in Romainville. Romainville is not one of the nicest parts of the eastern outskirts of Paris, located in the *département* of the Seine-Saint-Denis (93) and the writer is careful not to idealize the past or become nostalgic.

## laver les mains (s'en)

***

'To wash one's hands of an affair.' This is a reference to Pilate who, after having proposed to release Jesus, gave in to the demands of the priests and allowed Jesus to be crucified. 'So when Pilate saw that he prevailed nothing, but rather that a tumult was rising, he took water, and washed his hands before the multitude saying, I am innocent of the blood of this righteous man: see ye to it.' *Voyant alors qu'il n'aboutissait à rien, mais qu'il s'ensuivait plutôt du tumulte, Pilate prit de l'eau et se lava les mains en présence de la foule en disant: 'Je ne suis pas responsable de ce sang; à vous de voir!'* See Matthew 27: 24. *Parce que notre société, à la différence de plusieurs autres, veut à tout prix s'en laver les mains. Elle refuse d'accepter qu'elle en est largement responsable.* © *L'Express 3037.* This text refers to the recent spate of suicides that have occurred at France Telecom-Orange and the refusal of the France Telecom management to accept a share of the responsibility. NB: France Télécom and Orange are the same company but the name France

Télécom is the name of the landline division while Orange is the commercial name used for mobiles, internet and television.

## Lazare                                                            ( * )

Lazarus had been in his tomb for four days when Jesus arrived and said '"Lazarus, come forth." He that was dead came forth'. *Lazare, sors! Et le mort sortit. John 11: 43–44.* ***Et tout à coup des phrases bien senties de Martine Aubry font dire à chacun qu'à la manière de Lazare sortant du tombeau, le PS se dresse ragaillardi pour de nouvelles aventures.*** © *Les Echos 20 500.* The context of this quote is the apparent regaining of consciousness of the PS after months of being in a coma. NB: in English one is in 'a' coma, whereas in French one is in 'le' coma.

## légion adj                                                        ( *** )

This implies the plurality hidden behind what seems to be singular. When Jesus asked a man possessed by the devil what his name was, the man replied 'My name is Legion for we are many.' *Légion est mon nom … car nous sommes beaucoup.* See Mark 5. 9. See also Luke 8: 30. ***Une place est libre, et les candidats ne sont pas légion.*** © *Le Monde 19898.* With the departure of Xavier Bertrand from the government, to become secretary general of the UMP, a ministerial opening occurred, i.e. the ministry of labour and industrial relations. This is not considered to be a sinecure and there were few volunteers to fill the post.

## lentilles (un plat de) nfpl.                                      ( *** )

'A mess of pottage.' Esau (Esaü) was starving, and sold his birthright to Jacob for a mess of pottage. 'And Esau said to Jacob "Feed me, I pray thee with that same red pottage; for I am faint" … and Jacob said "Sell me this day thy birthright" … and he sware unto him and he sold his birthright unto Jacob.' *Esaü dit à Jacob: 'Laisse-moi avaler ce roux, ce roux là; je suis épuisé' … Jacob dit: 'Vends-moi d'abord ton droit d'aînesse ' … il prêta serment et vendit son droit d'aînesse à Jacob.* Genesis 25: 30–34 ***Esaü a vendu son droit d'aînesse pour un plat de lentilles. Nestlé, lui, vend ses lentilles.*** © *Les Echos 20 586.* This is a reference to the buyouts and sell-offs among the giants of the food industry, including Nestlé. NB: 'roux' is the translation of 'mess of pottage' in the Jerusalem Bible, the lentils being red.

## Lève-toi et marche                                                ( ** )

'Arise and walk.' The words of Christ to the man suffering from palsy. See Luke 5: 23, Mark 2: 9, and Matthew 9: 5. ***Lève-toi et cogne.*** © *Marianne 623.* This text refers to a general news item about a paraplegic in California who walked out of hospital after being treated for a spider sting. He was later arrested for conjugal violence. ('Cogner' is slang for 'to bash' or 'to beat up'.)

## Léviathan

`**`

This was supposed to be a monstrous sea creature that symbolized the forces of evil, the beast of the Apocalypse. 'The Lord … shall punish leviathan the swift serpent, and leviathan the crooked serpent and he shall slay the dragon of the sea.' *Yahvé châtiera … Léviathan, le serpent fuyard, Léviathan, le serpent tortueux; il tuera le dragon qui habite la mer.* See Isaiah 27: 1, Job 3: 8 and Psalms 74: 14. ***Ces dernières années, les dirigeants des deux groupes [La Caisse d'Épargne et Les Banques Populaires] ont tout fait pour s'émanciper de la tutelle de l'État. Et voilà que Léviathan effectue un retour fracassant.*** © *Le Point 1902.* By the appointment of a faithful follower of Nicolas Sarkozy at the head of the two banks, the State has reaffirmed its control over the two banks in question.

## limbes (dans les) nmpl.

`***`

'In limbo.' This is a term that does not appear in the Bible but dates from the thirteenth century. From the Latin term *limbus* meaning 'fringe', 'margin', 'edge' or 'border', it is a region bordering on hell and supposed to be the last abode of unbaptized children and of righteous people born before the time of Christ. Figuratively speaking, it refers to an indeterminate state, a midway place between two others, a no-man's-land. ***Le traité de Lisbonne demeure dans les limbes.*** © *Le Point 1910.*

## Mammon

`**`

'Ye cannot serve God and mammon.' *Vous ne pouvez pas servir Dieu et l'Argent.* See Matthew 6: 24. 'Mammon' has been variously interpreted as the false god of wealth, excessive materialism, and the demon of avarice. Its etymological origin is not so clear. ***Ruskin avait baptisé le culte du dieu Mammon 'une religion civile ratée'.*** © *Marianne 586.*

## manne nf.

`***`

'Manna.' From the Hebrew *mân hou* meaning literally 'What is it?' It was the food miraculously provided by God to the children of Israel during their wanderings in the wilderness over forty years. 'What is it? for they wist not what it was. And Moses said unto them, "It is the bread which the Lord hath given you to eat".' *'Qu'est-ce cela', car ils ne savaient pas ce que c'était. Moïse leur dit 'Cela c'est le pain que Yahvé vous a donné à manger'.* See Exodus, 16: 14–36, and Psalms 105: 40. Today, it refers to any providential windfall. ***Les dirigeants du football veulent éviter qu'Orange, manne essentielle, renonce à diffuser la Ligue 1.*** © *Le Monde 19 965.* This text refers to the possibility that the French telco might withdraw its sponsoring support from First Division football.

## marchands du temple nmpl.

`***`

This is a reference to Christ driving the money-changers and merchants out of the temple. 'And Jesus entered into the temple of God, and cast out all them that sold and bought in the temple, and overthrew the tables of the money-changers, and the seats of them who sold the doves.' *Puis Jésus entra dans le Temple et chassa tous les vendeurs et acheteurs qui s'y retrouvaient: il culbuta les tables des changeurs ainsi que les sièges des marchands de colombes.* See Matthew 21: 12–13. **Le Sénat pousse enfin dehors les marchands du temple! L'époque où les lobbies avaient un accès totalement libre à la buvette, au restaurant et aux salles des conférences du Palais du Luxembourg est révolue.** © *Le Nouvel Observateur 2345.* This is a reference to the fact that until now, lobbyists have had totally free access to the Senate café, restaurant and conference rooms. Since 1 January 2010 they have been obliged to wear a visitor's ID card.

### marcher sur l'eau     `*`
This is a reference to the miracle of Jesus walking on the water. 'And in the fourth watch of the night, he came unto them, walking upon the sea.' *A la quatrième veille de la nuit, Jésus alla vers eux, marchant sur la mer.* See Matthew 14: 25. See also Mark 6: 48–49 and John 6: 19. **Seul Dexia, marchant sur les eaux avec un résultat net bien plus solide qu'attendu, peut laisser accroire que les derniers du peloton boursier seront les premiers à s'en sortir.** © *Les Echos 20 424.* Dexia is a bank particularly active in the area of financing for local authorities that has made miraculous profits and avoided going under. See above 'derniers seront les premiers'.

### Mathusalem (l'age de/vieux comme)     `**`
'Mathuselah.' The oldest patriarch mentioned in the Old Testament. According to the Bible he is said to have lived 969 years. 'And all the days of Methuselah were nine hundred sixty and nine years: and he died.' *Toute la durée de la vie de Mathusalem fut de neuf cent soixante-neuf ans, puis il mourut.* See Genesis 5: 27. Today, it refers to either old age or a point in the very distant past. **L'économie de marché date de Mathusalem.** © *Le Point 1884.*

### Messie nm.     `***`
'Messiah.' From the Hebrew term 'the annointed one', the promised deliverer of the Jews. For Christians, it is Jesus. It is the concept rather than the word that we find in the Bible. Figuratively speaking, it refers to any saviour or liberator of a people or a country. **Steve Jobs, messie de la presse écrite?** © *Le Nouvel Observateur 2359.* This heading refers to the fact that the latest product from Apple, the 'iSlate' will enable the on-lining of newspaper articles but will open up the possibility of remuneration of on-line news. This is good news for the newspaper sector which is going through hard times.

### Moïse     `*`
Moses was the founder of the Jewish religion. He was the leader to whom God gave the Commandments and the one who led the Jewish people out of

Egypt. He is recognized by both the Christian and Islamic religions as a major prophet. The quote below refers to the miracle of the parting of the waves of the Dead Sea. The children of Israel had been allowed to leave Egypt after Moses had provoked the plagues. But after having given his permission for them to leave, Pharaoh changed his mind and sent his soldiers in pursuit of the Israelites. 'And lift thou up thy rod, and stretch out thine hand over the sea, and divide it: and the children of Israel shall go into the midst of the sea on dry ground.' *Toi, lève ton bâton, étends ta main sur la mer et fends-là, que les Israélites puissent pénétrer à pied sec au milieu de la mer.* Exodus 14: 16. *...l'écran tactile et sa réalité augmentée procurent un sentiment de puissance et de plénitude surnaturelles dont ne sont dignes que les divinités et les consommateurs ... Moïse employa un bâton pour entrouvrir la mer Morte: il aurait sans doute adoré la simplicité biblique d'un smartphone. L'Express 3064.* This is a remark about the magic quality of a smartphone.

## Moloch                                                            `**`

The Hebrew name for 'king' but also the name of a cruel Ammonite god and the name of a ritual sacrifice of children in his name. 'Then did Solomon build an high place for Chemosh the abomination of Moab, in the mount that is before Jerusalem, and for Molech the abomination of the children of Ammon.' *C'est alors que Solomon construisit un sanctuaire à Kemosh, l'abomination de Moab, sur la montagne à l'orient de Jérusalem et à Molèk, l'abomination des Ammonites.* See Kings (1) 11: 7. Today, it has come to mean anything which requires a very great sacrifice. *L'homme décentré, hier, par le socialisme au profit de l'État Léviathan est escamoté cette fois par le néolibéralisme au profit de l'argent Moloch.* © *Le Point 1876.* This text refers to man having been 'reduced' in the Soviet system and 'damaged' in the system of the market economy. See above 'Léviathan'.

## multiplication des petits pains. La                               `***`

This is a reference to one of the miracles (five loaves and two fishes) said to have been performed by Jesus. 'And he took the five loaves, and the two fishes, and looking up to heaven, he blessed, and brake; and gave to the disciples to set before the multitude. And they did all eat and were filled.' *Prenant alors les cinq pains et les deux poissons, il leva les yeux au ciel, les bénit, les rompit, il les donnait pour les servir à la foule. Ils mangèrent et furent tous rassasiés.* See Luke 9: 16–17. See also Matthew 14: 19–20, Mark 6: 41–42, and John 6: 11–12. *En Bourgogne les petits pains se multiplient.* © *Les Echos 20 517.* This is a reference to the fact that 50 per cent of the payroll of the industrial bread producer Jacquet can be found in the Burgundy region.

## Noé                                                               `**`
See above 'Arche de Noé'.

### œil pour œil

See 'Talion'.

### olivier (une branche d')

'Olive branch.' In western culture, this is the symbol of peace and goodwill. In the book of Genesis 8: 8–12, Noah released a dove from the ark in order to know if the flood waters had receded. On the second attempt, the dove returned with an olive leaf in its mouth. ***Le bec fermé, je vais porter la branche d'olivier.*** These are the words of the Ukranian politician, Ioulia Tymochenko quoted in © *Le Monde 19 709.* She lost the presidential elections in February 2010. See above 'colombe de la paix'.

### olivier (rameaux d') nm.

When Christ entered Jerusalem on Palm Sunday, his route was covered with palm branches. 'And the most part of the multitude spread their garments in the way and others cut branches from the trees and spread them in the way.' *Alors les gens en très nombreuse foule étendirent leurs manteaux sur le chemin; d'autres coupaient des branches aux arbres et en jonchaient le chemin.* See Matthew 21: 8. ***Mais les rameaux d'olivier américains se trouvent à présent engrenés sur la rivalité de plus en plus ouverte du président Medvedev et de son premier ministre … Poutine.*** © *Le Figaro 20 141.* This text refers to the fact that Obama has gained the respect of Chile and Brazil and has also moderated the American position on the nuclear shield. But for the moment, the American peace initiatives seem to have become pawns in the game of rivalry between the two Russian leaders.

### Ô mort, où est ta victoire?

'O death, where is thy victory, O death, where is thy sting?' *Ô mort, où est ta victoire, Ô mort, où est ton aiguillon?* See Corinthians (1) 15: 55. ***Oxymore, où est ta victoire.*** © *Le Canard Enchaîné 4612.* This was the heading of an article about a book entitled *La Politique de l'oxymore* by the intellectual Bertrand Méheust. See Chapter 4 'oxymore'.

### paille et la poutre nf.

This refers to the parable of the mote and the beam. 'And why beholdest thou the mote that is in thy brother's eye, but considerest not the beam that is in thine own eye.' *Qu'as-tu à regarder la paille qui est dans l'œil de ton frère? Et la poutre qui est dans ton œil à toi, tu ne la remarques pas!* See Luke 6: 41. ***…selon la vieille allégorie de la paille et de la poutre que vient d'illustrer avec brio Jean-Pierre Raffarin.*** © *Marianne 593.* During a visit to Peking, Raffarin was obliged to kow-tow to the Chinese while criticizing the mayor of Paris for having made the Dalai Lama an honorary citizen of the capital.

### Pandémonium nm.    `*`

Strictly speaking, this is not a biblical reference. It comes from the Greek *pan* (all) and *daimon* (demon) 'the abode of all demons.' The word was born of the pen of John Milton (1608–74) in *Paradise Lost*, written in 1663 shortly after the end of the Republic and the restoration of the monarchy in the person of Charles II. It was the name of the palace of Satan, the capital of hell. ***Matignon est un enfer, paraît-il, l'Élysée un pandémonium.*** © *Le Canard Enchaîné 4593.*

### pardon nm.    `***`

***La bonne foi sera proportionnelle au montant des capitaux cachés puis rapatriés. Donc, il sera beaucoup pardonné à ceux qui ont beaucoup fraudé. Il y a quelque chose de Jésus Christ en Eric Woerth.*** © *Marianne 625.* The context is the repatriation of the money placed in tax havens by tax evaders. The former minister of budget said that their 'good faith' would be taken into account if they repatriated their money. This text is the echo of 'Her sins, which are many, are forgiven; for she loved much.' *Ses péchés, ses nombreux péchés, lui sont remis, parce qu'elle a montré beaucoup d'amour.* See Luke 7: 47.

### pardonne-leur    `***`

'Forgive them.' 'Si y en a que ça les dérange d'augmenter les impôts' (the words of Nicolas Sarkozy). ***Et dire que c'est le même [Sarkozy] qui a osé s'incliner sur le cercueil de ce pauvre Druon Maurice [member of the Academie Française], pardonne-lui, il ne sait plus ce qu'il fait.*** © *Le Nouvel Observateur 2321.* This is yet another frightful example of Nicolas Sarkozy's poor level of French. The words of *Le Nouvel Observateur* are a reference to the words of Christ on the cross: 'Father, forgive them, for they know not what they do.' *Père, pardonne-leur, car ils ne savent pas ce qu'ils font.* See Luke 23: 34.

### parousie nf.    `*`

'Parousia.' From the Greek term meaning 'presence' or 'arrival', it is a synonym of 'the second coming'. ***Un rapide calcul convainc Newton qu'il est bien l'élu. Si l'on ajoute à 666 les mille ans prévus avant la parousie (le retour glorieux du Christ), cela donne 1666, l'année où voyant une pomme tomber, le jeune Isaac découvrit la loi de la gravitation universelle.*** © *Les Echos 20 636.* See above 'Bête de l'Apocalypse'.

### péché originel nm.    `***`

'Original sin.' In Christian teaching, this refers to the inherent sin or depravity of man stemming from Adam's original disobedience to God. ***Le péché originel*** [of Christine Lagarde, minister of finance] ***était son incapacité ... de présenter la loi Tepa comme autre chose qu'un cadeau aux riches.*** © *Le Point 1884.* See above 'faute originelle' and Chapter 14 'Tepa'.

### pierre d'achoppement nf.   ( \*\*\* )

'A stumbling block.' It was the stone of the Temple in Jerusalem that the unbeliever tripped over. A 'stone of stumbling' is mentioned in Isaiah 8: 14–15, and we can find 'Get thee behind me, Satan, thou art a stumbling block unto me'. *Arrière de moi, Satan! tu m'es en scandale.* See Matthew 16: 23. See also Romans 9: 32–33. *Le dialogue s'impose autour des principaux points d'achoppement du projet de statut qui n'ont rien d'insurmontable.* © *Le Point 1909.*

### pierre angulaire nf.   ( \*\*\* )

The corner stone is the fundamental stone that is the symbolic mark of the beginning of the construction of a building. 'Behold, I lay in Zion for a foundation, a stone, a tried stone, a precious corner stone of sure foundation.' *Voici que je vais poser en Sion une pierre, une pierre de granit, pierre angulaire, précieuse pierre de fondation bien assise.* See Isaiah 28: 16. *...la maîtrise du français est à ses yeux la pierre angulaire d'une éducation réussie.* © *Les Echos 20 598.* These were the words of Jean-Michel Blanquer, former *Recteur* of Créteil who maintains that mastering one's mother tongue is the basis of a sound education. See Chapter 10 'Académie'.

### pierre (jeter la première)   ( \*\*\* )

'To cast the first stone.' This refers to the lesson Christ gave the scribes and the Pharisees who were about to stone an adulturous woman to death. 'He that is without sin among you, let him first cast a stone at her.' *Que celui d'entre vous qui n'a jamais péché lui jette la première pierre.* See John 8: 7. *Que celui qui n'a jamais marivaudé par e-mail ou SMS lui jette la première pierre.* © *L'Express 3020.* This sentence was taken from an article about infidelity in France and flirting by SMS. See Chapter 5 'marivaudage'.

### plaies d'Egypte nfpl.   ( \*\*\* )

'Plagues of Egypt.' *Quant à François Bayrou, qui avait évoqué la décadence de l'Empire romain lorsque le Prince Jean avait été nommé à la tête de l'EPAD, il parle maintenant des dix plaies d'Egypte.* © *Le Monde 20 130.* The various plagues included an invasion of frogs, hailstones, an invasion of locust, the tenth plague being the death of the firstborn. See Exodus 9: 10, 11. This text refers to the row provoked, at the time, by the proposed nomination of Jean Sarkozy (the president's son) as head of the Epad. See Chapter 14 'Epad'.

### Ponce Pilate   ( \*\*\* )

'Pontius Pilate.' *Ponce Pilate ne peut demeurer impuni.* The words of Jean-Claude Marin, the Public Prosecutor in the Clearstream trial quoted in © *Le Monde 20 140.* The Pontius Pilate in question is Dominique de Villepin. See above 'laver les mains (S'en)'.

**porter sa croix**                                                                 <div>*</div>

'To bear one's burden', to endure suffering with patience. ***Pendant des années, Généreux porte ainsi ses deux croix.*** © *Marianne 615.* This refers to Jacques Généreux, a socialist, who not only refused the lucrative opportunities to earn more money giving speeches to the financial community (instead of his teaching responsiblities at Sciences Po) but who was also marginalized within the socialist hierarchy at Solférino. So he has lost on both counts. 'And he that doth not take his cross and follow after me, is not worthy of me.' *Qui ne prend pas sa croix et ne suit pas derrière moi n'est pas digne de moi.* See Matthew 10: 38, Mark 8: 34 and Luke 9: 23.

**prêcher dans le désert**                                                          <div>***</div>

*Vox clamantis in deserto.* 'The voice of one crying in the wilderness.' *C'est ici la voix de celui qui crie dans le désert.* See Matthew 3: 3, Mark 1: 3, Luke 3: 4 and John 1: 23. ***Ils ont prêché dans le désert pendant des années. Ils dénonçaient le capitalisme dévoyé. Qui les a entendus?*** © *Marianne 598.* Many specialists had been whistle-blowing about the imminence of a financial crisis but their warnings went unheeded. This expression means to speak without being heard. But see also Isaiah 40: 3 which gives another complexion to this saying with a small punctuation change. Compare the traditional 'a voice crying in the wilderness', with Isaiah 'A voice cries: in the wilderness prepare the way for Yahve.'

**prophète dans son pays (nul n'est)**                                              <div>**</div>

*Nemo propheta in patria.* When Jesus preached in Nazareth, his home town, he was met by the sarcastic remarks of those who had known him in the past, and he replied: 'A prophet is not without honour save in his own country and in his own house.' *Un prophète n'est méprisé que dans sa patrie et dans sa maison.* See Matthew 13: 57, and Luke 4: 24. ***Nul n'est prophète.*** © *Le Point 1949.* This refers to the artist William Bouguereau (1825–1905) who was never a great name in France but whose work is very well known and appreciated by American collectors.

**prophète de malheur nm.**                                                         <div>***</div>

Jeremiah, the Old Testament prophet, was constantly predicting doom and destruction and was put to death by his fellow citizens. ***...mais comme personne ne veut être le prophète de malheur, la Banque de France n'évoque pour l'heure qu'un scénario de récession limitée.*** © *Marianne 600.* All of the predictions about the end of the recession have been optimistic because nobody wants to tell the unsavoury truth, not even the Bank of France. See above 'jérémiades'.

**Purgatoire nm.**                                                                  <div>***</div>

'Purgatory.' A place of purification. This is not mentioned as such in the Bible but can be inferred. It was developed as part of Catholic dogma. ***À gauche, le Parlement européen est plutôt considéré comme un purgatoire,*** *avant que les instances du parti ou les hasards de la vie politique vous ramène dans le giron national.* © *Les Echos 20 437.* The European Parliament is seen by some politicians as a period of punishment inflicted on MPs who, after purification, can return to pick up their national career.

## Rendre à César
See above 'César'.

## Rois Mages nmpl.
'The Three Magi'. *...on voit tous les faux Rois Mages se pencher au-dessus du berceau.*© *Marianne 613.* This text refers to the new French football idol Yoann Gourcuff and the football business that threatens to destroy him now that he has become an icon adored by everyone. See above 'Épiphanie'.

## Salomé
The name 'Salome' comes from the Hebrew *shalom* or 'peace'. Salome was the beautiful, lascivious step daughter of Herod Antipas. He had married his brother's wife Herodias and provoked the criticism of John the Baptist whom he imprisoned. John the Baptist's criticism provoked the anger of Herodias. She arranged for her daughter to dance in front of Herod. He was impressed and said that he would give her whatever she asked for. On her mother's advice, Salome asked for the head of John the Baptist. 'And she came in straight away with haste unto the king, and asked, saying "I will that thou forthwith give me in a charger the head of John the Baptist".' See Mark 6: 22–28. *Rentrant aussitôt en hâte auprès du roi, elle lui fit cette demande: 'je veux que tout de suite tu me donnes sur un plat la tête de Jean le Baptiste'.* Les femmes ... *peuvent être aussi redoutables qu'une Salomé.* © *Marianne 589.* See Chapter 7 'Circé', for the context of this quote.

## sauterelles (la plaie des) nfpl.
'The plague of locusts'. This was the eighth of the ten plagues sent by God to persuade the Pharaoh to allow the Israelites to leave Egypt. 'And the Lord said unto Moses, "Stretch out thine hand over the land of Egypt for the locusts, that they may come upon the land of Egypt, and eat every herb of the land, even all that the hail hath left"'. *Yahvé dit à Moïse: 'Etends ta main sur le pays d'Egypte pour que viennent les sauterelles; qu'elles montent sur le pays d'Egypte et qu'elles dévorent toute l'herbe du pays, tout ce qu'a épargné la grêle'.* See Exodus 10: 12–15. *Mais à en croire le Ministre de l'Économie, il était impossible d'y couper: ces hausses seraient une variété de catastrophe naturelle. Comme un tremblement de terre, ou une invasion de sauterelles.* © *Le Canard Enchaîné 4564.* This text refers to the significant increases in energy prices and likens them to an inevitable plague. NB: 'sauterelle' in the biblical context is translated by 'locust'. The usual translation of 'sauterelle' is 'grasshoper'. In the fable *La Cigale et la fourmi* by La Fontaine 'grasshopper' is translated by 'cigale', i.e. a 'cicada'.

## sème le vent, récolte la tempête (qui)    **

The words are based on the quotation that comes from the book of Hosea. 'For they sow the wind, and they shall reap the whirlwind.' *Puisqu'ils ont semé du vent, ils moissonneront la tempête.* See Hosea 8: 7. ***Qui sème la misère récolte la colère.*** © *Marianne 627.* These are the words of a CGT trades union leader (Xavier Mathieu) at the Continental tyre factory in Clairvoix; it was a reflection on the violence of French industrial relations in the wake of an alarming number of factory closures in 2009.

## Sodome et Gomorrhe    *

Sodom, in the Bible, is the name of a city destroyed by fire because of the sinfulness of its inhabitants, male homosexuality and anal sex. The neighbouring city of Gomorrah suffered the same fate. 'And he looked toward Sodom and Gomorrah, and toward all the land of the Plain, and beheld, and, lo, the smoke of the land went up as the smoke of a furnace.' *Et il jeta son regard sur Sodome et Gomorrhe et sur toute la Plaine, et voici, qu'il vit la fumée monter du pays comme la fumée d'une fournaise.* Genesis 19: 27. ***Procédure express de divorce, mariage homo, fin de catéchisme obligatoire dans l'enseignement public ... Bref, Sodome et Gomorrhe.*** © *Le Canard Enchaîné 4559.* This is a reflection on changing life styles which for some Catholic fundamentalists represent the summit of immorality: quick divorce, same-sex marriage and an end to religious instruction at school.

## Salomon (jugement de) nm.    **

Solomon was King of Israel *c.* 970–931 BC. His wisdom and sense of justice were proverbial. His judgement was solicited by two prostitutes who, living under the same roof, had both given birth to a son during the night. One of the newborn babies died of suffocation during the night. The mother of the dead child accused the other of having substituted her dead son and taken the living one. Solomon asked for a sword to be brought and gave orders that the child should be split into two and one half given to each of the mothers. The dead child's mother agreed to this proposition while the true mother of the child in question preferred to renounce her claim in order to save her child. On seeing this, Solomon concluded that she must indeed be the real mother and gave her the child. 'And all Israel heard of the judgement which the king had judged; and they feared the king: for they saw that the wisdom of God was in him to do judgement.' *Tout Israël apprit le jugement qu'avait rendu le roi, et ils révérèrent le roi car ils virent qu'il y avait en lui une sagesse divine pour rendre la justice.* This story can be found in Kings (1) 3: 16–28. ***Avant que ne tombe des plus hautes sphères un jugement de Salomon: 's'il n'y a pas de désordre, laissez-les filmer tranquillement.*** © *Le Monde 19 800.* This text refers to the delayed authorization for the shooting of a scene for the film *London Dreams* in front of the French National Assembly.

## stigmates nmpl.

'Stigmata.' The traces of the wounds suffered by Christ during his crucifixion. Today, it means a scar or mark of shame. *Il [le sportif] se targue parfois de porter les stigmates de sa foi ... tendinites, entorses et autres blessures.* © *Marianne 586.* In this text, a comparison is drawn between sport and religion. The sportsman, bearing his scars, is intolerant of those who do not share his passion and like all high priests of other religions he promises a cardiovascular hell to the non-believer.

## Tables de la Loi nfpl.

*Lex Duodecim Tabularum* (the Law of the Twelve Tables) represent the first body of written Roman law. They are also the tablets upon which were written the Ten Commandments that God gave to Moses. 'And the Lord said unto Moses, Hew thee two tables of stone like unto the first: and I will write upon the tables the words that were on the first tables which thou brakest.' *Yahvé dit à Moïse, Taille deux tables de pierre semblables aux premières, et j'écrirai sur les tables les paroles qui étaient sur les premières tables que tu as brisées.* See Exodus 34: 1–4. *Les tablettes et la loi.* © *Les Echos 20 627.* This was the heading of an article about the new iPad and the possible legal problems that its commercialization may raise because of anti-competition considerations.

## Talion (la loi du)

*Lex Talionis,* from the Latin word *talis* meaning 'such' or 'the same'. The law of the Talion can be found in the most ancient code of law, i.e. the Hamurabi Code of the kingdom of Babylon. It is a law that requires punishment in kind for the crime committed. It is thus represented by the expression 'an eye for an eye, a tooth for a tooth'. 'Eye for eye, tooth for tooth, hand for hand, foot for foot, burning for burning, wound for wound, stripe for stripe.' *Oeil pour œil, dent pour dent, pied pour pied, brûlure pour brûlure, meutrissure pour meurtrissure, plaie pour plaie.* See Exodus 21: 24–25. *Œil pour œil, vache pour vache.* © *Le Canard Enchaîné 4624.* In the conflict opposing milk producers and the Leclerc supermarket chain, during which the dairy farmers blocked the supermarket car park, Leclerc, playing tit for tat, cancelled the regular customer discount card enjoyed by the dairy farmers when they did their shopping at the Leclerc supermarket. NB: Hamurabi, king of Babylon (1793–1750 BC).

## temps pour toute chose (Il y a un)

'To every thing there is a season, and a time to every purpose under heaven.' *Il y a un moment pour tout, et un temps pour toute chose sous le ciel.* Ecclesiastes 3: 1. *Il y a un temps pour toute chose, dit l'Ecclésiaste et dans le cottage, on cultive les relations bibliques.* © *Marianne 641.* This text is a reference to a couple against whom an offical complaint had been lodged with the magistrates in Oxford, England, because of their noisy love-making. The judge dismissed the complaint on the grounds that the noise was normal for a fundamental domestic activity. NB: this text of Ecclesiastes was put to music in 1959 by Pete Seeger and later recorded by the Byrds. It remains one of the greatest American peace songs and hits of the 1960s.

### Terre Promise nf.      `**`

Israel was the Promised Land which God had promised the Israelites when they left Egypt. Before attaining the Promised Land they had to wander in the wilderness for forty years. 'In that day, the Lord made a covenant with Abraham, saying, Unto thy seed have I given this land from the river of Egypt unto the great river Euphrates.' *Ce jour-là, Dieu conclut avec Abram\* une alliance, en disant: À ta descendance J'ai donné cette terre, depuis le fleuve d'Egypte jusqu'au grand fleuve, le fleuve Euphrate.* See Genesis 15: 18. **The Guardian, The Observer … la France n'est plus cette terre promise.** © *Le Figaro 20 057.* This is a reference to the financial difficulties of English people living in France, in the wake of the financial crisis. Many have been forced to return to England. France is no longer the land flowing with milk and honey. See above 'Exodus' and 'lait et de miel'. \*Spelling of 'Abraham' used in the Jerusalem Bible.

### tohu-bohu nm.      `***`

Hubbub or noisy confusion. From the Hebrew term, *tôhû-wâbôhû,* which describes the original chaos before the creation of the world. 'And the earth was waste and void; and darkness was upon the face of the deep.' *Or la terre était vide et vague, les ténèbres couvraient l'abîme.* See Genesis 1: 2. **Imaginez Total parrainant Polytechnique … Joli tohu-bohu à la clé.** © *Le Point 1896.* This text refers to the eternal debate in France about ethics, scholarship and corporate sponsoring. See Chapter 10 'Polytechnique'.

### touche pas (ne me)      `*`

*X, X, ne me touche pas.* © *Dossier du Canard 105.* These are an echo of the words said by Christ to Mary Magdalene (*Noli me tangere*). 'Jesus saith to her, Touch me not; for I am not yet ascended unto the Father.' *Jésus lui dit: 'Ne me touche pas, car je ne suis pas encore monté vers le Père'.* See John 20: 17. The context of this quote is the pro-Sarko attitudes of the editorial boss and news editor of a French TV channel who has cut out news items proposed by her journalists that would have been unfavourable to Nicolas Sarkozy.

### traversée du désert nf.      `***`

Usually, time spent in the political wilderness. A reference to the wanderings of the children of Israel led by Moses for over forty years before they arrived in the Promised Land. This reminds us of the forty days Christ spent in the wilderness and of the time that Abraham spent there too. 'They took their journey from Elim, and all the congregation of the children of Israel came unto the wilderness of Sin, which is between Elim and Sinai.' *Ils partirent d'Elim, et toute la communauté des Israélites arriva au désert de Sîn, situé entre Elim et le Sinaï.* See Exodus 16: 1–2. It is a period of hardship and rejection to which a politician is condemned before coming to power. The examples of Churchill and de Gaulle spring to mind. ***Ferdinand Piëch, président du conseil de surveillance de Volkswagen, prédisait une 'traversée du désert' pour l'automobile.*** © *Le Nouvel Observateur 2295.*

### vaches grasses, les années de nfpl.
( ** )

'A period of wealth and plenty.' The seven fat kine and the seven lean kine were in Pharaoh's dream that was interpreted by Joseph. 'And behold, there came up out of the river seven kine, well favoured and fatfleshed.' *...il vit monter du Nil sept vaches de belle apparence et grasses de chair.* See Genesis 41: 2. ***Mais en France, vaches maigres ou grasses, ce n'est jamais le bon moment.*** © *Le Point 1914.* This text refers to the difficulty of introducing reform in France whatever the economic situation may be.

### vaches maigres nfpl.
( *** )

'Shortage and privation.' The years of lean kine in Pharaoh's dream were interpreted by Joseph as years of shortage. 'And behold seven other kine came up after them out of the river, ill favoured and leanfleshed.' *Mais voici que sept autres vaches montèrent du Nil derrière elles, laides d'apparence et maigres de chair.* See Genesis 41: 3. ***La question d'un second porte-avions français, que certains dans l'armée de terre, ne jugent pas indispensable en période de vaches maigres.*** © *Le Figaro 20 067.* As in this example, the term is frequently associated with shrinking budgets and austerity.

### vade retro Satana(s)
( *** )

'Get thee behind me, Satan.' *Passe derrière moi, Satan!* A medieval Catholic formula used in exorcism having as its origin the Gospel according to St Mark 8: 33. See also Matthew 16: 23. ***...les strauss-khaniens ont dressé les barricades; et tous ont sonné le rassemblement. Vade retro Ségolène.*** © *Marianne 604.* The socialist old guard is doing everything possible to sabotage Ségolène Royal's chances of regaining the party leadership.

### vanitas vanitatum omnia vanitas
( * )

'Vanity of vanities, all is vanity.' *Vanité des vanités, tout est vanité.* See Ecclesiastes 1: 2. ***'Sic transit gloria' comme dirait ce latiniste [Xavier Darcos] ' ... Vanitas, vanitatum ... ' aurait enchaîné cet agrégé de lettres.*** © *Marianne 613.* Xavier Darcos is a former Latin scholar and an *agrégé* in *lettres classiques*, former minister of education, and former minister of labour and industrial relations. These terms might sum up his disillusion about what promised to be his great political future. See Chapter 13 'sic transit gloria mundi' and 'vanitas vanitatum'.

## Veau d'or nm.    `***`

'The Golden Calf'. After leaving Egypt, Moses left the children of Israel and ascended Mount Sinai in order to receive the Tables of the Law. Impatient, the children of Israel pressed Aaron the priest, to build a golden calf with the jewellery of the women. Their jewellery was melted down and a golden calf was built and the children of Israel fell down in adoration before it. On seeing this, on his return, Moses smashed the Tables of the Law. Idols were expressly forbidden by the third commandment. 'And all the people brake off the golden rings which were in their ears and brought them unto Aaron. And he received it at their hand, and fashioned it with a graving tool, and made it a molten calf.' *Tout le peuple ôta les anneaux d'or qui étaient à leurs oreilles, et ils les apportèrent à Aaron. Il reçut l'or de leurs mains, le fit fondre dans un moule et en fit une statue de veau.* See Exodus 32: 3–4. Today, it refers to the adoration of money. ***Le bon sens s'effraie des brides lâchées à toute une génération d'agents de finance, mirliflores de la caste du Veau d'or.*** © *Le Point 1882.* This is a reflection about the young traders who have their share of responsibility in the financial crisis. The term *mirliflore* refers to a person who is young, elegant and very self-satisfied.

## veau sacré nm.    `**`

See 'Veau d'or' above. ***Nous voudrions tant partager ce combat contre l'avilissement des puissants devant le veau sacré.*** © *Marianne 586. Marianne* wishes to combat the debasing of the political elite which seems to believe that 'dough' and 'success' are synonymous.

## voie royale nf.    `**`

'The king's highway.' The safest and surest way. In ancient times this was the caravan 'ring road', an itinerary bordering the desert beyond the river Jordan and the Dead Sea. It was the route that the Israelites wanted to take to reach the Promised Land by going through the kingdom of Edom. 'We will go along the king's highway, we will not turn aside to the right hand, nor to the left until we have passed thy border.' *Nous suivrons la route royale sans nous écarter à droite ou à gauche, jusqu'à ce que nous ayons traversé ton territoire.* See Numbers 20: 17. One might say that going to l'ENA is the 'voie royale' for anyone thinking of working in the higher echelons of the French civil service. ***Décidément, Roland Barthès est très stimulant [...] il les encourage [writers] à parler de leur région par la voie royale de l'enfance.*** © *Le Nouvel Observateur 2359.* The best way to get people to write about a region is to elicit their childhood memories.

## voies du Seigneur nfpl.    `***`

'My kingdom is not of this world.' *Mon royaume n'est pas de ce monde.* See John 18: 36 and 'how unsearcheable are his judgements and his ways past tracing out'. *Que ses jugements sont insondables, et ses voies incompréhensibles.* See Romans 11: 33. ***Mon royaume n'est pas de ce monde, mais les voies du Seigneur sont à péage.*** © *Le Canard Enchaîné 4585.* This is a reference to the increase in motorways tolls in France. Notice the pun on 'ways of God' (voies de Dieu) and 'lanes' of a motorway, e.g. 'a three-lane motorway' ('une autoroute à trois voies').

### Voile (écarter la)

**\*\***

'To lift the veil' is the equivalent of 'to reveal' or 'to disclose' and comes from the Greek word *apokalupsis*. This word gives its name to the last book of the Bible, 'Apocalypse', i.e. 'Revelation'. *...l'architecte Caecilia Pieri a voulu écarter ce voile de mythes et de souffrances.* © *Marianne 625*. See above 'Apocalypse'. This is a reference to the architect Caecilia Pieri who has carried out extensive architectural research on Bagdad and wishes to put an end to the myth that Bagdad has always been a city of blood and violence with a nostalgia for its past glory of twelve centuries ago. Her aim is to reveal the harmony and interpenetration of oriental and western styles of architecture.

### Vulgate nf.

**\*\*\***

Latin version of the Bible by St Jerome in the fourth century serving as an authorized version for the Roman Catholic Church. In French, the term is used as 'commonly accepted' and can mean 'a doctrine'. *Ils n'ont connu que la vulgate néolibérale qui théorisait l'inutilité de réfléchir.* © *Marianne 602*. This is a reference to the neo-liberal economists who were brought up to believe that there was no point in reflecting about market forces because the invisible hand of the market would take care of everything.

### zizanie (semer la)

**\*\*\***

'To provoke discord.' 'Zizanie' is considered to be the bad grain in contrast to the good. 'But while men slept, his enemy came and sowed tares also among the wheat.' *Mais pendant que les gens dormaient, son ennemi vint, sema de l'ivraie parmi le blé.* See Matthew 13: 25. 'Semer la zizanie' is to create tension. *Les accords militaires sèment la zizanie en Amérique latine.* © *Le Figaro 20 258*. This quote concerns the enhanced cooperation between Bogota and Washington that has led to tension and remilitarization in Latin America. See above 'ivraie'.

## Additional notes

### Translations of the titles of the books of the Bible

| | |
|---|---|
| Acts of the Apostles | Actes des Apôtres |
| I Corinthians | La Première épître aux Corinthiens |
| Daniel | Daniel |
| Deuteronomy | Le Deutéronome |
| Ecclesiastes | L'Ecclésiaste |
| Exodus | L'Exode |

| | |
|---|---|
| Genesis | La Genèse |
| Hosea | Osée |
| Isaiah | Isaïe |
| Jeremiah | Jérémie |
| Job | Job |
| John (The Gospel according to …) | Jean (L'Evangile selon …) |
| Joshua | Josué |
| Jude | Epître de saint Jude |
| Judges | Le livre des Juges |
| Kings | Le livre des Rois |
| Leviticus | Le Lévitique |
| Luke (The Gospel according to …) | Luc (L'Évangile selon …) |
| Mark (The Gospel according to …) | Marc (L'Évangile selon …) |
| Matthew (The Gospel according to …) | Matthieu (L'Évangile selon …) |
| Numbers | Les Nombres |
| Proverbs. The | Les Proverbes |
| Psalms. The | Les Psaumes |
| Revelation (without an 's') | Apocalypse (no article) |
| Samuel (I & II) | Les livres de Samuel |

A few translation considerations for non-English speaking readers. The difference between modern French and biblical French is not so marked as the difference between modern English and biblical English.

| French term | Modern English term | English biblical term |
|---|---|---|
| à | to | unto |
| avancer | to come forward | to come forth |
| brisa | broke | brake |
| colère | anger | wrath |
| désert | desert | wilderness |
| descendance | descendants | seed |
| fait | does | doth |
| frappa | struck | smote |
| jeter | throw | cast |
| laissez les petits enfants | let the little children | suffer the little children |
| lança | threw | slang |
| ne viens pas | don't come | come not |
| paille | straw | mote |
| plat | platter | charger |
| plat de lentilles | dish of lentils | mess of pottage |
| près | near | nigh |
| prostituée | prostitute | harlot |
| regardez | look | lo |
| sauterelle | grasshopper | locust |
| savaient | knew | wist |
| soir | evening | eventide |
| tien/tienne | yours | thine |

| toi | you | thee |
|-----|-----|------|
| ton/ta | your | thy |
| tu | you | thou |
| vaches | cows | kine |
| voyez | see | behold |
| vous | you | ye |

NB 'thine' is usually the possessive pronoun but can be the possessive adjective when followed by a word beginning with a vowel. Thus, from The Lord's Prayer 'thy kingdom come' but from *Ode to the West Wind* by Shelley we have 'Thine azur sister of the Spring shall blow'.

# Chapter 9

# Who's who

In this section, it is hoped that the reader will learn much more than the names of politicians and corporate leaders. The attentive reader will perhaps grasp the ferocity of the competitive examination system in France, and the stereotypical career path that practically all of the makers and shakers have taken. The reader will perhaps be surprised to learn that university studies, generally speaking, rarely lead to the top in politics or industry. They will perhaps understand why the monoculture of the *grande école* is causing problems in some sectors of industry, why working in teams is so alien to the French corporate mind and why French companies are run the way they are, as pyramids, with power distance governing the top-down approach to management. Things are changing, but very slowly.

**Abbé Pierre**  ( * )
Henri Groués (1912–2007) was a French Catholic priest. He was a war hero of the French Resistance, member of parliament and founder of the charity organization Emmaüs that was set up with the aim of helping the poor and the homeless. The Foundation bearing his name was established in the wake of the extremely cold winter of 1954 during which many homeless people died.

**Allègre, Claude**  ( * )
Socialist politician, born in Paris in 1937 and a geophysicist by training. He is internationally recognized for his scientific research and was awarded the Crafoord Prize in 1986. He is a member of the Académie des Sciences. He was minister of education, research and technology in the first Jospin government (1997–2000). He is remembered for his provocative phrase 'il faut dégraisser le mammouth' referring to the need to downsize the national education organization and also for his remarks about climate change which go against the generally held theories. He has since left the socialist party.

**Alliot-Marie, Michèle**  ( ** )
Right-wing politician (UMP), born in 1946 in the Val-de-Marne (94). She trained as a lawyer. She has just resigned as minister of foreign affairs

amid the Tunisian affair. She was formerly secretary general of the Gaullist RPR party, the forerunner of the UMP. Prior to being appointed as minister of justice, she was minister of the interior. Her nickname is 'MAM' and 'l'amère Michèle'. See Chapter 1 '*Mère Michel*'.

## Amara, Fadela

Socialist politician, she was born in Clermont-Ferrand in 1964 of Algerian parents, one of eleven children. She trained as a bookkeeper and became president of the women's defence organization 'Ni putes, ni soumises'. She was junior minister for urban policy in the second Fillon government. See Chapter 1 'Ni putes, ni soumises'.

## Arlette

See 'Laguiller'.

## Arnault, Bernard

A French businessman born in 1949 in Roubaix in the north of France. Polytechnician, *promotion* X 1969. He is the owner of the luxury goods empire LVMH, the biggest fortune in France and the 15th biggest fortune in the world. He was a witness at Nicolas Sarkozy's wedding to his second wife.

## Attali, Jacques

Socialist politician, born in Algiers in 1943. Polytechnician *major de sa promotion* X 63. He is an *Ingénieur des mines*, holds the diploma of Sciences Po and graduated from l'ENA in 1970 (*promotion* Robespierre). Economist, prolific writer, senior civil servant and special advisor to François Mitterrand as of 1981. Founder and head of the BIRD in 1990, member of the Conseil d'État. Teaches economics at Polytechnique, the University of Paris Dauphine, and at the École des Ponts et Chaussées. In 2009 he was entrusted by Nicolas Sarkozy with writing a report on how to free up growth in France entitled 'The Attali Report'. See Chapter 4 'Attali, Jacques'.

## Aubry, Martine

Socialist politician, née Delors (her father was the minister of the economy, finance and budget between 1981–4), she was born in 1950 in the seventeenth *arrondissement* of Paris. She is a graduate of Sciences Po. She graduated from l'ENA in 1975 (*promotion* Léon Blum). She was minister of labour, employment and vocational training in the government of Édith Cresson and Pierre Beregevoy between 1991–3. She has been mayor of Lille since 2001 and first secretary of the socialist party since November 2008. She is the 'mother' of the 35 hour week and her dictatorial manner has earned her several nicknames: 'la mère emptoire' (péremptoire), 'Madame Véto' and 'Titine' which is the hypocoristic form of 'Martine'.

## Bachelot, Roselyne       `***`

Right-wing UMP politician, she was born in Nevers in 1946. She trained as a pharmaceutical chemist and holds a doctorate in this field. Minister of the environment in the first and second Raffarin governments between May and June 2002. Currently minister of Solidarity and Social Cohesion (Nov 2010). Notorious for her verbal blunders and gaudy-coloured clothes. Courageously defended the bill concerning the PACS (civil weddings for homosexuals) in Parliament against the members of her own party. She came under attack for her management of the flu epidemic and the huge orders placed for millions of vaccine doses in 2009/10 for an epidemic that did not happen. Accused of nepotism with the appointment of her son within her own ministry at the time she was minister of health. He holds a diploma awarded by a private art school! She survived the flu vaccine scandal.

## Balkany, Patrick       `**`

Founding member of the RPR and today a member of the UMP. Born in Neuilly-sur-Seine in 1948. He studied at the Geneva school of commerce. He is mayor of Levallois-Perret in the Hauts-de-Seine (92) and member of parliament for the fifth constituency. He was sentenced in 1996 for having used three municipal employees (who were designated as such) to take care of his flat in Levallois-Perret and his country home in Geverny. Their salaries were paid for by the taxpayers of Levallois-Perret. He received a 15-month suspended prison sentence, was fined 200,000 francs and made ineligible for two years. In 1999 the Regional Accounting Office sentenced him to repay €520,000 to the municipality. This debt was graciously waived by the then UMP minister of finance, Thierry Breton, in 2007. He has also been sentenced by the courts for public insult and defamation against a communist member of the town council. He was re-elected as mayor of Levallois-Perret in 2007 and as member of parliament.

## Balladur, Edouard       `**`

Right-wing UMP politician, born in Smyrna, Turkey in 1929. Studied at Sciences Po. Graduated from l'ENA in 1957 (*promotion* France Afrique). He left l'ENA *dans la botte* and chose the Conseil d'État to begin his career. He was advisor to President Georges Pompidou and under his presidency became secretary general of the Élysée. He was prime minister under François Mitterrand from 1993–5. Balladur stood against Jacques Chirac in the presidential election of 1995 in which he was eliminated in the first round. He was recently entrusted with making recommendations to modernize the institutions of the Fifth Republic. He has several nicknames, e.g. 'l'ami de trente ans' (the words of Jacques Chirac) and because of his condescending attitude, he is also called 'Sa Courtoise Suffisance'. Because of his Turkish birthplace (Smyrna, the former name of the Turkish town of Izmir) he is also known as 'Ballamou', 'Ballamouchi' and 'l'Ottoman'.

## Bayrou, François     `***`

A centre-right politician, born in 1951 in Bordères in the Pyrénées Atlantiques (64). He obtained his *agrégation* in *lettres classiques* at the University of Bordeaux at the age of 23. He is the author of a best-selling biography of Henri de Navarre. He has held several positions of town councillor or regional councillor in the Pyrénées Atlantiques. All of his ministerial positions have been in the area of education. After having scored over 18 per cent in the 2007 presidential election, he founded and became president of the Mouvement Démocratique (MoDem), a centre-right party. Several of his team members have since deserted him and have gone over to the UMP right-wing party. For tax purposes he is officially recognized as a 'farmer', hence the nickname and pun 'l'homme détracteur'. He is also known as the 'ego-centriste' because of his style of leadership of the centre party. His least flattering nickname is 'Lou Bayrou' (see below Gaudin). His nickname 'le Béarnais' or 'le prince du Béarn' comes from the fact that he was born in this region and that his political power base has always been there; the Béarn takes its name from an old province that today lies within the *département* of Pyrénées-Atlantiques (64).

## Bertrand, Xavier     `***`

Right-wing politician (UMP), born in 1965 in what was then known as Châlons sur Marne (51) (Châlons en Champagne since 1995). He studied at the University of Reims where he graduated with a master's degree in public law. He also holds a DESS (*diplôme d'études supérieures spécialisées*) in local administration. An insurance agent by profession, he is a member of the Grand Orient de France, the main French masonic organization. He is currently minister of health (Feb 2011). He is known as 'Chouchou' ('the pet' as in 'teacher's pet').

## Besancenot, Olivier     `*`

Extreme left-wing politician (NPA) born in 1974 in Levallois-Perret in the Hauts-de-Seine (92). A postman by trade, he holds a bachelor's degree in history from the University of Paris X Nanterre. He was head of the Ligue Communiste Révolutionnaire party (founded by Alain Krivine in 1968) and was this party's candidate in the 2007 presidential election. The party was dissolved in 2009 and became the Nouveau Parti Anticapitaliste, with Besancenot as its leader. He delivers the mail in the Neuilly area, hence his nickname 'le facteur de Neuilly'.

## Besson, Eric     `***`

Socialist politician, born in Morocco in 1958. Initially member of the socialist party and *député* of the Drôme 1997–2002. He used to be a virulent critic of Nicolas Sarkozy. On the eve of the first round of the presidential election of 2007, he deserted Ségolène Royal and went over to the Sarkozy camp. His name has since become a synonym of betrayal. He failed the entrance examination to l'ENA. He was formely minister of immigration and national identity. He has since earned the nickname of 'Iago-go boy', a play on words using 'go-go boy' and the name of the arch traitor in Shakespeare's play *Othello*. He is minister of industry, energy and digital economy (Nov 2010).

## Bettencourt, Liliane     ( \*\*\* )

Liliane Bettencourt was born in Paris in 1922. She is the richest woman in France, being the major shareholder in the l'Oréal cosmetics group founded by her father Eugène Schueller. Her name is now linked to one of the biggest scandals of the fifth Republic, Bettencourt–Woerth, involving tax evasion, possible illegal party funding, conflict of interest, influence peddling and political backstairs influence to pervert the course of justice.

## Bockel, Jean-Marie     ( \* )

Born in 1950, in Strasbourg, Bas-Rhin (67) he read law, obtaining a master's degree and passing the CAPA (the lawyers' examination). He was initially a member of the socialist party. After having been socialist *député* since 1981, he abandoned Ségolène Royal and went over to Nicolas Sarkozy's camp after the presidential election of 2007. He was junior minister for cooperation and the French-speaking community from 19 June 2007 to 18 March 2008. His remarks about African development cost him his job. He asserted, before a group of French journalists, that the real brake on the development of African countries was bad government, wastage of public money and the predation of certain rulers. He remarked that it was strange that with a barrel of oil at $100 the people were not reaping the rewards of their natural resources. This statement incurred the wrath of President Omar Bongo of Gabon who demanded Bockel's head. He was given it. Bockel then became junior minister in charge of prison reform under the then minister of justice Michèle Alliot Marie.

## Borloo, Jean-Louis     ( \*\*\* )

French politician born in Paris (75) in 1951. He is president of the radical party and vice president of the UMP. He was a brilliant student at the lycée Janson de Sailly in Paris. He holds various degrees in law, history, philosophy and political science. He became a member of the Paris bar and set up his own law firm specializing in companies in difficulty. He is notably the lawyer who defended the notorious businessman Bernard Tapie. He was a founder member of Génération Ecologie in 1991 and election campaign manager for François Bayrou in the 2002 presidential election. Between 1989 and 2008 he was mayor of Valenciennes and held a variety of ministerial portfolios under three different prime ministers: Raffarin, de Villepin and Fillon. His marriage to a TV newsreader raised questions about the unhealthy proximity of members of the French media and politicians. He was formely minister of ecology, energy and sustainable development.

### Boutin, Christine

Right-wing politician (UMP), born in 1944 in l'Indre (36). She read law at Assas and holds a master's degree in public law. She started her career as a journalist. She is well known for her traditional Catholic views against abortion, euthanasia, the marriage of homosexuals and the adoption of children by homosexual couples. She made a non-stop speech lasting over five hours in the national assembly against the civil wedding of homosexuals. Member of parliament for the Yvelines (78) for 20 years, she joined the UMP in 2002. She was minister of housing and has held a variety of positions in local government.

### Bouton, Daniel

Banker, born in 1950 in Paris. A brilliant student, he was the youngest of his *promotion* (Rabelais) at l'ENA. He joined the Inspection des Finances and became *Inspecteur des Finances* in 1974. He became director general of the bank Société Générale in 1993 and chairman in 1997. The bank was then one of the most profitable banks in Europe. In 2007, the bank posted a record €7 billion loss due, in part, to subprimes and also to rogue trading practices within the brokerage division of the bank. In spite of dozens of alerts, no action was taken against the rogue trader Jérôme Kerviel until it was too late. Bouton was forced to resign as chairman of the bank but still occupies the role of president of the board. He was forced to give up his stock options as a result of the public outcry. The public refused to fund this bonus via the public bailout. Daniel Bouton is *Chevalier de la Légion d'Honneur.*

### Bouygues, Martin

Businessman born in 1952. After working his way up through his father's company, he became chairman and CEO of the BTP group in 1989. The Bouygues company is one of the most important players in the building industry and mass media. Bouygues owns the TV channel TF1 which is pro right wing. He is godfather to Louis Sarkozy and was a witness at Nicolas Sarkozy's second wedding (to Cécilia). He is *Chevalier de la Légion d'Honneur* and *Officier de l'Ordre de Mérite.*

### Bové, José

Born in 1953, in La Gironde (33). Agricultural trades unionist, later to become the emblem of alter-globalization in France. Refused to do his military service, was involved in the successful demonstrations to prevent the extension of the military camp in Larzac 1973–81. Founder member of both La Conféderation Paysanne and Attac. He took part in the destruction of a

McDonald's fast food restaurant in Milhau and protested against US protectionist measures against Roquefort cheese taken in reprisal to France's refusal to import hormone-treated beef. Unsuccessful candidate at the presidential election in 2007, MEP since June 2009 on the Europe Ecologie ticket. See Chapter 14 'Attac'.

### Bruni, Carla
Carla Gilberta Bruni-Tedeschi born in Turin in 1967. Third wife of Nicolas Sarkozy. Began studying architecture but gave it up to become a model and had a successful career as such between 1985–97. Gave up modelling for music. She is a writer, composer and singer. She married Nicolas Sarkozy in 2008. She is the illegitimate daughter of Maurizio Remmert who had an adulterous affair with her mother. The family, of Italian origin, fled Turin in 1972 at the height of the terrorist attacks by the Red Brigade. She is known as 'Carlita' and, of course, as 'La Première Dame de France'.

### Buffet, Marie-George
Born in Sceaux, Hauts-de-Seine (92) in 1949. Holds a bachelor's degree in history and geography. Was employed at the town hall of Plessis-Robinson. Has had elective roles at municipal and regional level. Was minister of youth and sport in the Jospin governments between 1997 and 2002. She became national secretary of the communist party in 2001 and has recently handed over the leadership of the party to Pierre Laurent. She has been *député* for the fourth constituency of Seine-Saint-Denis since 1997.

### Chérèque, François
French trades union leader born in Nancy, in the Meurthe-et-Moselle (54) in 1956. Since 2002, he has been the secretary general of the trades union CFDT. By training, he is a teacher for children with special needs and used to work in the area of paedopsychiatry. See Chapter 14 'CFDT'.

### Chevènement, Jean-Pierre
French socialist politician born in Belfort (90) in 1939. Co-founder of the PS and of the Mouvement des Citoyens. He studied at Sciences Po and l'ENA (*promotion* Stendhal 1963–5). He was head of the left-wing socialist think tank CERES and over the years held some of the highest of ministerial responsibilities: minister of the interior, minister of education and minister of defence. He resigned from the Rocard government in 1991 to protest at France's decision to enter the Gulf War and resigned later from the Jospin government in 2000 over the Corsican question. Many jokes are made about his 'resurrection'. While in hospital for a benign gall bladder operation in 1998, he showed a critical reaction to the anaesthetic. He was in a coma for eight days. Today, he is a senator. He is known as 'le Ché', an allusion to Che Guevara, the Argentinian rebel. See Chapter 2 'démissionne'.

## Chirac, Jacques

He was born in Paris in 1932. He is a former student of Sciences Po (1951). He entered l'ENA in 1954. As a student of l'ENA he could have easily dodged the draft for Algeria. He didn't. Between 1956 and 1957 he served in an armoured division in Algeria. On returning to France, he returned to l'ENA (*promotion* Vauban). He was tenth in his year. His first career steps were taken at the Cour des Comptes. He was a junior minister under Pompidou (1967–74), prime minister under Giscard d'Estaing, mayor of Paris as of 1977, president of France 1995–2002, re-elected for a second term of office 2002–7. He was the founder and leader of the new right-wing party RPR, forerunner of the UMP. No fewer than nine judicial investigations have been launched against him for a variety of reasons: bogus jobs, misappropriation of funds, money laundering, illegal party funding. Some of these charges have been dropped because the offences are now covered by the statute of limitations. Since leaving the presidency, Jacques Chirac has been living in an apartment on the quai Voltaire, in a chic quarter of Paris, belonging to the family of the assassinated Lebanese leader Rafic Hariri. In December 2009, he was officially charged over the allegedly phoney jobs at the Paris town hall, i.e. people were theoretically employed and paid by the town hall whereas they were in fact working for Jacques Chirac's political party. Alain Juppé has already been sentenced for his part in this scandal that has been described as 'an organized system of corruption'. The Public Prosecutor of Nanterre, Philippe Courroye, asked for seven charges of bogus jobs to be dropped owing to lack of evidence. The mayor of Paris decided to drop the other charges against Chirac in return for the reimbursement of €2.2 million to the Paris town hall. Chirac was to pay back €500,000 of his own money, with the balance to be paid by the UMP party. Eva Joly described this 'arrangement' as equivalent to 'misappropriation of funds'. Chirac was always known as a man in a hurry; this apparently held true even for his amorous escapades for which he was nicknamed 'Dix minutes, douche comprise'. See below 'Joly, Eva'.

## Cohn-Bendit, Daniel

He is a German and French politician born in France in 1945 in Tarn-et-Garonne (82) of German Jewish parents who had fled Nazi Germany in 1933. As a student at Nanterre in 1967 he became an icon of the student demonstrations with the occupation of the Sorbonne in 1968. One of the most famous photos of 1968 shows a smiling and somewhat angelic Cohn-Bendit facing a member of the CRS riot police. He has since become active in the ecology movement and co-headed the successful green list for the European elections in June 2009 for the Île de France region. He has been a MEP since 1994 and co-president of the Green movement at the European Parliament since 2004. Because of his past left-wing political opinions he has the nickname 'Dany le Rouge'.

## Copé, Jean-François ***

Right-wing politician (UMP) born in 1964 in Boulogne Billancourt (92). Mayor of Meaux since 1995 and a part-time lawyer. He is president of the UMP group at the National Assembly and *député* of the sixth constituency of the *département* of the Seine-et-Marne. He is a former student of Sciences Po 1985–7 and *l'ENA* 1987–9 (*promotion* Liberté Egalité Fraternité). Has held a variety of governmental positions and has made it known that he will stand for the presidency in 2017. He is notorious for being a 'cumulard', i.e. having multiple mandates. He is the mayor of a large town, member of parliament of a big constituency, chief whip of the UMP and can still find the time to work as a lawyer for a famous Paris law firm. Copé has frequently expressed his distaste with regard to 4 August 1789 and the year 1793 and is periodically accused of 'conflict of interest'. See Chapter 6 'nuit du 4 août' and 'année 1793'. Now secretary general of the UMP (Nov 2010).

## Courroye, Philippe **

Magistrate, born in 1959 in the Rhône (69). Former student at Sciences Po and the École de la Magistrature. He was fourth out of 232 other students on leaving the school. He was appointed as *Procureur de la République* at the Court of Nanterre against the advice of the Conseil Supérieur de la Magistrature whose opinion is requested for such high-level appointments. The members of the Conseil expressed reserves about his relative inexperience and his proximity to the President of the Republic. He is a close friend of Nicolas Sarkozy. He has recently been criticized in the Woerth-Bettencourt affair, not having asked to be taken off the case in which he himself has been named. Eva Joly (See below) has expressed the opinion that he is a public prosecutor at the disposal of the political executive.

## Cresson, Édith *

Socialist politician born in 1934 in Boulogne-Billancourt (92). Atypical in that she was not a product of Sciences Po or *l'ENA*. She holds a diploma from the École de haut enseignement commercial pour les jeunes filles (HECJF). She was the first woman to have held the portfolio of agriculture and the first woman prime minister of France under François Mitterrand from May 1991 to March 1992. She provoked a lot of hostility by her clumsy announcements, e.g. 'Englishmen are all homosexuals', 'the Japanese are yellow ants' and 'I couldn't give a tinker's cuss about the stock exchange'. As European Commissioner she was accused and found guilty of favouritism for giving a bogus job to a male friend. She provoked the collective resignation of the whole European Commission in 1999. She has held various ministerial posts and roles in local government including that of mayor of Châtelerault. See Chapter 14 'HEC'.

## Darcos, Xavier

Senior civil servant and right-wing politician (UMP) born in Limoges in 1947 in the Haute-Vienne (87). He studied at the University of Bordeaux and holds an *agrégation* in *lettres classiques*. He has held a number of local government positions, and has been senator, mayor, minister of education and minister of labour and industrial relations.

## Dassault, Serge

Born in Paris in 1925, French businessman and right-wing politician (UMP) he was born in Paris in 1925. He studied at Polytechnique and the École Nationale Supérieur de l'Aéronautique et de l'Espace. At 83, he is the doyen of the Senate, mayor of Corbeil-Essonnes, chairman and CEO of the aeronautics group that bears his name. He is the owner of the daily right-wing newspaper *Le Figaro*. His election as UMP mayor of Corbeil-Essonnes in 2009 was invalidated by the Conseil d'État because of his 'vote buying'. He was seen distributing bank notes to people in the streets of Corbeil-Essonnes. He has been made ineligible for one year. He is a *Grand Officier* in the *Légion d'Honneur*. His nicknames are 'l'avionneur' and 'le beau Serge'. See Chapter 10 *'Supaéro'*.

## Dati, Rachida

French politician born in the Saône-et-Loire (71) in 1965 of a Moroccan father and Algerian mother who were North African immigrants. She was the tenth of twelve children. She obtained a master's degree from the University of Paris II in economics, studied for an MBA at HEC but did not obtain the diploma. She entered the École Nationale de la Magistrature by way of an *équivalence*. Originally a socialist, she joined the UMP and was spokesperson for Nicolas Sarkozy in the election year of 2007. She is a former minister of justice. She is mayor of the seventh *arrondissement* in Paris and has been a MEP since June 2009. She is often criticized for her 'bling-bling' image and her taste for the jet set and night life.

## de Gaulle, Charles

Charles de Gaulle (1890–1970) graduated from the officer's training school of St Cyr in 1912. In his writings in the 1930s, he predicted the critical use of armoured vehicles in modern warfare. Refusing the armistice of 1940, he fled to London where he made his famous appeal to his fellow Frenchmen to continue the fight. After the war, he left politics but was called back during the Algerian crisis. He founded the fifth Republic (1958) which gave enormous powers to the president, thus putting an end to the political instability that had characterized the fourth Republic. The first president of the fifth Republic, he was forced from power by the 'revolution' of 1968. He died at Colombey les Deux Églises in 1970. His most famous nickname is 'l'homme du 18 juin'. He is also known as 'le grand Charles', 'l'homme qui a dit "non"', 'l'homme de Colombey' and 'le connétable', the latter term referring to the title of supreme commander of the army from the twelfth to the sixteenth century.

### Debré, Jean-Louis

Born in Toulouse in the Haute-Garonne (31) in 1944. RPR-UMP politician. A magistrate by training. He never obtained his *baccalauréat* but was able to pursue his law studies with an *équivalence*. Over the years, he has been minister of the interior, president of the National Assembly, and is currently president of the Conseil Constitutionnel. He was one of the most faithful of Jacques Chirac's followers. His nickname is 'l'incapacitaire en droit'. *La capacité en droit* is a university diploma known as the diploma of the 'seconde chance' since it is considered to be the equivalent of the *baccalauréat* for those who do not pass it. The holder is known as 'capacitaire'. The term 'incapacitaire' was coined by Simone Weil for whom Jean-Louis Debré does not represent the highest level of intellectual attainment.

### Delanoë, Bertrand

Socialist politician born in Tunis in 1950. Studied at the University of Toulouse. Councillor of Paris since 1977, *député* for Paris between 1981–6, Senator from 1995–2001. Mayor of Paris since 2001, re-elected in 2008.

### Devedjian, Patrick

Right-wing politician, born in Fontainebleu, Seine-et-Marne (77) in 1944, of an Armenian father who had fled the Turkish genocide. He is a lawyer by training having read law and obtained a master's degree at Assas. He then studied at Sciences Po. Between the age of 19 and 22 he was an active member of the extreme right-wing movement called Occident and was involved (along with Alain Madelin and Gérard Longuet) in violent street clashes with left-wing students in 1968. He is currently president of the *Conseil Général* of the Hauts-de-Seine and was minister in charge of economic recovery in the second Fillon government. See Chapter 7 'Augias'.

### Duflot, Cécile

Politician, secretary general of the French ecologist party Les Verts since 2006. She was born on 1 April 1975 in Villeneuve-Saint-Georges, in the Val-de-Marne, (94). She is the eldest daughter of a railwayman (and trades unionist) and a physics and chemistry teacher. A town planner by training, she graduated from l'École supérieure des sciences économiques et commerciales and holds a postgraduate degree in geography.

### Emmanuelli, Henri

See Chapter 11 'Urba'.

## Estrosi, Christian

[ * ]

Right-wing politician, (UMP) *député* and mayor of Nice. Born in Nice, Alpes-Maritime (06) in 1955. He has held a large number of government and local government positions. The fact that he has no diplomas has led to his being nicknamed 'motodidacte' with a play on words 'autodidacte' meaning 'self-taught' and the fact that he is a former world motorcycle champion. He was formerly minister in charge of industry.

## Fabius, Laurent

[ *** ]

Socialist politician, born in Paris, sixteenth *arrondissement,* in 1946. Former student of the École Normale Supérieure, Sciences Po and *l'ENA* 1972/3 (*promotion* Rabelais). He left *l'ENA* in third place and chose the Conseil d'État. He was prime minister between 1984–6 during which two scandals rocked his premiership: the sinking of the Greenpeace ship *Rainbow Warrior* and the AIDS-contaminated blood scandal. He was minister of the economy between 2000–2. He is one of the 'éléphants' of the socialist party. See Chapter 11 'sang contaminé'. His nickname is 'Lolo' which is the hypocoristic form of Laurent.

## Fillon, François

[ *** ]

Right-wing politician, (UMP) born in Le Mans, in La Sarthe (72) in 1954. Educated at the University of Maine and the University of Paris, he holds a postgraduate degree in public law. He also studied at Sciences Po. He has held a variety of positions: mayor, *député* and senator. He was minister of labour (2002–4), and minister of education (2004–6). He has been prime minister since July 2007. His nickname, 'Droopy', is an allusion to the fact that he always looks sad. He is also known as 'l'ectoplasme de Matignon', an allusion to the non-existant role of the PM since the election of Nicolas Sarkozy. His political base is in the *département* of the Sarthe, hence his nickname 'le Sarthois'. As all prime ministers, he is known as 'le locataire de Matignon'.

## Finkielkraut, Alain

[ * ]

Writer, essayist, teacher and intellectual, born in Paris in 1949 of Jewish parents. He was a brilliant student at the Lycée Henri IV where he prepared the competitive entrance exam to Normale Supérieure. He obtained his *agrégation* brilliantly in 1972. He has published many books and articles on anti-Semitism as well as on the failure of the French school system (*La Defait de la Peusée*). He has been a teacher of social science at Polytechnique since 1989. He is a frequent guest on TV and radio talk shows.

## Foccart, Jacques

[ * ]

Gaullist politician (1913–97) known as 'Mr France-Afrique', the *éminence grise* behind the African policy of the Fifth Republic. A resistant and fervent supporter of de Gaulle, he was co-founder of the SAC, the organization which did the dirty work of Gaullism. From 1960 onwards, he was the most influential politician after de Gaulle. He was closely associated with the former secret services DST and SDECE. See Chapter 14 DST, SAC and DGSE.

### Gallois, Louis                                                    **

French corporate manager born in Montauban, in the Ille-et-Vilaine (35) in 1944. Educated at HEC and *l'ENA* 1970 (*promotion* Charles de Gaulle). He chose the Treasury to begin his career. Over the years he has held some of the most eminent corporate positions: chairman and CEO of Snecma, chairman and CEO of Aérospatiale, chairman of the SNCF, co-chairman of EADS, and currently chairman of EADS. See Chapter 14 EADS.

### Gaudin, Jean Claude                                               **

Right-wing politician (UMP) born in Marseilles in the Bouches du Rhône (13) in 1939. A history/geography teacher by training, he spent 15 years as a teacher in Marseilles. He has held a variety of posts in central and local government: minister of regional development 1995–7, *député* 1978–89, senator, mayor of Marseilles since 1995, and president of the *Conseil Régional* of PACA. He has the *Légion d'Honneur*. Nickname 'Lou Ravi'. 'Lou' is Provençal for 'the' and is frequently used to refer to '*lou Ravi*' the village idiot by *Le Canard Enchaîné*. The figurine of *Lou Ravi* is always present at the Christmas crèche where he is represented as a small boy with his arms raised in amazement in front of the manger. See Chapter 14 'PACA'.

### Giscard d'Estaing, Valéry                                         **

Centre-right politician, born in Koblenz (Germany) in 1926. Third president of the fifth Republic. Studied at the lycée Janson-de-Sailly, Louis le Grand, Polytechnique, and *l'ENA* in 1948 *promotion* Europe). Left *l'ENA dans la botte* and entered the Inspection des Finances. Minister of finance under de Gaulle 1962–6. President of France 1974–81. His presidency was marked by the first oil crisis, the beginning of mass unemployment and the end of the 'Les Trente Glorieuses'. See Chapter 6 'Trente Glorieuses'. His Presidency will be remembered for the legalization of abortion, divorce by mutual consent and the voting age being reduced from 21 to 18. It was under his presidency that French telecommunications were revolutionized. Giscard d'Estaing currently sits as an *ex officio* member of the Conseil Constitutionnel and is a member of the Académie Française.

### Guaino, Henri                                                     ***

Born in Arles, Bouches-du-Rhône (13) in 1957. Senior civil servant and special advisor to Nicolas Sarkozy. He read law and political science at the University of Paris IX (Dauphine) and Paris IV (Sorbonne) and at Sciences

Po. He failed the entrance examination for *l'ENA* three times. He had a variety of jobs: journalist (with *Les Echos* and *La Croix*), economist at the Crédit Lyonnais (1982–6), teacher at Sup de Co Paris (1984–7) and lecturer at Sciences Po (1988–2000). He is the man behind all of Nicolas Sarkozy's speeches, including the highly controversial Dakar speech of July 2007. He has been *Conseiller Maître* at the Cour des Comptes since 2006. Given his ghostwriting activities he is known as 'le barde', 'le plume' and as 'le fou du roi'. Some of the speeches he has written have not been well received. See Chapter 2 'homme africain'.

## Guéant, Claude                                          〔 *** 〕

Senior civil servant born in Vimy, in the Pas-de-Calais (62) in 1945. Read law at the University of Paris and studied at Sciences Po. Entered *l'ENA* in 1971, (*promotion* Thomas More). Among the positions he has held are: technical advisor to the minister of the interior (1977–81), deputy head of office to Charles Pasqua, minister of the interior, and then director general of the police in 1994. *Préfet* of Franche Comté in 1998 and of Brittany in 2000. Head of office to Nicolas Sarkozy at the ministry of the interior 2002–4 and again from 2005–7. He was Nicolas Sarkozy's campaign director in the presidential elections of 2007 and is currently Minister of the Interior (March 2011). He is *Chevalier de la Légion d'Honneur*. He is known as 'le Cardinal', i.e. the 'éminence grise' of Nicolas Sarkozy. See Chapter 6 'éminence'.

## Haberer, Jean-Yves                                       〔 * 〕

Senior civil servant, he was born in 1932. *Énarque*, he was second in his year, (*major de sa promotion* on leaving in 1959) and joined the Inspection des Finances. He was chairman and CEO of the Crédit Lyonnais from 1988 to 1993, during which time his stewardship was judged as risky and aggressive. The Crédit Lyonnais crashed. He was sentenced in 2005 to a suspended 18-month prison sentence for presenting inaccurate accounts and the dissemination of false information. His decorations (*La Légion d'Honneur* and *l'Ordre National de Mérite*) have been suspended for seven years following his decision not to challenge the sentence in the supreme court of appeal (Cour de Cassation).

## Henri-Lévy, Bernard                                      〔 ** 〕

French intellectual born in Algeria in 1948. He studied at Lycée Louis-le-Grand. Entered Normale Supérieure in 1968 and passed the *agrégation* in philosophy in 1971. A controversial writer and journalist he is part of the 'new philosopher' trend. He defended Salman Rushdie during the *Satanic Verses* controversy. He has a weekly column in the news magazine *Le Point*. NB: in France, if you write about philosophy or teach philosophy you are called 'un philosophe'.

## Hollande, François                                                                    ***
Socialist politician, born in Rouen, in the Seine-Maritime (76) in 1954. Studied at, and holds the diplomas of the University of Paris, Sciences Po, HEC and *l'ENA*. He was eighth on leaving *l'ENA* in 1980 (*promotion* Voltaire) and he chose the Cour des Comptes to begin his career. He has held various positions in local government and is *député* of the first constituency of the Corrèze. He was first secretary of the socialist party from 1997–2008. He was formerly the life partner of Ségolène Royal.

## Hortefeux, Brice                                                                     ***
Right-wing politician born in Neuilly-sur-Seine (92) in 1958. Holds the equivalent of a bachelor's degree in private law and a master's degree in public law from the University of Paris X. Minister of immigration and national identity 2007–9 and currently presidential advisor. Close to Nicolas Sarkozy since 1976, he was a witness at the latter's first wedding and is godfather to one of Sarkozy's sons. He is considered to be the number one henchman of the President. He has occupied many various positions at all levels of government. He was recently found guilty of racial abuse and fined for his remarks about Arabs. He has lodged an appeal. See Chapter 2 'Quand il y en a un ça va'.

## Huchon, Jean-Paul                                                                    **
Socialist politician born in Paris in 1946. He is a former student of Sciences Po and *l'ENA* 1969–71 (*promotion* Thomas More). He was head of office to Michel Rocard the prime minister, and mayor of Conflans Sainte Honorine 1994–2001. He has been president of the Île de France *Conseil Général* since 1998, re-elected in 2010. In 2007 He was found guilty of 'prise illegale d'intérêt' (a form of corruption) and given a six months' suspended prison sentence, a €60,000 fine and one year ineligibility. The affair involved contracts being awarded to a company in which his wife worked. The Court of Appeal has confirmed the sentence. He has since gone to the Supreme Court of Appeal (La Cour de Cassation). At the end of 2010 the case was still pending. He has the *Légion d'Honneur* and is *Chevalier de l'Ordre National du Mérite*.

## Joly, Eva                                                                            **
Gro Eva Farseth was born in Oslo, Norway in 1943. She came to France, hardly speaking French and worked as an *au pair*. She married Pascal Joly in 1967 and obtained French nationality. She entered the École Nationale de la Magistrature and came to national fame in the Elf affair in which she was the investigating magistrate. She was the victim of numerous death threats and for the duration of the affair lived under the protection of bodyguards around the clock. She sent the former head of Elf, Loïk Le Floch-Prigent, to prison and forced the resignation of the president of the Conseil Constitutionnel, Roland Dumas. She has consistently denounced the immaturity

of French democracy as well as the immunity and absence of accountability of the French elite. She has attacked the failure of France to respect the separation of powers. She returned to Norway in 2002 and has recently returned to France to stand for the European elections on the green 'Europe Ecology' ticket. See Chapter 12 'Elf'.

## Jospin, Lionel                                                        ⌈ * ⌉
Former socialist prime minister born in 1937 of protestant parents in Meudon, in the Hauts-de-Seine (92). Former student at the Lycée Janson-de-Sailly he studied at Sciences Po 1956–9 and *l'ENA* 1965 (*promotion* Stendhal). On leaving, he joined the Quai d'Orsay. He joined the Trotskyists in 1965. He was first secretary of the socialist party 1981–8. Over the years, he has held many positions at all levels of local government and was minister of education. After his election defeat in 2002 when he arrived in third position after the national front, he retired from active politics and went to live on the Île de Ré, an island off the west coast of France, facing La Rochelle in the *département* of the Charente-Maritime (17), hence his nickname 'l'exilé de l'Île de Ré'. He is also known as 'l'austère qui se marre' because of his over-serious expression.

## Juppé, Alain                                                        ⌈ *** ⌉
Right-wing politician (RPR then UMP), born in the Landes (40) in 1945. Educated at the Lycée Louis-le-Grand, Paris, Normale Supérieure (*agrégé* in *lettres clasiques*), Sciences Po and *l'ENA*. He joined the Inspection des Finances *on leaving* l'ENA (*promotion* Charles de Gaulle). Prime minister 1995–7 and mayor of Bordeaux between 1995 and 2004. He was charged and found guilty of 'prise illégale d'intérêt' (a form of corruption) in 2004, in the affair concerning the bogus jobs at the Paris town hall. Sentenced to 10 years' ineligibility and an 18-month suspended prison sentence. On appeal, this was reduced to 14 months and one year's ineligibilty. He has been mayor of Bordeaux since 2008. Currently minister of foreign affairs.

## Kouchner, Bernard                                                    ⌈ ** ⌉
Socialist politician born in Avignon, in the Vaucluse (84) in 1939. A doctor by training, he was a co-founder of the NGO, Médecins Sans Frontierès. Communist in the 1960s, socialist in the 1980s, former member of the right-wing Sarkozy government as minister of foreign affairs. He is married to the TV newsreader and journalist Christine Ockrent. He is known as 'l'homme au sac de riz', since he was photographed in the Somalian capital Mogadiscio with a sack of rice on his back during the famine of 1992 and as 'le French doctor' (sic). Left the second Fillon government (Nov 2010).

## Lagarde, Christine                                                   ⌈ *** ⌉
Right-wing politician (UMP), born in Paris in 1956. She went to the USA on a scholarship after obtaining her *baccalauréat*. Returning to France, she

obtained a master's degree in English and a postgraduate degree in industrial relations law. She did not obtain the diploma of Sciences Po and made two unsuccesful attempts to enter *l'ENA*. Lawyer at the Paris bar in 1981, she joined the prestigious legal firm Baker and McKenzie and rose to the top. She spent most of her career years in the USA. On returning to France in 2005, she became minister of overseas trade in the Villepin government 2005–7, was then minister of agriculture and fisheries for a brief period in 2007, and became minister of finance in June 2007. She is one of the rare French politicians to be perfectly at ease when speaking in English. She is *Chevalier de la Légion d'Honneur* and opposition councillor in the twelfth *arrondissement* of Paris. She is known as *Madame La Marquise de Bercy.* This is a reference to the famous music hall song. See Chapter 1 'Tout va très bien'. All ministers of finance have the nickname 'le grand argentier' or in this case 'la grande argentière'.

### Lagardère, Arnaud        `**`
Businessman, born in Boulogne-Billancourt in the Hauts-de-Seine (92) in 1961. Son and successor of Jean Lagardère, head of Matra Hachette, who died in 2003. Holds a master's degree in economics and a postgraduate diploma in organizational management. A close friend of Nicolas Sarkozy, he sacked the editor of *Paris Match* (of which he is the owner) for having used, as the cover photo, a picture of Cécilia Sarkozy in New York with her new boyfriend, Richard Attias, in 2006.

### Laguiller, Arlette        `*`
One of the rare, respected politicians in France. She was born of working-class parents in Lilas, in the Seine-Saint-Denis (93), a poor quarter on the outskirts of Paris. On obtaining her BEPC (a school leaving certificate taken at 16) she joined the Crédit Lyonnais bank, and worked in the data processing department. She was transferred to head office in 1963 and spent all of her career there until she retired in 2000. She became active in politics during the Algerian war and co-founded the left-wing trotskyist party Lutte Ouvrière. She became spokesperson for this movement in 1973. As union delegate of the Lutte Ouvrière, she was one of the main organizers of the strike at the bank during the great industrial unrest in France in 1974. She has been candidate for the presidency in every presidential election since 1974. She was town councillor for Les Lilas between 1995–2001, regional councillor for the Île de France between 1998–2004 and EMP from 1999–2004. She is gradually handing over responsibility to her successor Nathalie Arthaud.

### Lauvergeon, Anne       
She was born in Dijon in the Côte d'Or (21) in 1959. She entered Normale Supérieure where she obtained an *agrégation* in physics. At one point, she

was deputy secretary general of the Élysée under Mitterrand. She became chairperson and CEO of Areva, the nuclear energy company, resulting from the merger of Cogema and Framatome. According to Fortune 500, she is the most powerful woman in French industry.

### Le Pen, Jean-Marie
See Chapter 2 'détail de l'histoire de la Deuxième Guerre mondiale', Chapter 4 'Le Pen' and Chapter 6 'poujadisme'.

### Longuet, Gérard
Republican right-wing politician, born in Neuilly-sur-Seine (92) in 1946. He studied at Lycée Henri IV and Sciences Po. He holds a DESS in political science and studied at *l'ENA* 1971–3 (*promotion* Rabelais). Co-founder of Occident, an extreme right-wing movement, with Alain Madelin in 1964, he was sentenced in 1967 for complicity of violence and assault with weapons and premeditation. On leaving *l'ENA* he joined the *corps préfectoral*. He is a former minister of post and telecommunications, former *député* of the Meuse (55) in 1978. He joined the UMP in 2002. He has been senator since 2009 and is currently minister of defence.

### Margérie, Christophe de
Businessman, born in the Vendée (85) in 1951. CEO of the French petrol giant Total. Educated at Sup de Co Paris and the European School of Management Studies.

### Mauroy, Pierre                                                         *
He is a French socialist politician, born in Cartignies in the north of France in 1928 whose electoral base is in the north of France in the region of the 'ch'ti'. 'Quinquin' is a small child in the ch'ti patois of the north of France. Pierre Mauroy is a rather well-built man, hence his affectionate nickname 'le gros quinquin'. See Chapter 1 'p'tit quinquin'. He is a former mayor of Lille and the first prime minister of François Mitterrand 1981–4. He was first secretary of the socialist party 1988–92.

### Minc, Alain                                                       ***
Political and economic advisor and essayist, born in Paris in 1949. Educated at Sciences Po and *l'ENA*. He was *major de sa promotion* at *l'ENA* 1975 (*promotion* Léon Blum) and chose the Inspection des Finances on leaving. He co-wrote what is considered to be a brilliant report on the information society in 1978 which has left its mark. He worked for Saint Gobain where his results were not convincing. Advisor to a large number of businessmen, he has on several occasions been accused of being in a situation of conflict of interest. He was ejected from the committee of governance of the newpaper *Le Monde*, being seen as too close to President Sarkozy. In 2001, he was

sentenced to pay 100,000 francs in damages for having partially plagiarized the work of Roger Rödel on Spinoza. He was accused of *'reproduction servile'* and *'imitation'*. He has the *Légion d'Honneur*. He is the embodiment of the French elite; a brilliant intellectual whose concrete realizations are far from being examples of excellence, but adulated because of his original virtue of being *major de sa promotion*. Alain Peyrefitte wrote in 1976: *'Aux Etats Unis, un diplôme universitaire n'assure que le démarrage. Après cinq ans en moyenne, c'est l'homme que l'on juge: ce qu'il peut faire, non d'où il sort. En France, le diplôme est une fusée à longue portée qui, sauf accident, vous propulse jusqu'à la retraite'* (*Le Mal Français* 1976, reprinted in 2006).

### Mitterrand, François                                    `***`

French politician (1916–96). He was born in Jarnac, in the Charentes (16). He read law in Paris. In the early days he was an extreme right-wing politician and was decorated by the Vichy regime. He was one of the latter day resistants. He was elected as first secretary of the socialist party in 1971. President of France 1981–95. The ambiguity of the person may be summed up in this phrase; 'He was a man who could condemn the mass arrests of Jews during the Vél' d'Hiv' raid in the morning, while dining on the same evening with the man who had organized it,' i.e. René Bousquet. See Chapter 11 'Bousquet'. His nickname was *Le Florentin*, since he was known to be Machiavellian. His familiar nickname was 'Tonton' (nunky). He abolished the death penalty in France. See Chapter 11 'Observatoire'.

### Montebourg, Arnaud                                    `**`

Socialist politician, born in Clamecy, in the Nièvre (58) in 1962. He read law in Dijon and studied at Sciences Po. In 1997 he was elected as *député* in the sixth constituency of Seine-et-Loire (71). A lawyer by training, he proposed to impeach Jacques Chirac on a multitude of corruption charges. He founded the Convention pour la VI République in 2001. He is one of the young lions of today's socialist party. Because of his attitude towards Chirac, he is known as 'le Danton du Saône-et-Loire', a reference to Georges Jacques Danton, the French revolutionary, who was also a lawyer.

### Moscovici, Pierre                                    `**`

Socialist politician born in Paris in 1957. He holds two postgraduate degrees in economics and philosophy. Former student of Sciences Po and *l'ENA* (1984 *promotion* Louise Michel). Served as junior minister for European affairs under Lionel Jospin, from 1997 to 2002. He is the national secretary for international affairs of the socialist party. He has been *député* for the Doubs (25) since 2007. He teaches at Sciences Po and has held a variety of posts in local government at the regional and municipal level.

## Ockrent, Christine                                      [ ** ]

Belgian journalist born in 1944. Educated at Sciences Po Paris and the University of Cambridge. Life partner of Bernard Kouchner, former minister of foreign affairs. Became famous as TV newsreader on Channel 2. Currently CEO of *France Monde*, the holding in charge of all French overseas broadcasting. She was voted best newsreader in 1985. She was made *Chevalier de la Légion d'Honneur* in 2009 on the quota of decorations allocated to the ministry of foreign affairs, which was headed up by her own husband! Her nickname is 'femme de ménages'. Although *ménage* is 'housework', and *femme de ménage* is 'a cleaning lady', *les ménages* is also the journalistic jargon to refer to 'extras', i.e. jobs undertaken outside the normal professional framework in order to earn extra money. In her heyday, she was known as 'la Reine Christine'. She is sometimes referred to as 'haine' or 'vaine' Christine.

## Oudea, Frédéric                                        [ * ]

Corporate manager born in Paris in 1963. Studied at Polytechnique, (1981) *l' ENA* (*promotion* Fernand Braudel 1987). On leaving *l'ENA*, he joined the Inspection des Finance. He worked with Nicolas Sarkozy when the latter was minister of budget. He is currently the chairman and CEO of the Société Générale bank. In March 2009, faced with violent public discontent, he was forced to give up 150,000 stock options. The bank had recently been bailed out with tax payers' money.

## Parisot, Laurence                                      [ *** ]

Business woman born in the Haute Saône (70) in 1959. Educated at the University of Nancy (master's degree in public law) and Sciences Po Paris. She was chairperson and CEO of the opinion poll company Institut français d'opinion publique (IFOP) between 1990 and 2008. She is currently head of the French employers' association, the Medef. She has the *Légion d'Honneur* and *l'Ordre du Mérite*. Her nicknames include 'La cheftaine du patronat', ('cheftaine' is the 'Brown Owl' or girl guide troop leader) and 'Madame Niet'.

## Pasqua, Charles                                        [ ** ]

Right-wing politician born in Grasse, in the Alpes-Maritimes (06) in 1927. Read law and obtained a bachelor's degree. He joined the Paul Ricard group in 1952 and had risen to the no. 2 position by the time he left in 1967. He was co founder of the Gaullist parallel police force the SAC of which he was vice president. He left the organization in 1969. Over the years, he has been *député*, EMP, president of the *Conseil Général* of the Hauts-de-Seine (92), municipal councillor, senator and minister of the interior from 1986 to 1988 and again from 1993 to 1995. Several judicial enquiries have been opened against him. In 2006, in the non-ministerial aspect of the Annemasse casino scandal, he was given an 18-month suspended prison sentence (illegal party funding and corruption). This sentence was confirmed on appeal in 2008 and has become final in the light of the rejection of his appeal to the Supreme Court of Appeal (La Cour de Cassation). In 1994, he had given his permission for the opening of a casino, against the advice of his own department and that of the police. In the ministerial aspect of the affair, he was cleared of the charges by *La Cour de la République* in 2010. His own son has been sentenced to prison on bribery and corruption charges in the related Sofremi scandal, two years, one without remission, and a fine of €375,000. The sentence is definitive since the La Cour de Cassation has rejected his appeal. Charles Pasqua, on 30 April 2010, was found guilty of complicity in the misuse of company assets in the Sofremi affair and was given a one-year suspended prison sentence by La Cour de la République. He lodged an appeal (*former un pourvoir en cassation* or *se pourvoir en cassation*) with the Supreme Court of Appeal but his appeal was rejected and thus the sentence has been confirmed. He is known as 'Charlie', 'le vieux Charlie' and 'Môssieu Charles'. See Chapter 11 'Angolagate'.

### Pébereau, Michel
Born in 1942. Studied at Polytechnique X (1961), *major de sa promotion* (Marcel Proust) at *l'ENA* in 1967. He chose the Inspection des Finances on leaving. He is currently chairman of the board of BNP Paribas. He has the *Légion d'Honneur*.

### Pécresse, Valérie  [ * ]
Right-wing politician, (UMP) born in Neuilly-sur-Seine (92) in 1967. Obtained her *bac* at 16, prepared for HEC at the École Sainte Geneviève in Versailles. Graduated from HEC in 1988. Studied at *l'ENA* (1990–2 *promotion* Condorcet) then went to the Conseil d'État. Taught constitutional law at Sciences Po between 1992–8. *Député* for the second constituency of the Yvelines (78) and minister of higher education and research since 2007. She was the unsuccessful UMP candidate for the Île de France in the regional elections of 2010.

### Pinault, François
Breton businessman born in 1936. The archetypal self-made man. He is a billionaire and the third biggest fortune in France. He made his money by buying out companies on the verge of bankruptcy and reselling them. His business empire includes such names as Printemps (Paris department store), La Redoute (mail order company), Gucci (luxury leather goods), Fnac (distributor of books, records and culture-related products and services), Conforama (the distributor of home furnishings and electrical appliances). He was very close to Jacques Chirac. He recently acquired the seventeenth-century

Grassi palace on the Grand Canal in Venice to be the centre of his modern art collection.

### Poivre d'Arvor, Patrick    **

Writer, 'journalist' and star TV newsreader, born in Reims in the Marne (51) in 1947. He obtained his bac at 16, studied at Sciences Po and at the CFJ, the school of journalism. In 1996 he was given a suspended prison sentence of 15 months and a 200,000 franc fine for 'receiving' misappropriated company assets in the Michel Noir–Pierre Botton scandal. He has frequently been criticized for his proximity to the political jet set. He has worked for the main stations and TV channels and was the star newsreader at TF1 from 1987 until 2007 when a word displeased Nicolas Sarkozy during an interview that he was conducting. He was given the golden handshake. He is *Chevalier de la Légion d'Honneur* and the star 'spitting image' newsreader of the programme *Les Guignols de l'Info* on Canal+. He is often simply referred to by his initials PPDA.

### Raffarin, Jean-Pierre    **

Centre-right politician, born in the Vienne (86) in 1948. He read law at Assas and graduated from Sup de Co in 1972. Spokesman and then general secretary of the centre party UDF 1993–5. Prime Minister from 2002–5. He has given his name to an expression, *raffarinade*, coined during his premiership, which is either an obscure nonsense or a perfectly atrocious truism. He is *Chevalier de la Légion d'Honneur*. Over the years, he has held several local government positions in the *Conseil Régional* of Poitou-Charentes. His nickname is 'le phénix du Haut Poitou'.

### Rocard, Michel    *

Socialist politician born in 1930 in Courbevoie in the Hauts-de-Seine (92). Militant socialist since 1949. Educated at Sciences Po and *l'ENA* (*promotion* 18 juin 1958). Prime minister of François Mitterrand (1988–91). First secretary of the socialist party 1993–4. *Grand Officier de la Légion d'Honneur*. He was recently entrusted (with Alain Juppé) with the task of advising the government on the extent of the 'Great Loan' to be launched by Nicolas Sarkozy. He has recently been appointed by President Sarkozy as French ambassador for the international negotiations on the North and South Poles.

### Royal, Ségolène    ***

Socialist politician born in Dakar in 1953. Educated at the University of Nancy, Sciences Po and *l'ENA* (*promotion* Voltaire 1980). *Deputé* of the second constituency of the Deux Sevres and president of the *Conseil Régional* of Poitou-Charentes. She was the unsuccessful socialist candidate in the presidential election of 2007 during which she lost against Nicolas Sarkozy. She has held a number of junior ministerial positions (family, education, and the environment) as well as a number of positions in local government. The election for the nomination of the leader of the socialist party gave Ségolène Royal as winner just before midnight on the evening of the election. Strangely, Martine Aubry was declared the winner in the early hours of the morning. She coined the term 'bravitude' during a visit to the Great Wall of China in 2007, not being able to find the word 'bravoure'. Many words have since been coined with the 'itude' suffix. She is called 'Bécassine' by her enemies. (See Chapter 1 'Bécassine'). The adjective pertaining to Poitiers, the capital of the Poitou, is 'poitevin'. She is also known as 'la Poitevine', and 'la dame en blanc', since she is frequently dressed in white.

## Santini, André                                          ( * )

Centre-right politician born in Paris in 1940. He holds a doctorate in law. He entered politics with the UDF centre party, supporting Giscard d'Estaing. Since 1980, he has been the mayor of the Paris suburb Issy-les-Moulineaux. He was appointed as junior minister within the ministry of budget (in charge of the civil service). He is also recognized as one of the pioneers in the area of Internet use within the area of local government.

## Sarkozy, Jean                                           ( * )

Right-wing politician born in Neuilly-sur-Seine (92) in 1986, second son of Nicolas Sarkozy and his first wife. Member of the General Council of Neuilly-sur-Seine. He is also president of the UMP group within the *Conseil Général* of the Hauts-de-Seine. He married Jessica Darty, member of the Darty family, one of the biggest electrical appliance distribution groups in France. He was obliged to back down on his ambition to take over the head position at the Epad faced with the public outcry his nomination provoked. Many people thought that a student who had failed the exams of his second year of law school was a slightly lightweight contender for such a powerful position. He is known as 'Jean de Neuilly' and 'fiston à piston'. 'Fiston' is 'sonny' whereas 'piston' is the slang term for string-pulling and backstairs influence.

## Sarkozy, Nicolas                                        ( *** )

Nicolas Sarkozy de Nagy-Bocsa, right-wing politician, born in Paris in 1955 of Hungarian origin. President of France since 16 May 2007, and former mayor of Neuilly-sur-Seine, he has held several ministerial positions over the years: budget, communication, interior, finance and the presidency of the *Conseil Général* of the Hauts-de-Seine (92). His father left the family while he was still young. Mediocre scholar, he was forced to go into the Catholic private sector to repeat his first year at secondary school. He studied at Sciences Po but failed the exam due to (among other things) an eliminatory low mark in English. He studied law, and obtained a DEA in political science in 1980. A lawyer by training, he is an associate in the legal firm of

Leibici-Claude & Sarkozy. He has a variety of nicknames that can be broken down according to what is being referred to. The most common are the following: (*a*) tendency to show off and his narcissism: 'l' homme du Fouquet's'; (*b*) small stature: 'Naboléon' (*nabot* is a dwarf or midget); (*c*) hyper activity: 'l'idiot en colère' (the Chinese name for him) 'Sha Ke Qui' i.e. 'the angry idiot', 'l'omnipresident', 'Speedy Sarko', 'Louis de Funès' (as the Germans see him); and (*d*) miscellaneous: 'le Président du pouvoir d'achat' (an election promise), 'le Chanoine de Latran' (the title granted by the Pope to Sarkozy during the latter's visit to Rome on 20 December 2007), 'le VRP de l'Élysée', (the travelling salesman of the Élysée). This is a reference to his attempts at selling nuclear power stations, military aircraft and high speed trains when abroad on state visits.

### Sarnez, Marielle de                                                                    ⬡ *

Centre party politician born in the eighth *arrondissement* of Paris in 1951. MEP since 1999, she is no. 2 in the MoDem centre party of François Bayrou. She was his principle private secretary when he was minister of education. She is the first non-*énarque* to have held such a position. She is a town councillor of Paris.

### Strauss-Kahn, Dominique                                                              ⬡ ***

He is an economist and socialist politician, born in Neuilly-sur-Seine (92) in 1937. He was educated at *HEC*, Sciences Po Paris. He holds a doctorate and an *agrégation* in economics. He was minister of industry and overseas trade (1991–3) and minister of economy and finance (1997–9). He was *député*, mayor of Sarcelles and municipal councillor. He has also worked as a business lawyer, and taught economics at the University of Paris X from 1978–82. He is married to the journalist and TV newsreader Anne Sinclair. He is currently president of the International Monetary Fund. He is known as DSK.

### Tapie, Bernard                                                                         ⬡ *

Born in Paris in the twentieth *arrondissement*, in 1943. Jack of all trades. Businessman, singer, TV, theatre and cinema actor, former member of parliament, former minister, former manager of a football club, MEP. He received an eight-month prison sentence without remission for corruption (he rigged a match between OM and Valenciennes) and for suborning witnesses. In the affair concerning his yacht, he was given a four-month sentence without remission for tax evasion, misuse of company assets and bankruptcy. Tapie said in 2010 that he might be returning to politics.

### Tibéri, Jean                                                                           ⬡ **

A right-wing politician (RPR then UMP), he was born in Paris in the fifth *arrondissement* in 1937. He read law and became a magistrate. *Député* of the second constituency of Paris since 1968. He was deputy to Jacques Chirac when the latter was mayor of Paris. He was mayor of Paris himself between 1995 and 2001. He has been involved in several scandals such as attributing council houses to his own family. He stood trial for electoral fraud in the fifth *arrondissement*. A number of non-residents were given favours in return for their vote. In May 2009, he was given a ten-month suspended prison sentence, a €10,000 fine and made ineligible for three years. He has appealed.

### Tibéri, Xavière                                                                      ( * )

Xavière Tibéri, née Casanova, was born in Corsica. She is the wife of the French politician and former mayor of Paris, Jean Tibéri. In the 1990s she was under investigation for having held a bogus job; she was commissioned by the *Conseil Général* of the Essonne (Xavier Dugoin) to write a report on the French-speaking world. Apart from the fact that she has no qualifications in this area, the report was a mixture of copy and paste, commonplaces and numerous spelling mistakes. She was paid €30,000 for the report. She was finally acquitted on a technicality (*vice de forme*).

### Trichet, Jean-Claude                                                           ( *** )

Born in Lyon in 1943. Educated at Sciences Po and *l'ENA* (*promotion* Thomas Moore 1971). He joined the Inspection des Finances becoming the head of office of Edouard Balladur, the minister of finance in 1986. Between 1987 and 1993 he was director of the treasury with a right of overseeing the public sector. He stood trial for complicity in the dissemination of false financial information about the accounts of the Crédit Lyonnais in 1997. He benefitted from a discharge. Since 2003 he has been the president of the European Central Bank. He is *Commandeur de la Légion d'Honneur*. See Chapter 4 'Trichet, Jean-Claude'.

### Valls, Manuel                                                                      ( * )

Manuel Valls, socialist politician, born in Barcelona in 1962. Currently mayor of Evry (a 'new' town in the Essonne *département* (91). He is also *député* of the first constituency of the Essonne. French by naturalization, he studied history at the University of Paris I. He is known as *dervish tourneur* because of his rapid U-turn on the referendum for the European constitution in 2005. Within 24 hours his 'non' position became a 'oui' position.

### Veil, Simone                                                                       ( *** )

Simone Veil (née Jacob), French centre-right politician born in Nice (06) in 1927. She was arrested in 1944 and deported to Auschwitz with her mother in April. She survived the death march to Bergen-Belsen. Her mother died in Auschwitz. Simone Veil was liberated by the Allies on 15 April 1945. On returning to France she read law in Paris and studied at Sciences Po. On completing her studies she became a magistrate and served until 1974. Between 1974 and 1979 she was minister of health under Giscard d'Estaing and is best remembered for guiding through parliament the law on the liberalization of abortion. She was victim at that time of a disgusting smear campaign conducted by Catholic fundamentalists. She was minister of social affairs between 1993 and 1995. She is a member of the Académie Française. She is *Grand Officier de La Légion d'Honneur* and holds a British OBE. She is one of the very, very few respected politicians in France. 'Momone' as she is affectionately known, is the best-liked public figure in France.

### Villepin, Dominique de                                             ( *** )
Diplomat, politician, lawyer and writer, born in Rabat (Morocco) in 1953. Took his *bac* at 16, educated at Sciences Po and *l'ENA* (*promotion* Voltaire 1980). On leaving *l'ENA*, he joined the diplomatic corps and served in the French embassy in Washington and Delhi. Minister of foreign affairs under Edouard Balladur. In 2003, he delivered a speech in front of the Security Council of the UN against US intervention in Iraq, and was applauded, a rare occurence in this assembly. Secretary general of the Élysée and then prime minister under Jacques Chirac from 2005–7. He has written extensively and his latest work bears on the fall of Napoleon and the First Empire. In 2007, he was officially charged with complicity to defame Nicolas Sarkozy in the Clearstream affair. He was acquitted but the public prosecutor's office appealed against the decision and he will have to re-stand trial. The public prosecutor in question has just been elevated to the rank of *Officier* in the *Légion d'Honneur.*

### Villiers, Philippe de                                               ( * )
Philippe Le Jolis de Villiers de Saintignon, French right-wing politician born in the Vendée (85) in 1949. He read law at the University of Nantes, studied at Sciences Po and *l'ENA* (1976–8 *promotion* Pierre Mendès France). His political career has been followed in the Vendée in a number of different local government roles. He is notorious for being an absent MEP. His nickname is 'l'agité du bocage'. NB: 'l'agité du bocal' was the injurious nickname Céline gave Sartre, while 'bocage' is the patchwork farmland in the Vendée characterized by small fields enclosed by hedges.

### Voynet, Dominique                                                   ( * )
Green politician born in Montbéliard in the Doubs (25) in 1958. Senator of Seine-Saint-Denis (93) and mayor of Montreuil since 2008. She is one of the historical figures of the green party. She is an anaesthetist by training.

### Woerth, Eric                                                        ( *** )
Right-wing politician, born in 1956 in Creil, in l'Oise (60). Educated at *HEC* and Sciences Po. He has always been active in local politics and was mayor

of Chantilly and held several local government positions in the Conseil Régional of Picardie. He was campaign fund manager to Jacques Chirac and advisor at ministerial level. He was formerly minister of labour. He is at the centre of the 'Bettencourt scandal', a scandal of conflict of interest, tax evasion, possible illegal party funding, influence peddling and political interference in the due process of law. Two journalists working on this story have had their portable computers stolen. Until now, the affair has been in the hands of the Procureur de Nanterre, Philippe Courroye. Woerth left the second Fillon government in Nov. 2010.

## Yade, Rama                                                    **\*\***

This is the usual name used by Mame Ramatoulaye Yade, a young, black, right-wing politician born in 1976 in Senegal. She was formerly junior minister in charge of human rights within the ministry of foreign affairs, and for a short time was minister of sport.

# Chapter 10

# What's what

This is not a tourist's guide to Paris! It is an analysis of those institutions and monuments to which reference is constantly made in the press and for which bilingual dictionary translations are not enough. The traditional bilingual dictionary is of necessity concerned with the translation of words and not the translation of the cultural significance behind those words. If students look up the French body *La caisse des dépôts et consignations* in a bilingual dictionary, they will find the following translation; 'the deposit and consignment office'. This is not a great help in understanding what the CDC really is. It is the aim of this chapter to provide the reader with a more meaningful description of such terms.

### Académie. L' `[ ** ]`
The Académie is an administrative echelon of the ministry of education which enables application of national policy at the local level. It is represented at the level of the *département* by the *Recteur*. The Académie liaises with the local authorities for the various levels of education as follows: with the *communes* for nursery schools, with the *départements* for secondary schools up to the age of 14, with the *régions* for secondary education from age 14 up to school-leaving exam level.

### Académie des Sciences. L' `[ ** ]`
This is one of the five *Académies* that are collectively represented under the name Institut de France. It was founded in 1666 on the initiative of Colbert and was aimed at promoting scientific research. Today, it is made up of French scientists and foreign associates who publish findings, give conferences, and play the role of guardian of the French language in the scientific sphere. It also has a role in promoting international scientific relations.

### Académie Française. L' `[ ** ]`
The Académie Française was founded in 1634 by Cardinal Richelieu during the reign of Louis XIII. It is one of the oldest institutions in France. The

Académie is made up of 40 members who are elected by their peers. Its original role was to lay down the rules of the French language, to guarantee its purity and eloquence and to enable it to address the arts and the sciences. Today, it defines correct usage of the French language and produces the *Dictionnaire de l'Académie*, the first edition of which appeared in 1694. Via its recommendations, the Académie contributes to various commissions set up to determine specific terminology. The 40 members are known as *les Immortels*. This nickname derives from the motto on the seal granted to the Académie by Richelieu 'À l'immortalité' which refers to the French language and not to the members of the Académie. For official ceremonies, the Académie sessions take place under the *Coupole* of the Institut de France. Its members have a green uniform (l'habit vert) and a two-pointed cocked hat. Members come from the ranks of poets, novelists, statesmen and men of science who have, in some way, contributed to defending the French language. It is located on the quai de Conti in the sixth *arrondissement* of Paris. See below 'La Coupole'.

### agrégé(e) nmf.                                                        `**`

An 'agrégé' is someone who has passed the highly competitive university examination known as the *agrégation*. *Agrégés* are normally recruited as teachers, either in very good secondary schools or certain faculties. Familiarly known as the *agrég*, this diploma dates back to Colbert in the seventeenth century. NB: *la licence* and *la maîtrise* are obtained by passing an *examen*, whereas *l'agrégation* is obtained by way of a *concours*.

### Alsacienne. L'École                                                   `*`

This is a private, non-denominational school under contract with the state and situated in the rue Notre Dame des Champs in the sixth *arrondissement* in Paris. It was founded in 1874 by people from Alsace, from the 'gymnase' Jean Sturm, who fled Alsace after the defeat of the French army at the hands of the Prussians in 1870. It has always been famous for its avant-garde methods and teaches children from nursery up to school leaving age. Given the selection procedure, it is inevitably considered to be one of the best, but also one of the most socially selective schools in Paris.

### Ambroise-Paré                                                         `*`

A hospital located in Boulogne-Billancourt in the *département* of the Hauts-de-Seine (92). It takes its name from the father of modern surgery (1509–90) who was surgeon to Henry II, François II, Charles IX and Henri III. His first publication dealt mainly with the treatment of arrow wounds.

### arrondissement. L'                                                    `**`

The *arrondissements* as we know them today were created in 1800 and are the administrative subdivisions of the *département*. There are three types:

*arrondissements* of a big city such as Paris, *arrondissements* of the *départements*, and the special coastal zones. The *arrondissements* of the *département* are under the authority of the *sous-préfet*. There are 325 in France. It is to be noted that Paris is the only city to have the status of a *département* (75). *Arrondissement* comes from the verb 'arrondir'. In Paris, *arrondissement* 1 is in the very centre of Paris. If one draws a naive picture of a snail with a helix in the clockwise direction, each circle bigger than the one before, one can visualize the positions of the *arrondissements*; 1, 2, 3, 4, 5, 6 are in the centre, whereas 14, 16, 17, 18, 19 and 20 are on the periphery.

## Article 49.3. L'                                                     `**`

Briefly put, this is the article of the Constitution of the Fifth Republic that allows the government to push through legislation without a parliamentary vote.

## Assemblée Nationale. L'                                              `**`

This is the name of the lower house of the French Parliament (the upper house being *le Sénat*). The first Assemblée Nationale (the Constituent) was proclaimed in Versailles by the Third Estate on 17 June 1789 shortly after the reunion of the Estates General in May. Today's Assemblée Nationale is made up of 577 members called *députés* who are elected by direct universal suffrage, in a two-round election with a simple majority in the second ballot. The building that houses the lower chamber is known as the Palais Bourbon which is the metonymical name of the Assemblée Nationale. It is situated on the left bank of the Seine in the seventh *arrondissement*. Parliamentary debates take place in the *hémicycle* and the sessions are chaired by the president of the Assemblée who sits at a place called *le perchoir*.

## Association loi 1901 nf.                                             `**`

See below 'Loi de 1901'.

## Beaubourg                                                            `*`

Le centre national d'art et de culture is located in the first *arrondissement* of Paris, and is known as the Centre Beaubourg or Centre Pompidou after the late President Georges Pompidou (1911–74).

## Baumettes. Les                                                       `*`

The name of a famous prison located in the ninth *arrondissement* of Marseilles.

## cadre nm.                                                           `***`

This is one of the most difficult concepts to translate into English. One might translate the term by 'manager' and leave it at that, but this translation is very wide of the mark. *Cadre* refers more to the position in the corporate and social hierarchy than it does to the fact that one has people under one's authority. It carries social class connotations and has a big impact well outside of company hours. If one asks a bank for a loan, or takes out an insurance policy, invariably the first question is 'Êtes-vous cadre?' It affects retirement benefit and even life expectancy.

### café de Flore. Le      `**`

This is the name of a famous café in the Saint-Germain district of Paris, in the sixth *arrondissement*. It is the legendary name associated with the postwar intellectuals and artists in general, and of Simone de Beauvoir and Jean-Paul Sartre in particular. Other famous names associated with this café, established under the third Republic (1870–1940), are Camus and Prévert.

### Caisse des dépôts et consignations. La      `***`

This is a public, financial institution placed under the direct authority of Parliament. It was created in 1816 in an attempt to restore confidence in the public finances in the wake of the Napoleonic wars. The motto of this institution is 'Foi Publique' (Public Faith). It has a general interest role which it fulfills for the state and local authorities. It manages the savings deposited on the *livret A* savings account as well as funds deposited with the notary public in the course of real estate operations. It is also a big institutional investor. It can be seen as the financial arm of the state. It is located in the seventh *arrondissement* of Paris. See Chapter 12 'Vieille maison'.

### canton nm.      `*`

The *départements* are divided into *arrondissements départementaux* which in turn can be subdivided into *cantons* which we can describe as being the lowest unit in the electoral hierarchy. The canton elects the member who will represent the *canton* at the level of the *Conseil Général* of the *département*.

### chambre correctionnelle. La 17ème      `**`

This is a court of the Tribunal de Grande Instance de Paris. Whenever questions related to the press arise (e.g. cases of libel) this is the court that will usually try the case.

### Chambre Régionale des Comptes. La      `**`

With the movement towards decentralization that began in 1982, so were created the Chambres Régionales des Comptes which can be seen as the regional ramifications of the central Cour des Comptes in Paris. They are responsible for monitoring how public money is being spent in the regions by public authorities, the balance of the budget, the conformity of expenditure with accounting rules, and the truth and fairness of the accounts presented.

## Chancellerie. La     [ \*\*\* ]

This is another name for the central administration of the ministry of justice.

## Closerie des Lilas. La     [ \*\*\* ]

Bar, *brasserie* and restaurant located at 171 bld Montparnasse in the sixth *arrondissement* of Paris. Since 1847 it has been the haunt of artists and intellectuals. Names closely associated with this renowned place include Zola, Verlaine, Apollinaire, Baudelaire, Mallarmé, Joyce and Hemingway. Today, it is a trendy venue for the rich and famous.

## Collège de France. Le     [ \*\*\* ]

It was founded by François I$^{er}$ and was initially called the *Collège des Trois Langues* (Latin, Greek and Hebrew were taught there) and later became *Le Collège des Lecteurs Royaux*. In 1870, it was renamed *Collège de France*. It is one of the most illustrious institutions of French higher education that is dedicated to teaching and research which are aimed at being universal, hence the motto of the Collège *Docet omnia* (*Il enseigne tout*). Lectures of a very high level are given in a broad spectrum of subjects: maths, physics, natural science, philosophy, sociology. The courses are *non-diplômants*, i.e. they do not lead to any qualifications. They are open to the general public without any prior enrollment. To be appointed to teach at the *Collège de France* is one of the greatest honours for a teacher. Located in the Latin Quarter, the *Collège* is not far from the Sorbonne in the fifth *arrondissement* of Paris.

## Comédie Française. La     [ \* ]

The Comédie Française was founded by Louis XIV in 1680 by a merger of Molière's former troupe with that of *le théâtre du Marais*. It was dissolved during the French Revolution and restored in 1804. It was totally reorganized by Napoleon in 1812 during the Russian campaign, under the decree known as the Moscow decree. Its name is intimately associated with the work of Molière. It is located in the first *arrondissement* of Paris.

## commune nf.     [ \* ]

The *commune* is the smallest local government entity in the institutional hierarchy. It is governed by the town council headed by the mayor whose powers are extensive. *Communes* can differ enormously in geographical coverage, from the smallest village to a great urban area. There are 36,686 communes in France. They were created in 1789, during the Revolution, to replace the former parishes (*paroisses*). See Chapter 6 'Commune'.

## Congrès du Parlement. Le ⟨ * ⟩

This is the name given to the gathering of the two chambers of the French Parliament (*Sénat* and *Assemblée Nationale*) in the Palace of Versailles for a vote involving any change to the Constitution.

## Conseil Constitutionnel. Le ⟨ *** ⟩

*Le Conseil Constitutionnel* was set up by the Constitution of 1958 and is one of the V Republic's major institutions. Its main role is to ensure that the laws and processes of the republic are consistent with the Constitution. It is composed of nine members, three chosen by the president of the republic, three chosen by the Senate, and three chosen by the National Assembly. The period of office is nine years. All former presidents of the republic are *ex officio* members. Its members are known as *les Sages* (the wise elders). It is located in the *Palais Royal* in the first *arrondissement* of Paris. The metonymical term *Palais Royal* can refer to this institution.

## Conseil de l'Ordre. Le ⟨ *** ⟩

This is the name of the governing body of a given profession such as doctor, lawyer, dentist, chartered accountant, etc. They were set up in 1940 by Maréchal Pétain. They are also the disciplinary bodies to which complaints may be made by the general public, e.g. for breaches of the code of ethics.

## Conseil d'État. Le ⟨ *** ⟩

As its name suggests, one of the two main roles of the Conseil d'État is to advise the government. It is always consulted for its opinion on bills before they are submitted to the Council of Ministers. The second role is judicial. Just as the Cour de Cassation is the highest jurisdiction in the land (the supreme court of appeal), so the Conseil d'État is the highest 'administrative' jurisdiction in the land (i.e. for cases involving the government, administration and public authorities). It can act as a court of appeal in the case of disputed elections, and as a court of 'cassation' in other 'administrative' cases. The origins of the Conseil d'État go back to the thirteenth century. The old names dating from the *ancien régime* such as *Conseiller d'État* and *Maître des Requêtes* are still used. In its present form, the Conseil d'État dates from the Consulat 1799. There are approximately 350 members of the Conseil d'État most of whom have been recruited from *l'ENA*. Indeed, on leaving l'ENA, the very best students are allowed to choose the *corps* to which they wish to be sent. They invariably choose to go either to *l'Inspection des Finances* or *le Conseil d'État* or to *la Cour des Comptes*. The metonymical name for the Conseil d'État is the Palais Royal in which it has been head-quartered since 1874 in the first *arrondissement* of Paris. Some people become members by way of a discretionary decision called *tour extérieur* which is simply the will of the prince often exercised to reward faithful followers. See below 'l'ENA'.

## Conseil Général. Le

We may refer to this as a rough equivalent of a county council, its members having been elected by the population in the cantonal elections. Following the laws on decentralization in 1982 and 1983, the *Conseil Général* has become the executive and decision-making authority at the level of the *département*. Its powers of decision are very broad, involving areas such as schooling, roads, transport, employment, the environment and culture, etc.

## Conseil Régional. Le

The territorial organization of France is based on four levels; *l'État, la région, le département* and *la commune. Le Conseil Régional* is elected by universal suffrage and its scope of intervention, following the laws of decentralization mentioned above, is the same as that of the *Conseil Général*, but at the regional level.

## Conseil Supérieur de la Magistrature. Le

The CSM first made its appearance in France in 1883. Under the terms of article 64 of the Constitution of the Fifth Republic, the role of the CSM is to guarantee the independence of the French judiciary and to act as a disciplinary body vis-à-vis the magistrates. It is chaired by the president of the Republic and vice-chaired by the minister of justice (*Le Garde des Sceaux*). It is asked for its opinion whenever senior appointments in the legal system are made but its opinion may or may not be followed. The separation of powers – between the executive and the judiciary – is impossible to achieve in this situation.

## Constitution de 1958. La

It was against the backdrop of chronic political instability and of the political crisis provoked by the Algerian war, and the putsch of the generals, that de Gaulle returned to power in June 1958. He immediately organized a referendum on 28 September 1958 setting up a political system of a presidential type, with extended personal powers given to the president. Elections were held and de Gaulle, via direct universal suffrage, was elected president of the Fifth Republic and took office in January 1959. The architect of the Constitution was Michel Debré.

## corps constitués. Les

This is the name given to the various bodies set up under the terms of the Constitution or by the law of the land. At the national level it includes the National Assembly, the Senate, the Constitutional Council, etc. At a local level, the name refers to the legal, administrative and municipal authorities.

## corpsard nm.       **

This is the name of a senior civil servant belonging to one of the technical 'grands corps'. In Polytechnique slang, it refers to a graduate engineer who, being *dans la botte* (i.e. among the top best students on leaving the school), choses his or her *école d'application* among the most prestigious, i.e. Mines or Ponts et Chaussées. An *école d'application* is a school more specialized in a given field of study.

## Coupole. La       **

One of the most famous of the Parisian *brasseries* located in the fourteenth *arrondissement* in the Montparnasse quarter. It was built in 1927 and its name is intimately associated with such writers as Hemingway, Kessel, Simone de Beauvoir and Jean Paul Sartre. It is also the metonymical name of the Académie Française. See above 'Académie Française' and also Chapter 12. 'Coupole'.

## Cour de Cassation. La       ***

This is the supreme court of appeal. It is the highest level of jurisdiction in the French legal system and is the equivalent of the Conseil d'État which has authority for all cases involving the civil service, government, etc. It is not a third level court and does not 'retry' a court case. It merely verifies that the law has been abided by in the conduct of the proceedings at the lower levels of jurisdiction. If this has not been the case, the court *'casse'*, i.e. annuls the decision of the lower appeal court and imposes a retrial of the case at another appeal court known as the *cour d'appel de renvoi*. There is only one *Cour de Cassation* in France and it is located within the Palais de Justice, Quai de l'Horloge in the sixth *arrondissement* of Paris.

## Cour des Comptes. La       **

This is the name of the public accounting office, the origins of which can be traced back to the *curia regis* of the Middle Ages. Today, its role is to monitor the receipts and expenditures of government entities and to ensure that these have been carried out in conformity with public accounting rules. The CDC is the entity which supervises the management of public funds; this includes the accounts of the state, the department of social security, publicly owned companies, or even private companies enjoying state support. There are twenty-two metropolitan regional chambers of the court which verify the accounts of local authorities. The members of the CDC are magistrates recruited principally from *l'ENA*. The CDC publishes an annual report and can express reservations about the 'fairness and truth' of the accounts of the state. The implementation of its recommendations, however, is not mandatory. The metonymical name for the Cour des Comptes is *rue Cambon*, the name of the street in which it is located in the first *arrondissement* of Paris. See Chapter 12 Section Geographical names 'Cambon'.

### Dauphine                                                                                 [ ** ]

Originally known as l'Université de Paris IX, it was founded in 1971 and specializes in social sciences, management and economics. It is situated near la Porte Dauphine, in the sixteenth *arrondissement* of Paris, hence its adopted name. Over 9,000 students are enrolled of whom over 600 are '*doctorants*', i.e. Ph.D. (doctoral) students.

### Défense. La                                                                              [ *** ]

Directly in the axis of the Champs Élysées and straddling the two communes of Puteaux and Courbevoie (Hauts-de-Seine 92). Since 1958, La Défense has been the new business centre of Paris. It is the work of three French architects: Bernard Zehrfuss, Robert Camelot and Jean de Mailly. See Chapter 14 'Epad'.

### département nm.                                                                          [ *** ]

Under the *ancien régime*, France was divided into regions known as *généralités*. These were replaced by the *départements* under a decree issued by the National Constituent Assembly in 1790. The *département* was supposed to be small enough to allow anyone on the periphery to reach the *chef-lieu* (i.e. the most important town, generally located in the geographical centre, and the heart of the local administrative system) within 24 hours, on horseback. They frequently take their name from the names of rivers, e.g. le Cher, l'Essonne, l'Ardèche. They were supposed to break down the power blocks of the *ancien régime* and to contribute to a more balanced distribution of power. The government's representative in the *département* is the *Préfet*. Each *département* has a number related to the position of the first letter of its name in the alphabet. Thus, Ain (01), Finistère (29), Nord (59). This number corresponds both to the postal code and a car's registration plates. The last two digits on a number plate e.g. 91, indicate that the car was registered in the *département* of the Essonne. This is changing in 2010 as the new numbering plan is being introduced. Sentimental drivers will still be able to put the number of their *département* on their registration plates but this is no longer an integral part of the registration number of the car in question; this may or may not be the number of the *département* in which the vehicle is registered.

### Domaines. Les                                                                           [ * ]

This is the name given to the government department that manages all the property of the state including real estate, car fleets, etc.

### École des Mines. L'                                                                      [ * ]

During the eighteenth century, with the boom in the mining industry, it was obvious that specialized teaching in this area was needed. It was in 1783, by royal order, that the first École des Mines was created. Today, it is one of the most prestigious of France's technical *grandes écoles* and is located in the sixth *arrondissement* of Paris.

### Élysée. Le Palais de l'                                      `***`
Situated in the rue Faubourg St Honoré in the eighth *arrondissement*, this has been the official residence of the president of the Republic since 1873. It was here that Napoleon signed his second abdication after his defeat at Waterloo in 1815. See Chapter 7 'Élysées'.

### ENA. L'                                                     `***`
The École Nationale d'Administration is one of the most prestigious of the French *grandes écoles*. It was created in 1945 with a view to democratizing access to the higher echelons of the French civil service. Each 'year' or *promotion* bears a name chosen by the students themselves. Under the fifth Republic, *l'ENA* has produced two presidents (Valéry Giscard d'Estaing and Jacques Chirac), several prime ministers, (Laurent Fabius, Edouard Balladur, Michel Rocard, Alain Juppé, Dominique de Villepin, Lionel Jospin), and a host of various ministers and company chairmen. It has also produced an alarming number of people who have been sentenced by the courts of the republic for various forms of corruption, or who have been involved in corporate disasters. See Chapter 9. Originally located in the rue des Saints Pères in Paris, *l'ENA* has relocated to Strasbourg as part of a decentralization programme. The cream of the cream, i.e. the most brilliant students (*la botte*) can choose the most prestigious '*corps*' for their career, i.e. *l'Inspection des Finances, le Conseil d'État* or *la Cour des Comptes* ... in that order!

### École Normale Supérieure. L'                                `***`
See below 'Normale Supérieure'.

### Fleury-Mérogis                                              `*`
The name of a prison in the *département* of the Essonne (91) some 25 km to the south of Paris.

### Fresnes                                                     `*`
The name of a prison in the *département* of the Val-de-Marne (94). It is one of the three big prisons of the Paris region located a few kilometres to the south of Paris.

### Garde des Sceaux. Le                                        `***`
This is the equivalent of the minister of justice. British students are warned that this bears no relation to 'The Keeper of the Seals'.

### Garnier. L'Opéra

In 1858, Napoleon III decided to have an opera house built in Paris. A competition was organized and in 1861 the competition was won by a young and rather unknown architect, Charles Garnier (1825–98) who had been the prize-winner of the Prix de Rome in 1848. (See below 'Villa Médicis'.) The works lasted from 1862 to 1875, the site having been chosen by Haussmann as part of the general renovation of the capital. This is part of the legacy of the Second Empire. It was always known as the Paris Opera but since the building of the Opéra Bastille in 1989, the name Garnier has been used to avoid confusion. It is located in the second *arrondissement*.

### Gaveau. La salle
One of the most prestigious concert halls (piano and chamber music recitals) built between 1906 and 1907 and named after Étienne Gaveau (1872–1943) who had it built. It is located in the second *arrondissement* of Paris and was declared an historical monument in 1992.

### Ginette
'Ginette' is the affectionate nickname of one of the most illustrious of the *écoles préparatoires* in France, l'École Sainte Geneviève. It is situated in Versailles in the *département* of the Yvelines (78). It is a private *lycée* which prepares students for the highly competitive entrance examinations to France's top schools – the *grandes écoles* such as Polytechnique, St Cyr, HEC, Navale, ESSEC. 'Ginette' was originally managed and staffed by the Jesuits. This is no longer the case.

### Grand Palais. Le
Situated between the Seine and the Champs Élysées in the eighth *arrondissement*, its full name is *Le Grand Palais des Beaux Arts*. It was built in 1897 for the Universal Exhibition that was to take place in Paris in 1900. It is both an exhibition centre and an art gallery.

### Grandes Écoles. Les
France has the particularity of having universities (which do not have the same prestige as in England, the USA or Germany) and the *grandes écoles*. The most famous *grandes écoles* are: the 'engineers' schools (Polytechnique, Mines, Ponts et Chaussées), the business schools (HEC, ESSEC, ESCP, Insead), the schools specializing in the training of university teachers and researchers, i.e. École Normale Supérieure, the schools for training senior civil servants, Sciences Po and *l'ENA*. After the school-leaving examination (*le baccalauréat* or *bac*) students prepare for the highly competitive entrance examinations over two years, then two to three years are generally spent at a *grande école*. It is the route traditionally followed by the future elite of the country who are destined to hold the reins of power in government

and industry. The *major* refers to the best student leaving the school in a given year or *promotion*. Out of the 80 French chairmen and CEOs of the CAC 40, 23 are Polytechnicians, 16 are *énarques*, six have studied at both schools and 18 are former HEC and ESSEC students. See Chapter 9 and Chapter 14.

### Grands Corps de l'État. Les
These are the most prestigious government and technical corps of the republic staffed by the cream of the cream of students from the ENA. The best students traditionally choose *l'Inspection des Finances, le Conseil d'État* and finally *la Cour des Comptes*, while for the technical corps, the students choose Mines and then Ponts et Chaussées. There is no legal definition of the corps but its members are to be found at the very top echelons of the French civil service and private industry.

### Haute Assemblée. La
The upper house of the French parliament. The home of the *Sénat* is the Palais de Luxembourg, located in the sixth *arrondissement*, which is also the metonymical term used to refer to the upper house. The Senate exercises legislative power along with the National Assembly. Senators are elected for six years by indirect suffrage by the 150,000 *grands électeurs*, i.e. municipal councillors, regional councillors, etc. The Senate represents the overseas *départements* and *territoires*. In the event of illness or death of the president of France, it is the president of the Senate who becomes the de facto caretaker president. From the point of view of protocol, he is no. 2 in order of precedence. The political colour of the Senate is right wing but this might change in 2011. It is known to be the most expensive, comfortable and opaque retirement home in France. See below 'Sénat'. See Chapter 2 'anomalie institutionnelle'.

### Haute Cour. La
This Court was originally set up to deal with cases of high treason on the part of the president. In 2002, the term 'treason' was changed to 'manquement' (negligence, breach, default) 'à ses devoirs manifestement incompatible avec l'exercice de son mandat'. Under the Fifth Republic, the Court is composed of 12 *sénateurs* and 12 *députés*. For criminal acts committed during their term of office, ministers are judged by the Cour de Justice de la République.

### Henri IV. Le Lycée
One of the most prestigious secondary schools and *écoles préparatoires* in France situated on the Mont Sainte Geneviève, in the fifth *arrondissement* of Paris, in the heart of the Latin Quarter. NB: a student may prepare for the competitive exams of the *grandes écoles* in a specifically dedicated school, e.g. École Sainte Geneviève, or in the dedicated stream for *préparatoire* within certain (often prestigious) traditional *lycées*.

**Hôtel du Petit Luxembourg. L'**
This has been the official residence of the president of the Senate since 1825.

**Hôtel de Lassay. L'**          ( ** )
This is an eighteenth-century house located in the seventh *arrondissement* of
Paris and is the official residence of the president of the National Assembly.

**hypokhâgne**          ( * )
This name refers to the first year of a two-year preparatory course for the
competitive examination to enter the arts section of l'École Normale Supérieure. See below 'khâgne'.

**Île-de-France**          ( *** )
This may be written with or without a circumflex accent on the 'i'. It is the
name of an old French province that disappeared during the French Revolution. Today, it has been assimilated to the Greater Paris region and
includes Paris (75) and the surrounding *départements*, i.e. the Essonne (91),
the Hauts-de-Seine (92), Seine-Saint-Denis (93), Seine-et-Marne (77), Val-de-
Marne (94), Val d'Oise (95) and the Yvelines (78). Paris is the only city to
have the status of a *département* and a number of its own (75). There are
over 11 million inhabitants and the emblem of the Île de France is a blazon
(shield) with a blue background and golden *fleurs de lys*.

**Inspection Académique. L'**          ( ** )
Just as the *Académie* is the administrative echelon of the *Éducation
Nationale* facilitating implementation of national policy at the regional level,
so the Inspection Académique is the administrative echelon acting at the
level of the *département*. It is essentially concerned with the organization of
primary education and the organization of ordinary exams and competitive
examinations.

**Inspection Générale des Finances. L'**          ( *** )
If there is an elite in France, then the Inspecteurs des Finances are considered to be the cream of the cream of this elite. Members are recruited
essentially from the ENA and more specifically from those students who
were *dans la botte*, i.e. who were in the top fifteen places on leaving the
school. The best students invariably choose the Inspection des Finances or
the Conseil d'État. The role of the *inspecteurs* (who are under the authority
of the ministry of finance) is to guarantee good stewardship in so far as the
use of state funds is concerned. Some inspectors leave their *corps* to work on
secondment in publicly owned companies or *pantouflent* in private industry.
Some of the biggest scandals and corporate failures of the past few years have
implicated Inspecteurs des Finances, e.g. Jean Marie Messier (Vivendi Universal), Jean-Yves Haberer and Jean-Claude Trichet (Crédit Lyonnais).

### Inspection Générale des Services. L'

This is 'the police of the police'. A police department known as the IGS, it is concerned with investigating complaints by the public and internal disciplinary procedures. Its members are collectively known as *les bœuf-carottes* because they start by 'grilling' a suspect (*cuisiner*) and then let the suspect 'simmer' (*mijoter*) in his own juice for some time afterwards. NB: *bœuf* is written in the singular.

### Institut Catholique. L'       *

The Catholic 'university' of Paris founded in 1875 consists of several faculties and schools of higher education. Situated in the heart of Paris in the rue d'Assas in the Latin Quarter, in the sixth *arrondissement*. It is called *institut* because *université* is a term reserved for an academic body of the state which has the monopoly of awarding degrees. Affectionately referred to as *Le Catho*.

### Institut de France. L'       *

*L'Institut de France* is known as the Institute of the five academies. It was created in 1795 and includes the Académie Française (1635), the Académie des Inscriptions et des Belles Lettres (1663), the Académie des Sciences (1666), the Académie des Beaux Arts (1816), and the Académie des Sciences Morales et Politiques (1795). Briefly put, it is the parliament of the learned and is located in the sixth *arrondissement*. See above 'Académie Française'.

### Institut Pasteur. L'

Located in the fifteenth *arrondissement* of Paris, the Institute is a private, non-profit-making foundation (1887) devoted to research and teaching in the areas of microorganisms, infectious diseases and vaccine development. It is named after its founder, Louis Pasteur (1822–95) who was also its first director.

### Janson de Sailly. Le Lycée       *

One of the most prestigious secondary schools and *écoles préparatoires*, located in the sixteenth *arrondissement* of Paris.

### Jésuites nmpl.

The Society of Jesus was founded by Ignace de Loyola in 1540 after he had been seriously wounded in the battle of Pampluna. The Jesuits have always had an influential role in the area of education. It is no surpise that three of the most prestigious *écoles préparatoires* in France, are, or were originally, Jesuit institutions: St Louis de Gonzague, Lycée Louis le Grand in Paris, and Sainte Geneviève in Versailles.

## Jeu de Paume (Paris)

The building was erected in the nineteenth century in the Tuileries gardens in the eighth *arrondissement* of Paris. It was formerly the home of the French impressionist collection which crossed the river with the opening of the Orsay Museum. It has become a gallery dedicated to photography and sometimes hosts visiting exhibitions. Not to be confused with the *Jeu de Paume* in Versailles. See Chapter 6 Jeu de Paume.

## Journal Officiel. Le

The JO as it is known, is the official daily gazette of the French Republic, (published by the state since 1868 and as a monopoly since 1870) containing all of the information related to official texts, laws, decrees, orders, public tenders, the promotion/appointments of senior civil servants, etc. The date of publication is generally taken as the date on which the decrees and laws come into legal effect. Until it has been published in the JO, any information of this type is deemed to be unofficial.

## juge d'instruction nm

It is the examining magistrate, and not the police, who decides whether there are grounds for bringing sb. to trial. President Sarkozy has decided to abolish this post. If his reform is passed, investigations will henceforth be the responsibility of the *Parquet* (the public prosecutor's office) which is controlled by the political executive. The separation of powers, dear to Montesquieu, is no longer guaranteed under the Constitution of the fifth Republic. None of the scandals involving eminent politicians over the last few years would ever have come to light had the investigations been carried out by the the public prosecutor's office. The European Court of Justice has underlined the fact that the French *Procureur* is in fact a political nominee and cannot be considered as a true member of the French judicial system. The public outcry and the opposition of the judiciary to this reform has delayed its introduction. It might simply be dropped. He was called 'l'homme le plus puissant de France' by Balzac.

## khâgne

This name refers to the second year of a two-year preparatory course for the competitive examination to enter the arts section (*lettres*) of *l'École Normale Supérieure*. See above 'hypokhâgne'. A student in this stream is known as a 'khâgneux' or 'khâgnard'.

## Lanterne. La

This is the name of a hunting lodge built in Versailles in 1787. Since 1959, it has been reserved as the weekend residence of the French prime minister. President Sarkozy, having taken a liking to it, made a hostile takeover bid and evicted the PM François Fillon, who must now make do with the consolation prize of the domaine of Souzy-la-Briche to spend his weekends. See Chapter 12 'Souzy-la-Briche'.

## Légion d'Honneur. La    ***

This is the highest honorary distinction awarded in France in recognition of eminent military or civil service to the country. It was created on 19 May 1802 by Napoleon Bonaparte and was inspired by the *Legio honoratorum conscripta*. Certain people objected that this was a violation of the principle of equality. The French Revolution had abolished hereditary nobility and honorary distinctions (19 June 1790) but in Bonaparte's opinion, it is with such *hochets* (gongs) that one leads men. The first *Légion d'Honneur* was awarded on 14 July 1804 at the Invalides. There are five levels of distinction; Chevalier, Officier, Commandeur, Grand Officier and Grand Croix. The motto of the order is *Honneur et Patrie* and the decoration is awarded for 'Conduite civile irréprochable et méritante ou faits de guerre exceptionnels après enquête officielle'. An alarming number of its holders have been convicted by the French courts for a variety of offences including corruption, misuse of company funds, electoral fraud and cases involving conflicts of interest, knowingly presenting accounts that are not true and fair, handling misused company assets, etc. There are many related privileges in kind.

## Lipp    *

Founded in 1880, this famous *brasserie* is located in Saint-Germain in the sixth *arrondissement*. It has been a chic venue since the time of Proust, Gide, Hemingway, Camus and Saint-Exupéry.

## Loi du 29 juillet 1881. La    **

This is the law which contains the articles related to the freedom of the press that was inspired by article 11 of the Declaration of the Rights of Man approved on 26 August 1789. It is also the text that gives a legal framework for restrictions in this field, i.e. cases of libel. The public posting of bills is limited by this law. The words *Défense d'Afficher: Loi du 29 juillet 1881* can be seen, written in black letters two feet high, over a length of 10 metres, on otherwise pristine Parisian walls! Every newspaper, magazine and even a corporate publication includes the name of the *Directeur de la Publication* because he or she is ultimately liable in the event of legal action being taken against the newspaper or magazine in question.

## Loi 1901. La    **

This is the law governing the activities of non-profit making associations. Nothing was provided for in the texts of the French Revolution and the situation of associations was uncertain throughout the nineteenth century. This law gave a legal foundation upon which associations could be built. There are over one million such associations in France.

## Loi 1905. La ⟦**⟧

This is the law separating church and state. It effectively put an end to the Napoleonic Concordat and was the final chapter in the confrontation between Catholic, royalist France and the secular and anti-clerical republicans. Religious instruction in schools ceased. Article 2 of the law stipulates 'La République ne reconnaît, ne salarie ni ne subventionne aucun culte.'

## Loi Evin. La ⟦**⟧

Named after the socialist *député* who drew up this law in 1991 forbidding indirect or direct advertising of alcoholic beverages and tobacco.

## loi organique nf. ⟦**⟧

*Une loi organique* is a law that sets out the organization of public authorities. In the hierarchy, it is below the Constitution but above all other laws.

## Louis le Grand. Le Lycée ⟦*⟧

One of the great *lycées* of Paris, and one of the most prestigious of the *écoles préparatoires* situated in the fifth *arrondissement* in heart of the Latin Quarter. It is housed within the walls of the former Jesuit Collège de Clermont, founded by the Jesuits in the sixteenth century. A high percentage of its students enter the *grandes écoles* such as Normale Supérieure, HEC and Polytechnique. The students are known as *magnoludoviciens*. 'Louis le Grand' was the nickname of Louis XIV.

## Maison de l'Amérique Latine. La ⟦*⟧

Located in the heart of Paris, in the seventh *arrondisesment*, it was originally founded by General de Gaulle to foster relations between France and Latin America. It is in fact a mansion situated in beautiful grounds with a high-quality restaurant. It is the ideal venue for seminars.

## Maison de la Chimie. La ⟦**⟧

This is the oldest conference centre in France. It is an eighteenth-century mansion located in the seventh *arrondissement* of Paris a stone's throw from the National Assembly. Today, it is an international congress centre. Political meetings often take place here. It is also known as a good address to eat at.

## Marigny. L' Hôtel ⟦***⟧

This nineteenth-century palace situated in the eighth *arrondissement* has been used since 1972 to lodge visiting heads of state. It is very near the Palais de l'Élysée.

## math spé ⟦*⟧

*Mathématiques spéciales*, i.e. 'advanced mathematics'. Until the reform of *classes préparatoires* in 1997, this was the school stream that students followed to prepare for the great scientific schools. Today, the streams corresponding to the former 'spé' are MP (maths and physics), PC (physics and chemistry), PSI (physics and engineering science), PT (physics and technology). In student slang, *taupe* was the name given to this advanced mathematics year, the students being known as *taupins*.

### major de sa promotion. Être
See above '*grandes écoles*'.

### Matignon. L'Hôtel
This large eighteenth-century edifice is the official Paris residence of the French prime minister. It is located at no. 57, rue de Varenne in the seventh *arrondissement*. It is used metonymically to refer to the prime minister and his staff.

### Necker
One of the Paris hospitals located in the fifteenth *arrondissement*, it is particularly associated with the care of sick children and was founded in 1778 by Mme Necker, wife of the French politician and finance minister of Louis XVI, Jacques Necker (1732–1804).

### Normale Supérieure. L'École
*L'École Normale Supérieure* is one of the great *grandes écoles* of the Republic created in 1794 and consistently recognized as the number one institution of higher education on the continent. It is one of the three French higher education institutions in the top 100 of the Shanghai academic ranking. It is located in the fifth *arrondissement* in the rue d'Ulm hence its metonymical name 'Ulm'. The students (*normaliens*) are admitted after one of the most highly selective competitive examinations. Both arts and sciences are studied and 75 per cent of the students go into higher education as teachers or mostly into research while the others join the technical corps such as Mines, Ponts et Chaussées or the government administrations such as *l'Inspection des Finances, le Conseil d'État*, or *la Cour des Comptes*, etc.

### Observatoire. L'
The Royal Astronomical Observatory, located in the fourteenth *arrondissement*, was created in 1666 under Louis XIV and marks the Paris meridian. It is particularly known as having been the place where a curious attempt on the life of François Mitterrand took place in 1959. See Chapter 11 'Observatoire'.

### Olympia. L'
Opened in 1893, with 'La Goulue' and the French cancan, it is the oldest music hall in Paris located on the boulevard des Capucines in the ninth and

second *arrondissements*. To be top of the bill at l'Olympia is the ultimate accolade for an artiste and most of the great names in French entertainment have performed there. NB Frequently, the odd numbers side of an avenue can be in one *arrondissement*, while the even numbers side of the same avenue can be in a different *arrondissement*.

### Opéra-Comique. L'                                                    `( * )`
Also known as La Salle Favart, it is the name of a theatre located in the second *arrondissement* of Paris. It was founded in 1714. The genre is *opéra-bouffe* and pantomime, and one of the constraints under the articles of its foundation was that dialogues had to be punctuated by song.

### Opéra de Paris. L'                                                    `( * )`
See above 'Garnier'.

### Orsay                                                               `( * )`
The name of a nuclear research centre located to the south west of Paris in the *département* of the Essonne (91). Part of the University of Paris (Faculty of Science) is also located there and is called Paris XI-Orsay.

### Orsay. La Musée d'                                                    `( * )`
The building in which the museum is housed used to be one of the great mainline railway stations in Paris but is now one of the finest museums and art galleries in Europe. It is seen as something of a time-bridge between the Louvre and the Pompidou Centre and is located in the seventh *arrondissement* on the left bank of the Seine.

### Palais Bourbon. Le                                                    `( *** )`
It was built between 1722–8 and is located on the left bank of the Seine in the seventh *arrondissement* of Paris. It is the home of the French lower house of Parliament, i.e. the National Assembly, of which the metonymical name is le Palais Bourbon.

### Palais de la Découverte. Le                                           `( * )`
Located in the eigth *arrondissement*, this has been the official Paris science museum since 1937, a role it now shares with La Cité des Sciences de Paris la Villette.

### Palais de la Mutualité. Le                                            `( *** )`
La Maison de la Mutualité is a polyvalent hall in the fifth *arrondissement* of Paris (rue Saint Victor). It is the HQ of the French mutualist movement and is better known as the venue for shows, conferences, pop concerts and mass meetings of political parties, generally left wing.

### Palais des Congrès. Le　　　　　　　　　　　　　[ ** ]

One of the most important venues for party political meetings, conferences and pop concerts. It is located at la Porte Maillot in the seventeenth *arrondissement* of Paris.

### Palais des Sports. Le　　　　　　　　　　　　　　　[ * ]

Located in the fifteenth *arrondissement* at la Porte de Versailles. It is one of the most important venues for pop concerts, etc.

### Palais du Luxembourg. Le　　　　　　　　　　　　[ *** ]

This sixteenth-century palace is located in the sixth *arrondissement* of Paris on the north side of the Luxembourg Gardens. Today, it is home to the upper house of the French Parliament, i.e. the Senate. See below 'Petit Luxembourg'.

### Panthéon. Le　　　　　　　　　　　　　　　　　　[ ** ]

It is situated on the 'mountain' of Sainte Geneviève in the heart of the Paris Latin Quarter in the fifth *arrondissement*. 'Pantheon', in Greek, means 'all of the gods'. Today, the building serves to honour the great names in French history. In the crypt are the tombs of 71 famous French men and women: Voltaire, Rousseau, Marie Curie, Braille, Jean Moulin, Alexander Dumas. The inscription above the entrance, added in 1837, reads 'Aux grands hommes, la patrie reconnaissante'. See Chapter 2 'Aux grands hommes'.

### Parc des expositions Porte de Versailles. Le　　　[ * ]

This is the great exhibition centre in the west of Paris. Most of the big fairs and shows take place here, i.e. the Ideal Home Exhibition, the agricultural show, the car show, etc. It is located in the fifteenth *arrondissement* of Paris.

### Parc des Princes. Le　　　　　　　　　　　　　　[ ** ]

The futuristic stadium in the south-west of Paris straddling the *périphérique* ring road in the sixteenth *arrondissement* is one of the most beautiful examples of modern architecture using concrete structures in cantilever. It was designed by Roger Tallibert and inaugurated in 1972 replacing the old stadium built in 1897. It is home to the Paris Saint-Germain Football Club and has a capacity of 44,000.

### Paris IV　　　　　　　　　　　　　　　　　　　　[ * ]

The original university of Paris Sorbonne specialized in the arts and social sciences. It is one of the 13 universities of Paris. It is located in the heart of the Latin Quarter in the fifth *arrondissement*.

### Parquet nm.

This is the French equivalent of the Public Prosecutor's office. It is a noun referring collectively to all of the magistrates who plead in the name of the Republic for the application of the law. See above 'juge d'instruction'.

### Pavillon Dauphine. Le

Located in the sixteenth *arrondissement* of Paris, *Le Pavillon Dauphine* is one of the most prestigious addresses for wedding receptions, business congresses, etc.

### Pavillon Gabriel. Le

Located in the eighth *arrondissement* of Paris, this is another chic address for receptions and conferences.

### Père Lachaise. Le cimetière du

Perhaps the most famous of the Parisian cemeteries and certainly the biggest. It takes its name from the confessor of Louis XIV who lived in a house on this site in the early eighteenth century. Its construction was decided upon by Napoleon and the architecture was entrusted to Brongniart. The cemetery was inaugurated in 1804. Located in the twentieth *arrondissement* of Paris, it is also known as le Cimetière de l'Est. The Irish writer Oscar Wilde (1854–1900) and the American writer Richard Wright (1908–60) are both buried there.

### Petit Trianon. Le

At the request of his favourite, Mme de Pompadour, Louis XV had this château built within the grounds of the Palace of Versailles between 1762–68. She never lived there having died in 1764. See Chapter 6 'Trianon'.

### Pitié Salpêtrière. La

A teaching hospital of Paris, located in the thirteenth *arrondissement*. It takes it name from the manufacture of gunpowder and the storage facilities set up there during the reign of Louis XIII. NB: saltpeter (US) saltpetre (UK).

### Pleyel. La Salle

The name of a symphony concert hall in the eighth *arrondissement* of Paris inaugurated in 1927 and home to the Orchestre de France and L'Orchestre philharmonique de Radio France. 'Pleyel' was originally a name associated with the making of the finest pianos.

### Polytechnique. L'École

This school is one of the most prestigious of the *écoles d'ingénieurs* in France and has the role of selecting the very best students who will later occupy the key posts in government and industry. *Sortir dans la botte* means to be among the top best students on leaving. The nickname 'l'X' is supposed to derive from the symbol of the mathematical variable in view of the fact that mathematics forms a large part of the training of polytechnicians. Founded in 1794, the school was given military status in 1804 by Napoleon and the motto 'Pour la patrie, les sciences et la gloire'. Originally a Parisian school, it is now located in Palaiseau in the *département* of the Essonne (91). All students leave the school with the grade of second lieutenant.

### Ponts et Chaussées. L'École des                        [ *** ]
Ponts et Chaussées (bridges and highways) is one of the most prestigious of the *écoles d'application*. Although the corps of engineers of Ponts et Chaussées was constituted in 1716, it was only in 1747 that a royal decree set up formal training for engineers. During the Revolution, the idea of grouping students from *Mines, Monts and Génie* began to take form and this led to the creation of Polytechnique in 1795. Ponts et Chaussées was kept as an *école d'application*, i.e. dealing with concrete applications as opposed to pure, theoretical science. It is located in Marne-la-Vallée in the *département* of Seine-et-Marne (77).

### Port Royal                                            [ * ]
A famous maternity hospital located in the fourteenth *arrondissement* of Paris and associated with Baudeloque. This is not to be confused with Port Royal des Champs in the *département* of the Yvelines (78) that used to be a Cistercian abbey closely associated with the Counter-Reformation and the Jansenist movement.

### préfectoral. Le corps                                 [ ** ]
This corps includes all of the *préfets* and *sous-préfets* who are in fact senior civil servants reporting to the ministry of the interior. The term *préfet* is both a function and a grade within the French civil service. The *énarques* dominate this 'corps'.

### préfecture nf.                                        [ *** ]
The echelon of the *préfecture* represents the authority of the Republic at the level of the *département*; there are 96 *préfectures*. The *préfecture* and its services are located in the *chef lieu* of the *département*. *Départements* are subdivided into *arrondissements*, such entities being headed up by the *sous-préfets*. The *Préfet* is the only senior civil servant whose role and existence are defined by the Constitution of 1958. The position was originally created by Napoleon in 1800. Being the representative of the state in the *département*, the *préfet* is responsible for the security of people and property (contingency plans are triggered by the *préfet* in the event of emergency), the issuing of documents related to national identity (residence permits and

driving licences), social integration and the fight against exclusion and discrimination, economic and urban development (in liaison with the *préfet* of the *région*), and the organization of the various types of election, referendum, etc.

### Prix de Rome. Le

The Prix de Rome was a scholarship awarded to students in the arts, selected after a highly competitive examination. It was originally instituted by Louis XIV in 1663. The prizewinners won a four-year stay at the Villa Médicis in Rome at the King's expense. The competitive examination was scrapped by André Malraux, the minister of culture in 1968 and replaced by selection based on a student's file. Scholarships are now awarded for a broader spectrum of subjects than the original three: painting, sculpture and architecture. They now include archeology, literature, etc. See below Villa Médicis.

### Procureur nm.

The Public Prosecutor. See above 'juge d'instruction'.

### Prytanée National Militaire de La Flèche nm.

Founded in 1604, this *lycée* is one of the six military *lycées* preparing students for the military *grandes écoles*. The instruction was initially given by the Jesuits and the school was one of the most prestigious in seventeenth-century Europe. Descartes attended this school. One of its roles is to provide help to families by funding the secondary education of bright students whose financial situation would normally exclude them from such a school. It is located in the *département* of the Sarthe (72).

### quatrième pouvoir nm.

The press, and by extension, the media in general. The French term can be found in *De la Démocratie en Amérique* (1833) by Alexis de Tocqueville. The English expression 'the fourth estate' (the first being the Crown, the second, the House of Lords and the third, the House of Commons) was used by Lord Macaulay in 1843 when he said 'The gallery in which the reporters sit has become a fourth estate of the realm.' De Toqueville saw the four estates in the USA as follows: central power, local power, lobbies and the press.

### région nf.

France is currently divided into 26 *régions* including four for the overseas territories. The government of the *région* is entrusted to the *Conseil Régional*. The vast majority are currently held by the socialist party.

### Roland Garros

Pilot, cycling champion and inventor (1888–1918), he was the first pilot to cross the Mediterranean by air, flying from Fréjus to Bizert. He gave his name to the tennis stadium (clay court) near the Porte d'Auteuil in the sixteenth *arrondissement* of Paris where the French international tennis tournament has been held since 1928. He was killed in a dogfight over the Ardennes.

## Rungis                                                                      ┌──────┐ ┃ ** ┃ └──────┘

Rungis, a *commune* in the *département* of the Val-de-Marne (94), 7 km south of Paris, is the name of the biggest wholesale market for fresh produce in the world, with over 1,400 wholesalers providing fish, meat, vegetables and dairy produce intended for professionals from fresh produce sectors and restaurants in Paris. Opened in 1969, it replaced the former market that used to be located in Les Halles in Paris.

## Saint Denis                                                                 ┌──────┐ ┃ * ┃ └──────┘

The basilica of Saint Denis is located in the *département* of the Seine-Saint-Denis (93) and is famous for being one of the necropolis(es) of the kings of France. The tombs were badly damaged during the French Revolution.

## Saint Simon. La Fondation de                                                ┌──────┐ ┃ * ┃ └──────┘

A foundation set up in 1982 by François Furet and having as its members eminent businessmen, journalists, senior civil servants, etc. It was dissolved in 1999.

## Sainte Geneviève. L'École                                                   ┌──────┐ ┃ * ┃ └──────┘

See 'Ginette'.

## Saint Louis de Gonzague (Franklin)                                          ┌──────┐ ┃ * ┃ └──────┘

Named after an Italian Jesuit (1568–91) it is a private Catholic (Jesuit) school under contract with the state. It is one of the best *écoles* (up to 11 years old), *colleges* (11 to 15), *lycées* (15 to 18) and *écoles préparatoires* (18 to 20 years old) in France and is seen sociologically as the school of the French aristocracy. It was founded in 1894 and is located in the sixteenth *arrondissement* in the west of Paris. It became a co-educational school in 1980. A famous old boy was Charles de Gaulle. It is located at no. 12 rue Franklin in the sixteenth *arrondissement* of Paris.

## Saint Vincent de Paul                                                       ┌──────┐ ┃ * ┃ └──────┘

A university hospital located in the fourteenth *arrondissement* of Paris, taking its name from the priest Vincent de Paul (1576 or 81–1660).

## Santé. La                                                                   ┌──────┐ ┃ * ┃ └──────┘

This is the name of the famous prison of Paris, intra-muros, located in the fourteenth *arrondissement*. It has the particularity of receiving (among others) VIPs who have been sentenced or who are awaiting trial. Punning possibilities are high.

## Sciences Po                                                             [ *** ]

L'Institut des Études Politiques. This *grande école* is an institute of higher education and research originally founded in 1872. There are eight other institutes in France located in the main cities and founded after 1945 on the Paris model. It is located in the rue Saint-Guillaume (hence its metonymical name) in the seventh *arrondissement*. See Chapter 12 'Saint-Guillaume'. This is sometimes written as 'Sciences-Po'.

## Sénat. Le                                                               [ *** ]

The Senate is the upper chamber of the French Parliament. The 330 or so senators are elected by indirect suffrage by the 150,000 *grands électeurs*, e.g. mayors, regional councillors, members of Parliament. This chamber shares the legislative power with the lower chamber, the *Assemblée nationale*. The president of the Senate is the second most important person in the fifth Republic since he is the caretaker president in the event of the resignation or death of the serving president. The Senate also represents French citizens living in the overseas territories. The seat of the Senate is the Palais du Luxembourg in Paris. See Chapter 12 'Luxembourg' and above 'Le Palais du Luxembourg'. The presidency of the Senate is known as *le plateau*.

## Sorbonne. La                                                            [ * ]

Originally a school founded in 1257 by Robert de Sorbon, a French theologian (1201–74) and chaplain to the King, Saint Louis (Louis IX). It was originally intended to give poor children the possibility of studying. It was later to become one of the most prestigious institutions of higher education and a theological college. It was also an ecclesiastical court whose authority was second only to that of the Pope. It was closed during the French Revolution and was refounded in 1821. The original Sorbonne University is located in the heart of the Latin Quarter in Paris in the fifth *arrondissement* and has the name Paris IV.

## Supaéro                                                                 [ * ]

One of France's great *grandes écoles, l'École Nationale Supérieure de l'Aéronautique et de l'Espace*, is located in Toulouse.

## Trésor Public. Le                                                       [ *** ]

This refers to all of the financial resources available to the French state and equally to the government department responsible for administering it. Tax questions are generally within the scope of responsibility of the minister of budget who is usually (but not always) under the authority of the minister of finance.

## tribunal de police nm.                                                  [ * ]

This is a police court in charge of judging people guilty of minor misdemeanours called *contraventions*.

## tribunal correctionnel nm.      *

This court judges people accused of more serious infractions called *délits*, i.e. criminal offences.

## tribunal d'instance nm.      *

This is a court dealing with most of the minor civil conflicts arising between individuals where the amounts of money involved are below €10,000.

## Tribunal de Grande Instance nm.      **

'Instance' should be understood in the sense of 'importance'. It is the first level of jurisdiction responsible for judging the more serious civil matters. It is generally located in the *chef-lieu* of the *département* as is the *préfecture*.

## Val de Grâce. Le      *

This is the name of a military hospital located in the fifth *arrondissement* of Paris. During the French Revolution (the first one) it became a military hospital as it remains to this day. It is, however, open to the rich general public. It has seen many famous patients and in each department of the hospital there is a VIP room!

## Villa Médicis. La      ***

In 1663, during the reign of Louis XIV and on his initiative, a special scholarship was created (*Le Prix de Rome*) to enable talented architects, sculptors and painters to perfect their knowledge through a four-year stay in Rome at the Palais Mancini, all expenses being paid by the Crown. In 1803, Napoleon created the Académie de France à Rome which has since been housed in the Villa Médicis*. In 1968, the competition was reorganized to include a far broader spectrum of artistic activity and candidates are now chosen on the strength of a dossier. (*Medici in Italian). See above 'Prix de Rome'.

## X. L'      ***

See above 'Polytechnique'.

## Zouave de l'Alma. Le      **

Whenever there is heavy rainfall and a rise in the level of the water of the Seine, reference is systematically made to the *Zouave*. *Le Zouave du Pont de l'Alma* is a sculpture representing a French soldier from a North African regiment. He is situated on one of the piles of the Alma Bridge. It was during the Crimean War, at the battle of the Alma (1854), that this North African regiment fought with great distinction. Well known to Parisians, it is traditionally the yardstick used to judge the level of the Seine. In the great flood of 1910, the water reached the shoulders of *le Zouave*. In normal times, his feet are dry.

# Chapter 11

# The Skeletons in Marianne's cupboard

This chapter does not claim to present a comprehensive list of the scandals that have marred the history of France, nor does it claim to give a thorough explanation of each of the scandals mentioned. The commentaries are intended to be a brief introduction to a given scandal that will put the reader in the picture. The scandals listed here are those which frequently come back to hit the headlines in spite of the fact that many of them date from the very distant past. Most of these scandals are so well known that the allusions made to them in the press are frequently not developed and foreign readers find themselves somewhat in the dark.

**amiante nm.**                                               \*\*
Asbestos. The relationship between exposure to asbestos and lung cancer was established in England in 1900. As early as 1918, US insurance companies were refusing to insure people working in the asbestos industry. In 1960, the correlation between exposure to asbestos and lung cancer was clearly demonstrated and was included in the basic medical studies of student doctors. The powerful French asbestos lobby successfully succeeded in delaying introduction of legislation against asbestos, in France, until 1997. The potential asbestos-related death toll is put at 100,000.

**Angolagate**                                               \*\*
This affair involved illegal arms sales to Angola in 1994 during the civil war and has implicated several well-known figures such as Charles Pasqua, former minister of the interior, and the son of the late President Mitterrand, Jean-Christophe Mitterrand. Huge commissions were paid to many eminent French people and the charges against them include money laundering, misuse of company funds, influence peddling and breach of trust. On 27 October 2009, the criminal court sentenced Charles Pasqua to a three-year prison term with two years as a suspended sentence, and one year without remission, plus a fine of €100,000 for influence peddling. He has appealed. Pierre Falcone and Arcadi Gaydamak have both received a six-year prison sentence without remission. Jean-Christophe Mitterrand has

been given a two-year suspended prison sentence and a fine of 370,000 euros. The Public Prosecutor had asked for a one-year prison term without remission for Jean-Christophe Mitterrard. The former president's son has decided not to lodge an appeal.

### Auriol. Le massacre d'

A police inspector named Jacques Massié, the Marseilles area manager of the SAC, (see Chapter 14 'SAC') was assassinated with his wife, son, father-in-law, mother-in-law and a friend, at his house in Auriol on 19 July 1981. It was after this killing that the SAC was officially disbanded. Massié was thought to be on the point of passing sensitive information about the SAC to the socialists who had just come to power in May 1981 with the election of the late François Mitterrand.

### avions renifleurs nmpl.

This was the name given to the affair by *Le Canard Enchaîné* in 1983. In the wake of the oil crisis of 1974, two confidence tricksters 'sold' the idea to Elf Aquitaine, the French petroleum group, that they had invented a machine which could detect oilfields. The machine was placed on board an aircraft which then flew over certain areas. It was said to be able to detect the depth of the oilfield and its capacity. Between 1975 and 1979 a billion francs of Elf Aquitaine's money was spent on 'research'. The swindle was stopped in 1979. None of the money was ever recovered. Some of France's most brilliant engineers were hoodwinked by the two swindlers.

### barbouzes npl.

This is a slang term referring to members of the French secret service generally operating under a hidden identity; a false beard (*une fausse barbe*) being the origin of the term. They were largely recruited from the underworld, and their role was to fight against the anti-de Gaulle factions. The adjective 'barbouzard' refers to any dirty work carried out by such men for the French secret service as of 1958.

### Ben Barka

El Mehdi Ben Barka (1920–65) was a Moroccan politician hostile to the French protectorate of Morocco and the main opponent of the regime of Hassan II. He was kidnapped on 29 October 1965 in front of the *brasserie* Lipp, in the bld Saint-Germain in Paris, by two French police officers. He was taken to Fontenay-le-Vicomte in the *département* of the Essonne (91) and was never seen again.

### Boulin, Robert

Robert Boulin (1920–79), minister of labour at the time of his death, had a long political career and was a credible contender for the position of prime minister in the late 1970s. He was found dead in the lake of Rambouillet in 1979. The initial version of suicide was soon rejected by the general public and his own family in the light of many worrying inconsistencies and the 'disappearance' of key organic exhibits from the Institut Médico-Légal, i.e. the coroner's office. A post-mortem carried out at the request of the Boulin family, three years after the death, revealed that Robert Boulin had sustained several fractures to the face, totally inconsistent with the 'suicide' theory. All attempts by the family to get the case reopened have so far ended in failure. It is interesting to note that at the time of his death, Robert Boulin was the victim of a smear campaign intended to discredit him politically. In his attempt to fight back, he hinted that he was in possession of some files concerning illegal funding of political parties. He left home on the day of his disappearance, with a dossier. The dossier has never been found.

## Bousquet, René

[ * ]

René Bousquet (1909–93) was a senior French civil servant who rose to be secretary general of the police during the Vichy regime. He is notably remembered for having masterminded the rounding up of Parisian Jews in the infamous Vél d'Hiv' raid that took place on 16/17 July 1942. After the war he was simply sentenced to five years' loss of civil rights (*dégradation nationale*) but had an excellent career afterwards. He was given back his *Légion d'Honneur* decoration in 1957 and pardoned in 1958. He was a close friend of François Mitterrand and contributed to the latter's presidential campaign fund. As of 1986, accusations were made against him and a judicial inquiry was launched. In 1989, Bousquet was accused of crimes against humanity for his role in the deportation of 194 children from the south-west of France. He was officially charged in 1991 but just as the judicial inquiry had been completed and Bousquet was on the point of standing trial, he was assassinated by Christian Didier. See Chapter 6 'Vél' d'Hiv'.

## Carrefour du développement. Le

[ ** ]

In 1983, the minister of cooperation, the socialist Christian Nucci (a freemason) set up the association Carrefour du développement, the object of which was to fund the then upcoming Franco-African summit. When the Right returned to power in 1986, the new minister of cooperation unveiled a report made by the public accounting office (Cour des Comptes) which pinpointed the misappropriation of funds that had taken place under Nucci and even more so by Yves Chalier, his head of office (also a freemason). The latter fled the country with the help of Charles Pasqua the minister of the interior. Pasqua had the DST (counter-espionnage) fabricate an authentic counterfeit passport (*vrai-faux passeport*) to enable Chalier to leave the country under the assumed name of Navarro. The basic idea was to create difficulties for the socialists. This must be set in the context of the right–left tensions during the first 'cohabitation', i.e. socialist president and right-wing prime minister. After six months on the run, Chalier returned to France and was given a jail sentence of five years without remission. The socialist minister Nucci was granted a pardon and Charles Pasqua could not be prosecuted since he was protected by parliamentary immunity. 'Vrai-faux' is now used in a variety of contexts.

## Charonne. La station du métro                                   `*`

On 8 February 1962, an anti-OAS demonstration took place in Paris in spite of having been forbidden by the police. The demonstrators were savagely dispersed and nine of them were killed in the resulting panic, near the Charonne métro station in the eleventh *arrondissement*. The *préfet de police* at the time was Maurice Papon. See Chapter 14 'OAS'.

## Clearstream                                                     `***`

Clearstream is the name of a clearing house located in Luxembourg. The writer of a poison pen letter to the financial section of the ministry of justice sent a CD-ROM with the names and account numbers of clients of the bank to the judge in charge of the Taiwan Frigates affair, Renaud Van Ruymbeke. The names included several politicians, Nicolas Sarkozy among them. The listings were shown to have been tampered with and the names of eminent politicians added. This happened before the presidential election and seems to have been hatched by people who wanted to discredit Nicolas Sarkozy. Currently, several people including Dominique de Villepin, the former prime minister, are on trial for a number of offences including complicity in defamatory denunciation. Jacques Chirac who was president at the time has told the judges that he will not reply to any summons to be heard as a witness. There is no legal basis for his refusal. Every citizen has the obligation to contribute to the revelation of the truth in the judicial process. The trial is over. Dominique de Villepin was acquitted but the Public Prosecutor has appealed and consequently de Villepin will stand trial again, lending substance to the accusation that Nicolas Sarkozy is thirsty for revenge. See below 'Frégates de Taïwan'.

## Collier de la Reine                                             `*`

This scandal blew up in 1785 and succeeded in tarnishing the already damaged image of the French monarchy in general and that of Marie-Antoinette in particular. The Cardinal de Rohan, bishop of Strasbourg, was avid for recognition at the court of Louis XVI and wanted to gain the favour of Marie-Antoinette. The Comtesse de la Motte, an obscure bastard of the Valois line, succeeded in convincing Rohan that she was an intimate relation of the Queen and that she could intervene on his behalf. With the use of some forged letters (produced by her own brother) she was able to hoodwink the cardinal into thinking that he was indeed 'in touch' with the Queen. The Comtesse indicated that the Queen would cover him with favours if he would stand surety for the purchase of a diamond necklace that the Queen had seen. The necklace was bought but the diamonds were soon shared out among the swindlers. The brother tried to sell the precious stones in France but their quality was such and the price he asked for, so low, that the jeweller smelled a rat. The brother fled to England, where an English jeweller had the same reaction as his French counterpart and informed Paris. The Comtesse was branded and imprisoned for life. In 1785 Cardinal Rohan was arrested and tried for using the name of the Queen to obtain the necklace. The slap in the face for the Queen came when the Cardinal was acquitted, betraying the fact that the court found the Cardinal's explanations more than plausible, given the notorious frivolity of the Queen.

### corvée de bois nf.                                                      ⬚ *

A military euphemism which referred to the assassination of FLN or suspected FLN members arrested by the French army during the Algerian war of independence. It consisted of taking prisoners into the woods and killing them and burying them in common graves; this was an alternative to throwing their corpses into the sea from helicopters.

### Crédit Lyonnais. Le                                                     ⬚ **

In 1988 Jean-Yves Haberer (*major de sa promotion* at *l'ENA*), *Inspecteur des Finances* was appointed as president of the Crédit Lyonnais bank, one of the top three banks in France at the time. A hazardous policy of growth at any price plus the 'law of silence' on the part of the Inspection des Finances drove the bank into bankruptcy. On 5 May 1996 a strange fire broke out in the HQ of the Crédit Lyonnais, on bld des Italiens in Paris. A fortnight later, the banking archives stored in a warehouse in Le Havre went up in smoke. The crash of one of the biggest French banks cost the French taxpayer €50 billion in total. Jean-Yves Haberer was given a two-year suspended prison sentence. The Governor of the Bank of France, at the time, who had an overseeing role, was Jean-Claude Trichet (*énarque*). He was tried for having presented accounts that were not true and fair and for the dissemination of false financial information. He was acquitted and became Governor of the European Central Bank. The second part of the Crédit Lyonnais scandal is known by the name 'Executive Life'. See below.

### de Broglie                                                             ⬚ *

Prince Jean de Broglie (1921–76) was an eminent French politician who had consistently been returned to Parliament as MP for the *département* of the Eure (28). He was assassinated on 24 December 1976. Although three people were convicted as either killer or accessory, no one has ever found the real motive for his assassination. The police were at the crime scene before the crime took place and rumours had been circulating for weeks about the assassination. Shortly before his death, de Broglie had announced his intention of leaving the Giscard d'Estaing camp for that of Chirac. In 1995 and 1996 France was severely criticized by the European Court of Human Rights for the handling of this affair. Before the trial, the minister of the interior, in flagrant violation of the presumption of innocence, declared that the case was closed and that the guilty parties had been apprehended.

## de Grossouvre, François                                                  [ * ]

François de Grossouvre (1918–94) had been a resistant during the war and a member of the SDECE (see Chapter 14 'DGSE). He was the grey eminence of François Mitterrand and was in charge of the presidential hunt. He was the special advisor in parallel diplomacy for Tunisia, the Lebanon, Morocco and Syria. He was also in charge of the security surrounding the secrecy of the existence of Mitterrand's illegitimate daughter Mazarine, whose god-father he was. He left Mitterrand's cabinet in 1985 but still retained the role related to the hunt and to protecting Mazarine. He still had an office in the Élysée. He was disgusted by the drift that presidential power was taking and gave frequent interviews to the press. He was found dead in his office in the Élysée on 7 April 1994. Rumour had it that he was depressed but in fact there are very serious reasons to believe that he was assassinated:

1  The weapon used was a high calibre .357 magnum; it is impossible that nobody heard the shot. Nobody heard the shot.
2  His body bore signs of physical aggression, i.e. facial injuries, and during the post-mortem it was discovered that his shoulder had been dislocated, consistent with the idea that he had been held by force in the position in which he died.
3  He had spoken to his family about his fears of being eliminated.
4  His children, who started their own investigations, received death threats.
5  No serious investigation was ever made into his death.

## diamants de Bokassa/Giscard d'Estaing nmpl.                   [ * ]

The affair of the diamonds was revealed by *Le Canard Enchaîné* on 10 October 1979. The diamonds in question were gifts made to VGE by the then head of state of the Central African Republic, Jean-Bédel Bokassa. At the time the gifts were made, VGE was either minister of finance or president of the Republic. He knew Bokassa well for having spent several seasons hunting big game in the Central African Republic. Although the diamonds were ultimately valued at less than the million francs suggested by *Le Canard*, the value was well over 100,000 francs at the time.

## Dreyfus, Alfred                                                    

This is a story of the miscarriage of justice that took place against the backdrop of espionage and anti-Semitism during the Third Republic. In 1894, Captain Alfred Dreyfus (1859–1935) who worked in the statistics department of the army, was convicted (on extremely flimsy evidence) of passing information to the German enemy. He was sent to Devil's Island, a penal colony, for life in 1894. He was a victim of the anti-Semitism prevalent in France at the time. A new officer, Picquart, was appointed to the statistics office. He not only uncovered some inconsistencies in the affair but he also discovered that staff papers were still going missing and that a certain Esterhazy was probably the guilty party. On making his hunches known, Picquart was immediately transferred to Tunisia. The War Office continued to cover up the affair. It was in defence of Dreyfus that Zola wrote *J'accuse* in 1898, accusing the French War Office of a judicial crime. Intellectuals began to lobby for a retrial. Esterhazy fled to England and Colonel Henry, who had lied and covered up for the War Office during the whole affair, committed suicide. The affair divided the country into two camps; the Dreyfusards and the anti Dreyfusards, frequently splitting up families and associations. A retrial was held and Dreyfus was cleared of the charge and reinstated in the army with the grade of Commandant in 1906.

## Elf      `***`

This is the former name of the petrol company Total. This was an affair of corruption implicating the top management of the company (le Floch-Prigent, Alfred Sirven and André Tallaro), a host of go-betweens and several politicians, among them Roland Dumas. The Elf scandal was triggered by a small affair of misuse of company funds by the PDG of Elf, Loïk le Floch-Prigent, who had invested 800 million francs of Elf's money to help bail out a failing company run by one of his close friends, Maurice Bidermann. However, during the investigation of this affair, another huge affair was uncovered. The then minister of foreign affairs was accused of having accepted expensive presents from a top-class whore employed by Elf to seduce the minister and to persuade him to lift his veto on the sale of six La Fayette-class frigates to Taiwan. He was later forced to resign from the presidency of the Conseil d'État. 'Retro commissions' were paid to eminent French politicians but the case is covered by '*le secret défense*'. The truth concerning politicians who received kickbacks will thus never be known. Several prison sentences were given to the former Chairman, le Floch-Prigent and his slush fund manager, Alfred Sirven. On appeal, Dumas was found innocent of any wrong doing although his behaviour was declared 'blâmable'. See below 'Frégates de Taïwan'. See Chapter 9 'Eva Joly'.

### emplois fictifs de l'Hôtel de Ville nmpl.      `**`

This scandal concerns the phoney job positions at the Paris Hôtel de Ville, people who received salaries, paid for by taxpayers' money, but who were, in fact, working for the political party founded by Jacques Chirac, the RPR.

The offence of 'misappropriation of public funds' took place between 1988 and 1995, the period during which Jacques Chirac was president of the political party RPR and mayor of Paris. According to a police report, the amount of money involved was 30 million francs. While President of France, Chirac was protected by his presidential immunity. Since his departure from the Élysée, he has been charged with 'détournement de fonds publics'. The affair was ongoing in 2010. It was during this affair that Alain Juppé was given a 14-month suspended prison sentence and sentenced to one year's ineligibility as secretary general of the Paris Hôtel de Ville in charge of finance. Chirac's trial was scheduled to start on March 7 2011. See Chapter 9 'Chirac'.

### Executive Life      (   *   )

Under US law, a foreign bank is not allowed to buy an American life assurance company. In spite of this legislation, the head of the French bank Crédit Lyonnais, Jean-Yves Haberer, in flagrant defiance of US legislation, bought the US company, Executive Life, using another company as a front. The violation was discovered in 1998 and the US began to negotiate the 'fines' for the various protagonists involved. The ultimate cost for the French taxpayer will be huge and known only in 2014. His successor, Jean Peyrelevade was fined US $500,000 in this affair and forbidden entry to the USA.

### Euralair      (   *   )

During the investigation related to the 'lycées d'Île de France', a judge discovered that cash payments had been made to a travel agent in Neuilly-sur-Seine for the purchase of air tickets for Jacques Chirac. The value of the transactions amounted to 2,400,000 francs. Jacques Chirac claimed that the money came from secret funds he had kept from the time he was prime minister. Bernadette Chirac is said to have been given at least 40,000 francs' worth of free tickets between 1998 and 1999. The airline company has since gone out of business and its owner accused of fraudulent bankruptcy. It was on 14 July 2001 during a TV interview that Chirac used the term 'pschitt' when discussing the affair. See below 'lycées'. See Chapter 2 'pschitt'.

### faux électeurs      (   **   )

The trial (12 years after the event) of Jean Tibéri (former mayor of Paris) and his wife Xavière ended in 2009. They were both accused of electoral fraud (municipal in 1995 and legislative in 1997). Many electors, although they had been removed from the electoral roll, no longer lived in the fifth *arrondissement,* yet still voted in the 1997 election. They did so in return for favours in the form of a job at the town hall, a place for their child at the municipal nursery or a council flat. In 1998 the Conseil Constitutionnel noted 'serious and repeated irregularities', but refused to annul the election of 1997 on the grounds that the final result would not have been affected.

The maximum sentence had been requested, i.e. five-years ineligibility, a €10,000 fine and one-year suspended prison sentence. The couple were sentenced in May 2009 to a 10-month suspended prison sentence, a €10,000 fine and three years' ineligibility. The Tibéris appealed and consequently the ineligibility does not apply until all of the appeal procedure has been completed, i.e. *appel* and *cassation*. It is to be noted that Jean Tibéri is a magistrate by training.

### frais de bouche nmpl.                              `*`

Between 1987 and 1995, 14 million francs were spent by the Chiracs on their own food consumption while at the Hôtel de Ville. Although the new mayor Bertrand Delanoé lodged a complaint for misuse of public money, the case was dismissed on grounds of 'lack of evidence'. A large quantity of documentary evidence had been destroyed before the investigation began.

### Frégates de Taïwan nfpl.                          `***`

This is a sub-chapter of the Elf scandal. The scandal bears on 3 billion francs of under-the-table commissions paid at the time of operation Bravo, i.e. the sale to Taiwan of six La Fayette-class frigates manufactured by Thomson CSF (see 'Elf' above). Several people involved in the case have died in curious circumstances. Thierry Imbot, member of the DGSE in Peking, was on the point of meeting the French press when he fell from his Paris apartment on the fifth floor in the year 2000. He fell 'accidentally' while closing the shutters. The body of Yin Ching-Feng of the Taiwanese navy was found floating in the bay of Taipei in 1993; he was on the point of revealing the names of Taiwanese naval officers who had been 'bought' by Thompson. Jean-Claude Albessart, delegate of the international branch of Thomson in Taiwan, died from what was called 'lightning cancer'. Jacques Morisson, former French navy specialist who had joined Thomson CSF, threw himself out of his apartment window in Neuilly in 2001. The *'secret défense'* was the reply of the government to requests to access confidential information that would have revealed the names of those politicians who had received a slice of the cake.

### Gautier-Sauvagnac, Denis                          

Senior civil servant born in Paris in 1943. Former student at the Lycée Janson de Sailly, Sciences Po and *l'ENA* (1970 *promotion* Marcel Proust). Former head of the metallurgical employer's federation, he is accused of having withdrawn €15 million in cash from the UIMM bank account between 2000 and 2007. On his own admission, this money was used to 'fluidify industrial relations'. He has never said to whom this slush money was paid. He is currently under judicial investigation and has been charged with breach of trust. He has the *Légion d'Honneur*.

## gégène nf.

[   *   ]

This term is the diminutive of 'génératrice d'électricité'. It is military slang for torture by electrical generator that was practised in Algeria by French troops to obtain information from suspected members of the FLN.

## Harkis nmpl.

[   *   ]

The harkis were soldiers recruited locally in Algeria to back up the French army between 1957 and 1962 during the Algerian war of independence. 'Harki' comes from the Arab word 'harka' meaning 'movement'. They were in fact mobile territorial units. The name was later used to refer to those Algerian Muslims who supported Algeria's continued attachment to France and it was to become a synonym of 'traitor'. Under the terms of the Evian agreement putting an end to the war, the harkis were disarmed by the French army and left defenceless. Disciplinary measures were threatened against any French soldier trying to assist the repatriation of any harki. Estimates put the number of those massacred between spring and autumn 1962 at between 60,000 and 90,000. In 1962, thousands of harkis and their families were able to embark on ships bound for France, thanks to those French officers who had disobeyed orders.

## HLM de Paris

[   **   ]

From 1977 to 1995 there was a scandal of misuse of funds involving the HLM (the administration responsible for managing council housing) of Paris. Construction tenders were awarded in return for kickbacks to the RPR party of Jacques Chirac. The case came to trial in 2004 and in spite of the posthumous testimony of Jean Claude Méry (who had accused Jacques Chirac of being present when briefcases of money were exchanged), nothing significant emerged regarding Jacques Chirac.

## Juppé, Alain

[   **   ]

To be 'droit dans ses bottes' (standing straight in one's boots) means to be determined not to give way and to have a clear conscience. These words were used by former Prime Minister Alain Juppé following the scandal of his intervention in the affairs of the social housing department of the Ville de Paris to obtain a reduction of the rent paid by his son for a flat in the sixth *arrondissement* of Paris. Juppé also had a flat, (theoretically reserved for people with moderate incomes), for which he paid a very low rent. At the time, Juppé was in charge of the attribution of flats and the fixing of the rents at the Paris Town Hall. He had authority to sign in the name of Jacques Chirac, the then mayor of Paris. In the affair of the 'emplois fictifs', he went on trial for 'prise illégale d'intérêt' (one of the various forms of corruption) and in 2004 was given an 18-month suspended prison sentence, and sentenced to 10 years' ineligibility. On appeal this was reduced to a 14-month suspended prison sentence and he was made ineligible for one year. In his summing up of the case, the judge said that Alain Juppé had deceived the French people and had refused to admit what was self-evident. Alain Juppé is an *énarque* and currently mayor of Bordeaux. NB: to apply to join the civil service (even as a postman) one must have a clean police record. He is now minister of foreign affairs, March 2011. See Chapter 9 'Juppé, Alain'.

### Légions d'Honneur. L'affaire des                                              ( * )

The scandal of the trafficking of *Légions d'Honneur* decorations blew up amid general discontent with the government of President Jules Grévy, in 1887. It appeared that the president's son-in-law, Daniel Wilson, was using a presidential office at the Élysée as a sales office for the sale of presidential favours. The scandal broke on 7 October 1887 when the press revealed the affair. Grévy was forced out of office amid growing hostility towards the parliamentary regime of the third Republic. The subsequent enquiry revealed that several thousand decorations had been sold for 25,000 francs apiece (€90,000 in today's money). Daniel Wilson, as a member of parliament, was protected by his parliamentary immunity and continued to sit in the National Assembly. He was ultimately sentenced in 1888 for corruption of civil servants but was acquitted on appeal. He was re-elected in 1893 and 1896.

### Luchaire                                                                       ( * )

In spite of the arms embargo against Iran, between 1984 and 1986 Luchaire exported half a million artillery shells to Iran. The socialist party is said to have received three million francs in commission for turning a blind eye to these exports. In spite of months of investigation and the accusations against the then minister of defence, Charles Hernu, nothing came of the affair because *'le secret défense'* was invoked by those concerned.

### lycées d'Île de France nmpl.                                                  ( ** )

This was, at the time, the biggest corruption scandal of the Fifth Republic. The RPR (Rassemblement pour la République), the PS, the PCF, the CDS (Centre des démocrates sociaux) and the PR (Parti Républicain) collectively received 200 million francs in 'racket' money. In the 1990s, a vast programme was launched for the extension, renovation and construction of 470 secondary schools in the greater Paris region and involving 24 billion francs of investment. An illicit agreement resulted in 2 per cent of the value of the contracts signed with certain construction companies being paid back to political parties across practically the whole political spectrum. The scandal was denounced by the Green party who had turned down the offer of a slice of the cake. See Chapter 14 'PCF', 'PS'.

### Main Rouge nf.                                                                 ( * )

This was the name of a French terrorist organization active during the 1950s and early 1960s. Terrorist attacks were carried out in North Africa and in

Europe against militants for Algerian independence and arms manufacturers who were known to be supplying FLN forces. It was said to be the 'murder machine' of the French Secret Service, the former SDECE. See Chapter 14 'DGSE.

## Markovic

( \* )

This affair must be understood in the context of 1968. Georges Pompidou, the prime minister, had announced his intention to run for the presidency as de Gaulle's successor. Stevan Markovic, Alain Delon's odd-job man, was found dead on a Paris rubbish tip on 1 October 1968. It was thought that he had been blackmailing some show-business friends of Delon using photos taken during sexual orgies. Soon after the death of Markovic, rumours began to evoke the presence of Pompidou's wife, Claude, at such orgies. A bogus photo showing a woman vaguely resembling Mme Pompidou was in circulation. It is also thought that Markovic was an honorable correspondent of the French secret service (the then SDECE). Finally, Pompidou was elected president and heads began to roll at the SDECE. See Chapter 14 'DGSE.

## Massacre à Paris 1961

( \*\* )

On 17 October 1961, a demonstration by 30,000 Algerian supporters of Algerian independence marched through Paris. The *préfet de police* at the time, Maurice Papon, gave orders to disperse the demonstrators. They were savagely attacked by the police, and in the following days, dozens of dead Algerian bodies were pulled out of the Seine. Official figures gave the death toll of the Algerians as 'two'. Conservative estimates put the death toll at over 200. Many of them had been 'drowned by bullets' to quote the expression of the time. The contribution to the French language was the expression 'noyés par balles'.

## Nouvelle Calédonie. La

( \* )

In March 1986, the new minister of the French Overseas Territories decided to propose to the Caldoches (white inhabitants) a reform for New Caledonia which went back on promises made beforehand to give more power to the native Kanaks. Disturbances took place between April and May 1988. The Kanaks attacked a gendarmerie, several gendarmes were killed and a number of hostages taken. They were taken to a cave near Goossanah on the island of Ouvéa. The cave was located by the special troops of the French army who took the cave by storm. Two soldiers were killed and 16 kidnappers were killed in the battle. However, three Kanak kidnappers died in conditions that could be qualified as crimes. Alphonse Dianou, the leader of the commandos, died under torture, while Wenceslas Levelloi and Waina Amossa, who had already been taken prisoner and represented no threat, were liquidated. In 1989, Parliament voted a pardon for those responsible for the deaths of the three prisoners.

## OAS                                                                    ***

*L'Organisation de l'Armée Secrète*. This was a political and military terrorist organization created in 1961 by Salan and Lagaillarde to fight the FLN and preserve French Algeria. After the failed putsch by the four retired generals Salan, Challe, Zeller and Jouhaud, the opponents of de Gaulle's policy of withdrawing from Algeria went underground and formed the OAS. It carried out numerous attacks both in Algeria and in mainland France, the most spectacular being the attempt on the life of de Gaulle at Petit-Clamart in 1962. See below 'SAC' and Chapter 12 Section Geographical names 'Petit Clamart'.

## Observatoire. L'attentat de l'                                        **

During the height of the Algerian war, François Mitterrand, senator of the Nièvre (58), was driving home in the night of the 15/16 October 1959. He was under the impression that he was being followed by another car. He got out of his car and took cover behind the bushes on the avenue de l'Observatoire in the fourteenth *arrondissement*. Shortly after, his car was machine-gunned. Such was the version that he gave to the police. A few days later, Robert Pesquet, an extreme right-wing supporter of Algérie Française confessed to having carried out the 'assassination attempt' that he claimed had been planned with ... François Mitterrand, in the hope that this would rekindle favour among the public. Pesquet's parliamentary immunity was lifted and he was charged with contempt of court. The judicial enquiry was never completed because seven years later he was granted a pardon in the affair.

## Oussekine, Malik                                                      *

On 6 December 1986, a huge student demonstration was organized in Paris and violent clashes took place between the police and students. At midnight, a 22-year-old student Malik Oussekine, was leaving a jazz club when he was chased by two 'voltigeurs' (police on motorbikes). Typically such units were used to clear the streets of demonstrators after a 'demo'. The student took refuge in the hallway of an apartment building but the police came after him and, according to the eye witness, beat the student with extraordinary violence, hitting him with a truncheon and kicking him in the stomach and back. An ambulance was called but the student died soon after his admission to hospital, from the beating and kidney failure. A plaque now marks the place in Paris where Malik died, 'beaten to death'. There is no mention of the fact that he died from police brutality.

## Overney, Pierre                                                       *

He was a 24 year-old, left-wing activist working in the Renault car factory at Boulogne-Billancourt in the Paris suburbs. He was sacked because of his political activities. Soon after, on 25 February 1972, while handing out tracts outside the factory, tracts to commemorate the Massacre of Charonne (see above 'Charonne'), he was shot by a Renault vigilante, Jean-Antoine Tramoni. Tramoni was assassinated five years later by the Noyaux armés pour l'autonomie populaire. The name of Pierre Overney was also mentioned at the time of the assassination of the head of Renault, Georges Besse, in 1986. He was killed by Action Directe by the commando unit having as its name Pierre Overney.

## Panama. L'Affaire du canal de                            ( * )

In 1879, the Panama Canal Company was set up with a view to building a canal across the isthmus of Panama to link the Atlantic and the Pacific oceans. A loan was floated but the amount of funds collected was insufficient. Part of the money raised was used by Jacques de Reinach and Cornelius Herz, two financiers, to bribe journalists into 'selling' the idea to the public, and to obtain backing from the political establishment. The project fell behind schedule and finally the company went bankrupt in 1889, ruining hundreds of thousands of small shareholders. One billion francs were lost in the biggest financial scandal of the nineteenth century. Reinach was found dead in 1892 but he had given secret documents to the journalist Edouard Drumont. The affair exploded in 1892. In his anti-Semitic and anti-parliamentarian newspaper, *La Libre Parole*, Drumont published the names of over 100 members of parliament who had taken bribes in order to cover up the real financial situation of the ailing Panama Canal Company. The then minister of the interior, Loubet, was forced to resign and both de Lesseps and Eiffel were found guilty of bribery but never served a sentence. A parliamentary commission of enquiry was set up. Five senators and five members of parliament were put on trial on corruption charges. In 1893, the minister of public works served a three-year prison sentence. This scandal tarnished the image of the political establishment and the parliamentary regime and also fuelled the already prevalent anti-Semitism, given the fact that Herz and Reinach were both Jews. This paved the way for the Dreyfus affair and put an end to Clémenceau's political career.

## Papon, Maurice                                         ( ** )

Maurice Papon (1910–2007) secretary general of the *Préfecture* of the Gironde between 1942–4, was found guilty of involvement in organizing the deportation of dozens of Jewish families to Auschwitz. After the war, he miraculously escaped charges of collaboration and continued to be employed at the very highest echelons of the French government; he was minister of the budget between 1978 and 1981. In 1983, he was charged with crimes against humanity. It was only in 1998 that he was given a ten-year prison sentence and lost his civic rights and was no longer allowed to wear the *Légion d'Honneur* decoration. He only served three years and was released, apparently for health reasons. He died in 2007. See above 'Charonne'.

## Piat, Yann     [ ** ]

She was a French right-wing politician, born in 1949 in Hanoi. In her early political career she was on the extreme right wing but turned to the centre later on. She was UDF (*Union pour la démocratie française*) member of parliament for the *département* of the Var (83). She intended to stand for the position of mayor of Hyères in the municipal elections of 1995. Her declared intention was to put an end to the collusion between politicians and the mafia in the *département* of the Var. She was assassinated by two men on a motorbike in 1994. Those who commissioned the attack have never been found.

## poisons. L'Affaire des     [ * ]

This affair refers to a series of poisonings that took place between 1672 and 1682 that shook the court of Louis XIV and triggered a witch-hunt against a backdrop of infanticides and black masses. The affair began in 1672 with the death of a cavalry officer, Godin de Sainte-Croix. Among his papers certain documents were found indicating that his mistress, the Marquise de Brinvilliers, had poisoned half of her own family so as to receive the inheritance. Louis XIV ordered that a special court of enquiry be set up (known as *La Chambre ardente*) to look into this affair and try the people involved. In 1677, the enquiry revealed that a certain Marie Bosse had been supplying poison to the wives of members of the *Parlement* whom they wanted to get rid of. On arrest, she denounced a woman known as 'La Voisine'. Various people were arrested, and tortured. Out of these forced confessions came the names of the king's concubine, Madame de Montespan, the countess of Soissons and the countess of Polignac, among others. Thirty-six people were ultimately sentenced to death. Those people who had accused Madame de Montespan were imprisoned. 'La Voisine' was burned alive at the place du Grève in 1680. *La Chambre ardente* was dissolved in 1682. Madame de Montespan continued to frequent the king as before and there is no proof that she was ever involved in black mass ceremonies herself.

## Rainbow Warrior     [ ** ]

This was the name of the Greenpeace ship that intended to sail to the atoll of Murora to protest against nuclear testing by the French government in July 1985. To avoid such a scenario, François Mitterrand asked the DGSE to intervene. In spite of the protests of certain officers of the secret service who were aware of the dangers of precipitous action, the operation went ahead. Two explosive charges were placed on the hull of the ship by members of the French secret service. The attack took place on 16 August. The first explosion was intended to make the passengers leave the ship, the second was intended to sink it. Unfortunately, a Dutch photographer of Portuguese origin went back on board to retrieve some equipment after the first explosion, and died in the second. The members of the French secret service were arrested after having left a trail of clues behind them. Their amateurism was as much of a scandal as the intervention of the French secret service in New Zealand sovereign territory. The socialist minister of defence, Charles Hernu, resigned. Ségolène Royal's brother was part of the commando unit.

## SAC                                                                         **\*\*\***

The Service d'Action Civique was the association set up to promote the ideas of General de Gaulle and succeeding Gaullists. Between 1960 and 1981 it was an association under the law of 1901. It was in fact a parallel political police force set up to combat the OAS and to prevent a Bolshevik *coup d'état* in France. Its recruits came from the regular police force and the general riff-raff of the underworld. It was responsible for keeping order at political meetings or breaking up meetings of communist sympathizers. Its founding members were Charles Pasqua, Etienne Léandri, and Jacques Foccart. It was also responsible for finding financial resources for the Gaullist party. After the assassination of the family of the local SAC representative of the Marseilles region, Jacques Massié in 1981, the SAC was officially disbanded. See above 'Auriol'. See Chapter 9 'Pasqua'.

### sang contaminé nm.                                                          **\*\***

The National Blood Transfusion Centre (*Centre national de transfusion sanguine* – CNTS), issued blood products between 1985 and 1986 knowing full well that the products were contaminated with the AIDS virus. Most of the 5,000 people infected were haemophiliacs. Most have since died. Since 1985, the sales of AIDS screening tests developed by the American laboratory Abbot had been blocked by the French authorities to give time to the Institut Pasteur to put the finishing touches to its own test. The prime minister at the time of the scandal, Laurent Fabius and two ministers, Georgina Dufoix (social affairs) and Edmond Hervé (health) were tried by the Cour de la République for manslaughter. Fabius and Dufoix were acquitted, Hervé, although found guilty of manslaughter, was not obliged to serve his sentence. The words of Georgina Dufoix remain 'Je suis responsable mais pas coupable'. The French reader is invited to take note of three possible English translations of the single French word 'responsable': 'responsible', 'accountable' and 'answerable'.

### Sétif, le massacre de

While Europe was celebrating the capitulation of Nazi Germany on 8 May 1945, a massacre took place in Algeria that escaped public attention. A demonstration was organized to demand independence and the release of Messali Hadj, head of the Algerian popular party. The demonstration was put down with extreme violence. No reliable statistics are available but several thousand people are thought to have perished.

## Stavisky

[ * ]

The Stavisky affair blew up on Christmas Eve 1933, with the arrest of the director of Le Crédit Municipal bank of Bayonne. He had put bonds into circulation to the value of 235 million francs that were backed by less than 20 million francs, in order to float a loan. It was soon discovered that the director of the bank was merely an accomplice and that the real brains behind the swindle was a financier called Alexandre Stavisky (1886–1934). It came to light that Alexandre Stavisky had already been taken to court for similar offences but his murky past had been hushed up by ministers and other corrupt politicians. The police began looking for him but he fled. He had had close relations with many politicians, members of the press and of the justice department. The police official in charge of investigations concerning Stavisky was found dead on a railway line, tied up and poisoned. Many politicians were afraid that during his trial Stavisky would speak. He was found dead in a chalet in Chamonix on 7 January 1934 having committed suicide. He had shot himself at a distance of three metres. This led to a wave of anti-parliamentary feeling and riots took place during which over two dozen people were killed. The affair also saw a resurgence of anti-Semitism and xenophobia (Stavisky was of Russian origin and a Jew) and demonstrations by Action Française. The scandal brought down the government of Chautemps and then that of Edouard Deladier.

## Transnonain, le massacre de la rue

[ * ]

On 13 April 1834, while the canuts were rioting in Lyons, barricades were being set up in Paris and several other French towns. A squad of soldiers marching in the rue Transnonain in Paris were fired upon and an officer was killed. The shot came from house no. 12. The soldiers entered the building and indiscriminately killed everyone they could find, women and children included. This massacre was immortalized in the lithograph by Honoré Daumier (1808–79).

## Urba

[ ** ]

This was the name of a pseudo consultancy firm set up by the PS in 1971. Its object was to centralize the collection of money received at the moment of the awarding of public tenders to construction companies. Companies wishing to take part in a public tender had to pay from 2–4 per cent of the value of the contract to Urba. A system of false invoices was set up. The money thus collected was transferred to the socialist party to fund the upcoming election of 1974. A judicial inquiry was opened for extortion, corruption and the drawing up and use of false documents. Political interference slowed down the inquiry. The stubborn police inspector in charge of the investigation was 'transferred', then 'taken off the case', and finally 'dismissed' from the police force in 1991. Nevertheless, the inquiry proceded. Henri

Emmanuelli, the treasurer of the PS, was charged with influence peddling and complicity and was given an 18-month suspended prison sentence and two years' civic ineligibility.

**vrai-faux passeport. Le**
See above 'Carrefour du Développement'.

# Chapter 12

# Metonymy

Although this chapter has the umbrella title 'Metonymy' the contents go far beyond the strict meaning of the term. Apart from metonymy proper, this chapter includes a host of rather enigmatic names, expression, euphemisms, nicknames and periphrases as well as many geographical references that are of great significance to the French. The terms are very well known even to the man in the street but many of them are far from being obvious to the non-native reader. These terms are so well known that their meaning is never developed.

### actions de maintien de l'ordre. Les nfpl. ***
The Algerian war of independence (1954–62) was never referred to as such by the French government. It was referred to as 'actions de maintien de l'ordre' or 'les événements'. See below 'événements'.

### Banque verte. La **
This is the nickname of the bank Le Crédit Agricole, so called because this bank, particularly present in the rural parts of France, has traditionally been the bank of the farmers and of the agricultural community.

### Beauvau. place ***
The metonymical name of the ministry of the interior. It is located in the eighth *arrondissement* of Paris.

### Bercy ***
The metonymical name of the ministry of finance. It is located in Bercy, in the twelfth *arrondissement* of Paris on the banks of the Seine. This is not to be confused with the abbreviated name of the stadium of the same name that is often used for sports events, mass meetings and rock concerts, i.e. le Palais Omnisports de Bercy. NB: rue de Rivoli was the previous name used to refer to the French ministry of finance before it moved to Bercy in 1989. This is useful to know for dating certain texts.

### blouses blanches. Les nfpl.

`**`

The white-uniformed members of the medical profession, i.e. doctors and nurses.

### Bonne Mère. La

`**`

This is the familiar and affectionate name given to Notre Dame de la Garde, the basilica overlooking Marseilles.

### Cambon. rue nf.

`***`

This is the metonymical name of *La Cour des Comptes*. See Chapter 10.

### Chancellerie. La

`**`

Another name for the French ministry of justice. Something of a false friend in that it has nothing to do with embassies or consulates.

### Château. Le

`***`

The Élysée or the president and his staff.

### château la pompe nm.

`*`

Water.

### chevrons. La marque aux

`*`

Citroën, the car manufacturer. Its logo is a double chevron.

### cité mariale. La

`**`

Lourdes, the city of Marie.

### cité phocéenne. La

`**`

Marseilles, known as the 'Phocaean' city, was founded in 600 BC by sailors who had originally come from Phocaea, an ancient Ionian village in western Asia Minor, on the Aegian Sea. The original name of Marseilles was Massilia. It is to be noted that Marseilles in French does not take a terminal 's'.

### Coupole. La (académie)

`*`

*L'Institut de France.* See Chapter 10 'La Coupole'.

### der des der. La (la dernière des dernières)

`**`

This is a reference to the First World War that was supposed to be the war to end all wars. Today, the expression refers to the ultimate, to the last of the last, sometimes to a final deciding game.

### deuxième personnage de l'État. Le

`**`

The president of the French Senate.

**Écureuil. L'**                                    `*`
The National Savings Bank, La Caisse d'Épargne, whose logo is a stylized squirrel.

**éléphants. Les**                                  `***`
The members of the socialist party old guard, i.e. Laurent Fabius, Domini-que Strauss-Kahn, Pierre Moscovici, Jacques Lang, Pierre Mauroy, etc.

**Élysée. L'**                                      `***`
The French president and/or his staff.

**Empire du Milieu. L'**                            `***`
China.

**énarques de la rue Cambon. Les**                 `***`
Members of *La Cour des Comptes*. See Chapter 10 'Cour des Comptes'.

**État hébreu. L'**                                 `***`
Israel.

**étrange lucarne. L'**                             `*`
A television set.

**événements. Les**                                 `***`
This is a euphemism for the war of Algerian independence. NB: the word *événement* may take a grave accent or an acute accent on the second 'e'. See above 'actions de maintien de l'ordre'.

**fille aînée de l'église catholique. La**         `**`
France. See Chapter 6 'Fille aînée de l'église'.

**grand argentier. Le**                             `**`
The minister of finance.

**Grande Boucle. La**                               `**`
Le Tour de France cycle race.

**Grande Muette. La**                               `**`
The French army and the ministry of defence. This is generally supposed to refer to the fact that until 1945 soldiers had no electoral rights. Furthermore, they were not allowed to join a trades union or belong to a political party.

**Grandes Oreilles. Les**                           `***`
This refers to the 'renseignements généraux' (the political police). This has now been merged with the Direction de la Surveillance du Territoire to form the new entity DCRI. See Chapter 14 'DCRI'.

### habit vert. L' nm.      **

The uniform of the members of the Académie Française.

### Hebdomadaire de l'actualité heureuse. L' nm.      *

The magazine *Jours de France*, founded by Marcel Dassault (1892–1996), in publication until 1989.

### Hémicycle. L'      ***

The National Assembly. It refers to the semi-circular construction of the *salle de séances* of the Palais Bourbon. This configuration contrasts singularly with the Westminster system where the parties are physically in a position of confrontation.

### herbe à nicot. L' nm.      *

Tobacco. Jean Nicot (1530–1600) introduced tobacco to the court of Catherine de Médici.

### Hexagone. L'      ***

France. A regular, six-sided geometrical figure into which the shape of France can be fitted. 'Hexagonal' is the corresponding adjective. See below 'outre-Quiévrain'.

### hirondelles nfpl.      ***

Ornithologically speaking, 'une hirondelle' is a 'swallow'. It can also be any form of police bugging, hidden microphones, telephone tapping, etc.

### homme le plus puissant de France. L'      ***

The opinion of Honoré de Balzac concerning the 'juge d'instruction'. See Chapter 10 'juge'. NB: *instruire* in this context means to conduct an investigation.

### hôte actuel. L' nm. (de Matignon ou de l'Élysée)      ***

The current prime minister or president.

### Hôtel de Lassay. L' nm.      ***

It is an eighteenth-century house, located in the seventh *arrondissement* of Paris and is the official residence of the president (Speaker) of the National Assembly.

### Hôtel Matigon. L' nm.      ***

The prime minister and/or his staff.

### Île de beauté. L' nf.      *

Corsica.

**Immortels. Les**     ✱✱

Members of the Académie Française.

**locataire de Matignon ou de l'Élysée. Le**     ✱

The prime minister or president.

**Lumières. Le pays des**     ✱

France. This is a reference to the period of Enlightenment in eighteenth-century France characterized by reason, tolerance, desacralization of the monarchy, the notion of a social contract and the primacy of intellectual enlightenment over divine illumination.

**Luxembourg. Le Palais du**     ✱✱✱

The French Senate. See Chapter 10.

**magistrats de la rue Cambon. Les nmpl**     ✱✱

Members of the Cour des Comptes. See Chapter 10 'Cour des Comptes'.

**magistrature suprême. La**     ✱✱✱

The presidency of the French Republic.

**maison rose. La**     ✱

The French socialist party.

**maréchaussée. La**     ✱

The police, especially when referring to the *gendarmerie*.

**Mère des guerres. La**     ✱

The First World War.

**métal jaune. Le**     ✱✱✱

Gold.

**nation arc-en-ciel. La**     ✱

South Africa.

**neuf-trois. Le**     ✱

The socially deprived *département* of Seine-Saint-Denis, the administrative number and postcode of which is 93.

**or noir. L'**     ✱✱

Crude oil.

## outre-Manche
\*\*

Another way of saying 'in England'. See below 'Perfide Albion'. The English are often referred to by the French as 'nos amis d'outre-Manche'. The 'amis' is sometimes used ironically.

## outre-Quiévrain
\*

Belgium or France. From the French standpoint, it refers to Belgium, but from the Belgian standpoint, it refers to France. Quiévrain is a commune in Belgium.

## outre-Rhin
\*

Germany.

## Palais Bourbon. Le

The lower house of the French Parliament, i.e. the National Assembly. See Chapter 10 'Palais Bourbon'.

## Palais Brongniart. Le
\*

The former Paris stock exchange La Bourse.

## Palais Royal. Le
\*\*\*

This can refer either to the Conseil d'État or to the Conseil Constitutionnel. See Chapter 10.

## Palais du Luxembourg. Le
\*\*\*

The French Senate. See Chapter 10.

## parti du poing et de la rose. Le
\*

The French socialist party.

## passé qui ne passe pas. Ce
\*\*\*

The collaborationist past of France symbolized by Vichy, from the title of a book by Eric Conan and Henry Rousso published in 1994.

## pays de Cyrano. Le
\*

France.

## pays de Rabelais. Le
\*

France.

## pays de Voltaire et des Lumières. Le
\*\*

France.

## pays des droits de l'homme. Le
\*\*

France.

**pays du jasmin. Le**                                  ( * )
Tunisia.

**Perfide Albion**                                      ( ** )
See Chapter 1 'Perfide Albion'.

**Petit Luxembourg. Le**                                ( * )
The official home of the president of the Senate since 1825. The building is
contiguous with the Palais du Luxembourg.

**Perchoir. Le**                                        ( *** )
The seat of the president of the National Assembly, i.e. the Speaker.

**petite reine. La**                                    ( ** )
The bicycle.

**Piscine. La**                                         ( ** )
The DGSE. See Chapter 14

**Plateau. Le**                                         ( *** )
The presidency of the French Senate.

**plus simple appareil. Dans le (en tenue d'Eve)**      ( * )
Naked.

**premier flic de France. Le**                          ( *** )
The minister of the interior.

**premier magistrat de France. Le**                     ( *** )
The president of the Republic.

**Quai Conti. Le**                                      ( * )
*L'Académie Française.*

**Quai des Orfèvres. Le**                               ( *** )
The regional headquarters of the 'police judiciaire de la Préfecture de Police de
Paris', located at no. 36, equivalent to the CID in England or the FBI in the USA.

**Quai d'Orsay. Le**                                    ( *** )
The French ministry of foreign affairs located in the seventh *arrondissement*
on the left bank in Paris. Frequently referred to simply as 'le Quai'.

**robes noires. Les**                                   ( * )
Lawyers.

**Rocher. Le**
The Rock, otherwise known as the Principality of Monaco.

**ruban rouge. Le**
The ribbon of the *Légion d'Honneur.*

**Sages de la rue Montpensier. Les**
Members of the Conseil Constitutionnel.

**Sainte Anne (l'hôpital de)**
A mad house, the 'loony bin', etc. The hospital of Saint Anne, in the four-teenth *arrondissement* of Paris, is particularly well known for treating patients with psychiatric problems.

**Saint-Guillaume. L'école de la rue**
Sciences Po, i.e. l'École des Sciences Politiques de Paris that is located at 27 rue Saint-Guillaume in the seventh *arrondissement* of Paris. See Chapter 10 'Sciences Po'.

**sale guerre. La**
The Algerian war of independence.

**salles obscures. Les**
Cinemas.

**Ségur, avenue de**
Ministry of health. An avenue in the seventh *arrondissement* of Paris. Today, it is the home of the ministry of health but for many years it was synon-ymous with the *Ministère des postes, télégraphes et télécommunications* (PTT). When the Direction Générale des Télécommunications became a commercial company, i.e. France Télécom in 1988, the telecom operator moved to 6, place d'Alleray in the fifteenth *arrondissement* of Paris. This fact can be important for dating certain texts.

**septième art. Le**
The cinema.

**Solférino**
The socialist party. Located in the seventh *arrondissement* of Paris, this is the headquarters of the PS.

**Sous ministre des cocotiers. Le**
The junior minister in charge of the overseas territories.

**télé de maçon. La**                    ⬭ * ⬭

TF1. France's most popular television channel. The owner of TF1, Bouygues, is also a giant construction group. A pejorative expression.

**têtes blondes. Nos chères nfpl.**                    ⬭ ** ⬭

Our children.

**Transalpin(e)**                    ⬭ *** ⬭

Italian.

**tricolore adj**                    ⬭ *** ⬭

French, after the French flag of three colours, red, white and blue, which in French is *bleu, blanc, rouge*.

**Ulm**                    ⬭ *** ⬭

The metonymical name for the École Normale Supérieure. See Chapter 10.

**Valois. rue de**                    ⬭ *** ⬭

The ministry of culture.

**Varennes. rue de**                    ⬭ *** ⬭

The French prime minister and/or his office and staff. They occupy no. 57.

**Veuve nf.**                    ⬭ * ⬭

The nickname of the guillotine.

**Vendôme. La place**                    ⬭ *** ⬭

The ministry of justice. Situated in the first *arrondissement* of Paris, it is the square where most of the prestigious jewellers' shops can be found. The ministry of justice is located here but 'Vendôme' is rarely used metonymically to refer to this ministry.

**ventre de Paris. Le**                    ⬭ * ⬭

Les Halles, the former wholesale market of Paris, now located in Rungis which inspired the title of a Zola novel, *Le Ventre de Paris* (1873).

**Vieille maison de la rue de Lille. La**                    ⬭ * ⬭

La Caisse des dépôts et consignations which is located at 56, rue de Lille in the seventh *arrondissement* in Paris. See Chapter 10.

**Vieux Continent. Le**

Europe.

**vieux métier du monde. Le plus**                    ⬭ *** ⬭

Prostitution.

**Vieux Port. Le**           \*\*\*
Marseilles.

**ville de Bernadette Soubirous. La**    \*\*
Lourdes.

**ville Lumière. La**           \*\*\*
Paris.

**ville phocéenne. La**          \*\*\*
Marseilles.

**ville rose. La**            \*
Toulouse.

**ville Sainte. La**           \*\*
Jerusalem.

## Geographical names of particular significance

### Albion. Le plateau d'         \*

The plateau saddles two *départements*, the Vaucluse (84) and the Drôme (26). It is the former launch site of ground-to-ground, nuclear, ballistic missiles of the French nuclear deterrent force. In 1996, President Chirac announced its closure and dismantling.

### Argenteuil. La dalle d'        \*\*

The Dalle d'Argenteuil is in the heart of the Val d'Argent quarter of Argenteuil located in the *département* of the Val d'Oise (95). It is a quarter with a high concentration of council flats. It was here that Nicolas Sarkozy, on 26 October 2005 (he was then minister of the interior), spoke about the local 'racaille' (rabble) that he was going to get rid of. His words contributed to a heightening of racial tension in the suburbs. When two youngsters died in Clichy-sous-Bois (in the *département* of Seine-Saint-Denis, (93)) seeking refuge in an EDF transformer while being chased by the police, there was an explosion of violence in the suburbs.

### Assas. rue d' nf.          \*

The rue d'Assas takes its name from the heroic French officer who died at the battle of Kloster-Kampen in Westphalia in 1760 while serving under Louis XV. Today, its name is synonymous with the faculty of law, the University of Paris II Panthéon Assas, located in the sixth *arrondissement*. Its name is closely associated with right-wing politics and

the street violence of 1968, opposing the right-wing students of the fac'
and those of the communist party. Three former students, Gérard Longuet,
Patrick Devedjian and Alain Madelin were members of the extreme
right-wing movement Occident of which Alain Madelin was a founding
member; they all spent some time in police custody after they had attacked
the Vietnam Committees on the campus of the University of Rouen in
1967. They are all lawyers and have all exercised ministerial responsibility
in right-wing governments of the fifth Republic. See Chapter 9 and Chapter 11.

## Baden-Baden                                                      ( * )
Amid the unrest of 1968, on 29 May, General de Gaulle disappeared; not
even the prime minister knew of his whereabouts. It transpired that he had
flown by helicopter to Baden-Baden in West Germany. He apparently went
there to visit General Massu, Commander-in-Chief of the French forces in
Germany, with a view to making sure that the army would remain faithful to
the Republic. This is the official version of the facts.

## Barbès                                                           ( * )
A poor quarter in the eighteenth *arrondissement* of northern Paris with a
high immigrant population, mainly from the Maghreb.

## Bièvre. rue de                                                   ( ** )
22, rue de Bièvre, situated in the fifth *arrondissement,* in the heart of the
Paris Latin Quarter, is the former private residence of the late President
François Mitterrand.

## Billancourt                                                      ( ** )
Boulogne-Billancourt is the home of the former Renault car plant created on
the Île de Seguin, in the *département* of the Hauts-de-Seine (92), in 1898 by
Louis Renault.

## Boétie. rue de la                                                ( ** )
The UMP, the right-wing political party, has its headquarters at 55, rue de la
Boétie in the eighth *arrondissement* of Paris. It is currently looking for new
premises.

## Bois de Boulogne nm.                                             ( * )
The name of a very big park in the west of Paris in the very chic sixteenth
*arrondissement* which is said to be the 'lung of Paris'. It is three times bigger
than London's Hyde Park. It is the notorious place where prostitutes and
transsexuals congregate at nightfall and is sometimes referred to as 'the
capital of Brazil', given the number of Brazilian transsexuals plying their
trade there.

## Boisserie. La ┌─*─┐

See below 'Colombey-les-Deux-Eglises'.

## Bormes-les-Mimosas ┌─**─┐

This is the name of a commune in the *département* of the Var (83), in the south of France, in which the Fort de Brégançon is situated. Since 1966, it has been the official holiday residence of the president of the French Republic.

## Brégançon. Fort de nm. ┌─**─┐

See above 'Bormes-les-Mimosas'.

## Caluire ┌─*─┐

*Préfet* and General de Gaulle's resistance coordinator of the Conseil National de Résistance in France, Jean Moulin (1899–1943) was arrested by the Gestapo on 21 June 1943 in Caluire in the suburbs of Lyons which is in the *département* of the Rhône (69). It is widely accepted that he had been betrayed and that the meeting in Caluire was in fact a trap. It has never been very clear who betrayed him. He was tortured in Paris and later died near Metz, on the train during his transfer to Berlin for further interrogation. Initially buried in the cemetery of Père-Lachaise, his presumed ashes were transferred to the Panthéon in 1964. See Chapter 2 'Entre ici, Jean Moulin'.

## Canebière. La ┌─**─┐

La Canebière is the name of a long street (and quarter) in the heart of Marseilles which goes from the Reformed Church and leads directly to the port of Marseilles, *le Vieux Port*. The name is said to derive from an Occitan word meaning 'hemp plantation'.

## Cap Nègre. Le ┌─***─┐

Carla Bruni-Sarkozy's vacation home on the Mediterranean coast, situated in the *commune* of Lavandou in the *département* of the Var (83).

## Chamalières ┌─*─┐

The name of a *commune* in the *département* of the Puy-de-Dôme (63) in the region of the Auvergne. The former mayor of Chamalières was Valéry Giscard d'Estaing, former president of the Republic. The current mayor of Chamalières is his son, Louis.

## Charleville-Mézières ┌─*─┐

Famous for being the birthplace of the poet Arthur Rimbaud (1854–91) in the *département* of the Ardennes (08).

## Clairefontaine

This is a small town situated 50 km south-west of Paris in the *département* of the Yvelines (78) and is the home of the Institut National de Football, a football training centre opened in 1988 and administered by the French Football Association.

## Clamart

See below 'Petit Clamart' and Chapter 2 'Je vous ai compris'.

## Colombey-les-Deux-Eglises

This is the name of a French *commune* located in the *département* of the Haute-Marne (52) in the region of Champagne-Ardennes. In 1934, General de Gaulle bought a property there called La Brasserie (the brewery) which he rapidly re-named La Boisserie. He chose this *commune* because it was equidistant from Paris and the north-eastern garrisons. He died there on 9 November 1970.

## Croisette. La

This famous promenade takes its name from the boulevard running along the sea front in Cannes in the *département* of the Alpes-Maritimes (06). It is synonymous with the Cannes film festival that traditionally takes place there in May.

## Drancy

See Chapter 6 'Vél' d'Hiv'.

## Épinay

The Congress of Épinay is the name given to the congress aimed at achieving socialist unification that was held between 11 and 13 June 1971 in the small town of Épinay-sur-Seine situated in the *département* of Seine-Saint-Denis (93). It was during this congress that a totally new member of the movement manoeuvred his way into the position of first secretary. His name was François Mitterrand. The new symbol of the socialist party, the fist and the rose, dates from this period.

## Faubourg Saint Honoré. 55, rue du

The address of the official residence of the president of the Republic, located in the eighth *arrondissement* of Paris. It is the official address of *Le Palais de l'Élysée*.

## Flamanville

One of the nuclear power stations in the French nuclear network, 25 km west of Cherbourg in the *département* of La Manche (50) in Normandy.

**Fleury-Mérogis**                                           ( * )

Fleury-Mérogis is the name of a famous prison in the *département* of the Essonne (91) some 35 km south of Paris.

**Fresnes**                                                   ( * )

A commune in the *département* of the Val-de-Marne (94) in the south suburbs of Paris which is famous for its prison. It is one of the three large prisons of the Paris region, the other two being 'La Santé' in Paris, and 'Fleury-Mérogis'. See above 'Fleury'.

**Foch. 84 avenue**                                          ( * )

Located on a beautiful residential avenue in the chic sixteenth *arrondissement* of Paris, this address was the headquarters of the Gestapo during the occupation of France in the Second World War. It was here that Pierre Brossolette, resistant and hero, was tortured and where he took his own life to avoid giving away any information.

**Forum des Halles. Le**                                     ( * )

Situated in the first *arrondissement* of Paris, this is the name of the underground leisure and shopping centre opened in 1979 on the site of the former wholesale market. The Pompidou Centre is part of this development. Several suburban railway lines and underground railway lines converge on this point with the accompanying 'importation' of suburban vandalism and violence.

**François I<sup>er</sup>. rue**                             ( * )

This street is located in the eighth *arrondissement* of Paris and is where Europe 1 is headquartered. Europe 1 is a private, French, general interest radio station, part of the Lagardère group.

**Gay-Lussac**                                               ( * )

This is the name of a street near the Sorbonne, in the Paris Latin quarter that was the scene of some of the most violent clashes between students and police in the riots of 1968. See 'St Michel' and 'Odéon'. Louis-Joseph Gay-Lussac was a French physicist (1778–1850).

**Glières. Plateau des nm.**                                 ( *** )

A mountainous area in the *massif des Bornes* in the *département* of the Haute Savoie (74). This plateau was chosen by the British Special Operations Executive as a parachuting zone for weapons and was the scene of a heroic stand by the *maquisard* against the Wehrmacht in March 1944. Two thirds of the *maquisards* defending the plateau were later captured after denunciation by local collaborators and died either under torture or during deportation.

### Goutte d'Or nf.

*

A poor quarter in the north-east of Paris in the eighteenth *arrondissement* with a high North African immigrant population. It is notorious for its drug trafficking and prostitution. See Chapter 2 'odeur'.

### Grenelle. rue de nf.

***

Astride the sixth and seventh *arrondissements* in Paris, 127, rue de Grenelle is remembered for having been the place where the industrial relations agreement ('les accords de Grenelle') was signed at the ministry of labour in May 1968. The agreement was reached in the wake of riots and unrest. The negotiations took place between the unions and the government representatives and the French employers' confederation then known as the CNPF. The name is now used as a generic term to describe any broad-scale discusssion among the *forces vives* of the nation. It can now be used with an indefinite article. 'Un Grenelle' designates a multipartite debate involving the government, associations and/or NGOs aimed at producing ideas for legislation. Note that 110, rue de Grenelle is the home of the ministry of education, and that the former ministry of immigration and national identity was also located in this street.

### Hauts-de-Seine

***

The *département* of the Hauts-de-Seine (92) is located to the west of Paris. Crescent in shape, it borders the western side of Paris. The GDP there is three times the national average. It is part of the Île de France (which may be equated with Greater London in terms of geographical extent). Given the political scandals associated with this *département* it has been called 'the Augean stables' by a right-wing politician. See Chapter 7 'Augias'.

### Invalides. Les

**

*L'Hôtel national des Invalides* was built on the initiative of Louis XIV in 1670 to house the war wounded of his armies. It still serves that purpose but is also a military museum and a military necropolis. It is the final resting place of Napoleon Bonaparte and some of France's most illustrious war leaders including Foch, Lyautey, Hautecloque (better known as Leclerc), Juin and Nivell. This edifice was to inspire Charles II of England to build the Chelsea pensioner's hospital in 1682.

### Jarnac (un coup de)

***

See Chapter 6 'Jarnac'.

### Latche

The private holiday home of François Mitterrand, located in the *département* of the Landes (40) in the region of Aquitaine in the south-west of France.

## Lauriston. rue nf.    `*`

The gang known as the Carlingue operated at this address. 93, rue Lauriston, was, in fact, the Parisian headquarters of the French Gestapo during
the Second World War. It was staffed by the dregs of the French underworld
aided and abetted by the collaborationist police. Other equally sinister streets
associated with police torture during the Second World War are rue des
Saussaies, rue de la Pompe, rue le Sueur and avenue Foch.

## Lourdes    `*`

This is a small *commune* located in the *département* of the Hautes-Pyrénées
(65) in the south-west of France. It was here, in 1858, that the Virgin Mary is
said to have appeared to Bernadette Soubirous. It is a place of Catholic pilgrimage, drawing 5 million visitors per year.

## Maisons-Alfort    `*`

Famous for being the home of the national veterinary school located in the
*département* of the Val-de-Marne (94).

## Marais. Le    `*`

A quarter that straddles the third and fourth *arrondissements* of Paris, on the
right bank. It is one of the oldest quarters in Paris and has become, over the
years, the *arrondissement* of the gay community in Paris.

## Montaigne. avenue nf.    `**`

An avenue situated in the chic eighth *arrondissement* of Paris famous for its
shops selling luxury goods. Many of the major brand names have shops on
this avenue, e.g. Dior, Chanel, Vuitton, Gucci, Prada, etc.

## Montparnasse    `***`

The home of the Muses in Greek mythology. The quarter of Montparnasse
is situated essentially in the fourteenth *arrondissement* in the south of Paris.
It has always been related to the artistic and intellectual community. Famous
names associated with Montparnasse early in the century include Modigliani,
Picasso, Soutine, Foujita, Matisse and Leger. In the 1950s and 1960s it was
frequented by Sartre and de Beauvoir at their famous haunts *Le Dôme, Les
Deux Magots*, and *Le Café de Flore*.

## Montpensier. 2 rue (au Palais Royal)    `**`

*Le Conseil Constitutionnel*. See Chapter 10.

## Mureaux. Les    `*`

Situated 40 km to the west of Paris in the *département* of the Yvelines (78) it is
the town in which the huge metallic structures of the Ariane rocket are assem-
bled. Over the recent past it has become a name that evokes urban violence.

## Muroroa

The name of the atoll in French Polynesia, located in the south Pacific, used as an underground nuclear testing site by the French government. The last test took place in 1995.

## Neuilly Auteuil Passy

Auteuil and Passy are very rich quarters which together constitute the very chic sixteenth *arrondissement*. Neuilly is an extremely affluent town in the *département* of the Haut-de-Seine (92). The former mayor of Neuilly was Nicolas Sarkozy. As an adjective, NAP could be translated into English by 'Sloaney'. The term connotes affluence and snobbery. See Chapter 14 'BCBG'.

## Odéon/Panthéon

In the Latin Quarter of Paris, the Odéon (sixth *arrondissement*) and the Panthéon (fifth *arrondissement*) were the scenes of some of the most violent clashes between students and the CRS in the student riots of 1968. (See 'Gay-Lussac' and 'St Michel'.) The Odéon is the name of the theatre located near the Luxembourg Gardens. See Chapter 14 'CRS'.

## Orléans

In 1429, against all expectations, Jeanne d'Arc succeeded in forcing the English to abandon their siege of Orleans. Since then, the name of Orleans, has been intimately associated with her. Her nickname is *La Pucelle d'Orléans*, i.e. the Maid of Orleans.

## Palais du Pharo. Le

The Pharo Palace in Marseilles was built on the initiative of Napoleon III. He wanted a residence similar to his residence in Biarritz for the empress Eugénie. Construction began in 1858 but the palace was never occupied. In 1870 the property of Napoleon III was confiscated but Eugénie retained the palace which she gave back to the town of Marseilles in 1884. It overlooks the port of Marseilles and today is used as a conference centre. The *Communauté Urbaine de Marseille Provence Métropole* is headquartered there.

## Petit Clamart

On 22 August 1962, under the code name Charlotte Corday, the OAS, led by Lieutenant Colonel Bastien Thiry (polytechnician), machine-gunned the car taking General de Gaulle and his wife to the military airfield of Villacoublay, his final destination being Colombey-les-Deux-Églises. As the car drove through Petit Clamart in the *département* of the Hauts-de-Seine (92) de Gaulle's car came under fire from the gunmen waiting in ambush. De Gaulle and his wife were unscathed in the attack; de Gaulle saying contemptuously 'ils tirent comme des cochons'. Bastien Thiry was found guilty of making an attempt on the life of the head of state and shot by firing squad on 11 March at the Fort d'Ivry in the *département* of the Val-de-Marne (94). See Chapter 2 'Je vous ai compris'. And Chapter 14 'OAS'.

### Pigalle     [ * ]
This quarter straddles the ninth and eighteenth *arrondissements* in Paris, and is famous for its striptease establishments, sex shops and clip joints. This red-light district takes its name from the architect Jean-Baptiste Pigalle (1714–85).

### Place de la Concorde nf.     [ * ]
Situated at the eastern end of the Champs Élysées in the eighth *arrondissement* in Paris, it was built in 1776 and originally called Place Louis XV. During the Revolution of 1789, it was the square at which the guillotine was erected. After the Revolution it was renamed Place Louis XVI (in 1826), but renamed Place de la Concorde after the Revolution of 1830. It is often used as a venue for political demonstrations.

### Plateau du Vercors nm.     [ * ]
A symbolic site in the Rhône-Alpes region that straddles the *départements* of the Isère (38) and the Drôme (26). It was the scene of the heroic resistance by the Free French forces who fought a losing battle against the German troops in June 1944. Vercors was also the pseudonym of the resistant Jean Bruller (1902–92).

### Plateau des Glières nm.     [ *** ]
See above 'Glières'.

### Pompe. rue de la     [ * ]
Another notorious address in the sixteenth *arrondissement* of Paris, associated with Gestapo torture during the German occupation of France during the Second World War.

### Porte de Versailles nf.    
In former times, access to Paris was possible only via one of the many gates surrounding the city. Each gate was in fact a customs post and it was here that the tax known as the 'octroi' was levied on certain goods entering the city. Many of the Paris métro termini are 'gates', e.g. *Porte d'Orléans, Porte des Lilas, Porte de Clignancourt*, etc. The name of the *Porte de Versailles* is synonymous with one of the biggest of the seven exhibition centres in Paris. *La Foire de Paris* (somewhat like an Ideal Home Exhibition) is held here every year in May. It is also used for political conventions.

## Quartier Latin nm.     ***

The Latin Quarter straddles the fifth and sixth *arrondissements* of Paris and is situated on the left bank of the Seine. It was here that Robert de Sorbon (1201–74) founded a school for the poor in 1257. Latin, in the Middle Ages, was both a lingua franca and the language of learning, which gave its name to the district. Apart from the Sorbonne, the Latin Quarter is home to many of the most prestigious grammar schools and institutes of higher education. The Latin Quarter, being the student quarter, was the scene of much violence during the unrest of 1968 with frequent clashes between students and the anti-riot police, the CRS. The names of St Michel, Panthéon, Odéon, Gay-Lussac all come to mind in this respect. See Chapter 14 'CRS'.

## Reims     *

Reims is a town situated in the *département* of the Marne (51) in the region of Champagne-Ardennes, some 129 km to the north east of Paris. This name is inevitably associated with Jeanne d'Arc because after she forced the English to lift the siege of Orleans in 1428/9, she conducted the *dauphin* Charles VII, to be crowned in Reims cathedral in 1429. NB: the former English (and the ancient French) spelling of Reims 'Rheims' is still current in the Champagne region.

## Saints-Pères. rue des nf.     **

Part of the premises of Sciences Po are located here.

## Saussaies. rue des nf.     *

One of the notorious addresses at which the Gestapo tortured French resistants. It is located in the eighth *arrondissement* of Paris.

## Seine-Saint-Denis     ***

The *département* of Seine-Saint-Denis (93) is situated to the north east of Paris and is part of the region known as Île-de-France. It has a high rate of unemployment and a high immigrant population. Its name is associated with chronic urban violence and social discrimination. See above 'neuf-trois'.

## Septimanie nf.     *

This is a fifth-century term for the region, in the south of France that roughly corresponds to the current region known as Languedoc-Roussillon. The president of this region was Georges Frêche who used to be known as the 'Néron de la Septimanie'. As a simplification, one may say that *Langue d'oc* refers to the Occitan language spoken in the more southern regions of France, while *Langue d'oïl* refers to the language spoken in the more northern regions of France.

## Solutré. Roche de nf.    `***`

A few kilometres west of Mâcon, this rocky escarpment, altitude 493 metres, looks over the vineyards of the mâconnais at the heart of the Pouilly-fuissé vineyards in the *département* of Saône et Loire (71) in the Burgundy region. It became famous through the annual pilgrimage made by the late President Mitterrand, accompanied by his close friends and family. The climb (one hour) used to take place on Whit Sunday, accompanied by the media.

## Souzy la Briche    `**`

This is the name of a small town in the *département* of the Essonne (91) to the south of Paris in which a private domain, reserved for the use of the president of the Republic, is located. It was here that the former President François Mitterrand used to spend his weekends in the company of his mistress and illegitimate daughter. Since taking over the Lanterne in Versailles, the president has left Souzy-la-Briche to the prime minister for his use at weekends.

## Saint-Germain-des-Près    `***`

This is the name of the affluent quarter surrounding the church of the same name in the sixth *arrondissement*. In 558, Childebert I died and was buried in the church that he had had built on the advice of Bishop Germain, who was later canonized. The inhabitants are known as 'germanopratins'. After the Second World War, the quarter became the intellectual and artistic centre of Paris, and many book publishers were located here. Philosophers, artists, musicians, writers and actors congregated in this quarter, frequenting the bars and cafés such as *Lipp, Les Deux Magots*, and *Café de Flore*. Among the famous names associated with the quarter are Jean-Paul Sartre, Simone de Beauvoir, Boris Vian and Juliette Greco.

## St Michel. bld nm.    `**`

The main street in the Latin quarter, which passes on a north-south axis in front of the Sorbonne was the scene of some of the most violent clashes between students and the police during the student riots of 1968 (see 'Assas', 'Gay-Lussac', 'Odéon/Panthéon'). It marks the boundary between the fifth and the sixth *arrondissements*.

## Tarterets. Les    `***`

The notorious name of a council estate-type quarter built in the 1960s in the town of Corbeil-Essonnes (with an 's') in the *département* (91) of the Essonne (without an 's') some 35 km south of Paris. It is known for its acute social problems, chronic unemployment, juvenile delinquency as well as urban violence.

### Varenne. 78, rue de                                    `**`
The address of the ministry of agriculture in Paris in the seventh *arrondissement*.

### Vél' d'Hiv'. Le                                    `***`
See Chapter 6 'Vél' d'Hiv'.

### Verdun                                    `**`
See Chapter 6.

### Vichy                                    `***`
A spa town in the *département* of the Allier (03), in the Auvergne, which was the seat of the French collaborationist government of Maréchal Pétain between 1940 and 1944.

### Villacoublay                                    `*`
A military aerodrome in the *département* of the Essonne (91), south-west of Paris. See above 'Petit Clamart'.

### Villa Médicis. La                                    `***`
See Chapter 10 'Villa'.

### Villers-Cotterêts, l'Ordonnance de nf.                                    `**`
See Chapter 6 'Villers'.

# Chapter 13

# Foreign words and expressions

## English

The English words and expressions listed below can be broken down into three broad categories:

(A) Words for which there is no concise translation and that are consequently never translated into French, e.g. 'boycott'.

(B) Words that are in vogue but for which there is a perfectly good translation and one that is recommended to the student for examination purposes, even though the English expression may be more usual: 'benchmarking' (*étalonnage concurrentiel*). The recommended French term is written in italics.

(C) Badly translated terms: 'happy end' being the most frequent among them and pseudo-English words such as: *un brushing, un lifting*, etc. In this case, the proper English term is given.

**baby-blues nm.**     `*`
*une dépression post-natale.*

**baby-boom nm.**     `***`
idem

**baby-boome(u)r nm.**     `***`
idem

**baby business nm.**     `**`
idem

**baby-foot nm.**     `**`
table football

**babysitter/sitting nm.**     `**`
idem

**background nm.**     **\*\***

This tends to be restricted to HR jargon meaning *parcours professionnel* or the more familiar term of *bagage.*

**back office nm.**     **\*\***

*les activités de post marché* nfpl.

**bad boy nm.**     **\*\***

*un mauvais garçon.*

**bankable adj.**     **\*\*\***

*une valeur sûre,* e.g. when speaking of a showbiz personality

**bashing nm.**     **\*\***

This term is never used in the meaning of physical violence but in the sense of severe criticism, for which the verb *taper sur* would be equivalent in meaning.

**benchmarking nm.**     **\*\***

*l'étalonnage concurrentiel* nm.

**best of nm.**     **\***

a collection of the best songs, episodes, etc.

**best-seller nm.**     **\*\*\***

*un succès en librairie.*

**beautiful people nmpl.**     **\*\***

idem

**big bang nm.**     **\*\***

idem. Not necessarily the beginning of the world but any cataclysmic event such as the financial crisis of 2008.

**big boss nm.**     **\*\*\***

*le grand patron.*

**Big Brother**     **\*\*\***

in the Orwellian meaning of *1984.*

**black (travailler au) vi.**     **\***

*travailler au noir* (to moonlight).

**blackbouler vt.**     **\***

idem (to blackball sb.).

**blacklisté adj., blacklister vt.**　　　　　　　**\*\***

blacklisted, to blacklist.

**black out nm.**　　　　　　　　　　　　　　**\*\***

*le silence radio.* Used in a context of censorship. Also used to describe a total electricity distribution failure. One word in English.

**bling-(bling) adj.**　　　　　　　　　　　**\*\*\***

*tape à l'œil.*

**blockbuster nm.**　　　　　　　　　　　**\*\*\***

*un film à grand succès.*

**blog nm.**　　　　　　　　　　　　　　**\*\*\***

idem

**blues. Les nmpl.**　　　　　　　　　　　**\*\*\***

*un coup de cafard.* Not translated in the case of music.

**boat people nmfpl.**　　　　　　　　　　**\*\***

idem. One may say *un/une boat people.*

**body building nm.**　　　　　　　　　　　**\***

*la musculation, le culturisme,* or *la gonflette* (slang).

**boom nm.**　　　　　　　　　　　　　　**\*\*\***

*une forte progression* or *un essor rapide.*

**booster vt.**　　　　　　　　　　　　　　**\*\*\***

*stimuler,* e.g. sales.

**borderline adj.**　　　　　　　　　　　　**\*\***

*limite.*

**boss nm.**　　　　　　　　　　　　　　　**\*\***

*le patron.*

**box nm.**　　　　　　　　　　　　　　　**\***

the dock in a court in which the accused person stands.

**box-office nm.**　　　　　　　　　　　**\*\*\***

frequently refers to the number of cinema-goers who have seen a given film. One could say *le nombre d'entrées.* It is not used in the meaning of the sales window at the cinema. Two words in English.

## boycott/boycottage nm., boycotter vt.    `***`

From Captain Boycott (1832–97), an estate agent working in Ireland for an absentee landlord, at the time of the Irish Land League agitation. In 1879, Boycott evicted some Irish tenants from the lord's land in response to their demand for fairer rents. He was ostracized by his neighbours and they acted collectively and refused to have anything to do with him. The term was first coined by the English newspaper *The Times* in November 1880 and entered the French language a year later.

## boy scout adj.    `***`

*naïve.*

## boys nmpl.    `***`

*acolytes.* Sometimes used in the military sense of 'our young soldiers' which might be translated by the familiar term *nos gars.*

## brain drain nm.    `*`

*la fuite des cerveaux.*

## brain trust nm.    `**`

*un groupe d'experts,* but notice that in English usage the word is 'brains' trust.

## break nm.    `*`

*une pause.* Also used in tennis score terminology without translation.

## briefer vt.    `***`

To brief.

## brunch nm.    `***`

idem

## brushing nm.    `**`

a blow-dry.

## bug nm.    `***`

*un bogue* in the IT context.

## building nm.    `**`

*un immeuble.* Often used in the meaning of a high-rise building.

## bulldozer nm.    `***`

attributed to sb. who has more force than tact. It can also be used as a verb in which case the French equivalent recommended would be *faire du forcing.* See below 'forcing'.

### bullish and bearish adj.

*un marché haussier* and *un marché baissier* in stock market jargon.

### burnout nm.

*épuisement professionnel.*

### business nm.

*affaire/s* nfpl. This term is frequently used with a negative connotation. It is often related to an activity that is illegal.

### business as usual

*nous restons ouverts pendant les travaux.* This is a reference to the Second World War and the Blitz when shopkeepers put up this sign outside of their bomb-damaged shop fronts. The English expression is never translated.

### business is business

*les affaires sont les affaires* nfpl.

### businessman nm.

*un homme d'affaires.*

### business model nm.

*un modèle d'activité/d'affaires.*

### business plan nm.

*un plan de développement.*

### buzz nm.

*le bruit médiatique.*

### bye-bye excl

*salut (au revoir).*

### call-girl nf.

idem, but not hyphenated in English usage.

### camping nm.

camp/camping site.

### cash adv.

This can either mean *en espèces* or *au comptant* or, in familiar register, to say something straight out, in a very frank manner. See Chapter 2 'cash, Monsieur le Président'.

### cashflow nm.

*la marge brute d'autofinancement.*

### casting nm.

In the theatrical sense, the translation of 'the cast' is *la distribution*. In French, 'casting' is often used with an indefinite article and has the meaning of 'an audition'. Frequently used in the figurative sense, e.g. *une erreur de casting*.

### catch-up tv nm.
\*
*la télévision de rattrapage.*

### challenge nm.
\*\*\*
*un défi*. There is no real justification for using the English term. That being said, it can *sometimes* have the specific meaning of an internal competition among certain members of a company, e.g. sales staff, for the prize of 'Salesperson of the Year', etc.

### challenger nm.
\*\*
idem

### chat nm.
\*\*\*
idem, in the context of the Internet.

### checkpoint nm.
\*\*
*un point de contrôle.*

### check-up nm.
\*\*\*
*une visite médicale de routine.*

### chewing gum nm.
\*\*
idem

### churn nm.
\*\*
*le taux de rotation des clients* particularly in the telecoms sector.

### clash nm.

*un heurt, un affrontement, un conflit.*

### class action nm.
\*\*\*
*une action de groupe, une action collective* or *un recours collectif.*

### clean adj.

in the sense of people who are not taking drugs, or have no criminal record or scandal attached to their name.

**clip (video) nm.**
idem

**cloud computing nm.**
*informatique distribuée* nf.

**coach nm.**
*un accompagnateur* (HR), *un entraineur* (in sport).

**coacher v**
*accompagner.* In the corporate context, this has a connotation of psychological support and mentoring.

**coaching nm.**
*accompagnement* nm. In the corporate environment, this implies personal development of one's team members and team-leading and is frequently used in cases of retraining, mobility and outplacement.

**cockpit nm.**
*le poste de pilotage.*

**come-back nm.**
*un retour sur scène* nm.

**coming-out nm.**
idem, in the meaning of a public declaration about one's homosexuality.

**cookies nmpl**
*mouchards* nmpl (IT).

**cool! adj. and interj.**
*genial!, super!*

**copyright nm.**
there is also the term *droits d'auteur* or *royalties* for the remuneration aspect.

**corner nm.**
only used in a football context.

**corporate adj.**
*de l'entreprise,* especially used in the sense of *au niveau de la direction générale,* i.e. 'at the headquarters level of a company' or 'affecting the company as a whole'.

**cost-killer nm.**
*un chasseur de coûts.*

**cow-boys nmpl**
especially used in the meaning of gun-happy policemen or maverick busi-nessmen. NB: cowboy is one word in English.

**crash nm.**
*un accident* (e.g. car, plane) or *un effondrement du marché.*

**crasher. se**
*s'abîmer* (*en mer*), *s'écraser* (*sur terre*) for aircraft.

**credit crunch nm.**
*un assèchement du crédit.*

**credit default swaps**
idem, in the stockmarket sector.

**customisé adj.**
*fait sur mesure.*

**dandy nm.**
idem

**deal nm.**
*un accord, une transaction, un marché.*

**dealer nm.**
idem, in the narcotics meaning.

**debriefing nm.**
*un compte rendu de fin de mission.*

**disc-jockey nm.**
idem. Two words in English.

**discount nm.** 
*une remise.*

**downsizing nm.** 
(HR not IT) *la compression du personnel.*

**draft nm.** 
*un projet de texte.*

**dream team nm.**    ⬜ *
*l'équipe des meilleurs, une équipe de rêve.*

**drone nm.**    ⬛ ***
*un avion de reconnaissance sans pilote.*

**dumping social nm.**    ⬛ ***
by analogy with commercial dumping, this refers to the employment of very low paid workers.

**Ebitda nm.**    ⬛ **
earnings before interest, taxation, depreciation and amortization, i.e. *excédent brut d'exploitation* nm. Constantly used in corporate accounting.

**embedded adj.**    ⬜ *
idem, as in the case of a photographer working with the army in the field. The recommended French term is *embarqué.*

**establishment nm.**    ⬛ ***
*le sérail.*

**fair play nm. or adj.**    ⬛ ***
*déloyal* would be appropriate in the expression *pas très fair play.*

**fan club nm.**    ⬛ **
*un club de fans.*

**fashion victim/addict nm.**    ⬛ ***
*une victime/un drogué de la mode.*

**fast food nm.**    ⬛ ***
*la restauration rapide.*

**feedback nm.**    ⬛ ***
*un retour d'information.*

**feeling, au adv**    ⬜ *
*par intuition.*

**finish, au loc. adv.**    ⬜ *
e.g. *combat au finish* (fight to the finish).

**flash-back nm.**    ⬛ ***
*un retour en arrière* in the cinema context.

**flirt nm, flirter vi**    \*\*\*
idem But originally French *conter fleurette*.

**flop nm.**    \*\*\*
*un bide, un four* (slang terms).

**folklore nm.**    \*\*\*
idem.

**foot business nm.**    \*
all of the business activities surrounding football, e.g. the sale of tee shirts, stickers, photos of team members, transfer fees, etc.

**forcing (faire du) vi.**    \*\*
*mettre la pression*.

**free-lance nm. adj.**    \*\*\*
but freelance journalist could be *un journaliste indépendant*, or *un pigiste*. One word in English.

**french doctor nm. (sic)**    \*\*
used ironically and exclusively as a name for Bernard Kouchner. See Chapter 9.

**french lover nm. (sic)**    \*
*Latin lover*.

**french touch nm. (sic)**    \*
*une note française* or *le sceau français*.

**fuel nm.**    \*\*
used in the sense of fuel oil. Never in the sense of the French term 'combustible'.

**fun nm. adj.**    \*\*
*amusement* or *amusant*

**gadget nm.**    \*
idem

**gag nm.**    \*\*\*
idem, in the sense of a 'joke', but also *plaisanterie*.

**garden-party nm.**    \*\*
idem. Two words in English

**gay adj.**     \*\*
*homosexuel.*

**geek nm.**     \*
idem

**gentleman nm.**     \*\*
idem

**gentleman's/gentlemen's agreement nm.**     \*\*
idem

**glamour adj.**     \*
this corresponds to the English 'glam' or 'glitzy'.

**golden boy nm.**     \*\*\*
idem

**golden hello nm.**     \*\*\*
*indemnité/prime d'arrivée* nf.

**golden parachute nm.**     \*\*\*
*un parachute d'or* or *un parachute doré.*

**golden share nm.**     \*
*une action privilégiée.*

**gore adj.**     \*
gory.

**green business nm.**     \*\*
idem

**groggy adj.**     \*
*sonné* (slang).

**guest-star nm.**     \*
idem. Two words in English.

**half-track nm.**     \*
idem. A military vehicle.

**happening nm.**     \*
idem, but also *un événement branché et exceptionnel.*

346

**happy end (sic) nm.**
happy ending.

**happy few nmpl**
*une poignée de privilégiés* or *les heureux élus.*

**happy hours nmpl**
idem, in the catering context.

**hard adj.**
used to qualify severe criticism.

**hard adj.**
idem (pornography). *Une hardeuse* is a hard porn actress.

**hard discount(er) nm.**
idem

**has been nm.**
*une célébrité sur le déclin.*

**hat-trick nm.**
*trois buts marqués dans un match par le même joueur.*

**hedge fund nm.**
*un fonds d'investissements spéculatifs.*

**high-tech adj.**
*technologie de pointe, de haute technologie.*

**hit-parade nm.**
idem. Two words in English.

**hobby nm.**
*un passe-temps, un violon d'Ingres.*

**hold up nm.**
*braquage* nm. is the term for a hold-up at a bank. In French usage, the English term 'hold up' is used in the sense of 'daylight robbery', *un vol manifeste.* Thus 'hold-up' in French usage would be more 'rip off' in English.

**holding nm.**
*une société de portefeuille.*

**home-grown players nmpl**
*joueurs formés localement* nmpl.

`*`

**home sweet home dict**
never translated.

`***`

**hooligan/houligan nm.**
restricted to the football context.

`**`

**hot-line nm.**
*un n° du service après vente 24/7.*

`***`

**hub nm.**
*une plate-forme* in distribution, but *un point de concentration* in civil aviation
or telecommunications.

`**`

**in adj.**
*à la mode.*

`**`

**insider nm.**
*un initié* (insider trading is *délit d'initié*).

`***`

**jackpot nm.**
*le gros lot.*

`***`

**jean nm.**
a pair of jeans.

`*`

**jet nm.**
idem

`***`

**jet-set nm.**
idem. Two words in English.

`***`

**jet-lag nm.**
*fatigue provoquée par le décalage horaire.* Two words in English.

`***`

**jet-ski nm.**
*un scooter des mers.*

`*`

**jingle nm.**
*un sonal publicitaire.*

`**`

**job nm.**    `***`

*un emploi, un travail.* Initially used in the sense of temporary or student-vacation employment, the sense is now broadening towards the English sense of the word but is still familiar in terms of linguistic register.

**jockey nm.**    `*`

idem

**jogging nm.**    `***`

*un survêtement,* as an item of clothing. Equivalent to the English 'track suit'. *Faire son jogging* means 'to go jogging'.

**joker nm., interj.**    `***`

idem. in the card game meaning, or used as a synonym of replacement. Frequently used as an interjection to say 'pass' when one is asked an embarrassing question which one does not wish to answer.

**junk bonds nmpl.**    `***`

*obligations pourries* nfpl.

**junk food nm.**    `***`

*la malbouffe.*

**junkie nm.**    `*`

*un camé* (from *de la camelote* meaning 'junk' in the sense of worthless bric à brac).

**kidnapping nm.**    `***`

*un rapt d'enfant, une abduction,* from 'kid' (*gamin*) and 'nap' (*enlever*). The term was originally used to describe the illegal capture of children for use in slavery. Now used irrespective of the kidnapped person's age. The term was first coined in 1672.

**killer nm.**    `***`

*tueur* nm, corporate speak, and 'serial killer' (*un tueur en série*).

**last but not least loc. adv.**    `***`

never translated.

**latin lover (sic) nm.**    `*`

idem, but with a capital 'L' for Latin in English usage.

**leader nm.**    `***`

Frequently used in the sense of 'number one' in a given field. The more appropriate term if used in the sense of 'leader' of a political party would be *chef de file* nm.

**leadership nm.** `***`

the 'number one' position rather than the abstract qualities of a leader.

**leasing** `*`

*le crédit bail.*

**leveraged management buyout nm.** `***`

*un rachat par endettement.*

**lifting nm.** `***`

a facelift.

**light adj.** `***`

*allégé, à faible teneur en calories.*

**listing nm.** `***`

*un listage,* but in the Clearstream affair 'listing' is systematically used, never *listage.* See Chapter 11 'Clearstream'.

**live adj.** `**`

*en direct* in a broadcasting context.

**lobby nm.** `***`

*un groupe de pression.*

**lobbying nm.** `***`

idem

**lobbyiste nm.** `**`

lobbyist.

**loft nm.** `*`

Not equivalent to an attic but used in the meaning of a rather trendy, up-market conversion of, for example, a stable or barn.

**look nm.** `***`

used fashion-wise, this refers to a person's *allure* nf, *style* nm, or *image* nm.

**looping nm.** `*`

idem, in aeronautics.

**loser nm.** `***`

*un perdant.* Often misspelt as 'looser' because of the apparently appropriate spelling.

**low-cost adj.**

`***`

*à bas prix*, particularly used for airline companies.

**low profile nm.**

`*`

*profil bas* nm.

**Made in China**

`***`

*Fabriqué en Chine.*

**mail nm.**

`***`

*un courriel* or *un mél.*

**making of nm.**

`**`

A documentary about how a film was made. Frequently mispronounced 'off'.

**manager nm.**

`***`

*un cadre* (See Chapter 10 'cadre').

**marketing nm.**

`***`

idem

**match nm.**

`***`

idem, in a sports context, but could also be translated by *une rencontre.*

**meeting nm.**

`***`

Used in the sense of a 'mass meeting', the venue often being a sports stadium. 'Meeting' in the English sense of the term is generally translated by *une réunion.*

**melting pot nm.**

`***`

idem

**merchandising nm.**

`*`

idem

**must nm.**

`**`

the noun could become the adjective *incontournable.*

**name-dropping nm.**

`***`

idem

**new deal nm.**

`***`

*la nouvelle donne.*

**new look nm.**    **\*\***
*une nouvelle allure.*

**new wave nm.**    **\*\***
*la nouvelle vague.*

**no comment**    **\*\*\***
*pas de commentaire.*

**no man's land nm.**    **\*\*\***
Never translated. Hyphenated in English.

**off adj.**    **\*\*\***
off the record.

**off (voix) nf.**    **\*\***
voice-over.

**offshore adj.**    **\*\*\***
*extraterritoriale* (banking).

**offshore adj**    **\*\*\***
*au large de/en mer* (oil rig).

**old school nm.**    **\***
*la vieille école.*

**one-man-show nm.**    **\*\*\***
idem. One-man show in Engish

**open space nm.**    **\*\***
*une plateforme de bureaux décloisonnée.*

**out adj.**    **\***
*hors circuit, hors du coup,* i.e. no longer being in favour or unable to keep up with the game. Idem. in tennis.

**outing nm.**    **\***
idem. in the meaning of a public announcement, without the consent of the person concerned, about his or her homosexuality.

**outplacement nm.**    **\*\*\***
idem

**outsider nm.**        ***

idem, in the competition sense of the word. *L'Étranger* in the sense of the novel by Camus.

**outsourcing nm.**        ***

*externalisation* nf.

**overdose nm.**        *

*une surdose.*

**pacemaker nm.**        *

*un stimulateur cardiaque.*

**package nm.**        ***

*une offre commerciale groupée.*

**packaging nm.**        **

*le conditionnement.*

**paddock nm.**        *

idem, for Formula One cars and for horses. In the latter case *enclos* nm is recommended.

**parking nm.**        ***

parking lot (US) car park (UK).

**patchwork nm.**        **

idem for a quilt, but *bigarré* for a landscape.

**peanuts nmpl.**        *

*des cacahuètes/cacahouètes* nfpl, when referring to a trifling sum of money.

**peer-to-peer nm.**        **

idem, but *station à station.*

**people ('pipole') nm. adj.**        ***

the 'celebs'.

**pickpocket nm.**        *

idem

**pick-up nm.**        **

a pick-up truck.

**pin-up nm.**

*

idem

**pipeline nm.**

***

*un oléoduc, un gazoduc.*

**playback, en loc. adv.**

**

idem

**playboy nm.**

***

idem

**pom-pom girls nfpl**

*

idem

**pool nm.**

*

idem, in the meaning of a certain group of people, e.g. investors.

**press-book nm.**

*

portfolio of a model or artiste. Not hyphenated in English.

**prime time nm.**

***

*les heures de grande écoute.*

**profit warning nm.**

**

idem

**punch nm.**

*

idem, in the sense of 'vigour'.

**punching ball nm.**

*

'punch ball' in the proper sense, but figuratively can be translated by *un souffre-douleur*, or *une tête de Turc*, i.e. someone who regularly serves as a bully's target for verbal or physical attacks.

**pure player nm.**

**

idem (telecom).

**puzzle nm.**

**

specifically 'a jigsaw puzzle'. The English word 'puzzle' could be translated by *un casse-tête* or *une énigme*.

**racket nm.**

***

*extorsion* nf.

**raider nm.**     `**`
idem, in the buyout context.

**raid financier nm.**     `**`
*le lancement d'une OPA hostile.* See Chapter 14 'OPA'.

**recordman/woman nmf**     `**`
record holder.

**relooker vt**     `**`
to give a new look to sb. or st.

**relooking nm.**     `*`
see above 'relooker'.

**remake nm.**     `***`
*une nouvelle version d'un film.*

**revolving (crédit) nm.**     `**`
*un crédit (documentaire) renouvelable.*

**ring nm.**     `*`
idem, in a boxing context.

**road-movie nm.**     `***`
idem. Two words in English

**roadshow nm.**     `*`
*une tournée de conférences, reservée aux analystes financiers.*

**roaming nm.**     `**`
*itinérance* (telecom).

**rock nm. (danse)**     `*`
rock and roll.

**rock-star nm.**     `*`
idem. Two words in English.

**round nm.**     `**`
*une reprise* in the boxing sense of the word.

**royalties nfpl**     `*`
*droits d'auteur* nmpl.

**rugbyman nm.**
*un joueur de rugby.*

$*$

**rushes nmpl.**
idem, in a cinema context.

**sandwich nm.**
idem

$**$

**scoop nm.**
idem (journalism).

$***$

**sea, sex and sun**
idem

$***$

**self nm.**
self-service café or restaurant.

$**$

**self control nm.**
*la maîtrise de soi.*

$*$

**self-made man/woman nmf**
idem

$***$

**self service adj.**
*en libre service.*

$***$

**serial killer nm.**
*un tueur en série.*

$**$

**sex-appeal nm.**
idem. Two words in English.

$*$

**sex toys nmpl.**
*jouets/gadgets sexuels* nmpl.

$*$

**sexy adj.**
*séduisant(e).*

$**$

**shocking! interj**
used ironically when referring to the prudes that the English are considered to be. It is used in the sense of 'oh my goodness'.

$**$

**shopping (faire du) nm.**                    `***`

*du lèche-vitrine.* In French, the word 'shopping' is often understood as 'window shopping' without necessarily involving a purchase. Otherwise the appropriate term would be *faire des courses, faire des achats* or *faire des emplettes* (the latter being of a higher register).

**short list nf.**                    `**`
idem

**short listé(e) adj.**                    `**`
shortlisted.

**short lister vt**                    `**`
to shortlist.

**show nm.**                    `***`
*un spectacle.*

**showbiz nm.**                    `***`
idem

**show-business nm.**                    `***`
idem. Two words in English.

**show must go on. The dict.**                    `***`
never translated.

**sit-in nm.**                    `*`
*une occupation d'usine* or *d'une faculté*

**small is beautiful dict.**                    `**`
idem. From the title of a book published in 1973 by the British economist E. F. Schumacher. Never translated.

**smoking nm.**                    `*`
evening or dinner suit/jacket (UK), tuxedo (US).

**snack nm.**                    `*`
a snack bar, the place rather than the quick meal.

**snacking nm.**                    `*`
The fact of having a snack rather than a sit-down meal. It can sometimes pejoratively refer to *grignotage* which means 'nibbling' between meals.

**sniper nm.**     **

*un tireur isolé.*

**snob adj.**     **

snobbish.

**snober vt.**     *

to snub sb.

**so british! (sic)**     **

often used with a slightly mocking tone towards the British.

**soap nm.**     ***

a soap opera (the original sponsors were soap and detergent companies in the USA).

**soft adj.**     *

for pornography but *atténué* for criticism or *édulcoré* when speaking about a watered-down or sweetened version.

**spin doctor nm.**     ***

un spécialiste en communication chargé de l'image d'un candidat ou d'un parti politique.

**sponsor nm.**     ***

*un parrain* or *un mécène.*

**sponsoring nm.**     ***

*le parrainage,* or *le mécénat d'entreprise.*

**spread nm.**     **

idem in the stock market context.

**squat nm.**     **

idem in the homeless context.

**squatter vi.**     **

to squat.

**squatteur nm.**     **

a squatter.

**staff nm.**     **

in the sense of senior advisors or directors at the headquarters level of a company. Not equivalent to 'personnel'.

**standing nm.**    `**`
*le statut social.*

**standing ovation nm.**    `***`
idem

**star nf.**    `***`
*une vedette.*

**start-up nm.**    `***`
*une jeune pousse.*

**starting blocks nmpl.**    `**`
*les blocs de départ* nmpl.

**stock-options nf.**    `***`
idem. Two words in English.

**streaming nm.**    `***`
idem, in the Internet context.

**stress nm.**    `***`
*la pression* or *la tension nerveuse.*

**stress test nm.**    `**`
*un test de résistance,* e.g. in car design, and more recently in the banking sector.

**stretching nm.**    `*`
stretches in the keep-fit context.

**string nm.**    `**`
G-string.

**striptease/strip-tease nm.**    `**`
idem. *Effeuillage* is the theoretical translation but is never used.

**subprimes nmpl.**    `***`
*crédits hypothécaires à haut risque* nmpl. NB: 'subprime mortgages' in English.

**success story nm.**    `***`
idem

**sunlights nmpl.**    `***`
*des projecteurs puissants* nmpl (in a cinema studio).

**superstar nf.** ***
idem.

**surbooké adj.** **
overbooked.

**swing nm.** *
idem, in golf or dancing.

**talk-show nm.** ***
idem. Two words in English.

**talkie-walkie nm.** *
walkie-talkie.

**tanker nm.** **
*un camion/bateau citerne.*

**tarmac nm.** *
tarmac (*au sol*, e.g. 'to taxi along the tarmac' *rouler lentement au sol).*

**task-force nf.** **
*un détachement* or *une équipe spéciale.*

**tea for two** **
This should never be translated; immortalized in the film *La Grande Vadrouille.* See Chapter 1 'Grande Vadrouille'.

**teasing nm.** **
idem, in the advertising context. See Chapter 1 'Demain j'enlève le bas'.

**tee-shirt nm.** ***
idem

**tennisman nm.** ***
tennis player.

**testing nm.** ***
This is used in the context of showing up discriminatory practices at the moment of recruitment, applying for an apartment, or of accessing a night-club. A black person will attempt to enter a night club and be turned away on the grounds that the club is full. A hidden camera will film subsequent white nightclub-goers who are granted admittance to the club a few minutes

later. This can sometimes lead to prosecution on the grounds of racial discrimination.

**think tank nm.**      ***

*un groupe/une cellule de réflexion.*

**thriller nm.**      **

*un film à suspense.*

**tie-break nm.**      *

idem, in tennis.

**timing nm.**      ***

*le choix du moment opportun.*

**top model nf.**      **

idem

**top secret adj.**      **

*ultra secret.*

**trader nm.**      ***

*un courtier en bourse.*

**trading nm.**      ***

*activité boursière* nf.

**tramway nm.**      *

idem

**trash adj.**      **

idem, e.g. in the meaning of trash TV.

**treadmill nm.**      *

*un tapis de jogging.*

**trendy adj.**      *

*à la mode.*

**triple player nm.**      *

idem. A telco offering telephone, Internet, and TV.

**trust nm.**      ***

*un cartel.*

**turnover nm.**     \*\*\*
*la rotation du personnel* (not used as an accounting term).

**underground adj.**     \*
idem, in the meaning of 'subversive'.

**understatement nm.**     \*\*\*
*une litote.*

**uppercut nm.**     \*\*
idem, in boxing.

**user-friendly adj.**     \*\*
*convivial pour l'utilisateur.*

**venture capital nm.**     \*\*
*capital-risque* nm.

**wagon nm.**     \*
idem, in the railway context.

**war lords nmpl.**     \*\*
*seigneurs de guerre* nmpl.

**war room nm.**     \*
idem

**week-end nm.**     \*\*\*
the French term *fin de semaine* is quite rare. Not hyphenated in English.

**Who's Who nm.**     \*\*\*
*le Bottin mondain.*

**workaholic nm.**     \*\*
*un bourreau de travail.*

**yes! interj.**
frequently used as an exclamation of satisfaction accompanied by a downward, vertical pulling action of the clenched fist.

**zoom nm.**     \*\*
a close-up shot, *un gros plan* in the cinema or TV context

## Latin terms

In reading the list of common Latin expressions used in French, English readers will be surprised by the absence of such familiar terms as e.g., *in absentia* and *in camera*, that are never used in the language of Molière. They will also be surprised by certain spelling differences between English and French usage and by the different use that is made of certain terms, for example *post mortem*, used as a noun in English but as an adverb in French. The following Latin terms have been translated into English and the French translation has been given in italics only where the French term is commonly used as an alternative. It is not within the scope of this book to give extensive details about the origin of the quote but there are one or two interesting exceptions to this rule.

**a contrario *loc. adv.***   `***`
inversely.

**a fortiori *loc. adv.***   `***`
all the more so.

**a maxima *loc. adj.***   `*`
at the highest possible level.

**a minima *loc. adj.***   `***`
at the lowest possible level.

**a posteriori *loc. adv., adj.***   `***`
from the latter, related to reasoning from observed facts.

**a priori *loc. adv., loc. adj. nm.***   `***`
from the former, without examination, conceived beforehand.

**abyssus abyssum invocat *loc. prov., cit.***   `*`
*L'abîme appelle l'abîme.* 'Deep calleth unto deep'. One fault leads to another. See The Psalm of David, Psalms 42: 7.

**accessit (s/he approached). *nm.***   `*`
A distinction given to a student who, although not coming first, came near to doing so.

**ad hoc *loc. adj.***   `***`
for this specific purpose.

### ad hominem *loc. adj.*                                    \*\*\*

an argument *ad hominem* is a means of contradicting opponents by quoting either their own words or citing their own actions which are in contradiction with their argument.

### ad majorem Dei gloriam *dev.*                               \*

'to the greater glory of God', the motto of the Society of Jesus (the Jesuits).

### ad nauseam *loc. adv.*                                     \*\*

*à la nausée*, to the point of causing disgust.

### ad patres *exp. adv.*                                      \*\*

*mort*, towards one's ancestors, i.e. dead.

### ad usum Delphini *loc. adj.*                               \*

*à l'usage du Dauphin*, 'for the use of the Dauphin'. A special series of texts by Latin authors was commissioned by Louis XIV for his son's use. All of the unchaste words and expressions were replaced by more innocuous terms. Le Dauphin in the French royal family was the heir to the throne. 'Bowdlerized' could be used as a translation of this Latin expression.

### ad vitam aeternam *loc. adv.*                              \*\*\*

*pour toujours*, for eternity.

### affectio societatis *nm.*                                  \*

the will to form a company. A commercial company results from a contract in which two or more people decide to pool their resources with a view to sharing the profits and, if necessary, assuming liability for the possible losses.

### Agnus Dei *nm.*                                           \*

*l'Agneau de Dieu*, the Lamb of God.

### aléa *nm.*                                                \*\*

game of dice, of chance. In modern French, it is used in the plural to designate unpredictable events. This term is sometimes confused with 'avatar'. See below 'Miscellaneous foreign words'.

### alea jacta est *cit.*                                     \*\*

*les dés sont jetés*, 'the die is cast'. See Chapter 7 'Rubicon'.

### alias *adv.*                                              \*\*\*

otherwise known as.

**alibi *nm.***

the plea in law of having been elsewhere at the time of a crime.

**Alma Mater *nf.***

*mère nourricière*, 'bounteous mother'. A rather archaic term used by former students to refer to their university or college. The university is seen as a foster mother and the students (alumni) as foster children.

**alter ego *nm.***

one's other self.

**annus horribilis *loc. nom.***

*une année horrible*, 'a horrible year'. This expression was used by Queen Elizabeth II in her speech at the Guildhall in 1992 after a year of family misfortune.

**ars longa, vita brevis *loc. prov.***

'The art is long, life is short.' This is the Latin translation of the Greek aphorism of Hippocrates. He was referring to the long time required to learn the 'art' of medicine compared to the brevity of human existence.

**au prorata *loc. adv.***

proportionally.

**auri sacra fames *loc. nom.***

*l'exécrable soif de l'or*, execrable lust for gold.

**Ave Maria *cit.***

*Je vous salue, Marie.* 'Hail, Mary.' The first words of the Latin version of a prayer to the Virgin Mary used in the Roman Catholic Church. See The Gospel according to Saint Luke 1:28.

**bis *adv.***

'twice', 'repeat'. It can be used as 'encore' in the theatrical meaning, and in addresses '12 bis' would be '12a' in English. It is used on roads (*itinéraire bis*) to advise drivers to take an alternative route to avoid congestion.

**bis repetita *ax.***

*les choses répétées.* It's the same story, all over again.

**bonus *nm.***

anything given in addition to the customary amount. Frequently used today as a coefficient for calculating the reduction in the insurance premium based on a driver's accident-free record. A no-claims bonus.

### carpe diem *loc. prov.*

*profitez du jour présent*, 'seize the day'. From Horace. The idea here is to take advantage of the present without thinking unduly about the future. See Chapter 5 'Mignonne, allons voir si la rose'.

### casus belli *nm.*

a situation that could constitute reasons for declaring war

### collapsus *nm.*

generally used as a medical term to describe a dramatic drop in blood pressure accompanied by cold sweating and a feeling of faintness. In popular usage it can simply mean 'collapse', e.g. of an economic system.

### confer *imp.*

compare; abbreviated to cf. or Cf.

### corpus *nm.*

body, particularly of a text.

### credo *nm.*

'The Creed' takes its name from the fact that it begins with the words 'I believe'. Today, it is used as a statement of belief or a principle in which one believes.

### curriculum vitae *nm.*

the course of one's life, a résumé. Frequently abbreviated to 'CV'

### cursus honorum *nm.*

the sequence of offices held by a Roman official before attaining the consulate. Consequently, any sequence of junior posts leading to a position of high authority.

### de facto *loc. adv.*

*de fait.* 'In fact', existing, whether legal or not. Used in opposition to *de jure.*

### de profundis *cit.*

*Des profondeurs je crie vers toi, Yahvé.* 'Out of the depths have I cried unto thee, O Lord.' A cry of appeal from the opening words of Psalm 130.

### de visu *loc. adv.*

for having seen it with one's own eyes

### decorum *nm.*

*étiquette*

**delirium tremens** *nm.*

\*

trembling delirium characterized by optical delusions and terror induced by excessive consumption of alcohol.

**desiderata** *nmpl.*

\*\*

things desired or needed.

**deus ex machina** *nm.*

\*\*

this expression literally means 'god out of a machine', and refers to an artificial, or improbable character, device, or event, introduced suddenly to resolve a situation or contribute to the dénouement of a play.

**distinguo** *nm.*

\*\*\*

distinction, from 'I draw a distinction'.

**dixit** *conjug.*

\*\*\*

'he said'. Used when quoting the exact words said by sb.

**dura lex, sed lex** *loc. prov.*

\*\*\*

*la loi est dure, mais c'est la loi,* 'the law is hard, but the law is the law'.

**errare humanum est** *dict.*

\*\*

*l'erreur est humaine,* 'to err is human'.

**et al.** *abr.*

\*

*et alii,* and others. Frequently used in publishing when one author's name is given although several authors contributed to the work.

**etc.** *abr.*

\*\*

*et c(a)etera*; and the rest.

**ex aequo** *loc. adv.*

\*\*\*

equal position; a tie in sport.

**ex nihilo** *adv., adj.*

\*\*\*

*à partir de rien,* 'from out of nothing'.

**exit** *conjug.*

\*\*

*il/elle sort,* 'he/she leaves the stage' (stage direction). NB: not used in the meaning of 'way out'.

**facsimile** *nm.*

\*\*\*

to make similar, an exact copy.

**fiat lux *loc. subj., cit.***    ( ** )
*que la lumière soit*, 'Let there be light'. See the Book of Genesis 1: 3.

**fluctuat nec mergitur *dev.***    ( *** )
*il est battu par les flots, mais ne sombre pas*, 'although it be tossed by the waves, yet it does not sink'. The motto of the city of Paris, the emblem of which is a ship.

**forum *nm.***    ( * )
forum, public place equivalent to the Greek 'agora'.

**grosso modo *adv.***    ( *** )
approximately.

**habeas corpus *loc. jurid.***    ( ** )
literally 'thou shalt have the body'. 'A writ requiring a person under arrest to be brought before a judge, especially to secure the person's release unless lawful grounds are shown for their detention' (*The Oxford Dictionary of Quotations*).

**hic *nm.***    ( *** )
*voilà le hic*; 'there's the rub', 'that's the snag'.

**hic et nunc *loc. adv.***    ( ** )
*ici et maintenant*, 'here and now', immediately.

**hic jacet *loc. verb.***    ( ** )
*ci-gît*, from the verb *gésir*, 'Here lies'. Typically engraved on tombstones.

**homo homini lupus *loc. prov.***    ( * )
*l'homme est un loup pour l'homme*, 'Brother will turn on brother'. See Matthew 10: 21.

**homo sapiens *nm.***    ( ** )
rational man.

**honoris causa *loc. adj.***    ( ** )
'for the sake of honour'; related to the awarding of a university degree.

**horresco referens *loc. verb.***    ( ** )
*je frémis en le racontant*, 'I shudder at the telling'.

**ibidem *adv.***    ( *** )
in the same place.

**idem *adv.***     ***

the same thing.

**imperium *nm.***     *

the power or the command over.

**imprimatur *nm.***     *

'let it be printed'. Authorization given by a bishop for a book about the Catholic faith to be printed.

**incognito *adv.***     **

disguised or under an assumed name, with one's true identity hidden.

**in cauda venenum *loc. prov.***     **

*dans la queue le venin*, 'the venom is in the tail'.

**in extenso *loc. adv.***     **

*intégralement*, 'in its complete form'.

**in extremis *loc. adv., loc. adj.***     ***

in extreme circumstances.

**in fine *loc. adv.***     ***

*à la fin*, 'in short'.

**in situ *loc. adv.***     *

at the place itself.

**in utero *loc. adv.***     *

within the womb.

**in vino veritas *loc. prov.***     *

there is truth in wine.

**in vivo *loc. adv.***     **

in the living organism.

**in vitro *loc. adv.***     **

in a test tube, in artificial conditions, as opposed to *in vivo*.

**intra muros adv., adj.**     **

within the walls of the city.

**intuitu personae *loc. adv.***     **

dependent on a particular person. A term used in the law of contract.

**ipso facto *loc. adv.***            \*\*\*
by that very fact.

**Ite, missa est *imp.***            \*\*\*
*Allez, la messe est dite.* It is with these words that the priest dismisses the faithful after Holy Communion. In idiomatic French, the expression is used in the meaning of 'there is nothing more to be said'.

**lapsus calami *nm.***            \*
a slip of the pen. 'Calamus' is a reed pen.

**lapsus (linguae) *nm.***            \*\*\*
a slip of the tongue.

**magnum opus *nm.***            \*
*l'œuvre majeure.* The greatest or most important work of an author, composer, etc.

**malus *nm.***            \*\*
coefficient for calculating the increase in the insurance premium based on a driver's bad accident record.

**manu militari *loc. adv.***            \*\*\*
by physical force.

**mater semper certa est *loc. prov.***            \*
*la mère est sûre.* 'One is always sure of who the mother is'. See below 'pater'.

**Mater Dolorosa *nf.***            \*
*La mère de douleur,* the sorrowful mother, 'the Lady of Sorrows'.

**Mare Nostrum *nf.***            \*\*
'Our sea', the name given to the Mediterranean by the Romans.

**mea culpa *nm.***            \*\*\*
'my fault'. An admission of one's error. From the prayer of confession in Latin Mass but frequently used as a noun, e.g. *Il a fait son mea culpa.*

**memento mori *nm.***            \*
a reminder of death, e.g. a skull is frequently used as a symbol of mortality.

**memorandum *nm.***
a note or summary made for future use and in order to remember the content. Frequently used in French in the term MOU Memorandum of Understanding (*un protocole d'accord*).

**mens sana in corpore sano *cit.***    *
*un esprit sain dans un corps sain*, 'a healthy mind in a healthy body' (Juvenal).

**missi dominici *nmpl.***    **
envoys of the Lord. Royal inspectors of the Carolingian period.

**modus operandi *nm.***    ***
the way of working or operating, especially of a criminal.

**modus vivendi *nm.***    ***
a practical arrangement or compromise which makes it possible to work/live together.

**mordicus *adv.***    ***
'in biting', e.g. *prétendre mordicus que* is 'to claim stubbornly that.

**morituri te salutant *cit.***    *
*ceux qui vont mourir te saluent*, 'those who are about to die, salute thee'. According to the Roman historian Suetonius, these words were said to the Roman emperors by each gladiator before combat commenced.

**motu proprio *nm.***    **
in the diplomatic language of the Vatican, it is an apostolic letter issued by the Pope on his own initiative, i.e. a papal decree.

**motus *excl.***    **
*motus et bouche cousue*, Mum's the word.

**multi sunt vocati, pauci vero electi *cit.***    **
See Chapter 8 'appelés'.

**mutatis mutandis *loc. adv.***    **
with any necessary change of detail.

**nec pluribus impar *dev.***    *
the motto of Louis XIV, the Sun King. The expression is not clear but understood to mean 'above (superior to) all others'.

**nec plus ultra *nm.***    ***
'no more beyond'. The highest point of perfection. 'ne' in English usage.

**nolens volens *adv.***    ***
*bon gré, mal gré*; 'unwilling or willing' i.e. 'whether one likes it or not'. NB: the sequence change between Latin and French.

### numerus clausus *nm.*

**\*\***

a fixed or limited number, e.g. taxis in Paris or chemists within a certain geographical radius, medical students, etc.

### opus *nm.*

**\*\*\***

an important literary or musical work. Sometimes used ironically.

### Opus Dei *nm.*

**\*\***

'The work of God'. A Catholic association.

### opus magnum *nm.*

**\***

a rather obsolete form of *magnum opus*. See *magnum opus* above.

### O tempora, o mores! *cit.*

**\*\*\***

*Ô temps, ô mœurs*, 'Oh the times, oh the manners!' (Cicero).

### panem et circenses *cit.*

**\*\***

*du pain et des jeux*, 'bread and circuses' (Juvenal).

### para bellum. Si vis pacem *loc. prov.*

**\*\***

*si tu veux la paix, prépare-toi à la guerre*, 'if you wish for peace, prepare for war'.

### pater semper incertus est *loc. prov.*

**\***

*le père n'est jamais certain*, 'one is never sure who the father is'.

### Pater Noster *nm.*

**\***

*Notre Père*, 'Our Father'; opening words of the Lord's Prayer. See Matthew 6: 9–14.

### paterfamilias *nm.*

**\*\***

*père de famille*, 'the head of a family'.

### Pax Americana *nm.*

**\***

American peace.

### pensum *nm.*

**\*\***

'task', or 'chore'. Often in the meaning of punishment at school, e.g. writing lines.

### persona *nf.*

**\***

'mask' in the theatrical meaning.

### persona non grata *nf.*

**\*\*\***

an undesirable or unwanted person, often used in diplomatic circles.

**post mortem *loc. adv.***

after death. Not used in the nominal sense of an 'autopsy' for which the French term is 'autopsie' but in the adverbial sense, e.g. 'le corps de la victime a été déplacé *post mortem*'.

**post scriptum *nm.***

written after. PS.

**pretium doloris *nm. jurid.***

a standard compensatory payment awarded to the victims of an accident to cover the pain and inconvenience they suffered as a result. In French law, there is no concept of 'punitive damages'. Three broken ribs are worth so much, one broken finger has a price, etc.

**primo *adv.***

firstly, to begin with.

**primus inter pares *loc. adj.***

first among equals.

**pro domo *loc. adv, adj.***

'for one's own house'. To plead in one's own interest.

**quid *interr.***

*qu'en est-il de?*, 'what about'?

**quidam *nm.***

an individual, an unspecified person, a chap.

**quiproquo *nm.***

a confusion whereby one thing or person is mistaken for another.

**quitus *nm.***

full discharge.

**quo non ascendet *dev.***

*Où ne montera-t-il pas?* 'To what heights may he not rise?' Motto of Nicolas Fouquet 1615–80. See Chapter 2 'Où ne montera-t-il pas?'

**quod erat demonstrandum (QED) abrév.**

CQFD-*ce qu'il fallait démontrer*, 'which was to be proved'.

**quota *nm.***

a share or determined amount.

**recto *nm.***                                                    ⟨ *** ⟩
the right-hand page of a book, the front side of a page.

**referendum *nm.***                                               ⟨ *** ⟩
from the Latin verb *referre*; to submit a question to an assembly.

**res publica *nf.***                                              ⟨ * ⟩
*la chose publique*, affairs relating to the community, state or nation.

**satisfecit *nm.***                                               ⟨ *** ⟩
a testimonial given by a teacher to a student who has done well.

**scenario *nm.***                                                 ⟨ * ⟩
*scénario*.

**secundo *adv.***                                                 ⟨ ** ⟩
secondly.

**senior *nm.***                                                   ⟨ ** ⟩
senior citizen.

**sic *adv.***                                                     ⟨ ** ⟩
*ainsi;* it is thus. When quoting a sentence in which there is a mistake, *sic* is
used to indicate that there is no error in the reproduction of the quotation.

**sic transit gloria mundi *cit.***                                ⟨ *** ⟩
*ainsi passe la gloire du monde* 'thus passes the glory of the world'. These words
are traditionally spoken during the coronation of a new Pope (Kempis).

**sine die *loc. adv.***                                           ⟨ *** ⟩
without day. Without any future date being designated, often used in legal
proceedings. A case is often 'renvoyé sine die'.

**sine qua non *loc. adj.***                                       ⟨ *** ⟩
without which not. A prerequisite.

**statu quo *nm.***                                                ⟨ *** ⟩
in the same state, 'status quo' in English usage.

**statu quo ante *nm.***                                           ⟨ ** ⟩
in the former state.

**stricto sensu *loc. adv.***                                      ⟨ *** ⟩
in the strict meaning of the word.

**subito *adv.***      `*`

suddenly, rapidly. The register here is familiar.

**sui generis *loc. adj.***      `*`

belonging to a single, unique class.

**summum *nm.***      `**`

the highest point, the highest degree, the acme.

**tabula rasa *nf.***      `**`

*table rase.* A blank surface ready to receive new impressions, related to the philosophical idea that the human mind, at birth, is a virgin blank receiving the impressions of life.

**Te Deum (laudamus) *nm.***      `*`

Christian hymn. 'God, we sing thy praise.' Frequently used to celebrate special occasions, e.g. the coronation of a new Pope, the signing of a peace treaty, etc.

**terra incognita *nf.* (terrae incognitae)**      `***`

*terre(s) inconnue(s)*, 'unknown territory/territories'.

**tertio *adv.***      `**`

*troisièmement*, third(ly).

**triumvirat *nm.***      `**`

power held by a group of three men.

**tu quoque, fili *cit.***      `**`

See Chapter 2 'toi aussi mon fils'.

**ultima cena *nf.***      `*`

*la Cène*, 'the Last Supper'.

**ultima ratio regum *nm.***      `*`

'The final argument of kings.' This was engraved on cannon cast for Louis XIV after 1650.

**urbi et orbi *loc. adv.***      `***`

'to the city and the world'. From the blessing of the Pope given from the balcony of the basilica of Saint Peter in Rome and particularly associated with his Easter and Christmas message to the world. Idiomatically, it is used in French to 'tell everyone everywhere'.

**vade mecum *nm.*** `***`
go with me. An *aide-mémoire*.

**vade retro Satana *imp, cit.*** `**`
*passez derrière moi Satan*, 'get thee behind me Satan'. See Chapter 8 'Vade' (Bible).

**vae victis *dict.*** `*`
*malheur aux vaincus*, 'woe to the vanquished'.

**vanitas vanitatum *loc. prov., cit.*** `*`
*Vanité, vanité, tout n'est que vanité*, 'Vanity of vanities, all is vanity'. See Chapter 8 'vanitas' (Bible).

**verbatim *nm, loc. adv.*** `***`
*mot à mot*, 'word for word', in the exact words, as originally spoken.

**verso *nm.*** `***`
the left-hand page of a book, the back of a page.

**veto (I forbid) *nm.*** `***`
An authoritative ban.

**via *prép.*** `***`
It can frequently be replaced by the French expression *par le biais de* or *par l'intermédiaire de.*

**vice versa *adv*** `**`
with the relations reversed.

**vis comica *nm.*** `*`
*la force comique*, 'the power to make people laugh'.

**vivats *nmpl.*** `*`
'vivat' means 'may he/she live'. Pluralised form of the term. A shouted wish for long life and prosperity. *Les vivats* are 'cheers' or 'cheering'.

**vox populi, vox dei *loc. prov.*** `***`
*la voix du people est la voix de Dieu*, 'the voice of the people is the voice of God'.

**vulgum pecus *nm.*** `***`
A very pejorative (and un-Latin) expression referring to the common herd or hoi polloi.

# Italian, German, North African

## *Italian terms*

### aggiornamento nm.      `*`
a bringing up to date or modernization. Term used to describe the policy of church reform implemented by the Second Vatican Council (1962–5).

### allegro *adv. mus.*      `*`
in quick time.

### basta! excl.      `**`
an exclamatory and familiar term meaning 'that's enough'.

### bel canto nm.      `*`
This refers to the singing associated with opera from the seventeenth century onwards, in which the virtuosity of the solo singer is highlighted.

### bravo! excl.      `**`
'well done'!

### brio (avec) loc. adv.      `*`
brilliantly, with flying colours.

### combinazione nf.      `*`
a crafty way, more or less honest, of achieving one's ends.

### Commedia dell'Arte nf.      `**`
This was a highly popular Italian theatrical genre which had its heyday in the sixteenth and seventeenth centuries and was to inspire Molière. The same stock characters may be found in such a play, each corresponding to the wily valet, the scheming lady's maid, the braggart, the miser, the old man in love with a young girl, etc. Among such characters we can mention Harlequin (Arlequin), Punch (Punchinello, formerly Polichinello), Pierrot (idem), Columbine (Colombine) and Pantaloon (Pantalone).

### condottiere nm.      `*`
the leader of a troop of mercenaries.

### cosa nostra nf.      `*`
'that which belongs to us'. The Sicilian mafia.

### crescendo adv. mus.      `*`
literally 'growing'. A gradual increase in the loudness of music.

**diva nf.**      `**`

a goddess or a distinguished female opera singer.

**dolce vita nf.**      `*`

a life of luxury, sensuality and hedonism. This word gained in popularity after the release of the film of the same name by Federico Fellini in 1960.

**Eppur, si muove! (apocryphal)**      `**`

*Et pourtant, elle tourne,* 'And yet it does move'. On 22 June 1633, Galileo was sentenced by the Inquisition to life imprisonment and forced to abjure the heliocentric system of Copernicus. On recanting, Galileo is said to have murmured these words.

**fiasco nm.**      `**`

literally a 'bottle', but usually used in the meaning of an ignominious failure.

**fortissimo adv. mus.**      `*`

with very high volume.

**ghetto nm.**      `***`

originally a Jewish quarter or Jewry in Italy. Its meaning has broadened to designate any neighbourhood inhabited only by persons of a given race, colour, creed or social class.

**graffiti nmpl**      `**`

a drawing or writing scribbled on a wall, often obscene in nature.

**illico presto adv.**      `***`

familiar expression equivalent to 'pdq, pretty damn quick'.

**imbroglio nm.**      `**`

a mix-up, a tangle, a mess, a state of confusion.

**in petto adv.**      `*`

'in the secret of one's heart', i.e. something one says to oneself and not out loud.

**lazzi nmpl.**      `*`

from the Italian 'lazzo' meaning 'link'. It refers to the grotesque and sarcastic buffoonery of improvised theatre. See above 'Comedia dell'arte'. It can also refer to a gibe or heckling.

**lingua franca nf.**      `**`

Frankish tongue. A hybrid language used in the Levant and by extension any language used for communication between people of different nationalities.

### ma non troppo adv. mus.

musical direction meaning 'not too much'.

### maestria (avec) nf.
brilliantly, with great skill.

### maestro nm.
a master in the area of music. Sometimes used as a facetious reference to a band leader.

### mezza voce adv. mus.
literally, this term means 'half-voice', i.e. with medium volume, neither loud nor soft.

### moderato adv. mus.
the tempo of moderate time.

### omertà nf. (Sicilian dialect)
a code of conduct that involves keeping silent about crimes and refusing to cooperate with the police.

### paparazzi nmpl.
a word invented by Fellini. It was the name of the young photographer in the film *La Dolce Vita*. Today, it refers to the photo-journalists who hunt the rich and famous for dubious scoops.

### razzia nf.
a foray, a raid.

### se non è vero è ben(e) trovato dict.
*si cela n'est pas vrai, c'est bien trouvé*, 'even if the story is not true, it is nevertheless a nice story'.

### tempo nm.
from the Latin *tempus,* time. The pace at which a musical piece is supposed to be played, indicated by such terms as *allegro, andante*, etc.

### tutti quanti, et loc. adv.
and all the rest of the same bunch.

### vendetta nf.
a hereditary blood feud, particularly in Corsica and southern Italy.

### German terms

German nouns should normally take a capital letter but this rule is not always adhered to when the word is used in French. The most common spelling has been given.

### Bildungsroman nm.

   ( \* )

a novel concerned with the moral and emotional development of the hero

### Blitzkrieg nm.

   ( \*\*\* )

*la guerre éclair*, 'lightning war'.

### diktat nm.

   ( \*\*\* )

a settlement imposed on a defeated enemy by the victor. Hence, any authoritarian order or decree.

### ersatz nm.

   ( \* )

a substitute or inferior quality article or product. It first made its appearance during the First World War but was extensively used during the Second World War.

### Leitmotiv nm.

   ( \*\* )

a dominant, recurrent theme or underlying pattern. A thread running through a literary or musical composition.

### Nach Paris! prep.

   ( \* )

'To Paris!' Particularly used by the invading German troops.

### putsch nm.

   ( \*\*\* )

an attack aimed at eliminating political opponents with a view to seizing power, popularized by Hitler's abortive putsch in Munich in 1933

### Realpolitik nf.

   ( \*\*\* )

pragmatic politics. A realistic policy that has little to do with values or morals.

### schuss (faire) loc. adv.

   ( \* )

to make a straight run down a ski slope at full speed.

### spiel nm.

   ( \* )

a game, e.g. Kriegsspiel, i.e. 'war game'.

### Sturm und Drang

   ( \* )

literally 'storm and passion'. It was the name given to the romantic, literary movement in Germany in the second half of the eighteenth century. Passion is prized over reason. Goethe and Schiller are the most famous representatives of this movement which takes its name from a play of the same name written by Friedrich Klinger in 1776.

**zeitgeist nm.**                                                          ⬚ * ⬚
the spirit of the times.


### North African terms

It is to be remembered that during and after the Algerian War of Independence (1954–62), many French Algerians known as *les pieds noirs* returned en masse to mainland France, bringing with them a host of terms that have now become an integral part of modern French.

**baraka nf.**                                                          ▐ *** ▌
chance, luck.

**bazar nm. (Persian origin)**                                         ⬚ ** ⬚
a mess or a shambles.

**bled nm.**                                                           ▐ *** ▌
refers to the hinterland of North Africa, i.e. the countryside, although it usually means a godforsaken place, a village in the middle of nowhere.

**caïd nm.**                                                           ▐ *** ▌
in North Africa, it was originally the name given to a civil servant who held judicial and police powers. Today, it usually refers to a big shot or gang leader.

**chouïa nm.**                                                         ▐ *** ▌
a little, a very small quantity.

**djebel nm.**                                                          ⬚ * ⬚
mountainous terrain in north Africa.

**djellaba nf.**                                                        ⬚ * ⬚
a long, loose outer garment worn by either men or women.

**fissa adv. and interj.**                                             ⬚ * ⬚
at once, rapidly, 'be snappy about it', 'get a move on!'

**gourbi nm.**                                                          ⬚ * ⬚
a slum or a shack.

### kebab nm. (Turkish origin)          `*`

generally speaking, this consists of small pieces of seasoned meat, roasted on a skewer.

### kif-kif loc. adj. (Arabic)          `**`

'same' in Arabic. *Bonnet blanc et blanc bonnet*; 'six of one and half a dozen of the other'.

### scoumoune nf. (Algerian slang)          `**`

rotten luck, jinx.

### smala nf.          `*`

from the Arab term 'Zmâla' which literally means a gathering of tents in which the clan chief's family and retinue lived while travelling. *Toute la smala* means 'the whole tribe' or 'the whole gang'.

### souk nm.          `*`

an Arabic term for the Persian or Turkish 'bazar'. Used figuratively in the same way as 'bazar', i.e. to indicate a mess or a shambles.

### toubib nm. (Algerian)          `***`

the pronunciation of this word is 'two-beeb', a familiar term for a doctor. This gives rise to one of the corniest puns in the French language: 'toubib or not toubib, zat is ze question'.


## Miscellaneous foreign terms

### aficionado nm. (Spanish)          `*`

having a great interest in any pursuit. Originally sb. passionately fond of bull-fighting.

### agora nf. (Greek)          `**`

a public place of assembly, especially a market place or pedestrian concourse.

### apparatchik nm. (Russian)          `***`

originally, a member of the soviet bureaucracy. Now, it refers to any rather senior member of the establishment or political party.

### autodafé nm. (Portuguese)          `***`

from the Latin term *actus fidei*, an 'act of faith'. It originally involved the burning of books deemed to be immoral, blasphemous or heretical, etc. In the Middle Ages, it came to mean the solemn proclamation of the sentence passed by the Inquisition especially for the burning of the condemned person at the stake.

### avatar nm. (Sanskrit)
*\*\*\**

the incarnation of a deity. Any metamorphosis.

### bakchich nm. (Persian)
*\*\**

*baksheesh,* or *bakshish,* a tip or gratuity. It now has the connotation of a bribe or a backhander.

### Banzai! interj. (Japanese)
*\**

the Japanese word for '10,000 years'. A cry used by the Japanese before going into battle, or on greeting the Emperor.

### boomerang nm. (Australian)
*\*\*\**

a curved wooden missile which, on being thrown, returns to the thrower. It is often used in the form *avoir un effet boomerang.*

### brouhaha nm. (Hebrew)
*\*\**

deformation of *barukh ha ba* which means 'blessed be he who comes'. Today, it means a hubbub or a confused noise coming from a crowd.

### burka nf. (bourka) burqa (Pachtou)
*\*\*\**

traditional dress of women in Afghanistan covering the whole of the body and equipped with a grill enabling the person to see and not be seen. Contrary to popular belief, this item of clothing has nothing whatsoever to do with Islam.

### commando nm. (Portuguese)
*\*\**

a small unit of highly mobile soldiers, skilled in the art of hand-to-hand fighting and frequently operating behind enemy lines

### diaspora nf. (Greek)
*\**

the dispersion or scattering, particularly of the Jews after the Babylonian exile but also used especially for the Armenian and Chinese exiles in Europe today.

### djihad nf. (Arabic)
*\*\*\**

Arabic for 'supreme effort'. A holy war.

### doxa nf. (Greek)
*\*\*\**

opinion, hence 'orthodox', i.e. conforming or in line with doctrinal belief.

### eldorado nm. (Spanish)
*\*\**

'the gilded'. An imaginary country rich in gold that the sixteenth-century Spaniards believed to exist in the upper Amazonian region. Thus, any region of great wealth.

### embargo nm. (Spanish)
'arrest'. An order forbidding commerce between two countries.

### fatwa nf. (Arabic)
In the Islamic faith, a fatwa is an edict or ruling on Islamic law issued by an Islamic scholar often to give guidance where Islamic jurisprudence is not clear. To the general public, particularly since the Salman Rushdie affair in 1988, it has come to mean a death sentence passed on sb. who has offended the Islamic faith.

### Fellagha nm. (Arabic)
bandit, highwayman, used in Tunisia and later in Algeria to refer to a rebel against French imperialism. From the French standpoint, this word meant 'FLN terrorist'. See Chapter 14 'FLN'.

### gouru nm. (Hindi)
guru. In Hinduism, this refers to one's spiritual advisor or teacher. It is often used with irony in the field of corporate management.

### guérilla nf. (Spanish)
guerrilla. Warfare conducted by a small group of irregular troops, often behind enemy lines. This term entered the English language at the time of the Peninsular War 1809–14, launched by the British to encourage Portuguese and Spanish resistance to Napoleon I.

### Halal adj. (Arabic)
Specialists claim that this word should not be written 'hallal' although it is frequently used in French with this spelling. It comes from the Arabic word meaning 'permitted'. It is generally used to describe meat that has been killed in accordance with Islamic rites, i.e. the animal is killed by slitting its throat and bleeding it to death, without prior stunning, and carried out in the name of Allah.

### hara-kiri nm. (Japanese)
ceremonial suicide by disembowelling often to preserve one's honour. Frequently and erroneously written 'hari'.

### hidjâb nm. (Arabic)
Hijab. The Islamic veil worn by Muslim women, covering the head but leaving the face visible.

### imam nm. (Arabic)
a Muslim spiritual guide.

**Inch'Allah interj. (Arabic)**
*si Dieu le veut*, 'God willing'.

**intifada nf. (Arabic)**
uprising.

**iota nm. (Greek)**
the ninth letter of the Greek alphabet, synonymous with a very small quantity.
See Chapter 8 'iota'.

**jihad nm. (Arabic)**
See above 'djihad'.

**junte nf. (Spanish)**
junta. An administrative and political council or assembly in Spain, Portugal
or Latin America. Frequently used in the expression *junte militaire*.

**kamikaze nm. adj. (Japanese)**
a Japanese suicide pilot of the Second World War. The word literally means
'divine wind'. *Kami* means 'divinity' and *kaze* means wind. Japan was saved
from invasion in 1281 when a violent and providential wind sprang up and
destroyed the invading Mongol fleet.

**karma nm. (Sanskrit)**
the whole of a person's actions in a given phase of his existence believed to
have an influence on his fate in the next. Loosely used, it means fate or
destiny.

**lambda nm. adj. (Greek)**
the eleventh letter of the Greek alphabet, which has twenty-four letters.
'Lamda' being nearly the middle letter, it is used to designate the average
person, the man on the Clapham omnibus.

**maelström nm. (Dutch)**
a whirlpool. In French, it may be written with or without the umlaut.

**mantra nm. (Sanskrit)**
a sacred text usually from the Vedas and used as a prayer or incantation.
Frequently used in relation to corporate speak. The latest management
mantra is 'Think global, act local'.

**moudjahiddin nmpl. (Arabic)**
fighters, resistants, in the name of religion.

### nabab nm. (Hindi)

nabob. A native provincial governor of the old Mogul empire in India. By extension, sb. who is rich and important.

### nada excl. (Spanish)

nothing! no way! nothing doing!

### niet excl. (Russian)

nothing! no way! nothing doing!

### nippon adj. (Japanese)
the word 'Nippon' is the Japanese name for 'Japan'. It literally means 'rising sun'.

### niqab nm. (Arabic)
a veil worn by Muslim women covering the head and leaving only the eyes visible.

### nirvana nm. (Sanskrit)

a 'blowing out' or 'extinction of human life', a 'blending with Brahma'. This Buddhist concept refers to a situation in which human desires and passions and even individual existence disappear into oblivion. It is supposed to be the reward for great holiness. It is a place or condition of peace or bliss.

### no pasarán (Spanish)

'They shall not pass.' See Chapter 2 'Ils ne passeront pas'.

### nomenklatura nf. (Russian)

a list of people enjoying exceptional prerogatives; the privileged elite.

### oukase nm. (Russian)
See below 'ukase'.

### paria(h) nm. (Tamil)
from the Tamil word 'paraiyan' meaning 'a hereditary drumbeater'. It is one of the lowest and most despised of the Indian castes. It now means anyone who is despised and outcast.

### pasionaria nf. (Spanish)
Somebody who is passionate about a cause to a degree which can involve spectacular and violent action.

### perestroika nf. (Russian)
a term for 'reconstruction', popularized by Mikhail Gorbatchev in the 1980s.

### pistolero nm. (Spanish)

a politician's henchman, a gunslinger.

### pogrom nm. (Russian)

total destruction. Aggression (supported or at least tolerated by the authorities) carried out with a view to destroying a people or class, etc.; particularly associated with the attacks against the Jewish community at various times during the history of Europe.

### safari nm. (Swahili)

a journey, on foot, especially in search of big game, now synonymous with a hunting expedition.

### sérail nm. (Persian-Turkish serâi)

the Sultan's Palace in the Ottoman Empire, now used to refer to the inner sanctum of the political establishment.

### Sherpa nm.

The Sherpa constitute an ethnic group of Tibetan origin living on the southern slopes of the Himalayas. Sherpas are bearers and guides who accompany mountaineers. In French, the term is very clearly defined as a person who takes part in the preparation of a political summit meeting and/ or who represents the head of state.

### Shoah nf. (Hebrew)

In Hebrew, the term means catastrophe. It has come to mean the extermination of the Jews by the German Nazis during the Second World War.

### sieste nf. (siesta Spanish)

from the Latin *sexta hora,* the sixth hour (dawn was considered to be zero hour). A short nap after the midday meal taken in many warm countries.

### skipper nm. (Dutch)

the captain, usually of a small sailing boat.

### tabou nm. adj. (Tonga)
taboo. What is forbidden or prohibited to a certain class of persons. Other spellings are found in other Polynesian languages.

### taliban nm. (Arabic-Persian)
'student of theology'.

### tohu-bohu nm. (Hebrew)
term qualifying the original chaos before the creation of the world. Hubbub or noisy confusion. See Chapter 8 'tohu-bohu'.

### totem nm. (Algonquin)     *

the emblem (frequently an animal) of a tribe or clan of American Indians.

### troïka nf. (Russian)     *

a carriage drawn by three horses abreast. Hence, a group of three political leaders.

### tsunami nm. (Japanese)     ***

a word of Japanese origin from 'tsu' (port) and 'nami' (wave). Apart from the natural disaster, today it is used in French to designate any figuratively catastrophic occurrence.

### tycoon nm. (Japanese)     ***

derived from Chinese, this word means 'prince' or 'great man'. The term has come to mean 'magnat' or highly successful businessman.

### Yom Kippour nm. (Hebrew)     **

*Le Jour du Grand Pardon*; 'The Day of Atonement'.

### ukase/oukase nm. (Russian)     ***

In Tsarist Russia, it was an imperial order having the force of law. Hence, any arbitrary proclamation or decree. Synonymous with diktat.

### zombie nm. (West African)     *

from 'zumbi' meaning 'image'. A revitalized corpse acting under the magical influence of voodoo (*vaudou* nm).

# Chapter 14

# Acronyms and abbreviations

We have witnessed an explosion in the use of acronyms and abbreviated forms over the past few years and it would have been quite fastidious, and not very helpful, to give a comprehensive list of acronyms used in the French press. In this chapter, we have concentrated on acronyms that not only occur frequently but on those that have become lexicalized, i.e. used as words in their own right. Most of these acronyms are recognized on sight by any French person and the original words represented by the individual letters of the acronym have often been forgotten. Everyone knows what the CAC 40 is, few French people know what it stands for! It will be noticed that usage of capitalization is not always consistent.

# A

## AB
`**`

Agriculture Biologique. nf.
Organic agriculture.

## ABS
`***`

Abus de Biens Sociaux. nm.
Misuse of corporate funds and/or property.

## ADN
`***`

Acide Désoxyribonucléique. nm.
DNA deoxyribonucleic acid.

## AFNOR
`**`

Association française de normalisation. nf.
The French industrial standards authority.

## AFP
`***`

Agence France Presse. nf.
The French news agency.

## AFSSA
`**`

Agence française de sécurité sanitaire des aliments. nf.
The French food safety agency has three tasks: monitoring, warning and research in the areas of public health, animal health and welfare, and phytoenvironmental protection.

## AFSSAPS
`*`

Agence française de sécurité sanitaire des produits de santé. nf.
A public authority whose mission is to guarantee the safe use and quality of health-related products including medicines and cosmetics.

## AG

Assemblée Générale. nf.
AGM Annual General Meeting.

## AGIRC

Association Générale des Institutions de Retraite des Cadres. nf.

This organization is in charge of the coordination of the various retirement funds for the complementary pensions paid out to former management-level staff.

## AMF

Autorité des marchés financiers. nf.

French watchdog of the financial markets equivalent to the SEC (Securities and Exchange Commission) in the USA and the FSA (Financial Services Authority) in the UK.

## ANPE

Agence Nationale pour l'Emploi. nf.

French equivalent of the British Job Centre that has recently merged with the Assedic to become 'Le Pôle Emploi'. See ASSEDIC.

## AOC

Appelation d'Origine Contrôlée. nf.

This is a quality label indicating the geographical origin of a product and guarantees its authenticity. It is frequently (but not exclusively) attributed to traditional products such as wine and dairy produce.

## ASSEDIC

Association pour l'emploi dans l'industrie et le commerce. nf.

This is the organization that pays out unemployment benefit. (See UNEDIC and ANPE.)

## ATTAC

Association pour la taxation des transactions financières pour l'aide aux citoyens. nf.

An association whose objective is to put a brake on speculation by instituting democratic control over the financial markets and their institutions, by way of taxing financial transactions. The motto of the association is 'the world is not for sale'.

# B

## BAC  ⟨ ** ⟩

Brigade Anti-Criminalité. nf.

A special police unit set up in 1994 to deal more successfully with urban delinquency and violence.

## BBC  ⟨ *** ⟩

Bâtiments Basse Consommation. nm.

Buildings with low energy consumption.

## BCBG  ⟨ * ⟩

Bon Chic, Bon Genre.

This term refers to the French upper middle class who stereotypically attach importance to sartorial elegance and outward signs of respectability. Similar to NAP, this expression may be translated into British English by 'Sloaney'.

## BCG  ⟨ * ⟩

Bacille Calmette-Guérin nm. or vaccin Bilié de Calmette-Guérin nm.

The BCG vaccine comes from 'bacille bilié' and the names of the research biologist Albert Calmette (1863–1933) and the vetinary surgeon Camille Guérin (1872–1961) who developed it. The culture of the tuberculin bacillus was carried out in the sterile bile of an ox, hence the term 'bilié'. The 'b' can thus stand for either 'bacille' or 'bilié'.

## BIRD  ⟨ ** ⟩

Banque Internationale de Reconstruction et de Développement. nf.

A bank whose objective is to help poor but solvent countries reduce poverty and achieve equitable growth by facilitating their access to financial resources.

## BNP

Banque Nationale de Paris. nf.

One of the biggest retail and investment banks in France. The new name is BNP Paribas.

**bobo**

An abbreviation of 'bourgeois bohème', i.e. a middle-class person who has a Bohemian lifestyle.

**BTP**

Bâtiment, Travaux Publics. nm.

An economic sector including the building industry and public works.

**BTS**

Brevet de Technicien Supérieur. nm.

A vocational diploma taken after two years of full-time and specialized study, after the age of 18, usually (but not necessarily) after the *bacca-lauréat*, the school-leaving examination.

**BVP**

Bureau de la Vérification de la Publicité. nm.

An advertising watchdog whose objective is to act in favour of fair and true advertising in the interests of advertising professionals, consumers and the public at large.

# C

### CAC 40 ***

Cotation Assistée en Continu. nf.
The main index on the Paris stock exchange.

### CAP *

Certificat d'Aptitude Professionnelle. nm.
A diploma certifying technical job competence, obtained after 16 years of age in a technical school with a period of in-company training plus theory.

### CDD ***

Contrat à Durée Déterminée. nm.
A fixed-term labour contract.

### CDI ***

Contrat à durée indéterminée. nm.
An unlimited term labour contract.

### CFDT ***

Confédération Française Démocratique du Travail. nf.
The biggest French trades union in terms of membership, the second largest in terms of union election impact.

### CFTC *

Confédération Française des Travailleurs Chrétiens. nf.
French union having a Christian outlook in its activities.

### CGC *

Confédération Générale des Cadres. nf.
A trades union for managerial staff.

## CGT

Confédération Générale du Travail. nf.
One of the biggest French trades unions founded in 1895, with clear communist sympathies.

## CHU

Centre Universitaire Hospitalier. nm.
A university/teaching hospital.

## CIMADE

Comité inter-mouvements auprès des évacués. nm.
A voluntary, non-profit-making support organization bringing help to illegal immigrants being held in detention centres by providing them with legal advice, interpreting services, etc.

## CNAM

Caisse Nationale d'Assurance Maladie. nf.
The health insurance branch of the French social security system.

## CNAV

Caisse Nationale d'Assurance Vieillesse. nf.
The retirement pension branch of the French social security system.

## CNES

Centre National d'Études Spatiales. nm.
The French space research centre.

## CNIL

Commission Nationale de l'Informatique et des Libertés. nf.
French watchdog for computer files and civil liberties.

## CNPF

Conseil National du Patronat Français. nm.
The former French employers' confederation that has since been renamed the Medef. See below 'Medef'.

## CNRS

Centre National de la Recherche Scientifique. nm.
The biggest French scientific research agency, founded in 1939.

## CQFD

Ce qu'il fallait démontrer.
Which was to be proved. See Chapter 13 'quod erat demonstrandum'.

## CREDOC ***

Centre de Recherche pour l'Étude et l'Observation des Conditions de Vie. nm.

A research centre oriented towards sociological observations about living conditions and economic and statistical measurements.

## CRIF ***

Conseil représentatif des institutions juives de France. nm.

A council representing the numerous Jewish institutions in France.

## CRIIRAD **

Commission de recherche et d'informations indépendantes sur la radio-activité. nf.

Criirad is an independent, non-profit-making organization whose objective is to provide the public with unbiased information about nuclear risks and pollution and to combat state censorship and disinformation.

## CRS ***

Compagnie Républicaine de Sécurité. nf.
The name of the French anti-riot police.

## CSA ***

Conseil Supérieur de l'Audiovisuel. nm.
The French regulatory authority for TV and radio broadcasting.

## CSG *

Contribution Sociale Généralisée. nf.
A tax introduced in 1990 to reduce the deficit of the social security fund.

## CV **

Curriculum Vitae. nm.
Idem. or résumé.

# D

**DAB**                                                              `*`

Distributeur Automatique de Billets. nm.

Although this is often translated by ATM, the term corresponding to
ATM is GAB ('guichet automatic de banque') where the services offered
are more enhanced than the simple distribution of banknotes which is the
case for the DAB.

**DAL**                                                              `*`

Droit Au Logement. nm.

The right to be housed; the name of an association that defends the
homeless.

**DASS**                                                             `***`

Direction des Affaires Sanitaires et Sociales. nf.

The social services department. The common expression *enfant de la
DASS* refers to a child brought up in care e.g. in a state orphanage.

**DCRI**                                                             `**`

Direction Centrale du Renseignement Intérieur. nf.

This organization is the result of the merger of the DST and the RG. See
below 'DST' and 'RG'. It is headquartered in Levallois-Perret in the
*département* of the Hauts-de-Seine (92).

**DDE**                                                              `*`

Direction Départementale de l'Équipement. nf.

A decentralized structure (there is one per *département*) depending on
the ministries of ecology and regional development, particularly in charge
of the repair and maintenance of the roads within a *département* and
questions involving secondary schools (*collèges*).

**DEA**                                                              `*`

Diplôme d'Études Approfondies. nm.

This is a postgraduate diploma at the 'bac plus 5' level, i.e. beyond Master's degree level. It is taken before a Ph.D.

### DESS                                                              [ ** ]

Diplôme d'Études Supérieures Spécialisées. nm.
A one-year postgraduate vocational diploma.

### DEUG                                                              [ * ]

Diplôme d'Études Universitaires Générales. nm.
A university diploma granted after two years of study.

### DGA                                                              [ *** ]

Délégation Générale pour l'Armement. nf.
This is the contracting authority for French arms programmes. This covers design, acquisition and evaluation of the systems which will equip the French armed forces.

### DGCCRF                                                              [ *** ]

Direction Générale de la Concurrence, de la Consommation et de la Répression des Fraudes. nf.
This is an agency concerned with the regulation of competition, consumer protection and safety, and unfair business practices, etc. Most of its former responsibilities have been taken over by the newly created 'Autorité de la Concurrence'.

### DGSE                                                              [ *** ]

Direction Générale de la Sécurité Extérieure. nf.
The French intelligence-gathering agency, part of the ministry of defence. The successor of the SDECE, (Service de Documentation et de Contre Espionnage), is called La Piscine since its HQ is located in bld. Mortier in the twentieth *arrondissement* near the swimming pool of Tourelles.

### DOM                                                              [ ** ]

Départements d'Outre-Mer. nm.
Those French overseas territories having the status of *départements*, i.e. la Guadeloupe, la Martinique, la Guyane, and la Réunion.

### DRE                                                              [ ** ]

Direction Régionale de l'Équipement. nf.
This is the decentralized echelon which implements national policy in the area of regional development regarding infrastructure, roads, railways, waterways, etc.

## DRH

[ ** ]

Directeur/Directrice des Ressources Humaines. nfm.
Human resources manager.

## DST

[ *** ]

Direction de la Surveillance du Territoire. nf.
Internal intelligence service. Also in charge of anti-terrorist actions and protecting French economic intelligence. Merged with the 'Renseignements Généraux' on 1 July 2008 to form the DCRI. See above 'DCRI'.

## DUT

[ ** ]

Diplôme Universitaire de Technologie. nm.
This is a higher education diploma created in 1966 and taken at the end of a two-year period of study at an IUT, Institut Universitaire de Technologie. It is equivalent in level to the BTS. See above 'BTS'.

## DVD

[ *** ]

Digital Video Disc nm.

# E

## EADS  `***`

European Aeronautic Defence and Space company.

## EBITDA  `**`

Earnings before interest, taxation, depreciation and amortization.
Excédent brut d'exploitation. nm.

## EDF  `***`

Électricité de France.
The French electricity generating company.

## ENA  `***`

École Nationale d'Administration. nf.
See Chapter 10 'ENA' and 'Grandes Écoles'.

## EPAD  `***`

Établissement public pour l'aménagement de la région de la Défense. nm.
A public agency whose mission is the development of the business quarter to the west of Paris, known as La Défense. The name of a polemical affair surrounding the 'election' of Nicolas Sarkozy's son to the head of this body. He is unqualified for the job and failed his second year exams at the faculty of law. He was obliged to withdraw his candidacy faced with the quasi unanimous outcry at this example of blatant nepotism.

## EPO  `**`

Erythropoïétine. nf.
Erythropoietin, also known as hematopoietin, is a drug stimulating the production of red blood cells. Frequently implicated in drug scandals on the Tour de France, given its capacity to improve oxygenation of the body tissue.

## EPR

`***`

European Pressurized Reactor
Réacteur pressurisé européen. nm.

## ERDF

`**`

Électricité Réseau Distribution France. nf.
The distribution arm of the French electricity company.

## ESB

`**`

Encéphalopathie Spongiforme Bovine. nf. (la maladie de la vache folle)
BSE Bovine Spongiform Encephalopathy (mad cow disease)

## ESSEC

`**`

École Supérieure des Sciences Économiques et Commerciales. nf.
One of the most famous French business schools. See Chapter 10
'Grandes Écoles'.

## ETA

`**`

Euzkadi Ta Azkatasunra.
'Basque homeland and freedom.' The name of the basque separatist
movement.

## ETP

`**`

Équivalent Temps Plein. nm.
The equivalent of one full-time job position.

# F

## FAI     ***

Fournisseur d'Accès Internet. nm.
IAP Internet access provider.

## FARC     **

Forces Armées Révolutionnaires de Colombie. nfpl.
The Columbian Revolutionary Army.

## FLNC     **

Front de Libération Nationale de la Corse. nm.
The Corsican National Liberation Front.

## FMI     ***

Fonds Monétaire International. nm.
IMF International Monetary Fund.

## FN     **

Front National. nm.
The French national front.

## FNAC     *

Fédération nationale d'achats des cadres. nf.
This is the name of the leader of distribution chains in the area of culture-related and electronic products.

## FNSEA     **

Fédération Nationale des Syndicats d'Exploitants Agricoles. nf.
This is the biggest French farmers' union with 320,000 members.

## FO     **

Force Ouvrière.
The third biggest French trades union after the CGT and the CFDT.

# G

## GIA

Groupes Islamiques Armés. nmpl.

Al-Jama'ah al-Islamiyah al-Musallaha. An armed organization whose goal is to overthrow the Algerian government and replace it with an Islamic state.

## GIGN

Groupe d'Intervention de la Gendarmerie Nationale. nm.

This is an elite unit of the French army specialized in anti-terrorist activity and the liberation of hostages. It is to be remembered that *gendarmes* are policemen with military status and therefore they are under the authority of the ministry of defence and not the ministry of the interior.

# H

## HALDE

`***`

Haute Autorité de Lutte contre les Discriminations et pour l'Égalité. nf.
This is the name of the body in charge of fighting against discrimination
and in charge of promoting equality of opportunity.

## HD

`**`

Haute Définition
High definition

## HEC

`**`

Hautes Études Commerciales. nfpl.
See Chapter 10 'Grandes Écoles'.

## HLM

`***`

Habitation à Loyer Modéré. nf.
Very roughly equivalent to council accommodation in England.
Although HLM connotes social accomodation for low income groups,
some of these premises are located in very pleasant Parisian quarters and bear
no resemblance whatsoever to social housing in England. Several scandals
have been associated with the name of HLM in Paris. See Chapter 11 'HLM
de Paris'.

## HQE

`**`

Haute Qualité Environnementale.
HEQ High environmental quality.
An approach used in the building industry with a view to limiting the
environmental impact of a building, particularly through energy savings
thanks to improved insulation.

# I

## IFOP

Institut Français d'Opinion Publique. nm.

Company specializing in marketing intelligence. The chairperson and chief executive officer is currently Laurence Parisot who is also the chairperson of the Medef, the French employers' confederation.

## IGAS

Inspection générale des affaires sociales. nf.

This is an authority which monitors any social body that receives public funding in the areas of employment, social security, training, etc. and checks that the activities of such bodies are compliant with the regulations, and that public money is being used appropriately.

## IGS

Inspection Générale des Services. nf.

'The police of the police.' A police department concerned with investigating complaints by the public and internal disciplinary procedures. See Chapter 10 'Inspection Générale des Services'.

## INSEAD

Institut Européen d'Administration des Affaires. nm.

A prestigious business school located in Fontainebleau, in the Seine-et-Marne (77).

## INSEE

Institut National de la Statistique et des Études. nm.
French national institute of statistics and economic studies.

## IRM

Imagerie par Résonance Magnétique (nucléaire) nf.
(N)MRI (Nuclear) Magnetic Resonance Imaging.

## ISF

Impôt de Solidarité sur la Fortune. nm.
Tax on high wealth.

## ITT

Interruption Temporaire de Travail. nf.
This is not a medical certificate to justify an employee's absence from work but rather a certificate establishing the fact that the employee cannot carry out the usual tasks of daily life. This has particular importance in the field of justice. After any physical assault, a victim will invariably be given an ITT of a few days or weeks.

## IUFM

Institut Universitaire de Formation des Maîtres. nm.
Equivalent to a teacher training college for primary school teachers. These *Instituts* have replaced the former *Écoles Normales d'Instituteurs.*

## IUT

Institut Universitaire de Technologie. nm.
This can be broadly compared with a British polytechnic.

## IVG

Interruption Volontaire de Grossesse. nf.
Elective abortion, termination of pregnancy.

# J

**JO**                                                              `***`

Journal Officiel. nm.

The official gazette published on a daily basis by the French Republic.
See Chapter 10 'Journal'.

# L

## LICRA ⟨ * ⟩

Ligue Internationale Contre le Racisme et l'Antisémitisme. nf.

The International League against Racism and Anti-Semitism, founded in 1926 to combat intolerance, xenophobia and exclusion.

## LVMH ⟨ *** ⟩

Louis Vuitton Moët Hennessy.

The world leader in the sale of luxury goods. See Chapter 9 'Arnault, Bernard'.

# M

### MBA     ( ** )

Marge Brute d'Autofinancement. nf.
Cash flow.

### Medef     ( *** )

Mouvement des entreprises de France. nm.
The French employers' confederation. It has replaced the former
CNPF Conseil National du Patronat Français and represents over 700,000
companies and 90 per cent of small and medium-sized companies.

### Mildt     ( ** )

Mission interministérielle de lutte contre la drogue et la toxicomanie. nf.
This is a permanent mission, placed under the authority of the prime
minister that is at the heart of the government's fight against drug abuse. It
prepares the government's plans and monitors implementation.

### MoDem     ( *** )

Mouvement Démocrate. nm.
The centre party, founded by its current president, François Bayrou, in
2007. It is the successor to the UDF party.

### Miviludes     ( * )

Mission interministérielle de vigilance et de lutte contre les dérives sec-
taires. nf.
An interministerial mission with the job of monitoring and fighting
against the activities of sects in France.

# N

## NDLR

Note De La Rédaction. nf.

In the press, this refers to any inserted note which is not part of the original text. It is either preceded by or followed by this abbreviation. It is generally placed within brackets.

# O

## OAS
*

Organisation armée secrète.

A clandestine political *cum* military organization set up to defend 'Algérie Française' after the referendum of 8 January 1961 in which 75% of the population of Algeria voted for self-determination. Terrorist attacks were carried out in Algeria and on mainland France culminating in the assassination attempt against de Gaulle at Petit Clamart on 22 August 1962. See Chapter 12 'Petit Clamart'.

## OCDE
***

Organisation de Coopération et de Développement Économique. nf.
OECD Organization for Economic Co-operation and Development.

## OGM
***

Organisme Génétiquement Modifié. nm.
GMO Genetically Modified Organism.

## OLP
***

Organisation de la Libération de la Palestine. nf.
PLO Palestine Liberation Organization.

## OMC
***

Organisation Mondiale du Commerce. nf.
WTO World Trade Organization.

## OMS
**

Organisation Mondiale de la Santé. nf.
WHO World Health Organization.

## ONG
**

Organisation Non Gouvernementale. nf.
NGO non-governmental organization.

## ONU                                                                `**`

Organisation des Nations Unies. nf.
UNO United Nations Organization.

## OPA                                                                `***`

Offre Publique d'Achat. nf.
A takeover bid.

## OPEP                                                               `**`

Organisation des Pays Exportateurs de Pétrole. nf.
OPEC Organization of Petroleum Exporting Countries.

## ORL                                                                `*`

Oto-rhino-laryngologiste. nm.
An ear, nose and throat specialist.

## ORTF                                                               `**`

Office de Radiodiffusion Télévision Française. nm.
The former French radio and television broadcasting authority. It was
dismantled in 1974. It was synonymous with rigid state control and censorship but also with quality programmes.

## OS                                                                 `*`

Ouvrier spécialisé. nm.
In spite of the appearance, this word refers to an unskilled worker who is
at the very bottom of the industrial worker's ladder.

## OTAN                                                               `***`

Organisation du Traité de l'Atlantique Nord. nf.
NATO North Atlantic Treaty Organization.

## OVNI                                                               `**`

Objet Volant Non-Identifié. nm.
UFO Unidentified Flying Object
Frequently used to describe people who are strange and who do not fit in.

# P

**PACA**

`*`

The region of Provence-Alpes-Côte d'Azur.

**PACS**

`*`

Pacte Civil de Solidarité. nm.

A contract intended for people who enter a long-term relationship. Not necessarily (but frequently) homosexual relationships.

**PAF**

`***`

Paysage Audiovisuel Français. nm.
The French broadcasting world.

**PCF**

`**`

Parti Communiste Français. nm.
The French Communist Party.

**PDG**

`***`

Président Directeur Général. nm.
Chairman and Chief Executive Officer.

**PDM**

`*`

Part du marché. nf.
Market share. Frequently used on presentation visual aids, etc.

**PEA**

`*`

Plan d'Épargne en Actions. nm.

This is a type of share cum savings account intended to foster stock market investments among private individuals and to enhance employee participation in the company they work for.

**PIB**

`***`

Produit Intérieur Brut. nm.
GDP Gross Domestic Product.

### PJ

***

Police Judiciaire. nf.
Equivalent to the CID (UK) or FBI (US).

### PLU

*

The main urban planning document of a given urban area.

### PME

***

Petites et Moyennes Entreprises. nfpl.
Small and medium-sized companies.

### PMU

*

Pari Mutuel Urbain. nm.
The organization in charge of horse-racing and the punting network in France.

### PNB

***

Produit National Brut. nm.
GNP Gross National Product.

### POS

*

Plan d'Occupation des Sols. nm.
The former name of the current PLU. See above.

### PS

***

Parti Socialiste. nm.
The French socialist party.

### PSG

*

Paris Saint-Germain.
Parisian football team.

### PV

**

Procès Verbal. nm.
A report, proceedings, minutes of a meeting. In its abbreviated form, it generally means a fine for a driving offence, speeding, irregular parking, etc. In this case it may be translated by 'a ticket' or an FPN (fixed penalty notice) in the UK.

# Q

## QCM

`***`

Questionnaire/Questions à Choix Multiples. nm.
Multiple choice questionnaire.

## QG

`***`

Quartier Général. nm.
HQ Headquarters.

## QI

`**`

Quotient Intellectuel. nm.
IQ Intelligence Quotient.

# R

**RAS**  `**`

Rien à Signaler.
A military expression meaning 'nothing to report'.

**RATP**  `***`

Régie Autonome des Transports Parisiens. nf.
The Paris Transport Authority.

**RER**  `**`

Réseau Express Régional. nm.
The Paris regional suburban express train network.

**RDA**  `**`

République Démocratique Allemande. nf.
GDR German Democratic Republic. Formerly known as East Germany.

**RFF**  `*`

Réseau Ferré de France. nm.
That part of the French railway system in charge of infrastructure, as
opposed to the SNCF which is the commercial operator of the system.

**RG**  `***`

Renseignements Généraux. nmpl.
Part of the French police force, under the control of the ministry of the
interior in charge of informing the government of threats to internal security.
It came into existence under the Third Republic in 1911. It has now been
merged with the Direction de la Surveillance du Térritoire to form the
Direction Centrale du Renseignement Intérieur (DCRI). See above 'DCRI'.

**RMC**  `*`

Radio Monte Carlo. nf.

## RMI

[ ✳✳✳ ]

Revenu Minimum d'Insertion. nm.

An allowance paid out by the Family Allowance administration to people of working age who are either without resources, or who are in receipt of income deemed to be below a minimum level. The recipient of such an allowance is known as an 'érémiste'.

## RSA

[ ✳✳✳ ]

Revenu de Solidarité Active. nm.

An unemployment allowance intended to replace the existing forms of assistance such as the RMI, PRE and PPE.

## RTL

[ ✳✳✳ ]

Radio Télévision Luxembourg nf.
The no. 1 radio station in France.

## RTT

[ ✳✳✳ ]

Réduction du Temps de Travail. nf.

RTT days are days taken in the form of leave, to compensate for the hours worked over the legal 35 hour limit.

# S

## SA    ( * )

Société Anonyme. nf.
This corresponds to a joint stock company in the UK.

## SAC

Service d'action civique. See Chapter 11.

## SARL    ( * )

Société à Responsabilité Limitée. nf.
A limited liability company.

## S.A.V.    ( ** )

Service Après Vente. nm.
After sales service. Given the old fashioned ring to this word, the term 'customer care' is sometimes preferred.

## SCI    ( * )

Société Civile Immobilière. nf.
This is a 'civil company' of which the object is real estate. A husband and wife may set up an SCI for the management of their real estate holdings. There are tax advantages and it is easier to transfer property to their heirs.

## SDECE    ( * )

Service de Documentation Extérieure et de Contre-Espionnage. nm.
See 'DGSE'.

## SDF    ( *** )

Sans Domicile Fixe. nm.
NFA, a person of No Fixed Abode.

## SFIO

( * )

Section Française de l'Internationale Ouvrière. nf.

Founded in 1905, it was to become the French socialist party in 1969, following the congress in Issy-les-Moulineaux.

## SFR

( ** )

Société Française de Radiotéléphonie. nf.

One of the three major mobile telephone operators in France, the other two being 'Bouygues Telecom' and 'Orange'.

## SGEN

( * )

Syndicat Général de l'Éducation Nationale. nm.

A teachers' union.

## SICAV

( ** )

Société d'Investissement à Capital Variable. nf.

This is a financial instrument enabling people to invest in shares and bonds via a fund without the risk of investing directly in shares.

## SMIC

( *** )

Salaire Minimum Interprofessionnel de Croissance. nm.

The minimum guaranteed wage. The recipient of such an allowance is known as a 'smicard'.

## SNCF

( *** )

Société Nationale des Chemins de Fer. nf.

The French national railway company in charge of the commercial running of the French railways. See above 'RFF'.

## SNES

( ** )

Syndicat national des enseignants du second degré. nm.

One of the most influential of the French secondary level teachers' trade unions.

## SRAS

( * )

Syndrome Respiratoire Aigu Sévère. nm.

SARS Severe Acute Respiratory Syndrome.

## SSII

( ** )

Société de Services en Ingénierie Informatique. nf.

Computer engineering and maintenance company.

## STO     `**`

Service du Travail Obligatoire. nm.

During the Nazi occupation of France, hundreds of thousands of Frenchmen were requisitioned and sent to work in Germany to take part in the German war effort. They were lodged in work camps on German soil.

## SUD     `***`

Solidaires, Unitaires et Démocratiques

A left-wing trades union whose motto is 'Solidarity, Unity and Democracy'.

# T

## TEPA

La Loi du 21 août 2007 en faveur du 'travail, de l'emploi et du pouvoir d'achat'.

The law of 21 August 2007 to encourage work, employment and buying power.

## TER                                                                            ⬭ * ⬭

Transport Express Régional. nm.
Part of the French express regional railway network.

## TFI                                                                            ⬛ *** ⬛

Télévision française 1. nf.
French television channel one. Part of the Bouygues group.

## TGI                                                                            ⬛ ** ⬛

Tribunal de Grande Instance. nm.

This is roughly equivalent to a county court having general jurisdiction and staffed by professional magistrates and, for the citizen, requiring the services of a lawyer.

## TGV                                                                            ⬛ *** ⬛

Train à Grande Vitesse. nm.
The French high-speed train.

## TIP                                                                            ⬭ * ⬭

Titre Interbancaire de Paiement. nm.

This is a document given to a debtor by his or her creditor. It is signed and dated by the debtor and sent back to the creditor. It authorizes a single automatic withdrawal of a given sum from a bank account for the amount marked on the TIP. It frequently replaces a cheque and must not be confused with direct debit (*prélèvement automatique*).

## TIPP ⟨ ** ⟩

Taxe Intérieure (de consommation) sur les Produits Pétroliers. nf.
The main excise tax levied on petroleum products.

## TNT ⟨ ** ⟩

Télévison Numérique Terrestre. nf.
Digital terrestrial television.

## TOC ⟨ ** ⟩

Troubles Obsessionnels Compulsifs. nmpl.
OCD obsessive compulsive disorder.

## TOM ⟨ * ⟩

Territoires d'Outre-Mer. nmpl.
French overseas territories that do not have the status of a *département*.

## TPG ⟨ ** ⟩

Trésorier-Payeur Général. nm.

This is one of the most highly paid (and sought after) positions in the French civil service. In the field, the TPG (paymaster general) is a treasurer, accountant and controller, the state's bank manager in the localities. It is one of the juiciest jobs (fromages) in the Republic given that the variable bonus of a TPG is based on the amounts of money under management.

## TRACFIN ⟨ *** ⟩

Traitement du renseignement et action contre les circuits financiers clandestins. nm.
The anti-money laundering unit within the ministry of finance at Bercy.

## TTC ⟨ ** ⟩

Toutes Taxes Comprises.
Inclusive of tax, tax included.

## TVA ⟨ *** ⟩

Taxe à la Valeur Ajoutée. nf.
VAT Value added tax.

# U

### UE

Union Européenne. nf
EU European Union.

### UFC

Union Fédérale des Consommateurs. nf.
A consumer defence association which regularly publishes a magazine called *Que Choisir.*

### UIMM

Union des Industries et Métiers de la Métallurgie. nf.
The metal industry employers' union. One of the most powerful unions within the Medef and recently involved in a slush fund scandal which provoked the resignation of its President Denis Gautier-Sauvagnac.

### UMP

Union pour un Mouvement Populaire. nf.
The party of the French right.

### UNEDIC

Union Nationale interprofessionnelle pour l'Emploi Dans l'Industrie et le Commerce. nf.
Unlike the ASSEDIC, which is concerned with paying out unemployment insurance benefit, the UNEDIC is concerned with all of the back-up paper work involved in making such payments, a kind of back-office of the ASSEDIC.

### URSSAF

Union de Recouvrement des Cotisations de Sécurité Sociale et d'Allocations Familiales. nf.
The social security contribution collection agency.

## UV

Unité de Valeur. nf.
The basic credit unit, for a given course, used in French universities.

# V

### VAB

[ \* ]

Véhicule à l'Avant Blindé. (blindé de transport de troupe) nm.
Armoured personnel carrier.

### VIH

[ \*\*\* ]

Virus d'Immunodéficience Humaine. nm.
HIV Human Immunodeficiency Virus.

### VRP

[ \*\*\* ]

Voyageur, Représentant, Placier. nm.
A term covering all travelling sales personnel.

### VTT

[ \* ]

Vélo Tout Terrain. nm.
Mountain bike.

### VSD

[ \* ]

Vendredi, Samedi, Dimanche.
A French popular weekly photo news magazine with a 'celeb' orientation.

# Z

## ZAC $\boxed{*}$

Zone d'Aménagement Concerté. nf.

An administrative mechanism to facilitate the urban development of areas declared a priority by facilitating the cooperation between local authorities and private developers.

## ZEP $\boxed{***}$

Zone d'Éducation Prioritaire. nf.

Certain difficult social areas have been declared ZEP. They enjoy more generous financial resources and more favourable teacher-student ratios.

## ZRR $\boxed{*}$

Zone de Revitalisation Rurale. nf.

The name given to a rural area that may enjoy a series of measures designed to redynamize the local economy, e.g. by way of tax breaks for companies setting up business there.

## ZUP $\boxed{*}$

Zone d'Urbanisation Prioritaire. nf.

Forerunner of the ZAC. See above.

# Chapter 15

# Tests

In this chapter, the reader will find 600 questions mostly based on the contents of the book and testing the whole spectrum of cultural references in the French press. For the general reader, these tests can be seen as an entertaining way to check on their general knowledge about France and the French language. For the student working alone, these tests can be a useful tool for self-assessment. For the teacher, these tests can be useful in several ways. They can be used as 'entry' or upstream 'diagnostic' tests for students starting a new course, or as tests for continued assessment. They may also be used as exit tests at the end of a given course, the teacher being free to fix what he or she considers to be a 'pass' mark in the light of previous students' results.

## Test 1: Popular cultural references

1) Which of the following is not an expression associated with French childhood?

a) Jeu de main, jeu de vilain
b) C'est celui qui dit, qui l'est
c) La souris verte
d) Droit dans mes bottes

2) Which of the following is not a song by Serge Gainsbourg?

a) *Sea, sex and sun*
b) *Je t'aime moi non plus*
c) *Le Poinçonneur des Lilas*
d) *Foule sentimentale*

3) Which of the following is not the title of a famous film?

a) *La Grande Vadrouille*
b) *La Bonne du curé*
c) *Elle court, elle court la banlieue*
d) *Le Bonheur est dans le pré*

4) Which of the following is not associated with Sartre and de Beauvoir?

a) La Coupole
b) Les Deux Magots
c) Le Café de Flore
d) Le Pavillon Gabriel

5) Which of the following is not a French cinema classic?

a) *Quai des brumes*
b) *Hôtel du Nord*
c) *La Guerre des Boutons*
d) *Le Passager de la pluie*

6) Find the odd man out among the following slang words.

a) godasses
b) schnouf
c) flingueurs
d) grisbi

7) Which of the following is not a comic strip character?

a) Lucky Luke
b) Astérix
c) Casimir
d) Les Bidochon

8) Programmes unsuitable for young viewers used to be indicated on the TV screen by a

a) colour
b) letter
c) number
d) geometrical form

9) Which is not a supermarket chain in France?

a) Les Mousquetaires
b) U
c) Leclerc
d) FNAC

10) The French prize for the best cinema performances is known as a/an

a) Oscar
b) Molière
c) César
d) 7 d'or

11) Which of the following is a typical cry of the French waiter?

a) 'On a gagné!'
b) 'Approchez Mesdames, Messieurs!'
c) 'Chaud devant!'
d) 'Sous vos applaudissements!'

12) Which of the following is not a famous advertising slogan?

a) 'Le contrat de confiance'
b) 'Sans une Rolex tu as raté ta vie'
c) 'X lave plus blanc'
d) 'Ça déménage'

13) Which of the following is not a famous publicity slogan?

a) 'Tu t'es vu quand t'as bu?'
b) 'Un verre ça va'
c) 'Elle est pas belle la vie?'
d) 'Boire ou conduire il faut choisir'

14) Which is the odd man out?

a) 'Crac, boum, hue'
b) *Et moi et moi et moi*
c) *Paris s'éveille*
d) *Tous les garçons et les filles*

15) Which of the following is not a charitable organization?

a) Les Enfants du marais
b) Emmaüs
c) Les Restos du cœur
d) Le Secours Catholique

16) Which Latin expression is unrelated to France?

a) *e pluribus unum*
b) *fluctuat nec mergitur*

c) *ultima ratio regum*
d) *Docet omnia*

17) What did young French servicemen shout on being demobilized?

a) Merde!
b) Bordel!
c) C'est la quille!
d) L'adjudant aux chiottes!

18) Which is the odd man out among the following prizes? Le Prix

a) Goncourt
b) de Rome
c) Renaudot
d) Interallié

19) Find the odd man out.

a) Theresa
b) Emmanuelle
c) Fouettard
d) Poulard

20) Find the odd man out among the following boulevards.

a) de la Madeleine
b) des Capucines
c) Haussmann
d) Suchet

21) From which famous film does the following (ungrammatical) quote
come: 'Si j'aurais su, j'aurais pas venu?'

a) *La Guerre des Boutons*
b) *Les Allumettes suédoises*
c) *Les Noisettes sauvages*
d) *Quai des brumes*

22) La Loi Carrèze is related to

a) violence on TV
b) real estate surveyance
c) smoking in public places
d) prostitution

23) La Loi Evin is related to

a) the numerus clausus concerning supermarkets
b) the numerus clausus concerning chemists
c) advertising of tobacco and alcohol
d) homosexual relations between consenting adults

24) La Loi Veil is related to

a) racism
b) sects
c) abortion
d) undenominational education

25) Find the odd man out among the following songs.

a) *Le Gorille*
b) *Une Jolie Fleur*
c) *Quand Margot dégrafait son corsage*
d) *Papa Mambo*

26) Traditionally, the lily of the valley is sold on

a) Labour Day
b) Whit Monday
c) 8 May
d) Easter Sunday

27) The operation known as 'pièces jaunes' was launched by Bernadette Chirac to raise money for

a) people with reduced mobility
b) funding hospital infrastructure for children and teenagers
c) AIDS research
d) the homeless

28) 'Poujadisme' was a

a) political movement founded by Pierre Poujade
b) trend in modern art
c) tropical disease
d) royalist political current

29) Find the odd man out.

a) *Prend l'oseille et tire-toi*
b) *On achève bien les chevaux*
c) *Le Train sifflera trois fois*
d) *La Grande Vadrouille*

30) Political demonstrations traditionally start from place de la République and terminate at place

a) de la Concorde
b) de la Bastille
c) de l'Étoile (Charles de Gaulle)
d) de Stalingrad

31) The period of pop music in France corresponding to that of the 1960s in England was known as the

a) go-go
b) chi-chi
c) yé-yé
d) ba-ba

32) The song *Le Temps des cerises* is associated with which historical event? The ...

a) execution of Louis XVI
b) Commune of 1871
c) troop departures of 1914
d) victory of 1918

33) 'La tentation de Venise' refers to

a) an elderly man's desire to have children
b) the desire to have an adulterous affair
c) the wish to drop everything and leave
d) the desire to marry at a ripe old age

34) Find the odd man out.

a) *L'École des Fans*
b) *La tête et les jambes*
c) *Les cinq dernières minutes*
d) *Peur sur la ville*

35) Which song title by La Compagnie Créole has since become a cult phrase?

a) *La Vie en rose*
b) *Je t'aime, moi non plus*
c) *C'est bon pour le moral*
d) *Le Plat Pays*

36) *Le Coup d'État permanent* was written by

a) Charles de Gaulle
b) François Mitterrand
c) Daniel Cohn-Bendit
d) Alain Krivine

37) *La Défaite de la pensée* was written by

a) Alain Minc
b) Emmanuel Todd
c) Alain Finkielkraut
d) Bernard-Henri Lévy

38) The *brasserie* 'La Closerie des Lilas' is associated with which literary name?

a) Verlaine
b) Zola
c) Balzac
d) Flaubert

39) What is the motto of the city of Paris?

a) *fluctuat nec mergitur*
b) *ars longa vita brevis*
c) *Docet omnia*
d) *in cauda venenum*

40) Find the 'Académicien'

a) Zola
b) Molière
c) Descartes
d) Giscard d'Estaing

## Test 2: Famous words

1) Who said 'La propriété, c'est le vol'?

a) Voltaire
b) Jean-Jacques Rousseau
c) Pierre-Joseph Proudhon
d) Louise Michel

2) 'Que d'eau, que d'eau'. These were the words of

a) Napoleon III
b) Jules Grévy
c) Georges Clémenceau
d) Maréchal Mac-Mahon

3) Who reputedly said 'Le 21ème siècle sera spirituel ou il ne sera pas'?

a) André Malraux
b) Jean-Paul Sartre
c) Alain Finkielkraut
d) Simone de Beauvoir

4) Who said 'Les Français sont des veaux'?

a) Charles de Gaulle
b) Napoleon Bonaparte
c) François Mitterrand
d) Jacques Chirac

5) 'Aux grands hommes, la patrie reconnaissante'. On which public building in Paris are these words written?

a) La Madeleine
b) Les Invalides
c) Le Panthéon
d) L'Opéra

6) Who said that the French army was ready 'jusqu'au dernier bouton de guêtre'?

a) Napoleon III
b) Maréchal Massena
c) Napoleon Bonaparte
d) Edmond le Boeuf

7) 'C'est l'histoire d'un mec.' This was the pet phrase of which French comic?

a) Coluche
b) Guy Bedos
c) Fernand Raynaud
d) Louis de Funès

8) 'À l'insu de mon plein gré.' With which sportsman is this phrase associated?

a) Lance Armstrong
b) Richard Virenque
c) Zinedine Zidane
d) Didier Drogba

9) Which sentence is not associated with the revolution of 1968?

a) 'Sous les pavés la plage'
b) 'Il est interdit d'interdire'
c) 'Pour vivre heureux vivons cachés'
d) 'Soyons réalistes, demandons l'impossible'

10) 'La justice militaire est à la justice ce que la musique militaire est à la musique.' These are the words of

a) Talleyrand
b) Clémenceau
c) Daladier
d) Châteaubriand

11) 'J'y suis, j'y reste.' Who said these words?

a) Général Nivelle
b) Maréchal Soult
c) Maréchal Massena
d) Maréchal Mac-Mahon

12) Who said 'Le cœur a ses raisons que la raison ne connaît point'?

a) René Descartes
b) Blaise Pascal
c) Auguste Comte
d) Antoine-Laurent de Lavoisier

13) 'Il faut dégraisser le mammouth.' Which minister of education said these words?

a) François Bayrou
b) Luc Ferry
c) Lionel Jospin
d) Claude Allègre

14) Who said 'La France ne peut accueillir toute la misère du monde'?

a) Michel Rocard
b) Jacques Chirac
c) François Mitterrand
d) Jean-Marie Le Pen

15) Who said 'Donnez-moi dix hommes sûrs et je tiens l'Etat'?

a) Joseph Fouché
b) Cardinal Richelieu
c) Cardinal Mazarin
d) Napoleon Bonaparte

16) Who said 'Enrichissez-vous'?

a) Napoleon III
b) François Guizot
c) Georges Clémenceau
d) Pierre Mendès-France

17) Who said 'Familles, je vous hais'?

a) André Gide
b) Jean-Paul Sartre
c) Simone de Beauvoir
d) Louis Aragon

18) 'La force tranquille' was the election slogan of which French president?

a) François Mitterrand
b) Jacques Chirac
c) Giscard d'Estaing
d) Nicolas Sarkozy

19) Who reputedly said 'La garde meurt mais ne se rend pas'?

a) Napoléon Bonaparte
b) Général Cambronne
c) Maréchal Mac-Mahon
d) Général Nivelle

20) Who said 'Mon Dieu, gardez-moi de mes amis, mes ennemis, je m'en charge'?

a) Rousseau
b) Gide
c) Bernanos
d) Voltaire

21) Who wrote 'Couvrez ce sein que je ne saurais voir'?

a) Beaumarchais
b) Molière
c) La Fontaine
d) Diderot

22) 'Ce n'est pas la girouette qui tourne, mais le vent.' These words by Camille Desmoulins were popularized by which politician of the Vth Republic?

a) Edgar Faure
b) Jacques Chirac
c) Georges Pompidou
d) Charles de Gaulle

23) Which comic wrote 'Construisons la ville à la campagne'?

a) Raymond Devos
b) George Bernanos
c) Jules Renard
d) Alphonse Allais

24) Who had as his motto 'jusqu'où ne montera-il pas'?

a) Charles Pasqua
b) Nicolas Sarkozy
c) Jean Tibéri
d) Nicolas Fouquet

25) Who wrote 'Il faut cultiver son jardin'?

a) Voltaire
b) Rousseau

c) Louis XIV

d) Louis XVIII

26) Who said 'Un ministre ça ferme sa gueule ou ça démissionne'?

a) Charles de Gaulle

b) Jean-Pierre Chevènement

c) Giscard d'Estaing

d) François Mitterrand

27) 'Casse-toi, pauvre con.' These words were said by Nicolas Sarkozy

a) at the Paris Agricultural Show

b) in the port of Guilvinec

c) in Argenteuil

d) in the town of Gandrange

28) Who wrote 'Quand la Chine s'éveillera, le monde tremblera'?

a) Alain Peyrefitte

b) Charles de Gaulle

c) Napoleon Bonaparte

d) André Malraux

29) Who said 'La Bourse, j'en ai rien à cirer!'?

a) Édith Cresson

b) Pierre Bérégovoy

c) Laurent Fabius

d) François Mitterrand

30) 'Un détail de l'histoire' is associated with which politician?

a) François Mitterrand

b) Jean-Marie Le Pen

c) Talleyrand

d) Charles de Gaulle

31) Which politician popularized the term, first coined by Rimbaud, 'abra-cadabrantesque'?

a) Nicolas Sarkozy

b) Alain Juppé

c) Jacques Chirac
d) Martine Aubry

32) Who said 'l'actionnaire, c'est moi'?

a) Louis XIV
b) Nicolas Sarkozy
c) Charles de Gaulle
d) Alain Juppé

33) Who said 'mon adversaire, celui de la France, n'a jamais cessé d'être l'argent'?

a) Nicolas Sarkozy
b) Jacques Delors
c) Pierre Mendès-France
d) Charles de Gaulle

34) Who is supposed to have said 'Trouvez-moi un normalien qui sache écrire'?

a) Charles de Gaulle
b) Georges Pompidou
c) Jacques Chirac
d) Giscard d'Estaing

35) Who called the Senate 'une anomalie démocratique'?

a) Robert Hue
b) Pierre Mendès-France
c) Lionel Jospin
d) Marie-George Buffet

36) Who wrote the words of the motto of the newpaper *Le Figaro* 'Sans la liberté de blâmer il n'est point d'éloge flatteur'?

a) Victor Hugo
b) Molière
c) Albert Camus
d) Beaumarchais

37) Who said 'Je suis droit dans mes bottes'?

a) Jean Tibéri
b) Charles Pasqua

c) Alain Juppé

d) Bernard Tapie

38) Who said 'La guerre est une affaire trop sérieuse pour être confiée à des aux militaires'?

a) Georges Clémenceau

b) Charles de Gaulle

c) Napoleon

d) Philippe Pétain

39) Who said 'Remember that there is not one of you who does not carry in his cartridge pouch the marshal's baton of the Duke of Reggio'? Louis

a) XIV

b) XV

c) XVI

d) XVIII

40) Who said 'La politique de la France ne se fait pas à la corbeille'?

a) Jacques Delors

b) Édith Cresson

c) Charles de Gaulle

d) François Mitterrand

41) 'Les copains et les coquins' was a reference to which political party?

a) PC

b) RPR

c) PS

d) UDF

42) Which expression is not associated with a scandal of the Vth Republic?

a) 'Donnez le temps au temps'

b) 'Pschitt!'

c) 'Pour fluidifier les relations sociales'

d) 'Je suis droit dans mes bottes'

43) Which sentence was not used by a modern French politician?

a) 'Lui c'est lui, moi c'est moi'

b) 'Parce que c'était lui, parce que c'était moi'

c) 'Qui va garder les enfants?'
d) 'Le meilleur d'entre nous'

44) Which sentence did General de Gaulle not say?

a) 'Je vous ai compris'
b) 'Il n'est de richesse que d'hommes'
c) 'La réforme oui, la chienlit, non'
d) 'Un quarteron de généraux'

45) Which sentence was not said by a socialist politician?

a) 'Les têtes vont tomber'
b) 'Responsable mais pas coupable'
c) 'Tous les matins en me rasant'
d) 'La France ne peut accueillir toute la misère du monde'

46) Which sentence was not said by Jacques Chirac?

a) 'On aperçoit le bout du tunnel'
b) 'Trop d'impôts tuent l'impôt'
c) 'Travailler plus pour gagner plus'
d) 'Mangez des pommes'

47) The term 'aller au charbon' is associated with which politician?

a) Jacques Delors
b) Pierre Mauroy
c) Pierre Bérégovoy
d) Raymond Barre

48) Who said 'When I want to bury a question, I create a commission'?

a) Georges Clémenceau
b) Napoleon III
c) Charles de Gaulle
d) Valéry Giscard d'Estaing

49) Who said 'J'ai survécu' in reply to the question 'What did you do during
the Revolution'?

a) Vidocq
b) Fouché

c) Talleyrand
d) Louis XVIII

50) Which sentence was not spoken by Nicolas Sarkozy?

a) 'J'irai chercher la croissance avec les dents'
b) 'Je serai le président du pouvoir d'achat'
c) 'C'est tout de même incroyable'
d) 'Les Français ont la mémoire courte'

## Test 3: Figurative expressions

1) Find the odd man out.

a) à bride abattue
b) tailler des croupières
c) prendre le mors aux dents
d) un pied à l'étrier

2) Find the odd man out.

a) sonner l'hallali
b) être aux abois
c) entrer en lice
d) lâcher la meute

3) Find the odd man out.

a) le branle-bas de combat
b) battre en brèche
c) convoquer le ban et l'arrière-ban
d) blanchi sous le harnois/harnais

4) Find the odd man out.

a) de but en blanc
b) à brûle pourpoint
c) ne pas aller par quatre chemins
d) une levée de boucliers

5) Find the odd man out.

a) Jarnac
b) pied de l'âne

c) citron
d) bas

6) Find the odd man out.

a) crier haro sur le …
b) tirer à boulets …
c) une volée de bois …
d) cousu de fil …

7) Find the odd man out.

a) boire en Suisse
b) en catimini
c) filer à l'anglaise
d) avoir du plomb dans l'aile

8) Find the odd man out.

a) jeter de l'huile sur le …
b) … d'escampette
c) mettre le feu aux …
d) …aux yeux

9) Find the odd man out.

a) tirer au flanc
b) coincer la bulle
c) glander
d) pousser des cris d'orfraie

10) Find the odd man out.

a) les ballets …
b) soigné aux petits …
c) la pièce était un …
d) les … sont cuites

11) Find the odd man out.

a) passer à tabac
b) tourner casaque
c) passer armes et bagages
d) retourner sa veste

12) Find the odd man out.

a) passer l'arme à gauche
b) revenir bredouille
c) clamser
d) lâcher la rampe

13) L'auberge espagnole is a place where

a) the food is exceptionally bad
b) one can only drink
c) one eats and drinks what one brings
d) prices are exceptionally high

14) Find the odd man out.

a) un coup de Jarnac
b) à fleurets mouchetés
c) d'estoc et de taille
d) vendre la mèche

15) Find the odd man out.

a) ne pas être dans son …
b) s'en laver les …
c) changer son fusil d' …
d) casser du sucre sur le …

16) Find the odd man out: comme

a) à la parade
b) de sa première chaussette
c) de l'an 40
d) d'une guigne

17) Find the odd man out.

a) battre de l'aile
b) avoir du plomb dans l'aile
c) tourner casaque
d) prendre l'eau

18) Un secret de Polichinelle is

a) an absolute secret
b) a secret that is common knowledge

c) a secret that only a few people know
d) a secret which is known by everybody but individually

19) payer 'rubis sur l'ongle' means

a) to pay late
b) never to pay
c) to pay cash
d) to pay in kind

20) Find the odd man out.

a) couleuvre
b) chapeau
c) pilule
d) cravate

21) 'avoir du pain sur la planche' means to

a) have a lot of money
b) have one's work cut out
c) be in a critical situation
d) owe a big debt

22) Find the common word

a) faire flèche de tout ...
b) le ... dont on fait des flûtes
c) le ... dont je me chauffe
d) langue de ...

23) Which is the odd man out?

a) âne
b) phrygien
c) blanc
d) bleu

24) Une 'bouchée de pain' is a small

a) snack
b) price
c) child
d) prize

25) The word 'braquet' means

a) a hold-up
b) stale water
c) a musical instrument
d) a cycle gear

26) Find the common element

a) debout
b) avoir
c) marées
d) brasser

27) Find the common element

a) sœur
b) blague
c) pâte
d) étoile

28) Find the odd man out.

a) caïd
b) toubib
c) bled
d) burka

29) Find the common element.

a) … de commandes
b) … d'adresses
c) … de chèques
d) … de notes

30) Find the odd man out.

a) butin
b) agapes
c) apôtres
d) cénacle

31) Find the odd man out.

a) courgettes
b) épinards

c) choux
d) carottes

32) Find the common element.

a) canif
b) balai
c) cœur
d) chaleur

33) 'il y a de l'eau dans le gaz' means

a) there is trouble brewing
b) one has to tone down one's pretensions
c) two things are irreconcilable
d) the weather is going to be stormy

34) 'n'y voir que du feu' means

a) to be pessimistic
b) to be the life and soul of the party
c) to be totally taken in
d) to look at life through rose-coloured glasses.

35) 'C'est l'hôpital qui se moque ...' Complete this expression.

a) du dispensaire
b) de la charité
c) de l'aumône
d) de la générosité

36) 'avoir des oursins dans les poches' means to be

a) prudential
b) stingy
c) frightened
d) generous

37) Which is the odd man out?

a) nez
b) voiture
c) jeton
d) cul

38) What is the common element among the following?

a) croiser le …
b) battre le …
c) porter le …
d) un bras de …

39) Which is the odd man out?

a) le bâton
b) cuites
c) les bœuf- (*sic*)
d) les poireaux

40) To get one's kicks is 'prendre son

a) pied
b) doigt
c) miel
d) jus

## Test 4: Headline punning

Puns are frequently based on the use of homophones. Find one homophone for each of the following words:

1) air
2) fin
3) saint
4) maire
5) gêne
6) coût
7) tante
8) heure
9) faux taux
10) maux
11) Anvers
12) mâle
13) de boue
14) chant
15) Delhi
16) tromper
17) d'hiver

18) voit
19) hasch
20) faucon

Puns are frequently based on the use of homonyms. Find a second meaning for the following words.

21) 'traite' a credit repayment or ...
22) 'action' movement or ...
23) 'bidon' phoney or ...
24) 'noir' darkness or ...
25) 'bretelle' slip road or ...

What should the word in bold type have originally been?

26) '**Paix** de lapin'.
27) '**Show** et froid'.
28) '**Délit** réalité'.
29) 'La chasse à la baleine ... **cétacé**'.
30) 'Le **veilleur** entre nous'.

## Test 5: Literary references

1) *La Clémence d'Auguste* was written by

a) Corneille
b) Racine
c) Molière
d) Diderot

2) *On ne badine pas avec l'amour* is tinged with

a) political intrigue
b) chivalry
c) adultery
d) anti-clericalism

3) Which work was not written by Proust?

a) *Du côté de chez Swann*
b) *Les Filles en fleur*
c) *Contre Sainte Beuve*
d) *Le Bateau ivre*

4) From which of La Fontaine's fables are the following sentences taken: 'quand la bise fut venue', 'dansez maintenant', 'crier famine'?

a) *La Cigale et la Fourmi*
b) *Le Vieux Lion*
c) *Le Lièvre et la Tortue*
d) *Les Animaux malades de la peste*

5) Who wrote the words 'luxe, calme et volupté'?

a) Baudelaire
b) Rimbaud
c) Lamartine
d) Hugo

6) Complete the sentence from Cyrano de Bergerac's 'tirade du nez'. 'Que dis-je c'est un cap C'est

a) une île
b) un continent
c) une péninsule
d) un isthme

7) In which play by Corneille does the character of Chimène appear?

a) *Le Cid*
b) *Horace*
c) *Médée*
d) *Polyeucte*

8) 'Le cœur a ses raisons, que la raison ne connaît point' comes from

a) *Les Pensées*
b) *Les Femmes savantes*
c) *Le Cid*
d) *Phèdre*

9) 'Tu me fends le cœur.' These words are spoken by which character in Marcel Pagnol's trilogy *Marius, Fanny, César*?

a) Fanny
b) Panisse
c) Escartefigue
d) César

10) 'Ô rage! Ô désespoir!' In *Le Cid* these words are spoken by

a) Don Arias
b) Don Rodrigue
c) Don Diègue
d) Chimène

11) The character of Cosette in *Les Misérables* evokes

a) a simpleton
b) a thief
c) frivolity
d) material deprivation

12) 'Le coup de pied de l'âne' is an expression that comes from which fable of La Fontaine?

a) *L'Âne et le Vieillard*
b) *L'Âne et le Cheval*
c) *Le Lion devenu vieux*
d) *Les Animaux malades de la peste*

13) 'Couvrez ce sein que je ne saurais voir' comes from

a) *Les Femmes savantes*
b) *Le Bourgeois Gentilhomme*
c) *L'École des femmes*
d) *Tartuffe*

14) 'Il faut cultiver son jardin.' This comes from which book by Voltaire?

a) *Candide*
b) *Zadig*
c) *Mahomet*
d) *Micromégas*

15) 'Demain, dès l'aube, à l'heure où blanchit la campagne.' These words of Victor Hugo were addressed to his

a) brother
b) sister
c) daughter
d) wife

16) Who was the author of this line: 'un seul être vous manque et tout est dépeuplé'?

a) Rimbaud
b) Lamartine
c) Hugo
d) de Musset

17) Diafoirus is a character in which play by Molière?

a) *Le Malade imaginaire*
b) *Tartuffe*
c) *Le Bourgeois Gentilhomme*
d) *Les Fourberies de Scapin*

18) *L'Éducation sentimentale* was written by

a) Honoré de Balzac
b) Gustave Flaubert
c) Victor Hugo
d) André Gide

19) 'Puisque ces mystères nous dépassent, feignons d'en être les organisateurs.' These words were written by

a) Georges Bernanos
b) Jean Cocteau
c) Alphonse Allais
d) Jules Romains

20) *Les Fleurs du Mal* was written by

a) Baudelaire
b) Rimbaud
c) Gide
d) Lamartine

21) Which phrase was not written by Molière?

a) 'qu'allait-il faire dans cette galère?'
b) 'purgare, saignare'
c) 'couvrez ce sein'
d) 'je suis né vraiment de ta lèvre'

22) The words of Jules Romains in the play *Knock* 'Ça vous chatouille ou ça vous gratouille?' were immortalized by which French actor?

a) Raimu
b) Louis de Funès
c) Louis Jouvet
d) Jean-Louis Barrault

23) The most frequently quoted of La Fontaine's fables is *Les Animaux malades de la peste*. Which words below do not come from this fable?

a) 'crier haro sur le baudet'
b) 'tous ne mouraient pas'
c) 'que vous serez puissant ou misérable'
d) 'la part du lion'

24) Harpagon is a character in which of Molière's plays?

a) *Le Malade imaginaire*
b) *Les Fourberies de Scapin*
c) *Tartuffe*
d) *L'Avare*

25) *L'Invitation au Voyage* was written by

a) Rimbaud
b) Proust
c) Baudelaire
d) de Musset

26) Who wrote the words 'qu'importe le flacon pourvu que l'on ait l'ivresse'?

a) Lamartine
b) Rimbaud
c) Baudelaire
d) de Musset

27) *J'irai cracher sur vos tombes* was written by

a) André Gide
b) Boris Vian
c) Jean-Paul Sartre
d) Baudelaire

28) Which phrase was not written by La Fontaine?

a) 'sur un arbre perché'
b) 'tous étaient affectés'
c) 'tirer les marrons du feu'
d) 'mignonne, allons voir si la rose'

29)'La madeleine de Proust' refers to

a) a close lady friend
b) an alcoholic beverage
c) a small sweet
d) the trigger of childhood memories

30) Which animal is closely associated with the poetry of Stéphane Mallarmé? The

a) eagle
b) swan
c) lamb
d) dove

31) 'Mon père, … au sourire si doux'. Complete this line.

a) ce héros
b) ce géant
c) ce soldat
d) cet homme

32) Which animals are associated with Panurge?

a) sheep
b) calves
c) cows
d) chickens

33) 'OTAN suspend ton vol.' This is a pun on the words of

a) Lamartine
b) de Musset
c) Proust
d) Rimbaud

34) *La Peau de chagrin* is the title of a book by

a) Hugo
b) Flaubert

c) Balzac

d) Gide

35) 'On a souvent besoin de plus petit que soi.' From which fable by La Fontaine does this expression come?

a) *Le Lion et le Rat*

b) *L'Hirondelle et les Petits Oiseaux*

c) *La Cigale et la Fourmi*

d) *Le Savetier et le Financier*

36) Pomponette is the name of a cat in which Pagnol novel?

a) *César*

b) *Marius*

c) *Fanny*

d) *La Femme du boulanger*

37) Which politician spoke disparagingly about *La Princesse de Clèves?*

a) Alain Juppé

b) Nicolas Sarkozy

c) Jean Tibéri

d) Jacques Chirac

38) Which of Molière's characters had been speaking prose for 40 years without knowing it?

a) Diafoirus

b) Harpagon

c) Géronte

d) M. Jourdain

39) Which English quotation in French translation is not used in French?

a) 'être ou ne pas être'

b) 'il y a quelque chose de pourri au royaume de'

c) 'des larmes et du sang'

d) 'confiture hier, confiture demain, jamais confiture aujourd'hui'

40) In the novel by Victor Hugo, *Les Misérables*, what does the couple Thénardier evoke?

a) generosity

b) exploitation

c) bravery

d) fervent spiritual beliefs

41) The expression 'tour d'ivoire' was used by

a) Sainte Beuve
b) de Vigny
c) M. Villemin
d) Lamartine

42) Who wrote 'Heureux qui comme Ulysse a fait un grand voyage'?

a) Ronsard
b) du Bellay
c) de Vigny
d) Rabelais

43) Complete the words of Victor Hugo: 'Waterloo, Waterloo, Waterloo ... plaine'.

a) triste
b) pale
c) morne
d) aigre

44) In the fable *La Lièvre et la Tortue* we can read: 'Rien ne sert de courir, il faut partir...'

a) à point
b) pile à l'heure
c) de bonheur
d) à temps

45) Which play was not written by Molière?

a) *Polyeucte*
b) *Le Malade imaginaire*
c) *L'Avare*
d) *Le Bourgeois Gentilhomme*

46) 'Là bas, tout n'est ... et beauté'. Complete the phrase.

a) qu'ordre
b) qu'art

c) que joie
d) que paix

47) Which of La Fontaine's fables illustrates the moral that it is better to have a wise enemy than a stupid friend?

a) *Le Lion et le Rat*
b) *La Cigale et la Fourmi*
c) *Les Animaux malades de la peste*
d) *Le Pavé de l'ours*

48) The French title *Le Meilleur des mondes*, which is the translation of the English title *Brave New World*, comes from

a) *Zadig*
b) *Mahomet*
c) *Mérope*
d) *Candide*

49) Which author is associated with the motif of *carpe diem*?

a) Rabelais
b) Ronsard
c) Gide
d) Sartre

50) Which book was not written by Simone de Beauvoir?

a) *Bonjour tristesse*
b) *Mémoires d'une jeune fille rangée*
c) *L'Invitée*
d) *La Force de l'âge*

## Test 6: Historical references

1) Find the odd one out

a) Transnonain
b) Sétif
c) Saint Barthélemy
d) Saint Germain

2) The national workshops were set up in

a) 1789
b) 1830

c) 1848

d) 1945

3) Find the odd man out among these feudal terms.

a) le droit de cuissage

b) la dime

c) la corvée

d) la gabelle

4) On the storming of the Bastille, how many prisoners were released?

a) Under a half dozen

b) 50

c) 100

d) 300

5) *La Belle Époque* corresponds to which decade?

a) 1880–90

b) 1890–1900

c) 1900–10

d) 1910–20

6) If Waterloo is figuratively speaking 'a final defeat', which battle is synonymous with 'rout'?

a) Salamanca

b) Ciudad Rodrigo

c) Bérézina

d) Bayonne

7) In the French Revolutionary calendar, 'Brumaire' was

a) foggy

b) rainy

c) blowy

d) flowery

8) *La Cagoule* was

a) a pro *Algérie Française* organization

b) an extreme right-wing movement active in the 1930s

c) an anti-terrorist movement of the 1960s
d) a movement for the liberation of Corsica

9) To make a pilgrimage to Canossa means

a) to flee
b) to take French leave
c) to make a humiliating apology
d) to be sent to Coventry

10) The 'canuts'

a) were agricultural labourers in the Vendée
b) were mutineers in the French navy
c) were workers in revolt in the Lyons silk industry
d) is a slang expression for 'shoes'

11) The Abbé Cauchon is famous for having been

a) the president of the ecclesiastical court that sentenced Jeanne d'Arc to death
b) a Catholic martyr shot by the Communards in 1871
c) a hero of the resistance in the Second World War
d) the name of an orange-flavoured liqueur

12) Champollion

a) invented a new weaving machine
b) was three-times winner of the Tour de France
c) was the first to decrypt the hieroglyphs on the Rosetta Stone
d) is a famous brand of Savoy cheese

13) In which year did Napoleon III carry out his *coup d'état*?

a) 1847
b) 1848
c) 1850
d) 1851

14) *Le Discours de la méthode* was written by

a) Le Cardinal de Retz
b) Blaise Pascal
c) René Descartes
d) Émile Durkheim

15) 'Je fais à la France le don de ma personne pour atténuer son malheur.'
When were these words spoken?

a) During the Festival of the Supreme Being in 1794
b) On the coronation of Napoleon as Emperor in 1804
c) When full powers were given to the régime of Vichy in 1940
d) At the time when de Gaulle became the first president of the Vth Republic
in 1958

16) Under the terms of which 'edict' or 'ordonnance' was the French language made the official language of France?

a) Nantes 1598
b) l'Union 1532
c) Saint Germain 1679
d) Villers-Cotterêts 1539

17) The *éminence grise* was a Capuchin father who was the discreet advisor of

a) Catherine de Médici
b) François I$^{er}$
c) le Cardinal Richelieu
d) le Cardinal Mazarin

18) François Mitterrand became leader of the socialist party at the
Congrès de

a) Rennes
b) Épinay
c) Lyon
d) Strasbourg

19) 'Les Rois Fainéants' were of which dynasty?

a) Merovingian
b) Carolingian
c) Capetitian
d) Valois

20) Félix Faure, 'le Président du Conseil', died in rather amusing circumstances; he

a) fell from a train in his sleep
b) died after the exertions of a session with his mistress

c) died in a brothel

d) died during an orgy with underage boys

21) Who built the château of Vaux le Vicomte?

a) Nicolas Fouquet

b) François I<sup>er</sup>

c) Louis XIV

d) Napoleon Bonaparte

22) In which luxury restaurant did Nicolas Sarkozy celebrate his victory in the 2007 presidential election?

a) Maxim's

b) Le Doyen

c) Le Véfour

d) Fouquet's

23) Which historical reference is used as a synonym of revolt? La

a) claque

b) fronde

c) cabale

d) dupe

24) *Le Grand Siècle* was the century of

a) Hugues Capet

b) François I<sup>er</sup>

c) Louis XIV

d) Napoleon Bonaparte

25) Napoleon's soldiers were known as les

a) grognards

b) barbouzes

c) poilus

d) hussards

26) The Jacobins were so called because

a) their meetings were held in a building in the rue Jacob in Paris

b) their leader's first name was Jacob

c) their leader's first name was Jacques (derived from the Hebrew Jacobus)
d) they used to meet in the convent of Saint Jacques run by the Dominicans

27) The famous French law related to the press was passed in

a) 1794
b) 1881
c) 1901
d) 1905

28) Undenominational education is associated with the name of

a) Georges Clémenceau
b) Napoleon III
c) Jules Ferry
d) Pierre Mendès-France

29) Which king succeeded Louis XVIII?

a) Louis XIX
b) Charles X
c) Louis Philippe
d) Napoleon III

30) 'La Veuve Scarron' is better known by the name of

a) Joséphine Béarnais
b) Madame de Pompadour
c) Madame de Maintenon
d) Madame de Staël

31) Marthe Richard is famous for having been

a) an emblematic figure of the Commune
b) the first woman minister
c) the person behind the law closing brothels in France
d) the woman who promoted women's rights to abortion

32) Mers el Kébir was

a) the place where the Algerian war of independence broke out in 1954
b) the rallying point for the free French forces in North Africa in 1940
c) one of Napoleon's naval victories against the English in 1802
d) the port where the French fleet was sunk by the British navy in 1940

33) Who is supposed to have said 'Paris is worth a mass'?

a) Henri III
b) Henri IV
c) Louis XI
d) Louis XIII

34) 'La nuit du 4 août' refers to which famous event: the

a) storming of the Bastille?
b) execution of Louis XVI?
c) interception of Louis XVI at Varennes?
d) abolition of privileges in 1789?

35) 'Le panache blanc' is supposed to have been the rallying point of the soldiers of

a) Henri IV
b) Saint Louis
c) François I$^{er}$
d) Louis XIV

36) Which army did Charles Martel defeat in Poitiers? The

a) English
b) Dutch
c) Spaniards
d) Muslims

37) Which king is associated with the dish 'poule au pot'?

a) Louis IX
b) Henri IV
c) François I$^{er}$
d) Louis XVIII

38) Which king was known as 'the locksmith king'? Louis

a) XIII
b) XIV
c) XVI
d) XVIII

39) Which King Louis had the nickname 'Saint' Louis?

a) IX
b) X

c) XI

d) XIII

40) 'Surcouf' was the name of a

a) French quisling

b) secret society

c) famous soldier

d) famous corsair

41) Which French defeat is the odd man out?

a) Waterloo

b) Sedan

c) Bérézina

d) Trafalgar

42) 'Les Trente Glorieuses' cover the period

a) 1840–70

b) 1870–1900

c) 1900–30

d) 1945–75

43) In what year did Louis XVI flee to Varennes?

a) 1792

b) 1791

c) 1790

d) 1789

44) In July 1942, the Jews rounded up in the raids in Paris were taken to which sports stadium before being deported to Auschwitz? Le

a) Vélodrome d'Hiver

b) Stade de France

c) Stade Charlety

d) Parc des Princes

45) Vercingétorix died

a) at the battle of Alésia

b) in bed of old age

c) beheaded by Caesar
d) strangled in prison

46) Find the odd man out.

a) Vidocq
b) Fouché
c) Pasqua
d) Jospin

47) Paul de Gondi is better known by the name

a) Le Cardinal Mazarin
b) Le Cardinal Richelieu
c) L'éminence grise
d) Le Cardinal de Retz

48) In which cathedral were the kings of France traditionally crowned?

a) Notre Dame de Paris
b) Chartres
c) Strasbourg
d) Reims

49) The patron saint of Paris is Saint

a) Barthélemy
b) Denis
c) Jacques
d) Augustin

50) Sophie Rostopchine is better known by the name

a) Madame de Staël
b) Madame Necker
c) Madame de Montespan
d) La Comtesse de Ségur

## Tests 7 and 8: Mythological, Classical and Biblical references

1) Les 'agapes' was originally a meal taken together by the early Christians.
(T)rue or (F)alse?

2) 'Babylone' literally means 'gate of heaven'. T or F?

3) Un 'boisseau' is a measure of grain. T or F?

4) The 'bouc émissaire' was killed to atone for the sins of the children of Israel. T or F?

5) Each of the four horsemen of the Apocalypse had a horse of a different colour. T or F?

6) The 'cénacle' was the chest in which the Covenant was kept. T or F?

7) 'Tohu-bohu' is the term referring to the original chaos. T or F?

8) 'Semer la zizanie' originally meant to sow tares in the field of wheat. T or F?

9) A 'crible' is a kind of sieve. T or F?

10) A long journey during which a spiritual conversion takes place is known as 'the road to Canossa'. T or F?

11) 'Épiphanie' derives form Greek meaning 'appearance'. T or F?

12) 'Golgotha' is the Greek term meaning 'place of the skeleton'. T or F?

13) 'Sauterelles' were the seventh plague of Egypt. T or F?

14) 'Iota' is the smallest letter in the Greek alphabet. T or F?

15) Although Job was poor, he had once been very rich. T or F?

16) 'Un plat de lentilles' is translated by 'a mess of pottage'. T or F?

17) 'La paille' can be translated by the word 'mote'. T or F?

18) 'Pandemonium' originally meant 'abode of all the demons'. T or F?

19) 'Sicaires' was the name given to terrorist zealots in Palestine who fought against the Romans. T or F?

20) Find the odd man out.

a) Jupiter
b) Achille
c) Morphée
d) Protée

21) Who broke her promise to Apollo and as a punishment was never believed, whatever she said?

a) Circé
b) Cassandre
c) Pandore
d) Clytemnestre

22) Find the odd man out.

a) pactole
b) Midas
c) Crésus
d) mânes

23) Which group designates the sons or followers of a great man or woman? Les

a) thébaïdes
b) épigones
c) Atrides
d) Pléiades

24) Who was created as a punishment for man?

a) Pandore
b) Orphée
c) Thémis
d) Clio

25) Find the odd man out.

a) Les Fourches Caudines
b) Etre voué aux gémonies
c) La roche Tarpéienne
d) Le Toison d'or

26) Who is the odd man out?

a) Homer
b) Jupiter
c) Titan
d) Icare

27) Which mythical animal is associated with the name of a French politician?

a) le phénix
b) le cerbère
c) l'hydre
d) le centaure

28) Which classical character is associated with defying the law in favour of one's conscience?

a) Hélène
b) Antigone
c) Diogène
d) Cincinnatus

29) Find the odd man out.

a) Ariane
b) Dédale
c) Labyrinthe
d) Chimère

30) Find the odd man out.

a) Phryné
b) Egérie
c) Cerbère
d) Harpie

## Test 9a: Who's who

1) Who among the following has never been president of France?

a) Jacques Chirac
b) François Mitterrand
c) Valéry Giscard d'Estaing
d) Lionel Jospin

2) Which of the following politicians is not an *énarque*?

a) Giscard d'Estaing
b) Jacques Chirac
c) Nicolas Sarkozy
d) François Hollande

3) Only one woman has ever been prime minister of France; who was she?

a) Elisabeth Guigou
b) Édith Cresson
c) Martine Aubry
d) Ségolène Royal

4) What do these politicians have in common?

a) Claude Allègre
b) Jack Lang
c) Lionel Jospin
d) Xavier Darcos

5) Who was the 'Garde des Sceaux' when the death penalty was abolished in France?

a) Robert Badinter
b) Alain Peyrefitte
c) Rachida Dati
d) Michèle Alliot-Marie

6) Who, among the following, was the only politician not to have committed suicide or been 'suicided'?

a) Edgar Faure
b) François de Grossouvre
c) Robert Boulin
d) Pierre Bérégovoy

7) President Georges Pompidou was an *agrégé*. T or F?

8) Who is the odd woman out?

a) Claire Chazal
b) Dominique Voynet
c) Christine Ockrent
d) Marie Drucker

9) Who was not a member of the extreme right-wing organization Occident?

a) Alain Madelin
b) Patrick Devedjian
c) Gérard Longuet
d) François Léotard

10) Who is the odd man out among the following *énarques*?

a) Laurent Fabius
b) François Hollande
c) François Léotard
d) Gérard Longuet

11) Who is the odd man out?

a) Daniel Cohn-Bendit
b) Dominique Voynet
c) Noël Mamère
d) Yves Jego

12) One of these sentences is not true, which one?

a) Jean-Paul Huchon is an *énarque*
b) His *promotion* at l'ENA was Rabelais
c) He is president of the *Conseil Général* of Île de France
d) His appeal to the Supreme Court is pending

13) Anne Pingeot was

a) at school with François Mitterrand
b) the name of his first wife
c) the mother of his illegitimate daughter
d) minister of labour in the first government of Pierre Mauroy

14) What do the following politicians have in common?

a) Nicolas Sarkozy
b) Patrick Devedjian
c) Arnaud Montebourg
d) Jean-Louis Borloo

15) The name of the head of the French employers' confederation is

a) Roselyne Bachelot
b) Nadine Moreno
c) Laurence Parisot
d) Christine Boutin

16) One of the sentences concerning Ségolène Royal is wrong; which one?

a) She was in the same year at *l'ENA* (Voltaire) as Dominique de Villepin
b) She was born in what was then French West Africa

c) She divorced François Hollande in 2007
d) Many new humorous substantives have been created thanks to her

17) The luxury goods empire LVMH belongs to

a) François Pinault
b) Bernard Arnault
c) Francis Bouygues
d) Arnaud Lagardère

18) Which politician's name do the following words evoke?

a) le vrai-faux passeport
b) le SAC
c) the accent of the midi
d) Angolagate

19) One of the sentences is incorrect; which one?

a) Alain Minc was 'major' of his year at *l'ENA*
b) The name of his year at l'ENA was Rabelais
c) He was sentenced to a fine of 100,000 francs for plagiarism
d) His father was a Polish dentist

20) One of the sentences concerning François Bayrou is incorrect; which one? He

a) is an *agrégé*
b) has written a best-seller about the life of Henri IV de France
c) is a pig breeder in the south west of France
d) was once minister of education

## Test 9b: Nicknames

1) 'L'agité du bocage' refers to

a) Jean-Pierre Raffarin
b) Charles Pasqua
c) Philippe de Villiers
d) François Bayrou

2) Anastasie is another name for

a) a bigot
b) a Bible thumper

c) a hypocrite
d) censorship

3) Which of these nicknames is not a nickname of Lionel Jospin?

a) Lolo
b) Yo-yo
c) L'austère qui se marre
d) L'exilé de l'Île de Ré

4) 'L'Avionneur' is the nickname of

a) Arnaud Lagardère
b) Serge Dassault
c) Jean-Luc Lagardère
d) Louis Schweitzer

5) 'Le Turc de Smyrne' refers to

a) Patrick Balkany
b) Nicolas Sarkozy
c) Patrick Devedjian
d) Edouard Balladur

6) 'Le barde', 'le scribe' and 'le fou du roi' are the nicknames of

a) François Bayrou
b) Jean-Pierre Chevènement
c) Henri Guaino
d) Jacques Attali

7) Which of these nicknames is not a nickname of François Bayrou?

a) Le Béarnais
b) motodidacte
c) L'homme des tracteurs
d) L'égocentriste

8) Which of these nicknames is not a nickname of Ségolène Royal?

a) La dame en blanc
b) La Madone du Poitou
c) Mme Michou
d) Mme Veto

9) 'Le Florentin' was a nickname of which president?

a) Valéry Giscard d'Estaing
b) Charles de Gaulle
c) François Mitterrand
d) Jacques Chirac

10) The 'french doctor' (*sic*) and 'l'homme au sac de riz' are the nicknames of

a) François Hollande
b) Bernard Tapie
c) Bernard Kouchner
d) Bernard Debré

11) Les Grimaldi refers to

a) A famous French circus family
b) The royal family of Monaco
c) A group of bank robbers of the 1960s
d) A 5-star restaurant in the sixteenth *arrondissement* of Paris

12) 'Gros Quinquin' refers to

a) Raymond Barre
b) Pierre Mauroy
c) Charles Pasqua
d) Jean-Claude Gaudin

13) 'l'homme du 18 juin' refers to

a) Napoleon Bonaparte
b) General Giroud
c) General de Gaulle
d) Philippe Pétain

14) The expression 'Les hussards noirs de la République' refers to

a) conscripts
b) primary school teachers
c) students at the military academy of St Cyr
d) students at the military school, Polytechnique

15) 'Le journal le mieux informé de France' is

a) *Le Figaro*
b) *Le Canard Enchaîné*

c) *Les Echos*
d) *Le Monde*

16) 'La femme des ménages' refers to

a) Martine Aubry
b) Ségolène Royal
c) Christine Ockrent
d) Christine Boutin

17) 'Le Cardinal' is the nickname of

a) Claude Guéant
b) Henri Guaino
c) Xavier Bertrand
d) Jean-Louis Debré

18) 'Le Phénix du Haut Poitou' refers to

a) Philippe de Villiers
b) François Bayrou
c) Jean-Pierre Raffarin
d) Alain Juppé

19) 'Dix minutes, douche comprise' was the nickname of

a) François Mitterrand
b) Valéry Giscard d'Estaing
c) Jacques Chirac
d) Dominique Strauss-Kahn

20) 'Le premier flic de France' refers to Le

a) Président de la République
b) Premier Ministre
c) Ministre de l'Intérieur
d) Préfet de police de Paris

21) 'Tante Yvonne' was the wife of

a) General de Gaulle
b) François Mitterrand
c) Valéry Giscard d'Estaing
d) Vincent Auriol

22) 'Talonnette' is the nickname of

a) Nicolas Sarkozy
b) Michel Charasse
c) Jacques Attali
d) Xavier Bertrand

23) 'Flanby' is the nickname of

a) Lionel Jospin
b) Nicolas Sarzozy
c) François Hollande
d) Jean-Pierre Raffarin

24) 'Chouchou' is the nickname of

a) Xavier Bertrand
b) Jack Lang
c) Michel Rocard
d) Brice Hortefeux

25) 'La Grande Muette' refers to the

a) army
b) navy
c) air force
d) secret police

## Test 10: What's what

1) Which famous institution was founded by Richelieu in 1634?

a) *Le Collège de France*
b) *L'Académie Française*
c) *La Comédie-Française*
d) *La Cour des Comptes*

2) Arrange the following academic diplomas in growing order of importance

a) *le CAPES*
b) *la licence*
c) *la maîtrise*
d) *l'agrégation*

3) The article of the Constitution which enables the government to push through legislation without a parliamentary vote is article

a) 49.3
b) 49.4
c) 49.5
d) 49.6

4) The rue d'Assas is synonymous with the faculty of

a) medicine
b) law
c) theology
d) music

5) The building in which the National Assembly is housed is known as Le Palais

a) du Luxembourg
b) Bourbon
c) Royal
d) Brogniart

6) An association set up as a non-profit-making organization is regulated under the terms of the law of

a) 1848
b) 1881
c) 1901
d) 1905

7) Which one of the following is not a famous Parisian hospital?

a) Necker
b) Cochin
c) Baudeloque
d) Le Marais

8) The Caisse des dépôts et consignations was originally a financial institution set up to

a) finance the revolutionary wars
b) finance the Napoleonic wars
c) fund French industry
d) restore confidence in French finances after the war years 1792–1815

9) Arrange the following in growing order of importance

a) *Le Tribunal d'Instance*
b) *La Cour de Cassation*
c) *La Cour d'Appel*
d) *La Tribunal de Grande Instance*

10) Arrange the following in growing order of size

a) *l'arrondissement*
b) *la région*
c) *le département*
d) *le canton*

11) The 17ème Chambre Correctionnelle is usually the court handling cases involving

a) driving offences
b) debts and repossessions
c) the press
d) illegal immigrants

12) Which sentence is incorrect?

a) The diploma of the Collège de France is one of the most prestigious
b) The Collège de France was founded by François I$^{er}$
c) Its motto is *Docet omnia*
d) It is located near the Sorbonne

13) Which sentence is incorrect?

a) *La Comédie-Française* was founded by Louis XIV
b) It was dissolved during the French Revolution
c) It was refounded by Napoleon under the Moscow decree
d) It was closely associated with the name of Corneille and Racine

14) Which sentence is incorrect?

a) *Le Conseil Constitutionnel* was set up in 1958
b) Its role is to ensure the consistency of laws with the Constitution
c) It is made up of nine members
d) It is located in the Palais du Luxembourg

15) Which grade is not a grade of members of the Conseil d'État?

a) *inspecteur*
b) *conseiller*
c) *conseiller maître*
d) *maître des requêtes*

16) *Le Conseil Général* is the executive decision-making body at the level of the

a) *arrondissement*
b) *région*
c) *département*
d) *commune*

17) Which sentence is incorrect?

a) The French Constitution of 1958 was the brainchild of Michel Debré
b) It provides for the election of the president by universal suffrage
c) It was born in a time of severe political instability
d) The powers of the president are limited by parliamentary vote

18) *La Cour des Comptes* is located in

a) rue Cambon
b) le Palais Royal
c) rue Grenelle
d) Bercy

19) Which sentence is incorrect?

a) The *départements* were set up during the French Revolution
b) They correspond roughly to a county
c) Their sizing was based on the distance a person could cover on horseback during a day
d) There are twenty-two *départements* in France.

20) Which organization is in charge of managing the property of the State?

a) *La Cour des Comptes*
b) *Le Ministère des Finances*
c) *Les Domaines*
d) *Le Conseil d'État*

21) Find the odd man out.

a) Nicolas Sarkozy
b) Valéry Giscard d'Estaing
c) Jacques Chirac
d) Edouard Balladur

22) Which sentence is correct: *Le Garde des Sceaux* is the

a) minister of justice
b) Keeper of the Seals
c) Speaker of the national assembly
d) minister of finance

23) Which former student of *l'ENA* has never been involved in a corporate disaster?

a) Alain Juppé
b) Jean-Yves Haberer
c) Jean-Marie Messier
d) Daniel Bouton

24) *L'Opéra Garnier* was founded during the

a) First Empire
b) reign of Louis Philippe
c) Second Empire
d) presidency of François Mitterrand

25) 'Ginette' is

a) the affectionate name given to one of the most famous *écoles préparatoires*
b) the name of the restaurant patronized by the MPs of the nearby National Assembly
c) a famous art school
d) the metonymical name for the faculty of medecine

26) Find the odd man out among the following schools

a) Mines
b) Ponts et Chaussées
c) Sup Télécom
d) École Boulle

27) Which *département* is not part of the Île de France Region?

a) Essonne (91)
b) Yvelines (78)
c) Hauts-de-Seine (92)
d) Cher (45)

28) The fifteen best students leaving *l'ENA* are known as

a) *corpsard*
b) *pantouflards*
c) *la botte*
d) *les taupins*

29) Which sentence is incorrect?

a) The Jesuit order was founded by Ignace de Loyala after losing his sight
b) It was the dominant intellectual force of the Counter-Reformation
c) It is also known as the Society of Jesus
d) Its motto is 'Ad majorem Dei gloriam'

30) Which school is not an *école préparatoire*?

a) Louis le Grand
b) Sainte Geneviève
c) Lycée Hoche
d) École des Chartes

31) The French equivalent of the Ideal Home Exhibition takes place every year in May and is held at the Porte

a) des Lilas
b) d'Orléans
c) de Versailles
d) de Pantin

32) Which sentence is incorrect?

a) Polytechnique is one of the greatest *écoles d'ingénieurs*
b) It is also known as 'l'Y'
c) It is a school that has military status
d) A former student tried to assassinate Charles de Gaulle

33) Which is the correct sentence? *Le Prix de Rome* is a

a) scholarship offered to the most gifted student of Italian
b) cash prize granted by the Italian ministry of culture
c) scholarship for students studying modern languages
d) competitive examination; the winner has an all expenses paid stay of six to 18 months in Rome

34) Which sentence is incorrect?

a) Roland Garros was the name of a French pilot
b) He was the first pilot to cross the Mediterranean
c) The tennis stadium of the same name has clay courts
d) The majority of the courts are covered

35) Which sentence is incorrect?

a) The president of the Sénat is the second most important person of the French State
b) He assumes caretaker responsibility if the president is incapacitated
c) Senators are elected by universal suffrage
d) Their term of office is six years

36) Find the odd man out among the following hospitals.

a) Val de Grâce
b) Cochin
c) Les Enfants Malades
d) St Vincent de Paul

37) *Le Prix de Rome* is associated with which of the Italian palaces below?

a) Palais Farnèse
b) Villa Médicis
c) Palais Ferrata
d) Palais Chigi

38) What do these names have in common? Les Baumettes, Fresnes, Fleury Mérogis, La Santé are all

a) hospitals
b) museums
c) castles
d) prisons

39) *La Chancellerie* refers to the

a) ministry of foreign affairs
b) administration of embassies
c) central administration of the ministry of justice
d) ministry of finance

40) Which sentence is incorrect?

a) La Cour de Cassation is the supreme court of appeal in France
b) It retries cases heard by courts of lower jurisdiction
c) There is only one Cour de Cassation in France
d) It is located on the Quai de l'Horloge in Paris

## Test 11: Skeletons in Marianne's cupboard

1) The first medical report establishing a correlation between asbestos and lung cancer dates back to

a) 1900
b) 1918
c) 1960
d) 1997

2) The son of the late President François Mitterrand was charged and found guilty in the Angolagate scandal. T or F?

3) The massacre in Auriol in 1981 was

a) a settling of accounts between two mafia gangs
b) an internal war among members of the SAC
c) a contract killing to silence an informer
d) a burglary that went wrong

4) The scandal of the 'sniffer planes' took place during the presidency of

a) Pompidou
b) Giscard d'Estaing
c) Mitterrand
d) Chirac

5) El Mehdi Ben Barka was an opponent of which regime?

a) Algerian
b) Tunisian

c) Moroccan
d) Libyan

6) Which statement is false?

a) Robert Boulin committed suicide
b) Several critically important exhibits were stolen from the coroner's office
c) His face bore signs of an aggression
d) He was found in 50 cm of water

7) René Bousquet: which of the following sentences is incorrect?

a) He was a close friend of François Mitterrand
b) He was secretary general of the police in the Vichy regime
c) He died in his sleep at a ripe old age
d) He organized the 'rafles' of the Vél' d'Hiv'

8) Which statement is incorrect concerning the scandal of the Carrefour du Développement?

a) Both Christian Nucci and Yves Chalier were freemasons
b) Charles Pasqua was protected by *le secret défense*
c) Nucci was pardoned
d) Chalier initially escaped thanks to the *vrai-faux passeport* to Paraguay

9) François Mitterrand was decorated by the Vichy régime. T or F?

10) Which of the following affairs did not involve Jacques Chirac?

a) les emplois fictifs de l'hôtel de ville de Paris
b) les chargés de mission de l'hôtel de ville
c) le compte secret au Japon
d) les frégates de Taïwan

11) The demonstration that ended in nine people being killed at the Charonne métro station was a demonstration

a) against police brutality
b) of Action Française against communist students
c) in support of the OAS
d) against the OAS

12) Which politician was not involved in the Clearstream affair?

a) Lionel Jospin
b) Nicolas Sarkozy

c) Dominique de Villepin
d) Jacques Chirac

13) Which sentence is incorrect concerning the scandal of the crash of the Crédit Lyonnais?

a) No *énarques* were involved in the crash of the bank
b) A fire broke out in the Paris HQ of the bank
c) Another fire destroyed the archives stocked in Le Havre
d) The governor of the Bank of France at the time was Jean-Claude Trichet

14) In the de Broglie scandal, which statement is incorrect?

a) He was related to Giscard d'Estaing
b) He was killed because of debts he owed
c) France was blamed by the European Court of Human Rights in this affair
d) He was killed on Christmas Eve

15) In the Elf affair, which sentence is incorrect?

a) The affair provoked the resignation of the minister of foreign affairs
b) French politicians received huge kickbacks
c) A high-class prostitute became the mistress of the minister of foreign affairs
d) Several people were assassinated in the wake of the affair

16) The diamonds given to Giscard d'Estaing were a present from the head of state of which African republic?

a) Zimbabwe
b) Malawi
c) The Central African Republic
d) Tanzania

17) The number of judicial inquiries in which Jacques Chirac has been implicated amounts to

a) 3
b) 6
c) 9
d) 12

18) The name of the French bank involved in the Executive Life scandal was the

a) La Caisse d'Épargne
b) Le Crédit Agricole

c) Le Crédit Lyonnais
d) La Société Générale

19) The case against Xavière Tibéri in the 'rapport de la Francophonie' scandal was dismissed because of lack of evidence. T or F?

20) In the Elf scandal, Alfred Sirven was

a) the regional manager for Elf in Taiwan
b) the human resources manager in Paris
c) the general slush fund manager for the group
d) an innocent fall guy

21) In the false electors scandal, which statement is incorrect?

a) Jean Tibéri's wife is co-accused of fraud
b) Jean Tibéri used to be a magistrate
c) His name has been linked to several affairs
d) He risks a five-year prison sentence

22) The harkis were

a) Algerian brigands
b) terrorists fighting for Algerian independence
c) terrorist commandos fighting against the OAS
d) native back-up forces of the French army

23) In the *Lycées d'Île de France* scandal, which statement is incorrect?

a) The Green party was the only party not to have accepted bribes
b) Both the socialist party and the communist party were guilty of taking kickbacks
c) The racket concerned 5 per cent commissions on an investment of 24 billion francs
d) It was the biggest corruption scandal of the Vth Republic, at the time

24) The Main Rouge was

a) an Algerian independence terrorist movement
b) a group of bank robbers in Paris in the 1960s
c) a splinter group of the FLN
d) the murder machine of the SDECE

25) Which statement is correct? Malik Oussekine

a) died while demonstrating in a student protest march
b) was the name of the first Algerian martyr in the war of independence

c) was beaten to death by the Paris police after a demonstration
d) was a Maoist sympathizer

26) The Markovic affair was aimed at smearing the reputation of which first lady?

a) Yvonne de Gaulle
b) Anémone Giscard d'Estaing
c) Claude Pompidou
d) Danielle Mitterrand

27) Concerning the assassination attempt on the life of de Gaulle, which sentence is incorrect?

a) The plot was masterminded by a former Polytechnician
b) It was carried out by the OAS
c) The mastermind was later shot
d) The attack took place while de Gaulle was driving to Le Bourget

28) Which of the sentences concerning Maurice Papon is false? He was

a) involved in the deportation of Jewish children
b) the secretary general of the préfecture of the Gironde
c) decorated with the Légion d'Honneur
d) minister of foreign affairs between 1978 and 1981

29) Which of the sentences is incorrect?

a) Two explosions occurred on the Greenpeace ship 'The Rainbow Warrior'
b) Ségolène Royal's brother was part of the French commando unit involved
c) There were no human casualties
d) The minister of defence resigned in the wake of the affair

30) Which sentence concerning the SAC is incorrect?

a) It was a Gaullist movement created to combat the OAS
b) It was a hand-picked elite police organization
c) Some of its members were known criminals
d) It was dissolved after the massacre of Auriol

### Test 12a: Metonymy, periphrasis

1) Place Beauvau is the metonymical name of the French ministry of

a) foreign affairs
b) the interior

c) the environment
d) education

2) *La Belle Province* refers to

a) Aquitaine
b) Brittany
c) Quebec
d) La Côte d'Azur

3) Bercy is the metonymical name for the ministry of

a) finance
b) culture
c) overseas trade
d) public works

4) Which word below is usually associated with Boulogne-Billancourt?

a) planes
b) cars
c) plastics
d) computers

5) Which political party is headquartered in the rue de la Boétie?

a) Communist party
b) Socialist party
c) MoDem
d) UMP

6) *La Bonne Mère* is the affectionate name given to

a) Notre Dame de Paris
b) Notre Dame de la Garde (Marseilles)
c) La basilique de la Madeleine (Paris)
d) La cathédrale de Strasbourg

7) *La Cour des Comptes* is headquartered in which rue?

a) Cambon
b) Solférino
c) Montpensier
d) de Bercy

8) *Le Château* refers to

a) the Élysée
b) the prime minister's office
c) the ministry of foreign affairs
d) Versailles

9) *Château la pompe* refers to

a) rot-gut
b) water
c) water mixed with wine
d) sparkling water mixed with wine

10) *La Grande Muette* is another way of speaking about the French

a) army
b) navy
c) airforce
d) secret service

11) *La cité mariale* refers to

a) Paris
b) Rome
c) Lourdes
d) Jerusalem

12) *La cité phocéenne* refers to

a) Marseilles
b) Nice
c) Toulon
d) St Tropez

13) *Les événements* refers to the

a) First World War
b) Korean War
c) Indo-Chinese War
d) Algerian war of independence

14) The Tour de France is known affectionately as

a) *La reine*
b) *La Grande Boucle*

c) *La Grande Vadrouille*
d) *Le Grand Braquet*

15) The ministry of the environment is located in the rue

a) Royale
b) Grenelle
c) Solférino
d) Monsieur le Prince

16) *L'habit vert* refers to the uniform worn by

a) Former French presidents of the Republic
b) members of the Légion d'Honneur
c) ushers in the National Assembly
d) members of the Académie Française

17) *L'Île de beauté* refers to

a) Jersey
b) Belle Île en Mer
c) Corsica
d) Île d'Hyères

18) *Les Immortels* are

a) members of the Académie Française
b) members of the Collège de France
c) former French presidents of the Republic
d) authors who have been published in the collection of the Pléiade

19) The Hôtel de Lassay is the official residence of the

a) president of the National Assembly
b) president of the Senate
c) minister of finance
d) minister of justice

20) Which expression is not a synonym of France?

a) l'Hexagone
b) le pays des droits de l'homme
c) le pays des Lumières
d) le pays de cocagne

21) *Le Palais du Luxembourg* is the home of

a) *Le Conseil Constitutionnel*
b) *Le Sénat*
c) *L'Assemblée Nationale*
d) *La Cour des Comptes*

22) *La maréchaussée* refers to the

a) police (*Gendarmerie*)
b) fire brigade
c) corps of civil engineers
d) army

23) Hôtel Marigny is

a) a famous Parisian theatre
b) the home of the prime minister
c) the official residence of visiting heads of state
d) the residence of the president of the Senate

24) *Le Conseil Constitutionnel* is located in la rue

a) Montpensier
b) de la Pompe
c) de Rivoli
d) Monsieur Le Prince

25) 9–3

a) This is the number of an article of the French Constitution
b) It is the euphemism for a sexual position
c) These are the normal working hours of a French civil servant
d) It refers to the département Seine-Saint-Denis (93)

26) 36, Quai des Orfèvres is the metonymical term for

a) the French equivalent of the CID or FBI
b) the ministry of foreign affairs
c) the French mint
d) one of the most prestigious jewellery shops in Paris

27) The name of a type of street is sufficient to evoke the ministry of foreign affairs; which one?

a) *la rue*
b) *le quai*

c) *le boulevard*
d) *l'avenue*

28) *Le Palais Bourbon* is the name of the building that houses the

a) French Senate
b) French National Assembly
c) ministry of education
d) ministry of culture

29) The official residence of the president of the French Senate is known as

a) *Le Petit Luxembourg*
b) *Le Petit Trianon*
c) *La Petite Écurie*
d) *Le Petit Four*

30) *Le Perchoir* is the name given to the position occupied by the

a) French President
b) president of the National Assembly
c) president of the Senate
d) president of the French employers' confederation

31) *Le quai de Conti* is the address of the

a) Académie Française
b) ministry of education
c) ministry of foreign affairs
d) HQ of the French CID

32) Which street in Paris has become synonymous with a congress during which a fundamental problem is looked into and suggestions for legislation are made? This street has since become a substantive in its own right.

a) rivoli
b) solférino
c) grenelle
d) sébastopol

33) *Le Rocher* is the metonymical term for

a) Solutré
b) Le Mont Saint Michel

c) Monaco
d) Le Vercors

34) The hospital of Sainte Anne in Paris is well known for

a) treating severe burns
b) dealing with premature babies
c) the treatment of cancer
d) psychiatric treatment

35) The school of the rue Saint-Guillaume refers to

a) Sup de Co de Paris
b) Sciences Po
c) HEC
d) Polytechnique

36) Which metonymical name can refer to two distinct institutions?

a) *Hôtel Matignon*
b) *Le Palais Bourbon*
c) *Le Palais du Luxembourg*
d) *Le Palais Royal*

37) *La sale guerre* refers to

a) the First World War
b) the Indo-Chinese war
c) the Korean War
d) the Algerian War of Independence

38) *Le plateau* is the metonymical name of the

a) French president's weekend retreat in Versailles
b) presidency of the national assembly
c) kitchens of the Élysée
d) presidency of the French Senate

39) Rue Solférino is the address of which political party?

a) PC (Communist)
b) MoDem (Centre party)
c) PS (Socialist)
d) UMP (presidential right-wing party)

40) The expression 'télé de maçon' refers to which TV channel in France? Channel

a) 1
b) 2
c) 3
d) 5

41) The Normale Supérieure school is located in a street that takes its name from a famous military victory; which one?

a) Solférino
b) Ulm
c) Wagram
d) Marengo

42) Rue de Valois is associated with which ministry?

a) culture
b) education
c) defence
d) foreign affairs

43) Which *place* in Paris is associated with luxury goods, jewellery and perfume in particular? La place

a) de la Bastille
b) Vendôme
c) d'Alésia
d) de la Bourse

44) Until the recent past, *le Palais Brogniart* was a synonym of

a) the Paris stock exchange
b) a chic venue for cocktail parties and congresses
c) a famous Parisian brasserie
d) the seat of the French communist party

45) Which famous person lives in the rue de Varenne?

a) The president of the republic
b) The prime minister
c) The president of the senate
d) The Speaker of the national assembly

46) *Le Vieux Port* refers to

a) le Havre
b) Concarneau
c) Toulon
d) Marseilles

47) Villejuif is a town with a hospital closely associated with the treatment of

a) cancer
b) mental disorders
c) heart conditions
d) amputations

48) *La Ville rose* refers to

a) Marseilles
b) Toulouse
c) Toulon
d) Lyons

49) *La ville Sainte* refers to

a) Jerusalem
b) Lourdes
c) Rome
d) Bethlehem

50) Historically, *les accords de Grenelle* refer to agreements reached in the area of

a) public health
b) industrial relations and working conditions
c) schooling
d) new policing methods

## Test 12b: Significant geographical names

1) Find the odd man out.

a) Souzy la Briche
b) Bormes les Mimosas
c) La Lanterne
d) Latché

2) Solutré is associated with an annual pilgrimage made by which former president?

a) Mitterrand
b) Giscard d'Estaing
c) Chirac
d) Pompidou

3) One would translate NAP (Neuilly Auteil Passy) by

a) clumsy
b) impoverished
c) distant
d) Sloaney

4) Which atoll used to be the French nuclear testing site?

a) Maketea
b) Tuamoto
c) Muroroa
d) Temoe

5) Which one of the following was not a street associated with the Gestapo? La rue

a) Lauriston
b) de la Pompe
c) des Saussaies
d) Monsieur le Prince

6) Drancy is a name associated with

a) deportation
b) resistance
c) torture
d) collaboration

7) Find the odd man out.

a) Flamanville
b) Bourges
c) Tricastin
d) Golfech

8) *Le Plateau de Glières* is associated with

a) gardening
b) war
c) sport
d) photography

9) Which former president was mayor of Chamalières?

a) Chirac
b) Giscard d'Estaing
c) Mitterrand
d) Pompidou

10) Clairefontaine is a town associated with

a) football
b) rugby
c) basketball
d) athletics

11) The assassination attempt on the life of de Gaulle took place while he
   was driving to the airport, his ultimate destination being

a) Lyons
b) Baden-Baden
c) Colombey-les-Deux-Eglises
d) Versailles

12) The cross of Lorraine adopted as an emblem of the Free French forces
   most resembles the

a) Maltese cross
b) Greek cross
c) Latin cross
d) Patriarchal cross

13) Find the odd man out among the following airports.

a) Le Bourget
b) Villacoublay
c) Charles de Gaulle
d) Orly

14) *La Croisette* is associated with

a) the cinema
b) the theatre
c) the navy
d) photography

15) The name of General de Gaulle's private residence was called

a) Le Boisseau
b) La Boiserie
c) La Brasserie
d) La Boisserie

16) The official summer residence of the president of the Republic is

a) Versailles
b) Saint Tropez
c) Bormes-les-Mimosas
d) Cap Nègre

17) rue de Bièvre no. 22, was the private Parisian residence of which president?

a) Mitterrand
b) Giscard d'Estaing
c) Pompidou
d) Chirac

18) Which is the odd man out?

a) Bois de Boulogne
b) Pigalle
c) rue Saint Denis
d) boulevard des Italiens

19) The German town of Baden-Baden hit the headlines in

a) 1939
b) 1945
c) 1959
d) 1968

20) *Le Plateau d'Albion*

a) was the former central command of France's nuclear deterrent
b) was a training camp for the commandos

c) was the site of a heroic fight of the French Resistance in 1944
d) the French meridian passes through this location

## Tests 13: Foreign words and expressions used in French

1) Find the odd man out.

a) kamikaze
b) typhon
c) tsunami
d) banzai

2) Find the odd man out.

a) chouïa
b) caïd
c) Führer
d) condottiere

3) Find the odd man out.

a) avatar
b) nabab
c) mantra
d) nirvana

4) Find the odd man out.

a) Nach Paris!
b) blitzkrieg
c) Blockhaus
d) leitmotiv

5) Find the odd man out.

a) apparatchik
b) establishment
c) nomenklatura
d) skipper

6) Find the odd man out.

a) imam
b) intifada

c) gourou

d) jihad

7) Find the odd man out.

a) Sturm und Drang

b) baraka

c) macchabée

d) smala

8) Find the odd man out.

a) Agnus Dei

b) ad hominem

c) fiat lux

d) Ite, missa est

9) Which of the following is not used in French?

a) a posteriori

b) pro forma

c) ad hoc

d) in camera

10) Find the odd man out.

a) alea jacta est

b) annus horribilis

c) ars longa vita brevis

d) au pro rata temporis

11) 'Ad majorem Dei gloriam' is the motto of which religious order?

a) Cistercians

b) Jesuits

c) Dominicans

d) Franciscans

12) Which of the following is not used in the same way in French as in English?

a) post scriptum

b) post mortem

c) persona non grata

d) sine die

13) Which word is common to the four following terms?

a) business
b) brother
c) bang
d) boss

14) Which of the following is not used in French? Un

a) hugging
b) jogging
c) brushing
d) camping

15) Give the English words usually used to express the following business terms.

a) assèchement du crédit
b) marge brut d'autofinancement
c) étalonnage concurrentiel
d) rachat par endettement

16) Give the English word usually used to express the following financial terms.

a) extraterritorial
b) obligations pourries
c) crédits hypothécaires à haut risque
d) courtier en bourse

17) Give the English words usually used to express the following cinema terms.

a) gros plan
b) retour en arrière
c) source sonore hors champ
d) distribution

18) Which of the following is a false friend?

a) boycott
b) lobby
c) has been
d) puzzle

19) Give the English words usually used to express the following TV terms.

a) heures de grande écoute
b) télévision à péage
c) spectacle
d) mécène/parrain

20) Give the English words usually used to express the following management terms.

a) accompagnement
b) rotation du personnel
c) un défi en termes d'objectifs
d) aide à la réinsertion d'un cadre sur le point d'être licencié

## Test 14: Acronyms and abbreviations

1) Which French acronym of an international organization is frequently punned upon in relation to a famous quotation from Lamartine?

2) The SFIO is the ancestor of the French socialist party. True or False?

3) The French employers' confederation is the

a) CNPF
b) CNIT
c) FNSEA
d) Medef

4) The organization set up to deport Frenchmen for compulsory work in German industry during the Second World War was the

a) STO
b) TOA
c) SSOT
d) PCV

5) Which English abbreviation is used to translate the French 'rachat par endettement?

6) What is today's French equivalent of the British MI6 or American CIA?

a) SDECE
b) RG

c) DST
d) DGSE

7) Which of the following is not a political party?

a) PCF
b) PS
c) DAL
d) UMP

8) Which is the odd man out?

a) RER
b) RFF
c) RATP
d) CHU

9) Which among the following is the organization concerned with food health and security?

a) Afep
b) Ania
c) Afssa
d) Ademe

10) Which of the following is not a trades union?

a) SUD
b) ATTAC
c) CGT
d) FO

11) Which letter of the alphabet completes the following acronyms and abbreviations?

a) ... AC
b) ... EP
c) ... RR
d) ... UP

12) Which is the odd man out?

a) RSA
b) RMI

c) SMIC
d) RMC

13) What do the following have in common?

a) Tracfin
b) OCRGDF
c) DNIF
d) AMF

14) DST + RG = ?

15) Find the odd man out.

a) ETA
b) FLN
c) FLNC
d) ENA

16) Which abbreviation is associated with the name of Simone Veil?

a) ISF
b) IVG
c) TGV
d) CSG

17) What do the following have in common?

a) MRAP
b) Halde
c) Criif
d) LICRA

18) Which abbreviation is used in French to designate a takeover bid?

a) OPA
b) PBC
c) TVA
d) OPV

19) Which of the following is not a diploma?

a) DEUG
b) CAPES

c) BTS
d) BTP

20) The name of the French watchdog on computer files and civil liberty is known by which abbreviation?

a) CNSA
b) CNIL
c) CNPF
d) CNSA

21) What do the following have in common?

a) CNRS
b) CREDOC
c) INRA
d) INRS

22) What do the following have in common?

a) CEA
b) AIEA
c) ASN
d) IRSN

23) Find the missing element.

a) USA = Dow Jones
b) UK = FT index
c) Germany = DAX
d) France = ?

24) The misuse of company funds and property is known by the acronym

a) ADN
b) ABS
c) AFP
d) Agirc

25) Which is the odd man out?

a) ALD
b) SIDA
c) AOC

d) TOC

26) Which of the following is the French equivalent of 'Sloaney'

a) BAC
b) BCBG
c) BIRD
d) BRDP

27) The CROSS is

a) a fundamentalist Catholic movement
b) the national mountain bike club
c) the centre for directing maritime rescue
d) an anger management programme

28) Which abbreviated Latin form is not used in French

a) etc.
b) PS
c) cf.
d) e.g.

29) Find the odd man out.

a) SARL
b) FNAC
c) EURL
d) SA

30) Which is the odd man out?

a) PDG
b) DRH
c) PDM
d) SDF

# Solutions

## (1) Popular Cultural References

1d, 2d, 3b, 4d, 5d, 6a ('bcd' are words used in famous French film titles), 7c, 8d, 9d, 10c, 11c, 12b, 13c, 14d (the first three are titles of songs by Jacques Dutronc, the fourth is the title of a song by Françoise Hardy), 15a (is the title of a film), 16a, 17c, 18b (the others are literary prizes), 19c Père Fouet-tard (the others are 'mère' and 'soeur'), 20d (the others are Grands Boule-vards), 21a, 22b, 23c, 24c, 25d (the first three are titles of songs by Brassens, the last one is by Suchon), 26a, 27b, 28a, 29d (29d is a French film, the others are French translations of American film titles), 30b, 31c, 32b, 33c, 34d (the last one is a film title, the others are the names of famous TV pro-grammes), 35c, 36b, 37c, 38a, 39a, 40d.

## (2) Famous Words

1c, 2d, 3a, 4a, 5c, 6d, 7a, 8b, 9c, 10b, 11d, 12b, 13d, 14a, 15d, 16b, 17a, 18a, 19b, 20d, 21b, 22a, 23d, 24d, 25a, 26b, 27a, 28a, 29a, 30b, 31c, 32b, 33d, 34a, 35c, 36d, 37c, 38a, 39d, 40c, 41b, 42a, 43b, 44b, 45c, 46c, 47d, 48a, 49c, 50d.

## (3) Figurative Expressions

1b (1b, 'mors', 'étrier' and 'bride' are all parts of the riding equipment of a horse), 2c (the others are hunting terms), 3d (the others are military terms), 4d (the others refer to asking a question very frankly), 5c (the others can be used with 'coup'), 6a (the others are used with colours), 7d (the others mean doing something on the quiet), 8a (the others are used with 'poudre'), 9d (the others refer to 'skiving'), 10a (the other expressions use the name of vege-tables), 11a (the others refer to going over to the enemy), 12b (the other terms mean 'to die'), 13c, 14d (the others are related to swords and fencing), 15a (the others are used with parts of the body), 16a (the others are expres-sions to say that one couldn't care less), 17c (the others mean 'in a bad way'), 18d, 19c, 20d (one swallows the others), 21b, 22 bois, 23d (the others are used with the word 'bonnet'), 24b, 25d, 26 vent, 27 'bonne', 28d is Pachtou (the others are of North African origin), 29 carnet, 30a (the others have biblical associations), 31a (the others can be used figuratively), 32 coup de, 33a, 34c, 35b, 36b, 37b (the others can be used with the word 'faux'), 38 'fer', 39d (the others are related to expressions using 'carottes'), 40a.

## (4) Headline Punning

1 Eire, or ère, or hère, 2 faim, 3 sein, 4 mère or mer, 5 gène, 6 coup, 7 tente, 8 heurt 9 photo, 10 mots, 11 envers, 12 mal, or malle, 13 debout, 14 champ, 15 délit, 16 tremper, 17 divers, 18 voie, 19 hache, 20 faux con 21 milking, 22 share, 23 oil drum, 24 a black person, 25 braces (suspenders USA), 26 pet, 27 chaud, 28 télé, 29 c'est assez, 30 meilleur.

## (5) Literary References

1a, 2d, 3d, 4a, 5a, 6c, 7a, 8a, 9d, 10c, 11d, 12c, 13d, 14a, 15c, 16b, 17a, 18b, 19b, 20a, 21d (Aragon), 22c, 23d, 24d, 25c, 26d, 27b, 28d, 29d, 30b, 31a, 32a, 33a, 34c, 35a, 36d, 37b, 38d, 39d, 40b, 41a (this was a contrast between the 'ivory tower' attitude of de Vigny compared to Hugo who was very 'engagé'), 42b, 43c, 44a, 45a (Corneille), 46a, 47d, 48d, 49b, 50a (Sagan).

## (6) Historical References

1d (the others are the names of famous massacres), 2c, 3a (in the feudal system 'a' is a myth not a tax), 4a, 5c, 6c, 7a, 8b, 9c, 10c, 11a, 12c, 13d, 14c, 15c, 16d, 17c, 18b, 19a, 20b, 21a, 22d, 23b, 24c, 25a, 26d, 27b, 28c, 29b, 30c, 31c, 32d, 33b, 34d, 35a, 36d, 37b, 38c, 39a, 40d, 41b (Sedan is rarely used figuratively), 42d, 43b, 44a, 45d, 46d (Lionel Jospin was never in charge of the police), 47d, 48d, 49b, 50d.

## (7 and 8) Mythological, Classical and Biblical References

Solutions: 1T, 2F (gate of God), 3T, 4F, 5T, 6F, 7T, 8T, 9T, 10F (Damascus), 11T, 12F (skull), 13F (eighth), 14T, 15T, 16T, 17T, 18T,19T, 20d (the others are associated with parts of the body), 21b, 22d (the others are associated with great wealth), 23b, 24a, 25d (the others are associated with punishment), 26d (the others can all be made into adjectives), 27a, 28b, 29d (the others are related to complicated paths), 30a (others are related to behaviour or traits of character).

## (9a) Who's who

1d, 2c, 3b, 4 (they are all former ministers of education), 5a, 6a, 7T, 8b (the others are TV newsreaders), 9d, 10b (Voltaire) (the others were in the year group named after Rabelais), 11d (the others are 'green'), 12b (the year group Thomas More), 13c, 14 (they are all lawyers), 15c, 16c (they were never married), 17b, 18 Charles Pasqua, 19b (Blum), 20c (he breeds horses).

## (9b) Nicknames

1c, 2d, 3a, 4b, 5d, 6c, 7b (Estrosi), 8d (Aubry), 9c, 10c, 11b, 12b, 13c, 14b, 15b, 16c, 17a, 18c, 19c, 20c, 21a, 22a, 23c, 24a, 25a.

## (10) What's What

1b, 2 bcad, 3a, 4b, 5b, 6c, 7d, 8d, 9 adcb, 10 dacb, 11c, 12a, 13d (Molière), 14d (Palais Royal), 15a, 16c, 17d, 18a, 19d (there are 100 *départements*), 20c, 21a (Sarkozy is not an énarque), 22a, 23a, 24c, 25a, 26d (Boulle is not an *école d'ingénieurs*), 27d, 28c, 29a, 30d, 31c, 32b (l'X), 33d, 34d, 35c, 36a (it is a military hospital), 37b, 38d, 39c, 40b.

## (11) Skeletons in Marianne's Cupboard

1a, 2T, 3c, 4b, 5b, 6a, 7c (assassinated), 8d (Brazil), 9T, 10d, 11d, 12a, 13a, 14b, 15a (president of the Conseil Constitutionnel), 16c, 17c, 18c, 19 F (a legal technicality), 20c, 21d (one year), 22d, 23c (2 per cent), 24d, 25c, 26c, 27d (Villacoublay), 28d (minister of budget), 29c, 30b.

## (12a) Metonymy

1b, 2c, 3a, 4b, 5d, 6b, 7a, 8a, 9b, 10a, 11c, 12a, 13d, 14b, 15b, 16d, 17c, 18a, 19a, 20d, 21b, 22a, 23c, 24a, 25d, 26a, 27b, 28b, 29a, 30b, 31a, 32c, 33c, 34d, 35b, 36d (The Conseil Constitutionnel and the Conseil d'État are both located here), 37d, 38d, 39c, 40a, 41b, 42a, 43b, 44a, 45b, 46d, 47a, 48b, 49a, 50b.

## (12b) Significant geographical names

1d (Latche was Mitterrand's private holiday home; the others are State residences), 2a, 3d, 4c, 5d, 6a, 7b (the others are the sites of nuclear power stations), 8b, 9b, 10a, 11c, 12d, 13b (Villacoublay is a military airfield whereas the others are civil airports), 14a, 15d, 16c, 17a, 18d (the others are notorious for prostitution), 19d (General de Gaulle went to visit General Massu, Commander in Chief of the French forces in Germany, to receive his assurance that the army would be faithful to the Republic), 20a.

## (13) Foreign Words and Expressions

1b is Chinese, the others are Japanese

2a 'chouïa' means 'a little' whereas the others are types of leader

3b 'nabab' is Hindi whereas the others are Sanskrit

4d the others have a strong war connotation

5d the others refer to an elite

6c is Hindi whereas the others are Arabic

7a the others are slang expressions

8b the others have a religious connotation

9d the equivalent French term is 'à huis clos'

10d the others are quotations by famous people: Caesar, Queen Elizabeth II, Hippocrates

11b

12b post-mortem is an adverb, e.g. 'the body was moved post-mortem. The French term for the English use of the expression post-mortem is 'autopsie'.

13  big

14a

15  credit crunch; cashflow; benchmarking; leveraged buy-out

16 off-shore; junk bonds; subprimes; trader

17 zoom/close-up; flashback; voice-over; cast

18d in French this is not a generic term but refers to a jigsaw puzzle

19 prime time; toll TV; show; sponsor

20 coaching; staff turnover; challenge; outplacement

## (14) Acronyms

1 l'OTAN (NATO), 2T, 3d, 4a, 5 LMBO, 6d, 7c, 8d (hospital) the others are associated with transport, 9c, 10b, 11 Z, 12d (radio) the others are welfare payments, 13 fight against financial crime, 14 DCRI, 15d (school) the others are terrorist movements, 16b, 17 fight against racial discrimination, 18a, 19d, 20b, 21 research, 22 nuclear, 23 CAC 40, 24b, 25c (quality label for wine and foodstuffs) the others are illnesses, 26b, 27c, 28d, 29b (shop) the others are types of company, 30d (homeless) the others are related to the corporate world.

# Bibliography

Adamczewski, Henri (1991) *Le Français Déchiffré*, Paris: Armand Colin.
Attali, Jacques (2009) *Dictionnaire amoureux du Judaïsme*, Paris: Plon Fayard.
Barnard, H. C. (1968) *A History of English Education from 1760*, London: University of London Press.
Bible (1949) *The Holy Bible Revised Version*, Oxford: Oxford University Press.
——(1961) *Le Nouveau Testament*, Paris: Louis Segond (Docteur en théologie).
——(2001) *La Bible de Jérusalem*, Paris: Éditions du Mame, Cerf, Fleurus.
Bliss, Alain (1992) *A Dictionary of Foreign Words and Phrases*, New York: Warner Books.
Bloch, O. and Wartburg, W. (1994) *Dictionnaire étymologique de la langue française*, Paris: Presses Universitaires de France.
Boulogne, Jean-Claude (1989) *Les Allusions littéraires*, Paris: Larousse.
——(1994) *Les Allusions bibliques*, Paris: Larousse.
Dauzat, A., Dubois, J. and Mitterand, M. (1994) *Dictionnaire étymologique et historique du français*, Paris: Larousse.
Decoin, Didier (2009) *Dictionnaire amoureux de la Bible*, Paris: Plon.
Desalmand, Paul and Stalloni, Yves (2009) *Petit inventaire des citations malmenées*, Paris: Albin Michel.
Doré, Gustave *Les Fables de La Fontaine*
Duneton, Claude (2001) *La Puce à l'oreille*, Paris: Balland.
Esnault, Gaston (1965) *Dictionnaire historique des argots*, Paris: Larousse.
Grevisse, Maurice (1994) *Le Bon Usage*, Paris: Duculot.
Grimal, Pierre (1999) *Dictionnaire de la mythologie grecque et romaine*, Paris: Presses Universitaires de France.
Hofstede, Geert (1984) *Culture's Consequences*, London: Sage.
Huisman, Denis *et al.* (2002) *Histoire de la philosophie française*, (XVII siècle), Paris: Editions Perrin.
Jouet, Jacques (1990) *Les Mots du corps*, Paris: Larousse.
Kauffer, R., Lecadre, R., Malye, F., Orange, M. and Zamponi, F. (2007) *Histoire secrète de la Vème République*, Paris: La Découverte, Poche.
Nicholson, Kate and Pilard George (2007) *Harrap's Slang* (anglais-français, français-anglais), Edinburgh: Chambers Harrap.
Peyrefitte, Alain (2006) *Le Mal Français*, Paris: Fayard.
Ratcliff, Susan (ed.) (2002) *The Oxford Dictionary of Phrase, Saying and Quotation*, Oxford: Oxford University Press.

Rey, Alain (1989) *Dictionnaire universel des noms propres*, Paris: Le Robert.

Rey, Alain and Chantreau Sophie (1993) *Dictionnaire des expressions et des locutions*, Paris: Le Robert.

Stewart, J. H. (1966) *A Documentary Survey of the French Revolution*, New York: Macmillan.

Trompenaars, Fons (1993) *Riding the Waves of Culture: Understanding Cultural Diversity in Business*, London: Economist Books.

Walter, Henriette (2001) *Honni soit qui mal y pense*, Paris: Robert Laffont.

# Annex I

## Facts and figures about the research sources of the book

### Le Canard Enchaîné

Genre: Satirical (8-page broadsheet).
Owner: SA Les Éditions Maréchal-Le Canard Enchaîné.
Political colour: Neither right nor left but violently opposed to any forms of hypocrisy and corruption. Very anti-clerical.
Circulation: 500,000 +
Periodicity: weekly.
Founded: 1915.
Price: €1.20.
Published in Paris.
General remarks: This newspaper carries absolutely no advertising and it thus enjoys total editorial freedom. Its journalists are not allowed to receive any official decorations or titles. One journalist did so in the past, and he was fired. Known as 'the most well-informed newspaper in France' and 'Le palmipède' (web-footed).

### Les Echos

Genre: Economic, financial and corporate news (Berliner format i.e. 470 mm by 320 mm). This is the similar to the 'tabloïd' format but the latter term is so closely associated with the gutter press ('la presse à scandales') that the term Berliner is preferred.
Owner: LVMH, the group of Bernard Arnault.
Political colour: Right wing, pro-liberal economy.
Circulation: 120,000 +
Periodicity: daily.
Founded: 1908.
Price: €1.40.
Published in Paris.

General remarks: This is one of the two major French financial news-papers the other being *La Tribune*. NB there is no accent on the newspaper title.

## L'Express

Genre: General news magazine.
Owner: The Belgian media group Roularta.
Political colour: Centre
Circulation: 444,000 +
Periodicity: weekly.
Founded: 1953 by Françoise Giroud and Jean-Jacques Servan-Schreiber.
Price: €3.50.
Published in Paris.
General remarks: Initially set up to support the socialist politician Pierre Mendès-France. It was anti-Gaullist and was one of the first news magazines to denounce torture in Algeria. Over the past few years the magazine has moved more to the political centre.

## Le Figaro

Genre: General interest newspaper. (Berliner format).
Owner: Socopress (Dassault Communications).
Political colour: Right.
Circulation: 319,000 +
Periodicity: daily
Founded: 1826.
Price: 1.30 euros.
Published in Paris.
General remarks: Founded during the reign of Charles X, *Le Figaro* is the oldest French newspaper. It takes its name from the character in the *Marriage of Figaro* by Beaumarchais, and has as its motto the famous line spoken by Figaro 'Sans la liberté de blamer il n'est point d'éloge flatteur'.

## Libération

Genre: General news (Berliner format)
Owner: Main shareholder Edouard de Rothschild.
Political colour: Left.
Circulation: 111,000 +
Periodicity: daily
Founded: 1973 by Jean-Paul Sartre and Serge July.
Price: €1.30.

### Marianne

Genre: General interest and political news magazine.
Owner: Jean-François Kahn and Maurice Szafran hold 40 per cent of the capital.
Political colour: Republican, anti-socialist of the 1968 type, and anti-neoliberal.
Circulation: 220,000 + on average (with peaks of 500,000)
Periodicity: weekly.
Founded: 1997 by Jean-François Kahn and Maurice Szafran.
Price: €2.50.
Published in Paris.
General remarks: This magazine has been ostracised by the big commercial brands. Only 5 per cent of its revenues are generated by advertising. It consequently has great editorial freedom. Journalists from all parts of the political spectrum frequently contribute to the magazine.

### Le Monde

Genre: General interest newspaper (Berliner format)
Owner: New shareholders since 2010: Pierre Bergé, Xavier Niel and Matthieu Pigasse
Political colour: traditionally left of centre.
Circulation: 300,000 +
Periodicity: daily.
Founded: 1944 by Hubert Beuve-Méry.
Price: €1.40.
Published in Paris.
General remarks: It is published in the afternoon bearing the following day's date. Among the French dailies it has the biggest circulation abroad – 40,000 copies. It has, however, lost the prestigious reputation that it once enjoyed.

### Le Nouvel Observateur

Genre: General interest news magazine.
Owner: Groupe Perdriel.
Political colour:  Left.
Circulation: 540,000 +
Periodicity: weekly.
Founded: 1964 by Claude Perdriel, Jean Daniel and André Gorz.
Price: €3.50.
Published in Paris.
General remarks: It is the number one news magazine in France. Familiarly known as *Le Nouvel Obs.*

### Le Point

Genre: General interest news magazine.
Owner: Artemis (François Pinault).
Political colour: Centre right.
Circulation: 400,000 +
Periodicity: weekly
Founded: 1972 by Claude Imbert and Georges Suffert.
Price: €3.50.
Published in Paris.
General remarks: The magazine was created by journalists who had left *L'Express* over disagreements about the editorial line taken by Jean-Jacques Servan-Schreiber.

If any readers wish for more detailed information about the publications that were studied, they are invited to get in touch with me by e-mail: michael. mould@wanadoo.fr

# Index